P9-ELG-874

Philosophy
and
Contemporary Issues

Philosophy

and

Contemporary Issues

Eighth Edition

John R. Burr
Milton Goldinger
University of Wisconsin Oshkosh

PRENTICE HALL
UPPER SADDLE RIVER, NEW JERSEY 07458

Library of Congress Cataloging-in-Publication Data

Philosophy and contemporary issues / [edited by] John R. Burr, Milton
   Goldinger. — 8th ed.
        p.   cm.
   Includes bibliographical references.
   ISBN 0–13–020993–7
   1. Philosophy.   I. Burr, John Roy   II. Goldinger, Milton
BD41.P47   1999
190'.9'04—dc21   99–26270
                                                          CIP

Editorial Director: Charlyce Jones Owen
Acquisitions Editor: Karita France
Assistant Editor: Emsal Hasan
Production Editor: Louise Rothman
Editorial Assistant: Jennifer Ackerman
Manufacturing Manager: Nick Sklitsis
Manufacturing Buyer: Tricia Kenny
Cover Design: Bruce Kenselaar
Cover Photo: Anatoly Chernishov, *Man Sitting on Top of Database,*
   Stock Illustration Source

This book was set in 10/12 Palatino by Pub Set,
and was printed and bound by RR Donnelley & Sons Company.
The cover was printed by Phoenix Color Corp.

© 2000, 1996, 1992, 1988, 1984, 1980, 1976, 1972 by Prentice-Hall Inc.
A Pearson Education Company
Upper Saddle River, New Jersey 07458

All rights reserved. No part of this book may be
reproduced, in any form or by any means,
without permission in writing from the publisher.

Printed in the United States of America

10 9 8 7 6 5 4 3 2 1

ISBN 0-13-020993-7

Prentice-Hall International (UK) Limited, *London*
Prentice-Hall of Australia Pty. Limited, *Sydney*
Prentice-Hall Canada Inc., *Toronto*
Prentice-Hall Hispanoamerica, S.A., *Mexico*
Prentice-Hall of India Private Limited, *New Delhi*
Prentice-Hall of Japan, Inc., *Tokyo*
Pearson Education Asia Pte. Ltd., *Singapore*
Editora Prentice-Hall do Brasil, Ltda., *Rio de Janeiro*

CONTENTS

WITHDRAWN

v

AUG - - 1999

PART FOUR   State and Society   291

PART FIVE   Mind and Body   397

PART SIX   *Knowledge and Science   475*

PREFACE

The purpose of this anthology is to show how philosophy illuminates and in some measure helps solve some of the important problems troubling contemporary humankind. The editors intend it to be an introductory text. Unfortunately, many introductory texts in philosophy are flawed by one of two major defects: (1) they are too difficult for the beginning student, or (2) they are too simple for the beginning student. Some introductory philosophy texts are introductory in name only because they demand of the philosophically innocent student a mastery of technical philosophical language and a knowledge of the history of philosophy one could reasonably expect only from a professional philosopher. No wonder students struggling to understand such books become convinced of the truth of the popular view that philosophy is a subject that is wholly unintelligible to all except a few compulsive adepts and is completely irrelevant to life outside of the classroom. On the other hand, in an attempt to eliminate excessive philosophical sophistication, other introductory philosophy texts are philosophical in name only because they contain no technical philosophy. Not surprisingly, students reading such books in order to learn about philosophy as a distinct discipline find them hollow and conclude that philosophy is not worth serious study.

In designing the structure of this book, in selecting the readings, in writing the introductions to the various parts, and in choosing the books to be listed in the bibliographies, the editors have striven to produce a work avoiding both defective extremes. Throughout, the guiding aim has been to make philosophy interesting and intelligible to students undertaking their first sustained study of the subject and, above all, to encourage them to engage in philosophizing themselves. To achieve this end, each part of this volume contains pro and con articles on provocative contemporary issues, which in turn raise fundamental philosophical issues. In addition to the material dealing directly with contemporary issues, each part includes other selections discussing at length and in depth some of the philosophical problems raised by the contemporary controversies. Each part closes with a "Problems and Puzzles" section focusing on some deep logical disquietudes embedded in the earlier readings. These problems and puzzles have been chosen not only for their intrinsic fascination but also for their power to lure students into broader philosophical argument. Therefore, each part forms a coherent unit of mutually relevant sections rather than a miscellaneous grouping. Every effort has been made to pick readings as appropriate as possible for the beginning student of philosophy rather than for the advanced or professional student of the subject. Because the editors planned a single volume and not a library, not all philosophical issues, methods, and movements could be included. If should be pointed out also that the readings in one part often will throw light on the material discussed in other parts. Nevertheless, the readings are also numerous and diverse enough to enable individual instructors to select just those they deem most suitable for their courses.

This introductory text is a mutual enterprise, each editor sharing equally in its production and benefiting in the same proportion from the comments and suggestions of his colleague.

This new edition of *Philosophy and Contemporary Issues* is a revision, not a reprint. New readings replace some of those in previous editions, and the introductions have been rewritten accordingly. Changes have been made in the bibliographies. We believe our eighth collaboration has resulted in a fresh edition superior to its seven predecessors.

The editors thank particularly Karita France, Editor of Philosophy and Religion at Prentice Hall; the faculty of the Forrest R. Polk Library of the University of Wisconsin Oshkosh; the staff of the Oshkosh Public Library; and Ann M. Hoeft. We also thank Houston Craighead, Winthrop University, and Elias Baumgarten, University of Michigan–Dearborn, who reviewed this edition. Finally we have profited greatly from the thoughtful comments and criticisms of the many users of the previous seven editions of *Philosophy and Contemporary Issues* and take this opportunity to express our appreciation.

J. R.B.
M. G.

Philosophy
and
Contemporary Issues

General Introduction

WHAT PHILOSOPHY CAN BE

Western philosophy has performed many different functions in the course of its long history. Perhaps the most important of these philosophical activities has been the encouragement of intellectual independence. This introductory text, *Philosophy and Contemporary Issues*, focuses on this autonomy-enhancing function of philosophy. But what is intellectual independence? Immanuel Kant (1724–1804), a German philosopher called "great" because his philosophy still profoundly influences what and how educated people think today, succinctly defines it as "Enlightenment." Kant makes clear that Enlightenment is not a set of specific doctrines, a universal system of philosophical truths; rather, Enlightenment is a distinct, active state of being. In his essay "What Is Enlightenment," Kant expresses the essence of Enlightenment, or Intellectual Independence, in the following words:

> Enlightenment is the emergence of man from the immaturity for which he is himself responsible. Immaturity is the inability to use one's understanding without the guidance of another. Man is responsible for his own immaturity, when it is caused, by lack not of understanding, but of the resolution and the courage to use it without the guidance of another. Sapere aude! Have the courage to use your own reason! is the slogan of Enlightenment.

The first philosophical selection in this book, its overture, is Plato's *Apology*. Kant provides an abstract definition of intellectual autonomy; Plato, the great philosophical artist, gives a vivid, dramatic representation of intellectual autonomy in action. The *Apology* is Plato's account of his teacher Socrates's defense at his trial in Athens in 399 B.C. Socrates has been brought to trial, charged with corrupting the youth and introducing strange gods—in contemporary terms, with being a dangerous subversive. Socrates contends that he is on trial for more than a technical violation of the law. His ideas are on trial; philosophy itself is on trial. The court gives this claim justification when it tells Socrates that he will be acquitted on the condition that he stop philosophizing. Socrates adamantly refuses. His defense becomes a defense of his life of philosophizing.

Socrates defends reason as the supreme authority, as the ultimate court of appeal. He declares that "the unexamined life is not worth living." He vows that the only thing he will follow is reason. Socrates prepares the way for his defense by reminding the jurors that the god Apollo, speaking through the human channel of the Oracle at Delphi, declared that no one is wiser than Socrates. To the ancient Greeks, Apollo, the god of reason, was not a strange god but the son of Zeus, the chief god of the Olympian mythology.[1] To obey one's reason is to obey Apollo.

---

[1] Mythology is someone else's religion.

Socrates's steadfast reliance on his own reason in all things, including religion, is illustrated strikingly by his response to the Oracle at Delphi's declaration about his wisdom. The actual Oracle, a woman called Pythia, would utter weird sounds while in a frenzy. Popular belief held that her words really were those of the god Apollo. Temple priests interpreted her unintelligible utterances to the public. In the *Apology,* Socrates depicts himself as employing his own reason to arrive at his own interpretation of the meaning of what Apollo communicated through the Oracle. While he is convinced that the gods always tell the truth, the meaning of what they say is not self-evident; it must be elicited by rational analysis and observation. Socrates's immediate response to what the Delphic Oracle has said about him is skeptical: how can it be true that Socrates is the wisest of men and yet also true that many men know more than he does? What does Apollo really mean?

Socrates tests the truth of Apollo's statement by questioning others to learn the greater wisdom they claim to possess but which Socrates knows he lacks—only to discover that they really are as ignorant as he is. Socrates concludes that he is wiser than others because he knows that he doesn't know. Self-knowledge is the beginning of wisdom: no one questions, inquires, learns if he believes that he already knows the answers. Socrates sees himself as on a divine mission to ceaselessly question people to prove to them that they don't know the answers—that is, to philosophize. Socrates says that he is not a teacher in the usual sense because he has no set truths or system of doctrines to teach.

Socrates uses his interpretation of the meaning of the Delphic Oracle's pronouncement that there was no one wiser than Socrates to refute those whom he calls "my old accusers" and whom he fears more than he does his present accusers, Meletus, Anytus, and Lycon. Since the childhood of most of those hearing him, these anonymous "old accusers" have slandered him as "a wise man, who speculates about the heavens, and who investigates things that are beneath the earth, and who can make the weaker reason appear the stronger." Socrates indignantly denounces this guilt by association and denies that he is that *kind* of wise man or "sophist." He insists that he is not wise about nature and its workings nor about how to argue persuasively but fallaciously concerning what is good for individuals and communities. Those claiming to be wise about nature have a reputation for being atheists; those claiming to be wise about human affairs are deceivers, who charge tuition for teaching what they do not really know. Socrates is neither. He *is* a wise man or sophist, true enough. But his wisdom is unique; he alone does not believe that he knows what in fact he does not know. Consequently, Socrates, disavowing any knowledge of physical nature (natural science) or of the good life for human beings (social science), declares he is a philo-sophist, a philosopher, a *lover* of wisdom, a *seeker* of wisdom.

Turning next to a refutation of the current accusations that he does not believe in the gods in whom the state believes, but introduces new divinities and that he corrupts the youth, Socrates subjects his present accuser, Meletus, to a brief but devastating cross-examination, a cameo version of what he daily inflicted on anyone willing to talk with him. Illustrating his now famous maieutic method of question and answer in which the philosopher or lover of wisdom questions and the other person claiming to have wisdom answers, Socrates quickly ensnares Meletus in a net of contradictions, thereby revealing Meletus's true ignorance by proving that he does not know what he believes he knows. It is easy to imagine the embarrassment and anger of anyone experiencing the public humiliation of having his lack of wisdom so glaringly exposed to anyone overhearing such a "conversation," and the stinging laughter of the auditors.

Nevertheless, Socrates is not a complete skeptic. Not only does he know that he doesn't know many things, he soon declares that he knows "that it is evil and disgraceful to do wrong, and disobey my superior, whoever he is, whether man or god." Socrates then argues in defense of his philosophical life of ceaseless questioning that the god Apollo in effect commanded him to philosophize or seek wisdom; that a god is a commander superior to any human court or other human authority; and that, therefore, he should obey Apollo and continue to philosophize rather than disobey the god by heeding any order to stop philosophizing from the court or any other inferior commander. If this argument does not demonstrate the wisest course of action to take, then Meletus and the other accusers should educate him by refuting it and so prove that Socrates does not really know what he believes he does instead of forcing him to court and threatening him with punishment. Not even the threat of death can deter Socrates from his rational independence in following the argument wherever it may lead. He asserts that no one knows whether death is a great good or a great evil but that he does know one should avoid a known evil, such as disobeying Apollo and ceasing to philosophize, rather than be intimidated by something which might or might not be evil, such as death.

For the philosopher the most important issue is not whether one lives or dies but whether one is acting as a just or an unjust person would act. Here is impregnable independence. But Socrates goes further and exhorts everyone to make this just or unjust issue paramount in his or her life. Know thyself, Socrates urges, know what is most important. By questioning others and by questioning yourself discover the good, what is really most important, what you really want as seen by analysis and argument. In short, to love wisdom, to philosophize, is what the Socrates of the *Apology* means by obeying "Apollo, the superior commander," whatever the historical Socrates may have really believed about the existence or nonexistence of that deity of the Greek Olympian religion. Socrates is not only a thinker; he is also a reformer. He not only questions himself; he questions everyone, saying: "My good friend, you are a citizen of Athens, a city which is very great and very famous for its wisdom and strength—are you not ashamed of caring so much for the making of money and for fame and prestige when you neither think nor care about wisdom and truth and the improvement of your soul?" Socrates encourages everyone to philosophize, to obey the superior commander. By emulating Socrates you will become a true son or daughter of Apollo.

Philosophy and Contemporary Issues has been designed in the spirit of Socrates. This introductory philosophy text has two main goals: (1) to show students their ignorance and (2) to awaken their desire for wisdom. If it encourages its readers to be intellectually independent, it will have introduced them to philosophy. *Philosophy and Contemporary Issues* is an anthology of writings by many authors, of alleged wisdom from many people said to be wise, on such basic topics as freedom and determinism, God and religion, morality and society, state and society, mind and body, knowledge and science. These range over such traditional fields of philosophy as metaphysics, philosophy of religion, ethics, social and political philosophy, philosophy of mind, epistemology, and philosophy of science. To the beginning student these topics and their technical terms may well seem abstract, remote, even unintelligible. Therefore, each of the six parts of this book includes contemporary issues vigorously, even passionately, discussed by intelligent and educated people which raise such questions as: Are criminals responsible? Should you believe in God on faith alone? Is abortion right or wrong? Should the government censor art? Are men machines? and What is the value of science? Rational attempts to answer these questions inexorably lead to such traditional philosophical subjects as hard determinism, libertarianism, soft determinism, proofs of God's existence, ethical relativism, democracy, individualism, socialism, anarchism, materialism, interactionism, idealism, rationalism, empiricism, and the nature of science. Finally, each of the six parts of this book concludes with some profound, baffling problems and puzzles raised by the previous readings. Rational attempts to answer questions produce more refined questions. Ultimately all important questions end in bafflement. To philosophize is not to be baffled too soon.

Are all of the readings in *Philosophy and Contemporary Issues* examples of genuine wisdom? Hardly. They cannot possibly all be wise because they disagree. The design of this book emphasizes their controversial character in order to awaken readers from their sleep, much as Socrates sought to rouse his fellow Athenians from their dreams. Ultimately each of us is on his or her own. Each of us must dare to ask questions, resolve to use our reason to follow the argument wherever it may lead to discover truth.

To philosophize is no easy task. Socrates's accusers have many contemporary descendants. A prominent American educator has declared:

> There seems to be nothing in the study of chemistry that makes you feel like a superior order of being, but you study Plato and you begin to believe you're a philosopher—and a philosopher should be king. This is a dangerous trend, and it jeopardizes the democratic principles on which this country was founded.[2]

The philosopher Socrates ignored his accusers and steadfastly obeyed the command of Apollo, the god of reason. The philosopher Kant ignored the accusers of his day and called for the courage to use one's own reason. The philosopher Bertrand Russell (1872–1970) interpreted the meaning of Apollo for our own time:

---

[2] Dr. Samuel I. Hayakawa, "The Playboy Panel: Student Revolt," *Playboy*, September 1969, p. 98. Reprinted by permission of *Playboy*.

1. Do not feel certain of anything.
2. Do not think it worthwhile to produce belief by concealing evidence, for the evidence is sure to come to light.
3. Never try to discourage thinking, for you are sure to succeed.
4. When met with opposition, even if it should be from your husband or your children, endeavour to overcome it by argument and not by authority, for a victory dependent upon authority is unreal and illusory.
5. Have no respect for the authority of others, for there are always contrary authorities to be found.
6. Do not use power to suppress opinions you think pernicious, for if you do the opinions will suppress you.
7. Do not fear to be eccentric in opinion, for every opinion now accepted was once eccentric.
8. Find more pleasure in intelligent dissents than in passive agreement, for, if you value intelligence as you should, the former implies a deeper agreement than the latter.
9. Be scrupulously truthful, even when truth is inconvenient, for it is more inconvenient when you try to conceal it.
10. Do not feel envious of the happiness of those who live in a fool's paradise, for only a fool will think that it is happiness.[3]

---

[3] Bertrand Russell, "The Ten Commandments," *The Independent,* June 1965, p. 4. Reprinted by permission of *The Independent.*

1. The Apology

Plato

Plato (427–347 B.C.) was an Athenian aristocrat who early in life came under the influence of Socrates. He wrote more than twenty dialogues, many of which feature his teacher and hero, Socrates. When he was around forty years old, Plato founded the Academy, which was in effect the first university in Europe. So great has been Plato's influence that Alfred North Whitehead said that Western philosophy has been a succession of footnotes to Plato.

Socrates (470–399 B.C.) left no writings. What he says in The Apology *are words attributed to him by Plato. Socrates was neither wealthy nor an aristocrat but a common Athenian whose father was a stonecutter and mother a midwife. Instead of practicing his father's craft, he devoted himself to questioning his fellow citizens in order to learn the wisdom they claimed to possess, only to find they had no wisdom to teach him.* The Apology *and the Platonic dialogues the* Crito *and the* Phaedo *depict the most famous trial, imprisonment, and death in the West other than that of Jesus Christ.[1]*

CHARACTERS
SOCRATES   MELETUS
SCENE—THE COURT OF JUSTICE

SOCRATES   I cannot tell what impression my accusers have made upon you, Athenians. For my own part, I know that they nearly made me forget who I was, so believable were they; and yet they have scarcely uttered one single word of truth. But of all their many falsehoods, the one which astonished me most was when they said that I was a clever speaker, and that you must be careful not to let me mislead you. I thought that it was most impudent of them not to be ashamed to talk in that way; for as soon as I open my mouth they will be refuted, and I shall prove that I am not a clever speaker in any way at all—unless, indeed, by a clever speaker they mean a man who speaks the truth. If that is their meaning, I agree with them that I am a much greater orator than they. My accusers, then I repeat, have said little or nothing that is true; but from me you shall hear the whole truth. Certainly you will not hear an elaborate speech, Athenians, dressed up, like theirs, with words and phrases. I will say to you what I have to say, without preparation, and in the words which come first, for I believe that my

From Socrates, *The Apology*, trans. by Jowett, 3rd edition (Oxford: Oxford University Press) 1896.

[1]There are no alleged facts about the lives of Plato and Socrates that have not been questioned by at least some scholars.

cause is just; so let none of you expect anything else. Indeed, my friends, it would hardly be seemly for me, at my age, to come before you like a young man with his specious phrases. But there is one thing, Athenians, which I do most earnestly beg and entreat of you. Do not be surprised and do not interrupt with shouts if in my defense I speak in the same way that I am accustomed to speak in the marketplace, at the tables of the money changers, where many of you have heard me, and elsewhere. The truth is this. I am more than seventy years old, and this is the first time that I have ever come before a law court; so your manner of speech here is quite strange to me. If I had been really a stranger, you would have forgiven me for speaking in the language and the fashion of my native country; and so now I ask you to grant me what I think I have a right to claim. Never mind the style of my speech—it may be better or it may be worse—give your whole attention to the question, Is what I say just, or is it not? That is what makes a good judge, as speaking the truth makes a good advocate.

I have to defend myself, Athenians, first against the old false accusations of my old accusers, and then against the later ones of my present accusers. For many men have been accusing me to you, and for very many years, who have not uttered a word of truth; and I fear them more than I fear Anytus and his associates, formidable as they are. But, my friends, those others are still more formidable; for they got hold of most of you when you were children, and they have been more persistent in accusing me untruthfully and have persuaded you that there is a certain Socrates, a wise man, who speculates about the heavens, and who investigates things that are beneath the earth, and who can make the weaker reason appear the stronger. These men, Athenians, who spread abroad this report are the accusers whom I fear; for their hearers think that persons who pursue such inquiries never believe in the gods. Then they are many, and their attacks have been going on for a long time, and they spoke to you when you were at the age most readily to believe them, for you were all young, and many of you were children, and there was no one to answer them when they attacked me. And the most unreasonable thing of all is that I do not even know their names: I cannot tell you who they are except when one happens to be a comic poet. But all the rest who have persuaded you, from motives of resentment and prejudice, and sometimes, it may be, from conviction, are hardest to cope with. For I cannot call any one of them forward in court to cross-examine him. I have, as it were, simply to spar with shadows in my defense, and to put questions which there is no one to answer. I ask you, therefore, to believe that, as I say, I have been attacked by two kinds of accusers—first, by Meletus and his associates, and, then, by those older ones of whom I have spoken. And, with your leave, I will defend myself first against my old accusers; for you heard their accusations first, and they were much more forceful than my present accusers are.

Well, I must make my defense, Athenians, and try in the short time allowed me to remove the prejudice which you have been so long a time acquiring. I hope that I may manage to do this, if it be good for you and for me, and that my defense may be successful; but I am quite aware of the nature of my task, and I know that it is a difficult one. Be the outcome, however, as is pleasing to God, I must obey the law and make my defense.

Let us begin from the beginning, then, and ask what is the accusation which has given rise to the prejudice against me, which was what Meletus relied on when he brought his indictment. What is the prejudice which my enemies have been spreading about me? I must assume that they are formally accusing me, and read their indictment. It would run somewhat in this fashion: Socrates is a wrongdoer, who meddles with inquiries into things beneath the earth and in the heavens, and who makes the weaker reason appear the stronger, and who teaches others these same things. That is what they say; and in the comedy of Aristophanes [*Clouds*] you yourselves saw a man called Socrates swinging round in a basket and saying that he walked the air, and prattling a great deal of nonsense about matters of which I understand nothing, either more or less. I do not mean to disparage that kind of knowledge if there is anyone who is wise about these matters. I trust Meletus may never be able to prosecute me for that. But the truth is, Athenians, I have nothing to do with these matters, and almost all of you are yourselves my witnesses of this. I beg all of you who have heard me discussing, and they are many, to inform your neighbors and tell them if any of you have ever heard me discussing such matters, either more or less. That will show you that the other common stories about me are as false as this one.

But the fact is that not one of these is true. And if you have heard that I undertake to educate men, and make money by so doing, that is not true either, though I think that it would be a fine thing to be able to educate men, as Gorgias of Leontini, and Prodicus of Ceos, and Hippias of Elis do. For each of them, my friends, can go into any city, and persuade the young men to leave the society of their fellow citizens, with any of whom they might associate for nothing, and be only too glad to be allowed to pay money for the privilege of associating with themselves. And I believe that there is another wise man from Paros residing in Athens at this moment. I happened to meet Callias, the son of Hipponicus, a man who has spent more money on sophists than everyone else put together. So I said to him (he has two sons), Callias, if your two sons had been foals or calves, we could have hired a trainer for them who would have made them perfect in the virtue which belongs to their nature. He would have been either a groom or a farmer. But whom do you intend to take to train them, seeing that they are men? Who understands the virtue which belongs to men and to citizens? I suppose that you must have thought of this, because of your sons. Is there such a person, said I, or not? Certainly there is, he replied.

Who is he, said I, and where does he come from, and what is his fee? Evenus, Socrates, he replied, from Paros, five minae. Then I thought that Evenus was a fortunate person if he really understood this art and could teach so cleverly. If I had possessed knowledge of that kind, I should have been conceited and disdainful. But, Athenians, the truth is that I do not possess it.

Perhaps some of you may reply: But, Socrates, what is the trouble with you? What has given rise to these prejudices against you? You must have been doing something out of the ordinary. All these stories and reports of you would never have arisen if you had not been doing something different from other men. So tell us what it is, that we may not give our verdict in the dark. I think that that is a fair question, and I will try to explain to you what it is that has raised these prejudices against me and given me this reputation. Listen, then: some of you, perhaps, will think that I am joking, but I assure you that I will tell you the whole truth. I have gained this reputation, Athenians, simply by reason of a certain wisdom. But by what kind of wisdom? It is by just that wisdom which is perhaps human wisdom. In that, it may be, I am really wise. But the men of whom I was speaking just now must be wise in a wisdom which is greater than human wisdom, or else I cannot describe it, for certainly I know nothing of it myself, and if any man says that I do, he lies and speaks to arouse prejudice against me. Do not interrupt me with shouts, Athenians, even if you think that I am boasting. What I am going to say is not my own: I will tell you who says it, and he is worthy of your respect. I will bring the god of Delphi to be the witness of my wisdom, if it is wisdom at all, and of its nature. You remember Chaerephon. From youth upwards he was my comrade; and also a partisan of your democracy, sharing your recent exile and returning with you. You remember, too, Chaerephon's character—how vehement he was in carrying through whatever he took in hand. Once he went to Delphi and ventured to put this question to the oracle—I entreat you again, my friends, not to interrupt me with your shouts—he asked if there was any man who was wiser than I. The priestess answered that there was no one. Chaerephon himself is dead, but his brother here will confirm what I say.

Now see why I tell you this. I am going to explain to you how the prejudice against me has arisen. When I heard of the oracle I began to reflect: What can the god mean by this riddle? I know very well that I am not wise, even the smallest degree. Then what can he mean by saying that I am the wisest of men? It cannot be that he is speaking falsely, for he is a god and cannot lie. For a long time I was at a loss to understand his meaning. Then, very reluctantly, I turned to seek for it in this manner: I went to a man who was reputed to be wise, thinking that there, if anywhere, I should prove the answer wrong, and meaning to point out to the oracle its mistake, and to say, You said that I was the wisest of men, but this man is wiser than I am. So I examined the man—I need not tell you his name, he was a politician—but this was the result, Athenians. When I conversed with him I came to see that, though a great many persons, and most of all he himself, thought that he was wise, yet he was not wise. Then I tried to prove to him that he was not wise, though he fancied that he was; and by so doing I made him indignant, and many of the bystanders. So when I went away, I thought to myself, I am wiser than this man: neither of us knows anything that is really worthwhile, but he thinks that he has knowledge when he has not, while I, having no knowledge, do not think that I have. I seem, at any rate, to be a little wiser than he is on this point: I do not think that I know what I do not know. Next I went to another man who was reputed to be still wiser than the last, with exactly the same result. And there again I made him, and many other men, indignant.

Then I went on to one man after another, seeing that I was arousing indignation every day, which caused me much pain and anxiety. Still I thought that I must set the god's command above everything. So I had to go to every man who seemed to possess any knowledge, and investigate the meaning of the oracle. Athenians, I must tell you the truth; by the god, this was the result of the investigation which I made at the god's bidding: I found that the men whose reputation for wisdom stood highest were nearly the most lacking in it, while others who were looked down on as common people were much more intelligent. Now I must describe to you the wanderings which I undertook, like Heraclean labors, to prove the oracle irrefutable. After the politicians, I went to the poets, tragic, dithyrambic, and others, thinking that there I should find myself manifestly more ignorant than they. So I took up the poems on which I thought that they had spent most pains, and asked them what they meant, hoping at the same time to learn something from them. I am ashamed to tell you the truth, my friends, but I must say it. Almost anyone of the bystanders could have talked about the works of these poets better than the poets themselves. So I soon found that it is not by wisdom that the poets create their works, but by a certain innate power and by inspiration, like soothsayers and prophets, who say many fine things, but who understand nothing of what they say. The poets seemed to me to be in a similar situation. And at the same time I perceived that, because of their poetry, they thought that they were the wisest of men in other matters, too, which they were not. So I went away again, thinking that I had the same advantage over the poets that I had over the politicians.

Finally, I went to the artisans, for I knew very well that I possessed no knowledge at all worth speaking of, and I was sure that I should find that they knew many fine things. And in that I was not mistaken. They knew what I did not know, and so far they were wiser than I. But, Athenians, it seemed to me that the skilled artisans made the same mistake as the poets. Each of them believed himself to be extremely wise in matters of the greatest importance because he was skillful in his own art: and this presumption of theirs obscured their real wisdom. So I asked myself, on behalf of the oracle, whether I would choose to remain as I was, without either their wisdom or their ignorance, or to possess both, as they did. And I answered to myself and to the oracle that it was better for me to remain as I was.

From this examination, Athenians, has arisen much fierce and bitter indignation, and from this a great many prejudices about me, and people say that I am "a wise man." For the bystanders always think that I am wise myself in any matter wherein I refute another. But, my friends, I believe that the god is really wise, and that by this oracle he meant that human wisdom is worth little or nothing. I do not think that he meant that Socrates was wise. He only made use of my name, and took me as an example, as though he would say to men: He among you is the wisest who, like Socrates, knows that in truth his wisdom is worth nothing at all. Therefore I still go about testing and examining every man whom I think wise, whether he be a citizen or a stranger, as the god has commanded me; and whenever I find that he is not wise, I point out to him, on the god's behalf, that he is not wise. I am so busy in this pursuit that I have never had leisure to take any path worth mentioning in public matters or to look after my private affairs. I am in great poverty as the result of my service to the god.

Besides this, the young men who follow me about, who are the sons of wealthy persons and have the most leisure, take pleasure in hearing men cross-examined. They often imitate me among themselves; then they try their hands at cross-examining other people. And, I imagine, they find plenty of men who think that they know a great deal when in fact they know little or nothing. Then the persons who are cross-examined get angry with me instead of with themselves, and say that Socrates is an abomination and corrupts the young. When they are asked, Why, what does he do? what does he teach? they do not know what to say; but, not to seem at a loss, they repeat the stock charges against philosophers, and allege that he investigates things in the air and under the earth, and that he teaches people to disbelieve in the gods, and to make the weaker reason appear the stronger. For, I suppose, they would not like to confess the truth, which is that they are shown up as ignorant pretenders to knowledge that they do not possess. So they have been filling your ears with their bitter prejudices for a long time, for they are ambitious, energetic, and numerous; and they speak vigorously and persuasively against me. Relying on this, Meletus, Anytus, and Lycon have attacked me. Meletus is indignant with me on the part of the poets, Anytus on the part of the artisans and politicians, and Lycon on the part of the orators. And so, as I said at the beginning, I shall be surprised if I am able, in the short time allowed me for my defense, to remove from your minds this prejudice which has grown so strong. What I have told you, Athenians, is the truth: I neither conceal nor do I suppress anything, small or great. Yet I know that it is just this plainness of speech which rouses indignation. But that is only a proof that my words are true, and that the prejudice against me, and the causes of it, are what I have said. And whether you look for them now or hereafter, you will find that they are so.

What I have said must suffice as my defense against the charges of my first accusers. I will try next to defend myself against Meletus, that "good patriot," as he calls himself, and my later accusers. Let us assume that they are a new set of accusers, and read their indictment, as we did in the case of the others. It runs thus. He says that Socrates is a wrongdoer who corrupts the youth, and who does not believe in the gods whom the state believes in, but in other new divinities. Such is the accusation. Let us examine each point in it separately. Meletus says that I do wrong by corrupting the youth. But I say, Athenians, that he is doing wrong, for he is playing a solemn joke by lightly bringing men to trial, and pretending to have zealous interest in matters to which he has never given a moment's thought. Now I will try to prove to you that it is so.

Come here, Meletus. Is it not a fact that you think it very important that the young should be as excellent as possible?

MELETUS   It is.

SOCRATES   Come then, tell the judges who is it who improves them? You care so much, you must know. You are accusing me, and bringing me to trial, because, as you say, you have discovered that I am the corrupter of the youth. Come now, reveal to the gentlemen who improves them. You see, Meletus, you have nothing to say; you are silent. But don't you think that this is shameful? Is not your silence a conclusive proof of what I say—that you have never cared? Come, tell us, my good sir, who makes the young better citizens?

MELETUS   The laws.

SOCRATES   That, my friend, is not my question. What man improves the young, who starts with the knowledge of the laws?

MELETUS   The judges here, Socrates.

SOCRATES   What do you mean, Meletus? Can they educate the young and improve them?

MELETUS   Certainly.

SOCRATES   All of them? or only some of them?

MELETUS   All of them.

SOCRATES   By Hera, that is good news! Such a large supply of benefactors! And do the listeners here improve them, or not?

MELETUS   They do.

SOCRATES   And do the senators?

MELETUS   Yes.

SOCRATES Well then, Meletus, do the members of the assembly corrupt the young or do they again all improve them?

MELETUS They, too, improve them.

SOCRATES Then all the Athenians, apparently, make the young into good men except me, and I alone corrupt them. Is that your meaning?

MELETUS Most certainly; that is my meaning.

SOCRATES You have discovered me to be most unfortunate. Now tell me: do you think that the same holds good in the case of horses? Does one man do them harm and everyone else improve them? On the contrary, is it not one man only, or a very few—namely, those who are skilled with horses—who can improve them, while the majority of men harm them if they use them and have anything to do with them? Is it not so, Meletus, both with horses and with every other animal? Of course it is, whether you and Anytus say yes or no. The young would certainly be very fortunate if only one man corrupted them, and every one else did them good. The truth is, Meletus, you prove conclusively that you have never thought about the youth in your life. You exhibit your carelessness in not caring for the very matters about which you are prosecuting me.

Now be so good as to tell us, Meletus, is it better to live among good citizens or bad ones? Answer, my friend. I am not asking you at all a difficult question. Do not the bad harm their associates and the good do them good?

MELETUS Yes.

SOCRATES Is there any man who would rather be injured than benefited by his companions? Answer, my good sir; you are obliged by the law to answer. Does any one like to be injured?

MELETUS Certainly not.

SOCRATES Well then, are you prosecuting me for corrupting the young and making them worse, intentionally or unintentionally?

MELETUS For doing it intentionally.

SOCRATES What, Meletus? Do you mean to say that you, who are so much younger than I, are yet so much wiser than I that you know that bad citizens always do evil, and that good citizens do good, to those with whom they come in contact, while I am so extraordinarily stupid as not to know that, if I make any of my companions evil, he will probably injure me in some way, and as to commit this great evil, as you allege, intentionally? You will not make me believe that, nor anyone else either, I should think. Either I do not corrupt the young at all or, if I do, I do so unintentionally: so that you are lying in either case. And if I corrupt them unintentionally, the law does not call upon you to prosecute me for an error which is unintentional, but to take me aside privately and reprove and instruct me. For, of course, I shall cease from doing wrong involuntarily, as soon as I know that I have been doing wrong. But you avoided associating with me and educating me; instead you bring me up before the court, where the law sends persons, not for instruction, but for punishment.

The truth is, Athenians, as I said, it is quite clear that Meletus has never cared at all about these matters. However, now tell us, Meletus, how do you say that I corrupt the young? Clearly, according to your indictment, by teaching them not to believe in the gods the state believes in, but other new divinities instead. You mean that I corrupt the young by that teaching, do you not?

MELETUS   Yes, most certainly I mean that.

SOCRATES   Then in the name of these gods of whom we are speaking, explain yourself a little more clearly to me and to these gentlemen here. I cannot understand what you mean. Do you mean that I teach the young to believe in some gods, but not in the gods of the state? Do you accuse me of teaching them to believe in strange gods? If that is your meaning, I myself believe in some gods, and my crime is not that of absolute atheism. Or do you mean that I do not believe in the gods at all myself, and I teach other people not to believe in them either?

MELETUS   I mean that you do not believe in the gods in any way whatever.

SOCRATES   You amaze me, Meletus! Why do you say that? Do you mean that I believe neither the sun nor the moon to be gods, like other men?

MELETUS   I swear he does not, judges; he says that the sun is a stone, and the moon earth.

SOCRATES   My dear Meletus, do you think that you are prosecuting Anaxagoras? You must have a very poor opinion of these men, and think them illiterate, if you imagine that they do not know that the works of Anaxagoras of Clazomenae are full of these doctrines. And so young men learn these things from me, when they can often buy places in the theatre for a drachma at most, and laugh at Socrates were he to pretend that these doctrines, which are very peculiar doctrines, too, were his own. But please tell me, do you really think that I do not believe in the gods at all?

MELETUS   Most certainly I do. You are a complete atheist.

SOCRATES   No one believes that, Meletus, not even you yourself. It seems to me, Athenians, that Meletus is very insolent and reckless, and that he is prosecuting me simply out of insolence, recklessness and youthful bravado. For he seems to be testing me, by asking me a riddle that has no answer. Will this wise Socrates, he says to himself, see that I am joking and contradicting myself? or shall I outwit him and everyone else who hears me? Meletus seems to me to contradict himself in his indictment: it is as if he were to say, Socrates is a wrongdoer who does not believe in the gods, but who believes in the gods. But that is mere joking.

Now, my friends, let us see why I think that this is his meaning. Do you answer me, Meletus; and do you, Athenians, remember the request which I made to you at the start, and do not interrupt me with shouts if I talk in my usual way.

Is there any man, Meletus, who believes in the existence of things pertaining to men and not in the existence of men? Make him answer the question, my friends, without these interruptions. Is there any man who believes in the existence of horsemanship and not in the existence of horses? or in flute-playing and not in flute-players? There is not, my friend. If you will not answer, I will tell both you and the judges. But you must answer my next question. Is there any man who believes in the existence of divine things and not in the existence of divinities?

MELETUS   There is not.

SOCRATES   I am very glad that these gentlemen have managed to extract an answer from you. Well then, you say that I believe in divine beings, whether they be old or new ones, and that I teach others to believe in them; at any rate, according to your statement, I believe in divine beings. That you have sworn in your indictment. But if I believe in divine beings, I suppose it follows necessarily that I believe in divinities. Is it not so? It is. I assume that you grant that, as you do not answer. But do we not believe that divinities are either gods themselves or the children of the gods? Do you admit that?

MELETUS   I do.

SOCRATES   Then you admit that I believe in divinities. Now, if these divinities are gods, then, as I say, you are joking and asking a riddle, and asserting that I do not believe in the gods, and at the same time that I do, since I believe in divinities. But if these divinities are the illegitimate children of the gods, either by the nymphs or by other mothers, as they are said to be, then, I ask, what man could believe in the existence of the children of the gods, and not in the existence of the gods? That would be as strange as believing in the existence of the offspring of horses and asses, and not in the existence of horses and asses. You must have indicted me in this manner, Meletus, either to test me or because you could not find any crime that you could accuse me of with truth. But you will never contrive to persuade any man with any sense at all that a belief in divine things and things of the gods does not necessarily involve a belief in divinities, and in the gods, and in heroes.

But in truth, Athenians, I do not think that I need say very much to prove that I have not committed the crime for which Meletus is prosecuting me. What I have said is enough to prove that. But I repeat it is certainly true, as I have already told you, that I have aroused much indignation. That is what will cause my condemnation if I am condemned; not Meletus nor Anytus either, but that prejudice and suspicion of the multitude which have been the destruction of many good men before me, and I think will be so again. There is no fear that I shall be the last victim.

Perhaps someone will say: Are you not ashamed, Socrates, of leading a life which is very likely now to cause your death? I should answer him with justice, and say: My friend, if you think that a man of any worth at all ought to reckon the chances of life and death when he acts, or that he ought to think of anything but whether he is acting rightly or wrongly, and as a good or a bad man would act, you are mistaken. According to you, the demigods who died at Troy would be foolish, and among them the son of Thetis, who thought nothing of danger when the alternative was disgrace. For when his mother—and she was a goddess—addressed him, when he was burning to slay Hector, in this fashion, "My son, if you avenge the death of your comrade Patroclus and slay Hector, you will die yourself, for 'fate awaits you straightaway after Hector's death'"; when he heard this, he scorned danger and death; he feared much more to live a coward and not to avenge his friend. "Let me punish the evil-doer and straightaway die," he said, "that I may not remain here by the beaked ships jeered at, encumbering the earth." Do you suppose that he thought of danger or of death? For this, Athenians, I believe to be the truth. Wherever a man's station is, whether he has chosen it of his own will, or whether he has been placed at it by his commander, there it is his duty to remain and face the danger without thinking of death or of any other thing except dishonor.

When the generals whom you chose to command me, Athenians, assigned me my station at Potidaea and at Amphipolis and at Delium, I remained where they placed me and ran the risk of death, like other men. It would be very strange conduct on my part if I were to desert my station now from fear of death or of any other thing when God has commanded me—as I am persuaded that he has done—to spend my life in searching for wisdom, and in examining myself and others. That would indeed be a very strange thing: then certainly I might with justice be brought to trial for not believing in the gods, for I should be disobeying the oracle, and fearing death and thinking myself wise when I was not wise. For to fear death, my friends, is only to think ourselves wise without really being wise, for it is to think that we know what we do not know. For no one knows whether death may not be the greatest good that can happen to man. But men fear it as if they knew quite well that it was the greatest of evils. And what is this but that shameful ignorance of thinking that we know what we do not know? In this matter, too, my friends, perhaps I am different from the multitude; and if I were to claim to be at all wiser than others, it would be because, not knowing very much about the other world, I do not think I know. But I do know very well that it is evil and disgraceful to do wrong, and to disobey my superior, whoever he is, whether man or god. I will never do what I know to be evil, and shrink in fear from what I do not know to be good or evil. Even if you acquit me now, and do not listen to Anytus' argument that, if I am to be acquitted, I ought never to have been brought to trial at all, and that, as it is, you are bound to put me to death because, as he said, if I escape, all your sons will be utterly corrupted by practicing what Socrates teaches. If you were therefore to say to me: Socrates, this time we will not listen to Anytus; we will let you go, but on this condition, that you give up this investigation of yours, and philosophy; if you are found following those pursuits again, you shall die. I say, if you offered to let me go on these terms, I should reply: Athenians, I hold you in the highest regard and affection, but I will be persuaded by the god rather than by you; and as long as I have breath and strength I will not give up philosophy and exhorting you and declaring the truth to every one of you whom I meet, saying, as I am accustomed, "My good friend, you are a citizen of Athens, a city which is very great and very famous for its wisdom and strength—are you not ashamed of caring so much for the making of money and for fame and prestige, when you neither think nor care about wisdom and truth and the improvement of your soul?" And if he disputes my words and says that he does care about these things, I shall not at once release him and go away: I shall question him and cross-examine him and test him. If I think that he does not possess virtue, though he says that he does, I shall reproach him for undervaluing the most valuable things, and overvaluing those that are less valuable. This I shall do to everyone whom I meet, young or old, citizen or stranger, but especially to citizens, for they are more nearly akin to me. For know that the god has commanded me to do so. And I think that no greater good has ever befallen you in Athens than my service to the god. For I spend my whole life in going about and persuading you all to give your first and greatest care to the improvement of your souls, and not till you have done that to think of your bodies or your wealth; and telling you that virtue does not come from wealth, but that wealth, and every other good thing which men have, whether in public or in private, comes from virtue. If then I corrupt the youth by this teaching, these things must be harmful; but if any man says that I teach anything else, there is nothing in what he says. And therefore, Athenians, I say, whether you are persuaded by Anytus or not, whether you acquit me or not, be sure I shall not change my way of life; no, not if I have to die for it many times.

Do not interrupt me, Athenians, with your shouts. Remember the request which I made to you, and do not interrupt my words. I think that it will profit you to hear them. I am going to say something more to you, at which you may be inclined to protest, but do not do that. Be sure that if you put me to death, who am what I have told you that I am, you will do yourselves more harm than me. Meletus and Anytus can do me no harm: that is impossible, for I am sure it is not allowed that a good man be injured by a worse. They may indeed kill me, or drive me into exile, or deprive me of my civil rights; and perhaps Meletus and others think those things great evils. But I do not think so. I think it is a much greater evil to do what he is doing now, and to try to put a man to death unjustly. And now, Athenians, I am not arguing in my own defense at all, as you might expect me to do, but rather in yours in order you may not make a mistake about the gift of the god to you by condemning me. For if you put me to death, you will not easily find another who, if I may use a ludicrous comparison, clings to the state as a sort of gadfly to a horse that is large and well-bred but rather sluggish from its size, and needing to be aroused. It seems to me that the god has attached me like that to the state, for I am constantly alighting upon you at every point to rouse, persuade, and reproach each of you all day long. You will not easily find anyone else, my friends, to fill my place; and if you are persuaded by me, you will spare my life. You are indignant, as drowsy persons are, when they are awakened, and, of course, if you are persuaded by Anytus, you could easily kill me with a single blow, and then sleep on undisturbed for the rest of your lives, unless the god in his care for you sends another to rouse you. And you may easily see that it is the god who has given me to your city; for it is not human the way in which I have neglected all my own interests and permitted my private affairs to be neglected now for so many years, while occupying myself unceasingly in your interests, going to each of you privately, like a father or an elder brother, trying to persuade him to care for virtue. There would have been a reason for it, if I had gained any advantage by this, or if I had been paid for my exhortations; but you see yourselves that my accusers, though they accuse me of everything else without shame, have not had the impudence to say that I ever either exacted or demanded payment. Of that they have no evidence. And I think that I have sufficient evidence of the truth of what I say—my poverty.

Perhaps it may seem strange to you that, though I go about giving this advice privately and meddling in others' affairs, yet I do not venture to come forward in the assembly and advise the state. You have often heard me speak of my reason for this, and in many places: it is that I have a certain divine sign, which is what Meletus has caricatured in his indictment. I have had it from childhood. It is a kind of voice which, whenever I hear it, always turns me back from something which I was going to do, but never urges me to act. It is this which forbids me to take part in politics. And I think it does well to forbid me. For, Athenians, it is quite certain that, if I had attempted to take part in politics, I should have perished at once and long ago without doing any good either to you or to myself. And do not be indignant with me for telling the truth. There is no man who will preserve his life for long, either in Athens or elsewhere, if he firmly opposes the multitude, and tries to prevent the commission of much injustice and illegality in the state. He who would really fight for justice must do so as a private citizen, not as an office-holder, if he is to preserve his life, even for a short time.

I will prove to you that this is so by very strong evidence, not by mere words, but by what you value highly, actions. Listen then to what has happened to me, that you may know that there is no man who could make me consent to do wrong from the fear of death, but that I would perish at once rather than give way. What I am going to tell you may be a commonplace in the law court; nevertheless it is true. The only office that I ever held in the state, Athenians, was that of Senator. When you wished to try the ten generals who did not rescue their men after the battle of Arginusae, as a group, which was illegal, as you all came to think afterwards, the tribe Antiochis, to which I belong, held the presidency. On that occasion I alone of all the presidents opposed your illegal action and gave my vote against you. The speakers were ready to suspend me and arrest me; and you were clamoring against me, and crying out to me to submit. But I thought that I ought to face the danger, with law and justice on my side, rather than join with you in your unjust proposal, from fear of imprisonment or death. That was when the state was democratic. When the oligarchy came in, the Thirty sent for me, with four others, to the council-chamber, and ordered us to bring Leon the Salaminian from Salamis, that they might put him to death. They were in the habit of frequently giving similar orders, to many others, wishing to implicate as many as possible in their crimes. But, then, I again proved, not by mere words, but by my actions, that, if I may speak bluntly, I do not care a straw for death; but that I do care very much indeed about not doing anything unjust or impious. That government with all its powers did not terrify me into doing anything unjust; but when we left the council-chamber, the other four went over to Salamis and brought Leon across to Athens; and I went home. And if the rule of the Thirty had not been destroyed soon afterwards, I should very likely have been put to death for what I did then. Many of you will be my witnesses in this matter.

Now do you think that I could have remained alive all these years if I had taken part in public affairs, and had always maintained the cause of justice like an honest man, and had held it a paramount duty, as it is, to do so? Certainly not, Athenians, nor could any other man. But throughout my whole life, both in private and in public, whenever I have had to take part in public affairs, you will find I have always been the same and have never yielded unjustly to anyone; no, not to those whom my enemies falsely assert to have been my pupils. But I was never anyone's teacher. I have never withheld myself from anyone, young or old, who was anxious to hear me discuss while I was making my investigation; neither do I discuss for payment, and refuse to discuss without payment. I am ready to ask questions of rich and poor alike, and if any man wishes to answer me, and then listen to what I have to say, he may. And I cannot justly be charged with causing these men to turn out good or bad, for I never either taught or professed to teach any of them any knowledge whatever. And if any man asserts that he ever learned or heard anything from me in private which everyone else did not hear as well as he, be sure that he does not speak the truth.

Why is it, then, that people delight in spending so much time in my company? You have heard why, Athenians. I told you the whole truth when I said that they delight in hearing me examine persons who think that they are wise when they are not wise. It is certainly very amusing to listen to that. And, I say, the god has commanded me to examine men, in oracles and in dreams and in every way in which the divine will was ever declared to man. This is the truth, Athenians, and if it were not the truth, it would be easily refuted. For if it were really the case that I have already corrupted some of the young men, and am now corrupting others, surely some of them, finding as they grew older that I had given them bad advice in their youth, would have come forward today to accuse me and take their revenge. Or if they were unwilling to do so themselves, surely their relatives, their fathers or brothers, or others, would, if I had done them any harm, have remembered it and taken their revenge. Certainly I see many of them in Court. Here is Crito, of my own deme and of my own age, the father of Critobulus; here is Lysanias of Sphettus, the father of Aeschines; here is also Antiphon of Cephisus, the father of Epigenes. Then here are others whose brothers have spent their time in my company—Nicostratus, the son of Theozotides and brother of Theodotus—and Theodotus is dead, so he at least cannot entreat his brother to be silent; here is Paralus, the son of Demodocus and the brother of Theages; here is Adeimantus, the son of Ariston, whose brother is Plato here; and Aeantodorus, whose brother is Aristodorus. And I can name many others to you, some of whom Meletus ought to have called as witnesses in the course of his own speech; but if he forgot to call them then, let him call them now—I will yield the floor to him—and tell us if he has any such evidence. No, on the contrary, my friends, you will find all these men ready to support me, the corrupter, the injurer, of their relatives, as Meletus and Anytus call me. Those of them who have been already corrupted might perhaps have some reason for supporting me, but what reason can their relatives have who are grown up, and who are uncorrupted, except the reason of truth and justice—that they know very well that Meletus is a liar, and that I am speaking the truth?

Well, my friends, this, and perhaps more like this, is pretty much what I have to say in my defense. There may be some one among you who will be indignant when he remembers how, even in a less important trial than this, he begged and entreated the judges, with many tears, to acquit him, and brought forward his children and many of his friends and relatives in Court in order to appeal to your feelings; and then finds that I shall do none of these things, though I am in what he would think the supreme danger. Perhaps he will harden himself against me when he notices this: it may make him angry, and he may cast his vote in anger. If it is so with any of you—I do not suppose that it is, but in case it should be so—I think that I should answer him reasonably if I said: My friend, I have relatives, too, for, in the words of Homer, "I am not born of an oak or a rock" but of flesh and blood; and so, Athenians, I have relatives, and I have three sons, one of them a lad, and the other two still children. Yet I will not bring any of them forward before you and implore you to acquit me. And why will I do none of these things? It is not from arrogance, Athenians, nor because I lack respect for you—whether or not I can face death bravely is another question—but for my own good name, and for your good name, and for the good name of the whole state. I do not think it right, at my age and with my reputation, to do any thing of that kind. Rightly or wrongly, men have made up their minds that in some way Socrates is different from the mass of mankind. And it will be shameful if those of you who are thought to excel in wisdom, or in bravery, or in any other virtue, are going to act in this fashion. I have often seen men of reputation behaving in an extraordinary way at their trial, as if they thought it a terrible fate to be killed, and as though they expected to live for ever if you did not put them to death. Such men seem to me to bring shame upon the state, for any stranger would suppose that the best and most eminent Athenians, who are selected by their fellow citizens to hold office, and for other honors, are no better than women. Those of you, Athenians, who have any reputation at all ought not to do these things, and you ought not to allow us to do them; you should show that you will be much more ready to condemn men who make the state ridiculous by these pitiful pieces of acting, than men who remain quiet.

But apart from the question of reputation, my friends, I do not think that it is right to entreat the judge to acquit us, or to escape condemnation in that way. It is our duty to convince him by reason. He does not sit to give away justice as a favor, but to pronounce judgment; and he has sworn, not to favor any man whom he would like to favor, but to judge according to law. And, therefore, we ought not to encourage you in the habit of breaking your oaths; and you ought not to allow yourselves to fall into this habit, for then neither you nor we would be acting piously. Therefore, Athenians, do not require me to do these things, for I believe them to be neither good nor just nor pious; and, more especially, do not ask me to do them today when Meletus is prosecuting me for impiety. For were I to be successful and persuade you by my entreaties to break your oaths, I should be clearly teaching you to believe that there are no gods, and I should be simply accusing myself by my defense of not believing in them. But, Athenians, that is very far from the truth. I do believe in the gods as no one of my accusers believes in them: and to you and to God I commit my cause to be decided as is best for you and for me.

(He is found guilty . . .)

I am not indignant at the verdict which you have given, Athenians, for many reasons. I expected that you would find me guilty; and I am not so much surprised at that as at the numbers of the votes. I certainly never thought that the majority against me would have been so narrow. But now it seems that if only thirty votes had changed sides, I should have escaped. So I think that I have escaped Meletus, as it is; and not only have I escaped him, for it is perfectly clear that if Anytus and Lycon had not come forward to accuse me, too, he would not have obtained the fifth part of the votes, and would have had to pay a fine of a thousand drachmae.

So he proposes death as the penalty. Be it so. And what alternative penalty shall I propose to you, Athenians? What I deserve, of course, must I not? What then do I deserve to pay or to suffer for having determined not to spend my life in ease? I neglected the things which most men value, such as wealth, and family interests, and military commands, and popular oratory, and all the political appointments, and clubs, and factions, that there are in Athens; for I thought that I was really too honest a man to preserve my life if I engaged in these matters. So I did not go where I should have done no good either to you or to myself. I went, instead, to each one of you privately to do him, as I say, the greatest of services, and tried to persuade him not to think of his affairs until he had thought of himself and tried to make himself as good and wise as possible, nor to think of the affairs of Athens until he had thought of Athens herself; and to care for other things in the same manner. Then what do I deserve for such a life? Something good, Athenians, if I am really to propose what I deserve; and something good which it would be suitable to me to receive. Then what is a suitable reward to be given to a poor benefactor who requires leisure to exhort you? There is no reward, Athenians, so suitable for him as a public maintenance in the Prytaneum. It is a much more suitable reward for him than for any of you who has won a victory at the Olympic games with his horse or his chariots. Such a man only makes you seem happy, but I make you really happy; and he is not in want, and I am. So if I am to propose the penalty which I really deserve, I propose this—a public maintenance in the Prytaneum.

Perhaps you think me stubborn and arrogant in what I am saying now, as in what I said about the entreaties and tears. It is not so, Athenians; it is rather that I am convinced that I never wronged any man intentionally, though I cannot persuade you of that, for we have discussed together only a little time. If there were a law at Athens, as there is elsewhere, not to finish a trial of life and death in a single day, I think that I could have persuaded you; but now it is not easy in so short a time to clear myself of great prejudices. But when I am persuaded that I have never wronged any man, I shall certainly not wrong myself, or admit that I deserve to suffer any evil, or propose any evil for myself as a penalty. Why should I? Lest I should suffer the penalty which Meletus proposes when I say that I do not know whether it is a good or an evil? Shall I choose instead of it something which I know to be an evil, and propose that as a penalty? Shall I propose imprisonment? And why should I pass the rest of my days in prison, the slave of successive officials? Or shall I propose a fine, with imprisonment until it is paid? I have told you why I will not do that. I should have to remain in prison, for I have no money to pay a fine with. Shall I then propose exile? Perhaps you would agree to that. Life would indeed be very dear to me if I were unreasonable enough to expect that strangers would cheerfully tolerate my discussions and reasonings when you who are my fellow citizens cannot endure them, and have found them so irksome and odious to you that you are seeking now to be relieved of them. No, indeed, Athenians, that is not likely. A fine life I should lead for an old man if I were to withdraw from Athens and pass the rest of my days in wandering from city to city, and continually being expelled. For I know very well that the young men will listen to me wherever I go, as they do here; and if I drive them away, they will persuade their elders to expel me; and if I do not drive them away, their fathers and kinsmen will expel me for their sakes.

Perhaps someone will say, "Why cannot you withdraw from Athens, Socrates, and hold your peace?" It is the most difficult thing in the world to make you understand why I cannot do that. If I say that I cannot hold my peace because that would be to disobey the god, you will think that I am not in earnest and will not believe me. And if I tell you that no better thing can happen to a man than to discuss virtue every day and the other matters about which you have heard me arguing and examining myself and others, and that an unexamined life is not worth living, then you will believe me still less. But that is so, my friends, though it is not easy to persuade you. And, what is more, I am not accustomed to think that I deserve any punishment. If I had been rich, I would have proposed as large a fine as I could pay: that would have done me no harm. But I am not rich enough to pay a fine unless you are willing to fix it at a sum within my means. Perhaps I could pay you a *mina*, so I propose that. Plato here, Athenians, and Crito, and Critobulus, and Apollodorus bid me propose thirty minae, and they will be sureties for me. So I propose thirty minae. They will be sufficient sureties to you for the money.

(He is condemned to death.)

You have not gained very much time, Athenians, and, as the price of it, you will have an evil name for all who wish to revile the state, and they will say that you put Socrates, a wise man, to death. For they will certainly call me wise, whether I am wise or not, when they want to reproach you. If you would have waited for a little while, your wishes would have been fulfilled in the course of nature; for you see that I am an old man, far advanced in years, and near to death. I am saying this not to all of you, only to those who have voted for my death. And to them I have something else to say. Perhaps, my friends, you think that I have been convicted because I was wanting in the arguments by which I could have persuaded you to acquit me, if, that is, I had thought it right to do or to say anything to escape punishment. It is not so. I have been convicted because I was wanting, not in arguments, but in impudence and shamelessness—because I would not plead before you as you would have liked to hear me plead, or appeal to you with weeping and wailing, or say and do many other things which I maintain are unworthy of me, but which you have been accustomed to from other men. But when I was defending myself, I thought that I ought not to do anything unworthy of a free man because of the danger which I ran, and I have not changed my mind now. I would very much rather defend myself as I did, and die, than as you would have had me do, and live. Both in a lawsuit and in war, there are some things which neither I nor any other man may do in order to escape from death. In battle, a man often sees that he may at least escape from death by throwing down his arms and falling on his knees before the pursuer to beg for his life. And there are many other ways of avoiding death in every danger if a man is willing to say and to do anything. But, my friends, I think that it is a much harder thing to escape from wickedness than from death, for wickedness is swifter than death. And now I, who am old and slow, have been overtaken by the slower pursuer: and my accusers, who are clever and swift, have been overtaken by the swifter pursuer—wickedness. And now I shall go away, sentenced by you to death; and they will go away, sentenced by truth to wickedness and injustice. And I abide by this award as well as they. Perhaps it was right for these things to be so; and I think that they are fairly measured.

And now I wish to prophesy to you, Athenians, who have condemned me. For I am going to die, and that is the time when men have most prophetic power. And I prophesy to you who have sentenced me to death that a far more severe punishment than you have inflicted on me will surely overtake you as soon as I am dead. You have done this thing, thinking that you will be relieved from having to give an account of your lives. But I say that the result will be very different. There will be more men who will call you to account, whom I have held back, though you did not recognize it. And they will be harsher toward you than I have been, for they will be younger, and you will be more indignant with them. For if you think that you will restrain men from reproaching you for not living as you should, by putting them to death, you are very much mistaken. That way of escape is neither possible nor honorable. It is much more honorable and much easier not to suppress others, but to make yourselves as good as you can. This is my parting prophecy to you who have condemned me.

With you who have acquitted me I should like to discuss this thing that has happened, while the authorities are busy, and before I go to the place where I have to die. So, remain with me until I go: there is no reason why we should not talk with each other while it is possible. I wish to explain to you, as my friends, the meaning of what has happened to me.

A wonderful thing has happened to me, judges—for you I am right in calling judges. The prophetic sign has been constantly with me all through my life till now, opposing me in quite small matters if I were not going to act rightly. And now you yourselves see what has happened to me—a thing which might be thought, and which is sometimes actually reckoned, the supreme evil. But the divine sign did not oppose me when I was leaving my house in the morning, nor when I was coming up here to the court, nor at any point in my speech when I was going to say anything; though at other times it has often stopped me in the very act of speaking. But now, in this matter, it has never once opposed me, either in my words or my actions. I will tell you what I believe to be the reason. This thing that has come upon me must be a good; and those of us who think that death is an evil must needs be mistaken. I have a clear proof that that is so; for my accustomed sign would certainly have opposed me if I had not been going to meet with something good.

And if we reflect in another way, we shall see that we may well hope that death is a good. For the state of death is one of two things: either the dead man wholly ceases to be and loses all consciousness or, as we are told, it is a change and a migration of the soul to another place. And if death is the absence of all consciousness, and like the sleep of one whose slumbers are unbroken by any dreams, it will be a wonderful gain. For if a man had to select that night in which he slept so soundly that he did not even dream, and had to compare with it all the other nights and days of his life, and then had to say how many days and nights in his life he had spent better and more pleasantly than this night, I think that a private person, nay, even the great King himself, would find them easy to count, compared with the others. If that is the nature of death, I for one count it a gain. For then it appears that all time is nothing more than a single night. But if death is a journey to another place, and what we are told is true—that there are all who have died—what good could be greater than this, my judges? Would a journey not be worth taking, at the end of which, in the other world, we should be released from the self-styled judges here and should find the true judges who are said to sit in judgment below, such as Minos and Rhadamanthus and Aeacus and Triptolemus, and the other demigods who were just in their own lives? Or what would you not give to discuss with Orpheus and Musaeus and Hesiod and Homer? I am willing to die many times if this be true. And for my own part I should find it wonderful to meet there Palamedes, and Ajax, the son of Telamon, and the other men of old who have died through an unjust judgment, and in comparing my experiences with theirs. That I think would be no small pleasure. And, above all, I could spend my time in examining those who are there, as I examine men here, and in finding out which of them is wise, and which of them thinks himself wise when he is not wise. What would we not give, my judges, to be able to examine the leader of the great expedition against

Troy, or Odysseus, or Sisyphus, or countless other men and women whom we could name? It would be an infinite happiness to discuss with them and to live with them and to examine them. Assuredly there they do not put men to death for doing that. For besides the other ways in which they are happier than we are, they are immortal, at least if what we are told is true.

And you, too, judges, must face death hopefully, and believe this as a truth that no evil can happen to a good man, either in life or after death. His fortunes are not neglected by the gods; and what has happened to me today has not happened by chance. I am persuaded that it was better for me to die now, and to be released from trouble; and that was the reason why the sign never turned me back. And so I am not at all angry with my accusers or with those who have condemned me to die. Yet it was not with this in mind that they accused me and condemned me, but meaning to do me an injury. So far I may blame them.

Yet I have one request to make of them. When my sons grow up, punish them, my friends, and harass them in the same way that I have harassed you, if they seem to you to care for riches or for any other thing more than virtue; and if they think that they are something when they are really nothing, reproach them, as I have reproached you, for not caring for what they should, and for thinking that they are great men when really they are worthless. And if you will do this, I myself and my sons will have received justice from you.

But now the time has come, and we must go away—I to die, and you to live. Whether life or death is better is known to God, and to God only.

PART ONE

Freedom and Determinism

INTRODUCTION

As currently discussed, the issue of whether human behavior is free or determined has been generated by the development of the natural sciences since the sixteenth century. A basic assumption of the evolving sciences was universal causation: i.e., the principle that every event has a cause. Further, it was thought that events occurred in orderly patterns, which could be formulated as causal or natural laws. On the basis of these laws and knowledge of the actual causes at work, accurate predictions would be made. In principle, any event could be predicted; it was only the lack of knowledge of the laws or of the present causes that limited prediction. The theory asserting universal causation and total predictability traditionally has been called *determinism.*

For the determinist, human actions are events as predictable as any other type of event. Just as the behavior of water heated to 212 degrees Fahrenheit can be predicted, so, in principle, can the behavior of a person given a million dollars. The determinist would admit that, at the moment, the latter sort of prediction cannot be made reliably because we lack the necessary exact laws of human behavior. Someday, however, the social sciences may find such laws, and correct predictions will become possible.

Determinism is rejected by a group of theorists holding a position called *libertarianism.* Although libertarians present a number of specific criticisms of determinism, most of these objections are concerned primarily with what appears to be a consequence of that position. Libertarians contend that if all actions are the result of causes (and those causes of other causes, and so on), then no actions are ones for which anyone can be held morally responsible. The robber sticking up a bank today does so as a result of a series of causes that can be traced back prior to his birth. His behavior results from such factors as his education, a lack of parental love, and the nutritional quality of the food he ate as a child. In turn, these causes flow from the kind of education his parents received, their lack of parental love, and other such elements. How can the robber justifiably be held responsible or blamed for his behavior? He could not help the way his parents treated him nor the manner in which they were educated. For the libertarian, to be considered responsible for an act is to be free to have acted otherwise; but such freedom apparently cannot exist when all human actions are the predictable outcome of various causes. In "Freedom of Choice and Human Responsibility," Corliss Lamont presents a detailed defense of libertarianism. He maintains that we have an immediate, powerful, common-sense intuition that we are free. While such an intuition could be false, it puts the burden of proving that is so on the determinists. Also, Lamont maintains that determinism must be considered false because if it were true it would imply that all deliberation is illusory since one never can

The free will party seem to think of the will as something independent of the man, as something outside him. They seem to think that the will decides without the control of the man's reason.

If that were so, it would not prove the man responsible. "The will" would be responsible, and not the man. It would be as foolish to blame a man for the act of a "free" will, as to blame a horse for the action of its rider.

But I am going to prove to my readers, by appeals to their common sense and common knowledge, that the will is not free; and that it is ruled by heredity and environment.

To begin with, the average man will be against me. He knows that he chooses between two courses every hour, and often every minute, and he thinks his choice is free. But that is a delusion: his choice is not free. He can choose, and does choose. But he can only choose as his heredity and his environment cause him to choose. He never did choose and never will choose except as his heredity and his environment—his temperament and his training—cause him to choose. And his heredity and his environment have fixed his choice before he makes it.

The average man says, "I know that I can act as I wish to act." But what causes him to wish?

The free will party say, "We know that a man can and does choose between two acts." But what settles the choice?

There is a cause for every wish, a cause for every choice; and every cause of every wish and choice arises from heredity, or from environment.

For a man acts always from temperament, which is heredity, or from training, which is environment.

And in cases where a man hesitates in his choice between two acts, the hesitation is due to a conflict between his temperament and his training, or, as some would express it, "between his desire and his conscience."

A man is practicing at a target with a gun, when a rabbit crosses his line of fire. The man has his eye and his sights on the rabbit, and his finger on the trigger. The man's will is free. If he presses the trigger the rabbit will be killed.

Now, how does the man decide whether or not he shall fire? He decides by feeling, and by reason.

He would like to fire, just to make sure that he could hit the mark. He would like to fire, because he would like to have the rabbit for supper. He would like to fire, because there is in him the old, old hunting instinct, to kill.

But the rabbit does not belong to him. He is not sure that he will not get into trouble if he kills it. Perhaps—if he is a very uncommon kind of man—he feels that it would be cruel and cowardly to shoot a helpless rabbit.

Well. The man's will is free. He can fire if he likes: he can let the rabbit go if he likes. How will he decide? On what does his decision depend?

His decision depends upon the relative strength of his desire to kill the rabbit, and of his scruples about cruelty, and the law.

Not only that, but, if we knew the man fairly well, we could guess how his free will would act before it acted. The average sporting Briton would kill the rabbit. But we know that there are men who would on no account shoot any harmless wild creature.

Broadly put, we may say that the sportsman would will to fire, and that the humanitarian would not will to fire.

Now, as both their wills are free, it must be something outside the wills that makes the difference.

Well. The sportsman will kill, because he is a sportsman: the humanitarian will not kill, because he is a humanitarian.

And what makes one man a sportsman and another a humanitarian? Heredity and environment: temperament and training.

One man is merciful, another cruel, by nature; or one is thoughtful and the other thoughtless, by nature. That is a difference of heredity.

One may have been taught all his life that to kill wild things is "sport"; the other may have been taught that it is inhuman and wrong: that is a difference of environment.

Now, the man by nature cruel or thoughtless, who has been trained to think of killing animals as sport, becomes what we call a sportsman, because heredity and environment have made him a sportsman.

The other man's heredity and environment have made him a humanitarian.

The sportsman kills the rabbit, because he is a sportsman, and he is a sportsman because heredity and environment have made him one.

That is to say the "free will" is really controlled by heredity and environment.

Allow me to give a case in point. A man who had never done any fishing was taken out by a fisherman. He liked the sport, and for some months followed it eagerly. But one day an accident brought home to his mind the cruelty of catching fish with a hook, and he instantly laid down his rod, and never fished again.

Before the change he was always eager to go fishing if invited: after the change he could not be persuaded to touch a line. His will was free all the while. How was it that his will to fish changed to his will not to fish? It was the result of environment. He had learnt that fishing was cruel. The knowledge controlled his will.

But, it may be asked, how do you account for a man doing the thing he does not wish to do?

No man ever did a thing he did not wish to do. When there are two wishes the stronger rules.

Let us suppose a case. A young woman gets two letters by the same post; one is an invitation to go with her lover to a concert, the other is a request that she will visit a sick child in the slums. The girl is very fond of music, and is rather afraid of the slums. She wishes to go to the concert, and to be with her lover; she dreads the foul street and the dirty home, and shrinks from the risk of measles or fever. But she goes to the sick child, and she foregoes the concert. Why?

Because her sense of duty is stronger than her self-love.

Now, her sense of duty is partly due to her nature—that is, to her heredity—but it is chiefly due to environment. Like all of us, this girl was born without any kind of knowledge, and with only the rudiments of a conscience. But she has been well taught, and the teaching is part of her environment.

We may say that the girl is free to act as she chooses, but she *does* act as she has been *taught* that she *ought* to act. This teaching, which is part of her environment, controls her will.

We may say that a man is free to act as he chooses. He is free to act as *he* chooses, but *he* will choose as heredity and environment cause *him* to choose. For heredity and environment have made him that which he is.

A man is said to be free to decide between two courses. But really he is only free to decide in accordance with his temperament and training. . . .

Macbeth was ambitious; but he had a conscience. He wanted Duncan's crown; but he shrank from treason and ingratitude. Ambition pulled him one way, honour pulled him the other way. The opposing forces were so evenly balanced that he seemed unable to decide. Was Macbeth free to choose? To what extent was he free? He was so free that he could arrive at no decision, and it was the influence of his wife that turned the scale to crime.

Was Lady Macbeth free to choose? She did not hesitate. Because her ambition was so much stronger than her conscience that she never was in doubt. She chose as her over-powering ambition compelled her to choose.

And most of us in our decisions resemble either Macbeth or his wife. Either our nature is so much stronger than our training, or our training is so much stronger than our nature, that we decide for good or evil as promptly as a stream decides to run down hill; or our nature and our training are so nearly balanced that we can hardly decide at all.

In Macbeth's case the contest is quite clear and easy to follow. He was ambitious, and his environment had taught him to regard the crown as a glorious and desirable possession. But environment had also taught him that murder, and treason, and ingratitude were wicked and disgraceful.

Had he never been taught these lessons, or had he been taught that gratitude was folly, that honour was weakness, and murder excusable when it led to power, he would not have hesitated at all. It was his environment that hampered his will. . . .

In all cases the action of the will depends upon the relative strength of two or more motives. The stronger motive decides the will; just as the heavier weight decides the balance of a pair of scales. . . .

How, then, can we believe that free will is outside and superior to heredity and environment? . . .

"What! Cannot a man be honest if he choose?" Yes, if he choose. But that is only another way of saying that he can be honest if his nature and his training lead him to choose honesty.

"What! Cannot I please myself whether I drink or refrain from drinking?" Yes. But that is only to say you will not drink because it pleases *you* to be sober. But it pleases another man to drink, because his desire for drink is strong, or because his self-respect is weak.

And you decide as you decide, and he decides as he decides, because you are *you,* and he is *he;* and heredity and environment made you both that which you are.

And the sober man may fall upon evil days, and may lose his self-respect, or find the burden of his trouble greater than he can bear, and may fly to drink for comfort, or oblivion, and may become a drunkard. Has it not been often so?

And the drunkard may, by some shock, or some disaster, or some passion, or some persuasion, regain his self-respect, and may renounce drink, and lead a sober and useful life. Has it not been often so?

And in both cases the freedom of the will is untouched: it is the change in the environment that lifts the fallen up, and beats the upright down.

We might say that a woman's will is free, and that she could, if she wished, jump off a bridge and drown herself. But she cannot *wish.* She is happy, and loves life, and dreads the cold and crawling river. And yet, by some cruel turn of fortune's wheel, she may become destitute and miserable; so miserable that she hates life and longs for death, and *then* she can jump into the dreadful river and die.

Her will was as free at one time as at another. It is the environment that has wrought the change. Once she could not wish to die: now she cannot wish to live.

The apostles of free will believe that all men's wills are free. But a man can only will that which he is able to will. And one man is able to will that which another man is unable to will. To deny this is to deny the commonest and most obvious facts of life. . . .

We all know that we can foretell the action of certain men in certain cases, because we know the men.

We know that under the same conditions Jack Sheppard would steal and Cardinal Manning would not steal. We know that under the same conditions the sailor would flirt with the waitress, and the priest would not; that the drunkard would get drunk, and the abstainer would remain sober. We know that Wellington would refuse a bribe, that Nelson would not run away, that Buonaparte would grasp at power, that Abraham Lincoln would be loyal to his country, that Torquemada would not spare a heretic. Why? If the will is free, how can we be sure, before a test arises, how the will must act?

Simply because we know that heredity and environment have so formed and moulded men and women that under certain circumstances the action of their wills is certain.

Heredity and environment having made a man a thief, he will steal. Heredity and environment having made a man honest, he will not steal.

That is to say, heredity and environment have decided the action of the will, before the time has come for the will to act.

This being so—and we all know that it is so—what becomes of the sovereignty of the will?

Let any man that believes that he can "do as he likes" ask himself *why* he *likes,* and he will see the error of the theory of free will, and will understand why the will is the servant and not the master of the man: for the man is the product of heredity and environment, and these control the will.

As we want to get this subject as clear as we can, let us take one or two familiar examples of the action of the will.

Jones and Robinson meet and have a glass of whisky. Jones asks Robinson to have another. Robinson says, "no thank you, one is enough." Jones says, "all right: have another cigarette." Robinson takes the cigarette. Now, here we have a case where a man refuses a second drink, but takes a second smoke. Is it because he would like another cigarette, but would not like another glass of whisky? No. It is because he knows that it is *safer* not to take another glass of whisky.

How does he know that whisky is dangerous? He has learnt it—from his environment.

"But he *could* have taken another glass if he wished."

But he could not wish to take another, because there was something he wished more strongly—to be safe.

And why did he want to be safe? Because he had learnt—from his environment—that it was unhealthy, unprofitable, and shameful to get drunk. Because he had learnt—from his environment—that it is easier to avoid forming a bad habit than to break a bad habit when formed. Because he valued the good opinion of his neighbours, and also his position and prospects.

These feelings and this knowledge ruled his will, and caused him to refuse the second glass.

But there was no sense of danger, no well-learned lesson of risk to check his will to smoke another cigarette. Heredity and environment did not warn him against that. So, to please his friend, and himself, he accepted.

Now suppose Smith asks Williams to have another glass. Williams takes it, takes several, finally goes home—as he often goes home. Why?

Largely because drinking is a habit with him. And not only does the mind instinctively repeat an action, but, in the case of drink, a physical craving is set up, and the brain is weakened. It is easier to refuse the first glass than the second; easier to refuse the second than the third; and it is very much harder for a man to keep sober who has frequently got drunk.

So, when poor Williams has to make his choice, he has habit against him, he has a physical craving against him, and he has a weakened brain to think with.

"But, Williams could have refused the first glass."

No. Because in his case the desire to drink, or to please a friend, was stronger than his fear of the danger. Or he may not have been so conscious of the danger as Robinson was. He may not have been so well taught, or he may not have been so sensible, or he may not have been so cautious. So that his heredity and environment, his temperament and training, led him to take the drink, as surely as Robinson's heredity and environment led him to refuse it.

And now, it is my turn to ask a question. If the will is "free," if the conscience is a sure guide, how is it that the free will and the conscience of Robinson caused him to keep sober, while the free will and the conscience of Williams caused him to get drunk?

Robinson's will was curbed by certain feelings which failed to curb the will of Williams. Because in the case of Williams the feelings were stronger on the other side.

It was the nature and the training of Robinson which made him refuse the second glass, and it was the nature and the training of Williams which made him drink the second glass.

What had free will to do with it?

We are told that *every* man has a free will, and a conscience.

Now, if Williams had been Robinson, that is to say if his hereditary and his environment had been exactly like Robinson's, he would have done exactly as Robinson did.

It was because his heredity and environment were not the same that his act was not the same.

Both men had free wills. What made one do what the other refused to do?

Heredity and environment. To reverse their conduct we should have to reverse their heredity and environment. . . .

Two boys work at a hard and disagreeable trade. One leaves it, finds other work, "gets on," is praised for getting on. The other stays at the trade all his life, works hard all his life, is poor all his life, and is respected as an honest and humble working man; that is to say, he is regarded by society as Mr. Dorgan was regarded by Mr. Dooely—"he is a fine man, and I despise him."

What causes these two free wills to will so differently? One boy knew more than the other boy. He "knew better." All knowledge is environment. Both boys had free wills. It was in knowledge they differed: environment!

Those who exalt the power of the will, and belittle the power environment, belie their words by their deeds.

For they would not send their children amongst bad companions or allow them to read bad books. They would not say the children have free will and therefore have power to take the good and leave the bad.

They know very well that evil environment has power to pervert the will, and that good environment has power to direct it properly.

They know that children may be made good or bad by good or evil training, and that the will follows the training.

That being so, they must also admit that the children of other people may be good or bad by training.

And if a child gets bad training, how can free will save it? Or how can it be blamed for being bad? It never had a chance to be good. That they know this is proved by their carefulness in providing their own children with better environment.

As I have said before, every church, every school, every moral lesson is a proof that preachers and teachers trust to good environment, and not to free will, to make children good.

In this, as in so many other matters, actions speak louder than words.

That, I hope, disentangles the many knots into which thousands of learned men have tied the simple subject of free will; and disposes of the claim that man is responsible because his will is free. But there is one other cause of error, akin to the subject, on which I should like to say a few words.

We often hear it said that a man is to blame for his conduct because "he knows better."

It is true that men do wrong when they know better. Macbeth "knew better" when he murdered Duncan. But it is true, also, that we often think a man "knows better," when he does not know better.

For a man cannot be said to know a thing until he believes it. If I am told that the moon is made of green cheese, it cannot be said that I *know* it to be made of green cheese.

Many moralists seem to confuse the words "to know" with the words "to hear."

Jones reads novels and plays opera music on Sunday. The Puritan says Jones "knows better," when he means that Jones has been told that it is wrong to do those things.

But Jones does not know that it is wrong. He has heard someone say that it is wrong, but does not believe it. Therefore it is not correct to say that he knows it.

And, again, as to that matter of belief. Some moralists hold that it is wicked not to believe certain things, and that men who do not believe those things will be punished.

But a man cannot believe a thing he is told to believe: he can only believe a thing which he *can* believe; and he can only believe that which his own reason tells him is true.

It would be no use asking Sir Roger Ball to believe that the earth is flat. He *could not* believe it.

It is no use asking an agnostic to believe the story of Jonah and the whale. He *could not* believe it. He might pretend to believe it. He might try to believe it. But his reason would not allow him to believe it.

Therefore it is a mistake to say that a man "knows better," when the fact is that he has been told "better" and cannot believe what he has been told.

That is a simple matter, and looks quite trivial; but how much ill-will, how much intolerance, how much violence, persecution, and murder have been caused by the strange idea that a man is wicked because *his* reason *cannot* believe that which to another man's reason [is] quite true.

Free will has no power over a man's belief. A man cannot believe by will, but only by conviction. A man cannot be forced to believe. You may threaten him, wound him, beat him, burn him; and he may be frightened, or angered, or pained; but he cannot *believe,* nor can he be made to believe. Until he is convinced.

Now, truism as it may seem, I think it necessary to say here that a man cannot be convinced by abuse, nor by punishment. He can only be convinced by *reason.*

Yes. If we wish a man to believe a thing, we shall find a few words of reason more powerful than a million curses, or a million bayonets. To burn a man alive for failing to believe that the sun goes round the world is not to convince him. The fire is searching, but it does not seem to him to be relevant to the issue. He never doubted that fire would burn; but perchance his dying eyes may see the sun sinking down into the west, as the world rolls on its axis. He dies in his belief. And knows no "better."

LIBERTARIANISM

3. Freedom of Choice and Human Responsibility

Corliss Lamont

Corliss Lamont (1902–1995) was an American philosopher who combined his philosophical defense of humanism with active participation in human affairs. Secretary-Treasurer of the Journal of Philosophy, *he was also Chairman of the National Emergency Civil Liberties Committee.*

It is my thesis that a man who is convinced he possesses freedom of choice or free will has a greater sense of responsibility than a person who thinks that total determinism rules the universe and human life. Determinism in the classic sense means that the flow of history, including all human choices and actions, is completely predetermined from the beginning of time. He who believes that "whatever is, was to be" can try to escape moral responsibility for wrongdoing by claiming that he was compelled to act as he did because it was predestined by the iron laws of cause and effect.

But if free choice truly exists at the moment of choosing, men clearly have full moral responsibility in deciding between two or more genuine alternatives, and the deterministic alibi has no weight. The heart of our discussion, then, lies in the question of whether free choice or universal determinism represents the truth. I shall try to summarize briefly the main reasons that point to the existence of free will.

First, there is the immediate, powerful, common-sense intuition shared by virtually all human beings that freedom of choice is real. This intuition seems as strong to me as the sensation of pleasure or pain; and the attempt of the determinists to explain the intuition away is as artificial as the Christian Scientist claim that pain is not real. The intuition of free choice does not, of course, in itself prove that such freedom exists, but that intuition is so strong that the burden of proof is on the determinists to show that it is based on an illusion.

Second, we can defuse the determinist argument by admitting, and indeed insisting, that a great deal of determinism exists in the world. Determinism

Reprinted from *Religious Humanism*, Vol. III, No. 3, Summer, 1969. This paper was followed by a discussion by Professors Van Meter Ames, Robert Atkins, John Herman Randall, Williard Enteman, James Gould, Milic Capek, and Sterling Lamprecht. A copy of these papers can be obtained from the Fellowship of Religious Humanists, Yellow Springs, Ohio.

in the form of if-then causal laws governs much of the human body's functioning and much of the universe as a whole. We can be glad that the automatic system of breathing, digestion, circulation of the blood, and beating of the heart operate deterministically—until they get out of order. Determinism *versus* free choice is a false issue; what we always have is *relative* determinism and *relative* free choice. Free will is ever limited by the past and by the vast range of if-then laws. At the same time, human beings utilize free choice to take advantage of those deterministic laws embodied in science and man-made machines. Most of us drive cars, but it is we and not the autos that decide when and where they are to go. Determinism wisely used and controlled—which is by no means always the case—can make us freer and happier.

Third, determinism is a relative thing, not only because human free choice exists, but also because contingency or chance is an ultimate trait of the cosmos. Contingency is best seen in the intersection of mutually independent event-streams between which there was no previous causal connection. My favorite example here is the collision of the steamship *Titanic* with an iceberg off Newfoundland, in the middle of the night on April 14, 1912. It was a terrible accident, with more than 1,500 persons lost. The drifting of the iceberg down from the north and the steaming of the *Titanic* west from England clearly represented two causal streams independent of each other.

Even if a team of scientific experts had been able, *per impossible,* to trace back the two causal streams and ascertain that the catastrophe had been predestined from the moment the steamship left Southampton, that would not upset my thesis. For the space-time relation of the iceberg and the *Titanic,* as the ship started on its voyage, would have been itself a matter of contingency, since there was no relevant cause to account for that precise relation.

The pervasive presence of contingency in the world is also proved by the fact that all natural laws, as I have observed, take the form of if-then sequences or relations. The *if* factor is obviously conditional and demonstrates the continual coexistence of contingency with determinism. The actuality of contingency negates the idea of total and all-inclusive necessity operating throughout the universe. As regards human choice, contingency ensures that at the outset the alternatives one faces are indeterminate in relation to the act of choosing, which proceeds to make one of them determinate.

My fourth point is that the accepted meaning of *potentiality,* namely, that every object and event in the cosmos possesses plural possibilities of behavior, interaction, and development, knocks out the determinist thesis. From the determinist viewpoint, multiple potentialities are an illusion. If you want to take a vacation trip next summer, you will no doubt think over a number of possibilities before you make a final decision. Determinism logically implies that such deliberation is mere playacting, because you were destined all the time to choose the trip you did choose. When we relate the causal pattern to potentiality, we find that causation as mediated through free choice can have its appropriate effect in the actualization of any one of various possibilities.

Fifth, the normal processes of human thought are tied in with potentiality as I have just described it, and likewise tend to show that freedom of choice is real. Thinking constantly involves general conceptions, universals, or abstractions under which are classified many varying particulars. In the case that I discussed under my fourth point, "vacation travel" was the general conception and the different places that might be visited were the particulars, the alternatives, the potentialities, among which one could freely choose. Unless there is free choice, the function of human thought in solving problems becomes superfluous and a mask of make-believe.

Sixth, it is clarifying for the problem of free choice to realize that only the present exists, and that it is always some present activity that builds up the past, as a skier leaves a trail behind him in the snow as he weaves down the hill. Everything that exists—the whole vast aggregate of inanimate matter, the swarming profusion of earthly life, man in his every aspect—exists only as an event or events taking place at this instant moment, which is now. The past is dead and gone; it is efficacious only as it is embodied in present structures and activities.

The activity of former presents establishes the foundations upon which the immediate present operates. What happened in the past creates both limitations and potentialities, always conditioning the present. But conditioning in this sense is not the same as determining; and each day sweeps onward under its own momentum, actualizing fresh patterns of existence, maintaining other patterns and destroying still others. Thus a man choosing and acting in the present is not wholly controlled by the past, but is part of the unending forward surge of cosmic power. He is an active, initiating agent, riding the wave of the present, as it were, and deliberating among open alternatives to reach decisions regarding the many different phases of his life.

My seventh point is that the doctrine of universal and eternal determinism is seen to be self-refuting when we work out its full implications in the cases of *reductio ad absurdum* implied. If our choices and actions today were all predestined yesterday, then they were equally predestined yesteryear, at the day of our birth, and at the birth of our solar system and earth some five billion years ago. To take another instance: for determinism, the so-called *irresistible impulse* that the law recognizes in assessing crimes by the insane must hold with equal force for the actions of the sane and virtuous. In the determinist philosophy, the good man has an irresistible impulse to tell the truth, to be kind to animals, and to expose the graft in City Hall.

Eighth, in the novel dialect of determinism many words lose their normal meaning. I refer to such words as *refraining, forbearance, self-restraint,* and *regret.* If determinism turns out to be true, we shall have to scrap a great deal in existing dictionaries and do a vast amount of redefining. What meaning, for example, is to be assigned to *forbearance* when it is determined in advance that you are going to refuse that second Martini cocktail? You can truly forbear only when you refrain from doing something that it is possible for you to do. But under the determinist dispensation it is not possible for you to accept the second cocktail because fate has already dictated your "No." I am not saying that nature necessarily conforms to our linguistic usages, but human language habits that have evolved over aeons of time cannot be neglected in the analysis of free choice and determinism.

Finally, I do not think that the term *moral responsibility* can retain its traditional meaning unless freedom of choice exists. From the viewpoint of ethics, law, and criminal law, it is difficult to understand how a consistent determinist would have a sufficient sense of personal responsibility for the development of decent ethical standards. But the question remains whether there have ever been or can be any consistent determinists or whether free choice runs so deep in human nature as an innate characteristic that, as Jean Paul Sartre suggests, "We are not free to cease being free."

SOFT DETERMINISM

4. The Problem of Free Will

W. T. Stace

*Walter Terence Stace (1886–1967) was born in Britain and served in the British
Civil Service in Ceylon before coming to the United States to teach at
Princeton University in 1932. He wrote widely acclaimed books in many
areas of philosophy.*

[A] great problem which the rise of scientific naturalism has created for the modern mind concerns the foundations of morality. The old religious foundations have largely crumbled away, and it may well be thought that the edifice built upon them by generations of men is in danger of collapse. A total collapse of moral behavior is, as I pointed out before, very unlikely. For a society in which this occurred could not survive. Nevertheless, the danger to moral standards inherent in the virtual disappearance of their old religious foundations is not illusory.

I shall first discuss the problem of free will, for it is certain that if there is no free will there can be no morality. Morality is concerned with what men ought and ought not to do. But if a man has no freedom to choose what he will do, if whatever he does is done under compulsion, then it does not make sense to tell him that he ought not to have done what he did and that he ought to do something different. All moral precepts would in such case be meaningless. Also if he acts always under compulsion, how can he be held morally responsible for his actions? How can he, for example, be punished for what he could not help doing?

It is to be observed that those learned professors of philosophy or psychology who deny the existence of free will do so only in their professional moments and in their studies and lecture rooms. For when it comes to doing anything practical, even of the most trivial kind, they invariably behave as if they and others were free. They inquire from you at dinner whether you will choose this dish or that dish. They will ask a child why he told a lie, and will punish him for not having chosen the way of truthfulness. All of which is inconsistent with a disbelief in free will. This should cause us to suspect that the problem is not a real one; and this, I believe, is the case. The dispute is merely verbal, and is due to nothing but a confusion about the meanings of words. It is what is now fashionably called a semantic problem.

Selected excerpts from pages 248–258 from *Religion and the Modern Mind* by W. T. Stace. Copyright © 1952 by W. T. Stace. Copyright renewed. Reprinted by permission of HarperCollins Publishers, Inc.

How does a verbal dispute arise? Let us consider a case which, although it is absurd in the sense that no one would ever make the mistake which is involved in it, yet illustrates the principle which we shall have to use in the solution of the problem. Suppose that someone believed that the word "man" means a certain sort of five-legged animal; in short that "five-legged animal" is the correct *definition* of man. He might then look around the world, and rightly observing that there are no five-legged animals in it, he might proceed to deny the existence of men. This preposterous conclusion would have been reached because he was using an incorrect definition of "man." All you would have to do to show him his mistake would be to give him the correct definition; or at least show him that his definition was wrong. Both the problem and its solution would, of course, be entirely verbal. The problem of free will, and its solution, I shall maintain, is verbal in exactly the same way. The problem has been created by the fact that learned men, especially philosophers, have assumed an incorrect definition of free will, and then finding that there is nothing in the world which answers to their definition, have denied its existence. As far as logic is concerned, their conclusion is just as absurd as that of the man who denies the existence of men. The only difference is that the mistake in the latter case is obvious and crude, while the mistake which the deniers of free will have made is rather subtle and difficult to detect.

Throughout the modern period, until quite recently, it was assumed, both by the philosophers who denied free will and by those who defended it, that *determinism is inconsistent with free will.* If a man's actions were wholly determined by chains of causes stretching back into the remote past, so that they could be predicted beforehand by a mind which knew all the causes, it was assumed that they could not in that case be free. This implies that a certain definition of actions done from free will was assumed, namely that they are actions *not* wholly determined by causes or predictable beforehand. Let us shorten this by saying that free will was defined as meaning indeterminism. This is the incorrect definition which has led to the denial of free will. As soon as we see what the true definition is we shall find that the question whether the world is deterministic, as Newtonian science implied, or in a measure indeterministic, as current physics teaches, is wholly irrelevant to the problem.

Of course there is a sense in which one can define a word arbitrarily in any way one pleases. But a definition may nevertheless be called correct or incorrect. It is correct if it accords with a *common usage* of the word defined. It is incorrect if it does not. And if you give an incorrect definition, absurd and untrue results are likely to follow. For instance, there is nothing to prevent you from arbitrarily defining a man as a five-legged animal, but this is incorrect in the sense that it does not accord with the ordinary meaning of the word. Also it has the absurd result of leading to a denial of the existence of men. This shows that *common usage is the criterion for deciding whether a definition is correct or not.* And this is the principle which I shall apply to free will. I shall show that indeterminism is not what is meant by the phrase "free will" *as it is commonly used.* And I shall attempt to discover the correct definition by inquiring how the phrase is used in ordinary conversation.

Here are a few samples of how the phrase might be used in ordinary conversation. It will be noticed that they include cases in which the question whether a man acted with free will is asked in order to determine whether he was morally and legally responsible for his acts.

JONES   I once went without food for a week.

SMITH   Did you do that of your own free will?

JONES   No. I did it because I was lost in a desert and could find no food.

But suppose that the man who had fasted was Mahatma Gandhi. The conversation might then have gone:

GANDHI   I once fasted for a week.

SMITH   Did you do that of your own free will?

GANDHI   Yes. I did it because I wanted to compel the British Government to give India its independence.

Take another case. Suppose that I had stolen some bread, but that I was as truthful as George Washington. Then, if I were charged with the crime in court, some exchange of the following sort might take place:

JUDGE   Did you steal the bread of your own free will?

STACE   Yes. I stole it because I was hungry.

Or in different circumstances the conversation might run:

JUDGE   Did you steal of your own free will?

STACE   No. I stole because my employer threatened to beat me if I did not.

At a recent murder trial in Trenton some of the accused had signed confessions, but afterwards asserted that they had done so under police duress. The following exchange might have occurred:

JUDGE   Did you sign the confession of your own free will?

PRISONER   No. I signed it because the police beat me up.

Now suppose that a philosopher had been a member of the jury. We could imagine this conversation taking place in the jury room.

FOREMAN OF THE JURY   The prisoner says he signed the confession because he was beaten, and not of his own free will.

PHILOSOPHER   This is quite irrelevant to the case. There is no such thing as free will.

FOREMAN   Do you mean to say that it makes no difference whether he signed because his conscience made him want to tell the truth or because he was beaten?

PHILOSOPHER   None at all. Whether he was caused to sign by a beating or by some desire of his own—the desire to tell the truth, for example—in either case his signing was causally determined, and therefore in neither case did he act of his own free will. Since there is no such thing as free will, the question whether he signed of his own free will ought not to be discussed by us.

The foreman and the rest of the jury would rightly conclude that the philosopher must be making some mistake. What sort of a mistake could it be? There is only one possible answer. The philosopher must be using the phrase "free will" in some peculiar way of his own which is not the way in which men usually use it when they wish to determine a question of moral responsibility. That is, he must be using an incorrect definition of it as implying action not determined by causes. Suppose a man left his office at noon, and were questioned about it. Then we might hear this:

JONES   Did you go out of your own free will?

SMITH   Yes. I went out to get my lunch.

But we might hear:

JONES   Did you leave your office of your own free will?

SMITH   No. I was forcibly removed by the police.

We have now collected a number of cases of actions which, in the ordinary usage of the English language, would be called cases in which people have acted of their own free will. We should also say in all these cases that they *chose* to act as they did. We should also say that they could have acted otherwise, if they had chosen. For instance, Mahatma Gandhi was not compelled to fast; he chose to do so. He could have eaten if he had wanted to. When Smith went out to get his lunch, he chose to do so. He could have stayed and done some work, if he had wanted to. We have also collected a number of cases of the opposite kind. They are cases in which men were not able to exercise their free will. They had no choice. They were compelled to do as they did. The man in the desert did not fast of his own free will. He had no choice in the matter. He was compelled to fast because there was nothing for him to eat. And so with the other cases. It ought to be quite easy, by an inspection of these cases, to tell what we ordinarily mean when we say that a man did or did not exercise free will. We ought therefore to be able to extract from them the proper definition of the term. Let us put the cases in a table:

Free Acts	Unfree Acts
Gandhi fasting because he wanted to free India.	The man fasting in the desert because there was no food.
Stealing bread because one is hungry.	Stealing because one's employer threatened to beat one.
Signing a confession because one wanted to tell the truth.	Signing because the police beat one.
Leaving the office because one wanted one's lunch.	Leaving because forcibly removed.

It is obvious that to find the correct definition of free acts we must discover what characteristic is common to all the acts in the left-hand column, and is, at the same time, absent from all the acts in the right-hand column. This characteristic which all free acts have, and which no unfree acts have, will be the defining characteristic of free will.

Is being uncaused, or not being determined by causes, the characteristic of which we are in search? It cannot be, because although it is true that all the acts in the right-hand column have causes, such as the beating by the police or the absence of food in the desert, so also do the acts in the left-hand column. Mr. Gandhi's fasting was caused by his desire to free India, the man leaving his office by his hunger, and so on. Moreover there is no reason to doubt that these causes of the free acts were in turn caused by prior conditions, and that these were again the results of causes, and so on back indefinitely into the past. Any physiologist can tell us the causes of hunger. What caused Mr. Gandhi's tremendously powerful desire to free India is no doubt more difficult to discover. But it must have had causes. Some of them may have lain in peculiarities of his glands or brain, others in his past experiences, others in his heredity, others in his education. Defenders of free will have usually tended to deny such facts. But to do so is plainly a case of special pleading, which is unsupported by any scrap of evidence. The only reasonable view is that all human actions, both those which are freely done and those which are not, are either wholly determined by causes, or at least as much determined as other events in nature. It may be true, as the physicists tell us, that nature is not as deterministic as was once thought. But whatever degree of determinism prevails in the world, human actions appear to be as much determined as anything else. And if this is so, it cannot be the case that what distinguishes actions freely chosen from those which are not free is that the latter are determined by causes while the former are not. Therefore, being uncaused or being undetermined by causes, must be an incorrect definition of free will.

What, then, is the difference between acts which are freely done and those which are not? What is the characteristic which is present to all the acts in the left-hand column and absent from all those in the right-hand column? Is it not obvious that, although both sets of actions have causes, the causes of those in the left-hand column are *of a different kind* from the causes of those in the right-hand column?

The free acts are all caused by desires, or motives, or by some sort of internal psychological states of the agent's mind. The unfree acts, on the other hand, are all caused by physical forces or physical conditions, outside the agent. Police arrest means physical force exerted from the outside; the absence of food in the desert is a physical condition of the outside world. We may therefore frame the following rough definitions. *Acts freely done are those whose immediate causes are psychological states in the agent. Acts not freely done are those whose immediate causes are states of affairs external to the agent.*

It is plain that if we define free will in this way, then free will certainly exists, and the philosopher's denial of its existence is seen to be what it is—nonsense. For it is obvious that all those actions of men which we should ordinarily attribute to the exercise of their free will, or of which we should say that they freely chose to do them, are in fact actions which have been caused by their own desire, wishes, thoughts, emotions, impulses, or other psychological states.

In applying our definition we shall find that it usually works well, but that there are some puzzling cases which it does not seem exactly to fit. These puzzles can always be solved by paying careful attention to the ways in which words are used, and remembering that they are not always used consistently. I have space for only one example. Suppose that a thug threatens to shoot you unless you give him your wallet, and suppose that you do so. Do you, in giving him your wallet, do so of your own free will or not? If we apply our definition, we find that you acted freely, since the immediate cause of the action was not an actual outside force but the fear of death, which is a psychological cause. Most people, however, would say that you did not act of your own free will but under compulsion. Does this show that our definition is wrong? I do not think so. Aristotle, who gave a solution of the problem of free will substantially the same as ours (though he did not use the term "free will") admitted that there are what he called "mixed" or borderline cases in which it is difficult to know whether we ought to call the acts free or compelled. In the case under discussion, though no actual force was used, the gun at your forehead so nearly approximated to actual force that we tend to say the case was one of compulsion. It is a borderline case.

Here is what may seem like another kind of puzzle. According to our view an action may be free though it could have been predicted beforehand with certainty. But suppose you told a lie, and it was certain beforehand that you would tell it. How could one then say, "You could have told the truth"? The answer is that it is perfectly true that you could have told the truth *if* you had wanted to. In fact you would have done so, for in that case the causes producing your action, namely your desires, would have been different, and would therefore have produced different effects. It is a delusion that predictability and free will are incompatible. This agrees with common sense. For if, knowing your character, I predict that you will act honorably, no one would say when you do act honorably, that this shows you did not do so of your own free will.

Since free will is a condition of moral responsibility, we must be sure that our theory of free will gives a sufficient basis for it. To be held morally responsible for one's actions means that one may be justly punished or rewarded, blamed or praised, for them. But it is not just to punish a man for what he cannot help doing. How can it be just to punish him for an action which it was certain beforehand that he would do? We have not attempted to decide whether, as a matter of fact, all events, including human actions, are completely determined. For that question is irrelevant to the problem of free will. But if we assume for the purposes of argument that complete determinism is true, but that we are nevertheless free, it may then be asked whether such a deterministic free will is compatible with moral responsibility. For it may seem unjust to punish a man for an action which it could have been predicted with certainty beforehand that he would do.

But that determinism is incompatible with moral responsibility is as much a delusion as that it is incompatible with free will. You do not excuse a man for doing a wrong act because, knowing his character, you felt certain beforehand that he would do it. Nor do you deprive a man of a reward or prize because, knowing his goodness or his capabilities, you felt certain beforehand that he would win it.

Volumes have been written on the justification of punishment. But so far as it affects the question of free will, the essential principles involved are quite simple. The punishment of a man for doing a wrong act is justified, either on the ground that it will correct his own character, or that it will deter other people from doing similar acts. The instrument of punishment has been in the past, and no doubt still is, often unwisely used; so that it may often have done more harm than good. But that is not relevant to our present problem. Punishment, if and when it is justified, is justified only on one or both of the grounds just mentioned. The question then is how, if we assume determinism, punishment can correct character or deter people from evil actions.

Suppose that your child develops a habit of telling lies. You give him a mild beating. Why? Because you believe that his personality is such that the usual motives for telling the truth do not cause him to do so. You therefore supply the missing cause, or motive, in the shape of pain and the fear of future pain if he repeats his untrustful behavior. And you hope that a few treatments of this kind will condition him to the habit of truth-telling, so that he will come to tell the truth without the infliction of pain. You assume that his actions are determined by causes, but that the usual causes of truth-telling do not in him produce their usual effects. You therefore supply him with an artificially injected motive, pain and fear, which you think will in the future cause him to speak truthfully.

The principle is exactly the same where you hope, by punishing one man, to deter others from wrong actions. You believe that the fear of punishment will cause those who might otherwise do evil to do well.

We act on the same principle with non-human, and even with inanimate, things, if they do not behave in the way we think they ought to behave. The rose bushes in the garden produce only small and poor blooms, whereas we want large and rich ones. We supply a cause which will produce large blooms, namely fertilizer. Our automobile does not go properly. We supply a cause which will make it go better, namely oil in the works. The punishment for the man, the fertilizer for the plant, and the oil for the car, are all justified by the same principle and in the same way. The only difference is that different kinds of things require different kinds of causes to make them do what they should. Pain may be the appropriate remedy to apply, in certain cases, to human beings, and oil to the machine. It is, of course, of no use to inject motor oil into the boy or to beat the machine.

Thus we see that moral responsibility is not only consistent with determinism, but requires it. The assumption on which punishment is based is that human behavior is causally determined. If pain could not be a cause of truth-telling there would be no justification at all for punishing lies. If human actions and volitions were uncaused, it would be useless either to punish or reward, or indeed to do anything else to correct people's bad behavior. For nothing that you could do would in any way influence them. Thus moral responsibility would entirely disappear. If there were no determinism of human beings at all, their actions would be completely unpredictable and capricious, and therefore irresponsible. And this is in itself a strong argument against the common view of philosophers that free will means being undetermined by causes.

CONTEMPORARY ISSUES
The Control of Men

5. *Walden Two: Selections*

B. F. Skinner

Burrhus Frederic Skinner (1904–1990), who taught psychology at Harvard University, was one of America's most prominent psychologists. He was known both for his defense of behaviorism and his experimentation with modern teaching devices.

[The participants in the following discussion are Frazier, the founder of Walden Two; Castle, a philosopher who is skeptical of the society's achievements and purposes; and Professor Burris, the narrator of the discussion, who is trying objectively to evaluate Frazier's new society. -Ed.]

"Each of us," Frazier began, "is engaged in a pitched battle with the rest of mankind."

"A curious premise for a Utopia," said Castle. "Even a pessimist like myself takes a more hopeful view than that."

"You do, you do," said Frazier. "But let's be realistic. Each of us has interests which conflict with the interest of everybody else. That's our original sin, and it can't be helped. Now, 'everybody else' we call 'society.' It's a powerful opponent, and it always wins. Oh, here and there an individual prevails for a while and gets what he wants. Sometimes he storms the culture of a society and changes it slightly to his own advantage. But society wins in the long run, for it has the advantage of numbers and of age. Many prevail against one, and men against a baby. Society attacks early, when the individual is helpless. It enslaves him almost before he has tasted freedom. The 'ologies' will tell you how it's done. Theology calls it building a conscience or developing a spirit of selflessness. Psychology calls it the growth of the super-ego.

"Considering how long society has been at it, you'd expect a better job. But the campaigns have been badly planned and the victory has never been secure. The behavior of the individual has been shaped according to revelations of 'good conduct,' never as the result of experimental study. But why not experiment? The questions are simple enough. What's the best behavior for the individual so far as the

From *Walden Two* by B. F. Skinner, © 1976. Reprinted by permission of Prentice-Hall, Inc., Upper Saddle River, NJ.

group is concerned? And how can the individual be induced to behave in that way? Why not explore these questions in a scientific spirit?

"We could do just that in Walden Two. We had already worked out a code of conduct—subject, of course, to experimental modification. The code would keep things running smoothly if everybody lived up to it. Our job was to see that everybody did. Now, you can't get people to follow a useful code by making them into so many jacks-in-the-box. You can't foresee all future circumstances, and you can't specify adequate future conduct. You don't know what will be required. Instead you have to set up certain behavioral processes which will lead the individual to design his own 'good' conduct when the time comes. We call that sort of thing 'self-control.' But don't be misled, the control always rests in the last analysis in the hands of society.

"One of our Planners, a young man named Simmons, worked with me. It was the first time in history that the matter was approached in an experimental way. Do you question that statement, Mr. Castle?"

"I'm not sure I know what you are talking about," said Castle.

"Then let me go on. Simmons and I began by studying the great works on morals and ethics—Plato, Aristotle, Confucius, the New Testament, the Puritan divines, Machiavelli, Chesterfield, Freud—there were scores of them. We were looking for any and every method of shaping human behavior by imparting techniques of self-control. Some techniques were obvious enough, for they had marked turning points in human history. 'Love your enemies' is an example—a psychological invention for easing the lot of an oppressed people. The severest trial of oppression is the constant rage which one suffers at the thought of the oppressor. What Jesus discovered was how to avoid these inner devastations. His technique was to *practice the opposite emotion.* If a man can succeed in 'loving his enemies' and 'taking no thought for the morrow,' he will no longer be assailed by hatred of the oppressor or rage at the loss of his freedom or possessions. He may not get his freedom or possessions back, but he's less miserable. It's a difficult lesson. It comes late in our program."

"I thought you were opposed to modifying emotions and instincts until the world was ready for it," said Castle. "According to you, the principle of 'love your enemies' should have been suicidal."

"It would have been suicidal, except for an entirely unforeseen consequence. Jesus must have been quite astonished at the effect of his discovery. We are only just beginning to understand the power of love because we are just beginning to understand the weakness of force and aggression. But the science of behavior is clear about all that now. Recent discoveries in the analysis of punishment—but I am falling into one digression after another. Let me save my explanation of why the Christian virtues—and I mean merely the Christian techniques of self-control—have not disappeared from the face of the earth, with due recognition of the fact that they suffered a narrow squeak within recent memory.

"When Simmons and I had collected our techniques of control, we had to discover how to teach them. That was more difficult. Current educational practices were of little value, and religious practices scarcely any better. Promising paradise or threatening hell-fire is, we assumed, generally admitted to be unproductive. It is based upon a fundamental fraud which, when discovered, turns the individual against society and nourishes the very thing it tries to stamp out. What Jesus offered in return for loving one's enemies was heaven *on earth*, better known as peace of mind.

"We found a few suggestions worth following in the practices of the clinical psychologist. We undertook to build a tolerance for annoying experiences. The sunshine of midday is extremely painful if you come from a dark room, but take it in easy stages and you can avoid pain altogether. The analogy can be misleading, but in much the same way it's possible to build a tolerance to painful or distasteful stimuli, or to frustration, or to situations which arouse fear, anger or rage. Society and nature throw these annoyances at the individual with no regard for the development of tolerances. Some achieve tolerances, most fail. Where would the science of immunization be if it followed a schedule of accidental dosages?

"Take the principle of 'Get thee behind me, Satan,' for example," Frazier continued. "It's a special case of self-control by altering the environment. Subclass A 3, I believe. We give each child a lollipop which has been dipped in powdered sugar so that a single touch of the tongue can be detected. We tell him he may eat the lollipop later in the day, provided it hasn't already been licked. Since the child is only three or four, it is a fairly diff—"

"Three or four!" Castle exclaimed.

"All our ethical training is completed by the age of six," said Frazier quietly. "A simple principle like putting temptation out of sight would be acquired before four. But at such an early age the problem of not licking the lollipop isn't easy. Now, what would you do, Mr. Castle, in a similar situation?"

"Put the lollipop out of sight as quickly as possible."

"Exactly. I can see you've been well trained. Or perhaps you discovered the principle for yourself. We're in favor of original inquiry wherever possible, but in this case we have a more important goal and we don't hesitate to give verbal help. First of all, the children are urged to examine their own behavior while looking at the lollipops. This helps them to recognize the need for self-control. Then the lollipops are concealed, and the children are asked to notice any gain in happiness or any reduction in tension. Then a strong distraction is arranged—say, an interesting game. Later the children are reminded of the candy and encouraged to examine their reaction. The value of the distraction is generally obvious. Well, need I go on? When the experiment is repeated a day or so later, the children all run with the lollipops to their lockers and do exactly what Mr. Castle would do—a sufficient indication of the success of our training."

"I wish to report an objective observation of my reaction to your story," said Castle, controlling his voice with great precision. "I find myself revolted by this display of sadistic tyranny."

"I don't wish to deny you the exercise of an emotion which you seem to find enjoyable," said Frazier. "So let me go on. Concealing a tempting but forbidden object is a crude solution. For one thing, it's not always feasible. We want a sort of psychological concealment—covering up the candy by paying no attention. In a later experiment the children wear their lollipops like crucifixes for a few hours."

> Instead of the cross, the lollipop,
> About my neck was hung.

said Castle. . . .

"How do you build up a tolerance to an annoying situation?" I said.

"Oh, for example, by having the children 'take' a more and more painful shock, or drink cocoa with less and less sugar in it until a bitter concoction can be savored without a bitter face."

"But jealousy or envy—you can't administer them in graded doses," I said.

"And why not? Remember, we control the social environment, too, at this age. That's why we get our ethical training in early. Take this case. A group of children arrive home after a long walk tired and hungry. They're expecting supper; they find, instead, that it's time for a lesson in self-control: they must stand for five minutes in front of steaming bowls of soup.

"The assignment is accepted like a problem in arithmetic. Any groaning or complaining is a wrong answer. Instead, the children begin at once to work upon themselves to avoid any unhappiness during the delay. One of them may make a joke of it. We encourage a sense of humor as a good way of not taking an annoyance seriously. The joke won't be much, according to adult standards—perhaps the child will simply pretend to empty the bowl of soup into his upturned mouth. Another may start a song with many verses. The rest join in at once, for they've learned that it's a good way to make time pass."

Frazier glanced uneasily at Castle, who was not to be appeased.

"That also strikes you as a form of torture, Mr. Castle?" he asked.

"I'd rather be put on the rack," said Castle.

"Then you have by no means had the thorough training I supposed. You can't imagine how lightly the children take such an experience. It's a rather severe biological frustration, for the children are tired and hungry and they must stand and look at food; but it's passed off as lightly as a five-minute delay at curtain time. We regard it as a fairly elementary test. Much more difficult problems follow."

"I suspected as much," muttered Castle.

"In a later stage we forbid all social devices. No songs, no jokes—merely silence. Each child is forced back upon his own resources—a very important step."

"I should think so," I said."And how do you know it's successful? You might produce a lot of silently resentful children. It's certainly a dangerous stage."

"It is, and we follow each child carefully. If he hasn't picked up the necessary techniques, we start back a little. A still more advanced stage"—Frazier glanced again at Castle, who stirred uneasily—"brings me to my point. When it's time to sit down to the soup, the children count off—heads and tails. Then a coin is tossed and if it comes up heads, the 'heads' sit down and eat. The 'tails' remain standing for another five minutes."

Castle groaned.

"And you call that envy?" I asked.

"Perhaps not exactly," said Frazier. "At least there's seldom any aggression against the lucky ones. The emotion, if any, is directed against Lady Luck herself, against the toss of the coin. That, in itself, is a lesson worth learning, for it's the only direction in which emotion has a surviving chance to be useful. And resentment toward things in general, while perhaps just as silly as personal aggression, is more easily controlled. Its expression is not socially objectionable." . . .

"May you not inadvertently teach your children some of the very emotions you're trying to eliminate?" I said. "What's the effect, for example, of finding the anticipation of a warm supper suddenly thwarted? Doesn't that eventually lead to feelings of uncertainty, or even anxiety?"

"It might. We had to discover how often our lessons could be safely administered. But all our schedules are worked out experimentally. We watch for undesired consequences just as any scientist watches for disrupting factors in his experiments.

"After all, it's a simple and sensible program," he went on in a tone of appeasement. "We set up a system of gradually increasing annoyances and frustrations against a background of complete serenity. An easy environment is made more and more difficult as the children acquire the capacity to adjust."

"But *why?*" said Castle. "Why these deliberate unpleasantnesses—to put it mildly? I must say I think you and your friend Simmons are really very subtle sadists."

"You've reversed your position, Mr. Castle," said Frazier in a sudden flash of anger with which I rather sympathized. Castle was calling names, and he was also being unaccountably and perhaps intentionally obtuse. "A while ago you accused me of breeding a race of softies," Frazier continued. "Now you object to toughening them up. But what you don't understand is that these potentially unhappy situations are never very annoying. Our schedules make sure of that. You wouldn't understand, however, because you're not so far advanced as our children."

Castle grew black.

"But what do your children get out of it?" he insisted, apparently trying to press some vague advantage in Frazier's anger.

"What do they get out of it!" exclaimed Frazier, his eyes flashing with a sort of helpless contempt. His lips curled and he dropped his head to look at his fingers, which were crushing a few blades of grass.

"They must get happiness and freedom and strength," I said, putting myself in a ridiculous position in attempting to make peace.

"They don't sound happy or free to me, standing in front of bowls of Forbidden Soup," said Castle, answering me parenthetically while continuing to stare at Frazier.

"If I must spell it out," Frazier began with a deep sigh, "what they get is escape from the petty emotions which eat the heart out of the unprepared. They get the satisfaction of pleasant and profitable social relations on a scale almost undreamed of in the world at large. They get immeasurably increased efficiency, because they can stick to a job without suffering the aches and pains which soon

beset most of us. They get new horizons, for they are spared the emotions characteristic of frustration and failure. They get—" His eyes searched the branches of
the trees. "Is that enough?" he said at last.

"And the community must gain their loyalty," I said, "when they discover
the fears and jealousies and diffidence in the world at large."

"I'm glad you put it that way," said Frazier. "You might have said that they
must feel superior to the miserable products of our public schools. But we're at
pains to keep any feeling of superiority or contempt under control, too. Having
suffered most acutely from it myself, I put the subject first on our agenda. We carefully avoid any joy in a personal triumph which means the personal failure of somebody else. We take no pleasure in the sophistical, the disputative, the dialectical."
He threw a vicious glance at Castle. "We don't use the motive of domination,
because we are always thinking of the whole group. We could motivate a few
geniuses that way—it was certainly my own motivation—but we'd sacrifice some
of the happiness of everyone else. Triumph over nature and over oneself, yes. But
over others, never."

"You've taken the mainspring out of the watch," said Castle flatly.

"That's an experimental question, Mr. Castle, and you have the wrong
answer." . . .

"Are your techniques really so very new?" I said hurriedly. "What about the
primitive practice of submitting a boy to various tortures before granting him a
place among adults? What about the disciplinary techniques of Puritanism? Or of
the modern school, for that matter?"

"In one sense you're right," said Frazier, "And I think you've nicely
answered Mr. Castle's tender concern for our little ones. The unhappinesses we
deliberately impose are far milder than the normal unhappinesses from which
we offer protection. Even at the height of our ethical training, the unhappiness
is ridiculously trivial—to the well-trained child.

"But there's a world of difference in the way we use these annoyances,"
he continued. "For one thing, we don't punish. We never administer an unpleasantness in the hope of repressing or eliminating undesirable behavior. But there's
another difference. In most cultures the child meets up with annoyances and
reverses of uncontrolled magnitude. Some are imposed in the name of discipline
by persons in authority. Some, like hazings, are condoned though not authorized.
Others are merely accidental. No one cares to, or is able to, prevent them.

"We all know what happens. A few hardy children emerge, particularly
those who have got their unhappiness in doses that could be swallowed. They
become brave men. Others become sadists or masochists of varying degrees of
pathology. Not having conquered a painful environment, they become preoccupied with pain and make a devious art of it. Others submit—and hope to inherit the
earth. The rest—the cravens, the cowards—live in fear for the rest of their lives.
And that's only a single field—the reaction to pain. I could cite a dozen parallel
cases. The optimist and the pessimist, the contented and the disgruntled, the loved
and the unloved, the ambitious and the discouraged—these are only the extreme
products of a miserable system.

"Traditional practices are admittedly better than nothing," Frazier went on. "Spartan or Puritan—no one can question the occasional happy result. But the whole system rests upon the wasteful principle of selection. The English public school of the nineteenth century produced brave men—by setting up almost insurmountable barrier and making the most of the few who came over. But selection isn't education. Its crops of brave men will always be small, and the waste enormous. Like all primitive principles, selection serves in place of education only through a profligate use of material. Multiply extravagantly and select with rigor. It's the philosophy of the 'big litter' as an alternative to good child hygiene.

"In Walden Two we have a different objective. We make every man a brave man. They all come over the barriers. Some require more preparation than others, but they all come over. The traditional use of adversity is to select the strong. We control adversity to build strength. And we do it deliberately, no matter how sadistic Mr. Castle may think us, in order to prepare for adversities which are beyond control. Our children eventually experience the 'heartache and the thousand natural shocks that flesh is heir to.' It would be the cruelest possible practice to protect them as long as possible, especially when we *could* protect them so well."

Frazier held out his hands in an exaggerated gesture of appeal.

"What alternative *had* we?" he said, as if he were in pain. "What else could we do? For four or five years we could provide a life in which no important need would go unsatisfied, a life practically free of anxiety or frustration or annoyance. What would *you* do? Would you let the child enjoy this paradise with no thought for the future—like an idolatrous and pampering mother? Or would you relax control of the environment and let the child meet accidental frustrations? *But what is the virtue of accident?* No, there was only one course open to us. We had to design a series of adversities, so that the child would develop the greatest possible self-control. Call it deliberate, if you like, and accuse us of sadism; there was no other course." . . .

"A modern, mechanized, managerial Machiavelli—that is my final estimate of you, Mr. Frazier," he [Castle] said, with the same challenging stare.

"It must be gratifying to know that one has reached a 'final estimate,'" said Frazier:

"An artist in power," Castle continued, "whose greatest art is to conceal art. The silent despot."

"Since we are dealing in 'M's.' why not sum it all up and say 'Mephistophelian'?" said Frazier, curiously reviving my fears of the preceding afternoon.

"I'm willing to do that!" said Castle. "And unless God is very sure of himself, I suspect He's by no means easy about this latest turn in the war of the angels. So far as I can see, you've blocked every path through which man was to struggle upward toward salvation. Intelligence, initiative—you have filled their places with a sort of degraded instinct, engineered compulsion. Walden Two is a marvel of efficient coordination—as efficient as an anthill!"

"Replacing intelligence with instinct—" muttered Frazier. "I had never thought of that. It's an interesting possibility. How's it done?" It was a crude maneuver. The question was a digression, intended to spoil Castle's timing and to direct our attention to practical affairs in which Frazier was more at home.

"The behavior of your members is carefully shaped in advance by a Plan," said Castle, not to be taken in, "and it's shaped to perpetuate that Plan. Intellectually Walden Two is quite as incapable of a spontaneous change of course as the life within a beehive."

"I see what you mean," said Frazier distantly. But he returned to his strategy. "And have you discovered the machinery of my power?"

"I have, indeed. We were looking in the wrong place. There's no *current* contact between you and the members of Walden Two. You threw us off the track very skillfully on that point last night. But you were behaving as a despot when you first laid your plans—when you designed the social structure and drew up the contract between community and member, when you worked out your educational practices and your guarantees against despotism—What a joke! Don't tell me you weren't in control *then!* Burris saw the point. What about your career as organizer? *There* was leadership! And the most damnable leadership in history, because you were setting the stage for the withdrawal of yourself as a personal force, knowing full well that everything that happened would still be your doing. Hundreds—you predicted millions—of unsuspecting souls were to fall within the scope of your ambitious scheme."

Castle was driving his argument home with great excitement, but Frazier way lying in exaggerated relaxation, staring at the ceiling, his hands cupped behind his head.

"Very good, Mr. Castle," he said softly. "I gave you the due, of course, when we parted last night."

"You did, indeed. And I've wondered why. Were you led into that fatal error by your conceit? Perhaps that's the ultimate answer to your form of despotism. No one could enjoy the power you have seized without wishing to display it from time to time."

"I've admitted neither power nor despotism. But you're quite right in saying that I've exerted an influence and in one sense will continue to exert it forever. I believe you called me a *primum mobile*—not quite correctly, as I found upon looking the term up last night. But I did plan Walden Two—not as an architect plans a building, but as a scientist plans a long-term experiment, uncertain of the conditions he will meet but knowing how he will deal with them when they arise. In a sense, Walden Two is predetermined, but not as the behavior of a beehive is determined. Intelligence, no matter how much it may be shaped and extended by our educational system, will still function as intelligence. It will be used to puzzle out solutions to problems to which a beehive would quickly succumb. What the plan does is to keep intelligence on the right track, for the good of society rather than of the intelligent individual—or for the eventual rather than the immediate good of the individual. It does this by making sure that the individual will not forget his personal stake in the welfare of society."

"But you are forestalling many possibly useful acts of intelligence which aren't encompassed by your plan. You have ruled out points of view which may be more productive. You are implying that T. E. Frazier, looking at the world from the middle of the twentieth century, understands the best course for mankind forever."

"Yes, I suppose I do."

"But that's absurd!"

"Not at all. I don't say I foresee the course man will take a hundred years hence, let alone forever, but I know which he should take now."

"How can you be sure of it? It's certainly not a question you have answered experimentally."

"I think we're in the course of answering it," said Frazier. "But that's beside the point. There's no alternative. We must take that course."

"But that's fantastic. You who are taking it are in a small minority."

Frazier sat up.

"And the majority are in a big quandary," he said. "They're not on the road at all, or they're scrambling back toward their starting point, or sidling from one side of the road to the other like so many crabs. What do you think two world wars have been about? Something as simple as boundaries or trade? Nonsense. The world is trying to adjust to a new conception of man in relation to men."

"Perhaps it's merely trying to adjust to despots whose ideas are incompatible with the real nature of man."

"Mr. Castle," said Frazier very earnestly, "let me ask you a question. I warn you, it will be the most terrifying question of your life. *What would you do if you found yourself in possession of an effective science of behavior?* Suppose you suddenly found it possible to control the behavior of men as you wished. What would you do?"

"That's an assumption?"

"Take it as one if you like. I take it as a fact. And apparently you accept it as a fact too. I can hardly be as despotic as you claim unless I hold the key to an extensive practical control."

"What would I do?" said Castle thoughtfully. "I think I would dump your science of behavior in the ocean."

"And deny men all the help you could otherwise give them?"

"And give them the freedom they would otherwise lose forever!"

"How could you give them freedom?"

"By refusing to control them!"

"But you would only be leaving the control in other hands."

"Whose?"

"The charlatan, the demagogue, the salesman, the ward heeler, the bully, the cheat, the educator, the priest—all who are now in possession of the techniques of behavioral engineering."

"A pretty good share of the control would remain in the hands of the individual himself."

"That's an assumption, too, and it's your only hope. It's your only possible chance to avoid the implications of a science of behavior. If man is free, then a technology of behavior is impossible. But I'm asking you to consider the other case."

"Then my answer is that your assumption is contrary to fact and any further consideration idle."

"And your accusations—?"

"—were in terms of intention, not of possible achievement."

Frazier sighed dramatically.

"It's a little late to be proving that a behavioral technology is well advanced. How can you deny it? Many of its methods and techniques are really as old as the hills. Look at their frightful misuse in the hands of the Nazis! And what about the techniques of the psychological clinic? What about education? Or religion? Or practical politics? Or advertising and salesmanship? Bring them all together and you have a sort of rule-of-thumb technology of vast power. No, Mr. Castle, the science is there for the asking. But its techniques and methods are in the wrong hands—they are used for personal aggrandizement in a competitive world or, in the case of psychologist and educator, for futilely corrective purposes. My question is, have you the courage to take up and wield the science of behavior for the good of mankind? You answer that you would dump it in the ocean!"

"I'd want to take it out of the hands of the politicians and advertisers and salesmen, too."

"And the psychologists and educators? You see, Mr. Castle, you can't have that kind of cake. The fact is, we not only *can* control human behavior, we *must*. But who's to do it, and what's to be done?"

"So long as a trace of personal freedom survives, I'll stick to my position," said Castle, very much out of countenance.

"Isn't it time we talked about freedom?" I said. "We parted a day or so ago on an agreement to let the question of freedom ring. It's time to answer, don't you think?"

"My answer is simple enough," said Frazier "I deny that freedom exists at all. I must deny it—or my program would be absurd. You can't have a science about a subject matter which hops capriciously about. Perhaps we can never *prove* that man isn't free; it's an assumption. But the increasing success of a science of behavior makes it more and more plausible."

"On the contrary, a simple personal experience makes it untenable," said Castle. "The experience of freedom. I *know* that I'm free."

"It must be quite consoling," said Frazier.

"And what's more—you do, too," said Castle hotly. "When you deny your own freedom for the sake of playing with a science of behavior, you're acting in plain bad faith. That's the only way I can explain it." He tried to recover himself and shrugged his shoulders." At least you'll grant that you *feel* free."

"The 'feeling of freedom' should deceive no one," said Frazier. "Give me a concrete case."

"Well, right now," Castle said. He picked up a book of matches. "I'm free to hold or drop these matches."

"You will, of course, do one or the other," said Frazier. "Linguistically or logically there seem to be two possibilities, but I submit that there's only one in fact. The determining forces may be subtle but they are inexorable. I suggest that as an orderly person you will probably hold—ah! you drop them! Well, you see, that's all part of your behavior with respect to me. You couldn't resist the temptation to prove me wrong. It was all lawful. You had no choice. The deciding factor entered rather late, and naturally you couldn't foresee the result when you first held them up. There was no strong likelihood that you would act in either direction, and so you said you were free."

"That's entirely too glib," said Castle. "It's easy to argue lawfulness after the fact. But let's see you predict what I will do in advance. Then I'll agree there's law."

"I didn't say that behavior is always predictable, any more than the weather is always predictable. There are often too many factors to be taken into account. We can't measure them all accurately, and we couldn't perform the mathematical operations needed to make a prediction if we had the measurements. The legality is usually an assumption—but none the less important in judging the issue at hand."

"Take a case where there's no choice, then," said Castle. "Certainly a man in jail isn't free in the sense in which I am free now."

"Good! That's an excellent start. Let us classify the kinds of determiners of human behavior. One class, as you suggest, is physical restraint—handcuffs, iron bars, forcible coercion. These are ways in which we shape human behavior according to our wishes. They're crude, and they sacrifice the affection of the controller, but they often work. Now, what other ways are there of limiting freedom?"

Frazier had adopted a professorial tone and Castle refused to answer.

"The threat of force would be one," I said.

"Right. And here again we shan't encourage any loyalty on the part of the controller. He has perhaps a shade more of the feeling of freedom, since he can always 'choose to act and accept the consequences,' but he doesn't feel exactly free. He knows his behavior is being coerced. Now what else?"

I had no answer.

"Force or the threat of force—I see no other possibility," said Castle after a moment.

"Precisely," said Frazier.

"But certainly a large part of my behavior has no connection with force at all. There's my freedom!" said Castle.

"I wasn't agreeing that there was no other possibility—merely that *you* could see no other. Not being a good behaviorist—or a good Christian, for that matter—you have no feeling for a tremendous power of a different sort."

"What's that?"

"I shall have to be technical," said Frazier. "But only for a moment. It's what the science of behavior calls 'reinforcement theory.' The things that can happen to us fall into three classes. To some things we are indifferent. Other things we like—we want them to happen, and we take steps to make them happen again. Still other things we don't like—we don't want them to happen and we take steps to get rid of them or keep them from happening again.

"*Now,*" Frazier continued earnestly, "if it's in our power to create any of the situations which a person likes or to remove any situation he doesn't like, we can control his behavior. When he behaves as we want him to behave, we simply create a situation he likes, or remove one he doesn't like. As a result, the probability that he will behave that way again goes up, which is what we want. Technically it's called 'positive reinforcement.'

"The old school made the amazing mistake of supposing that the reverse was true, that by removing a situation a person likes or setting up one he doesn't like—in other words by punishing him—it was possible to *reduce* the probability that he would behave in a given way again. That simply doesn't hold. It has been established beyond question. What is emerging at this critical stage in the evolution of society is a behavioral and cultural technology based on positive reinforcement alone. We are gradually discovering—at an untold cost in human suffering—that in the long run punishment doesn't reduce the probability that an act will occur. We have been so preoccupied with the contrary that we always take 'force' to mean punishment. We don't say we're using force when we send shiploads of food into a starving country, though we're displaying quite as much power as if we were sending troops and guns."

"I'm certainly not an advocate of force," said Castle. "But I can't agree that it's not effective."

"It's *temporarily* effective, that's the worst of it. That explains several thousand years of bloodshed. Even nature has been fooled. We 'instinctively' punish a person who doesn't behave as we like—we spank him if he's a child or strike him if he's a man. A nice distinction! The immediate effect of the blow teaches us to strike again. Retribution and revenge are the most natural things on earth. But in the long run the man we strike is no less likely to repeat his act."

"But he won't repeat it if we hit him hard enough," said Castle.

"He'll still *tend* to repeat it. He'll *want* to repeat it. We haven't really altered his potential behavior at all. That's the pity of it. If he doesn't repeat it in our presence, he will in the presence of someone else. Or it will be repeated in the disguise of a neurotic symptom. If we hit hard enough, we clear a little place for ourselves in the wilderness of civilization, but we make the rest of the wilderness still more terrible.

"Now, early forms of government are naturally based on punishment. It's the obvious technique when the physically strong control the weak. But we're in the throes of a great change to positive reinforcement—from a competitive society in which one man's reward is another man's punishment, to a cooperative society in which no one gains at the expense of anyone else.

"The change is slow and painful because the immediate, temporary effect of punishment overshadows the eventual advantage of positive reinforcement. We've all seen countless instances of the temporary effect of force, but clear evidence of the effect of not using force is rare. That's why I insist that Jesus, who was apparently the first to discover the power of refusing to punish, must have hit upon the principle by accident. He certainly had none of the experimental evidence which is available to us today, and I can't conceive that it was possible, no matter what the man's genius, to have discovered the principle from casual observation."

"A touch of revelation, perhaps?" said Castle.

"No, accident. Jesus discovered one principle because it had immediate consequences, and he got another thrown in for good measure."

I began to see light.

"You mean the principle of 'love your enemies'?" I said.

"Exactly! To 'do good to those who despitefully use you' has two unrelated consequences. You gain the peace of mind we talked about the other day. Let the stronger man push you around—at least you avoid the torture of your own rage. *That's* the immediate consequence. What an astonishing discovery it must have been to find that in the long run you could *control the stronger man* in the same way!"

"It's generous of you to give so much credit to your early colleague," said Castle, "but why are we still in the throes of so much misery? Twenty centuries should have been enough for one piece of behavioral engineering."

"The conditions which made the principle difficult to discover made it difficult to teach. The history of the Christian Church doesn't reveal many cases of doing good to one's enemies. To inoffensive heathens, perhaps, but not enemies. One must look outside the field of organized religion to find the principle in practice at all. Church governments are devotees of *power*, both temporal and bogus."

"But what has all this got to do with freedom?" I said hastily.

Frazier took time to reorganize his behavior. He looked steadily toward the window, against which the rain was beating heavily.

"Now that we *know* how positive reinforcement works and why negative doesn't," he said at last, "we can be more deliberate, and hence more successful, in our cultural design. We can achieve a sort of control under which the controlled, though they are following a code much more scrupulously than was ever the case under the old system, nevertheless *feel free*. They are doing what they want to do, not what they are forced to do. That's the source of the tremendous power of positive reinforcement—there's no restraint and no revolt. By a careful cultural design, we control not the final behavior, but the inclination to behave—the motives, the desires, the wishes.

"The curious thing is that in that case *the question of freedom never arises*. Mr. Castle was free to drop the matchbook in the sense that nothing was preventing him. If it had been securely bound to his hand he wouldn't have been free. Nor would he have been quite free if I'd covered him with a gun and threatened to shoot him if he let it fall. The question of freedom arises when there is restraint—either physical or psychological.

"But restraint is only one sort of control, and absence of restraint isn't freedom. It's not control that's lacking when one feels 'free,' but the objectionable control of force. Mr. Castle felt free to hold or drop the matches in the sense that he felt no restraint—no threat of punishment in taking either course of action. He neglected to examine his positive reasons for holding or letting go, in spite of the fact that these were more compelling in this instance than any threat of force.

"We have no vocabulary of freedom in dealing with what we want to do," Frazier went on. "The question never arises. When men strike for freedom they strike against jails and the police, or the threat of them—against oppression. They never strike against forces which make them want to act the way they do. Yet, it seems to be understood that governments will operate only through force or the threat of force, and that all other principles of control will be left to education, religion, and commerce. If this continues to be the case, we may as well give up. A government can never create a free people with the techniques now allotted to it.

"The question is: Can men live in freedom and peace? And the answer is: Yes, if we can build a social structure which will satisfy the needs of everyone and in which everyone will want to observe the supporting code. But so far this has been achieved only in Walden Two. Your ruthless accusations to the contrary, Mr. Castle, this is the freest place on earth. And it is free precisely because we make no use of force or the threat of force. Every bit of our research, from the nursery through the psychological management of our adult membership, is directed toward that end—to exploit every alternative to forcible control. By skillful planning, by a wise choice of techniques we *increase* the feeling of freedom.

"It's not planning which infringes upon freedom, but planning which uses force. A sense of freedom was practically unknown in the planned society of Nazi Germany, because the planners made a fantastic use of force and the threat of force.

"No, Mr. Castle, when a science of behavior has once been achieved, there's no alternative to a planned society. We can't leave mankind to an accidental or biased control. But by using the principle of positive reinforcement—carefully avoiding force or the threat of force—we can preserve a personal sense of freedom."

6. Ignoble Utopias

Joseph Wood Krutch

Joseph Wood Krutch (1893–1970) was a philosopher, essayist, and naturalist. He taught English at Columbia until the early 1950s, when he moved to the Arizona desert. The Measure of Man *is generally considered his most important philosophical work.*

Walden Two is a utopian community created by an experimental psychologist named Frazier who has learned the techniques for controlling thought with precision and who has conditioned his subjects to be happy, obedient and incapable of antisocial behavior. Universal benevolence and large tolerance of individual differences reign—not because it is assumed, as the founders of such utopias generally do assume, that they are natural to all innocent men uncorrupted by society—but because an experimental scientist, having at last mastered the "scientific ability to control men's thoughts with precision," has caused them to think benevolently and tolerantly.

An appeal to reason in contradistinction to passion, habit, or mere custom has been the usual basis of utopias from Plato to Sir Thomas More and even down to Samuel Butler. Mr. Skinner's is, on the other hand, distinctly modern in that it puts its faith in the conditioned reflex instead, and proposes to perfect mankind by making individual men incapable of anything except habit and prejudice. At Walden Two men behave in a fashion we are accustomed to call "reasonable," not because they reason, but because they do not; because "right responses" are automatic. At the very beginning of the story we are shown a flock of sheep confined to the area reserved for them by a single thread which long ago replaced the electric fence once employed to condition them not to wander. As predicted in official Communist theory, the State—represented here by electricity—has "withered away" and no actual restraint is necessary to control creatures in whom obedience has become automatic. Obviously the assumption is that what will work with sheep will work with men.

Now, though men can reason, they are not exclusively reasoning creatures. None, therefore, of the classic utopias could be realized because each is based on the assumption that reason alone can be made to guide human behavior. Moreover—and what is perhaps more important—few people have ever seriously wished to be exclusively rational. The good life which most desire is a life warmed by passions and touched with that ceremonial grace which is impossible without some affectionate loyalty to traditional forms and ceremonies. Many have, nevertheless, been

Reprinted with permission of Simon & Schuster from *The Measure of Man* by Joseph Wood Krutch. Copyright © 1954 by Joseph Wood Krutch, renewed 1982 by Marcelle Krutch.

very willing to grant that a little more reason in the conduct of private and public affairs would not be amiss. That is why, as fantasies, the utopias of Plato and Sir Thomas More have seemed interesting, instructive, even inspiring. But who really wants, even in fancy, to be, as Walden Two would make him, more unthinking, more nearly automatic than he now is? Who, even in his imagination, would like to live in a community where, instead of thinking part of the time, one never found it possible to think at all?

Is it not meaningful to say that whereas Plato's Republic and More's Utopia are noble absurdities, Walden Two is an ignoble one; that the first two ask men to be more than human, while the second urges them to be less? When, in the present world, men behave well, that is no doubt sometimes because they are creatures of habit as well as, sometimes, because they are reasonable. But if one proposes to change Man as Professor Skinner and so many other cheerful mechanists propose, is it really so evident that he should be changed in the direction they advocate? Is he something which, in Nietzsche's phrase, "must be surpassed," or is he a creature to whom the best advice one can give is the advice to retreat—away from such reasoned behavior as he may be capable of and toward that automatism of which he is also capable.

Obviously Walden Two represents—glorified, perfected, and curiously modernized—that ideal of a "cloistered virtue" which European man has tended to find not only unsatisfactory as an ideal but almost meaningless in terms of his doubtless conflicting aspirations. Nevertheless it must be admitted that Thomas Henry Huxley, a protomodern, once admitted in an often quoted passage that "if some great power would agree to make me always think what is true and do what is right, on condition of being turned into a sort of clock and wound up every morning before I got out of bed, I should instantly close with the offer." And what a Huxley would have agreed to, prospective candidates for admission into Walden Two might also find acceptable.

Frazier himself is compelled to make a significant confession: the motives which led him to undertake his successful experiment included a certain desire to exercise power over his fellows. That is not admirable in itself and is obviously not without its dangers. But he insists that the danger will disappear with him because those who succeed to his authority and inherit his techniques will have enjoyed, as he did not, the advantages of a scientific conditioning process and that therefore such potentially antisocial impulses as his will no longer exist. In other words, though the benevolent dictator is a rare phenomenon today, the happy chance which produced this one will not have to be relied on in the future. Walden Two will automatically produce the dictators necessary to carry it on.

Nevertheless and even if the skeptical reader will grant for the sake of argument that automatic virtue represents an ideal completely satisfactory, a multitude of other doubts and fears are likely to arise in his mind. He will remember of course that Brook Farm and the rest failed promptly and decisively. Perhaps he will remember also that Russian communism achieved at least some degree of permanence only by rejecting, more and more completely, everything which in any way parallels the mildness, the gentleness, and the avoidance of all direct restraints and pressures which is characteristic of Walden Two; that the makers of Soviet policy came to denounce and repress even that somewhat paradoxical enthusiasm for the culture of a different world which was as much encouraged in the earliest days of the experiment as it is at Walden Two.

Hence, if a Walden Two is possible it obviously has become so only because—and this is a point which presumably Mr. Skinner himself wishes to emphasize—it differs in several respects from all superficially similar projects. Like the Russian experiment it assumes that, for all practical purposes, man is merely the product of society; but it also assumes a situation which did not exist when the Communist state was set up: namely one in which "the scientific ability to control men's thoughts with precision" has fully matured.

Thus if the man upon whom the experiment is performed is nothing but the limitlessly plastic product of external processes operating upon him and is, by definition, incapable of any significant autonomous activity, he is also, in this case, a creature who has fallen into the hands of an ideally competent dictator. His desires, tastes, convictions and ideals are precisely what the experimenter wants to make them. He is the repository of no potentialities which can ever develop except as they are called forth by circumstances over which he has no control. Finally, of course, his happy condition is the result of the fortunate accident which determined that the "engineer" who created him and, indirectly, will create all of his progeny, was an experimenter whose own random conditioning happened to produce, not the monster who might just as likely have been the first to seize the power that science offered, but a genuinely benevolent dictator instead.

A propos this last premise it might, in passing, be remarked as a curious fact that though scientific method abhors the accidental, the uncontrollable and the unpredicted; though Mr. Skinner's own ideal seems to be to remove for ever any possible future intrusion of it into human affairs; yet the successful establishment of the first utopia depended ultimately on the decisive effect of just such an accident as will henceforth be impossible.

Critics of the assumption that technological advance is the true key to human progress have often urged that new powers are dangerous rather than beneficial unless the question of how they should be used is at least opened before the powers become available. With more than usual anxiety they might contemplate the situation in which we are now placed if it is true that only chance will answer the question by whom and in the interest of what "our approaching scientific ability to control men's thoughts with precision" is to be used. But this is only one of several desperate questions which the premises of *Walden Two* provoke. Most of them can also be related to points made by Mr. Skinner in less fanciful contexts and to one or two of them we may turn in connection with a more general consideration of problems raised if we are ready to assume that we actually do stand at the threshold of a world in which men's thoughts will be controlled scientifically and as a matter of course.

To begin with, we must, of course, abandon the old platitude, "You can't change human nature," and accept its opposite, "You can change human nature as much and in whatever direction you wish"—because "human nature" does not exist in the sense which the phrase implies. Whatever desires, tastes, preferences, and tendencies have been so general and so persistent as to create the assumption that they are innate or "natural" must be, as a matter of fact, merely the most ancient and deeply graven of the conditioning to which the human animal has been subjected. As Pascal—an odd thinker to be invoked in defense of a mechanistic and completely relativist ethic—once exclaimed in one of those terrifying speculations of which, no doubt, his own conditioning made him capable: "They say that habit is Second Nature; but perhaps Nature is only First Habit."

By eager reformers "You can't change human nature" has often been denounced as both a counsel of despair and a convenient excuse for lazy indifference in the face of the world's ills. Yet the fact or alleged fact which the phrase attempts to state has also its positive aspect. To say that human nature cannot be changed means that human nature is something in itself and there is at least the possibility that part of this something is valuable. If we say that it cannot be changed we are also saying that it cannot be completely corrupted; that it cannot be transformed into something which we would not recognize as human at all. This is what the eighteenth century allowed Pope to say for it, and as long as one holds the doctrine that the term Nature actually describes some enduring set of possibilities and values, then some limit is set, not only to human perfectibility, but also, and more encouragingly, to things which it can become or be made.

But once this view of "Nature" has been dismissed as an illusion and even what appear to be the most persistent of its traits are thought of as merely the result of conditioning, then there is no limit to the extent to which men may become different from what they now are. There is nothing against which it may be assumed that human nature will revolt. Only by a temporarily established convention is any kind of vice a "creature of so frightful mien." Anything can be made to seem "natural." Cruelty, treachery, slander and deceit might come generally to seem not frightful but beautiful. And if it be said that the successful putting into practice of certain recent political philosophies supports the contention of determinists that man may, indeed, be taught to believe precisely this, it must be added that something more is also implied: namely that we must abandon—along with the conviction that human nature cannot be changed—all the hopes expressed in such phrases as "human nature will in the end revolt against" this or that.

Since no human nature capable of revolting against anything is now presumed to exist, then some other experimenter—conditioned perhaps as the son of the commandant of a Nazi labor camp—might decide to develop a race of men who found nothing more delightful than the infliction of suffering, and to establish for them a colony to be called Walden Three. By what standards could the dictator of Walden Two presume to judge that his utopia was any more desirable than its new rival? He could not appeal to God's revealed word; to the inner light of conscience; or to that eighteenth-century stand-by, the voice of Nature. He could say only that the accidents of his previous existence in a world where accident still played its part in determining how an individual should be conditioned had conditioned him to prefer what he would, in full realization of the unjustifiability of the metaphor, call "light rather than darkness." The life in Walden Two appears to him as "good" but the adjective would, of course, have no meaning in relation to anything outside himself.

In the light of such possibilities those who have not yet been molded by either Walden Two or Walden Three will tend to feel that before the "scientific ability to control men's thoughts with precision" has been fully utilized by whoever may seize the limitless power it will confer, we had better take a last look around—if not for that way of escape which may not exist, then at least in order to grasp certain implications and possible consequences as they appear to the minds of men who are still "free"—free at least in the limited sense that they are the product of conditions which were brought about, in part, through the presence of random factors destined to play a smaller and smaller part in determining human personality. That second generation of dictators to whom the dictator of Walden Two expects to pass on the control of affairs will be conditioners who have themselves been conditioned. The circle of cause and effect will have been closed and no man will ever again be anything which his predecessor has not consciously willed him to be.

According to the mechanist's own theories, everything which happened in the universe from its beginning down, at least until yesterday, was the result of chance. The chemical molecule didn't "want" or "plan" to grow more complex until it was a protein; the protein did not plan to become protoplasm; and the amoeba did not plan to become man. As a matter of fact, a theory very popular at the moment explains the fact that life seems to have arisen on our earth but once in all the billions of years of the planet's existence by saying that it could arise only as the result of a combination of circumstances so fantastically improbable that they have never occurred again. Yet though they owe to chance both their very existence and all progress from the protozoan to civilization, they are eager to take a step which would make it forever impossible for the unexpected and the unplanned to erupt again into the scheme which will pass completely under their own control.

No doubt many practical-minded people will object that such speculations as these are a waste of time. After all, they will say, even Walden Two does not exist except in fancy and no one has yet claimed that the "approaching scientific ability to control men's thoughts with precision" has already arrived. Logical dilemmas and metaphysical difficulties are cobwebs which will not entangle those who refuse to take seriously their gossamer threads. We have work to do and practical problems to solve.

But to all such it may be replied that practical problems and the metaphysical forms to which they may be reduced are not so unrelated as they may think, and that the logical extreme sometimes serves to make clear the real nature of a purely practical problem. It is true that no man has yet established a Walden Two or Walden Three, and that neither has any man yet controlled *with precision* men's thoughts. But it is also true that there has been a movement in a direction which suggests Walden Two as an ideal. Moreover, statesmen, educators and publicists have already achieved considerable success in their frankly admitted attempts to use the techniques already developed to control and condition large sections of the public and have increasingly declared their faith in the desirability and practicality of such methods in contradistinction to what used to be called education, on the one hand, and appeals to the enlightened understanding of the public, on the other. Already it has quite seriously and without any conviction of cynicism been proposed that the advertisers' principle, "say a thing often enough and it will be believed," be utilized by those who have what they regard as "correct" or "healthy" or "socially useful" ideas to sell. Every time it is proposed that schools should develop certain attitudes in their pupils or that the government should undertake propaganda along a certain line, the question of the difficult distinction between education in some old-fashioned sense and "conditioning" definitely arises.

Moreover, it is because the techniques of the social scientist and the experimental psychologists do to some extent work that some attempt must be made to understand their implications. By their methods many men may be made to do and think many things. Already in the relatively simple case of education versus "useful conditioning," the difficult distinction ceases to be difficult once a border line has been definitely crossed. Writing to George Washington not long after our particular democracy had been founded, Thomas Jefferson remarked, "It is an axiom in my mind that our liberty can never be safe but in the hands of the people themselves, and that, too, of the people with a certain degree of instruction." What would Jefferson have thought of the suggestion that "a certain degree of instruction" be interpreted to mean "a certain degree of conditioning?" Would he not have pointed out that the distinction between the two is clear and fundamental; that "conditioning" is achieved by methods which by-pass or, as it were, short-circuit those very reasoning faculties which education proposes to cultivate and exercise? And would he not have added that democracy can have no meaning or no function unless it is assumed that these faculties do lie within a realm of freedom where the sanctions of democracy arise?

Thus the whole future of mankind may well depend not only on the question whether man is entirely or only in part the product of conditioning, but also on the extent to which he is treated as though he were. Will we come ultimately to base what we call "education," in and out of schools, on the assumption that conditioning by propaganda as well as other methods is the most effective, even if it is not the only, method of influencing human beings?

To all such questions an answer in pragmatic terms has already been given at least positively enough to make it very pertinent to ask into whose hands the power already being exercised is to fall; to ask who is to decide in what direction the citizen is to be conditioned, and on the bases of what standards of value those decisions are to be made. That is simply the practical aspect of the theoretical question, "Who shall be master of Walden Two?"

In the totalitarian countries, where deterministic theories have been accepted in their most unqualified form and the techniques of control most systematically practiced, the question just posed has been answered in the simplest possible manner, and very much the same way that it was answered at Walden Two. Power is exercised by those who seized it and, theoretically at least, this seizure was the last event which could "happen" because henceforward human destiny will be in the hands of those who are now in a position to control it. The question whether they ought to have done so and whether it is well for humanity that they did was either always meaningless or soon to become so since all the value judgments made in the future will be made by those who have been conditioned to approve what has happened to them.

One result of all this is that during the transition period while there are still survivors from the age when men's minds had not yet been controlled with precision and a conflict of wills is still possible—i.e., under the conditions prevailing in the totalitarian states as they actually exist—a sharp distinction has to be made between those in possession of the power which they have seized and those who are subject to their manipulations. As a catchword the old term "classless society" may be used, but it is evident that no two classes could be more widely separated than the class of those who decide what shall be done and the class of those who are conditioned and controlled.

Obviously such a situation cannot arise either in Germany, Russia or Walden Two until the seizure of power has actually occurred and the power seized must include not only the classic essential, "the instruments of production," but also those "instruments of thought control" which seem to be assuming a more crucial importance than Marx assigned them.

No less obviously this seizure has not yet been made in the countries still called "democratic." Power may be drifting into the hands of certain groups but most of the members of these groups are not quite so completely committed as the totalitarian leaders were to the theories by which they justified their acts and are therefore not so ready to assume the dictatorship which may possibly be already within their reach. In such countries it is, therefore, still possible to consider certain questions, both practical and metaphysical, which even those still capable of considering them are forbidden to raise publicly in totalitarian states. We can still think—or at least go through those mental motions which were formerly called thinking—about the direction in which our own society seems to be moving, about certain large questions of values and ethics, even about the possibilities that under certain conditions men may not be the automata they are more and more assumed to be and that therefore their thoughts never can be controlled either completely or "with precision." Even more specifically we may ask whether totalitarianism on either the model of Soviet Russia or Walden Two is what we wish for or must inevitably accept.

It has sometimes been said that the totalitarian state is merely what democracy must in time become. Enthusiastically in the one case, reluctantly in the other, the same premises lead to the same methods and the same methods to the same results. What one proclaims definitively as dogma is the same as what the other drifts toward and this distinction is the only one which can be made, no matter where we attempt to draw it. In this view a "people's democracy" is only a "welfare state" which has fully accepted its implications. In theory as well as in practice the difference is always merely in the degree to which the logic of any position has been followed to its ultimate conclusion.

No doubt reality is much less simple. But after this large proviso has been accepted much can be said to support the contention that what we of the democracies toy with and lean toward are the same scientific hypotheses and the same philosophical notions that totalitarians proclaim as truths it is forbidden to question.

Roman Catholic doctrine makes the useful distinction between those beliefs which are *de fide* and those which are no more than *pia sententia*. The one must be accepted without dispute by all who wish to remain within the fold; the other, though part of commonly held opinion, have the weight of no authority behind them. In many cases the distinction between what the Communist state proclaims concerning the real nature of man and the proper methods of dealing with it differs from what many of our own psychologists and sociologists tend to assume only as an article of belief which has been proclaimed *de fide* differs from *pia sententia*. What we may tend to deduce from, say, the Pavlovian experiments does not differ too significantly from what an orthodox Russian scientist would say that these same experiments have proved with ultimate finality.

In what the sociologist previously quoted was pleased to call "today's thinking" man tends to appear very much what the Russian version of Marxist science would make him and those who follow such lines of thought are inevitably led to the same next step. If man is the product of the conditioning to which chance has subjected him, why should we not make him what we would like him to be?

We have, it is said, already effectively asserted our control over nature, animate and inanimate. Technology has already entered its mature phase and biology is entering it. We have mastered the atom; we have also learned how both to breed and to train animals. Since man is part of nature he also should be subject to control and no more should be necessary to make him so than easy extensions of the methods already successfully applied. We boast that we have mastered nature but that mastery can hardly be called complete until human nature is at least as completely under our control as the other phenomena of animate nature have become.

Perhaps the most general aspect of this subtle but inclusive shift of emphasis is revealed in the almost unconscious substitution of one term for another when the characteristics of a good social order are discussed. At the beginning of the democratic movement the watchword was "opportunity." Social and political evils were thought of as impediments to the free development of aspirations and abilities. But because "opportunity" as an ideal implies faith in the autonomous powers of the individual it has given way to others embodied in words which suggest in one way or another, not what men may be permitted to do for themselves, but what with benevolent intentions of course may be done to them.

The most brutally frank of such words is of course "control" but it is used most freely by those who have come frankly to accept a barely disguised totalitarian ideal. In those who wish still to pay lip service at least to some sort of faith in democracy and freedom the preferred words are "education," "adjustment" and, with a closer approach to frankness, "conditioning." But the difference is one of degree, not in the fundamental assumption, which is that men should not be left to develop but must have their characters and temperaments, as well as their daily lives, somehow "planned" for them. The most benign aspect of this assumption is revealed in the desire for a "welfare state" which will assure the physical well-being of its citizens. The most sinister aspect is that more fully revealed in the speculations of the most advanced and theoretical social psychologists who have passed on, as the author of *Walden Two* has, to consider how the character, opinions and tastes of the individual may also be "planned" for him.

No doubt many of those who agree with that Dean of the Humanities to whose happy phrase we find ourselves again and again recurring would speak with the customary horror of the frankly totalitarian states which have, to date, achieved the greatest success in controlling men's thoughts with precision. They would carefully avoid such frank terms as "brain washing" which the Communists use to state clearly their intentions. But it is difficult to see what difference there is except the difference between a philosophy which is still tentative and somewhat reluctant to admit its ultimate implications and one which, facing those implications, proceeds confidently to put into practice the techniques which it has found effective. If "adjustment" is not to become "control" and "conditioning" is to stop short of "brain washing," some limits must be set which are not defined or even hinted at in such statements as those made by some psychologists.

Even those of us whose convictions permit us to doubt that men's thoughts will ever be completely controlled with absolute "precision" must realize, nevertheless, that the "scientific ability" to control them to some considerable degree has been growing and that in all probability it will grow still further. The terrifying extent to which many (if not all) the individuals in a group may be made to act and think in ways which we would once have thought inconceivable is already all too evident. Hence the question of how that power, whether it be limited or unlimited, will be used in our own society is of immediate as well as remote importance. It is no longer merely a metaphysical one.

It does no good to say that the democracy to which we assure ourselves we are committed safeguards us against the arbitrary use of that power. To say anything of the sort is merely to beg the question because an essential part of the question has to do with the reasonable doubt whether what we call democracy can survive the maturing techniques for determining in advance what "the voice of the people" will say. "Democracy," as the West defined it and in contradistinction to the new definition which totalitarianism has attempted to formulate, is meaningless except on the assumption that the individual man's thoughts and desires are to some extent uncontrollable and unpredictable. There can be no possible reason for taking a vote if the results can either be determined or even predicted in advance. In a society which assures, rightly or wrongly, that events are predictably determined, elections can be no more than those rituals with only a formal, ceremonial significance which, in Soviet Russia and Nazi Germany, they actually became.

In Walden Two this fact is tacitly recognized. Its founding dictator expects authority to "wither away" at the time of his death if not before, precisely as, in Communist theory, the dictatorship of the party will some day wither. But before withering away has occurred, the whole future history of mankind will have been set in a pattern which can never suffer any fundamental change because it must correspond to the pattern of conditionings which are self-perpetuating once they have been firmly and universally established. It is hard to see how we can accept even pragmatically the convictions and ideals of Walden Two without incurring consequences which correspond in the realm of the actual to the theoretical consequences of its theoretical premises. The question whether our own society is in the process of turning itself into some sort of Walden Two is far from being merely fantastic.

The Responsibility of Criminals

7. *An Address Delivered to the Prisoners in the Chicago County Jail*

Clarence Darrow

Clarence Seward Darrow (1857–1938) was one of America's outstanding criminal and trial lawyers. Among his famous cases were the Leopold and Loeb murder trial and the Scopes evolution trial in Tennessee. He was an outspoken agnostic and an opponent of traditional penal practices.

If I looked at jails and crimes and prisoners in the way the ordinary person does, I should not speak on this subject to you. The reason I talk to you on the question of crime, its cause and cure, is because I really do not in the least believe in crime. There is no such thing as a crime as the word is generally understood. I do not believe there is any sort of distinction between the real moral condition of the people in and out of jail. One is just as good as the other. The people here can no more help being here than the people outside can avoid being outside. I do not believe that people are in jail because they deserve to be. They are in jail simply because they can not avoid it on account of circumstances which are entirely beyond their control and for which they are in no way responsible.

I suppose a great many people on the outside would say I was doing you harm if they should hear what I say to you this afternoon, but you can not be hurt a great deal anyway, so it will not matter. Good people outside would say that I was really teaching you things that were calculated to injure society, but it's worth while now and then to hear something different from what you ordinarily get from preachers and the like. These will tell you that you should be good and then you will get rich and be happy. Of course we know that people do not get rich by being good, and that is the reason why so many of you people try to get rich some other way, only you do not understand how to do it quite as well as the fellow outside.

There are people who think that everything in this world is an accident. But really there is no such thing as an accident. A great many folks admit that many of the people in jail ought not to be there, and many who are outside ought to be in. I think none of them ought to be here. There ought to be no jails, and if it were

Reprinted from *Crime and Criminals* by Clarence Darrow, published by Charles H. Kerr & Company, 1902.

not for the fact that the people on the outside are so grasping and heartless in their dealings with the people on the inside, there would be no such institutions as jails.

I do not want you to believe that I think all you people here are angels. I do not think that. You are people of all kinds, all of you doing the best you can, and that is evidently not very well—you are people of all kinds and conditions and under all circumstances. In one sense everybody is equally good and equally bad. We all do the best we can under the circumstances. But as to the exact things for which you are sent here, some of you are guilty and some of you are not guilty. Some of you did the particular act because you needed the money. Some of you did it because you are in the habit of doing it, and some of you because you are born to it, and it comes to be as natural as it does, for instance, for me to be good.

Most of you probably have nothing against me, and most of you would treat me the same as any other person would; probably better than some of the people on the outside would treat me, because you think I believe in you and they know I do not believe in them. While you would not have the least thing against me in the world you might pick my pockets. I do not think all of you would, but I think some of you would. You would not have anything against me, but that's your profession, a few of you. Some of the rest of you, if my doors were unlocked, might come in if you saw anything you wanted—not out of any malice to me, but because that is your trade. There is no doubt there are quite a number of people in this jail who would pick my pockets. And still I know this, that when I get outside pretty nearly everybody picks my pocket. There may be some of you who would hold up a man on the street, if you did not happen to have something else to do, and needed the money; but when I want to light my house or my office the gas company holds me up. They charge me one dollar for something that is worth twenty-five cents, and still all these people are good people; they are pillars of society and support the churches, and they are respectable.

When I ride on the street cars, I am held up—I pay five cents for a ride that is worth two and a half cents, simply because a body of men have bribed the city council and the legislature, so that all the rest of us have to pay tribute to them.

If I do not want to fall into the clutches of the gas trust and choose to burn oil instead of gas, then good Mr. Rockefeller holds me up, and he uses a certain portion of his money to build universities and support churches which are engaged in telling us how to be good.

Some of you are here for obtaining property under false pretenses—yet I pick up a great Sunday paper and read the advertisements of a merchant prince—"Shirt waists for 39 cents, marked down from $3.00."

When I read the advertisements in the paper I see they are all lies. When I want to get out and find a place to stand anywhere on the face of the earth, I find that it has all been taken up long ago before I came here, and before you came here, and somebody says, "Get off, swim into the lake, fly into the air; go anywhere, but get off." That is because these people have the police and they have the jails and the judges and the lawyers and the soldiers and all the rest of them to take care of the earth and drive everybody off that comes in their way.

A great many people will tell you that all this is true, but that it does not excuse you. These facts do not excuse some fellow who reaches into my pocket and takes out a five dollar bill; the fact that the gas company bribes the members of the legislature from year to year, and fixes the law, so that all you people are compelled to be "fleeced" whenever you deal with them; the fact that the street car companies and the gas companies have control of the streets and the fact that the landlords own all the earth, they say, has nothing to do with you.

Let us see whether there is any connection between the crimes of the respectable classes and your presence in the jail. Many of you people are in jail because you have really committed burglary. Many of you, because you have stolen something: in the meaning of the law, you have taken some other person's property. Some of you have entered a store and carried off a pair of shoes because you did not have the price. Possibly some of you have committed murder. I can not tell what all of you did. There are a great many people here who have done some of these things who really do not know themselves why they did them. I think I know why you did them—every one of you; you did these things because you were bound to do them. It looked to you at the time as if you had a chance to do them or not, as you saw fit, but still after all you had no choice. There may be people here who had some money in their pockets and who still went out and got some more money in a way society forbids. Now you may not yourselves see exactly why it was you did this thing, but if you look at the question deeply enough and carefully enough you would see that there were circumstances that drove you to do exactly the thing which you did. You could not help it any more than we outside can help taking the positions that we take. The reformers who tell you to be good and you will be happy, and the people on the outside who have property to protect—they think that the only way to do it is by building jails and locking you up in cells on week-days and praying for you Sundays.

I think that all of this has nothing whatever to do with right conduct. I think it is very easily seen what has to do with right conduct. Some so-called criminals—and I will use this word because it is handy, it means nothing to me—I speak of the criminals who get caught as distinguished from the criminals who catch them—some of these so-called criminals are in jail for the first offenses, but nine-tenths of you are in jail because you did not have a good lawyer and of course you did not have a good lawyer because you did not have enough money to pay a good lawyer. There is no very great danger of a rich man going to jail.

Some of you may be here for the first time. If we would open the doors and let you out, and leave the laws as they are today, some of you would be back tomorrow. This is about as good a place as you can get anyway. There are many people here who are so in the habit of coming that they would not know where else to go. There are people who are born with the tendency to break into jail every chance they get, and they can not avoid it. You can not figure out your life and see why it was, but still there is a reason for it, and if we were all-wise and knew all the facts we could figure it out.

In the first place, there are a good many more people who go to jail in the winter time than in summer. Why is this? Is it because people are more wicked in winter? No, it is because the coal trust begins to get us in its grip in the winter. A few gentlemen take possession of the coal, and unless the people will pay $7 or $8 a ton for something that is worth $3, they will have to freeze. Then there is nothing to do but to break into jail, and so there are many more in jail in the winter than in summer. It costs more for gas in the winter because the nights are longer, and people go to jail to save gas bills. The jails are electric-lighted. You may not know it, but these economic laws are working all the time, whether we know it or do not know it.

There are more people who go to jail in hard times than in good times—few people comparatively go to jail except when they are hard up. They go to jail because they have no other place to go. They may not know why, but it is true all the same. People are not more wicked in hard times. That is not the reason. The fact is true all over the world that in hard times more people go to jail than in good times, and in winter more people go to jail than in summer. Of course it is pretty hard times for people who go to jail at any time. The people who go to jail are almost always poor people—people who have no other place to live first and last. When times are hard then you find large numbers of people who go to jail who would not otherwise be in jail.

Long ago, Mr. Buckle, who was a great philosopher and historian, collected facts and he showed that the number of people who are arrested increased just as the price of food increased. When they put up the price of gas ten cents a thousand I do not know who will go to jail, but I do know that a certain number of people will go. When the meat combine raises the price of beef I do not know who is going to jail, but I know that a large number of people are bound to go. Whenever the Standard Oil Company raises the price of oil, I know that a certain number of girls who are seamstresses, and who work night after night long hours for somebody else, will be compelled to go out on the streets and ply another trade, and I know that Mr. Rockefeller and his associates are responsible and not the poor girls in the jails.

First and last, people are sent to jail because they are poor. Sometimes, as I say, you may not need money at the particular time, but you wish to have thrifty forehanded habits, and do not always wait until you are in absolute want. Some of you people are perhaps plying the trade, the profession, which is called burglary. No man in his right senses will go into a strange house in the dead of night and prowl around with a dark lantern through unfamiliar rooms and take chances of his life if he has plenty of the good things of the world in his own home. You would not take any such chances as that. If a man had clothes in his clothes-press and beefsteak in his pantry, and money in a bank, he would not navigate around nights in houses where he knows nothing about the premises whatever. It always requires experience and education for this profession, and people who fit themselves for it are no more to blame than I am for being a lawyer. A man would not hold up another man on the street if he had plenty of money in his own pocket. He might do it if he had one dollar or two dollars, but he wouldn't if he had as much money as Mr. Rockefeller has. Mr. Rockefeller has a great deal better hold-up game than that.

The more that is taken from the poor by the rich, who have the chance to take it, the more poor people there are who are compelled to resort to these means for a livelihood. They may not understand it, they may not think so at once, but after all they are driven into that line of employment.

There is a bill before the legislature of this State to punish kidnapping children, with death. We have wise members of the Legislature. They know the gas trust when they see it and they always see it,—they can furnish light enough to be seen, and this Legislature thinks it is going to stop kidnapping children by making a law punishing kidnappers of children, with death. I don't believe in kidnapping children, but the Legislature is all wrong. Kidnapping children is not a crime, it is a profession. It has been developed with the times. It has been developed with our modern industrial conditions. There are many ways of making money—many new ways that our ancestors knew nothing about. Our ancestors knew nothing about a billion dollar trust; and here comes some poor fellow who has no other trade and he discovers the profession of kidnapping children.

This crime is born, not because people are bad; people don't kidnap other people's children because they want the children or because they are devilish, but because they see a chance to get some money out of it. You cannot cure this crime by passing a law punishing by death kidnappers of children. There is one way to cure it. There is one way to cure all these offenses, and that is to give the people a chance to live. There is no other way, and there never was any other way since the world began, and the world is so blind and stupid that it will not see. If every man and woman and child in the world had a chance to make a decent, fair, honest living, there would be no jails, and no lawyers and no courts. There might be some persons here or there with some peculiar formation of their brain, like Rockefeller, who would do these things simply to be doing them; but they would be very, very few, and those should be sent to a hospital and treated, and not sent to jail; and they would entirely disappear in the second generation, or at least in the third generation.

I am not talking pure theory. I will just give you two or three illustrations.

The English people once punished criminals by sending them away. They would load them on a ship and export them to Australia. England was owned by lords and nobles and rich people. They owned the whole earth over there, and the other people had to stay in the streets. They could not get a decent living. They used to take their criminals and send them to Australia—I mean the class of criminals who got caught. When these criminals got over there, and nobody else had come, they had the whole continent to run over, and so they could raise sheep and furnish their own meat, which is easier than stealing it; these criminals then became decent, respectable people because they had a chance to live. They did not commit any crimes. They were just like the English people who sent them there, only better. And in the second generation the descendants of those criminals were as good and respectable a class of people as there were on the face of the earth, and then they began building churches and jails themselves.

A portion of this country was settled in the same way, landing prisoners down on the southern coast; but when they got here and had a whole continent to run over and plenty of chances to make a living, they became respectable citizens, making their own living just like any other citizen in the world; but finally these descendants of the English aristocracy, who sent the people over to Australia, found out they were getting rich, and so they went over to get possession of the earth as they always do, and they organized land syndicates and got control of the land and ores, and then they had just as many criminals in Australia as they did in England. It was not because the world had grown bad; it was because the earth had been taken away from the people.

Some of you people have lived in the country. It's prettier than it is here. And if you have ever lived on a farm you understand that if you put a lot of cattle in a field, when the pasture is short they will jump over the fence; but put them in a good field where there is plenty of pasture, and they will be law-abiding cattle to the end of time. The human animal is just like the rest of the animals, only a little more so. The same thing that governs in the one governs in the other.

Everybody makes his living along the lines of least resistance. A wise man who comes into a country early sees a great undeveloped land. For instance, our rich men twenty-five years ago saw that Chicago was small and knew a lot of people would come here and settle, and they readily saw that if they had all the land around here it would be worth a good deal, so they grabbed the land. You can not be a landlord because somebody has got it all. You must find some other calling. In England and Ireland and Scotland less than five percent own all the land there is, and the people are bound to stay there on any kind of terms the landlords give. They must live the best they can, so they develop all these various professions—burglary, picking pockets and the like.

Again, people find all sorts of ways of getting rich. These are diseases like everything else. You look at people getting rich, organizing trusts, and making a million dollars, and somebody gets the disease and he starts out. He catches it just as a man catches the mumps or the measles; he is not to blame, it is in the air. You will find men speculating beyond their means, because the mania of money-getting is taking possession of them. It is simply a disease; nothing more, nothing less. You can not avoid catching it; but the fellows who have control of the earth have the advantage of you. See what the law is; when these men get control of things, they make the laws. They do not make the laws to protect anybody; courts are not instruments of justice; when your case gets into court it will make little difference whether you are guilty or innocent; but it's better if you have a smart lawyer. And you can not have a smart lawyer unless you have money. First and last it's a question of money. Those men who own the earth make the laws to protect what they have. They fix up a sort of fence or pen around what they have, and they fix the law so the fellow on the outside can not get in. The laws are really organized for the protection of the men who rule the world. They were never organized or enforced to do justice. We have no system for doing justice, not the slightest in the world.

Let me illustrate: Take the poorest person in this room. If the community had provided a system of doing justice the poorest person in this room would have as good a lawyer as the richest, would he not? When you went into court you would have just as long a trial, and just as fair a trial as the richest person in Chicago. Your case would not be tried in fifteen or twenty minutes, whereas it would take fifteen days to get through with a rich man's case.

Then if you were rich and were beaten, your case would be taken to the Appellate Court. A poor man can not take his case to the Appellate Court; he has not the price; and then to the Supreme Court, and if he were beaten there he might perhaps go to the United States Supreme Court. And he might die of old age before he got into jail. If you are poor, it's a quick job. You are almost known to be guilty, else you would not be there. Why should any one be in the criminal court if he were not guilty? He would not be there if he could be anywhere else. The officials have no time to look after all these cases. The people who are on the outside, who are running banks and building churches and making jails, they have no time to examine 600 or 700 prisoners each year to see whether they are guilty or innocent. If the courts were organized to promote justice the people would elect somebody to defend all these criminals, somebody as smart as the prosecutor—and give him as many detectives and as many assistants to help, and pay as much money to defend you as to prosecute you. We have a very able man for State's Attorney, and he has many assistants, detectives and policemen without end, and judges to hear the cases—everything handy.

Most of all our criminal code consists in offenses against property. People are sent to jail because they have committed a crime against property. It is of very little consequence whether one hundred people more or less go to jail who ought not to go—you must protect property, because in this world property is of more importance than anything else.

How is it done? These people who have property fix it so they can protect what they have. When somebody commits a crime it does not follow that he had done something that is morally wrong. The man on the outside who has committed no crime may have done something. For instance: to take all the coal in the United States and raise the price two dollars or three dollars when there is no need of it, and thus kill thousands of babies and send thousands of people to the poorhouse and tens of thousands to jail, as is done every year in the United States,—this is a greater crime than all the people in our jails ever committed, but the law does not punish it. Why? Because the fellows who control the earth make the laws. If you and I had the making of the laws, the first thing we would do would be to punish the fellow who gets control of the earth. Nature put this coal in the ground for me as well as for them and nature made the prairies up here to raise wheat for me as well as for them, and then the great railroad companies came along and fenced it up.

Most all of the crimes for which we are punished are property crimes. There are a few personal crimes, like murder—but they are very few. The crimes committed are mostly those against property. If this punishment is right the criminals must have a lot of property. How much money is there in this crowd? And yet you are all here for crimes against property. The people up and down the Lake Shore have not committed crime, still they have so much property they don't know what to do with it. It is perfectly plain why these people have not committed crimes against property; they make the laws and therefore do not need to break them. And in order for you to get some property you are obliged to break the rules of the game. I don't know but what some of you may have had a very nice chance to get rich by carrying the hod for one dollar a day, twelve hours. Instead of taking that nice, easy profession, you are a burglar. If you had been given a chance to be a banker you would rather follow that. Some of you may have had a chance to work as a switchman on a railroad where you know, according to statistics, that you can not live and keep all your limbs more than seven years, and you get fifty dollars or seventy-five dollars a month for taking your lives in your hands, and instead of taking that lucrative position you choose to be a sneak thief, or something like that. Some of you made that sort of choice. I don't know which I would take if I was reduced to this choice. I have an easier choice.

I will guarantee to take from this jail, or any jail in the world, five hundred men who have been the worst criminals and law-breakers who ever got into jail, and I will go down to our lowest streets and take five hundred of the most abandoned prostitutes, and go out somewhere where there is plenty of land, and will give them a chance to make a living, and they will be as good people as the average in the community.

There is a remedy for the sort of condition we see here. The world never finds it out, or when it does find it out it does not enforce it. You may pass a law punishing every person with death for burglary, and it will make no difference. Men will commit it just the same. In England there was a time when one hundred different offenses were punishable with death, and it made no difference. The English people strangely found out that so fast as they repealed the severe penalties and so fast as they did away with punishing men by death, crime decreased instead of increased; that the smaller the penalty the fewer the crimes.

Hanging men in our county jails does not prevent murder. It makes murderers.

And this has been the history of the world. It's easy to see how to do away with what we call crime. It is not so easy to do it. I will tell you how to do it. It can be done by giving the people a chance to live—by destroying special privileges. So long as big criminals can get the coal fields, so long as the big criminals have control of the city council and get the public streets for street cars and gas rights, this is bound to send thousands of poor people to jail. So long as men are allowed to monopolize all the earth, and compel others to live on such terms as these men see fit to make, then you are bound to get into jail.

The only way in the world to abolish crime and criminals is to abolish the big ones and the little ones together. Make fair conditions of life. Give men a chance to live. Abolish the right of the private ownership of land, abolish monopoly, make the world partners in production, partners in the good things of life. Nobody would steal if he could get something of his own some easier way. Nobody will commit burglary when he has a house full. No girl will go out on the streets when she has a comfortable place at home. The man who owns a sweatshop or a department store may not be to blame himself for the condition of his girls, but when he pays them five dollars, three dollars, and two dollars a week, I wonder where he thinks they will get the rest of their money to live. The only way to cure these conditions is by equality. There should be no jails. They do not accomplish what they pretend to accomplish. If you would wipe them out, there would be no more criminals than now. They terrorize nobody. They are a blot upon any civilization, and a jail is an evidence of the lack of charity of the people on the outside who make the jails and fill them with the victims of their greed.

8. The Humanitarian Theory of Punishment

C. S. Lewis

Clive Staples Lewis (1898–1963) was professor of Medieval and Renaissance English at Cambridge University from 1954 until his death. He is most famous for his numerous books and essays that defend various aspects of Christianity.

In England we have lately had a controversy about capital punishment. I do not know whether a murderer is more likely to repent and make a good end on the gallows a few weeks after his trial or in the prison infirmary thirty years later. I do not know whether the fear of death is an indispensable deterrent. I need not, for the purpose of this article, decide whether it is a morally permissible deterrent. Those are questions which I propose to leave untouched. My subject is not Capital Punishment in particular, but that theory of punishment in general which the controversy showed to be almost universal among my fellow-countrymen. It may be called the Humanitarian Theory. Those who hold it think that it is mild and merciful. In this I believe that they are seriously mistaken. I believe that the "Humanity" which it claims is a dangerous illusion and disguises the possibility of cruelty and injustice without end. I urge a return to the traditional or Retributive theory not solely, nor even primarily, in the interests of society but in the interests of the criminals.

According to the Humanitarian theory, to punish a man because he deserves it, and as much as he deserves, is mere revenge, and, therefore, barbarous and immoral. It is maintained that the only legitimate motives for punishing are the desire to deter others by example or to mend the criminal. When this theory is combined, as frequently happens, with the belief that all crime is more or less pathological, the idea of mending tails off into that of healing or curing and punishment becomes therapeutic. Thus it appears at first sight that we have passed from the harsh and self-righteous notion of giving the wicked their deserts to the charitable and enlightened one of tending the psychologically sick. What could be more amiable? One little point which is taken for granted in this theory needs, however, to be made explicit. The things done to the criminal, even if they are called cures, will be just as compulsory as they were in the old days when we called them punishments. If a tendency to steal can be cured by psychotherapy, the thief will no doubt be forced to undergo the treatment. Otherwise, society cannot continue.

From *God in the Dock*. Copyright 1970 by C. S. Lewis Pte Ltd. Reprinted with permission.

My contention is that this doctrine, merciful though it appears, really means that each one of us, from the moment he breaks the law, is deprived of the rights of a human being.

The reason is this. The Humanitarian theory removes from Punishment the concept of Desert. But the concept of Desert is the only connecting link between punishment and justice. It is only as deserved or undeserved that a sentence can be just or unjust. I do not here contend that the question "Is it deserved?" is the only one we can reasonably ask about a punishment. We may very properly ask whether it is likely to deter others and to reform the criminal. But neither of these two last questions is a question about justice. There is no sense in talking about a "just deterrent" or a "just cure." We demand of a deterrent not whether it is just but whether it will deter. We demand of a cure not whether it is just but whether it succeeds. Thus when we cease to consider what the criminal deserves and consider only what will cure him or deter others, we have tacitly removed him from the sphere of justice altogether; instead of a person, a subject of rights, we now have a mere object, a patient, a "case."

The distinction will become clearer if we ask who will be qualified to determine sentences when sentences are no longer held to derive their propriety from the criminal's deserving. On the old view the problem of fixing the right sentence was a moral problem. Accordingly, the judge who did it was a person trained in jurisprudence; trained, that is, in a science which deals with rights and duties, and which, in origin at least, was consciously accepting guidance from the Law of Nature, and from Scripture. We must admit that in the actual penal code of most countries at most times these high originals were so much modified by local custom, class interests, and utilitarian concessions, as to be very imperfectly recognizable. But the code was never in principle, and not always in fact, beyond the control of the conscience of the society. And when (say, in Eighteenth Century England) actual punishments conflicted too violently with the moral sense of the community, juries refused to convict and reform was finally brought about. This was possible because, so long as we are thinking in terms of Desert, the propriety of the penal code, being a moral question, is a question on which every man has a right to an opinion, not because he follows this or that profession, but because he is simply a man, a rational animal enjoying the Natural Light. But all this is changed when we drop the concept of Desert. The only two questions we may now ask about a punishment are whether it deters and whether it cures. But these are not questions on which anyone is entitled to have an opinion simply because he is a man. He is not entitled to an opinion even if, in addition to being a man, he should happen also to be a jurist, a Christian, and a moral theologian. For they are not questions about principle but about matter of fact; and for such *cuiquam in sua arte credendum.** Only the expert "penologist" (let barbarous things have barbarous names), in the light of previous experiment, can tell us what is likely to deter: only

* ["Experts must be believed."-Ed.]

the psychotherapist can tell us what is likely to cure. It will be in vain for the rest of us, speaking simply as men, to say, "but this punishment is hideously unjust, hideously disproportionate to the criminal's deserts." The experts with perfect logic will reply, "but nobody was talking about deserts. No one was talking about *punishment* in your archaic vindictive sense of the word. Here are the statistics proving that this treatment cures. What is your trouble?"

The Humanitarian theory, then, removes sentences from the hands of jurists whom the public conscience is entitled to criticize and places them in the hands of technical experts whose special sciences do not even employ such categories as Rights or Justice. It might be argued that since this transference results from an abandonment of the old idea of punishment, and therefore, of all vindictive motives, it will be safe to leave our criminals in such hands. I will not pause to comment on the simple minded view of fallen human nature which such a belief implies. Let us rather remember that the "cure" of criminals is to be compulsory; and let us then watch how the theory actually works in the mind of the Humanitarian. The immediate starting point of this article was a letter I read in one of our Leftist weeklies. The author was pleading that a certain sin, now treated by our Laws as a crime, should henceforward be treated as a disease. And he complained that under the present system the offender, after a term in gaol, was simply let out to return to his original environment where he would probably relapse. What he complained of was not the shutting up but the letting out. On his remedial view of punishment the offender should, of course, be detained until he was cured. And of course the official straighteners are the only people who can say when that is. The first result of the Humanitarian theory is, therefore, to substitute for a definite sentence (reflecting to some extent the community's moral judgment on the degree of ill-desert involved) an indefinite sentence terminable only by the word of those experts—and they are not experts in the moral theology nor even in the Law of Nature—who inflict it. Which of us, if he stood in the dock, would not prefer to be tried by the old system?

It may be said that by the continued use of the word Punishment and the use of the verb "inflict" I am misrepresenting the Humanitarians. They are not punishing, not inflicting, only healing. But do not let us be deceived by a name. To be taken without consent from my home and friends; to lose my liberty; to undergo all those assaults on my personality which modern psychotherapy knows how to deliver; to be remade after some pattern of "normality" hatched in a Viennese laboratory to which I never professed allegiance; to know that this process will never end until either my captors have succeeded or I have grown wise enough to cheat them with apparent success—who cares whether this is called Punishment or not? That it includes most of the elements for which any punishment is feared—shame, exile, bondage, and years eaten by the locust—is obvious. Only enormous ill-desert could justify it; but ill-desert is the very conception which the Humanitarian theory has thrown overboard.

If we turn from the curative to the deterrent justification of punishment we shall find the new theory even more alarming. When you punish a man *in terrorem*, make of him an "example" to others, you are admittedly using him as a means to an end; someone else's end. This, in itself, would be a very wicked thing to do. On the classical theory of Punishment it was of course justified on the ground that the man deserved it. That was assumed to be established before any question of "making him an example" arose. You then, as the saying is, killed two birds with one stone; in the process of giving him what he deserved you set an example to others. But take away desert and the whole morality of the punishment disappears. Why, in Heaven's name, am I to be sacrificed to the good of society in this way?—unless, of course, I deserve it.

But that is not the worst. If the justification of exemplary punishment is not to be based on desert but solely on its efficacy as a deterrent, it is not absolutely necessary that the man we punish should even have committed the crime. The deterrent effect demands that the public should draw the moral, "If we do such an act we shall suffer like that man." The punishment of a man actually guilty whom the public think innocent will not have the desired effect; the punishment of a man actually innocent will, provided the public think him guilty. But every modern State has powers which make it easy to fake a trial. When a victim is urgently needed for exemplary purposes and a guilty victim cannot be found, all the purposes of deterrence will be equally served by the punishment (call it "cure" if you prefer) of an innocent victim, provided that the public can be cheated into thinking him guilty. It is no use to ask me why I assume that our rulers will be so wicked. The punishment of an innocent, that is, an undeserving, man is wicked only if we grant the traditional view that righteous punishment means deserved punishment. Once we have abandoned that criterion, all punishments have to be justified, if at all, on other grounds that have nothing to do with desert. Where the punishment of the innocent can be justified on those grounds (and it could in some cases be justified as a deterrent) it will be no less moral than any other punishment. Any distaste for it on the part of a Humanitarian will be merely a hangover from the Retributive theory.

It is, indeed, important to notice that my argument so far supposes no evil intentions on the part of the Humanitarian and considers only what is involved in the logic of his position. My contention is that good men (not bad men) consistently acting upon that position would act as cruelly and unjustly as the greatest tyrants. They might in some respects act even worse. Of all tyrannies a tyranny sincerely exercised for the good of its victims may be the most oppressive. It may be better to live under robber barons than under omnipotent moral busybodies. The robber baron's cruelty may sometimes sleep, his cupidity may at some point be satiated; but those who torment us for our own good will torment us without end for they do so with the approval of their own conscience. They may be more likely to go to Heaven yet at the same time likelier to make a Hell of earth. Their very kindness stings with intolerable insult. To be "cured" against one's will and cured of states which we may not regard as disease is to be put on a level with those who have not yet reached the age of reason or those who never will; to be classed with infants, imbeciles, and domestic animals. But to be punished, however severely, because we have deserved it, because we "ought to have known better," is to be treated as a human person made in God's image.

In reality, however, we must face the possibility of bad rulers armed with a Humanitarian theory of punishment. A great many popular blue prints for a Christian society are merely what the Elizabethans called "eggs in moonshine" because they assume that the whole society is Christian or that the Christians are in control. This is not so in most contemporary States. Even if it were, our rulers would still be fallen men, and, therefore, neither very wise nor very good. As it is, they will usually be unbelievers. And since wisdom and virtue are not the only or the commonest qualifications for a place in the government, they will not often be even the best unbelievers. The practical problem of Christian politics is not that of drawing up schemes for a Christian society, but that of living as innocently as we can with unbelieving fellow-subjects under unbelieving rulers who will never be perfectly wise and good and who will sometimes be very wicked and very foolish. And when they are wicked the Humanitarian theory of Punishment will put in their hands a finer instrument of tyranny than wickedness ever had before. For if crime and disease are to be regarded as the same thing, it follows that any state of mind which our masters choose to call "disease" can be treated as crime; and compulsorily cured. It will be vain to plead that states of mind which displease government need not always involve moral turpitude and do not therefore always deserve forfeiture of liberty. For our masters will not be using the concepts of Desert and Punishment but those of disease and cure. We know that one school of psychology already regards religion as a neurosis. When this particular neurosis becomes inconvenient to government what is to hinder government from proceeding to "cure" it? Such "cure" will, of course, be compulsory; but under the Humanitarian theory it will not be called by the shocking name of Persecution. No one will blame us for being Christians, no one will hate us, no one will revile us. The new Nero will approach us with the silky manners of a doctor, and though all will be in fact as compulsory as the *tunica molesta* or Smithfield or Tyburn, all will go on within the unemotional therapeutic sphere where words like "right" and "wrong" or "freedom" and "slavery" are never heard. And thus when the command is given every prominent Christian in the land may vanish overnight into Institutions for the Treatment of the Ideologically Unsound, and it will rest with the expert Fablers to say when (if ever) they are to re-emerge. But it will not be persecution. Even if the treatment is painful, even if it is life-long, even if it is fatal, that will be only a regrettable accident; the intention was purely therapeutic. Even in ordinary medicine there were painful operations and fatal operations; so in this. But because they are "treatment," not punishment, they can be criticized only by fellow-experts and on technical grounds, never by men as men and on grounds of justice.

This is why I think it essential to oppose the Humanitarian theory of Punishment, root and branch, wherever we encounter it. It carries on its front a semblance of Mercy which is wholly false. That is how it can deceive men of good will. The error began, perhaps, with Shelley's statement that the distinction between Mercy and Justice was invented in the courts of tyrants. It sounds noble, and was indeed the error of a noble mind. But the distinction is essential. The older view was that Mercy "tempered" Justice, or (on the highest level of all) that Mercy and Justice had met and kissed. The essential act of Mercy was to pardon; and pardon in its very essence involves the recognition of guilt and ill-desert in the recipient. If crime is only a disease which needs cure, not sin which deserves punishment, it cannot be pardoned. How can you pardon a man for having a gum-boil or a club foot? But the Humanitarian theory wants simply to abolish Justice and substitute Mercy for it. This means that you start being "kind" to people before you have considered their rights, and then force upon them supposed kindnesses which they in fact had a right to refuse, and finally kindnesses which no one but you will recognize as kindnesses and which the recipient will feel as abominable cruelties. You have overshot the mark. Mercy, detached from Justice, grows unmerciful. That is the important paradox. As there are plants which will flourish only in mountain soil, so it appears that Mercy will flower only when it grows in the crannies of the rock of Justice; transplanted to the marshlands of mere Humanitarianism, it becomes a man-eating weed, all the more dangerous because it is still called by the same name as the mountain variety. But we ought long ago to have learned our lesson. We should be too old now to be deceived by those humane pretensions which have served to usher in every cruelty of the revolutionary period in which we live. These are the "precious balms" which will "break our heads."

There is a fine sentence in Bunyan: "It came burning hot into my mind, whatever he said, and however he flattered, when he got me home to his house, he would sell me for a slave." There is a fine couplet, too, in John Ball:

> Be ware ere ye be wo
> Know your friend from your foe.

One last word. You may ask why I send this to an Australian periodical. The reason is simple and perhaps worth recording; I can get no hearing for it in England.

PROBLEMS AND PUZZLES

9. *God, the Arch-Hypnotist*

Jonathan Harrison

Jonathan Harrison, a professor at the University of Nottingham in England, is a prominent philosopher. He has published many books and articles on a variety of philosophical topics.

Once upon a time Dr. Thomas Svengali was walking by the side of a lake when he saw some children playing with their boats. They were model boats of course, but it was possible to control them by short-wave radio. In this way they could be made to go through all the manoeuvres which life-sized boats could execute, but in an unrealistically jerky way, like mice pretending to be elephants.

This gave Dr. Svengali an idea. It was not an original one. Even some twentieth-century philosophers had had it before him. Had he not spent so much of his life immersed in his study of the human brain he would probably have had it before. He had recently been experiencing a great deal of trouble with his housekeeper, a Mrs. Geraldine O'Farrell. He had never liked the new-fangled practice of having his house run by a computer, but being as unversed in the ways of the opposite sex as he was knowledgeable about brain physiology and electronics, he had not the faintest idea how to manage a woman. And the fact that Mrs. O'Farrell considered that she would not have been compelled to occupy her present poorly paid position had it not been for the deplorably inequitable way in which her sex was treated made her quite exceptionally and often quite deliberately incompetent.

It occurred to Dr. Svengali that if he could not make her perform her household duties in any other way he might insert a device into her skull which would enable her to be controlled by a short-wave radio transmitter, which Dr. Svengali prudently kept locked in a cupboard when not in use, out of Mrs. O'Farrell's reach. Though this transmitter could, if necessary, be worked manually, doing so would save Dr. Svengali only labour, but no time. Hence, when familiarity caused him no longer to regard it as a plaything, he built into it a programmer which, at the appointed hours, caused Mrs. O'Farrell to cook, shop and clean, without any further intervention on his part. When these things were not necessary the transmitter

From "Tom & Jerry, or What Price Pelagius?" by Jonathan Harrison. *Religious Studies*, Vol. 17 (December, 1981). Reprinted with the permission of Cambridge University Press.

automatically switched itself off, and left Mrs. O'Farrell to do what she thought she pleased.

Dr. Svengali found, however, that this way of solving the problem presented by Mrs. O'Farrell's intransigence had a drawback. Though her limbs went through the movements of polishing and bed-making in a highly efficient and satisfactory way, the expression on her face was disturbingly resentful, and her language so appalling as to be quite unacceptable to someone as gently nurtured as Dr. Svengali. It was also extremely embarrassing to him when he had visitors.

To a man of Dr. Svengali's ability the task of modifying the controlling device in Mrs. O'Farrell's brain in such a way as to produce a more pleasing facial expression and a less colourful vocabulary was easily accomplished. Dr. Svengali, however, was a sensitive man, and he found the mere knowledge of the resentment that Mrs. O'Farrell felt, but could not express, extremely disturbing to him. And though a very poor housekeeper, she had been a good companion, and resentment at being forced to do her work in such a humiliating manner made her extremely disagreeable to Dr. Svengali in the evenings. Most of these she spent in reproaching him bitterly for the way in which he treated her, and in trying to bring home to him how dreadful it was to find one's limbs manipulated from without—just as if, as Mrs. O'Farrell herself strikingly and originally put it, she was possessed.

Dr. Svengali took longer to solve this second problem. He reasoned that just as he could move Mrs. O'Farrell's limbs, so he could produce or eradicate the desires which normally made her move them. Hence he thought he might make her a better housekeeper without at the same time making her a worse companion if he built a modified device, which would make her *want* to cook, shop and clean at the required times.

Promising though this idea seemed to Dr. Svengali when it first occurred to him, it in fact turned out to be a complete failure. Mrs. O'Farrell did, at the times the controlling device decided that she should, want to cook, clean and shop. But by now she had become so incensed that no such inducement would make her perform these duties well. However intensely Dr. Svengali's machine made her want to do things, she regarded the desires so produced as akin to temptations from the devil. A calvinistic upbringing and a naturally obdurate disposition aided her in her determination to resist, and she very rarely succumbed. When the strength of her wants became overwhelming and, for a short while she did her work in a satisfactory way, she was subsequently so overcome with exasperation and remorse that she treated Dr. Svengali in the evenings in a way which he found nearly unendurable.

Clearly, Dr. Svengali thought, he must modify his device a second time. He decided that the easiest thing to do was simply to combine the first two versions of it, and insert in Mrs. O'Farrell's brain a dual instrument which both made her limbs adequately perform her external tasks, and which also made her want to do, and enjoy doing, them, though it was in fact the instrument, and not the wants, which produced the movements. But Mrs. O'Farrell's fanaticism was so implacable that even the knowledge that in caring for Dr. Svengali, she was simply doing what she herself wanted to do, did little, if anything, to diminish the hostility with which she treated him when the transmitter was switched off.

Since a remote ancestor of hers had once read philosophy in a twentieth-century British university, her mother had inherited some books and journals. One of them, she had been told, contained an article by someone called Harrison, arguing that a man was free so long as he was doing what he wanted to do. In a rare philosophical moment, Mrs. O'Farrell reasoned that, in cooking, shopping and cleaning she was doing what she wanted to do. Nevertheless, so far from being free, she was even more helpless than when she had been controlled by Dr. Svengali's first device, which had made her look after him, even when she did not want to. She at first thought that the reason why she could not be free, although she both wanted to keep house and did, was that she would still be keeping house even though she did not want to. A little reflection, however, made her realise that this was not so. For Dr. Svengali had so constructed his radio control that the only dial setting which made Mrs. O'Farrell *want* to make the beds, for example, also caused the control to direct her to move her limbs to go through the external motions of making them. Hence had she not wanted to make the beds, she would not have. Mrs. O'Farrell failed to find consolation in philosophy and efficiently though his household was run, Dr. Svengali's evenings were as miserable as before.

The intractable nature of his problem caused Dr. Svengali also to engage in unwonted philosophical reflection. After all, he thought, Geraldine (he was not a man to insist in superficial ways upon the superiority of his position) must want not to be made to do the housework, for whatever absurd reason, or she would not resist my attempts to make her do it. So if I can make her want to do the housework, why cannot I eradicate those more central and recalcitrant impulses which make her want not to want to do the housework, and which motivate her prolonged and determined resistance to all my efforts to manage her? Perhaps if I could learn to control those impulses which lie at the very core of her being, I might be able so to manipulate her that I can get my house looked after and some agreeable conversation and pleasant companionship in the evenings.

Trial and error showed that he was right in his surmise. The correct dial setting on his radio control blotted out Mrs. O'Farrell's sense of her duty to the community of women, and she happily did everything Dr. Svengali wished to his entire satisfaction. But success had whetted Dr. Svengali's appetite, and Faustus-like he looked about for more worlds to conquer. In the days when Mrs. O'Farrell was controlled by Mark I of his device, he had made her steal the notes of some experiments from a colleague, to whose study she, but not he, had access. A man naturally prone to make other people bear the guilt which he incurred by his own actions, Dr. Svengali had tried to put the blame upon her, but without success. She had not, she always insisted, stolen the papers. Her feet had gone to the study and her hands taken them against her will. She had even threatened to inform the police of what she considered Dr. Svengali had done, and at one time only doubts about the possibility of convicting him had prevented her from doing so. Now, however, Dr. Svengali saw the chance of having her a willing accomplice to his schemes. He did not consider that Mrs. O'Farrell would make a very effective criminal, but at least, if she were found out, his machine could eradicate any inclination she might have to turn informer.

After a surprisingly successful criminal career, Mrs. O'Farrell was eventually apprehended, tried, convicted and sentenced to a long term of imprisonment. The sentence proved not to be nearly as onerous as intended. She died a week after entering prison from a brain tumour caused by Dr. Svengali's insertion of the control. She herself felt, as was only to be expected, no inclination to blame him, or to feel anything other than that she was herself responsible for what she had apparently done. No-one, she now argued, had compelled her to do it. She had simply done what she herself pleased, and had she not wanted to steal it was by no means outside her power to refrain. She had simply not tried. The remote causes of her want to steal, she thought, were irrelevant. For her wanting to steal must have been caused by something, and the fact that it was actually caused by Dr. Svengali, though highly relevant to what moral judgements ought to be passed upon him, were quite beside the point when it came to passing moral judgements about her.

The prison chaplain, with whom she discussed the matter agreed. He did not try to get Mrs. O'Farrell pardoned, but instead informed the police of Dr. Svengali's complicity, if one could call it that, in the matter. The latter, however, had by this time vanished.

He reappeared a few months later, a changed man, in a country whose police force had the reputation of being weak and internationally uncooperative. But Mrs. O'Farrell's apprehension, conviction and subsequent demise made him realise that he was in fact deeply fond of her. Remorse at the way in which he had treated her overcame him, and he was consumed by a desire to be a better person. To a man of Dr. Svengali's outlook and training, the obvious way to accomplish this difficult feat was to alter the physiology of his own brain in such a manner as to secure the desired improvement. He found an assistant to insert Mrs. O'Farrell's control into his own skull, and himself set the dial on his short-wave radio transmitter, which he had prudently taken with him, in such a manner as to eradicate from himself any further desire towards similar misbehaviour.

Unfortunately, however, his hand slipped, and the dial fell back to the slightly worn place where it had been set to control the behaviour of Mrs. O'Farrell. From that time forward Dr. Svengali stole for himself, and his exploits became progressively more and more dangerous.

Though he, unlike Mrs. O'Farrell, had the knowledge to alter the dial setting so as to eliminate his desire to steal or, at any rate, so as to produce a counter-desire to avoid prison or a stronger dislike of his addiction to such dishonourable conduct, the machine itself, by causing him to be quite satisfied with his behaviour, brought it about that he had no motive for doing so. His very desire to steal prevented him from ordering its own extinction. Inevitably he was eventually apprehended, and the laws of his new country, which tried to make up by their extreme severity for the inefficiency of its police force, condemned him to death.

The imminence of his decease did what the death of his now beloved Geraldine had been unable to do, and he became at last overwhelmed with a readily effective remorse. Even the knowledge that he would not have been in his present plight but for a quite inadvertent slip of his fingers on the control could not prevent him from deciding to hang himself. A stool and a piece of rope had been left in his cell by thoughtful and economically minded prison authorities, but Dr. Svengali had always been a little clumsy, and in climbing on to the stool his foot slipped, and his consequent fall jolted the control in such a way as to make it function in a highly erratic manner, and Dr. Svengali to behave as one demented. The cell, of course, was not padded, and he so damaged himself against its stone sides that the prison authorities, perhaps a little inconsistently, took him to hospital to prevent him doing himself any further injury.

In the course of his treatment doctors discovered the controlling device inside his skull and removed it. His behaviour instantly became as normal as it had ever been. His solicitor appealed against the conviction on the ground that the person who was to be hanged was a different person from the person who had committed the crimes and, alternatively, on the ground that Dr. Svengali was not responsible for his actions, which were caused by the control, not by Dr. Svengali himself. The appeal court found in his favour, though one judge disagreed, on the ground that Dr. Svengali had put the control inside his own skull.

Dr. Svengali thanked God, whom he imagined in his own augmented image as a supremely powerful brain physiologist without much moral character, for his good fortune, for since his belief in the deity manifested itself only in moments of stress, he did not notice the impropriety of ascribing anything at all to luck. On his release from prison, he returned to his own country, where Mrs. O'Farrell had cached most of their booty.

His first act upon retaking up his abode in his former lodgings was to advertise for another housekeeper.

10. *Fate*

Richard Taylor

*Richard Taylor (1919–   ), emeritus professor of philosophy at the University
of Rochester, has written highly acclaimed books and articles on a variety of
philosophical problems.*

We are all, at certain moments of pain, threat, or bereavement, apt to entertain the
idea of fatalism, the thought that what is happening at a particular moment is
unavoidable, that we are powerless to prevent it. Sometimes we find ourselves in
circumstances not of our own making, in which our very being and destinies are so
thoroughly anchored that the thought of fatalism can be quite overwhelming, and
sometimes consoling. One feels that whatever then happens, however good or ill,
will be what those circumstances yield, and we are helpless. Soldiers, it is said, are
sometimes possessed by such thoughts. Perhaps everyone would feel more inclined
to them if they paused once in a while to think of how little they ever had to do with
bringing themselves to wherever they have arrived in life, how much of their fortunes and destinies were decided for them by sheer circumstance, and how the entire course of their lives is often set, once and for all, by the most trivial incidents,
which they did not produce and could not even have foreseen. If we are free to
work out our destinies at all, which is doubtful, we have a freedom that is at best
exercised within exceedingly narrow paths. All the important things—when we
are born, of what parents, into what culture, whether we are loved or rejected,
whether we are male or female, our temperament, our intelligence or stupidity,
indeed everything that makes for the bulk of our happiness and misery—all these
are decided for us by the most casual and indifferent circumstances, by sheer coin-
cidences, chance encounters, and seemingly insignificant fortuities. One can see
this in retrospect if he searches, but few search. The fate that has given us our
very being has given us also our pride and conceit, and has thereby formed us so
that, being human we congratulate ourselves on our blessings, which we call our
achievements; blame the world for our blunders, which we call our misfortunes; and
scarcely give a thought to that impersonal fate that arbitrarily dispenses both.

FATALISM AND DETERMINISM

Determinism, it will be recalled, is the theory that all events are rendered unavoidable by their causes. The attempt is sometimes made to distinguish this from fatalism by saying that, according to the fatalist, certain events are going to happen *no*

From *Metaphysics* 3rd ed. by Richard Taylor © 1974. Reprinted by permission of Prentice-Hall Inc., Upper
Saddle River, NJ.

matter what, or in other words, regardless of causes. But this is enormously contrived. It would be hard to find in the whole history of thought a single fatalist, on that conception of it.

Fatalism is the belief that whatever happens is unavoidable. That is the clearest expression of the doctrine, and it provides the basis of the attitude of calm acceptance that the fatalist is thought, quite correctly, to embody. One who endorses the claim of universal causation, then, and the theory of the causal determination of all human behavior, is a kind of fatalist—or at least he should be, if he is consistent. For that theory, as we have seen, once it is clearly spelled out and not hedged about with unresolved "ifs," does entail that whatever happens is rendered inevitable by the causal conditions preceding it, and is therefore unavoidable. One can indeed think of verbal formulas for distinguishing the two theories, but if we think of a fatalist as one who has a certain attitude, we find it to be the attitude that a thoroughgoing determinist should, in consistency, assume. That some philosophical determinists are not fatalists does not so much illustrate a great difference between fatalism and determinism but rather the humiliation to one's pride that a fatalist position can deliver, and the comfort that can sometimes be found in evasion.

FATALISM WITH RESPECT TO THE FUTURE AND THE PAST

A fatalist, then, is someone who believes that whatever happens is and always was unavoidable. He thinks it is not up to him what will happen a thousand years hence, next year, tomorrow, or the very next moment. Of course he does not pretend always to *know* what is going to happen. Hence, he might try sometimes to read signs and portents, as meteorologists and astrologers do, or to contemplate the effects upon him of the various things that might, for all he knows, be fated to occur. But he does not suppose that whatever happens could ever have really been avoidable.

A fatalist thus thinks of the future in the way we all think of the past, for everyone is a fatalist as he looks *back* on things. To a large extent we know what has happened—some of it we can even remember—whereas the future is still obscure to us, and we are therefore tempted to imbue it, in our imagination, with all sorts of "possibilities." The fatalist resists this temptation, knowing that mere ignorance can hardly give rise to any genuine possibility in things. He thinks of both past and future "under the aspect of eternity," the way God is supposed to view them. We all think of the past this way, as something settled and fixed, to be taken for what it is. We are never in the least tempted to try to modify it. It is not in the least up to us what happened last year, yesterday, or even a moment ago, any more than are the motions of the heavens or the political developments in Tibet. If we are not fatalists, then we might think that past things once *were* up to us, to bring about or prevent, as long as they were still future—but this expresses our attitude toward the future, not the past.

Such is surely our conception of the whole past, whether near or remote. But the consistent fatalist thinks of the future in the same way. We say of past things that they are no longer within our power. The fatalist says they never were.

THE SOURCES OF FATALISM

A fatalistic way of thinking most often arises from theological ideas, or from what are generally thought to be certain presuppositions of science and logic. Thus, if God is really all-knowing and all-powerful, it is not hard to suppose that He has arranged for everything to happen just as it is going to happen, that He already knows every detail of the whole future course of the world, and there is nothing left for you and me to do except watch things unfold, in the here or the hereafter. But without bringing God into the picture, it is not hard to suppose, as we have seen, that everything that happens is wholly determined by what went before it, and hence that whatever happens at any future time is the only thing that can then happen, given what precedes it. Or even disregarding that, it seems natural to suppose that there is a body of truth concerning what the future holds, just as there is such truth concerning what is contained in the past, whether or not it is known to any person or even to God, and hence, that everything asserted in that body of truth will assuredly happen, in the fullness of time, precisely as it is described therein.

No one needs to be convinced that fatalism is the only proper way to view the past. That it is also the proper way to view the future is less obvious, due in part, perhaps, to our vastly greater ignorance of what the future holds. The consequences of holding such fatalism are obviously momentous. To say nothing of the consolation of fatalism, which enables a person to view all things as they arise with the same undisturbed mind with which he contemplates even the most revolting of history's horrors, the fatalist teaching also relieves one of all tendency toward both blame and approbation of others and of both guilt and conceit in himself. It promises that a perfect understanding is possible and removes the temptation to view things in terms of human wickedness and moral responsibility. This thought alone, once firmly grasped, yields a sublime acceptance of all that life and nature offer, whether to oneself or one's fellows; and although it thereby reduces one's pride, it simultaneously enhances the feelings, opens the heart, and expands the understanding.

DIVINE OMNISCIENCE

Suppose for the moment, just for the purpose of this discussion, that God exists and is omniscient. To say that God is omniscient means that He knows everything that is true. He cannot, of course, know that which is false. Concerning any falsehood, an omniscient being can know that it is false; but then it is a truth that is known, namely, the truth that the thing in question is a falsehood. So if it is false that the moon is a cube, then God can, like you or me, know that this is false; but He cannot know the falsehood itself, that the moon is a cube.

Thus, if God is omniscient He knows, as you probably do, the date of your birth. He also knows, as you may not, the hour of your birth. Furthermore, God knows, as you assuredly do not, the date of your conception—for there is such a truth, and we are supporting that God knows every truth. Moreover, He knows as you surely do not, the date of your death, and the circumstances thereof—whether at that moment, known already to Him, you die as the result of accident, a fatal malady, suicide, murder, whatever. And, still assuming God exists and knows everything, He knows whether any ant walked across my desk last night, and if so, what ant it was, where it came from, how long it was on the desk, how it came to be there, and so on, to every truth about this insect that there is. Similarly, of course, He knows when some ant will again appear on my desk, if ever. He knows the number of hairs on my head, notes the fall of every sparrow, knows why it fell, and why it was going to fall. These are simply a few of the consequences of the omniscience that we are for the moment assuming. A more precise way of expressing all this is to say that God knows, concerning any statement whatever that anyone could formulate, that it is true, in case it is, and otherwise, that it is false. And let us suppose that God, at some time or other, or perhaps from time to time, vouchsafes some of his knowledge to people, or perhaps to certain chosen persons. Thus prophets arise, proclaiming the coming of certain events, and things do then happen as they have foretold. Of course it is not surprising that they should, on the supposition we are making, namely, that the foreknowledge of these things comes from God, who is omniscient.

The Story of Osmo

Now, then, let us make one further supposition, which will get us squarely into the philosophical issue these ideas are intended to introduce. Let us suppose that God has revealed a particular set of facts to a chosen scribe who, believing (correctly) that they came from God, wrote them all down. The facts in question then turned out to be all the more or less significant episodes in the life of some perfectly ordinary man named Osmo. Osmo was entirely unknown to the scribe, and in fact to just about everyone, but there was no doubt concerning whom all these facts were about, for the very first thing received by the scribe from God, was: "He of whom I speak is called Osmo." When the revelations reached a fairly voluminous bulk and appeared to be completed, the scribe arranged them in chronological order and assembled them into a book. He at first gave it the title *The Life of Osmo, as Given by God,* but thinking that people would take this to be some sort of joke, he dropped the reference to God.

The book was published but attracted no attention whatsoever, because it appeared to be nothing more than a record of the dull life of a very plain man named Osmo. The scribe wondered, in fact, why God had chosen to convey such a mass of seemingly pointless trivia.

The book eventually found its way into various libraries, where it gathered dust until one day a high school teacher in Indiana, who rejoiced under the name of Osmo, saw a copy on the shelf. The title caught his eye. Curiously picking it up and blowing the dust off, he was thunderstruck by the opening sentence: "Osmo is born in Mercy Hospital in Auburn, Indiana, on June 6, 1942, of Finnish parentage, and after nearly losing his life from an attack of pneumonia at the age of five, he is enrolled in the St. James school there." Osmo turned pale. The book nearly fell from his hands. He thumbed back in excitement to discover who had written it. Nothing was given of its authorship nor, for that matter, of its publisher. His questions of the librarian produced no further information, he being as ignorant as Osmo of how the book came to be there.

So Osmo, with the book pressed tightly under his arm, dashed across the street for some coffee, thinking to compose himself and then examine this book with care. Meanwhile he glanced at a few more of its opening remarks, at the things said there about his difficulties with his younger sister, how he was slow in learning to read, of the summer on Mackinac Island, and so on. His emotions now somewhat quieted, Osmo began a close reading. He noticed that everything was expressed in the present tense, the way newspaper headlines are written. For example, the text read, "Osmo is born in Mercy Hospital," instead of saying he was born there, and it recorded that he quarrels with his sister, is a slow student, is fitted with dental braces at age eight, and so on, all in the journalistic present tense. But the text itself made quite clear approximately when all these various things happened, for everything was in chronological order, and in any case each year of its subject's life constituted a separate chapter and was so titled—"Osmo's Seventh Year," "Osmo's Eighth Year," and so on through the book.

Osmo became absolutely engrossed, to the extent that he forgot his original astonishment, bordering on panic, and for a while even lost his curiosity concerning authorship. He sat drinking coffee and reliving his childhood, much of which he had all but forgotten until the memories were revived by the book now before him. He had almost forgotten about the kitten, for example, and had entirely forgotten its name, until he read, in the chapter called "Osmo's Seventh Year," this observation: "Sobbing, Osmo takes Fluffy, now quite dead, to the garden, and buries her next to the rose bush." Ah yes! And then there was Louise, who sat next to him in the eighth grade—it was all right there. And how he got caught smoking one day. And how he felt when his father died. On and on. Osmo became so absorbed that he quite forgot the business of the day, until it occurred to him to turn to Chapter 26, to see what might be said there, he having just recently turned twenty-six. He had no sooner done so than his panic returned, for lo! what the book said was *true!* That it rains on his birthday for example, that his wife fails to give him the binoculars he had hinted he would like, that he receives a raise in salary shortly thereafter, and so on. Now how in God's name, Osmo pondered, could anyone know that apparently before it had happened? For these were quite recent events, and the book had dust on it. Quickly moving on, Osmo came to this: "Sitting and reading in the coffee shop across from the library, Osmo, perspiring copiously, entirely forgets, until it is too late, that he is supposed to collect his wife at the hairdresser's at four." Oh my god! He had forgotten all about that. Yanking out his watch, Osmo discovered that it was nearly five o'clock—too late. She would be on her way home by now, and in a very sour mood.

Osmo's anguish at this discovery was nothing, though, compared with what the rest of the day held for him. He poured more coffee, and it now occurred to him to check the number of chapters in this amazing book: only twenty-nine! But surely, he thought, that doesn't mean anything. How anyone could have gotten all this stuff down so far was puzzling enough, to be sure, but no one on God's earth could possibly know in advance how long this or that person is going to live. (Only God could know that sort of thing, Osmo reflected.) So he read along; though not without considerable uneasiness and even depression, for the remaining three chapters were on the whole discouraging. He thought he had gotten that ulcer under control, for example. And he didn't see any reason to suppose his job was going to turn out that badly, or that he was really going to break a leg skiing; after all, he could just give up skiing. But then the book ended on a terribly dismal note. It said: "And Osmo, having taken Northwest flight 569 from O'Hare, perishes when the aircraft crashes on the runway at Fort Wayne, with considerable loss of life, a tragedy rendered the more calamitous by the fact that Osmo had neglected to renew his life insurance before the expiration of the grace period." And that was all. That was the end of the book.

So *that's* why it had only twenty-nine chapters. Some idiot thought he was going to get killed in a plane crash. But, Osmo thought, he just wouldn't get on that plane. And this would also remind him to keep his insurance in force.

(About three years later our hero, having boarded a flight for St. Paul, went berserk when the pilot announced they were going to land at Fort Wayne instead. According to one of the flight attendants, he tried to hijack the aircraft and divert it to another airfield. The Civil Aeronautics Board cited the resulting disruptions as contributing to the crash that followed as the plane tried to land.)

FOUR QUESTIONS

Osmo's extraordinary circumstances led him to embrace the doctrine of fatalism. Not quite completely, perhaps, for there he was, right up to the end, trying vainly to buck his fate—trying, in effect, to make a fool of God, though he did not know this, because he had no idea of the book's source. Still, he had the overwhelming evidence of his whole past life to make him think that everything was going to work out exactly as described in the book. It always had. It was, in fact, precisely this conviction that terrified him so.

But now let us ask these questions, in order to make Osmo's experiences more relevant to our own. First, why did he become, or nearly become, a fatalist? Second, just what did his fatalism amount to? Third, was his belief justified in terms of the evidence he had? And finally, is that belief justified in terms of the evidence we have—or in other words, should we be fatalists too?

This last, of course, is the important metaphysical question, but we have to approach it through the others.

Why did Osmo become a fatalist? Osmo became a fatalist because there existed a set of true statements about the details of his life, both past and future, and he came to know what some of these statements were and to believe them, including many concerning the future. That is the whole of it.

No theological ideas entered into his conviction, nor any presuppositions about causal determinism, the coercion of his actions by causes, or anything of this sort. The foundations of Osmo's fatalism were entirely in logic and epistemology, having to do only with truth and knowledge. Ideas about God did not enter in, for he never suspected that God was the ultimate source of those statements. And at no point did he think God was *making* him do what he did. All he was concerned about was that someone seemed somehow to *know* what he had done and was going to do.

What, then, did Osmo believe? He did not, it should be noted, believe that certain things were going to happen to him *no matter what.* That does not express a logically coherent belief. He did not think he was in danger of perishing in an airplane crash even in case he did not get into any airplane, for example, or that he was going to break his leg skiing, whether he went skiing or not. No one believes what he considers to be plainly impossible. If anyone believes that a given event is going to happen, he does not doubt that those things necessary for its occurrence are going to happen too. The expression "no matter what," by means of which some philosophers have sought an easy and even childish refutation of fatalism, is accordingly highly inappropriate in any description of the fatalist conviction.

Osmo's fatalism was simply the realization that the things described in the book were unavoidable.

Of course we are all fatalists in this sense about some things, and the metaphysical question is whether this familiar attitude should not be extended to everything. We know the sun will rise tomorrow, for example, and there is nothing we can do about it. Each of us knows he is sooner or later going to die, too, and there is nothing to be done about that either. We normally do not know just when, of course, but it is mercifully so! For otherwise we would sit simply checking off the days as they passed, with growing despair, like a man condemned to the gallows and knowing the hour set for his execution. The tides ebb and flow, and heavens revolve, the seasons follow in order, generations arise and pass, and no one speaks of taking preventive measures. With respect to those things each of us recognizes as beyond his control, we are of necessity fatalists.

The question of fatalism is simply: Of all the things that happen in the world, which, if any, are avoidable? And the philosophical fatalist replies: None of them. They never were. Some of them only seemed so.

Was Osmo's fatalism justified? Of course it was. When he could sit right there and read a true description of those parts of his life that had not yet been lived, it would be idle to suggest to him that his future might, nonetheless, contain alternative possibilities. The only doubts Osmo had were whether those statements could really be true. But here he had the proof of his own experience, as one by one they were tested. Whenever he tried to prevent what was set forth, he of course failed. Such failure, over and over, of even the most herculean efforts, with never a single success, must surely suggest, sooner or later, that he was *destined* to fail. Even to the end, when Osmo tried so desperately to save himself from the destruction described in the book, his effort was totally in vain—as he should have realized it was going to be had he really known that what was said there was true. No power in heaven or earth can render false a statement that is true. It has never been done, and never will be.

Is the doctrine of fatalism, then, true? This amounts to asking whether our circumstances are significantly different from Osmo's. Of course we cannot read our own biographies the way he could. Only people who become famous ever have their lives recorded, and even so, it is always in retrospect. This is unfortunate. It is too bad that someone with sufficient knowledge—God, for example—cannot set down the lives of great men in advance, so that their achievements can be appreciated better by their contemporaries, and indeed, by their predecessors— their parents, for instance. But mortals do not have the requisite knowledge, and if there are any gods who do, they seem to keep it to themselves.

None of this matters, as far as our own fatalism is concerned. For the important thing to note is that, of the two considerations that explain Osmo's fatalism, only one of them was philosophically relevant, and that one applies to us no less than to him. The two considerations were: (1) there existed a set of true statements about his life, both past and future, and (2) he came to know what those statements were and to believe them. Now the second of these two considerations explains why, as a matter of psychological fact, Osmo became fatalistic, but it has nothing to do with the validity of that point of view. Its validity is assured by (1) alone. It was not the fact that the statements happened to be written down that rendered the things they described unavoidable; that had nothing to do with it at all. Nor was it the fact that, because they had been written, Osmo could read them. His reading them and coming to believe them likewise had nothing to do with the inevitability of what they described. This was ensured simply by there being such a set of statements, whether written or not, whether read by anyone or not, and whether or not known to be true. All that is required is that they should *be* true.

Each of us has but one possible past, described by that totality of statements about us in the past tense, each of which happens to be true. No one ever thinks of rearranging things there; it is simply accepted as given. But so also, each of us has but one possible future, described by that totality of statements about oneself in the future sense, each of which happens to be true. The sum of these constitutes one's biography. Part of it has been lived. The main outlines of it can still be seen, in retrospect, though most of its details are obscure. The other part has not been lived, though it most assuredly is going to be, in exact accordance with the set of statements just referred to. Some of its outlines can already be seen, in prospect, but it is on the whole more obscure than the part belonging to the past. We have at best only premonitory glimpses of it. It is no doubt for this reason that not all of this part, the part that awaits us, is perceived as given, and people do sometimes speak absurdly of altering it—as though what the future holds, as identified by any true statement in the future tense, might after all *not* hold.

Osmo's biography was all expressed in the present tense because all that mattered was that the things referred to were real events; it did not matter to what part of time they belonged. His past consisted of those things that preceded his reading of the book, and he simply accepted it as a given. He was not tempted to revise what was said there, for he was sure it was true. But it took the book to make him realize that his future was also something given. It was equally pointless for him to try to revise what was said there, for it, too, was true. As the past contains what has happened, the future contains what will happen, and neither contains, in addition to these things, various other things that did not and will not happen.

Of course we know relatively little of what the future contains. Some things we know. We know the sun will go on rising and setting, for example, that taxes will be levied and wars will rage, that people will continue to be callous and greedy, and that people will be murdered and robbed. It is only the details that remain to be discovered. But the same is true of the past; it is only a matter of degree. When I meet a total stranger, I do not know, and will probably never know, what his past has been, beyond certain obvious things—that he had a mother, and things of this sort. I know nothing of the particulars of that vast realm of fact that is unique to his past. And the same for his future, with only this difference—that *all* people are strangers to me as far as their futures are concerned, and here I am even a stranger to myself.

Yet there is one thing I know concerning any stranger's past and the past of everything under the sun; namely, that whatever it might hold, there is nothing anyone can do about it now. What has happened cannot be undone. The mere fact that it has happened guarantees this.

And so it is, by the same token, of the future of everything under the sun. Whatever the future might hold, there is nothing anyone can do about it now. What will happen cannot be altered. The mere fact that it is going to happen guarantees this.

THE LAW OF EXCLUDED MIDDLE

The presupposition of fatalism is therefore nothing but the commonest presupposition of all logic and inquiry; namely, that there is such a thing as truth, and that this has nothing at all to do with the passage of time. Nothing *becomes* true or *ceases* to be true; whatever is truth at all simply *is* true.

It comes to the same thing, and is perhaps more precise, to say that every meaningful statement, whether about oneself or anything else, is either true or else it is false; that is, its denial is true. There is no middle ground. The principle is thus appropriately called *the law of excluded middle*. It has nothing to do what tense a statement happens to express, nor with the question of whether anyone, man or god, happens to know whether it is true or false.

Thus no one knows whether there was an ant on my desk last night, and no one ever will. But we do know that either this statement is true or else its denial is true—there is no third alternative. If we say it *might* be true, we mean only that we do not happen to know. Similarly, no one knows whether or not there is going to be an ant there tonight, but we do know that either it will or else it will not be there.

In a similar way we can distinguish two mutually exclusive but exhaustive classes of statements about any person; namely, the class of all those that are true, and the class of all that are false. There are no others in addition to these. Included in each are statements never asserted or even considered by anyone, but such that, if anyone were to formulate one of them, it would either be a true statement or else a false one.

Consider, then, that class of statements about some particular person—you, let us suppose—each of which happens to be true. Their totality constitutes your biography. One combination of such statements describes the time, place, and circumstances of your birth. Another combination describes the time, place, and circumstances of your death. Others describe in detail the rises and falls of your fortunes, your achievements and failures, your joys and sorrows—absolutely everything that is true of you.

Some of these things you have already experienced, others await you. But the entire biography is there. It is not written, and probably never will be; but it is nevertheless there, all of it. If, like Osmo, you had some way of discovering those statements in advance, then like him you could hardly help becoming a fatalist. But foreknowledge of the truth would not create any truth, nor invest your philosophy with truth, nor add anything to the philosophical foundations of the fatalism that would then be so apparent to you. It would only serve to make it apparent.

OBJECTIONS

This thought, and the sense of its force, have tormented and frightened people from the beginning, and thinkers whose pride sometimes exceeds their acumen and their reverence for truth have attempted every means imaginable to demolish it. There are few articles of faith upon which virtually everyone can agree, but one of them is certainly the belief in their cherished free will. Any argument in opposition to the doctrine of fate, however feeble, is immediately and uncritically embraced, as though the refutation of fatalism required only the denial of it, supported by reasons that would hardly do credit to a child. It will be worthwhile, therefore, to look briefly at some of the arguments most commonly heard.

1. One can neither foresee the future nor prove that there is any god, or even if there is, that he could know in advance the free actions of men.

The reply to this is that it is irrelevant. The thesis of fatalism rests on no theory of divination and on no theology. These ideas were introduced only illustratively.

2. True statements are not the cause of anything. Statements only entail; they do not cause, and hence threaten no man's freedom.

But this, too, is irrelevant, for the claim here denied is not one that has been made.

3. The whole argument just conflates fact and necessity into one and the same thing, treating as unavoidable that which is merely true. The fact that a given thing is going to happen implies only that it is *going* to happen, not that it *has* to. Someone might still be able to prevent it—though of course no one will. For example, President Kennedy was murdered. This means it was true that he was going to be murdered. But it does not mean his death at that time and place was unavoidable. Someone *could* have rendered that statement false; though of course no one did.

That is probably the commonest "refutation" of fatalism ever offered. But how strong is the claim that something *can* be done, when in fact it never *has* been done in the whole history of the universe, in spite, sometimes, of the most strenuous efforts? No one has ever rendered false a statement that was true, however hard some have tried. When an attempt, perhaps a heroic attempt, is made to avoid a given calamity, and the thing in question happens anyway, at just the moment and in just the way it was going to happen, we have reason to doubt that it could have been avoided. And in fact great effort was made to save President Kennedy, for example, from the destruction toward which he was heading on that fatal day, a whole legion of bodyguards having no other mission. And it failed. True, we can say that *if* more strenuous precautions had been taken, the event would not have happened. But to this we must add *true,* they were not taken, and hence *true,* they were not going to be taken—and we have on our hands again a true statement of the kind that no man has ever had the slightest degree of success in rendering false.

4. The fatalist argument just rests on a "confusion of modalities." The fact that something is true entails only that its denial is false, not that its denial is impossible. All that is impossible is that both should be true, or both false. Thus, if the president is going to be murdered, it is certainly false that he is not—but not impossible. What is impossible is that he will be both murdered and spared.

Here again we have only a distracting irrelevancy, similar to the point just made. The fatalist argument has nothing to do with impossibility in those senses familiar to logic. It has to do with unavoidability. It is, in other words, concerned with human abilities. The fact that a statement is true does not, to be sure, entail that it is necessary, nor do all false statements express impossibilities. Nonetheless, no one is able to avoid what is truly described, however contingently, in any statement, nor to bring about what is thus falsely described. Nor can anyone convert the one to the other, making suddenly true that which was false, or vice versa. It has never been done, and it never will be. It would be a conceit indeed for someone now to suggest that he, alone among men, might be able to accomplish that feat. This inability goes far beyond the obvious impossibility of making something both true and false at once. No metaphysics turns on that simple point.

5. Perhaps it would be best, then, to discard the presupposition underlying the whole fatalist philosophy; namely, the idea that statements are true in advance of the things they describe. The future is the realm of possibilities, concerning any of which we should neither say it is true that it will happen, nor that it is false.

But, in reply, this desperate move is nothing but arbitrary fiction, resorted to for no other reason than to be rid of the detested doctrine of fatalism. What is at issue here is the very law of excluded middle, which, it is suggested, we shall be allowed to affirm only up to that point at which it threatens something dear. We shall permit it to hold for one part of time, but suddenly retract it in speaking of another, even though the future is continuously being converted to the past through sheer temporal passage.

Most surely, if the statement, made now, that President Kennedy has been murdered, is a true one, then the prediction, made before the event, that he was going to be murdered, was true too. The two statements have exactly the same content, and are in fact one and the same statement; except for the variation of tense. The fact that this statement is more easily known in retrospect than in prospect casts no doubt on its truth but only illustrates a familiar fact of epistemology. A prediction, to be sure, must await fulfillment, but it does not thereupon for the first time acquire its truth. Indeed, had it not been true from the start, it could not have been fulfilled, nor its author congratulated for having it right. Fulfillment is nothing but the occurrence of what is correctly predicted.

The law of excluded middle is not like a blank check into which we can write whatever values we please, according to our preferences. We can no more make ourselves metaphysically free and masters of our destinies by adding qualifications to this law than a poor person can make himself rich just by adding figures to his bankbook. That law pronounces every meaningful statement true, or, if not true, then false. It leaves no handy peg between these two on which one may hang his beloved freedom of will for safekeeping, nor does it say anything whatever about time.

Every single philosophical argument against the teaching of fatalism rests upon the assumption that we are free to pursue and realize various alternative future possibilities—the very thing, of course, that is at issue. When some of these possibilities have become realized and moved on into the past, the supposed alternative possibilities usually appear to have been less real than they had seemed; but this somehow does not destroy the fond notion that they were there. Metaphysics and logic are weak indeed in the face of an opinion nourished by invincible pride, and most people would sooner lose their very souls than be divested of that dignity that they imagine rests upon their freedom of will.

INVINCIBLE FATE

We shall say, therefore, of whatever happens that it was going to be that way. And this is a comfort, both in fortune and in adversity. We shall say of him who turns out bad and mean that he was going to; of him who turns out happy and blessed that he was going to; neither praising nor berating fortune, crying over what has been, lamenting what was going to be, or passing moral judgments.

Shall we, then, sit idly by, passively observing the changing scene without participation, never testing our strength and our goodness, having no hand in what happens, or in making things come out as they should? This is a question for which each will find his own answer. Some people do little or nothing with their lives and might as well never have lived, they make such a waste of it. Others do much, and the lives of a few even shine like the stars. But we knew this before we ever began talking about fate. In time we will all know of which sort we were destined to be.

SUGGESTIONS
FOR FURTHER READING

ANTHOLOGIES

Enteman, Willard F., ed. *The Problem of Free Will.* New York: Scribners, 1967. A collection of important articles on various aspects of the free will–determinism controversy. Since most of the articles are easily readable, this is a good book for the beginning student to turn to for additional reading.

Hook, Sidney, ed. *Determinism and Freedom in the Age of Modern Science.* New York: New York Univ. Press, 1958. A collection of twenty-seven articles that analyze the concepts of determinism and freedom and the significance of these concepts in physics, law, and ethics. Most of the articles will be difficult for the beginning student.

INDIVIDUAL WORKS

Clemens, Samuel. "What Is Man?" in *What Is Man? and Other Essays.* New York: Harper, 1917. An interesting and amusing statement of the determinist position by a famous writer.

Cranston, Maurice. *Freedom: A New Analysis.* London: Longmans, 1953. The latter half of this book is a good discussion of the main positions and a defense of libertarianism.

D'Angelo, Edward. *The Problem of Freedom and Determinism.* Columbia, Mo.: Univ. of Missouri Press, 1968. A good, clear discussion of the three major positions.

Darrow, Clarence. *Crime: Its Cause and Treatment.* New York: Crowell, 1922. A famous discussion of criminal treatment from the hard determinist viewpoint.

Dennett, Daniel C. *Elbow Room.* Cambridge: MIT Press, 1984. A prominent contemporary philosopher attempts to clarify the notion of free will.

Lamont, Corliss. *Freedom of Choice Affirmed.* New York: Horizon, 1967. A clear statement and defense of libertarianism.

Matson, Floyd W. *The Broken Image.* New York: George Braziller, 1964. A good discussion of how the hard determinist position has affected man's image of himself. There is also an examination of Skinner and other behaviorists in this connection.

O'Connor, D.J. *Free Will.* Garden City, N.Y.: Doubleday, 1971. A careful survey of the main arguments both for and against determinism.

Schopenhauer, Arthur. "Free-Will and Fatalism" in *The Pessimist's Handbook (Parerga und Paralipomena).* Translated by T. Bailey Saunders, edited by Hazel E. Barnes. Lincoln: Univ. of Nebraska Press, 1964. A concise and forceful defense of fatalism. Schopenhauer, a clear stylist, uses many illustrations drawn from everyday human behavior and world literature in this essay intended for the general reading public.

Taylor, Richard. *Metaphysics.* 4th ed. Englewood Cliffs, N.J.: Prentice-Hall, 1992. Chapter Five contains a clearly written attack on hard and soft determinism and a defense of a version of libertarianism.

Thorton, Mark. *Do We Have Free Will?* New York: St. Martin's Press, 1989. An introductory account of the major positions on the free will versus determinism controversy.

Trusted, Jennifer. *Free Will and Responsibility.* Oxford: Oxford Univ. Press, 1984. The clear style and thorough coverage make this an excellent text for undergraduates.

Dictionary of the History of Ideas: Studies of Selected Pivotal Ideas. Philip P. Weiner, editor-in-chief. New York: Scribner's, 1973. Substantial and clearly written essays emphasizing the historical development of topics discussed in this part. Designed to inform the nonspecialist, each essay concludes with a select bibliography.

Encyclopedia of Philosophy. Paul Edwards, editor-in-chief. New York: Macmillan, 1967. The student will find many worthwhile articles on the subject treated in this part and excellent bibliographies.

PART TWO

God and Religion

INTRODUCTION

A question troubling many students is whether they should believe in religion. One reason for their hesitation simply to follow in the paths of their parents in this matter is their conviction that religion has failed to bring about a better world for humankind. Perhaps an even more important reason is that there appears to be no scientific manner by which the basic religious tenets can be established. The desire that one's beliefs be supported by science has its roots in the movement of Western civilization away from a religious view of the world to a scientific one. The great success of science has led many to the view that we should believe only those things that can be established in a proper scientific manner. Further, the advance of science has certainly tended to undermine any simplistic acceptance of religious doctrines and writings. The scientifically trained no longer accept, for example, the biblical accounts of creation and the Garden of Eden as literally true. Thus, it is easy to understand why so many of today's students are dubious about accepting traditional orthodox religion. In the light of modern science it appears to be a remnant of ancient superstition that will one day be completely replaced by a scientific view of the world.

Contemporary religious thinkers generally deplore the tendency to view science and religion as competing views of the world. For them, religion and science are concerned with different issues. Science is concerned with discovering the laws that are operative in the physical universe, whereas religion is concerned with issues beyond the scope of science, such as the reason for the existence of the universe, the existence of God, and the purpose of life. Since the issues with which religion is concerned are not within the scope of science, it is held to be inappropriate to demand that religious beliefs should be substantiated by scientific facts.

Must religious beliefs be supported by scientific evidence, or is it acceptable to believe without proof? Do the discoveries of modern science show that the views of the major religions are untenable? These are some of the questions that the philosopher seeks to answer about religion. The philosopher's interest in such questions arises out of the fact that religion gives answers to many of humanity's most fundamental questions about themselves and their place in the world. The philosopher wants to know if the answers are true. Thus, in examining religious views, the philosopher is concerned with their accurate assessment rather than their defense or destruction. The readings in this section show that a great diversity of opinion exists among philosophers regarding the truth and value of religion. Some hold that only in a religious framework can a foundation for morality and a meaning to life be found. Others see various religious views as not only false but a great detriment to the happiness of human beings. The student's job is to assess carefully the various positions and arguments to determine which, if any, are sound.

The basic tenet of the major Western religions is that there exists a supernatural being called "God." God is defined as being an all-good, all-knowing, all-powerful creator of the universe. God is viewed as concerned with our affairs rather than being withdrawn and aloof. For the most part, religious believers are convinced that such a God exists without inquiring into the question of scientific or rational proofs for their conviction. Yet many religious theorists believe it important to show, if possible, that the existence of God can be proven or at least shown to be probable on the basis of scientific evidence or other rational arguments. If God's existence could be proven, not only could the skeptics and atheists be converted but many who believe would feel more confident in their belief.

Numerous proofs have been offered for the existence of God. Most are of little interest to philosophers since they are clearly unsound. Typical of these widely used but unsound arguments are the argument from agreement and the argument from Scripture. The *argument from agreement* consists in attempting to show that God exists on the basis of the fact that so many people throughout the world have believed in the existence of God. It is claimed that such a widespread belief cannot be explained on any other basis than the actual existence of God. One problem with arguing in this manner is that it makes the majority opinion the basis of truth; but it is certainly well known that large majorities have been wrong. At one time there was widespread agreement that the earth was flat. Another difficulty with this argument is that the widespread belief in God can perhaps be explained as the result of superstition, wishful thinking, or fear. If so, the belief in God would not indicate his existence but the psychological characteristics or the lack of scientific knowledge of the majority of humankind. The *argument from Scripture* attempts to prove God's existence on the basis of the fact that we have some writings (Old Testament, New Testament, Koran, and so on) that tell of God. These writings are assumed to have been inspired by God and therefore reliable. The obvious difficulty with attempting to prove God in this manner is that the events recorded in the writings must be proved to be accurate and such proof seems impossible to get. Those who doubt the existence of God will also be doubtful that the Bible was inspired by God and that the events given there are accurately reported.

In the readings that follow, some of the arguments that philosophers have considered more plausible are presented. The one that will probably be most familiar to the student is the *argument from design.* According to this argument the world is so intricately put together to maintain the existence of various types of life that it must have been designed by an extremely rational being. This argument is presented in a simple, straightforward manner by A. Cressy Morrison, a highly respected American scientist. Morrison argues that life does not exist by chance because the probability of all the necessary factors existing in the proper relationship would be too slight. Also, he claims that the fact that nature is so balanced that no species can conquer all the others indicates that some great intelligence planned the world. The soundness of the argument is attacked by Clarence Darrow, who argues that the universe shows no clear order or design. He goes on to say that even if it did, it was apparently not designed for human life since we could easily imagine ways in which the world could have been made to provide a better habitation for human beings.

D. E. Trueblood presents another frequently encountered argument for the existence of God, the *argument from religious experience.* Since many people have experiences which they attribute to the existence of a God, a problem for the philosopher is to determine whether such experiences can have any evidential value. Trueblood recognizes that our experience can be delusory, but he maintains that religious experiences provide no less evidence of objective reality than ordinary sensory experiences which are the basis of science. In any assessment of the strength of Trueblood's argument, it is important to decide which experiences are religious ones and the kind of Deity for which these experiences could be evidence.

In "The Basis of the Moral Law," C. S. Lewis presents a version of the *moral argument* for God. He maintains that humans have a sense of moral obligation, which they feel as a claim coming from outside themselves. No naturalistic account of this sense of obligation in terms of human needs or interests satisfactorily explain it. It can be explained, Lewis argues, only by assuming the existence of a lawgiver outside the universe. The crucial issue in assessing this argument is whether he is correct in denying that the sense of obligation can be given an alternative explanation.

Many of the arguments for the existence of God, including the argument from design, are discussed by Bertrand Russell. Russell maintains that none of the arguments for the existence of God are convincing. Further, he attacks all religions, not just Christianity, on several grounds. Religion, he maintains, is born of fear and a desire to have a protector. We must not give in to such feelings but must learn to stand on our own feet and conquer the world by intelligence. Further, the various organized religions have hindered progress by defending a morality that is not conducive to human happiness. Human institutions can be improved and moral progress allowed for only if the morality of the churches is opposed.

Some philosophers have maintained not only that God's existence is unprovable but also that we can show that God does not exist. The main attempt to show that an all-good, all-powerful God does not exist arises from a consideration of the evil that exists in the world. It seems undeniably true that bad or evil things happen. Hurricanes and floods destroy houses and crops; children are born crippled or deformed; and murderers and thieves plague our cities. The question that must be answered is this: Why does a God who has the power to eliminate such evils allow them to occur? If God is indifferent to or powerless to prevent such evils, then he is not the kind of good and all-powerful being that Western religions worship. Many theologians have argued that all of the things we call evils are allowed to occur by God for some good purpose. To defend this view, one must show that God could not have produced equally good results without these evils.

The existence of evil and its bearing on God's existence are discussed by B. C. Johnson and John Hick. In "God and the Problem of Evil," Johnson examines the traditional explanations of an all-good God's purpose for allowing evil to exist and concludes that these explanations are inadequate. He argues that a careful assessment of the possible alternatives leads to the conclusion that the existence of an all-good God is unlikely. John Hick rejects the claim that no adequate explanation for the evil in the world is possible. He argues that evil is allowed to exist because God's purpose for humans in this world is not to provide them with a carefree, happy existence but to continue the process of "soul-making." To achieve full development, humans must experience and learn to overcome the problems that exist in this world.

When confronted with the difficulty of proving the existence of God, many philosophers and theologians fall back on faith as the basis for religious belief. Faith is usually thought of as belief unsupported by evidence. The contention that it is acceptable to believe the claims of religion or any other topic without evidence has not gone unchallenged. In "The Ethics of Belief," W. K. Clifford argues that it is always wrong to believe anything without evidence since such a belief could either produce some harm or lead the holder to accept too readily other unsupported and potentially harmful beliefs. Our beliefs should be determined by an assessment of the evidence and probabilities involved, not by unfounded hopes and wishes. In contrast to this view of the value of faith, William James argues that belief without evidence is sometimes justified. James is careful to point out, however, that such belief is justified only in certain types of situations. He does not want to encourage the holding of unsupported beliefs in every instance where evidence is not available. Ultimately, James believes that to withhold belief on an important matter such as religion just because there is insufficient evidence of God's existence would be too cautious. Since withholding belief might cut one off from God's grace, he believes that one should run the risk of error in hopes that one's belief may be true. In assessing James's position, the student should consider whether it rests on a conception of God as a wrathful being. Would James's argument be correct if God would not punish those who do not believe without evidence? Also, it is interesting to decide if there are any areas outside of religion where one should believe without evidence.

The "Problems and Puzzles" section contains two articles that raise important issues. In his autobiography, *My Confession,* Leo Tolstoy vividly describes how he reached a state of utter despair because he thought that death, which is destructive of everyone and everything one loves, makes confronting and overcoming the problems of living pointless. He believed that life was a "stupid joke" and that the courageous and consistent course to end his despair was to commit suicide. He was saved from suicide and acquired a renewed interest in life only when he returned to his faith in God. His experience convinced him that such faith was the only way to provide life with any significance and value. In "Cacodaemony," Steven Cahn objects to the reasoning used by John Hick to support his contention that an omnipotent, good God could allow evil as a means to produce greater good. Relying on an argument that parallels the one used by Hick, Cahn shows that an omnipotent demon could be allowing good to occur to produce greater evil. According to Cahn, the kinds of objections that can be raised against the claim that good is ultimately a source of greater evil can also be raised against the claim that evil leads to greater good.

DOES GOD EXIST?

11. Seven Reasons Why a Scientist Believes in God

A. Cressy Morrison

A. Cressy Morrison (1884–1951) was an astronomer and president of the New York Academy of Sciences from 1938 to 1939. He wrote a number of books on scientific topics, as well as Man Does Not Stand Alone, *from which the following article was condensed.*

We are still in the dawn of the scientific age and every increase of light reveals more brightly the handiwork of an intelligent Creator. In the 90 years since Darwin we have made stupendous discoveries; with a spirit of scientific humility and of faith grounded in the knowledge we are approaching even nearer to an awareness in God.

For myself, I count seven reasons for my faith:

First: *By unwavering mathematical law we can prove that our universe was designed and executed by a great engineering Intelligence.*

Suppose you put ten pennies, marked from one to ten, into your pocket and give them a good shuffle. Now try to take them out in sequence from one to ten, putting back the coin each time and shaking them all again. Mathematically we know that your chance of first drawing number one is one to ten; of drawing one and two in succession, one to 100; of drawing one, two, and three in succession, one in a thousand, and so on; your chance of drawing them all from number one to number ten in succession, would reach the unbelievable figure of one chance in ten billion.

By the same reasoning, so many exacting conditions are necessary for life on the earth that they could not possibly exist in proper relationship by chance. The earth rotates on its axis one thousand miles per hour; if it turned at one hundred miles an hour, our days and nights would be ten times as long as now, and the hot sun would then burn up our vegetation each long day while in the long night any surviving sprout would freeze.

Copyright 1946, 1960 by The Reader's Digest Assn., Inc. Adapted from the book *Man Does Not Stand Alone,* by A. Cressy Morrison. Copyright 1944 by Fleming H. Revell Company.

Again, the sun, source of our life, has a surface temperature of 12,000 degrees Fahrenheit, and our earth is just far enough away so that this "eternal fire" warm us *just enough and not too much!* If the sun gave off only one half its present radiation, we would freeze and if it gave half as much more, we would roast.

The slant of the earth, tilted at an angle of 23 degrees, gives us our seasons; if it had not been so tilted, vapors from the ocean would move north and south, piling up for us continents of ice. If our moon was, say, only 50 thousand miles away instead of its actual distance, our tides would be so enormous that twice a day all continents would be submerged; even the mountains would soon be eroded away. If the crust of the earth had been only ten feet thicker, there would be no oxygen, without which animal life must die. Had the ocean been a few feet deeper, carbon dioxide and oxygen would have been absorbed and no vegetable life could exist. Or if our atmosphere had been much thinner, some of the meteors, now burned in space by the millions every day, would be striking all parts of the earth, setting fires everywhere.

Because of these and a host of other examples, there is not one chance in millions that life on our planet is an accident.

Second: *The resourcefulness of life to accomplish its purpose is a manifestation of all-pervading Intelligence.*

What life itself is, no man has fathomed. It has neither weight nor dimensions; but it does have force; a growing root will crack a rock. Life has conquered water, land and air, mastering the elements, compelling them to dissolve and reform their combinations.

Life, the sculptor, shapes all living things; an artist, it designs every leaf of every tree, and colors every flower. Life is a musician and has taught each bird to sing its love songs, the insects to call each other in the music of their multitudinous sounds. Life is a sublime chemist, giving taste to fruits and spices, and perfume to the rose, changing water and carbonic acid into sugar and wood, and, in so doing, releasing oxygen that animals may have the breath of life.

Behold an almost invisible drop of protoplasm, transparent, jellylike, capable of motion, drawing energy from the sun. This single cell, this transparent mistlike droplet, holds within itself the germ of life, and has the power to distribute this life to every living thing, great and small. The powers of this droplet are greater than our vegetation and animals and people, for all life came from it. Nature did not create life; fire-blistered rocks and a saltless sea could not meet the necessary requirements.

Who, then, has put it here?

Third: *Animal wisdom speaks irresistibly of a good Creator who infused instinct into otherwise helpless little creatures.*

The young salmon spends years at sea, then comes back to his own river, and travels up the very side of the river into which flows the tributary where he was born. What brings him back so precisely? If you transfer him to another tributary he will know at once that he is off his course and he will fight his way down and back to the main stream and then turn up against the current to finish his destiny accurately.

Even more difficult to solve is the mystery of eels. These amazing creatures migrate at maturity from all ponds and rivers everywhere—those from Europe across thousands of miles of ocean—all bound for the same abysmal deeps near Bermuda. There they breed and die. The little ones, with no apparent means of knowing anything except that they are in a wilderness of water, nevertheless start back and find their way not only to the very shore from which their parents came but thence to the rivers, lakes or little ponds—so that each body of water is always populated with eels. No American eel has ever been caught in Europe, no European eel in American waters. Nature has even delayed the maturity of the European eel by a year or more to make up for its longer journey. Where does the directing impulse originate?

A wasp will overpower a grasshopper, dig a hole in the earth, sting the grasshopper in exactly the right place so that he does not die but becomes unconscious and lives on as a form of preserved meat. Then the wasp will lay her eggs handily so that her children when they hatch can nibble without killing the insect on which they feed; to them dead meat would be fatal. The mother then flies away and dies; she never sees her young. Surely the wasp must have done all this right the first time and every time, else there would be no wasps. Such mysterious techniques cannot be explained by adaptation; they were bestowed.

Fourth: *Man has something more than animal instinct—the power of reason.*

No other animal has ever left a record of its ability to count ten, or even to understand the meaning of ten. Where instinct is like a single note of a flute, beautiful but limited, the human brain contains all the notes of all the instruments in the orchestra. No need to belabor this fourth point; thanks to human reason we can contemplate the possibility that we are what we are only because we have received a spark of Universal Intelligence.

Fifth: *Provision for all living is revealed in phenomena which we know today but which Darwin did not know—such as the wonders of genes.*

So unspeakably tiny are these genes that, if all of them responsible for all living people in the world could be put in one place, there would be less than a thimbleful. Yet these ultramicroscopic genes and their companions, the chromosomes, inhabit every living cell and are the absolute keys to all human, animal, and vegetable characteristics. A thimble is a small place in which to put all the individual characteristics of two billions of human beings. However, the facts are beyond question. Well, then—how do genes lock up all the normal heredity of a multitude of ancestors and preserve the psychology of each in such an infinitely small space?

Here evolution really begins—at the cell, the entity which holds and carries the genes. How a few million atoms, locked up as an ultramicroscopic gene, can absolutely rule all life on earth is an example of profound cunning and provision that could emanate only from a Creative Intelligence; no other hypothesis will serve.

Sixth: *By the economy of nature, we are forced to realize that only infinite wisdom could have foreseen and prepared with such astute husbandry.*

Many years ago a species of cactus was planted in Australia as a protective fence. Having no insect enemies in Australia the cactus soon began a prodigious growth; the alarming abundance persisted until the plants covered an area as long and wide as England, crowding inhabitants out of towns and villages, and destroying their farms. Seeking a defense, the entomologists scoured the world; finally they turned up an insect which lived exclusively on cactus, and would eat nothing else. It would breed freely, too; and it had no enemies in Australia. So animal soon conquered vegetable and today the cactus pest has retreated, and with it all but a small protective residue of the insects, enough to hold the cactus in check forever.

Such checks and balances have been universally provided. Why have not fast-breeding insects dominated the earth? Because they have no lungs such as man possesses; they breathe through tubes. But when insects grow large, their tubes do not grow in ratio to the increasing size of the body. Hence there never has been an insect of great size; this limitation on growth has held them all in check. If this physical check had not been provided, man could not exist. Imagine meeting a hornet as big as a lion!

Seventh: *The fact that man can conceive the idea of God is in itself a unique proof.*

The conception of God rises from a divine faculty of man, unshared with the rest of our world—the faculty we call imagination. By its power, man and man alone can find the evidence of things unseen. The vista that power opens up is unbounded; indeed, as man's perfected imagination becomes a spiritual reality, he may discern in all the evidences of design and purpose the great truth that heaven is wherever and whatever; that God is everywhere and in everything but nowhere so close as in our hearts.

It is scientifically as well as imaginatively true, as the Psalmist said: *The heavens declare the glory of God and the firmament showeth His handiwork.*

12. The Delusion of Design and Purpose

Clarence Darrow

Seldom do the believers in mysticism fail to talk about the evidence of purpose and design shown in the universe itself. This idea runs back at least one hundred and five years, to Paley's "Natural Theology." There was a time when this book was a part of the regular course in all schools of higher learning, which then included theology; but the book is now more likely to be found in museums.

Paley points out that if a man travelling over the heath should find a watch and commence examining it he would soon discover in the watch itself abundant evidence of purpose and design. He would observe the wheels that fit into each other and turn the hour hand and the minute hand, the crystal made to fit over the face, etc., etc.

What the hypothetical man would observe and conclude would depend on the man. Most men that we know would think that the watch showed a design to accomplish a certain purpose, and therefore must have had a maker. They would reach that conclusion because they are familiar with tools and their use by man. But, suppose the watch had been picked up by a bushman or some other savage or an ape? None of them would draw an inference, for the article would be new to them. Supposing, instead of a man, a coyote or wolf came upon the watch, turned it over and examined it, would the animal read or sense any design? Most assuredly not. Suppose the civilized man should pick up an unfamiliar object, a stone, or a piece of quartz; he might view it and examine it, but it would never enter his head that it was designed, and yet on close inspection and careful study the stone or quartz is just as marvelous as the watch.

Paley passes from the watch to the human structure and shows how the mouth and teeth are adjusted to prepare the food for man's digestion, and how his stomach is formed to digest it; how the eye and ear were made to carry sensations to the brain, etc. Many of the clergy say the same thing today, in spite of the fact that the organs of man were never made for any such purpose. In fact, man never was made. He was evolved from the lowest form of life. His ancestor in the sea slowly threw its jellylike structure around something that nourished it and absorbed it. Slowly through ages of continued development and change and mutations the present man was evolved, and with him the more perfect and adaptable and specialized structure, with which he sees and hears and takes his food, and digests it

From Clarence Darrow, *The Story of My Life* (Charles Scribners, Sons, 1932). By Permission of the Estate of Clarence Darrow, All rights reserved.

and assimilates it to his structure. The stomach was not made first, and then food created for its use. The food came first, and certain forms of life slowly developed an organ that would absorb food to be utilized in the process of growth. By degrees, through the survival of the construction most fitted for life, the stomach and digestive apparatus for men and other animals gradually grew and unfolded in endless time.

To discover that certain forms and formations are adjusted for certain action has nothing to do with design. None of these developments are perfect, or anywhere near so. All of them, including the eye, are botchwork that any good mechanic would be ashamed to make. All of them need constant readjustment, are always out of order, and are entirely too complicated for dependable work. They are not made for any purpose; they simply grew out of needs and adaptations; in other words, they happened. Just as God must have happened, if he exists at all.

Turning from Paley and his wornout watch to the universe and the physical world in general, is there any more evidence here? First, the "design and order" sharks ought to tell what they mean by their terms, and how they find out what they think they understand. To say that a certain scheme or process shows order or system, one must have some norm or pattern by which to determine whether the matter concerned shows any design or order. We have a norm, a pattern, and that is the universe itself, from which we fashion our ideas. We have observed this universe and its operation and we call it order. To say that the universe is patterned on order is to say that the universe is patterned on the universe. It can mean nothing else.

The earth revolves around the sun in a long curve not far from a circle. Does that show order? Let us suppose that instead of going in a circle it formed a rectangle. Would this not have been accepted as order? Suppose it were a triangle, or any other figure. Suppose it took a toothlike course, would that, then, be considered order? As a matter of fact, the earth does not go regularly in the same path around the sun; it is drawn out into the universe with the whole solar system, and never travels the same course twice. The solar system really has an isolated place in space. The sun furnishes light and heat to nine different planets, of which the earth is one of the smallest and most insignificant. The earth has one satellite, the moon. Saturn and Jupiter have eight moons each, and, besides that, Saturn has a ring that looks very beautiful from here, running all around the planet. We do know that all the planets of the solar system, and the sun as well, are made of the same stuff. It is most likely that every moving thing in the universe has the same constituents as the earth. What is the plan that gave Jupiter eight moons, while only one was lavished upon the earth, supposed to be the special masterpiece of the Almighty, and for whose benefit all the hosts of the heavens were made? Jupiter is three hundred and seventeen times the weight of the earth, and it takes four years for it to go around the sun. Perhaps the universe was made for inhabitants that will one day live on Jupiter.

It is senseless to talk about order and system and design in the universe. Sir James Jean's book published in 1931, *The Stars in Their Course*, tells us his theory of the origin of our solar system, which is of more interest to us than the Milky Way. The theory of Jeans, and most of the other astronomers is that there was a time when all the planets of the solar system were a part of the sun, and that some wandering star in its course across the heavens entered the sphere of the sun and dragged after it the planets and moons that make up the solar system by the power of gravitation. This is the planetismal theory, postulated by Professors Chamberlain and Moulton, of the University of Chicago. These mighty chunks of matter drawn from the sun rushed on through space at a terrific speed, and each was caught by gravitation and revolved around the sun. Their distance from the sun depended largely upon their size before gravitation held them in its grasp.

There is nothing in the solar system that could be called design and order. It came from a catastrophe of whose immensity no one could even dream. Religionists have pointed to the ability of an astronomer to fix the time of an eclipse as evidence of system. There are only a few heavenly bodies involved in an eclipse of the sun or moon, from the standpoint of the earth. The motions and positions of all these bodies are well known, and from this the passage of another heavenly planet or the moon between the earth and the sun can be easily determined. It matters not whether the date of an eclipse is far-off or near-by, the method is the same. To an astronomer the computation is as simple as the question propounded to the first-grade pupil: "If John had three apples and James gave him two more, how many apples would John then have?"

We know that gravitation caught the various planets at a certain point as they sped across space, and that these accidents of colliding bodies are very rare; the reason is that regardless of what seems to be the distance between the stars, they are so far apart that it is almost impossible for them ever to meet. To quote from Jeans: "For the most part, each voyage is in splendid isolation, like a ship on the ocean. In a scale model in which the stars are ships, the average ship will be well over a million miles from its neighbor."

Still, catastrophes have occurred and do occur. Our solar system was probably born from one. The moon was thrown from the earth by some pull of gravitation. The heavens are replete with dark planets, and parts of planets, and meteors hurrying through space. Now and then one drops onto the earth, and is preserved in some park or museum; so that in various parts of the world numerous specimens exist. If there was any purpose in the creation of the universe, or any part of it, what was it? Would any mortal dare to guess?

Our solar system is one of the smallest of the endless systems of which we have any knowledge. Our earth is eight thousand miles in diameter. The star Betelgeuse is so large that it would fill all the space occupied in the heavens in the whole orbit made by the earth going around the sun. There are many stars known to be much larger than Betelgeuse. The diameter of this sun is thirty-seven thousand times that of our little earth, for which all the universe is supposed to have been made, and whose inhabitants are endowed with everlasting life.

When the telescope is turned toward the heavens we learn another story. Leaving the sparsely settled section of eternity in which we live forever, and going out into the real main universe, we find worlds on worlds, systems upon systems, and nebula after nebula. No one can possibly imagine the dimensions of endless space. The great Nebula M. 31 in Andromeda is so far away from the earth that it takes light nine hundred thousand millions of years to reach our planet. The nebula itself is so vast that it takes fifty thousand years for light to cross it. To make it still more simple I have taken the pains to figure the distance of this nebula from our important planet, called the earth, which boasts a diameter of eight thousand miles. This nebula is 5,279,126,400,000,000,000 miles away from us, if my computations are right. I would not positively guarantee the correctness of the answer, but I think it is all right, although I did it by hand. I have gone over the figures three times, and got a different result each time, so I think the answer can be pretty well depended upon. I cannot help feeling sorry for the residents of Nebula M. 31 in Andromeda, when I think what a great deprivation they must suffer through living so far away from our glorious planet, which Mark Twain named "the wart," but which theology has placed at the centre of the universe and as the sole concern of gods and men.

What lies beyond Andromeda? No one can answer that question. And still there is every reason to believe that other worlds and systems and nebulae reach out into stellar space, without end. It is obvious that no one can form a conception of the extent of space or the infinite number of suns and planets with which the limitless sky is strewn. No one can vision a beginning or an end. If it were possible for any fertile mind to imagine a conception of the end of space, then we should wonder what lies beyond that limit. We cannot attain the slightest comprehension of the extent of our pygmy solar system, much less any of the greater ones. The planet which is the farthest from our sun is Pluto, one of the smallest in our system. The diameter of Pluto's orbit around the sun is only about 7,360,000,000 miles. This may be taken as the extent of our solar system. This can be compared with the distance to the nebula in Andromeda, which I hesitate to record again, showing the trifling importance of our whole solar system in so much of the universe as we can scan.

When the new telescope is completed and mounted on the top of Mount Wilson, it is hoped that we can produce figures of distance that are real figures.

Among the endless number of stars that whirl in the vastness of illimitable space, how many millions of billions of planets are likely to be in existence? How many of these may possibly have as much special and historical importance as the tiny globe to which we so frantically cling? To find that number, go and count the grains of sand on all the coasts of all the waters of the earth, and then think of the catastrophe that would result to the coasts if one grain were shattered or lost.

In spite of the countless numbers of bodies moving about in limitless space, and the distances between them so great that they seldom clash, still they do sometimes clash. What is our solar system in comparison with the great nebula out there in the beginning, or end, or middle stretch of real space? Compared with that part of the heavens the density of the stellar population of our solar system is like the prairies of Kansas compared with the city of New York. Can anything be inferred about the origin or arrangement of all this, so far as man can tell, except that it is the outcome of the merest, wildest chance?

But let us try to clear the cobwebs from our brains, and the dizziness from our stomachs, and come back to earth, as it were. Let us talk of something where we can deal with what at least approaches facts. Does the earth show design, and order, and system, and purpose? Again, it would be well for the designers to tell what the scheme really is. If the plan is so clear as to justify the belief in a master designer, then it must be plain that the believers should be able to give the world some idea of the purpose of it all. Knowing winks and Delphic utterances and cryptic insinuations are not enough. Was the earth ever designed for the home of man? Sir James Jeans, in his admirable book on astronomy, shows us in no uncertain way that it evidently was not; that the human race has made the most of a bad environment and a most unfortunate habitation. Strange that the high-priests of superstition should so convulsively clutch Jeans and Eddington; neither one believes in a future life of the individual; neither one believes in the God of the theologians; neither believes in a special revelation, although Jeans does manage to say that Venus is the planet that the religionists thought was the star that led the camels over the desert to the stable where Jesus was born. Is this science or religion?—this bit of hearsay.

Even had this planet been meant for life, it plainly was not meant for human life. Three-fourths of the surface is covered with water, which would show that if it was ever designed for life it was designed for fishes and not for men. But what about the dry land? Two-thirds of this is not fitted for human beings. Both the polar zones are too cold for the abode of man. The equatorial regions are too hot. Vast deserts are spread out in various sections, and impassable and invincible mountain ranges make human habitation and the production of food impossible over immense areas. The earth is small enough, to begin with; the great seas, the wide useless stretches of land and the hostile climates have shrunk the livable portion almost to the vanishing point, and it is continually shrinking day by day. The human race is here because it is here, and it clings to the soil because there is nowhere else to go.

Even a human being of very limited capacity could think of countless ways in which the earth could be improved as a home of man, and from the earliest time the race has been using all sorts of efforts and resources to make it more suitable for its abode. Admitting that the earth is a fit place for life, and certainly every place in the universe where life exists is fitted for life, then what sort of life was this planet designed to support? There are some millions of different species of animals on this earth, and one-half of these are insects. In numbers, and perhaps in other ways, man is in a great minority. If the land of the earth was made for life, it seems as if it was intended for insect life, which can exist almost anywhere. If no other available place can be found they can live by the million on man, and inside of him. They generally succeed in destroying his life, and, if they have a chance, wind up by eating his body.

Aside from the insects, all sorts of life infest the earth and sea and air. In large portions of the earth man can make no headway against the rank growths of jungles and the teeming millions of animals that are seeking his death. He may escape the larger and most important of these only to be imperilled and probably eaten by the microbes, which seem instinctively to have their own idea of the worth and purpose of man's existence. If it were of any importance, we might view man from the standpoint of the microbe and consider his utility as the microbe's "meal-ticket." Can any one find any reason for claiming that the earth was meant for man, any more than for any other form of life that is spawned from land and sea and air?

But, how well is the earth itself adapted to human life? Even in the best parts of this world, speaking from the standpoint of man, one-fourth of the time it is too cold and another fourth of the season it is too hot, leaving little time for comfort and pleasure of the worthiest product of the universe, or that small fraction of it that we have some limited knowledge about.

Passing up the manifold difficulties that confront man and his brief life and career upon this mundane sphere, let us look at the world itself. It is a very wobbly place. Every year, upon the surface of this globe, and in the seas that cover such a major part of it, there are ten thousand earthquakes, ranging from light shocks to the total destruction of large areas of territory and the annihilation of great numbers of human lives. Were these, too, designed? Then, there is no such meaning as is usually applied to the word "design." What "design" was there in the earthquake that destroyed Lisbon in 1755? The entire city was blotted out, together with the destruction of thirty thousand to forty thousand human beings. This earthquake occurred on a Sunday which was also a saint's day, and a large number were killed in a cathedral, which was also destroyed. And yet people talk about design and purpose and order and system as though they knew the meaning of the words.

Let us look at the earth as it exists today. It is not the same earth that came into some sort of separate existence millions of years ago. It has not only experienced vast and comparatively sudden changes, like the throwing up of mountain ranges in the cooling and contracting processes, but other changes not so sudden and acute have worked their way through ages of time, and changes are still going on all the time all over the earth. New lands keep rising, others sinking away. Volcanoes are sending out millions of tons of matter each year, new islands are rising above the surface of the sea, while other islands are lowered beneath the waves. Continents are divided by internal forces and the ruthless powers of the sea.

Great Britain was cut off from the mainland not so very long ago, according to geological time. The shores of America and Africa were once connected, as seems evident from looking at the maps, and countless other geological shiftings have happened all over the surface and inside the earth, so that the world was no more made as it is now than was man created as we find him today. The destruction of the island of Martinique, the Mont Pelee disaster, the earthquake of San Francisco, are all within the memory of many now living. Active volcanoes are continuously pouring solid matter into the waters and slowly or rapidly building up new land where once was only sea.

The various archipelagoes are instances of this formation of fairly recent times. The Allegheny Mountains were once thirty thousand feet high. The crevices of their rocks have been penetrated by rain, split by frost and ice, pulverized by friction, and every minute are moving off toward the Gulf of Mexico. This range of mountains, which once reached an altitude of thirty thousand feet at the highest point, now has its highest peak but six thousand feet above the sea. These mountains have been worn down day after day, and the Ohio and Tennessee and Mississippi Rivers, carrying off the sediment, are building up the delta on the Louisiana coast. The earth and its seas were never made; they are in constant flux, moved by cold and heat and rain, and with no design or purpose that can be fathomed by the wit of man.

The delta of the Nile has through the long ages been carried down in mud and sand and silt from two thousand miles away and deposited in the open sea; and this is also called design by those who look for things they wish to find.

Nature brings hordes of insects that settle over the land and destroy the farmers' crops. Who are the objects of the glorious design: the farmers who so patiently and laboriously raise the crops or the grasshoppers that devour them? It must be the insects, because the farmers hold prayer meetings and implore their God to kill the bugs, but the pests go on with their deadly work unmolested. Man prates glibly about design, but Nature furnishes not a single example or fact as proof. Perhaps the microbe who bores a hole into the vitals of man and brings him down to his death may believe in a Providence and a design. How else could he live so royally on the vitals of one of the lords of creation?

All that we know is that we were born on this little grain of sand we call the earth. We know that it is one of the smallest bits of matter that floats in the great scoreless sea of space, and we have every reason to believe that it is as inconsequential in every other respect. On board the same craft, sailing the same seas, are all sorts of living things, fighting each other, and us, that each may survive. Most of these specimens are living on the carcasses of the dead. The strongest instinct of most of our crew is to stay here and live. The strongest in intellect and prowess live the longest. Nature, in all her manifestations, is at war with life, and sooner or later will doubtless have her way. No one can give a reason for any or all of the manifestations which we call life. We are like a body of shipwrecked sailors clutching to a raft and desperately engaged in holding on.

Men have built faith from hopes. They have struggled and fought in despair. They have frantically clung to life because of the will to live. The best that we can do is to be kindly and helpful toward our friends and fellow passengers who are clinging to the same speck of dirt while we are drifting side by side to our common doom.

13. The Evidential Value of Religious Experience

D. E. Trueblood

David Elton Trueblood (1900–1994) was a professor of philosophy at Earlham College. He has written many books, including his popular The Logic of Belief, *in support of religion and Christianity.*

THE PRIMARY DATUM OF RELIGION

The fact that religious experience occurs is a fact with which every philosophy must eventually deal. The claim which such experience makes, the claim to actual contact, not merely with persons and things, but with the Creator and Sustainer of the universe, is so stupendous and so insistent that it cannot be neglected. Our philosophy must either explain it away or construct a world view consistent with it.

The reasonable procedure is to look at religious experience as we look at any other datum. It is the primary datum of religion, and it awaits analysis. If we are scientifically minded we approach experience without prejudice and with humility. The scientific temper demands that we neither *accept* the data of experience uncritically nor *reject* it uncritically. We do not know what any experience is worth in the verification of belief until we analyze it, subjecting it to all the appropriate tests available. The mere fact that millions have reported that they have known God directly is not absolute proof that they have really done so, but, on the other hand, to assume, prior to critical testing, that they have not really done so would be unscientific in the extreme.

It must be made clear that we are not referring to *belief* in this connection, but to *reported experience.* The two are different. Belief may arise from many sources, some of them intellectually respectable and some of them not respectable. There can be belief *because* of direct experience and there can be belief *apart from* direct experience. The point we are making is not that millions of men have believed in God, something almost too obvious to bother to mention, but rather that millions of men have reported and continue to report that they have known God with the directness and intimacy with which they know other persons or physical objects.

Not all religious experience is the same, but there are characteristic features which appear with astonishing regularity and which are not especially difficult to describe. Normally it is not some experience wholly separated from other

Selected excerpts from pp. 197–214 of *The Logic of Belief* by David Elton Trueblood. Copyright 1942, by Harper & Brothers; renewed 1969 by David Elton Trueblood. Reprinted by permission of HarperCollins Publishers, Inc.

experiences, but a particular way in which all reality is apprehended. It comes about most naturally in the mood of prayer or worship, but is by no means limited to stated times for these, either individually or collectively. Ordinarily religious experience has nothing to do with visions, ecstasies, raptures or other phenomena which are usually considered abnormal. It is true that some mystics have experienced these exalted states of consciousness or unconsciousness, but they are no part of *normative* religious experience.[1] It, on the contrary, is as unspectacular as breathing or sleeping. For most men and women religious experience has been a calm assurance of the reality of a relationship which gives meaning to existence.

The chief reason why the opinion has become current that religious experience is rare, and therefore of little evidential value, is that there has been a misunderstanding concerning what is denoted by the term "religious experience." This misunderstanding has been created in large measures by certain writers . . . who have claimed to study the empirical phenomena of religion, but in doing so have limited their study to the *bizarre*. The result is that they have made the discipline known as the psychology of religion sound like a branch of abnormal psychology. Even William James in his brilliant book *The Varieties of Religious Experience* lent some credence to this interpretation or misinterpretation. Some critics have maintained that the only mistake James made, in this regard, was in the *title* of his famous book. The cases he presents are not really varieties, for they are all queer.

THE CHARACTERISTICS OF RELIGIOUS EXPERIENCE

Interesting as may be the study of peculiar mental phenomena, that is no part of our present purpose. We are concerned with the logical structure of belief, and, for this purpose, we are interested in the unspectacular. This normative experience may be described by making certain definite propositions about it which are related to one another as steps in the progressive narrowing of the field.

(1) *Religious experience is perceptual.* By this we mean that experience, as reported, is not a matter of either speculation or imagination, but of something independent of the observer with which the observer has established contact. God might be either imagined or perceived, just as a tree might be imagined or perceived. We say the tree is perceived when the tree is experienced as external to the mind of the perceiver. Imagination is free to indulge in wishful thinking; perception is limited by the nature of the real as known. The point is that religious experience reports itself as so limited.

Perhaps it is necessary to remind the reader that perceptual and sensory are not identical concepts. Perception refers to a relation to an *object* and is thus distinct from *conception*, as well as from imagination. Sensation, on the other hand, refers to the kind of experience which comes through the instrumentality of end

---

[1] Unusual mental states such as "speaking in tongues," have frequently been minimized, even by those reporting them personally.

organs, of which ears and eyes are conspicuous examples. There can be nonperceptual sensation, as a blow on the head may easily demonstrate, and, unless normative religion is a delusion, there is a vast amount of non-sensory perception, i.e., real contact with a perceived object, *without* the instrumentality of the sensory end organs. If God is really known, as so many have claimed to know Him, it is clear that He is not known by means of our auditory, optic or tactual nerves. Sometimes the language of sense has been used in the reports of vivid religious experience, but nearly always such language is consciously figurative. This is well illustrated by the Psalmist's appeal, "O taste and see that the Lord is good." The very fact that men speak so often of an *inward* sense is evidence that they are not talking about the actual sensory apparatus. What they mean is that their awareness of God is *as vivid, as incontestable*, as any sensory experience ever is. One of the great seventeenth century interpreters of such experience attempted, in the following words, to tell his Dutch friend Heer Paets, what he meant by an "inward sense."

> An example of an inward, supernatural sense is when the heart or soul of a pious man feels in itself divine motions, influences and operations, which sometimes are as the voice or speech of God, sometimes as a most pleasant and glorious illustration or visible object to the inward eye, sometimes as a most sweet savour or taste, sometimes as a heavenly and divine warmness or (so to speak) melting of the soul in the love of God.[2]

It would be stupid to minimize the value of expressions like those of Barclay on the ground that they are figures of speech. The more important any disclosure is, the more necessary figures of speech become. The necessity for figures of speech arises from the fact that intelligible language is used for the purpose of making known what was formerly unknown, and this can only be done by establishing some similarity with what is already known. Thus we seek to make the experience of color understandable to the congenitally blind by comparing color with musical tone, though we are well aware that the two are not the same. Similarly, those who have tried to make religious experience understandable to others not conscious of it have used the language of sense, while recognizing that it is not really sensory. They mean that it has the vividness, the certitude, the striking quality of that which impinges on ears, eyes, and other organs. An impressive testimony to this effect is that of Newman, when, speaking of his *inward conversion*, he affirmed years later that he was still more certain of it "than that I have hands and feet."[3]

It was, apparently, in an effort to emphasize the perceptual character of his own religious experience that the celebrated French mathematician, Blaise Pascal, used the word "Fire" in capital letters, as the central feature of the record of his life-shaking experience. This record, which Pascal's servant found sewed into the scholar's coat, at the time of his death, was made up largely of interjections,

---

[2] Robert Barclay, *Truth Triumphant*, p. 897.

[3] John Henry Newman, *Apologia pro Vita Sua*, Everyman edition, p. 31.

the normal language of assured contact. The word "Fire" was most emphasized, probably in the effort to show that what he perceived had about the same indubitable quality that we find in the flame, which warms, lights, and even burns.

Perhaps there is need to remark in passing that when we speak of perception as *contact with an object*, we are not necessarily referring to a *physical* object. The object is that which is perceived, whatever it is. It would be both unphilosophical and unscientific to assert dogmatically that the only objects of perception are physical bodies. The kinds of objects in which we must believe depend wholly on the kind of evidence which is available. The correct method is not to decide in advance whether or not there are nonphysical objects of perception, but rather to begin with the data of experience and wait to see to what conclusions we are led by the analysis of this experience.

(2) *Religious experience is cognitive,* in that it claims to be the kind of perception which gives the perceiver actual knowledge of God. In short it is possible, in religious experience, to go beyond Pascal's memorable hour, when there was certainty of contact, but little more. The prophets, in all generations, claim that their experience of God is such that they learn something about His nature, and His will for men. We are not discussing now the correctness of this knowledge, since such discussion should come later in this chapter; we are saying merely that the primary datum of religion includes a "knowledge claim."

Naturally it is not easy for men to tell others *what* they know, since language here becomes more inadequate than it ordinarily is, and poetry becomes inevitable, but this is not the important point. The point is that knowledge is claimed, though never perfect knowledge. The devout man in all generations says with St. Paul, "I know in part." It has long been recognized that men, in their knowledge of God, can touch no more than the hem of His garment. But to know in part is to know something.

(3) *Religious experience is personal,* not in the sense that every devout man has consciously believed that God is a "Person," but that the experience characteristically recorded is of the kind which we normally associate with persons. The experience has about it, as aesthetic experience has, the augustness which we cannot expect contact with a mere "thing" to inspire. In many cases, and most strikingly in the experience of Jesus, the relationship is consciously personal. God is addressed in prayer as "O Father," and the second person is used when a pronoun is employed. . . .

Religion is not so much the thrill of discovery, as the awareness of being assaulted. The witness to this comes from testimonies as far apart as Francis Thompson's *Hound of Heaven* and Karl Barth's theology of crisis. Religion is not so much finding God, as reaction to the Reality which has found us. It is not so much man's bargain with God, as it is man's response to God's grace. But the point of all this, to which there is abundant testimony covering the greater part of three thousand years, is that this is the way we react to the tremendous, soul-stirring experience of *being loved. It is persons who do the loving.* . . .

Assuming that the foregoing brief description of religious experience is sufficient for our present purposes, we can proceed to show the main structure of the argument based upon it. All that we know arises in experience. Our reason for believing that there is a physical order is the fact that millions of men report an experience of such an order. In a similar manner millions of men in all times and places have experienced God as the Sustainer of their lives. Therefore, God is.

The only reason for not accepting this forthright empirical evidence is the fact that experience can be delusory. Not everything that men experience exists. Two experiences given at a court trial and referring to the same event are sometimes contradictory. Though we cannot dispense with the ultimate appeal to experience we cannot take experience at its face value. But this applies to sensory experience just as truly as it applies to religious experience. Why, then, are there so many who deny the evidential value of religious experience while they accept the evidential value of sensory experience? The fact that men may make mistakes about the interpretation of their sense perceptions does not lead the ordinary intelligent person to the conclusion that sense perception is a purely subjective affair, but the fact that some men have had religious experiences which we must regard as illusory has led a number of otherwise critical persons to the conclusion that religious experience is a purely subjective affair and no revelation of the real. It is indeed a curious leap to conclude, from the fact that men make mistakes, that there is no reality which they are making mistakes *about*.

This curious logic arises from an epistemological confusion, which in turn arises from an unrecognized metaphysical prejudice in favor of naturalism. Many theological writers have made the confusion easier by constantly referring to religion as an affair of the *inner* life. The consequence is that, for many, the serious question of the validity of religious experience is supposedly answered by pointing out that all religious experiences are mental—they are merely *in the mind*. How then, can they have evidential value? But all experiences are in the mind in this sense of the word. My perception of the bird in the tree is as much in my mind as is my perception of God. . . .

There are some persons who object to an empirical analysis which brackets sensory experience and religious experience, referring to the relation between them as an *analogy*. The facts to which we are now pointing show that this objection misses the mark. There is not an analogy between the two types of experiences in regard to the subjective predicament; there is an *identity*. The notion that sensory experience has some advantage in certainty of objective reference turns out to be a mere superstition.

Many people appear to suppose that there is some *absolute* test of veracity in ordinary sense experience, but reflection shows that none exists. I see a flaw in the windowpane and the question arises whether this is just a figment of my imagination or is really there. Accordingly, I go over and touch the glass. But does this prove my original contention? All I have is another experience which, indeed, increases the presumptive value of my first observation, but I can never escape the circle of subjectivity.

When this particular confusion is dispelled the greatest barrier to a fair estimate of the situation is removed. To list an experience as inner or subjective is not sufficient to deny its objectivity, for on that ground there would be no objective world at all. Though all experiences are subjectively known, they may be *occasioned* by objective stimuli. Thus the assertion of subjectivity is no denial of objectivity. The chief question is the question of reference. Ideas *in the mind* may refer to what is *outside the mind,* in that it exists independently, so far as the individual mind is concerned. The concept of objectivity, one of the most advanced of which the human mind is capable, involves not only the ability to distinguish between the self which experiences and the world which is experienced, but also the ability to distinguish between what the experient wishes were the case, and what he is forced to believe is the case.

THE TESTS OF VERACITY

To know precisely what belongs to the objective order is a problem of the greatest difficulty, and one never fully solved in any extended area. We solve the problem, insofar as we solve it at all, not by the application of some special *means,* but rather by the humble process of noting converging lines of agreement with experience as known. . . .

When people, who differ in many ways, have substantial agreement about one item, we consider it more reasonable to posit objective status than to accept a miracle of coincidence. In this we may be wrong, but we have no suitable alternative.

The agreement, of course, must be of a particular kind to have any value. In testing the veracity of religious experience four tests are of special importance.

(1) *Number of reporters.* Other things being equal an experience has more veracity if it is widely shared. One reason for doubting the objective status of the animals seen in *delirium tremens* is that those who see them are so badly outnumbered.

By the most conservative estimate the number of persons who have reported religious experience, not in the sense of ecstatic trance, and not in the sense of mere inference from the order of nature, but with a deep assurance of the divine undergirding, is many millions and, indeed, it is difficult to think of any similar data that are so numerous. The abundance of such reports in the Old and New Testament is enough to give us pause, but this is by no means the end of the story. When we think of the humble souls who have made their testimony in Christian lands in the intervening years, as well as many more quite outside the Christian tradition, we begin to see that we are dealing with one of the best attested experiences in the world. "The simple fact is," as Canon Raven has said, "that those who would explain away religion are hardly aware of the greatness of the task or of the qualifications necessary for it."[4]

[4] Charles E. Raven, *Jesus and the Gospel of Love,* London, 1931, p. 73.

The evidence upon which we can depend comes to us chiefly in three ways. (a) In the first place there is the vocal testimony, especially that which has appeared in gatherings similar to the Methodist "class meeting." Some of this can be discounted, especially when it follows the fashionable religious pattern of the day, but, taken as a whole, the vocal testimonies are so numerous and so sincere that it is impossible for a reasonable person to dismiss them as unworthy of attention.

(b) A second source of evidence is found in literary records, especially those of spiritual autobiography. This material, as is well known, is an important part of our literature from Augustine's *Confessions* to Newman's *Apologia* and beyond.[5] Even the Quaker journals alone make an impressive showing *and all of them were written in order to provide the very data with which we are here concerned.*

(c) If these two sources were the only ones the evidence would be impressive, but they do not exhaust the data. The experiences of most people cannot be known by their own direct report, since they are too modest or are lacking in facility of expression. Accordingly we must learn what their experience is from the worship in which they share, the reading which they prize, and the prayers to which they turn for the expression of their own devotional life. Thus the Hebrew Psalms tell us something, not merely about the experience of the few persons who originally composed them, but chiefly about the experience of the millions, of all creeds, who have found in the Psalms the best expression of what they would like to say and cannot. The satisfaction found in the use of hymns, many of which are forthright testimonies to divine acquaintance, gives us similar evidence. The testimony implicit in prayer is similarly great. We cannot know how many pray, but all will agree that the number is enormous. Anyone who believes in prayer is bearing witness thereby to direct contact between the human and the divine, inasmuch as God is supposed to hear our prayers. Of course this relationship need not be mutual, but the chief reasons for denying the objective reality of what devout men experience is already overcome, if there is the real contact which prayer entails.

Any thorough study of the number of the reports must include some reference to the fact that the report is not universal in the human race. There is not space here for an exhaustive treatment of this matter, but two relevant points can be made briefly. One is that no human experience, not even sight, is strictly universal, for experience depends in part on receptive powers. The higher we go, as in music for example, the less universal experience is. The other point is that failure to report experience has no evidential value, *unless* the individual concerned has met the appropriate conditions. The testimony of those who have not met the requirements has no logical weight and need not be seriously considered, whatever their qualifications in other ways. *The religious opinions of the unreligious are no more valuable than are the scientific opinions of the unscientific.*

(2) *The quality of the reporters* is more important than the numbers. Great numbers are not sufficient unless they include those who have qualitative fitness. The majority has frequently been wrong. Is there a substantial body of evidence

---

[5]Reliable modern studies of this rich deposit are available in Gaius Glenn Atkins' *Pilgrims of the Lonely Road* and Willard L. Sperry's Lowell Lectures, *Strangers and Pilgrims.*

coming from sensitive men, who are in command of their faculties, and properly qualified, on both moral and intellectual grounds, so that they inspire trust in that to which they bear testimony? We want to be sure of a substantial body of men and women of sufficiently good character not to engage in deliberate deceit and of sufficiently critical intelligence not to be self-deceived.

The answer is that there is a substantial body of evidence which meets these qualifications. That the great majority of reporters have been honest needs little support. It is not credible that the increase in personal effectiveness and power would come if men were consciously deceiving others in what they say on the deepest questions. This personal effectiveness is recognized even by those who reject the evidential value of the testimony. Furthermore, no serious reader can look at the written testimony of men like Pascal, Newman, and Fox and suppose that these men were engaged in a grand hoax.

The more important question concerns the sanity of the reporters and their capacity to resist delusion. Even if men are *honest*, their testimony is valueless if they are easily deluded. But the fact is that the reports come from a number of the most critical and sane persons the world has known, providing we use any standard test of sanity and critical power. . . .

The only way to avoid the weight of such testimony is to make religious experience an *evidence* of an unbalanced mind, but that is to beg the question in a flagrant manner. It is obviously true that some of those who have reported vivid religious experience have been mentally unbalanced, but this situation is by no means peculiar to religion. There are unbalanced people in every field. If some necessary connection between mental aberrations and religious experience could be demonstrated, the credibility of witnesses would be undermined, but no such demonstration is forthcoming. Undoubtedly there are some truths revealed to eccentrics which are hidden from the normal and prudent, but the overwhelming majority of those who participate in prayer are so sane as to be almost uninteresting. That is why their testimony so seldom finds its way into psychology books.

(3) *The agreement of the reports* is our third test of veracity. Even if the reports are numerous, and the reporters persons of proven integrity as well as critical judgment, the evidence is not good unless there is fundamental agreement in what is said. Part of the reason for doubting the objective reference to the animals "seen" by patients suffering from *delirium tremens* is that two or more patients do not "see" the same snakes.

Upon a superficial view, it is easy to conclude that the reports of the religious consciousness are more remarkable for their diversity than for their convergence. This conclusion is strengthened by the development of many sects. As we consider the matter carefully, however, we discover that the obvious differences, so easily recognized by the populace, refer chiefly to matters of organization and liturgical details, on the one hand, and to differences of creed on the other. It is when we concentrate on the actual record of experience that we are struck with the great degree of convergence in the testimony. There is, indeed, the most distressing divergency on all questions *about* religion, but not in the experience *of* religion. To use William James' familiar distinction, that on which men have argued is "knowledge about," and that on which they have agreed is "acquaintance with.". . .

Such conclusions are enforced by a simple experiment. Take a number of records of direct religious experience, read them to listeners, putting all into the same tongue, and see what success the listeners have in separating and locating them. In many cases there is no way to identify the reports at all, and an ancient Hindu testimony is sometimes mistaken for a modern Christian testimony. "We need not trouble ourselves to ask," writes Dr. Inge, "and we could seldom guess without asking, whether a paragraph describing the highest spiritual experiences was written in the Middle Ages or in modern times, in the north or south of Europe, by a Catholic or by a Protestant."[6] . . .

(4) *The fourth and final test of the veracity of religious experience is the difference it makes.* It is not necessary to be a pragmatist in order to recognize that the pragmatic test is one among others. That there has been a new quality of life in countless persons as a result of religious experience is beyond serious doubt.

In religion we cannot reasonably look for a mark on photographic plates, but we can reasonably look for a mark on human lives. If the experience of God is what men claim it is, we should expect to see a general change in their character; we should expect them to walk with a new step. It is this that we can check abundantly in a way that should be convincing to the open-minded. The evidence of altered lives, including both new strength and new tenderness, is so great that only a small portion of it has ever been committed to print. Not all of those who have reported religious experience have demonstrated "the fruits of the spirit," but, in considering evidence of this kind, we are concerned not so much with what is universal as with what is typical. We can show the typical verification through moral strength, by pointing to characteristic experiences in different settings.

The sense of God's presence has been sufficient to make men courageous in the face of persecution, to sensitize their consciences to social wrong, such as that of slavery and poverty, and, above all, has suffused entire lives with joy. . . .

The pragmatic test of the veracity of religious experience has seldom been more vividly illustrated than in the letters of German pastors, which have been written in concentration camps during the last few dreadful years. The following expressions are characteristic:

"I cannot tell you how thankful I am for the inner experience I have been permitted to have in these days. Though I walk through the valley of the shadow, I fear no evil, for Thou art with me. This presence of God in such a situation becomes even now a precious reality. And how good it is that our faith may now manifest itself really as faith, not merely in words, but in deeds and in the attitude in which we stand ready to take upon ourselves unpleasantness for the sake of the faith, if God thus permits it that men oppress us for our faith's sake. No one will be able to say any more what formerly in foolishness was sometimes said: He merely talks that way because he is paid for it. . . .

[6] W. R. Inge, *Studies of English Mystics*, p. 35.

"God's ways are wonderful. And where He leads through dark ways, there one experiences his glory the most. And again and again the experience is repeated: 'You thought to bring evil upon me, but God thought to turn it to good.' . . ."

What can we say in the face of testimonies so tremendous, testimonies repeated in so many generations? Drugs and delusions may sustain men for a time, but here is something which wears out all opposition. It makes weak men bold and proud men humble. Words seem impertinent and silence the only adequate response. If that which sustains men and makes them praise God in both bright and dark hours be not reality, where is reality to be found?

Thus we see that the empirical evidence for the hypothesis of God as real is the strongest evidence of all. It is the most difficult to escape, especially in a scientific age when experience is respected. We need, however, to integrate this evidence with the other evidence which comes from our knowledge of nature and our own being. The full strength of each line of evidence appears, not in isolation, but in conjunction.

The conclusion to which we are driven is that in religion we have a situation in which the evidence of objectivity is even better than it is in natural science because the corroboration comes from such a long time and from such widely separated areas. The miracle of coincidence is so great that it is bound to be unacceptable to thoughtful persons. Yet what other alternative is there unless belief in God as objectively real is accepted? Herein lies part of the deep significance of the ancient saying that it is hard to believe, but harder still to disbelieve.

14. The Basis of the Moral Law

C. S. Lewis

I now go back to what I said . . . that there were two odd things about the human race. First, that they were haunted by the idea of a sort of behaviour they ought to practice, what you might call fair play, or decency, or morality, or the Law of Nature. Second, that they did not in fact do so. Now some of you may wonder why I called this odd. It may seem to you the most natural thing in the world. In particular, you may have thought I was rather hard on the human race. After all, you may say, what I call breaking the Law of Right and Wrong or of Nature, only means that people are not perfect. And why on earth should I expect them to be? That would be a good answer if what I was trying to do was to fix the exact amount of blame which is due to us for not behaving as we expect others to behave. But that is not my job at all. I am not concerned at present with blame: I am trying to find out truth. And from that point of view the very idea of something being imperfect, of its not being what it ought to be, has certain consequences.

If you take a thing like a stone or a tree, it is what it is and there seems no sense in saying it ought to have been otherwise. Of course you may say a stone is "the wrong shape" if you want to use it for a rookery, or that a tree is a bad tree because it does not give you as much shade as you expected. But all you mean is that the stone or tree does not happen to be convenient for some purpose of your own. You are not, except as a joke, blaming them for that. You really know, that, given the weather and the soil, the tree could not have been any different. What we, from our point of view, call a "bad" tree is obeying the laws of its nature just as much as a "good" one.

Now have you noticed what follows? It follows that what we usually call the laws of nature—the way weather works on a tree for example—may not really be laws in the strict sense, but only in a manner of speaking. When you say that falling stones always obey the law of gravitation, is not this much the same as saying that the law only means "what stones always do"? You do not really think that when a stone is let go, it suddenly remembers that it is under orders to fall to the ground. You only mean that, in fact, it does fall. In other words, you cannot be sure that there is anything over and above the facts themselves, any law about what ought to happen, as distinct from what does happen. The laws of nature, as applied to stones or trees, may only mean "what Nature, in fact, does." But if you turn to the Law of Human Nature, the Law of Decent Behaviour, it is a different matter. That law certainly does not mean "what human beings, in fact, do"; for as

Reprinted with permission of HarperCollins Publishers Limited from *Mere Christianity* by C. S. Lewis. Copyright © C. S. Lewis 1943.

I said before, many of them do not obey this law at all, and none of them obey it completely. The law of gravity tells you what stones do if you drop them; but the Law of Human Nature tells you what human beings ought to do and do not. In other words, when you are dealing with humans, something else comes in above and beyond the actual facts. You have the facts (how men do behave) and you also have something else (how they ought to behave). In the rest of the universe there need not be anything but the facts. Electrons and molecules behave in a certain way, and certain results follow, and that may be the whole story. But men behave in a certain way and that is not the whole story, for all the time you know that they ought to behave differently.

Now this is really so peculiar that one is tempted to try to explain it away. For instance, we might try to make out that when you say a man ought not to act as he does, you only mean the same as when you say that a stone is the wrong shape; namely, that what he is doing happens to be inconvenient to you. But that is simply untrue. A man occupying the corner seat in the train because he got there first, and a man who slipped into it while my back was turned and removed my bag, are both equally inconvenient. But I blame the second man and do not blame the first. I am not angry—except perhaps for a moment before I come to my senses—with a man who trips me up by accident; I am angry with a man who tries to trip me up even if he does not succeed. Yet the first has hurt me and the second has not. Sometimes the behaviour which I call bad is not inconvenient to me at all, but the very opposite. In war, each side may find a traitor on the other side very useful. But though they use him and pay him they regard him as human vermin. So you cannot say that what we call decent behaviour in others is simply the behaviour that happens to be useful to us. And as for decent behaviour in ourselves, I suppose it is pretty obvious that it does not mean behaviour that pays. It means things like being content with thirty shillings when you might have got three pounds, doing school work honestly when it would be easy to cheat, leaving a girl alone when you would like to make love to her, staying in dangerous places when you could go somewhere safer, keeping promises you would rather not keep, and telling the truth even when it makes you look a fool.

Some people say that though decent conduct does not mean what pays each particular person at a particular moment, still, it means what pays the human race as a whole; and that consequently there is no mystery about it. Human beings, after all, have some sense; they see that you cannot have real safety or happiness except in a society where everyone plays fair, and it is because they see this that they try to behave decently. Now, of course, it is perfectly true that safety and happiness can only come from individuals, classes, and nations being honest and fair and kind to each other. It is one of the most important truths in the world. But as an explanation of why we feel as we do about Right and Wrong it just misses the point. If we ask: "Why ought I to be unselfish?" and you reply "Because it is good for society," we may then ask, "Why should I care what's good for society except when it happens to pay *me* personally?" and then you will have to say, "Because you ought to be unselfish"—which simply brings us back to where we started. You are saying what is true, but you are not getting any further. If a man asked what was the point of playing football, it would not be much good saying "in order to score goals," for trying to score goals is the game itself, not the reason for the game, and you would really only be saying that football was football—which is true, but not worth saying. In the same way, if a man asked what was the point of behaving decently, it is no good replying, "in order to benefit society," for trying to benefit society, in other words being unselfish (for "society" after all only means "other people"), is one of the things decent behaviour consists in; all you are really saying is that decent behaviour is decent behaviour. You would have said just as much if you had stopped at the statement, "Men ought to be unselfish."

And that is where I do stop. Men ought to be unselfish, ought to be fair. Not that men are unselfish, nor that they like being unselfish, but that they ought to be. The Moral Law, or Law of Human Nature, is not simply a fact about human behaviour in the same way as the Law of Gravitation is, or may be, simply a fact about how heavy objects behave. On the other hand, it is not a mere fancy, for we cannot get rid of the idea, and most of the things we say and think about men would be reduced to nonsense if we did. And it is not simply a statement about how we should like men to behave for our own convenience; for the behaviour we call bad or unfair is not exactly the same as the behaviour we find inconvenient, and may even be the opposite. Consequently, this Rule of Right and Wrong, or Law of Human Nature, or whatever you call it, must somehow or other be a real thing—a thing that is really there, not made up by ourselves. And yet it is not a fact in the ordinary sense, in the same way as our actual behaviour is a fact. It begins to look as if we shall have to admit that there is more than one kind of reality; that, in this particular case, there is something above and beyond the ordinary facts of men's behaviour, and yet quite definitely real—a real law, which none of us made, but which we find pressing on us.

Let us sum up what we have reached so far. In the case of stones and trees and things of that sort, what we call the Laws of Nature may not be anything except a way of speaking. When you say that nature is governed by certain laws, this may only mean that nature does, in fact, behave in a certain way. The so-called laws may not be anything real—anything above and beyond the actual facts which we observe. But in the case of Man, we saw that this will not do. The Law of Human Nature, or of Right and Wrong, must be something above and beyond the actual facts of human behaviour. In this case, besides the actual facts, you have something else—a real law which we did not invent and which we know we ought to obey.

I now want to consider what this tells us about the universe we live in. Ever since men were able to think, they have been wondering what this universe really is and how it came to be there. And, very roughly, two views have been held. First, there is what is called the materialist view. People who take that view think that matter and space just happen to exist, and always have existed, nobody knows why; and that the matter, behaving in certain fixed ways, has just happened, by a sort of fluke, to produce creatures like ourselves who are able to think. By one chance in a thousand something hit our sun and made it produce the planets; and by another thousandth chance the chemicals necessary for life, and the right temperature, occurred on one of these planets, and so some of the matter on this earth came alive; and then, by a very long series of chances, the living creatures developed into things like us. The other view is the religious view. According to it, what is behind the universe is more like a mind than it is like anything else we know. That is to say, it is conscious, and has purposes, and prefers one thing to another. And on this view it made the universe, partly for purposes we do not know, but partly, at any rate, in order to produce creatures like itself—I mean, like itself to the extent of having minds. Please do not think that one of these views was held a long time ago and that the other has gradually taken its place. Wherever there have been thinking men both views turn up. And note this too. You cannot find out which view is the right one by science in the ordinary sense. Science works by experiments. It watches how things behave. Every scientific statement in the long run, however complicated it looks, really means something like, "I pointed the telescope to such and such a part of the sky at 2:20 A.M. on January 15th and saw so-and-so," or, "I put some of this stuff in a pot and heated it to such-and-such a temperature and it did so-and-so." Do not think I am saying anything against science: I am only saying what its job is. And the more scientific a man is, the more (I believe) he would agree with me that this is the job of science—and a very useful and necessary job it is too. But why anything comes to be there at all, and whether there is anything behind the things science observes—something of a different kind—this is not a scientific question. If there is "Something Behind," then either it will have to remain altogether unknown to men or else make itself known in some different way. The statement that there is any such thing, and the statement that there is no such thing, are neither of them statements that science can make. And real scientists do not usually make them. It is usually the journalists and popular novelists who have picked up a few odds and ends of half-baked science from textbooks who go in for them. After all, it is really a matter of common sense. Supposing science ever became complete so that it knew every single thing in the whole universe. Is it not plain that the questions, "Why is there a universe?" "Why does it go on as it does?" "Has it any meaning?" would remain just as they were?

Now the position would be quite hopeless but for this. There is one thing, and only one, in the whole universe which we know more about than we could learn from external observation. That one thing is Man. We do not merely observe men, we *are* men. In this case we have, so to speak, inside information; we are in the know. And because of that, we know that men find themselves under a moral law, which they did not make, and cannot quite forget even when they try, and which they know they ought to obey. Notice the following point. Anyone studying Man from the outside as we study electricity or cabbages, not knowing our language and consequently not able to get any inside knowledge from us, but merely observing what we did, would never get the slightest evidence that we had this moral law. How could he? For his observations would only show what we did, and the moral law is about what we ought to do. In the same way, if there were anything above or behind the observed facts in the case of stones or the weather, we, by studying them from outside, could never hope to discover it.

The position of the question, then, is like this. We want to know whether the universe simply happens to be what it is for no reason or whether there is a power behind it that makes it what it is. Since that power, if it exists, would be not one of the observed facts but a reality which makes them, no mere observation of the facts can find it. There is only one case in which we can know whether there is anything more, namely our own case. And in that one case we find there is. Or put it the other way round. If there was a controlling power outside the universe, it could not show itself to us as one of the facts inside the universe—no more than the architect of a house could actually be a wall or staircase or fireplace in that house. The only way in which we could expect it to show itself would be inside ourselves as an influence or a command trying to get us to behave in a certain way. And that is just what we do find inside ourselves. Surely this ought to arouse our suspicions? In the only case where you can expect to get an answer, the answer turns out to be Yes; and in the other cases, where you do not get an answer, you see why you do not. Suppose someone asked me, when I see a man in a blue uniform going down the street leaving little paper packets at each house, why I suppose that they contain letters? I should reply, "Because whenever he leaves a similar little packet for me I find it does contain a letter." And if he then objected, "But you've never seen all these letters which you think the other people are getting," I should say, "Of course not, and I shouldn't expect to, because they're not addressed to me. I'm explaining the packets I'm not allowed to open by the ones I am allowed to open." It is the same about this question. The only packet I am allowed to open is Man. When I do, especially when I open that particular man called Myself, I find that I do not exist on my own, that I am under a law; that somebody or something wants me to behave in a certain way. I do not, of course, think that if I could get inside a stone or a tree I should find exactly the same thing, just as I do not think all the other people in the street get the same letters as I do. I should expect, for instance, to find that the stone had to obey the law of gravity—that whereas the sender of the letters merely tells me to obey the law of my human nature. He compels the stone to obey the laws of its stony nature. But I should expect to find that there was, so to speak, a sender of letters in both cases, a Power behind the facts, a Director, a Guide.

Do not think I am going faster than I really am. I am not yet within a hundred miles of the God of Christian theology. All I have got to is a Something which is directing the universe, and which appears in me as a law urging me to do right and making me feel responsible and uncomfortable when I do wrong. I think we have to assume it is more like a mind than it is like anything else we know—because after all the only other thing we know is matter and you can hardly imagine a bit of matter giving instructions. But, of course, it need not be very like a mind, still less like a person. . . .

15. Why I Am Not a Christian

Bertrand Russell

Bertrand Russell (1872–1970) was one of the most prominent philosophers of the twentieth century. He wrote numerous books on a wide variety of philosophical and social issues and was known to the general public for his outspoken stands on religion, marriage, and the banning of the nuclear bomb. In 1950 he was awarded the Nobel Prize for Literature.

As your chairman has told you, the subject about which I am going to speak to you tonight is "Why I Am Not a Christian." Perhaps it would be as well, first of all, to try to make out what one means by the word *Christian*. It is used these days in a very loose sense by a great many people. Some people mean no more by it than a person who attempts to live a good life. In that sense I suppose there would be Christians in all sects and creeds; but I do not think that that is the proper sense of the word, if only because it would imply that all the people who are not Christians—all the Buddhists, Confucians, Mohammedans, and so on—are not trying to live a good life. I do not mean by a Christian any person who tries to live decently according to his lights. I think that you must have a certain amount of definite belief before you have a right to call yourself a Christian. The word does not have quite such a full-blooded meaning now as it had in the times of St. Augustine and St. Thomas Aquinas. In those days, if a man said that he was a Christian it was known what he meant. You accepted a whole collection of creeds which were set out with great precision, and every single syllable of those creeds you believed with the whole strength of your convictions.

What Is a Christian?

Nowadays it is not quite that. We have to be a little more vague in our meaning of Christianity. I think, however, that there are two different items which are quite essential to anybody calling himself a Christian. The first is one of a dogmatic nature—namely, that you must believe in God and immortality. If you do not believe in those two things, I do not think that you can properly call yourself a Christian. Then, further than that, as the name implies, you must have some kind of belief about Christ. The Mohammedans, for instance, also believe in God and in immortality, and yet they would not call themselves Christians. I think you must have at the very lowest the belief that Christ was, if not divine, at least the best and

Reprinted with the permission of Simon & Schuster, Inc., and Routledge, from *Why I Am Not a Christian* by Bertrand Russell. Copyright © 1957 by George Allen & Unwin Ltd.

wisest of men. If you are not going to believe that much about Christ, I do not think you have any right to call yourself a Christian. Of course, there is another sense, which you find in *Whitaker's Almanack* and in geography books, where the population of the world is said to be divided into Christians, Mohammedans, Buddhists, fetish worshipers, and so on; and in that sense we are all Christians. The geography books count us all in, but that is a purely geographical sense, which I suppose we can ignore. Therefore I take it that when I tell you why I am not a Christian I have to tell you two different things: first, why I do not believe in God and immortality; and secondly, why I do not think that Christ was the best and wisest of men, although I grant him a very high degree of moral goodness.

But for the successful efforts of unbelievers in the past, I could not take so elastic a definition of Christianity as that. As I said before, in olden days it had a much more full-blooded sense. For instance, it included the belief in hell. Belief in eternal hell-fire was an essential item of Christian belief until pretty recent times. In this country, as you know, it ceased to be an essential item because of a decision of the Privy Council, and from that decision the Archbishop of Canterbury and the Archbishop of York dissented; but in this country our religion is settled by Act of Parliament, and therefore the Privy Council was able to override their Graces and hell was no longer necessary to a Christian. Consequently I shall not insist that a Christian must believe in hell.

THE EXISTENCE OF GOD

To come to this question of the existence of God: it is a large and serious question, and if I were to attempt to deal with it in any adequate manner I should have to keep you here until Kingdom Come, so that you will have to excuse me if I deal with it in a somewhat summary fashion. You know, of course, that the Catholic Church has laid it down as a dogma that the existence of God can be proved by the unaided reason. That is a somewhat curious dogma, but it is one of their dogmas. They had to introduce it because at one time the freethinkers adopted the habit of saying that there were such and such arguments which mere reason might urge against the existence of God, but of course they knew as a matter of faith that God did exist. The arguments and the reasons were set out at great length, and the Catholic Church felt that they must stop it. Therefore they laid it down that the existence of God can be proved by the unaided reason and they have to set up what they considered were arguments to prove it. There are, of course, a number of them, but I shall take only a few.

THE FIRST-CAUSE ARGUMENT

Perhaps the simplest and easiest to understand is the argument of the First Cause. (It is maintained that everything we see in this world has a cause, and as you go back in the chain of causes further and further you must come to a First Cause, and to that First Cause you give the name of God.) That argument, I suppose, does not carry very much weight nowadays, because, in the first place, cause is not quite what it used to be. The philosophers and the men of science have got going on cause, and it has not anything like the vitality it used to have; but, apart from that, you can see that the argument that there must be a First Cause is one that cannot have any validity. I may say that when I was a young man and was debating these questions very seriously in my mind, I for a long time accepted the argument of the First Cause, until one day, at the age of eighteen, I read John Stuart Mill's Autobiography, and I there found this sentence: "My father taught me that the question 'Who made me?' cannot be answered, since it immediately suggests the further question 'Who made God?'" That very simple sentence showed me, as I still think, the fallacy in the argument of the First Cause. If everything must have a cause, then God must have a cause. If there can be anything without a cause, it may just as well be the world as God, so that there cannot be any validity in that argument. It is exactly of the same nature as the Hindu's view, that the world rested upon an elephant and the elephant rested upon a tortoise; and when they said, "How about the tortoise?" the Indian said, "Suppose we change the subject." The argument is really no better than that. There is no reason why the world could not have come into being without a cause; nor, on the other hand, is there any reason why it should not have always existed. There is no reason to suppose that the world had a beginning at all. The idea that things must have a beginning is really due to the poverty of our imagination. Therefore, perhaps, I need not waste any more time upon the argument about the First Cause.

THE NATURAL-LAW ARGUMENT

Then there is a very common argument from natural law. That was a favorite argument all through the eighteenth century, especially under the influence of Sir Isaac Newton and his cosmogony. People observed the planets going around the sun according to the law of gravitation, and they thought that God had given a behest to these planets to move in that particular fashion, and that was why they did so. That was, of course, a convenient and simple explanation that saved them the trouble of looking any further for explanations of the law of gravitation. Nowadays we explain the law of gravitation in a somewhat complicated fashion that Einstein has introduced. I do not propose to give you a lecture on the law of gravitation, as interpreted by Einstein, because that again would take some time; at any rate, you no longer have the sort of natural law that you had in the Newtonian system, where, for some reason that nobody can understand, nature behaved in a uniform fashion. We now find that a great many things we thought were natural laws are really human conventions. You know that even in the remotest depths of stellar space there are still three feet to a yard. That is, no doubt, a very remarkable fact, but you would hardly call it a law of nature. And a great many things that have been regarded as laws of nature are of that kind. On the other hand, where you can get down to any knowledge of what atoms actually do, you will find they are much less subject to law than people thought, and that the laws at which you arrive are statistical averages of just the sort that would emerge from chance. There is, as we all know, a law that if you throw dice you will get double sixes only about once in thirty-six times, and we do not regard that as evidence that the fall of the dice is regulated by design; on the contrary, if the double sixes came every time we should think that there was design. The laws of nature are of that sort as regards a great many of them. They are statistical averages such as would emerge from the laws of chance; and that makes this whole business of natural law much less impressive than it formerly was. Quite apart from that, which represents the momentary state of science that may change tomorrow, the whole idea that natural laws imply a lawgiver is due to a confusion between natural and human laws. Human laws are behests commanding you to behave a certain way, in which way you may choose to behave, or you may choose not to behave; but natural laws are a description of how things do in fact behave, and being a mere description of what they in fact do, you cannot argue that there must be somebody who told them to do that, because even supposing that there were, you are then faced with the question "Why did God issue just those natural laws and no others?" If you say that he did it simply from his own good pleasure, and without any reason, you then find that there is something which is not subject to law, and so your train of natural law is interrupted. If you say, as more orthodox theologians do, that in all the laws which God issues he had a reason for giving those laws rather than others—the reason, of course, being to create the best universe, although you would never think it to look at it—if there were a reason for the laws which God gave, then God himself was subject to law, and therefore you do not get any advantage by introducing God as an intermediary. You have really a law outside and anterior to the divine edicts, and God does not serve your purpose, because he is not the ultimate lawgiver. In short, this whole argument about natural law no longer has anything like the strength that it used to have. I am traveling on in time in my review of the arguments. The arguments that are used for the existence of God change their character as time goes on. They were at first hard intellectual arguments embodying certain quite definite fallacies. As we come to modern times they become less respectable intellectually and more and more affected by a kind of moralizing vagueness.

THE ARGUMENT FROM DESIGN

The next step in this process brings us to the argument from design. You all know the argument from design: everything in the world is made just so that we can manage to live in the world, and if the world was ever so little different, we could not manage to live in it. That is the argument from design. It sometimes takes a rather curious form; for instance, it is argued that rabbits have white tails in order to be easy to shoot. I do not know how rabbits would view that application. It is an easy argument to parody. You all know Voltaire's remark, that obviously the nose was designed to be such as to fit spectacles. That sort of parody has turned out to be not nearly so wide of the mark as it might have seemed in the eighteenth century, because since the time of Darwin we understand much better why living creatures are adapted to their environment. It is not that their environment was made to be suitable to them but that they grew to be suitable to it, and that is the basis of adaptation. There is no evidence of design about it.

When you come to look into this argument from design, it is a most astonishing thing that people can believe that this world, with all the things that are in it, with all its defects, should be the best that omnipotence and omniscience have been able to produce in millions of years. I really cannot believe it. Do you think that, if you were granted omnipotence and omniscience and millions of years in which to perfect your world, you could produce nothing better than the Ku Klux Klan or the Fascists? Moreover, if you accept the ordinary laws of science, you have to suppose that human life and life in general on this planet will die out in due course: it is a stage in the decay of the solar system; at a certain stage of decay you get the sort of conditions of temperature and so forth which are suitable to protoplasm, and there is life for a short time in the life of the whole solar system. You see in the moon the sort of thing to which the earth is tending—something dead, cold, and lifeless.

I am told that that sort of view is depressing, and people will sometimes tell you that if they believed that, they would not be able to go on living. Do not believe it; it is all nonsense. Nobody really worries much about what is going to happen millions of years hence. Even if they think they are worrying much about that, they are really deceiving themselves. They are worried about something much more mundane, or it may merely be a bad digestion; but nobody is really seriously rendered unhappy by the thought of something that is going to happen to this world millions and millions of years hence. Therefore, although it is of course a gloomy view to suppose that life will die out—at least I suppose we may say so, although sometimes when I contemplate the things that people do with their lives I think it is almost a consolation—it is not such as to render life miserable. It merely makes you turn your attention to other things.

THE MORAL ARGUMENTS FOR DEITY

Now we reach one stage further in what I shall call the intellectual descent that the Theists have made in their argumentations, and we come to what are called the moral arguments for the existence of God. You all know, of course, that there used to be in the old days three intellectual arguments for the existence of God, all of which were disposed of by Immanuel Kant in the *Critique of Pure Reason;* but no sooner had he disposed of those arguments than he invented a new one, a moral argument, and that quite convinced him. He was like many people: in intellectual matters he was skeptical, but in moral matters he believed implicitly in the maxims that he had imbibed at his mother's knee. That illustrates what the psychoanalysts so much emphasize—the immensely stronger hold upon us that our early associations have than those of later times.

Kant, as I say, invented a new moral argument for the existence of God, and that in varying forms was extremely popular during the nineteenth century. It has all sorts of forms. One form is to say that there would be no right or wrong unless God existed. I am not for the moment concerned with whether there is a difference between right and wrong, or whether there is not: that is another question. The point I am concerned with is that, if you are quite sure there is a difference between right and wrong, you are then in this situation: Is that difference due to God's fiat or is it not? If it is due to God's fiat, then for God himself there is no difference between right and wrong, and it is no longer a significant statement to say that God is good. If you are going to say, as theologians do, that God is good, you must then say that right and wrong have some meaning which is independent of God's fiat, because God's fiats are good and not bad independently of the mere fact that he made them. If you are going to say that, you will then have to say that it is not only through God that right and wrong came into being, but that they are in essence logically anterior to God. You could, of course, if you liked, say that there was a superior deity who gave orders to the God who made this world, or could take up the line that some of the gnostics took up—a line which I often thought was a very plausible one—that as a matter of fact this world that we know was made by the devil at a moment when God was not looking. There is a good deal to be said for that, and I am not concerned to refute it.

The Argument for the Remedying of Injustice

Then there is another very curious form of moral argument, which is this: they say that the existence of God is required in order to bring justice into the world. In the part of this universe that we know there is great injustice, and often the good suffer, and often the wicked prosper, and one hardly knows which of those is the more annoying; but if you are going to have justice in the universe as a whole you have to suppose a future life to redress the balance of life here on earth. So they say that there must be a God, and there must be heaven and hell in order that in the long run there may be justice. That is a very curious argument. If you looked at the matter from a scientific point of view, you would say, "After all, I know only this world. I do not know about the rest of the universe, but so far as one can argue at all on probabilities one would say that probably this world is a fair sample, and if there is injustice here the odds are that there is injustice elsewhere also." Supposing you got a crate of oranges that you opened, and you found all the top layer of oranges bad, you would not argue, "The underneath ones must be good, so as to redress the balance." You would say, "Probably the whole lot is a bad consignment"; and that is really what a scientific person would argue about the universe. He would say, "Here we find in this world a great deal of injustice, and so far as that goes that is a reason for supposing that justice does not rule in the world; and therefore so far as it goes it affords a moral argument against deity and not in favor of one." Of course I know that the sort of intellectual arguments that I have been talking to you about are not what really moves people. What really moves people to believe in God is not any intellectual argument at all. Most people believe in God because they have been taught from early infancy to do it, and that is the main reason.

Then I think that the next most powerful reason is the wish for safety, a sort of feeling that there is a big brother who will look after you. That plays a very profound part in influencing people's desire for a belief to God.

THE CHARACTER OF CHRIST

I now want to say a few words upon a topic which I often think is not quite sufficiently dealt with by Rationalists, and that is the question whether Christ was the best and the wisest of men. It is generally taken for granted that we should all agree that that was so. I do not myself. I think that there are a good many points upon which I agree with Christ a great deal more than the professing Christians do. I do not know that I could go with Him all the way, but I could go with Him much further than most professing Christians can. You will remember that He said, "Resist not evil: but whosoever shall smite thee on thy right cheek, turn to him the other also." That is not a new precept or a new principle. It was used by Lao-tse and Buddha some 500 or 600 years before Christ, but it is not a principle which as a matter of fact Christians accept. I have no doubt that the present Prime Minister,[1] for instance, is a most sincere Christian, but I should not advise any of you to go and smite him on one cheek. I think you might find that he thought this text was intended in a figurative sense.

Then there is another point which I consider excellent. You will remember that Christ said "Judge not lest ye be judged." That principle I do not think you would find was popular in the law courts of Christian countries. I have known in my time quite a number of judges who were very earnest Christians, and none of them felt that they were acting contrary to Christian principles in what they did. Then Christ says, "Give to him that asketh of thee, and from him that would borrow of thee turn not thou away." That is a very good principle. Your Chairman has reminded you that we are not here to talk politics, but I cannot help observing that the last general election was fought on the question of how desirable it was to turn away from him that would borrow of thee, so that one must assume that the Liberals and Conservatives of this country are composed of people who do not agree with the teaching of Christ, because they certainly did very emphatically turn away on that occasion.

Then there is one other maxim of Christ which I think has a great deal in it, but I do not find that it is very popular among some of our Christian friends. He says, "If thou wilt be perfect, go and sell that which thou hast, and give to the poor."

---

[1] Stanley Baldwin.

That is a very excellent maxim, but as I say, it is not much practiced. All these, I think, are good maxims, although they are a little difficult to live up to. I do not profess to live up to them myself; but then, after all, it is not quite the same thing as for a Christian.

DEFECTS IN CHRIST'S TEACHING

Having granted the excellence of these maxims, I come to certain points in which I do not believe that one can grant either the superlative wisdom or the superlative goodness of Christ as depicted in the Gospels; and here I may say that one is not concerned with the historical question. Historically it is quite doubtful whether Christ ever existed at all, and if He did we do not know anything about Him, so that I am not concerned with the historical question, which is a very difficult one. I am concerned with Christ as He appears in the Gospels, taking the Gospel narrative as it stands, and there one does find some things that do not seem to be very wise. For one thing, He certainly thought that His second coming would occur in clouds of glory before the death of all the people who were living at that time. There are a great many texts that prove that. He says, for instance, "Ye shall not have gone over the cities of Israel till the Son of Man be come." Then He says, "There are some standing here which shall not taste death till the Son of Man comes into His Kingdom"; and there are a lot of places where it is quite clear that He believed that His second coming would happen during the lifetime of many then living. That was the belief of His earlier followers, and it was the basis of a good deal of His moral teaching. When He said, "Take no thought for the morrow," and things of that sort, it was very largely because He thought that the second coming was going to be very soon, and that all ordinary mundane affairs did not count. I have, as a matter of fact, known some Christians who did believe that the second coming was imminent. I knew a person who frightened his congregation terribly by telling them that the second coming was very imminent indeed, but they were much consoled when they found that he was planting trees in his garden. The early Christians did really believe it, and they did abstain from such things as planting trees in their gardens, because they did accept from Christ the belief that the second coming was imminent. In that respect, clearly He was not so wise as some other people have been, and He was certainly not superlatively wise.

THE MORAL PROBLEM

Then you come to moral questions. There is one very serious defect to my mind in Christ's moral character, and that is that He believed in hell. I do not myself feel that any person who is really profoundly humane can believe in everlasting punishment. Christ certainly as depicted in the Gospels did believe in everlasting punishment, and one does find repeatedly a vindictive fury against those people who would not listen to His preaching—an attitude which is not uncommon with preachers, but which does somewhat detract from superlative excellence. You do not, for instance, find that attitude in Socrates. You find him quite bland and urbane toward the people who would not listen to him; and it is, to my mind, far more worthy of a sage to take that line than to take the line of indignation. You probably all remember the sort of things that Socrates was saying when he was dying, and the sort of things that he generally did say to people who did not agree with him.

You will find that in the Gospels Christ said, "Ye serpents, ye generation of vipers, how can ye escape the damnation of hell." That was said to people who did not like His preaching. It is not really to my mind quite the best tone, and there are a great many of these things about hell. There is, of course, the familiar text about the sin against the Holy Ghost: "Whosoever speaketh against the Holy Ghost it shall not be forgiven him neither in this World nor in the world to come." That text has caused an unspeakable amount of misery in the world, for all sorts of people have imagined that they have committed the sin against the Holy Ghost, and thought that it would not be forgiven them either in this world or in the world to come. I really do not think that a person with a proper degree of kindliness in his nature would have put fears and terrors of that sort in the world.

Then Christ says, "The Son of Man shall send forth His angels, and they shall gather out of His kingdom all things that offend, and them which do iniquity, and shall cast them into a furnace of fire; there shall be wailing and gnashing of teeth"; and He goes on about the wailing and gnashing of teeth. It comes in one verse after another, and it is quite manifest to the reader that there is a certain pleasure in contemplating wailing and gnashing of teeth, or else it would not occur so often. Then you all, of course, remember about the sheep and the goats; how at the second coming He is going to divide the sheep from the goats, and He is going to say to the goats, "Depart from me, ye cursed, into everlasting fire." He continues, "And these shall go away into everlasting fire." Then He says again, "If thy hand offend thee, cut it off; it is better for thee to enter into life maimed, than having two hands to go into hell, into the fire that never shall be quenched; where the worm dieth not and the fire is not quenched." He repeats that again and again also. I must say that I think all this doctrine, that hell-fire is a punishment for sin, is a doctrine of cruelty. It is a doctrine that put cruelty into the world and gave the world generations of cruel torture: and the Christ of the Gospels, if you could take Him as His chroniclers represent Him, would certainly have to be considered partly responsible for that.

There are other things of less importance. There is the instance of the Gadarene swine, where it certainly was not very kind to the pigs to put devils into them and make them rush down the hill to the sea. You must remember that He was omnipotent, and He could have made the devils simply go away; but He chose to send them into the pigs. Then there is the curious story of the fig tree, which always rather puzzled me. You remember what happened about the fig tree. "He was hungry; and seeing a fig tree afar off having leaves, He came if haply He might find anything thereon; and when He came to it He found nothing but leaves, for the time of figs was not yet. And Jesus answered and said unto it: 'No man eat fruit of thee hereafter for ever' . . . and Peter . . . saith unto Him: 'Master, behold the fig tree which thou cursedst is withered away.'" This is a very curious story, because it was not the right time of year for figs, and you really could not blame the tree. I cannot myself feel that either in the matter of wisdom or in the matter of virtue Christ stands quite as high as some other people known to history. I think I should put Buddha and Socrates above Him in those respects.

THE EMOTIONAL FACTOR

As I said before, I do not think that the real reason why people accept religion has anything to do with argumentation. They accept religion on emotional grounds. One is often told that it is a very wrong thing to attack religion, because religion makes men virtuous. So I am told; I have not noticed it. You know, of course, the parody of that argument in Samuel Butler's book, *Erewhon Revisited.* You will remember that in *Erewhon* there is a certain Higgs who arrives in a remote country, and after spending some time there he escapes from that country in a balloon. Twenty years later he comes back to that country and finds a new religion in which he is worshiped under the name of the "Sun Child," and it is said that he ascended into heaven. He finds that the Feast of the Ascension is about to be celebrated, and he hears Professors Hanky and Panky say to each other that they never set eyes on the man Higgs, and they hope they never will; but they are the high priests of the religion of the Sun Child. He is very indignant, and he comes up to them, and he says, "I am going to expose all this humbug and tell the people of Erewhon that it was only I, the man Higgs, and I went up in a balloon." He was told, "You must not do that, because all the morals of this country are bound round this myth, and if they once know that you did not ascend into heaven they will all become wicked"; and so he is persuaded of that and he goes quietly away.

That is the idea—that we should all be wicked if we did not hold to the Christian religion. It seems to me that the people who have held to it have been for the most part extremely wicked. You find this curious fact, that the more intense has been the religion of any period and the more profound has been the dogmatic belief, the greater has been the cruelty and the worse has been the state of affairs. In the so-called ages of faith, when men really did believe the Christian religion in all its completeness, there was the Inquisition, with its tortures; there were millions of unfortunate women burned as witches; and there was every kind of cruelty practiced upon all sorts of people in the name of religion.

You find as you look around the world that every single bit of progress in humane feeling, every improvement in the criminal law, every step toward the diminution of war, every step toward better treatment of the colored races, or every mitigation of slavery, every moral progress that there has been in the world, has been consistently opposed by the organized churches of the world. I say quite deliberately that the Christian religion, as organized in its churches, has been and still is the principal enemy of moral progress in the world.

How the Churches Have Retarded Progress

You may think that I am going too far when I say that that is still so. I do not think that I am. Take one fact. You will bear with me if I mention it. It is not a pleasant fact, but the churches compel one to mention facts that are not pleasant. Supposing that in this world that we live in today an inexperienced girl is married to a syphilitic man; in that case the Catholic Church says, "This is an indissoluble sacrament. You must endure celibacy or stay together. And if you stay together, you must not use birth control to prevent the birth of syphilitic children." Nobody whose natural sympathies have not been warped by dogma, or whose moral nature was not absolutely dead to all sense of suffering, could maintain that it is right and proper that that state of things should continue.

That is only an example. There are a great many ways in which, at the present moment, the church, by its insistence upon what it chooses to call morality, inflicts upon all sorts of people undeserved and unnecessary suffering. And of course, as we know, it is in its major part an opponent still of progress and of improvement in all the ways that diminish suffering in the world, because it has chosen to label as morality a certain narrow set of rules of conduct which have nothing to do with human happiness; and when you say that this or that ought to be done because it would make for human happiness, they think that has nothing to do with the matter at all. "What has human happiness to do with morals? The object of morals is not to make people happy."

Fear, the Foundation of Religion

Religion is based, I think, primarily and mainly upon fear. It is partly the terror of the unknown and partly, as I have said, the wish to feel that you have a kind of elder brother who will stand by you in all your troubles and disputes. Fear is the basis of the whole thing—fear of the mysterious, fear of defeat, fear of death. Fear is the parent of cruelty, and therefore it is no wonder if cruelty and religion have gone hand in hand. It is because fear is the basis of those two things. In this world we can now begin a little to understand things, and a little to master them by help of science, which has forced its way step by step against the Christian religion, against the churches, and against the opposition of all the old precepts. Science can help us to get over this craven fear in which mankind has lived for so many generations. Science can teach us, and I think our own hearts can teach us, no longer to look around for imaginary supports, no longer to invent allies in the sky, but rather to look to our own efforts here below to make this world a fit place to live in, instead of the sort of place that the churches in all these centuries have made it.

WHAT WE MUST DO

We want to stand upon our own feet and look fair and square at the world—its good facts, its bad facts, its beauties, and its ugliness; see the world as it is and be not afraid of it. Conquer the world by intelligence and not merely by being slavishly subdued by the terror that comes from it. The whole conception of God is a conception derived from the ancient Oriental despotisms. It is a conception quite unworthy of free men. When you hear people in church debasing themselves and saying that they are miserable sinners, and all the rest of it, it seems contemptible and not worthy of self-respecting human beings. We ought to stand up and look the world frankly in the face. We ought to make the best we can of the world, and if it is not so good as we wish, after all it will still be better than what these others have made it in all these ages. A good world needs knowledge, kindliness, and courage; it does not need a regretful hankering after the past or fettering of the free intelligence by the words uttered long ago by ignorant men. It needs a fearless outlook and a free intelligence. It needs hope for the future, not looking back all the time toward a past that is dead, which we trust will be far surpassed by the future that our intelligence can create.

CONTEMPORARY ISSUES

The Problem of Evil

16. *God and the Problem of Evil*

B. C. Johnson

B. C. Johnson is a pen name for the author, who wishes to remain anonymous.

Here is a common situation: a house catches on fire and a six-month-old baby is painfully burned to death. Could we possibly describe as "good" any person who had the power to save this child and yet refused to do so? God undoubtedly has this power and yet in many cases of this sort he has refused to help. Can we call God "good"? Are there adequate excuses for his behavior?

First, it will not do to claim that the baby will go to heaven. It was either necessary for the baby to suffer or it was not. If it was not, then it was wrong to allow it. The child's ascent to heaven does not change this fact. If it was necessary, the fact that the baby will go to heaven does not explain why it was necessary, and we are still left without an excuse for God's inaction.

It is not enough to say that the baby's painful death would in the long run have good results and therefore should have happened, otherwise God would not have permitted it. For if we know this to be true, then we know—just as God knows—that every action successfully performed must in the end be good and therefore the right thing to do, otherwise God would not have allowed it to happen. We could deliberately set houses ablaze to kill innocent people and if successful we would then know we had a duty to do it. A defense of God's goodness which takes as its foundation duties known only after the fact would result in a morality unworthy of the name. Furthermore, this argument does not explain why God allowed the child to burn to death. It merely claims that there is some reason discoverable in the long run. But the belief that such a reason is within our grasp must rest upon the additional belief that God is good. This is just to counter evidence against such a belief by assuming the belief to be true. It is not unlike a lawyer defending his client by claiming that the client is innocent and therefore the evidence against him must be misleading—that proof vindicating the defendant will be found

From B. C. Johnson, *The Atheist Debater's Handbook* (Amherst, NY: Prometheus Books) Copyright 1981. Reprinted by permission of the publisher.

in the long run. No jury of reasonable men and women would accept such a defense and the theist cannot expect a more favorable outcome.

The theist often claims that man has been given free will so that if he accidentally or purposefully cause fires, killing small children, it is his fault alone. Consider a bystander who had nothing to do with starting the fire but who refused to help even though he could have saved the child with no harm to himself. Could such a bystander be called good? Certainly not. If we could not consider a mortal human being good under these circumstances, what grounds could we possibly have for continuing to assert the goodness of an all-powerful God?

The suggestion is sometimes made that it is best for us to face disasters without assistance, otherwise we would become dependent on an outside power for aid. Should we then abolish modern medical care or do away with efficient fire departments? Are we not dependent on their help? Is it not the case that their presence transforms us into soft, dependent creatures? The vast majority are not physicians or firemen. These people help in their capacity as professional outside sources of aid in much the same way that we would expect God to be helpful. Theists refer to aid from firemen and physicians as cases of man helping himself. In reality, it is a tiny minority of men helping a great many. We can become just as dependent on them as we can on God. Now the existence of this kind of outside help is either wrong or right. If it is right, then God should assist those areas of the world which do not have this kind of help. In fact, throughout history, such help has not been available. If aid ought to have been provided, then God should have provided it. On the other hand, if it is wrong to provide this kind of assistance, then we should abolish the aid altogether. But we obviously do not believe it is wrong.

Similar considerations apply to the claim that if God interferes in disasters, he would destroy a considerable amount of moral urgency to make things right. Once again, note that such institutions as modern medicine and fire departments are relatively recent. They function irrespective of whether we as individuals feel any moral urgency to support them. To the extent that they help others, opportunities to feel moral urgency are destroyed because they reduce the number of cases which appeal to us for help. Since we have not always had such institutions, there must have been a time when there was greater moral urgency than there is now. If such a situation is morally desirable, then we should abolish modern medical care and fire departments. If the situation is not morally desirable, then God should have remedied it.

Besides this point, we should note that God is represented as one who tolerates disasters, such as infants burning to death, in order to create moral urgency. It follows that God approved of these disasters as a means to encourage the creation of moral urgency. Furthermore, if there were no such disasters occurring, God would have to see to it that they occur. If it so happened that we lived in a world in which babies never perished in burning houses, God would be morally obliged to take an active hand in setting fire to houses with infants in them. In fact, if the frequency of infant mortality due to fire should happen to fall below a level necessary for the creation of maximum moral urgency in our real world, God would be justified in setting a few fires of his own. This may well be happening right now, for there is no guarantee that the maximum number of infant deaths necessary for moral urgency are occurring.

All of this is of course absurd. If I see an opportunity to create otherwise nonexistent opportunities for moral urgency by burning an infant or two, then I should *not* do so. But if it is good to maximize moral urgency, then I *should* do so. Therefore, it is not good to maximize moral urgency. Plainly we do not in general believe that it is a good thing to maximize moral urgency. The fact that we approve of modern medical care and applaud medical advances is proof enough of this.

The theist may point out that in a world without suffering there would be no occasion for the production of such virtues as courage, sympathy, and the like. This may be true, but the atheist need not demand a world without suffering. He need only claim that there is suffering which is in excess of that needed for the production of various virtues. For example, God's active attempts to save six-month-old infants from fires would not in itself create a world without suffering. But no one could sincerely doubt that it would improve the world.

The two arguments against the previous theistic excuse apply here also. "Moral urgency" and "building virtue" are susceptible to the same criticisms. It is worthwhile to emphasize, however, that we encourage efforts to eliminate evils; we approve of efforts to promote peace, prevent famine, and wipe out disease. In other words, we do value a world with fewer of (if possible) no opportunities for the development of virtue (when "virtue" is understood to mean the reduction of suffering). If we produce such a world for succeeding generations, how will they develop virtues? Without war, disease, and famine, they will not be virtuous. Should we then cease our attempts to wipe out war, disease, and famine? If we do not believe that it is right to cease attempts at improving the world, then by implication we admit that virtue-building is not an excuse for God to permit disasters. For we admit that the development of virtue is no excuse for permitting disasters.

It might be said that God allows innocent people to suffer in order to deflate man's ego so that the latter will not be proud of his apparently deserved good fortune. But this excuse succumbs to the arguments used against the preceding excuses and we need discuss them no further.

Theists may claim that evil is a necessary by-product of the laws of nature and therefore it is irrational for God to interfere every time a disaster happens. Such a state of affairs would alter the whole causal order and we would then find it impossible to predict anything. But the death of a child caused by an electrical fire could have been prevented by a miracle and no one would ever have known. Only a minor alteration in electrical equipment would have been necessary. A very large disaster could have been avoided simply by producing in Hitler a miraculous heart attack—and no one would have known it was a miracle. To argue that continued miraculous intervention by God would be wrong is like insisting that one should never use salt because ingesting five pounds of it would be fatal. No one is requesting that God interfere all of the time. He should, however, intervene to prevent especially horrible disasters. Of course, the question arises: where does one draw the line? Well, certainly the line should be drawn somewhere this side of infants burning to death. To argue that we do not know where the line should be drawn is no excuse for failing to interfere in those instances that would be called clear cases of evil.

It will not do to claim that evil exists as a necessary contrast to good so that we might know what good is. A very small amount of evil, such as a toothache, would allow that. It is not necessary to destroy innocent human beings.

The claim could be made that God has a "higher morality" by which his actions are to be judged. But it is a strange "higher morality" which claims that what we call "bad" is good and what we call "good" is bad. Such a morality can have no meaning to us. It would be like calling black "white" and white "black." In reply the theist may say that God is the wise Father and we are ignorant children. How can we judge God any more than a child is able to judge his parent? It is true that a child may be puzzled by his parents' conduct, but his basis for deciding that their conduct is nevertheless good would be the many instances of good behavior he has observed. Even so, this could be misleading. Hitler, by all accounts, loved animals and children of the proper race; but if Hitler had had a child, this offspring would hardly have been justified in arguing that his father was a good man. At any rate, God's "higher morality," being the opposite of ours, cannot offer any grounds for deciding that he is somehow good.

Perhaps the main problem with the solutions to the problem of evil we have thus far considered is that no matter how convincing they may be in the abstract, they are implausible in certain particular cases. Picture an infant dying in a burning house and then imagine God simply observing from afar. Perhaps God is reciting excuses in his own behalf. As the child succumbs to the smoke and flames, God may be pictured as saying: "Sorry, but if I helped you I would have considerable trouble deflating the ego of your parents. And don't forget I have to keep those laws of nature consistent. And anyway if you weren't dying in that fire, a lot of moral urgency would just go down the drain. Besides, I didn't start this fire, so you can't blame *me*."

It does no good to assert that God may not be all-powerful and thus not able to prevent evil. He can create a universe and yet is conveniently unable to do what the fire department can do—rescue a baby from a burning building. God should at least be as powerful as a man. A man, if he had been at the right place and time, could have killed Hitler. Was this beyond God's abilities? If God knew in 1910 how to produce polio vaccine and if he was able to communicate with somebody, he should have communicated this knowledge. He must be incredibly limited if he could not have managed this modest accomplishment. Such a God if not dead, is the next thing to it. And a person who believes in such a ghost of a God is practically an atheist. To call such a thing a god would be to strain the meaning of the word.

The theist, as usual, may retreat to faith. He may say that he has faith in God's goodness and therefore the Christian Deity's existence has not been disproved. "Faith" is here understood as being much like confidence in a friend's innocence despite the evidence against him. Now in order to have confidence in a friend one must know him well enough to justify faith in his goodness. We cannot have justifiable faith in the supreme goodness of strangers. Moreover, such confidence must come not just from a speaking acquaintance. The friend may continually assure us with his words that he is good but if he does not act like a good person, we would have no reason to trust him. A person who says he has faith in God's goodness is speaking as if he had known God for a long time and during that time had never seen Him do any serious evil. But we know that throughout history God has allowed numerous atrocities to occur. No one can have justifiable faith in the goodness of such a God. This faith would have to be based on a close friendship wherein God was never found to do anything wrong. But a person would have to be blind and deaf to have had such a relationship with God. Suppose a friend of yours had always claimed to be good yet refused to help people when he was in a position to render aid. Could you have justifiable faith in his goodness?

You can of course say that you trust God anyway—that no arguments can undermine your faith. But this is just a statement describing how stubborn you are; it has no bearing whatsoever on the question of God's goodness.

The various excuses theists offer for why God has allowed evil to exist have been demonstrated to be inadequate. However, the conclusive objection to these excuses does not depend on their inadequacy.

First, we should note that every possible excuse making the actual world consistent with the existence of a good God could be used in reverse to make that same world consistent with an evil God. For example, we could say that God is evil and that he allows free will so that we can freely do evil things, which would make us more truly evil than we would be if forced to perform evil acts. Or we could say that natural disasters occur in order to make people more selfish and bitter, for most people tend to have a "me-first" attitude in a disaster (note, for example, stampedes to leave burning buildings). Even though some people achieve virtue from disasters, this outcome is necessary if persons are to react freely to disaster—necessary if the development of moral degeneracy is to continue freely. But, enough; the point is made. Every excuse we could provide to make the world consistent with a good God can be paralleled by an excuse to make the world consistent with an evil God. This is so because the world is a mixture of both good and bad.

Now there are only three possibilities concerning God's moral character. Considering the world as it actually is, we may believe: (a) that God is more likely to be all evil than he is to be all good; (b) that God is less likely to be all evil than he is to be all good; or (c) that God is equally as likely to be all evil as he is to be all good. In case (a) it would be admitted that God is unlikely to be all good. Case (b) cannot be true at all, since—as we have seen—the belief that God is all evil can be justified to precisely the same extent as the belief that God is all good. Case (c) leaves us with no reasonable excuses for a good God to permit evil. The reason is as follows: if an excuse is to be a reasonable excuse, the circumstances it identifies as excusing conditions must be actual. For example, if I run over a pedestrian and my excuse is that the brakes failed because someone tampered with them, then the facts had better bear this out. Otherwise the excuse will not hold. Now if case *(c)* is correct and, given the facts of the actual world, God is as likely to be all evil as he is to be all good, then these facts do not support the excuses which could be made for a good God permitting evil. Consider an analogous example. If my excuse for running over the pedestrian is that my brakes were tampered with, and if the actual facts lead us to believe that it is no more likely that they were tampered with than that they were not, the excuse is no longer reasonable. To make good my excuse, I must show that it is a fact or at least highly probable that my brakes were tampered with—not that it is just a possibility. The same point holds for God. His excuse must not be a possible excuse, but an actual one. But case *(c)*, in maintaining that it is just as likely that God is all evil as that he is all good, rules this out. For if case *(c)* is true, then the facts of the actual world do not make it any more likely that God is all good than that he is all evil. Therefore, they do not make it any more likely that his excuses are good than that they are not. But, as we have seen, good excuses have a higher probability of being true.

Cases *(a)* and *(c)* conclude that it is unlikely that God is all good, and case *(b)* cannot be true. Since these are the only possible cases, there is no escape from the conclusion that it is unlikely that God is all good. Thus the problem of evil triumphs over the traditional theism.

17. The Problem of Evil

John Hick

John Hick (1922–   ), formerly lecturer in divinity at Cambridge University in England, is professor of world religions and cultures at the Claremont Graduate School in California. He is the author of several books on the philosophy of religion.

To many, the most powerful positive objection to belief in god is the fact of evil. Probably for most agnostics it is the appalling depth and extent of human suffering, more than anything else, that makes the idea of a loving Creator seem so implausible and disposes them toward one or another of the various naturalistic theories of religion.

As a challenge to theism, the problem of evil has traditionally been posed in the form of a dilemma: if God is perfectly loving, he must wish to abolish evil; and if he is all-powerful, he must be able to abolish evil. But evil exists; therefore God cannot be both omnipotent and perfectly loving.

Certain solutions, which at once suggest themselves, have to be ruled out so far as the Judaic-Christian faith is concerned.

To say, for example (with contemporary Christian Science), that evil is an illusion of the human mind, is impossible within a religion based upon the stark realism of the Bible. Its pages faithfully reflect the characteristic mixture of good and evil in human experience. They record every kind of sorrow and suffering, every mode of man's inhumanity to man and of his painfully insecure existence in the world. There is no attempt to regard evil as anything but dark, menacingly ugly, heart-rending, and crushing. In the Christian scriptures, the climax of this history of evil is the crucifixion of Jesus, which is presented not only as a case of utterly unjust suffering, but as the violent and murderous rejection of God's Messiah. There can be no doubt, then, that for biblical faith, evil is unambiguously evil, and stands in direct opposition to God's will.

Again, to solve the problem of evil by means of the theory (sponsored for example, by the Boston "Personalist" School) of a finite deity who does the best he can with a material, intractable and coeternal with himself, is to have abandoned the basic premise of Hebrew-Christian monotheism; for the theory amounts to rejecting belief in the infinity and sovereignty of God.

Indeed, any theory which would avoid the problem of the origin of evil by depicting it as an ultimate constituent of the universe, coordinate with good, has

From *Philosophy of Religion,* 1st ed. by John Hick, © 1965. Reprinted by permission of Prentice-Hall Inc., Upper Saddle River, NJ.

been repudiated in advance by the classic Christian teaching, first developed by Augustine, that evil represents the going wrong of something which in itself is good. Augustine holds firmly to the Hebrew-Christian conviction that the universe is *good*—that is to say, it is the creation of a good God for a good purpose. He completely rejects the ancient prejudice, widespread in his day, that matter is evil. There are, according to Augustine, higher and lower, greater and lesser goods in immense abundance and variety; but everything which has being is good in its own way and degree, except in so far as it may have become spoiled or corrupted. Evil—whether it be an evil will, an instance of pain, or some disorder or decay in nature has not been set there by God, but represents the distortion of something that is inherently valuable. Whatever exists is, as such, and in its proper place, good; evil is essentially parasitic upon good, being disorder and perversion in a fundamentally good creation. This understanding of evil as something negative means that it is not willed and created by God; but it does not mean (as some have supposed) that evil is unreal and can be disregarded. On the contrary, the first effect of this doctrine is to accentuate even more the question of the origin of evil.

Theodicy,[1] as many modern Christian thinkers see it, is a modest enterprise, negative rather than positive in its conclusions. It does not claim to explain, nor to explain away, every instance of evil in human experience, but only to point to certain considerations which prevent the fact of evil (largely incomprehensible though it remains) from constituting a final and insuperable bar to rational belief in God.

In indicating these considerations it will be useful to follow the traditional division of the subject. There is the problem of *moral evil* or wickedness: why does an all-good and all-powerful God permit this? And there is the problem of the *nonmoral evil* of suffering or pain, both physical and mental: why has an all-good and all-powerful God created a world in which this occurs?

Christian thought has always considered moral evil in its relation to human freedom and responsibility. To be a person is to be a finite center of freedom, a (relatively) free and self-directing agent responsible for one's own decisions. This involves being free to act wrongly as well as to act rightly. The idea of a person who can be infallibly guaranteed always to act rightly is self-contradictory. There can be no guarantee in advance that a genuinely free moral agent will never choose amiss. Consequently, the possibility of wrongdoing or sin is logically inseparable from the creation of finite persons, and to say that God should not have created beings who might sin amounts to saying that he should not have created people.

This thesis has been challenged in some recent philosophical discussions of the problem of evil, in which it is claimed that no contradiction is involved in saying that God might have made people who would be genuinely free

---

[1] The word "theodicy," from the Greek *theos* (God) and *dike* (righteous), means the justification of God's goodness in the face of the fact of evil.

and who could yet be guaranteed always to act rightly. A quote from one of these discussions follows:

> If there is no logical impossibility in a man's freely choosing the good on one, or on several occasions, there cannot be a logical impossibility in his freely choosing the good on every occasion. God was not, then, faced with a choice between making innocent automata and making beings who, in acting freely, would sometimes go wrong: there was open to him the obviously better possibility of making beings who would act freely but always go right. Clearly, his failure to avail himself of this possibility is inconsistent with his being both omnipotent and wholly good.[2]

A reply to this argument is suggested in another recent contribution to the discussion.[3] If by a free action we mean an action which is not externally compelled but which flows from the nature of the agent as he reacts to the circumstances in which he finds himself, there is, indeed, no contradiction between our being free and our actions being "caused" (by our own nature) and therefore being in principle predictable. There is a contradiction, however, in saying that God is the cause of our acting as we do but that we are free beings in relation to God. There is, in other words, a contradiction in saying that God has made us so that we shall of necessity act in a certain way, and that we are genuinely independent persons in relation to him. If all our thoughts and actions are divinely predestined, however free and morally responsible we may seem to be to ourselves, we cannot be free and morally responsible in the sight of God, but must instead be his helpless puppets. Such "freedom" is like that of a patient acting out a series of post-hypnotic suggestions: he appears, even to himself, to be free, but his volitions have actually been predetermined by another will, that of the hypnotist, in relation to whom the patient is not a free agent.

A different objector might raise the question of whether or not we deny God's omnipotence if we admit that he is unable to create persons who are free from risks inherent in personal freedom. The answer that has always been given is that to create such beings is logically impossible. It is no limitation upon God's power that he cannot accomplish the logically impossible, since there is nothing here to accomplish, but only a meaningless conjunction of words—in this case "person who is not a person." God is able to create beings of any and every conceivable kind; but creatures who lack moral freedom, however superior they might be to human beings in other respects, would not be what we mean by persons. They would constitute a different form of life which God might have brought into existence instead of persons. When we ask why God did not create such beings in place of persons, the traditional answer is that only persons could, in any meaningful sense, become "children of God," capable of entering into a personal relationship with their Creator by a free and uncompelled response to his love.

[2] J. L. Mackie, "Evil and Omnipotence," *Mind* (April 1955), 209.
[3] Flew, in *New Essays on Philosophical Theology.*

When we turn from the possibility of moral evil as a correlate of man's personal freedom to its actuality, we face something which must remain inexplicable even when it can be seen to be possible. For we can never provide a complete causal explanation of a free act; if we could, it would not be a free act. The origin of moral evil lies forever concealed within the mystery of human freedom.

The necessary connection between moral freedom and the possibility, now actualized, of sin throws light upon a great deal of the suffering which afflicts mankind. For an enormous amount of human pain arises either from the inhumanity or the culpable incompetence of mankind. This includes such major scourges as poverty, oppression and persecution, war, and all the injustice, indignity, and inequity which occur even in the most advanced societies. These evils are manifestations of human sin. Even disease is fostered to an extent, the limits of which have not yet been determined by psychosomatic medicine, by moral and emotional factors seated both in the individual and in his social environment. To the extent that all of these evils stem from human failures and wrong decisions, their possibility is inherent in the creation of free persons inhabiting a world which presents them with real choices which are followed by real consequences.

We may now turn more directly to the problem of suffering. Even though the major bulk of actual human pain is traceable to man's misused freedom as a sole or part cause, there remain other sources of pain which are entirely independent of the human will, for example, earthquake, hurricane, storm, flood, drought, and blight. In practice it is often impossible to trace a boundary between the suffering which results from human wickedness and folly and that which falls upon mankind from without. Both kinds of suffering are inextricably mingled together in human experience. For our present purpose, however, it is important to note that the latter category does exist and that it seems to be built into the very structure of our world. In response to it, theodicy, if it is wisely conducted, follows a negative path. It is not possible to show positively that each item of human pain serves the divine purpose of good; but, on the other hand, it does seem possible to show that the divine purpose as it is understood in Judaism and Christianity could not be forwarded in a world which was designed as a permanent hedonistic paradise.

An essential premise of this argument concerns the divine purpose in creating the world. The skeptic's assumption is that man is to be viewed as a completed creation and that God's purpose in making the world was to provide a suitable dwelling-place for this fully-formed creature. Since God is good and loving, the environment which he has created for human life to inhabit is naturally as pleasant and comfortable as possible. The problem is essentially similar to that of a man who builds a cage for some pet animal. Since our world, in fact, contains sources of hardship, inconvenience, and danger of innumerable kinds, the conclusion follows that this world cannot have been created by a perfectly benevolent and all-powerful deity.

Christianity, however, has never supposed that God's purpose in the creation of the world was to construct a paradise whose inhabitants would experience a maximum of pleasure and a minimum of pain. The world is seen, instead, as a place of "soul-making" in which free beings, grappling with the tasks and challenges of their existence in a common environment, may become "children of God" and "heirs of eternal life." A way of thinking theologically of God's continuing creative purpose for man was suggested by some of the early Hellenistic Fathers of the Christian Church, especially Irenaeus. Following hints from St. Paul, Irenaeus taught that man has been made as a person in the image of God but has not yet been brought as a free and responsible agent into the finite likeness of God, which is revealed in Christ. Our world, with all its rough edges, is the sphere in which this second and harder stage of the creative process is taking place.

This conception of the world (whether or not set in Irenaeus' theological framework) can be supported by the method of negative theodicy. Suppose, contrary to fact, that this world were a paradise from which all possibility of pain and suffering were excluded. The consequences would be very far-reaching. For example, no one could ever injure anyone else: the murderer's knife would turn to paper or his bullets to thin air; the bank safe, robbed of a million dollars, would miraculously become filled with another million dollars (without this device, on however large a scale, proving inflationary); fraud, deceit, conspiracy, and treason would somehow always leave the fabric of society undamaged. Again, no one would ever be injured by accident: the mountain-climber, steeplejack, or playing child falling from a height would float unharmed to the ground; the reckless driver would never meet with disaster. There would be no need to work, since no harm could result from avoiding work; there would be no call to be concerned for others in time of need or danger, for in such a world there could be no real needs or dangers.

To make possible this continual series of individual adjustments, nature would have to work by "special providence" instead of running according to general laws which men must learn to respect on penalty of pain or death. The laws of nature would have to be extremely flexible: sometimes gravity would operate, sometimes not; sometimes an object would be hard and solid, sometimes soft. There could be no sciences, for there would be no enduring world structure to investigate. In eliminating the problems and hardships of an objective environment, with its own laws, life would become like a dream in which, delightfully but aimlessly, we would float and drift at ease.

One can at least begin to imagine such a world. It is evident that our present ethical concepts would have no meaning in it. If, for example, the notion of harming someone is an essential element in the concept of a wrong action, in our hedonistic paradise there could be no wrong actions—nor any right actions in distinction from wrong. Courage and fortitude would have no point in an environment in which there is, by definition, no danger or difficulty. Generosity, kindness, the *agape* aspect of love, prudence, unselfishness, and all other ethical notions which presuppose life in a stable environment, could not even be formed. Consequently, such a world, however well it might promote pleasure, would be very ill adapted for the development of the moral qualities of human personality. In relation to this purpose it would be the worst of all possible worlds.

It would seem, then, that an environment intended to make possible the growth in free beings of the finest characteristics of personal life, must have a good deal in common with our present world. It must operate according to general and dependable laws: and it must involve real dangers, difficulties, problems, obstacles, and possibilities of pain, failure, sorrow, frustration, and defeat. If it did not contain the particular trials and perils which—subtracting man's own very considerable contribution—our world contains, it would have to contain others instead.

To realize this is not, by any means, to be in possession of a detailed theodicy. It is to understand that this world, with all its "heartaches and the thousand natural shocks that flesh is heir to," and environment so manifestly not designed for the maximization of human pleasure and the minimization of human pain, may be rather well adapted to the quite different purpose of "soul-making."

Should We Believe in God Without Evidence?

18. The Ethics of Belief

W. K. Clifford

William Kingdon Clifford (1845–1879) was a prominent English mathematician and philosopher who made important contributions to the theory of knowledge and the philosophy of science.

A shipowner was about to send to sea an emigrant ship. He knew that she was old, and not over-well built at the first; that she had seen many seas and climes, and often had needed repairs. Doubts had been suggested to him that possibly she was not seaworthy. These doubts preyed upon his mind and made him unhappy; he thought that perhaps he ought to have her thoroughly overhauled and refitted, even though this should put him to great expense. Before the ship sailed, however, he succeeded in overcoming these melancholy reflections. He said to himself that she had gone safely through so many voyages and weathered so many storms that it was idle to suppose she would not come safely home from this trip also. He would put his trust in Providence, which could hardly fail to protect all these unhappy families that were leaving their fatherland to seek for better times elsewhere. He would dismiss from his mind all ungenerous suspicions about the honesty of builders and contractors. In such ways he acquired a sincere and comfortable conviction that his vessel was thoroughly safe and seaworthy; he watched her departure with a light heart, and benevolent wishes for the success of the exiles in their strange new home that was to be; and he got his insurance money when she went down in midocean and told no tales.

What shall we say of him? Surely this, that he was verily guilty of the death of those men. It is admitted that he did sincerely believe in the soundness of his ship; but the sincerity of his conviction can in no wise help him, because *he had no right to believe on such evidence as was before him.* He had acquired his belief not by honestly earning it in patient investigation, but by stifling his doubts. And although in the end he may have felt so sure about it that he could not think otherwise, yet inasmuch as he had knowingly and willingly worked himself into that frame of mind, he must be held responsible for it.

Reprinted from *Lectures and Essays* by William K. Clifford, Macmillan & Co., London, 1879.

Let us alter the case a little, and suppose that the ship was not unsound after all; that she made her voyage safely, and many others after it. Will that diminish the guilt of her owner? Not one jot. When an action is once done, it is right or wrong forever; no accidental failure of its good or evil fruits can possibly alter that. The man would not have been innocent, he would only have been not found out. The question of right or wrong has to do with the origin of his belief, not the matter of it; not what it was, but how he got it; not whether it turned out to be true or false, but whether he had a right to believe on such evidence as was before him.

There was once an island in which some of the inhabitants professed a religion teaching neither the doctrine of original sin nor that of eternal punishment. A suspicion got abroad that the professors of this religion had made use of unfair means to get their doctrines taught to children. They were accused of wresting the laws of their country in such a way as to remove children from the care of their natural and legal guardians; and even of stealing them away and keeping them concealed from their friends and relations. A certain number of men formed themselves into a society for the purpose of agitating the public about this matter. They published grave accusations against individual citizens of the highest position and character, and did all in their power to injure those citizens in the exercise of their professions. So great was the noise they made, that a Commission was appointed to investigate the facts; but after the Commission had carefully inquired into all the evidence that could be got, it appeared that the accused were innocent. Not only had they been accused on insufficient evidence, but the evidence of their innocence was such as the agitators might easily have obtained, if they had attempted a fair inquiry. After these disclosures the inhabitants of that country looked upon the members of the agitating society, not only as persons whose judgment was to be distrusted, but also as no longer to be counted honorable men. For although they had sincerely and conscientiously believed in the charges they had made, *yet they had no right to believe on such evidence as was before them.* Their sincere convictions, instead of being honestly earned by patient inquiring, were stolen by listening to the voice of prejudice and passion.

Let us vary this case also, and suppose, other things remaining as before, that a still more accurate investigation proved the accused to have been really guilty. Would this make any difference in the guilt of the accusers? Clearly not; the question is not whether their belief was true or false, but whether they entertained it on wrong grounds. They would no doubt say, "Now you see that we were right after all; next time perhaps you will believe us." And they might be believed, but they would not thereby become honorable men. They would not be innocent, they would only be not found out. Every one of them, if he chose to examine himself *in foro conscientiae,* would know that he had acquired and nourished a belief, when he had no right to believe on such evidence as was before him; and therein he would know that he had done a wrong thing.

It may be said, however, that in both of these supposed cases it is not the belief which is judged to be wrong, but the action following upon it. The shipowner might say, "I am perfectly certain that my ship is sound, but still I feel it my duty to have her examined, before trusting the lives of so many people to her." And it might be said to the agitator, "However convinced you were of the justice of your cause and the truth of your convictions, you ought not to have made a public attack upon any man's character until you had examined the evidence on both sides with the utmost patience and care."

In the first place, let us admit that, so far as it goes, this view of the case is right and necessary; right, because even when a man's belief is so fixed that he cannot think otherwise, he still has a choice in regard to the action suggested by it, and so cannot escape the duty of investigating on the ground of the strength of his convictions; and necessary, because those who are not yet capable of controlling their feelings and thoughts must have a plain rule dealing with overt acts.

But this being premised as necessary, it becomes clear that it is not sufficient, and that our previous judgment is required to supplement it. For it is not possible so to sever the belief from the action it suggests as to condemn the one without condemning the other. No man holding a strong belief on one side of a question, or even wishing to hold a belief on one side, can investigate it with such fairness and completeness as if he were really in doubt and unbiased; so that the existence of a belief not founded on fair inquiry unfits a man for the performance of this necessary duty.

Nor is that truly a belief at all which has not some influence upon the actions of him who holds it. He who truly believes that which prompts him to an action has looked upon the action to lust after it, he has committed it already in his heart. If a belief is not realized immediately in open deeds, it is stored up for the guidance of the future. It goes to make a part of that aggregate of beliefs which is the link between sensation and action at every moment of all our lives, and which is so organized and compacted together that no part of it can be isolated from the rest, but every new addition modifies the structure of the whole. No real belief, however trifling and fragmentary it may seem, is ever truly insignificant; it prepares us to receive more of its like, confirms those which resembled it before, and weakens others; and so gradually it lays a stealthy train in our inmost thoughts, which may some day explode into overt action, and leave its stamp upon our character forever.

And no one man's belief is in any case a private matter which concerns himself alone. Our lives are guided by that general conception of the course of things which has been created by society for social purposes. Our words, our phrases, our forms and processes and modes of thought, are common property, fashioned and perfected from age to age; an heirloom which every succeeding generation inherits as a precious deposit and a sacred trust to be handed on to the next one, not unchanged but enlarged and purified, with some clear marks of its proper handiwork. Into this, for good or ill, is woven every belief of every man who has speech of his fellows. An awful privilege, and an awful responsibility, that we should help to create the world in which posterity will live.

In the two supposed cases which have been considered, it has been judged wrong to believe on insufficient evidence, or to nourish belief by suppressing doubts and avoiding investigation. The reason of this judgment is not far to seek; it is that in both these cases the belief held by one man was of great importance to other men. But for as much as no belief held by one man, however seemingly trivial the belief, and however obscure the believer, is ever actually insignificant or without its effect on the fate of mankind, we have no choice but to extend our judgment to all cases of belief whatever. Belief, that sacred faculty which prompts the decisions of our will, and knits into harmonious working all the compacted energies of our being, is ours not for ourselves, but for humanity. It is rightly used on truths which have been established by long experience and waiting toil, and which have stood in the fierce light of free and fearless questioning. Then it helps to bind men together, and to strengthen and direct their common action. It is desecrated when given to unproved and unquestioned statements, for the solace and private pleasure of the believer; to add a tinsel splendor to the plain straight road of our life and display a bright mirage beyond it; or even to drown the common sorrows of our kind by a self-deception which allows them not only to cast down, but also to degrade us. Whoso would deserve well of his fellows in this matter will guard the purity of his belief with a very fanaticism of jealous care, lest at any time it should rest on an unworthy object, and catch a stain which can never be wiped away.

It is not only the leader of men, statesman, philosopher, or poet, that owes this bounded duty to mankind. Every rustic who delivers in the village alehouse his slow, infrequent sentences, may help to kill or keep alive the fatal superstitions which clog his race. Every hard-worked wife of an artisan may transmit to her children beliefs which shall knit society together, or rend it in pieces. No simplicity of mind, no obscurity of station, can escape the universal duty of questioning all that we believe.

It is true that this duty is a hard one, and the doubt which comes out of it is often a very bitter thing. It leaves us bare and powerless where we thought that we were safe and strong. To know all about anything is to know how to deal with it under all circumstances. We feel much happier and more secure when we think we know precisely what to do, no matter what happens, than when we have lost our way and do not know where to turn. And if we have supposed ourselves to know all about anything, and to be capable of doing what is fit in regard to it, we naturally do not like to find that we are really ignorant and powerless, that we have to begin again at the beginning and try to learn what the thing is and how it is to be dealt with—if indeed anything can be learned about it. It is the sense of power attached to a sense of knowledge that makes men desirous of believing, and afraid of doubting.

This sense of power is the highest and best of pleasures when the belief on which it is founded is a true belief, and has been fairly earned by investigation. For then we may justly feel that it is common property, and holds good for others as well as ourselves. Then we may be glad, not that *I* have learned secrets by which I am safer and stronger, but that *we men* have got mastery over more of the world; and we shall be strong, not for ourselves, but in the name of Man and in his strength. But if the belief has been accepted on insufficient evidence, the pleasure is a stolen one. Not only does it deceive ourselves by giving us a sense of power which we do not really possess, but it is sinful, because it is stolen in defiance of our duty to mankind. That duty is to guard ourselves from such beliefs as from a pestilence, which may shortly master our own body and then spread to the rest of the town. What would be thought of one who, for the sake of a sweet fruit, should deliberately run the risk of bringing a plague upon his family and his neighbors?

And, as in other such cases, it is not the risk only which has to be considered; for a bad action is always bad at the time when it is done, no matter what happens afterwards. Every time we let ourselves believe for unworthy reasons, we weaken our power of self-control, of doubting, of judicially and fairly weighing evidence. We all suffer severely enough from the maintenance and support of false beliefs and the fatally wrong actions which they lead to, and the evil born when one such belief is entertained is great and wide. But a greater and wider evil arises when the credulous character is maintained and supported, when a habit of believing for unworthy reasons is fostered and made permanent. If I steal money from any person, there may be no harm done by the mere transfer of possession; he may not feel the loss, or it may prevent him from using the money badly. But I cannot help doing this great wrong towards Man, that I make myself dishonest. What hurts society is not that it should lose its property, but that it should become a den of thieves; for then it must cease to be society. This is why we ought not to do evil that good may come; for at any rate this great evil has come, that we have done evil and are made wicked thereby. In like manner, if I let myself believe anything on insufficient evidence, there may be no great harm done by the mere belief; it may be true after all, or I may never have occasion to exhibit it in outward acts. But I cannot help doing this great wrong toward Man, that I make myself credulous. The danger to society is not merely that it should believe wrong things, though that is great enough; but that it should become credulous, and lose the habit of testing things and inquiring into them; for then it must sink back into savagery.

The harm which is done by credulity in a man is not confined to the fostering of a credulous character in others, and consequent support of false beliefs. Habitual want of care about what I believe leads to habitual want of care in others about the truth of what is told to me. Men speak the truth to one another when each reveres the truth in his own mind and in the other's mind; but how shall my friend revere the truth in my mind when I myself am careless about it, when I believe things because I want to believe them, and because they are comforting and pleasant? Will he not learn to cry, "Peace," to me, when there is no peace? By such a course I shall surround myself with a thick atmosphere of falsehood and fraud, and in that I must live. It may matter little to me, in my cloud-castle of sweet illusions and darling lies; but it matters much to Man that I have made my neighbors ready to deceive. The credulous man is father to the liar and the cheat; he lives in the bosom of this his family, and it is no marvel if he should become even as they are. So closely are our duties knit together, that whoso shall keep the whole law, and yet offend in one point, he is guilty of all.

To sum up: it is wrong always, everywhere, and for anyone, to believe anything upon insufficient evidence.

If a man, holding a belief which he was taught in childhood or persuaded of afterwards, keeps down and pushes away any doubts which arise about it in his mind, purposely avoids the reading of books and the company of men that call in question or discuss it, and regards as impious those questions which cannot easily be asked without disturbing it—the life of that man is one long sin against mankind.

If this judgment seems harsh when applied to those simple souls who have never known better, who have been brought up from the cradle with a horror of doubt, and taught that their eternal welfare depends on what they believe, then it leads to the very serious question. Who hath made Israel to sin?. . .

Inquiry into the evidence of a doctrine is not to be made once for all, and then taken as finally settled. It is never lawful to stifle a doubt; for either it can be honestly answered by means of the inquiry already made, or else it proves that the inquiry was not complete.

"But," says one, "I am a busy man; I have no time for the long course of study which would be necessary to make me in any degree a competent judge of certain questions, or even able to understand the nature of the arguments." Then he should have no time to believe. . .

19. The Will to Believe

William James

William James (1842–1910) is considered one of America's greatest philosophers. He attended Harvard Medical School and later taught anatomy and physiology at Harvard. Later his interests were primarily in the fields of psychology and philosophy. He is considered one of the main developers of pragmatism.

. . . I have long defended to my own students the lawfulness of voluntarily adopted faith; but as soon as they have got well imbued with the logical spirit, they have as a rule refused to admit my contention to be lawful philosophically, even though in point of fact they were personally all the time chock-full of some faith or other themselves. I am all the while, however, so profoundly convinced that my own position is correct, that your invitation has seemed to me a good occasion to make my statements more clear. Perhaps your minds will be more open than those with which I have hitherto had to deal. I will be as little technical as I can, though I must begin by setting up some technical distinctions that will help us in the end.

Let us give the name of *hypothesis* to anything that may be proposed to our belief; and just as the electricians speak of live and dead wires, let us speak of any hypothesis as either *live* or *dead*. A live hypothesis is one which appeals as a real possibility to him to whom it is proposed. If I ask you to believe in the Mahdi, the notion makes no electric connection with your nature,—it refuses to scintillate with any credibility at all. As an hypothesis it is completely dead. To an Arab, however (even if he be not one of the Mahdi's followers), the hypothesis is among the mind's possibilities: it is alive. This shows that deadness and liveness in an hypothesis are not intrinsic properties, but relations to the individual thinker. They are measured by his willingness to act. The maximum of liveness in an hypothesis means willingness to act irrevocably. Practically, that means belief; but there is some believing tendency wherever there is willingness to act at all.

Next, let us call the decision between two hypotheses an *option*. Options may be of several kinds. They may be—1, *living* or *dead*; 2, *forced* or *avoidable*; 3, *momentous* or *trivial*; and for our purposes we may call an option a *genuine* option when it is of the forced, living, and momentous kind.

1. A living option is one in which both hypotheses are live ones. If I say to you: "Be a theosophist or be a Mohammedan," it is probably a dead option, because for you neither hypothesis is likely to be alive. But if I say: "Be an agnostic

Reprinted from *The Will to Believe and Other Essays in Popular Philosophy* by William James. Published by Longmans, Green (New York, 1896).

or be a Christian," it is otherwise: trained as you are, each hypothesis makes some appeal, however small, to your belief.

2. Next, if I say to you: "Choose between going out with your umbrella or without it," I do not offer you a genuine option, for it is not forced. You can easily avoid it by not going out at all. Similarly, if I say, "Either love me or hate me," "Either call my theory true or call it false," your option is avoidable. You may remain indifferent to me, neither loving nor hating, and you may decline to offer any judgment as to my theory. But if I say, "Either accept this truth or go without it," I put on you a forced option, for there is no standing place outside of the alternative. Every dilemma based on a complete logical disjunction, with no possibility of not choosing, is an option of this forced kind.

3. Finally, if I were Dr. Nansen and proposed to you to join my North Pole expedition, your option would be momentous; for this would probably be your only similar opportunity, and your choice now would either exclude you from the North Pole sort of immortality altogether or put at least the chance of it into your hands. He who refuses to embrace a unique opportunity loses the prize as surely as if he tried and failed. *Per contra*, the option is trivial when the opportunity is not unique, when the stake is insignificant, or when the decision is reversible if it later prove unwise. Such trivial options abound in the scientific life. A chemist finds an hypothesis live enough to spend a year in its verification: he believes in it to that extent. But if his experiments prove inconclusive either way, he is quit for his loss of time, no vital harm being done.

It will facilitate our discussion if we keep all these distinctions well in mind . . .

The thesis I defend is, briefly stated, this: *Our passional nature not only lawfully may, but must, decide an option between propositions, whenever it is a genuine option that cannot by its nature be decided on intellectual grounds; for to say, under such circumstances, "Do not decide, but leave the question open," is itself a passional decision,—just like deciding yes or no,—and is attended with the same risk of losing the truth.* . . .

Wherever the option between losing truth and gaining it is not momentous, we can throw the chance of *gaining truth* away, and at any rate save ourselves from any chance of *believing falsehood*, by not making up our minds at all till objective evidence has come. In scientific questions, this is almost always the case; and even in human affairs in general, the need of acting is seldom so urgent that a false belief to act on is better than no belief at all. Law courts, indeed, have to decide on the best evidence attainable for the moment, because a judge's duty is to make law as well as to ascertain it, and (as a learned judge once said to me) few cases are worth spending much time over: the great thing is to have them decided on *any* acceptable principle, and got out of the way. But in our dealings with objective nature we obviously are recorders, not makers, of the truth; and decisions for the mere sake of deciding promptly and getting on to the next business would be wholly out of place. Throughout the breadth of physical nature facts are what they are quite independently of us, and seldom is there any such hurry about them that the risks of being duped by believing a premature theory need be faced. The questions here are always trivial options, the hypotheses are hardly living (at any rate not living for us spectators), the choice between believing truth or falsehood is seldom forced. The attitude of sceptical balance is therefore the absolutely wise one if we would escape mistakes. What difference, indeed, does it make to most of us whether we have or have not a theory of the Röntgen rays, whether we believe or not in mind-stuff, or have a conviction about the causality of conscious states? It makes no difference. Such options are not forced on us. On every account it is better not to make them, but still keep weighing reasons *pro et contra* with an indifferent hand.

I speak, of course, here of the purely judging mind. For purposes of discovery such indifference is to be less highly recommended, and science would be far less advanced than she is if the passionate desires of individuals to get their own faiths confirmed had been kept out of the game. . . . On the other hand, if you want an absolute duffer in an investigation, you must, after all, take the man who has no interest whatever in its results: he is the warranted incapable, the positive fool. The most useful investigator, because the most sensitive observer, is always he whose eager interest in one side of the question is balanced by an equally keen nervousness lest he become deceived. Science has organized this nervousness into a regular *technique*, her so-called method of verification; and she has fallen so deeply in love with the method that one may even say she has ceased to care for truth by itself at all. It is only truth as technically verified that interests her. The truth of truths might come in merely affirmative form, and she would decline to touch it. Such truth as that, she might repeat with Clifford, would be stolen in defiance of her duty to mankind. Human passions, however, are stronger than technical rules. "Le coeur a ses raisons," as Pascal says, "que la raison ne connaît pas";* and however indifferent to all but the bare rules of the game the umpire, the abstract intellect, may be, the concrete players who furnish him the materials to judge of are usually, each one of them, in love with some pet 'live hypothesis' of his own. Let us agree, however, that wherever there is no forced option, the dispassionately judicial intellect with no pet hypothesis, saving us, as it does, from dupery at any rate, ought to be our ideal.

The question next arises: Are there not somewhere forced options in our speculative questions, and can we (as men who may be interested at least as much in positively gaining truth as in merely escaping dupery) always wait with impunity till the coercive evidence shall have arrived? It seems *a priori* improbable that the truth should be so nicely adjusted to our needs and powers as that. In the great boarding-house of nature, the cakes and the butter and the syrup seldom come out so even and leave the plates so clean. Indeed, we should view them with scientific suspicion if they did.

Moral questions immediately present themselves as questions whose solution cannot wait for sensible proof. A moral question is a question not of what

---

* [The heart has its reasons that reason does not know. —Ed.]

sensibly exists, but of what is good, or would be good if it did exist. Science can tell us what exists; but to compare the *worths,* both of what exists and of what does not exist, we must consult not science, but what Pascal calls our heart. Science herself consults her heart when she lays it down that the infinite ascertainment of fact and correction of false belief are the supreme goods for man. Challenge the statement, and science can only repeat it oracularly, or else prove it by showing that such ascertainment and correction bring man all sorts of other good which man's heart in turn declares. The question of having moral beliefs at all or not having them is decided by our will. Are our moral preferences true or false, or are they only odd biological phenomena, making things good or bad for us, but in themselves indifferent? How can your pure intellect decide? If your heart does not *want* a world of moral reality, your head will assuredly never make you believe in one. Mephistophelian scepticism, indeed, will satisfy the head's play-instincts much better than any rigorous idealism can. Some men (even at the student age) are so naturally cool-hearted that the moralistic hypothesis never has for them any pungent life, and in their supercilious presence the hot young moralist always feels strangely ill at ease. The appearance of knowingness is on their side, of *naiveté* and gullibility on his. Yet, in the inarticulate heart of him, he clings to it that he is not a dupe, and that there is a realm in which (as Emerson says) all their wit and intellectual superiority is no better than the cunning of a fox. Moral scepticism can no more be refuted or proved by logic than intellectual scepticism can. When we stick to it that there *is* truth (be it of either kind), we do so with our whole nature, and resolve to stand or fall by the results. The sceptic with his whole nature adopts the doubting attitude; but which of us is the wiser, Omniscience only knows.

Turn now from these wide questions of good to a certain class of questions of fact, questions concerning personal relations, states of mind between one man and another. *Do you like me or not?*—for example. Whether you do or not depends, in countless instances, on whether I meet you half-way, am willing to assume that you must like me, and show you trust and expectation. The previous faith on my part in your liking's existence is in such cases what makes your liking come. But if I stand aloof, and refuse to budge an inch until I have objective evidence, until you shall have done something apt, as the absolutists say, *ad extorquendum assensum meum,* ten to one your liking never comes. How many women's hearts are vanquished by the mere sanguine insistence of some man that they *must* love him! He will not consent to the hypothesis that they cannot. The desire for a certain kind of truth here brings about that special truth's existence; and so it is in innumerable cases of other sorts. Who gains promotions, boons, appointments, but the man in whose life they are seen to play the part of live hypotheses, who discounts them, sacrifices other things for their sake before they have come, and takes risks for them in advance? His faith acts on the powers above him as a claim, and creates its own verification.

A social organism of any sort whatever, large or small, is what it is because each member proceeds to his own duty with a trust that the other members will simultaneously do theirs. Wherever a desired result is achieved by the co-operation of many independent persons, its existence as a fact is a pure consequence of the precursive faith in one another of those immediately concerned. A government, an army, a commercial system, a ship, a college, an athletic team, all exist on this condition, without which not only is nothing achieved, but nothing is even attempted. A whole train of passengers (individually brave enough) will be looted by a few highwaymen, simply because the latter can count on one another, while each passenger fears that if he makes a movement of resistance, he will be shot before any one else backs him up. If we believed that the whole car-full would rise at once with us, we should each severally rise, and train-robbing would never even be attempted. There are, then, cases where a fact cannot come at all unless a preliminary faith exists in its coming. *And where faith in a fact can help create the fact,* that would be an insane logic which should say that faith running ahead of scientific evidence is the 'lowest kind of immorality' into which a thinking being can fall. Yet such is the logic by which our scientific absolutists pretend to regulate our lives!

In truths dependent on our personal action, then, faith based on desire is certainly a lawful and possibly an indispensable thing.

But now, it will be said, these are all childish human cases, and have nothing to do with great cosmical matters, like the question of religious faith. Let us then pass on to that. Religions differ so much in their accidents that in discussing the religious question we must make it very generic and broad. What then do we now mean by the religious hypothesis? Science says things are; morality says some things are better than other things; and religion says essentially two things.

First, she says that the best things are the more eternal things, the overlapping things, the things in the universe that throw the last stone, so to speak, and say the final word. "Perfection is eternal,"—this phrase of Charles Secretan seems a good way of putting this first affirmation of religion, an affirmation which obviously cannot yet be verified scientifically at all.

The second affirmation of religion is that we are better off even now if we believe her first affirmation to be true.

Now, let us consider what the logical elements of this situation are *in case the religious hypothesis in both its branches be really true.* (Of course, we must admit that possibility at the outset. If we are to discuss the question at all, it must involve a living option. If for any of you religion be a hypothesis that cannot, by any living possibility be true, then you need go no farther. I speak to the 'saving remnant' alone.) So proceeding, we see, first, that religion offers itself as a *momentous* option. We are supposed to gain, even now, by our belief, and to lose by our nonbelief, a certain vital good. Secondly, religion is a *forced* option, so far as that good goes. We cannot escape the issue by remaining sceptical and waiting for more light, because, although we do avoid error in that way *if religion be untrue,* we lose the good, *if it be true,* just as certainly as if we positively chose to disbelieve. It is as if a man should hesitate indefinitely to ask a certain woman to marry him because he was not perfectly sure that she would prove an angel after he brought her home. Would he not cut himself off from that particular angel-possibility as decisively as if he went and married some one else? Scepticism, then, is not avoidance of option; it is option of a certain particular kind of risk. *Better risk loss of truth than chance of error,*—that is your faith-vetoer's exact position. He is actively playing his stake as much as the believer is; he is backing the field against the religious hypothesis, just as the believer is backing the religious hypothesis against the field. To preach scepticism to us as a duty until "sufficient evidence" for religion be found, is tantamount therefore to telling us, when in presence of the religious hypothesis, that to yield to our fear of its being error is wiser and better than to yield to our hope that it may be true. It is not intellect against all passions, then; it is only intellect with one passion laying down its law. And by what, forsooth, is the supreme wisdom of this passion warranted? Dupery for dupery, what proof is there that dupery through hope is so much worse than dupery through fear? I, for one, can see no proof; and I simply refuse obedience to the scientist's command to imitate his kind of option, in a case where my own stake is important enough to give me the right to choose my own form of risk. If religion be true and the evidence for it be still insufficient, I do not wish, by putting your extinguisher upon my nature (which feels to me as if it had after all some business in this matter), to forfeit my sole chance in life of getting upon the winning side,—that chance depending, of course, on my willingness to run the risk of acting as if my passional need of taking the world religiously might be prophetic and right.

All this is on the supposition that it really may be prophetic and right, and that, even to us who are discussing the matter, religion is a live hypothesis which may be true. Now, to most of us religion comes in a still further way that makes a veto on our active faith even more illogical. The more perfect and more eternal aspect of the universe is represented in our religions as having personal form. The universe is no longer a mere *It* to us, but a *Thou*, if we are religious; and any relation that may be possible from person to person might be possible here. For instance, although in one sense we are passive portions of the universe, in another we show a curious autonomy, as if we were small active centres on our own account. We feel, too, as if the appeal of religion to us were made to our own active good-will, as if evidence might be forever withheld from us unless we met the hypothesis half-way. To take a trivial illustration: just as a man who in a company of gentlemen made no advances, asked a warrant for every concession, and believed no one's word without proof, would cut himself off by such churlishness from all the social rewards that a more trusting spirit would earn,—so here, one who should shut himself up in snarling logicality and try to make the gods extort his recognition willy-nilly, or not get it at all, might cut himself off forever from his only opportunity of making the gods' acquaintance. This feeling, forced on us we know not whence, that by obstinately believing that there are gods (although not to do so would be so easy both for our logic and our life) we are doing the universe the deepest service we can, seems part of the living essence of the religious hypothesis. If the hypothesis *were* true in all its parts, including this one, then pure intellectualism, with its veto on our making willing advances, would be an absurdity; and some participation of our sympathetic nature would be logically required. I, therefore, for one, cannot see my way to accepting the agnostic rules for truth-seeking, or willfully agree to keep my willing nature out of the game. I cannot do so for this plain reason, that *a rule of thinking which would absolutely prevent me from acknowledging certain kinds of truth if those kinds of truth were really there, would be an irrational rule.* That for me is the long and short of the formal logic of the situation, no matter what the kinds of truth might materially be.

I confess I do not see how this logic can be escaped. But sad experience makes me fear that some of you may still shrink from radically saying with me, *in abstracto,* that we have the right to believe at our own risk any hypothesis that is live enough to tempt our will. I suspect, however, that if this is so, it is because you have got away from the abstract logical point of view altogether, and are thinking (perhaps without realizing it) of some particular religious hypothesis which for you is dead. The freedom to "believe what we will" you apply to the case of some patent superstition; and the faith you think of is the faith defined by the schoolboy when he said, "Faith is when you believe something that you know ain't true." I can only repeat that this is misapprehension. *In concerto,* the freedom to believe can only cover living options which the intellect of the individual cannot by itself resolve; and living options never seem absurdities to him who has them to consider. When I look at the religious question as it really puts itself to concrete men, and when I think of all the possibilities which both practically and theoretically it involves, then this command that we shall put a stopper on our heart, instincts, and courage, and *wait*—acting of course meanwhile more or less as if religion were *not* true—till doomsday, or till such time as our intellect and senses working together may have raked in evidence enough,—this command, I say, seems to me the queerest idol ever manufactured in the philosophic cave. Were we scholastic absolutists, there might be more excuse. If we had an infallible intellect with its objective certitudes, we might feel ourselves disloyal to such a perfect organ of knowledge in not trusting to it exclusively, in not waiting for its releasing word. But if we are empiricists, if we believe that no bell in us tolls to let us know for certain when truth is in our grasp, then it seems a piece of idle fantasticality to preach so solemnly our duty of waiting for the bell. Indeed we wait if we will,—I hope you do not think that I am denying that,—but if we do so, we do so at our peril as much as if we believed. In either case *we act,* taking our life in our hands. No one of us ought to issue vetoes to the other, nor should we bandy words of abuse. We ought, on the contrary, delicately and profoundly to respect one another's mental freedom: then only shall we bring about the intellectual republic; then only shall we have that spirit of inner tolerance without which all our tolerance is soulless, and which is empiricism's glory; then only shall we live and let live, in speculative as well as in practical things. . . .

PROBLEMS AND PUZZLES

20. *My Confession*

Leo Tolstoy

Leo Tolstoy (1828–1910), author of such famous novels as War and Peace *and* Anna Karenina, *was also an important social and moral reformer in his native Russia.*

IV

My life came to a standstill. I could breathe, eat, drink, and sleep, and could not help breathing, eating, drinking, and sleeping; but there was no life, because there were no desires the gratification of which I might find reasonable. If I wished for anything, I knew in advance that, whether I gratified my desire or not, nothing would come of it. If a fairy had come and had offered to carry out my wish, I should not have known what to say. If in moments of intoxication I had, not wishes, but habits of former desires, I knew in sober moments that that was a deception, that there was nothing to wish for. I could not even wish to find out the truth, because I guessed what it consisted in. The truth was that life was meaningless. It was as though I had just been living and walking along, and had come to an abyss, where I saw clearly that there was nothing ahead but perdition. And it was impossible to stop and go back, and impossible to shut my eyes, in order that I might not see that there was nothing ahead but suffering and imminent death,—complete annihilation.

What happened to me was that I, a healthy, happy man, felt that I could not go on living,—an insurmountable force drew me on to find release from life. I cannot say that I *wanted* to kill myself.

The force which drew me away from life was stronger, fuller, more general than wishing. It was a force like the former striving after life, only in an inverse sense. I tended with all my strength away from life. The thought of suicide came as naturally to me as had come before the ideas of improving life. That thought was so seductive that I had to use cunning against myself, lest I should rashly execute it. I did not want to be in a hurry, because I wanted to use every effort to disentangle myself: if I should not succeed in disentangling myself, there would always be time for that. And at such times I, a happy man, hid a rope from myself

Reprinted from *The Complete Works of Count Tolstoy,* Vol. 13, translated and edited by Leo Wiener. Colonial Press Co., New York and Boston. Copyright, 1904.

so that I should not hang myself on a cross-beam between two safes in my room, where I was by myself in the evening, while taking off my clothes, and did not go out hunting with a gun, in order not to be tempted by an easy way of doing away with myself. I did not know myself what it was I wanted: I was afraid of life, strove to get away from it, and, at the same time, expected something from it.

All that happened with me when I was on every side surrounded by what is considered to be complete happiness. I had a good, loving, and beloved wife, good children, and a large estate, which grew and increased without any labour on my part. I was respected by my neighbours and friends, more than ever before, was praised by strangers, and, without any self-deception, could consider my name famous. With all that, I was not deranged or mentally unsound,—on the contrary, I was in full command of my mental and physical powers, such as I had rarely met with in people of my age: physically I could work in a field, mowing, without falling behind a peasant; mentally I could work from eight to ten hours in succession, without experiencing any consequences from the strain. And while in such condition I arrived at the conclusion that I could not live, and, fearing death, I had to use cunning against myself, in order that I might not take my life.

This mental condition expressed itself to me in this form: my life is a stupid, mean trick played on me by somebody. Although I did not recognize that "somebody" as having created me, the form of the conception that some one had played a mean, stupid trick on me by bringing me into the world was the most natural one that presented itself to me.

Involuntarily I imagined that there, somewhere, there was somebody who was now having fun as he looked down upon me and saw me, who had lived for thirty or forty years, learning, developing, growing in body and mind, now that I had become strengthened in mind and had reached that summit of life from which it lay all before me, standing as a complete fool on that summit and seeing clearly that there was nothing in life and never would be. And that was fun to him—

But whether there was or was not that somebody who made fun of me, did not make it easier for me. I could not ascribe any sensible meaning to a single act, or to my whole life. I was only surprised that I had not understood that from the start. All that had long ago been known to everybody. Sooner or later there would come diseases and death (they had come already) to my dear ones and to me, and there would be nothing left but stench and worms. All my affairs, no matter what they might be, would sooner or later be forgotten, and I myself should not exist. So why should I worry about all these things? How could a man fail to see that and live,—that was surprising! A person could live only so long as he was drunk; but the moment he sobered up, he could not help seeing that all that was only a deception, and a stupid deception at that! Really, there was nothing funny and ingenious about it, but only something cruel and stupid.

Long ago has been told the Eastern story about the traveller who in the steppe is overtaken by an infuriated beast. Trying to save himself from the animal, the traveller jumps into a waterless well, but at its bottom he sees a dragon who opens his jaws in order to swallow him. And the unfortunate man does not dare climb out, lest he perish from the infuriated beast, and does not dare jump down to the bottom of the well, lest he be devoured by the dragon, and so clutches the twig of a wild bush growing in a cleft of the well and holds on to it. His hands grow weak and he feels that soon he shall have to surrender to the peril which awaits him at either side; but he still holds on and sees two mice, one white, the other black, in even measure making a circle around the main trunk of the bush to which he is clinging, and nibbling at it on all sides. Now, at any moment, the bush will break and tear off, and he will fall into the dragon's jaws. The traveller sees that and knows that he will inevitably perish; but while he is still clinging, he sees some drops of honey hanging on the leaves of the bush, and so reaches out for them with his tongue and licks the leaves. Just so I hold on to the branch of life, knowing that the dragon of death is waiting inevitably for me, ready to tear me to pieces, and I cannot understand why I have fallen on such suffering. And I try to lick that honey which used to give me pleasure; but now it no longer gives me joy, and the white and the black mouse day and night nibble at the branch to which I am holding on. I clearly see the dragon, and the honey is no longer sweet to me. I see only the inevitable dragon and the mice, and am unable to turn my glance away from them. That is not a fable, but a veritable, indisputable, comprehensible truth.

The former deception of the pleasures of life, which stifled the terror of the dragon, no longer deceives me. No matter how much one should say to me, "You cannot understand the meaning of life, do not think, live!" I am unable to do so, because I have been doing it too long before. Now I cannot help seeing day and night, which run and lead me up to death. I see that alone, because that alone is the truth. Everything else is a lie.

The two drops of honey that have longest turned my eyes away from the cruel truth, the love of family and of authorship, which I have called an art, are no longer sweet to me.

"My family—" I said to myself, "but my family, my wife and children, they are also human beings. They are in precisely the same condition that I am in: they must either live in the lie or see the terrible truth. Why should they live? Why should I love them, why guard, raise, and watch them? Is it for the same despair which is in me, or for fullness of perception? Since I love them, I cannot conceal truth from them,—every step in cognition leads them up to this truth. And the truth is death."

"Art, poetry?" For a long time, under the influence of the success of human praise, I tried to persuade myself that that was a thing which could be done, even though death should come and destroy everything, my deeds, as well as my memory of them; but soon I came to see that that, too, was a deception. It was clear to me that art was an adornment of life, a decoy of life. But life lost all its attractiveness for me. How, then, could I entrap others? So long as I did not live my own life, and a strange life bore me on its waves; so long as I believed that life had some sense, although I was not able to express it,—the reflections of life of every description in poetry and in the arts afforded me pleasure, and I was delighted to look at life through this little mirror of art; but when I began to look for the meaning of life, when I experienced the necessity of living myself, that little mirror became either useless, superfluous, and ridiculous, or painful to me. I could no longer console myself with what I saw in the mirror, namely, that my situation was stupid and desperate. It was all right for me to rejoice so long as I believed in the depth of my soul that life had some sense. At that time the play of lights—of the comical, the tragical, the touching, the beautiful, the terrible in life—afforded me amusement. But when I knew that life was meaningless and terrible, the play in the little mirror could no longer amuse me. No sweetness of honey could be sweet to me, when I saw the dragon and the mice that were nibbling down my support.

That was not all. If I had simply comprehended that life had no meaning, I might have known that calmly,—I might have known that that was my fate. But I could not be soothed by that. If I had been like a man living in a forest from which he knew there was no way out, I might have lived; but I was like a man who had lost his way in the forest, who was overcome by terror because he had lost his way, who kept tossing about in his desire to come out on the road, knowing that every step got him only more entangled, and who could not help tossing.

That was terrible. And, in order to free myself from that terror, I wanted to kill myself. I experienced terror before what was awaiting me,—I knew that that terror was more terrible than the situation itself, but I could not patiently wait for the end. No matter how convincing the reflection was that it was the same whether a vessel in the heart should break or something should burst, and all should be ended, I could not wait patiently for the end. The terror of the darkness was too great, and I wanted as quickly as possible to free myself from it by means of a noose or a bullet. It was this feeling that more than anything else drew me on toward suicide. . . .

VII

Having found no elucidation in science, I began to look for it in life, hoping to find it in the men who surrounded me. I began to observe the people such as I, to see how they lived about me and what attitude they assumed to the question that had brought me to the point of despair.

This is what I found in people who were in the same position as myself through their education and manner of life.

I found that for people of my circle there were four ways out from the terrible condition in which we all are.

The first way out is through ignorance. It consists in not knowing, not understanding that life is evil and meaningless. People of this category—mostly women or very young or very dull persons—have not yet come to understand that question of life which presented itself to Schopenhauer, Solomon, and Buddha. They see neither the dragon that awaits them, nor the mice that are nibbling at the roots of the bushes to which they are holding on, and continue to lick the honey.

But they lick the honey only till a certain time: something will direct their attention to the dragon and the mice, and there will be an end to their licking. From them I can learn nothing,—it is impossible to stop knowing what you know.

The second way out is through Epicureanism. It consists in this, that, knowing the hopelessness of life, one should in the meantime enjoy such good as there is, without looking either at the dragon or the mice, but licking the honey in the best manner possible, especially if there is a lot of it in one spot. Solomon expresses this way out like this:

"Go thy way, eat thy bread with joy, and drink thy wine. Live joyfully with the wife whom thou lovest all the days of the life of thy vanity, which he hath given thee under the sun, all the days of thy vanity: for that is thy portion in this life, and in thy labour which thou takest under the sun. Whatsoever thy hand findeth to do, do it with thy might; for there is no work, nor device, nor knowledge, nor wisdom, in the grave, whither thou goest."

Thus the majority of the people of our circle support the possibility of life in themselves. The conditions in which they are give them more good than evil, and their moral dullness makes it possible for them to forget that the advantage of their situation is a casual one; that not everybody can have a thousand wives and palaces, like Solomon; that to every man with a thousand wives there are a thousand men without wives, and for every palace there are a thousand people who built it in the sweat of their brows; and that the accident which had made me a Solomon today, will tomorrow make me a slave of Solomon. The dullness of the imagination of these people makes it possible for them to forget that which gave no rest to Buddha,—the inevitableness of sickness, old age, and death, which sooner or later will destroy all those pleasures.

Thus think and feel the majority of men of our time and our manner of life. The fact that some of these people assert that the dullness of their comprehension and imagination is philosophy, which they call positive, in my opinion does not take them out of the category of those who, in order not to see the question, lick the honey. Such people I could not imitate: as I did not possess their dullness of comprehension, I could not artificially reproduce it in myself. Just like any live man, I could not tear my eyes away from the mice and the dragon, having once seen them.

The third way out is through force and energy. It consists in this, that, having comprehended that life is evil and meaningless, one should set out to destroy it. Thus now and then act strong, consistent people. Having comprehended all the stupidity of the joke which has been played upon them, and seeing that the good of the dead is better than that of the living, and that it is better not to be at all, they go and carry this out and at once put an end to that stupid joke, so long as there are means for it: a noose about the neck, the water, a knife to pierce the heart with, railway trains. The number of people of our circle who do so is growing larger and larger. These people commit the act generally at the best period of life, when the mental powers are in full bloom and few habits have been acquired that lower human reason.

I saw that that was the worthiest way out, and I wanted to act in that way.

The fourth way out is through weakness. It consists in this, that, comprehending the evil and the meaninglessness of life, one continues to drag it out, knowing in advance that nothing can come of it. People of this calibre know that death is better than life, but, not having the strength to act reasonably, to make an end to the deception, and to kill themselves, they seem to be waiting for something. This is the way of weakness, for if I know that which is better, which is in my power, why not abandon myself to that which is better? I belonged to that category.

Thus people of my calibre have four ways of saving themselves from the terrible contradiction. No matter how much I strained my mental attention, I saw no other way out but those four. The one way out was not to understand that life was meaningless, vanity, and an evil, and that it was better not to live. I could not help knowing it and, having once learned it, I could not shut my eyes to it. The second way out was to make use of life such as it is, without thinking of the future. I could not do that either. Like Sakya-Muni, I could not go out hunting, when I knew that there was old age, suffering, death. My imagination was too vivid. Besides, I could not enjoy the accident of the moment, which for a twinkling threw enjoyment in my path. The third way out was, having come to see that life was an evil and a foolishness, to make an end of it and kill myself. I comprehended that, but for some reason did not kill myself. The fourth way out was to live in the condition of Solomon, of Schopenhauer,—to know that life was a stupid joke played on me, and yet to live, wash and dress myself, dine, speak, and even write books. That was repulsive and painful for me, but still I persisted in that situation. . . .

XII

I remember, it was early in spring, I was by myself in the forest, listening to the sounds of the woods. I listened and thought all the time of one and the same thing that had formed the subject of my thoughts for the last three years. I was again searching after God.

"All right, there is no God," I said to myself, "there is not such a being as would be, not my concept, but reality, just like my whole life,—there is no such being. And nothing, no miracles, can prove him to me, because the miracles would be my concept, and an irrational one at that.

"But my idea about God, about the one I am searching after?" I asked myself. "Where did that idea come from?" And with this thought the joyous waves of life again rose in me. Everything about me revived, received a meaning; but my joy did not last long,—the mind continued its work.

"The concept of God is not God," I said to myself. "A concept is what takes place within me; the concept of God is what I can evoke or can not evoke in myself. It is not that which I am searching after. I am trying to find that without which life could not be." And again everything began to die around me and within me, and I wanted again to kill myself.

Then I looked at myself, at what was going on within me, and I recalled those deaths and revivals which had taken place within me hundreds of times. I remembered that I lived only when I believed in God. As it had been before, so it was even now: I needed only to know about God, and I lived; I needed to forget and not believe in him, and I died.

What, then are these revivals and deaths? Certainly I do not live when I lose my faith in the existence of God; I should have killed myself long ago, if I had not had the dim hope of finding him. "So what else am I looking for?" a voice called out within me. "Here he is. He is that without which one cannot live. To know God and live is one and the same thing. God is life."

"Live searching after God, and then there will be no life without God." And stronger than ever all was lighted up within me and about me, and that light no longer abandoned me.

Thus I was saved from suicide. When and how this transformation took place in me I could not say. Just as imperceptibly and by degrees as my force of life had waned, and I had arrived at the impossibility of living, at the arrest of life, at the necessity of suicide, just so by degrees and imperceptibly did that force of life return to me. Strange to say, the force of life which returned to me was not a new, but the same old force which had drawn me on in the first period of my life.

I returned in everything to the most remote, the childish and the youthful. I returned to the belief in that will which had produced me and which wanted something of me; I returned to this, that the chief and only purpose of my life was to be better, that is, to live more in accord with that will; I returned to this, that the expression of this will I could find in that which all humanity had worked out for its guidance in the vanishing past, that is, I returned to the faith in God, in moral perfection, and in the tradition which had handed down the meaning of life. There was only this difference, that formerly it had been assumed unconsciously, while now I knew that I could not live without it.

This is what seemed to have happened with me: I do not remember when I was put in a boat, was pushed off from some unknown shore, had pointed out to me the direction toward another shore, had a pair of oars given into my inexperienced hands, and was left alone. I plied my oars as well as I could, and moved on; but the farther I rowed toward the middle, the swifter did the current become which bore me away from my goal, and the more frequently did I come across oarsmen like myself, who were carried away by the current. There were lonely oarsmen, who continued to row; there were large boats, immense ships, full of people; some struggled against the current, others submitted to it. The farther I rowed, the more did I look down the current, whither all those boats were carried, and forget the direction which had been pointed out to me. In the middle of the current, in the crush of the boats and ships which bore me down, I lost my direction completely and threw down the oars. On every side of me sailing vessels and rowboats were borne down the current with merriment and rejoicing, and the people in them assured me and each other that there could not even be any other direction, and I believed them and went down the stream with them. I was carried away, so far away, that I heard the noise of the rapids where I should be wrecked, and saw boats that had already been wrecked there. I regained my senses. For a long time I could not understand what had happened with me. I saw before me nothing but ruin toward which I was rushing and of which I was afraid; nowhere did I see any salvation, and I did not know what to do; but, on looking back, I saw an endless number of boats that without cessation stubbornly crossed the current, and I thought of the shore, the oars, and the direction, and began to make my way back, up the current and toward the shore.

That shore was God, the direction was tradition, the oars were the freedom given me to row toward the shore,—to unite myself with God. Thus the force of life was renewed in me, and I began to live once more.

21. Cacodaemony: A Puzzle about God

Steven M. Cahn

Steven M. Cahn (1942–   ) is a philosophy professor and administrator at the City University of New York. He has written and edited books on a variety of philosophical topics.

For many centuries philosophers have grappled with what has come to be known as "the problem of evil." Succinctly stated, the problem is: Could a world containing evil have been created by an omnipotent, omniscient, omnibenevolent being?

Considering the vast literature devoted to this issue, it is perhaps surprising that there has been little discussion of an analogous issue that might appropriately be referred to as "the problem of goodness." Succinctly stated, the problem is: Could a world containing goodness have been created by an omnipotent, omniscient, omnimalevolent being?

This chapter has two aims. The first is to provide a reasonable solution to the problem of goodness. Traditional theists find the hypothesis of creation by a benevolent deity far more plausible than the hypothesis of creation by a malevolent demon, and they may, therefore, believe the problem of goodness to be irrelevant to their commitments. My second aim is to demonstrate that this belief is mistaken.

Before proceeding, it would be well to restate the problem of goodness in more formal fashion.

(1) Assume that there exists an omnipotent, omniscient, omnimalevolent Demon who created the world.

(2) If the Demon exists, there would be no goodness in the world.

(3) But there is goodness in the world.

(4) Therefore, the Demon does not exist.

Since the conclusion of the argument follows from the premises, those who wish to deny the conclusion must deny one of the premises. No demonist (the analogue to a theist) would question premise (1), so in order to avoid the conclusion of the argument, an attack would have to be launched against either premise (2) or premise (3).

What if a demonist attempted to deny premise (3)? Suppose it were claimed that goodness is an illusion, that there is nothing of this sort in the world. Would this move solve the problem?

From Steven M. Cahn, *Philosophical Explorations* (Amherst, NY: Prometheus Books) Copyright 1989. Reprinted by permission of the publisher.

I think not, for such a claim is either patently false or else involves a distortion of the usual meaning of the term "good." If the word is being used in its ordinary sense, then acts of kindness, expressions of love, and creations of beauty are good. Since obviously such things do occur, there is goodness in the world.

If one insists that such things are not good, then the expression "good" is being used eccentrically, and the claim loses its import. It is as though one were to defend the view that all persons are pigs by defining "persons" as "omnivorous hoofed mammals of the family Suidae." Such "persons" are not persons at all. Similarly, a supposedly omnimalevolent Demon who cherishes personal affection and great works of art is certainly not omnimalevolent and is probably no demon.

Premise (3) can thus be adequately defended, and if demonists are to find an answer to the problem of goodness, they must attack premise (2). How can there be goodness in the world if the creator is omnimalevolent and possesses the power and the knowledge to carry out evil intentions? To paraphrase Epicurus, is the Demon willing to prevent good, but not able? Then he is impotent. Is he able, but not willing? Then he is benevolent. Is he both able and willing? Whence then is goodness?

At this point it may appear to be a hopeless task to justify the Demon's malevolence in the face of the fact of goodness, an enterprise appropriately referred to as "cacodaemony" (the analogue of theodicy). But sophisticated demonists would realize there is much play left in their position. They would not agree that just because there is goodness in the world, it could not have been created by the omnimalevolent Demon. After all, isn't it possible that whatever goodness exists is logically necessary for this to be the most evil world that the Demon could have created? Not even an omnipotent being can contravene the laws of logic, for such a task is senseless, and so if each and every good in the world were logically tied to the achievement of the greatest evil, the omnimalevolent Demon, in order to bring about the greatest possible evil, would have been forced to allow the existence of these goods.

The demonist thus rejects premise (2) of the argument and argues instead for premise (2'):

(2') If the Demon exists, then every good in the world is logically necessary in order for this to be the most evil world that the Demon could have created.

Now if we substitute premise (2') for premise (2) in the original argument, that argument falls apart, for the conclusion no longer follows from the premises. One can affirm without contradiction both the existence of an omnipotent, omniscient, omnimalevolent Demon who created the world and the existence of goodness in the world, so long as one also affirms that every good is logically necessary in order for this to be the most evil world the Demon could have created. Demonists thus appear to have escaped the force of the problem of goodness.

Things are not so simple, for now demonists are faced by yet another argument that challenges their belief.

(1) Assume that there exists an omnipotent, omniscient, omnimalevolent Demon who created the world.

(2) If the Demon exists, then every good in the world is logically necessary in order for this to be the most evil world that the Demon could have created.

(3) But there is strong reason to believe that not every good in the world is logically necessary in order for this to be the most evil world the Demon could have created.

(4) Therefore, there is strong reason to believe that the Demon does not exist.

This second argument, unlike the first, does not claim that belief in the Demon is illogical; rather, it claims that such belief is unreasonable. Beautiful mountain ranges, spectacular sunsets, the plays of Shakespeare, and the quartets of Beethoven do not seem in any way to enhance the evils of the world. Acts of altruism, generosity, and kindheartedness certainly do not appear to increase the world's sinister aspects. In other words, this argument challenges demonists to suggest plausible reasons for their view that every good in the world makes possible a world containing even greater evils than would be possible without these goods.

The reader will, of course, have observed that thus far the discussion of the problem of goodness exactly parallels traditional discussions of the problem of evil; all the arguments and counterarguments that have been presented are equally applicable *mutatis mutandis* to either problem. What may be somewhat surprising, however, is that classic arguments in defense of the view that every evil in the world makes possible a world containing even greater goods can be exactly paralleled by arguments in defense of the view that every good in the world makes possible a world containing even greater evils. To illustrate this point, I shall proceed to construct a cacodaemony along the identical lines of the well-known theodicy constructed by John Hick.

We begin by dividing all goods into two sorts: moral goods and physical goods. Moral goods are those human beings do for each other; physical goods are those to be found in the human environment.

The justification of moral goods proceeds by logically tying the existence of such goods to human free will. Surely, performing a bad act freely is more evil than performing such an act involuntarily. The Demon could have ensured that human beings would always perform bad actions, but such actions would not have been free, since the Demon would have ensured their occurrence.[1] Because the actions would not have been free, their performance would not have produced the greatest possible evil, since greater evil can be produced by free persons than by unfree ones. The Demon, therefore, had to provide human beings with freedom, so that they might perform their bad actions voluntarily, thus maximizing evil.

---

[1] I here assume without argument that freedom and determinism are incompatible. Those who believe they are not face more difficulty in resolving the problem of goodness (or the problem of evil).

As for the justification of physical goods, we should not suppose that the Demon's purpose in creating the world was to construct a mere chamber of tortures in which the inhabitants would be forced to endure a succession of unrelieved pains. The world can be viewed, instead, as a place of "soul-breaking," in which free human beings, by grappling with the exhausting tasks and challenges of their existence in a common environment, can thereby have their spirits broken and their wills-to-live destroyed.

This conception of the world can be supported by what, following Hick, we may call "the method of negative cacodaemony." Suppose, contrary to fact, that this world were so arranged that nothing could ever go well. No one could help anyone else, no one could perform a courageous act, no one could complete any worthwhile project. Presumably, such a world could be created through innumerable acts of the Demon that would continually alter the laws of nature as necessary.

It is evident that our present ethical concepts would be useless in such a world, for "ought" implies "can," and if no good acts could be performed, it would follow that none ought to be performed. The whole notion of "evil" would seem to drop out, for to understand and recognize evils we must have some idea of goods. Consequently, such a world, however efficiently it might promote pains, would be ill-adapted for the development of the worst qualities of the human personality.

At this point, this cacodaemony, just as Hick's theodicy, points forward in two ways to the subject of life after death. First, although there are many striking instances of evil being brought forth from good through a person's reaction to it (witness the pollution of beautiful lakes or the slashing of great paintings), still there are many other cases in which the opposite has happened. Therefore, it would seem that any demonic purpose of soul-breaking at work in earthly history must continue beyond this life if it is ever to achieve more than a very partial and fragmentary success.

Second, if we ask whether the business of soul-breaking is so evil as to nullify all the goodness to be found in human life, the demonist's answer must be in terms of a future evil great enough to justify all that has happened on the way to it.

Have we now provided an adequate cacodaemony? It is, I think, just as strong as Hick's theodicy, but neither in my view is successful. Nor do I see any plausible ways of strengthening either one. What reason is there to believe in an afterlife of any particular sort? What evidence is there that the world would be either better without the beauty of a sunset or worse without the horrors of bubonic plague? What evidence is there either that the free will of a Socrates achieved greater evil than would have been achieved by his performing wrong actions involuntarily or that the free will of a Hitler achieved greater good than would have been achieved by his performing right actions involuntarily?

The hypothesis that all the good in the world is a necessary part of this worst of all possible worlds is not contradictory; nevertheless, it is highly unlikely.

Similarly, the hypothesis that all the evil in the world is a necessary part of this best of all possible worlds is not contradictory; but it, too, is highly unlikely. If this is neither the worst of all possible worlds nor the best of all possible worlds, then it could not have been created by either an all-powerful, all-evil demon or an all-powerful, all-good diety. Thus, although the problem of goodness and the problem of evil do not show either demonism or theism to be impossible views, they show them both to be highly improbable. If demonists or theists can produce any other evidence in favor of their positions, they may be able to increase the plausibility of their views, but unless they can produce such evidence, the reasonable conclusion appears to be that neither the Demon nor God exists.

SUGGESTIONS FOR FURTHER READING

ANTHOLOGIES

Brody, Baruch A. *Readings in the Philosophy of Religion.* 2nd ed. Englewood Cliffs, N.J.: Prentice-Hall, 1991. A comprehensive collection emphasizing contemporary essays in the recent analytical tradition.

Flew, Antony, and Alasdair Macintyre, eds. *New Essays in Philosophical Theology.* London: SCM Press, 1955. A collection of important writings on various aspects of the philosophy of religion. Many of these articles will be difficult for the beginning student.

Hick, John, ed. *The Existence of God.* New York: Macmillan, 1964. A good collection of classical and contemporary writings on the major arguments for the existence of God.

Kaufmann, Walter, ed. *Religion from Tolstoy to Camus.* New York: Harper, 1961. A collection of some of the most important writings on the philosophy of religion.

Pike, Nelson, ed. *God and Evil.* Englewood Cliffs, N.J.: Prentice-Hall, 1964. A collection of opposing views and arguments about the problem of evil. There is a good bibliography for the student who wishes to read further on this topic.

Sanders, Steven, and David R. Cheney, eds. *The Meaning of Life.* Englewood Cliffs, N.J.: Prentice-Hall, 1980. A collection of significant writings on the meaning and value of life.

INDIVIDUAL WORKS

Abraham, William J. *An Introduction to the Philosophy of Religion.* Englewood Cliffs, N.J.: Prentice-Hall, 1985. A readable introduction to the major topics in the philosophy of religion.

Collins, John. *God in Modern Philosophy.* Chicago: Regnery, 1959. A survey of many of the major issues in the philosophy of religion from a Catholic point of view.

Du Noüy, Lecomte. *Human Destiny.* New York: Longmans, 1947. A version of the argument from design. Du Noüy argues that the facts of biology cannot be adequately explained unless the existence of a Designer is accepted.

Hick, John. *Philosophy of Religion.* 4th ed. Englewood Cliffs, N.J.: Prentice-Hall, 1989. An excellent brief introduction to the philosophy of religion. The student will find this a valuable guide in organizing the issues raised by the readings in this text.

Hume, David. *Dialogues on Natural Religion,* edited by Norman Kemp Smith. Indianapolis: Bobbs, 1947. A classic discussion of the argument from design. The beginning student will find this difficult but very rewarding.

Mackie, J. L. *The Miracle of Theism.* Oxford: Clarendon Press, 1982. A careful presentation and criticism of the arguments for God's existence.

Matson, Wallace I. *The Existence of God.* Ithaca, N.Y.: Cornell Univ. Press, 1965. An excellent, detailed analysis of the major arguments for the existence of God.

Nielsen, Kai. *Philosophy and Atheism.* Buffalo, N.Y.: Prometheus, 1985. A collection of articles by a contemporary defender of atheism.

Paley, William. *Natural Theology: Selections,* edited by Frederick Ferré. Indianapolis: Bobbs, 1963. The classic statement of the argument from design.

Purtill, Richard L. *Thinking About Religion.* Englewood Cliffs, N.J.: Prentice-Hall, 1978. A clear, entertainingly written introduction to the main issues in the philosophy of religion.

Scriven, Michael. *Primitive Philosophy.* New York: McGraw-Hill, 1966. Chapter Four presents an interesting and detailed defense of atheism.

Smith, George H. *Atheism: The Case Against God.* Buffalo, N.Y.: Prometheus, 1979. A recent analysis and defense of atheism.

Warren, Thomas B., and Wallace I. Matson. *The Warren-Matson Debate on the Existence of God.* Jonesboro, Ark.: National Christian Press, 1978. This debate is especially noteworthy because of Matson's provocative arguments and emotionally moving appeals for tolerance.

Dictionary of the History of Ideas: Studies of Selected Pivotal Ideas. Philip P. Weiner, editor-in-chief. New York: Scribner's, 1973. Substantial and clearly written essays emphasizing the historical development of topics discussed in this part. Designed to inform the nonspecialist, each essay concludes with a select bibliography.

Encyclopedia of Philosophy. Paul Edwards, editor-in-chief. New York: Macmillan, 1967. The beginning student will find many worthwhile articles on the subjects treated in this part and excellent bibliographies.

PART THREE

Morality and Society

INTRODUCTION

Just about everyone seeks to distinguish right behavior from wrong and to determine what is worthwhile in life. In our society we frequently encounter discussions about the morality of the death penalty, the decline in current moral values, and the injustice done to minority groups. Also, at times, we are faced with personal moral decisions: Should we lie to get out of an unpleasant situation? Should we fight in a war if we think it unjust? Should we cheat on our income tax if we are sure we will not get caught? It is these kinds of questions that produce philosophical speculations about the basis of morality and the good life.

Although philosophers are concerned with the kinds of moral problems we face in daily life, they believe that primary concern should be given to a number of very basic problems that must be answered before it is possible to give a reasoned answer to any other moral issues. *Ethics* is that branch of philosophy that is concerned with finding answers to these basic problems. Some of the problems most often discussed in the study of ethics are: Is there a basis for deciding whether any act is right? How can we prove or disprove that there is such a basis? What kinds of things are most worth attaining? When does a person deserve to be praised or blamed? In answering these kinds of questions, the philosopher does not merely give an opinion or list a variety of opinions on the subject but rather attempts to find reasons that will show that a certain answer is correct. The student seeking to get much out of the readings must pay close attention to reasons that are offered and attempt to decide which philosophers, if any, have proved their case.

Many students approach ethics with the belief that there is little to be gained from the investigation because they believe that moral standards or principles are merely products of the society in which one lives. They believe that the moral views of people in other societies, no matter how much they differ from one's own, are correct for the people in those societies. Such a view is called *relativism*.

Two kinds of relativism, sociological and ethical, must be distinguished and defined before the topic can be clearly discussed. *Sociological relativism* is the name given to the factual claim that societies sometimes have different ultimate principles. An ultimate principle is one that is used as a basis for defending all other moral judgments and principles. It seems evident that societies do have different moral principles regarding a variety of matters such as marriage, raising the young, and the treatment of women. The crucial point, however, is whether societies that obviously differ in their moral practices also differ on their view of the correct ultimate principle. The observed differences may not indicate differences in ultimate principles but merely the necessity of different behavior to satisfy the same principle. For example, a society with insufficient food to feed everyone might kill the elderly when they are no longer productive in order to save the young. A society with abundant means to care for the elderly would probably consider killing them abhorrent. Yet if the latter society were suddenly to find its means reduced to that of the former, it might well consider the killing of the elderly as a necessity because, like the first society, it too wants to ensure survival of the group.

The belief in sociological relativism has been of great significance because for many it justifies ethical relativism. *Ethical relativism* is the view that there are different but equally correct ultimate principles. This position is opposed to that of *ethical absolutism*, a theory that holds that there is only one correct ultimate principle or set of principles. The conflict between the ethical absolutist and relativist is of crucial importance. If the relativist is right, it would be necessary to give up the criticism of other societies, and possibly each individual's ultimate moral principles, although one still could criticize the application of those principles.

W. T. Stace presents the arguments for and against both ethical relativism and absolutism. He shows that sociological relativism, even if true, would not require a belief in ethical relativism, for the absolutist could claim that those ultimate moral principles contrary to the "true" one were merely mistaken. Further, Stace argues that the consequences of ethical relativism are unacceptable and that absolutism, despite the difficulty of establishing the correct moral principle, is preferable.

Philosophers have presented a number of theories concerning the correct ultimate moral principles. Three of the most prominent views are *egoism, utilitarianism,* and *formalism.* The main tenet of *egoism* is that self-interest is the only proper standard of conduct. Egoists deny that they ever have a moral duty to sacrifice their own interests for the interests of others. Egoists may frequently act generously or charitably, but only because they find such acts to be in their own long-term interests. Many egoists defend their position by claiming that everyone is motivated solely by self-interest, and, thus, it would be pointless to urge people to act in a nonegoistic manner. In "The Morality Trap," Harry Browne presents a forceful statement of the egoist position. For him, a person should always strive to produce the best consequences for himself. To achieve this result, two traps must be avoided: the morality trap and the unselfishness trap. The morality trap is the belief that there is some nonegoistic basis (such as God's will or the good of society) on which one should base moral judgments. The unselfishness trap is the belief that one's own happiness should be sacrificed for the happiness of others. If these two traps are avoided, one is on the road to self-fulfillment and personal happiness.

Utilitarianism is a moral theory that holds that right acts are acts producing the greatest happiness. In deciding which acts are right, a utilitarian considers the consequences of all the acts open to him and performs the one that would produce the best consequences for everybody concerned. Although many would agree that this is generally a proper procedure, sometimes there is dissatisfaction with some kinds of acts that might turn out to be right on this basis. For example, if it would produce the best results for all concerned, then it would be right to lie, steal, and even murder. Jeremy Bentham presents a clear statement of the utilitarian position and attempts to work out some of the details required for its implementation. He maintains that in assessing the consequences of various possible acts, we should be concerned with the amounts of pleasure and pain produced and perform only those acts resulting in the most pleasure or the least pain. Bentham believed that the only thing ultimately worthwhile in life is pleasure. Such a view that the good is pleasure is called *hedonism*. The student should realize, however, that a utilitarian need not be a hedonist. He could believe that many things besides pleasure, such as intellectual growth, beauty, and integrity, are worthwhile and that these should be considered in assessing possible actions.

Unlike egoists and utilitarians, some moral theorists maintain that the rightness or wrongness of actions is not determined by the consequences produced by the actions. Such a view is called *formalism* in ethical theory. The kinds of ultimate principles that formalists have held have varied widely. One formalist principle that has had great appeal is the golden rule, "Do unto others as you would have others do unto you." R. M. MacIver defends this rule as the only one that can bring agreement out of the conflicting moral viewpoints because it lays down a procedure to follow in determining proper behavior rather than stating final goals and values. A problem for the student in considering MacIver's view is to decide on what basis the golden rule is being defended. Is MacIver appealing to the utility of accepting it, or is there some other basis of appeal?

A moral issue that has recently received increasing attention is what obligation, if any, people in affluent countries have to the poor throughout the world. Since many people in poor countries desire to live in richer countries, immigration policy is an important aspect of this issue. In "Lifeboat Ethics: The Case Against Helping the Poor," Garrett Hardin argues that so long as there is no world government to institute rational control of the world's resources, each nation should protect its citizens against encroachments on their resources by others. He contends that it is unwise either to feed the poor in other countries or to allow unrestricted immigration into our own. Peter Singer, who disagrees with Hardin, contends that it is unjustified to ignore the needy in other countries. In "Insiders and Outsiders," he argues that one way to aid the needy is to open our borders to larger numbers of refugees than we now accept.

An issue much debated at present is the morality of abortion. Opinions on this issue range from the extreme liberal view that women should be free to end unwanted pregnancies by abortion at any time to the extreme conservative view that all abortions are wrong since they involve killing an innocent person. Relevant to the assessment of the various views on abortion are a variety of metaphysical and moral issues: Is the fetus a human being? If so, when does it become one? Is it ever morally justified intentionally to kill one innocent person to save another? Should fetuses have the same rights as children? The two readings on this issue deal with these fundamental questions. In "An Almost Absolute Value in History," John T. Noonan contends that a fetus should be considered a human being at the moment of conception because at that time the genetic code which determines human potentialities is acquired. Noonan examines and rejects other proposed criteria for determining when a fetus should be considered human. If every fetus possesses full human rights, then abortion involves the taking of a human life. So, for Noonan, abortion would be justified only in those rare instances when the rights of others outweighed the fetus's right to life. In "A Defense of Abortion," Judith Jarvis Thomson argues that even if a fetus is a human being from the moment of conception, abortion is still morally permissible in many cases. She contends that women, having the right to use their bodies as they choose, need not allow a fetus to use it. Although a fetus needs a mother's body, its use of it must depend on the mother's good will.

The "Problems and Puzzles" section contains two provocative articles. In "A Case for Torture," Michael Levin contends that the use of torture should not be as strongly condemned as it is. Since most people would support the use of torture to prevent a disaster, it is not a type of act that is always wrong. Whether torture is justified to prevent harmful acts that are not disasters should be determined by a careful assessment of its consequences in a given case. The need to torture a terrorist to obtain information that would save lives is a case in which torture might be justified. In "People or Penguins: The Case for Optimal Pollution," William Baxter maintains that environmental policies should be concerned only with the welfare of humans. For him, the survival of plants and animals that are not helpful to man is unimportant. Baxter asserts that because some human goods cannot be achieved without permitting low levels of air and water pollution, the goal should not be to eliminate pollution, but to allow the level needed for the production of the greatest amount of human goods.

ARE ETHICAL VALUES RELATIVE?

22. *Ethical Relativism*

W. T. Stace

Any ethical position which denies that there is a single moral standard which is equally applicable to all men at all times may fairly be called a species of ethical relativity. There is not, the relativist asserts, merely one moral law, one code, one standard. There are many moral laws, codes, standards. What morality ordains in one place or age may be quite different from what morality ordains in another place or age. The moral code of Chinamen is quite different from that of Europeans, that of African savages quite different from both. Any morality, therefore, is relative to the age, the place, and the circumstances in which it is found. It is in no sense absolute.

This does not mean merely—as one might at first sight be inclined to suppose—that the very same kind of action which is *thought* right in one country and period may be *thought* wrong in another. This would be a mere platitude, the truth of which everyone would have to admit. Even the absolutist would admit this—would even wish to emphasize it—since he is well aware that different people have different sets of moral ideas, and his whole point is that some of these sets of ideas are false. What the relativist means to assert is, not this platitude, but that the very same kind of action which *is* right in one country and period may *be* wrong in another. And this, far from being a platitude, is a very startling assertion.

It is very important to grasp thoroughly the difference between the two ideas. For there is reason to think that many minds tend to find ethical relativity attractive because they fail to keep them clearly apart. It is so very obvious that moral ideas differ from country to country and from age to age. And it is so very easy, if you are mentally lazy, to suppose that to say this means the same as to say that no universal moral standard exists,—or in other words that it implies ethical relativity. We fail to see that the word "standard" is used in two different senses. It is perfectly true that, in one sense, there are many variable moral standards. We speak of judging a man by the standard of his time. And this implies that different times have different standards. And this, of course, is quite true. But when the word "standard" is used in this sense it means simply the set of moral ideas current during the period in question. It means what people *think* right, whether as a matter of

Reprinted with the permission of Simon & Schuster from *The Concept of Morals* by W. T. Stace. Copyright 1937 by Macmillan Publishing Company, renewed 1965 by Walter T. Stace.

fact it *is* right or not. On the other hand when the absolutist asserts that there exists a single universal moral "standard," he is not using the word in this sense at all. He means by "standard" <u>what *is* right as distinct from what people merely think right</u>. His point is that although what people think right varies in different countries and periods, yet what actually is right is everywhere and always the same. And it follows that when the ethical relativist disputes the position of the absolutist and denies that any universal moral standard exists he too means by "standard" what actually is right. But it is exceedingly easy, if we are not careful, to slip loosely from using the word in the first sense to using it in the second sense; and to suppose that the variability of moral beliefs is the same thing as the variability of what really is moral. And unless we keep the two senses of the word "standard" distinct, we are likely to think the creed of ethical relativity much more plausible than it actually is.

The genuine relativist, then, does not merely mean that Chinamen may think right what Frenchmen think wrong. He means that what *is* wrong for the Frenchman may *be* right for the Chinaman. And if one enquires how, in those circumstances, one is to know what actually is right in China or in France, the answer comes quite glibly. What is right in China is the same as what people think right in China; and what is right in France is the same as what people think right in France. So that, if you want to know what is moral in any particular country or age all you have to do is ascertain what are the moral ideas current in that age or country. Those ideas are, *for that age or country*, right. Thus what is morally right is identified with what is thought to be morally right, and the distinction which we made above between these two is simply denied. To put the same thing in another way, it is denied that there can be or ought to be any distinction between the two senses of the word "standard." There is only one kind of standard of right and wrong, namely, the moral ideas current in any particular age or country.

Moral right *means* what people think morally right. It has no other meaning. What Frenchmen think right is, therefore, right *for Frenchmen*. And evidently one must conclude—though I am not aware that relativists are anxious to draw one's attention to such unsavoury but yet absolutely necessary conclusions from their creed—that cannibalism is right for people who believe in it, that human sacrifice is right for those races which practice it, and that burning widows alive was right for Hindus until the British stepped in and compelled the Hindus to behave immorally by allowing their widows to remain alive.

When it is said that, according to the ethical relativists, what is thought right in any social group is right for that group, one must be careful not to misinterpret this. The relativist does not, of course, mean that there actually is an objective moral standard in France and a different objective standard in England, and that France and British opinions respectively give us correct information about these different standards. His point is rather that there are no objectively true moral standards at all. There is no single universal objective standard. Nor are there a variety of local objective standards. All standards are subjective. People's subjective feelings about morality are the only standards which exist.

To sum up. The ethical relativist consistently denies, it would seem, whatever the ethical absolutist asserts. For the absolutist there is a single universal moral standard. For the relativist there is no such standard. There are only local, ephemeral, and variable standards. For the absolutist there are two senses of the word "standard." Standards in the sense of sets of current moral ideas are relative and changeable. But the standard in the sense of what is actually morally right is absolute and unchanging. For the relativist no such distinction can be made. There is only one meaning of the word standard, namely, that which refers to local and variable sets of moral ideas. Or if it is insisted that the word must be allowed two meanings, then the relativist will say that there is at any rate no actual example of a standard in the absolute sense, and that the word as thus used is an empty name to which nothing in reality corresponds; so that the distinction between the two meanings becomes empty and useless. Finally—though this is merely saying the same thing in another way—the absolutist makes a distinction between what actually is right and what is thought right. The relativist rejects this distinction and identifies what is moral with what is thought by certain human beings or groups of human beings. . . .

I shall now proceed to consider, first, the main arguments which can be urged in favour of ethical relativity, and secondly, the arguments which can be urged against it. . . . The first is that which relies upon the actual varieties of moral "standards" found in the world. It was easy enough to believe in a single absolute morality in older times when there was no anthropology, when all humanity was divided clearly into two groups, Christian peoples and the "heathen." Christian peoples knew and possessed the one true morality. The rest were savages whose moral ideas could be ignored. But all this is changed. Greater knowledge has brought greater tolerance. We can no longer exalt our own morality as alone true, while dismissing all other moralities as false or inferior. The investigations of anthropologists have shown that there exist side by side in the world a bewildering variety of moral codes. On this topic endless volumes have been written, masses of evidence piled up. Anthropologists have ransacked the Melanesian Islands, the jungles of New Guinea, the steppes of Siberia, the deserts of Australia, the forests of central Africa, and have brought back with them countless examples of weird, extravagant, and fantastic "moral" customs with which to confound us. We learn that all kinds of horrible practices are, in this, that, or the other place, regarded as essential to virtue. We find that there is nothing, or next to nothing, which has always and everywhere been regarded as morally good by all men. Where then is our universal morality? Can we, in face of all this evidence, deny that it is nothing but an empty dream?

This argument, taken by itself, is a very weak one. It relies upon a single set of facts—the variable moral customs of the world. But this variability of moral ideas is admitted by both parties to the dispute, and is capable of ready explanation upon the hypothesis of either party. The relativist says that the facts are to be explained by the non-existence of any absolute moral standard. The absolutist says that they are to be explained by human ignorance of what the absolute moral standard is. And he can truly point out that men have differed widely in their opinions about all manner as topics—including the subject-matters of the physical sciences—just as much as they differ about morals. And if the various different opinions which men have held about the shape of the earth do not prove that it has no one real shape, neither do the various opinions which they have held about morality prove that there is no one true morality.

Thus the facts can be explained equally plausibly on either hypothesis. There is nothing in the facts themselves which compels us to prefer the relativistic hypothesis to that of the absolutist. And therefore the argument fails to prove the relativist conclusion. If that conclusion is to be established, it must be by means of other considerations.

This is the essential point. But I will add some supplementary remarks. The work of the anthropologists, upon which ethical relativists seem to rely so heavily, has as matter of fact added absolutely nothing *in principle* to what has always been known about the variability of moral ideas. Educated people have known all along that the Greeks tolerated sodomy, which in modern times has been regarded in some countries as an abominable crime; that the Hindus thought it a sacred duty to burn their widows; that trickery, now thought despicable, was once believed to be a virtue; that terrible torture was thought by our own ancestors only a few centuries ago to be a justifiable weapon of justice; that it was only yesterday that western peoples came to believe that slavery is immoral. Even the ancients knew very well that moral customs and ideas vary—witness the writings of Herodotus. Thus the principle of the variability of moral ideas was well understood long before modern anthropology was ever heard of. Anthropology has added nothing to the knowledge of this principle except a mass of new and extreme examples of it drawn from very remote sources. But to multiply examples of a principle already well known and universally admitted adds nothing to the argument which is built upon that principle. The discoveries of the anthropologists have no doubt been of the highest importance in their own sphere. But in my considered opinion they have thrown no new light upon the special problems of the moral philosopher.

Although the multiplication of examples has no logical bearing on the argument, it does have an immense *psychological* effect upon people's minds. These masses of anthropological learning are impressive. They are propounded in the sacred name of "science." If they are quoted in support of ethical relativity—as they often are—people *think* that they must prove something important. They bewilder and over-awe the simple-minded, batter down their resistance, make them ready to receive humbly the doctrine of ethical relativity from those who have acquired a reputation by their immense learning and their claims to be "scientific." Perhaps this is why so much ado is made by ethical relativists regarding the anthropological evidence. But we must refuse to be impressed. We must discount all this mass of evidence about the extraordinary moral customs of remote peoples. Once we have admitted—as everyone who is instructed must have admitted these last two thousand years without any anthropology at all—the principle that moral ideas vary, all this new evidence adds nothing to the argument. And the argument itself proves nothing for the reasons already given. . . .

The second argument in favour of ethical relativity is also a very strong one. And it does not suffer from the disadvantage that it is dependent upon the acceptance of any particular philosophy such as radical empiricism. It makes its appeal to considerations of a quite general character. It consists in alleging that no one has ever been able to discover upon what foundation an absolute morality could rest, or from what source a universally binding moral code could derive its authority.

If, for example, it is an absolute and unalterable moral rule that all men ought to be unselfish, from whence does this *command* issue? For a command it certainly is, phrase it how you please. There is no difference in meaning between the sentence "You ought to be unselfish" and the sentence "Be unselfish." Now a command implies a commander. An obligation implies some authority which obliges. Who is this commander, what this authority? Thus the vastly difficult question is raised of *the basis of moral obligation.* Now the argument of the relativist would be that it is impossible to find any basis for a universally binding moral law; but that it is quite easy to discover a basis for morality if moral codes are admitted to be variable, ephemeral, and relative to time, place, and circumstance.

In this book I am assuming that it is no longer possible to solve this difficulty by saying naively that the universal moral law is based upon the uniform commands of God to all men. There will be many, no doubt, who will dispute this. But I am not writing for them. I am writing for those who feel the necessity of finding for morality a basis independent of particular religious dogmas. And I shall therefore make no attempt to argue the matter.

The problem which the absolutist has to face, then, is this. The religious basis of the one absolute morality having disappeared, can there be found for it any other, any secular, basis? If not, then it would seem that we cannot any longer believe in absolutism. We shall have to fall back upon belief in a variety of perhaps mutually inconsistent moral codes operating over restricted areas and limited periods. No one of these will be better, or more true, than any other. Each will be good and true for those living in those areas and periods. We shall have to fall back, in a word, on ethical relativity.

For there is no great difficulty in discovering the foundations of morality, or rather of moralities, if we adopt the relativist hypothesis. Even if we cannot be quite certain *precisely* what these foundations are—and relativists themselves are not entirely agreed about them—we can at least see in a general way the *sort* of foundations they must have. We can see that the question on this basis is not in principle impossible to answer—although the details may be obscure; while, if we adopt the absolutist hypothesis—so the arguments runs—no kind of answer is conceivable at all. . . .

This argument is undoubtedly very strong. It *is* absolutely essential to solve the problem of the basis of moral obligation if we are to believe in any kind of moral standards other than those provided by mere custom or by irrational emotions. It is idle to talk about a universal morality unless we can point to the source of its authority—or at least to do so is to indulge in a faith which is without rational ground. To cherish a blind faith in morality may be, for the average man whose business is primarily to live aright and not to theorize, sufficient. Perhaps it is his wisest course. But it will not do for the philosopher. His function, or at least one of his functions, is precisely to discover the rational grounds of our everyday beliefs— if they have any. Philosophically and intellectually, then, we cannot accept belief in a universally binding morality unless we can discover upon what foundation its obligatory character rests.

But in spite of the strength of the argument thus posed in favour of ethical relativity, it is not impregnable. For it leaves open one loop-hole. It is always possible that some theory, not yet examined, may provide a basis for a universal moral obligation. The argument rests upon the negative proposition that *there is no theory which can provide a basis for a universal morality.* But it is notoriously difficult to prove a negative. How can you prove that there are no green swans? All you can show is that none have been found so far. And then it is always possible that one will be found tomorrow. . . .

It is time that we turned our attention from the case in favour of ethical relativity to the case against it. Now the case against it consists, to a very large extent, in urging that, if taken seriously and pressed to its logical conclusion, ethical relativity can only end in destroying the conception of morality altogether, in undermining its practical efficacy, in rendering meaningless many almost universally accepted truths about human affairs, in robbing human beings of any incentive to strive for a better world, in taking the life-blood out of every ideal and every aspiration which has ever ennobled the life of man. . . .

First of all, then, ethical relativity, in asserting that the moral standards of particular social groups are the only standards which exist, renders meaningless all propositions which attempt to compare these standards with one another in respect to their moral worth. And this is a very serious matter indeed. We are accustomed to think that the moral ideas of one nation or social group may be "higher" or "lower" than those of another. We believe, for example, that Christian ethical ideals are nobler than those of the savage races of central Africa. Probably most of us would think that the Chinese moral standards are higher than those of the inhabitants of New Guinea. In short we habitually compare one civilization with another and judge the sets of ethical ideas to be found in them to be some better, some worse. The fact that such judgments are very difficult to make with any justice, and that they are frequently made on very superficial and prejudiced grounds, has no bearing on the question now at issue. The question is whether such judgments have any *meaning.* We habitually assume that they have.

But on the basis of ethical relativity they can have none whatever. For the relativist must hold that there is no *common* standard which can be applied to the various civilizations judged. Any such comparison of moral standards implies the existence of some superior standard which is applicable to both. And the existence of any such standard is precisely what the relativist denies. According to him the

Christian standard is applicable only to Christians, the Chinese standard only to Chinese, the New Guinea standard only to the inhabitants of New Guinea.

What is true of comparisons between the moral standards of different races will also be true of comparisons between those of different ages. It is not unusual to ask such questions as whether the standard of our own day is superior to that which existed among our ancestors five hundred years ago. And when we remember that our ancestors employed slaves, practiced barbaric physical tortures, and burnt people alive, we may be inclined to think that it is. At any rate we assume that the question is one which has meaning and is capable of rational discussion. But if the ethical relativist is right, whatever we assert on this subject must be totally meaningless. For here again there is no common standard which could form the basis of any such judgments.

This in its turn implies that the whole notion of moral *progress* is a sheer delusion. Progress means an advance from lower to higher, from worse to better. But on the basis of ethical relativity it has no meaning to say that the standards of this age are better (or worse) than those of a previous age. For there is no common standard by which both can be measured. Thus it is nonsense to say that the morality of the New Testament is higher than that of the Old. And Jesus Christ, if he imagined that he was introducing into the world a higher ethical standard than existed before his time, was merely deluded. . . .

I come now to a second point. Up to the present I have allowed it to be taken tacitly for granted that, though judgments comparing different races and ages in respect of the worth of their moral codes are impossible for the ethical relativist, yet judgments of comparison between individuals living within the same social group would be quite possible. For individuals living within the same social group would presumably be subject to the same moral code, that of their group, and this would therefore constitute, as between these individuals, a common standard by which they could both be measured. We have not here, as we had in the other case, the difficulty of the absence of any common standard of comparison. It should therefore be possible for the ethical relativist to say quite meaningfully that President Lincoln was a better man than some criminal or moral imbecile of his own time and country, or that Jesus was a better man than Judas Iscariot.

But is even this minimum of moral judgment really possible on relativist grounds? It seems to me that it is not. For when once the whole of humanity is abandoned as the area covered by a single moral standard, what smaller areas are to be adopted as the *loci* of different standards? Where are we to draw the lines of demarcation? We can split up humanity, perhaps,—though the procedure will be very arbitrary—into races, races into nations, nations into tribes, tribes into families, families into individuals. Where are we going to draw the *moral* boundaries? Does the *locus* of a particular moral standard reside in a race, a nation, a tribe, a family, or an individual? Perhaps the blessed phrase "social group" will be dragged in to save the situation. Each such group, we shall be told, has its own moral code which is, for it, right. But what *is* a "group"? Can any one define it or give its boundaries? This is the seat of that ambiguity in the theory of ethical relativity to which reference was made on an earlier page.

The difficulty is not, as might be thought, merely an academic difficulty of logical definition. If that were all, I should not press the point. But the ambiguity has practical consequences which are disastrous for morality. No one is likely to say that moral codes are confined within the arbitrary limits of the geographical divisions of countries. Nor are the notions of race, nation, or political state likely to help us. To bring out the essentially practical character of the difficulty let us put it in the form of concrete questions. Does the American nation constitute a "group" having a single moral standard? Or does the standard of what I ought to do change continuously as I cross the continent in a railway train? Do different States of the Union have different moral codes? Perhaps every town and village has its own peculiar standard. This may at first sight seem reasonable enough. "In Rome do as Rome does" may seem as good a rule in morals as it is in etiquette. But can we stop there? Within the village are numerous cliques having their own set of ideas. Why should not each of these claim to be bound only by its own special and peculiar moral standards? And if it comes to that, why should not the gangsters of Chicago claim to constitute a group having its own morality, so that its murders and debaucheries must be viewed as "right" by the only standard which can legitimately be applied to it? And if it be answered that the nation will not tolerate this, that may be so. But this is to put the foundation of right simply in the superior force of the majority. In that case whoever is stronger will be right, however monstrous his ideas and actions. And if we cannot deny to any set of people the right to have its own morality, is it not clear that, in the end, we cannot even deny this right to the individual? Every individual man and woman can put up, on this view, an irrefutable claim to be judged by no standard except his or her own.

If these arguments are valid, the ethical relativist cannot really maintain that there is anywhere to be found a moral standard binding upon anybody against his will. And he cannot maintain that, even within the social group, there is a common standard as between individuals. And if that is so, then even judgments to the effect that one man is morally better than another become meaningless. All moral valuation thus vanishes. There is nothing to prevent each man from being a rule unto himself. The result will be moral chaos and the collapse of all effective standards. . . .

But even if we assume that the difficulty about defining moral groups has been surmounted, a further difficulty presents itself. Suppose that we have now definitely decided what are the exact boundaries of the social group within which a moral standard is to be operative. And we will assume—as is invariably done by relativists themselves—that this group is to be some actually existing social community such as a tribe or nation. How are we to know, even then, what actually *is* the moral standard within that group? How is anyone to know? How is even a member of the group to know? For there are certain to be within the group—at least this will be true among advanced peoples—wide differences of opinion as to what is right, what wrong. Whose opinion, then, is to be taken as representing *the* moral standard of the group? Either we must take the opinion of the majority within the group, or the opinion of some minority. If we rely upon the ideas of the majority, the results will be disastrous. Wherever there is found among a people a small band of select spirits, or perhaps one man, working for the establishment of higher and nobler ideals than those commonly accepted by the group, we shall be compelled to hold that, for that people at that time, the majority are right, and that the reformers are wrong and are preaching what is immoral. We shall have to maintain, for example, that Jesus was preaching immoral doctrines to the Jews. Moral goodness will have to be equated always with the mediocre and sometimes with the definitely base and ignoble. If on the other hand we said that the moral standard of the group is to be identified with the moral opinions of some minority, then what minority is this to be? We cannot answer that it is to be the minority composed of the best and most enlightened individuals of the group. This would involve us in a palpably vicious circle. For by what standard are these individuals to be judged the best and the most enlightened? There is no principle by which we could select the right minority. And therefore we should have to consider every minority as good as every other. And this means that we should have no logical right whatever to resist the claim of the gangsters of Chicago—if such a claim were made—that their practices represent the highest standards of American morality. It means in the end that every individual is to be bound by no standard save his own.

The ethical relativists are great empiricists. *What* is the actual moral standard of any group can only be discovered, they tell us, by an examination on the ground of the moral opinions and customs of that group. But will they tell us how they propose to decide, when they get to the ground, which of the many moral opinions they are sure to find there is *the* right one in that group? To some extent they will be able to do this for the Melanesian Islanders—from whom apparently all lessons in the nature of morality are in future to be taken. But it is certain that they cannot do it for advanced peoples whose members have learnt to think for themselves and to entertain among themselves a wide variety of opinions. They cannot do it unless they accept the calamitous view that the ethical opinion of the majority is always right. We are left therefore once more with the conclusion that, even within a particular social group, anybody's moral opinion is as good as anybody else's, and that every man is entitled to be judged by his own standards.

Finally, not only is ethical relativity disastrous in its consequences for moral theory. It cannot be doubted that it must tend to be equally disastrous in its impact upon practical conduct. If men come really to believe that one moral standard is as good as another, they will conclude that their own moral standard has nothing special to recommend it. They might as well then slip down to some lower and easier standard. It is true that, for a time, it may be possible to hold one view in theory and to act practically upon another. But ideas, even philosophical ideas, are not so ineffectual that they can remain for ever idle in the upper chambers of the intellect. In the end they seep down to the level of practice. They get themselves acted on.

HOW SHOULD WE BEHAVE?

23. *The Morality Trap*

Harry Browne

Harry Browne (1933–   ) is an ardent supporter of free enterprise and the author of several books on finance and investment.

I. THE MORALITY TRAP

The Morality Trap is the belief that you must obey a moral code created by someone else.

This trap is a variation of the Identity Trap in that it leads you to try to be something other than yourself. It's an easy trap to get caught in and an easy way to lose your freedom.

Morality is a powerful word. Perhaps even more powerful is the word *immoral.* In an attempt to avoid being labeled *immoral,* many people allow themselves to be manipulated by others.

What Is Morality?   At the same time, the concept of morality is very vague. What is it? Where does it come from? What purpose does it serve? How is it determined?

My dictionary defines *morality* as "Moral quality or character; rightness or wrongness, as of an action." Well then, let's refer to the definition of *moral*, which is: "Related to, serving to teach, or in accordance with, the principles of right and wrong."

Now we're getting somewhere; all we need is a definition of *right*. And I suppose you can guess what *that* is: "In accordance with justice, law, morality, etc."[1]

Unfortunately, this definitional merry-go-round is typical of the common understanding of morality. You should do something because it's "right" —but *by what standard?*

It seems to me that there are three different kinds of morality. I call them *personal, universal,* and *absolute.* By looking at each of them, I think we can get a clearer idea of what morality is and how it can be useful in helping you to achieve your freedom.

Reprinted from *How I Found Freedom in an Unfree World.* Copyright © 1973 by Harry Browne, by permission of Collier Associates, P.O. Box 20149, West Palm Beach, FL 33416, U.S.A.

[1]*Webster's New World Dictionary of the American Language,* 1966 edition: World Publishing Company, New York.

Personal Morality. We've seen that you act in ways that you hope will bring the best consequences to you. And the "best consequences" are those that bring you happiness.

You always have to consider the consequences of your actions; they're the point of anything you do. However, any given act will undoubtedly cause *many* consequences. You may see that a particular action will produce a consequence you want, but you might also be aware that it could produce other consequences that you don't want. . . .

Since you're always seeking numerous different goals, you try to foresee the ways in which something immediately desirable might get in the way of other things that are ultimately more desirable. You try to consider more than just what's immediately in front of you. You're placing things in a broader context.

Obviously, you can't expect to foresee *all* the consequences of a given act, but you can try to see all the significant ones. In some cases, such as the bank-robbing example, there are obvious consequences that immediately rule out a proposed course of action.

In other cases, more subtle possibilities will be recognized after a few minutes' thought. But there will also be cases in which you won't be aware of the specific consequences until *after* you've acted and begun to experience them.

Code of Conduct. Because you can't foresee all the specific consequences of what you do, there's a need to have some generalized rules available that can help keep you out of situations that could be troublesome. Those rules can be valuable if they do two things: (1) steer you away from potential disasters; and (2) remind you of the things you must do to satisfy your most important long-term desires.

The basic question is: "How can I get something I want without hurting my chances for other things that are more important to me?"

It is this generalized, long-term attitude that underlies an individual's basic code of conduct. And when we speak of morality, I can't think of any other sensible reason to be concerned about the subject. Its purpose is to keep you aimed in the direction you most want to go.

Personal morality is an attempt to consider all the relevant consequences of your actions.

"Relevant" means those consequences that will affect *you*. How your actions affect others is only important insofar as that, in turn, affects you.

A personal morality is basic to your overall view of how you'll find happiness. It's so important that a later chapter will be devoted entirely to questions that can help you form such a morality for yourself.

And it's important that you form it yourself. No one else (including me) is qualified to tell you how to live. A realistic morality has to consider many personal factors: your emotional nature, abilities, strengths, weaknesses, and, most important, your goals.

Your code of conduct has to be consistent with your goals so that you don't do anything that would make those goals unattainable. A code devised by someone else will necessarily be based upon the goals *he* believes possible and desirable.

To be useful, a morality shouldn't include rules for every possible situation. It shouldn't be concerned with minor questions involving only immediate consequences. It's devised to prevent big problems for you and to keep you aimed toward the ultimate goals that mean the most to you. Moral questions are concerned only with matters that involve large consequences.

There's a difference, for instance, between investing three dollars in a movie that might prove to be a dud and investing your life savings in a risky business venture. There's also a difference between tasting a different food that's commonly eaten (such as snails) and sampling toadstools in the forest. The first might cause a stomachache; the second could poison you.

A useful morality will prevent you from doing things that might take years to correct, while keeping you aimed in the direction of the things that are most important to you.

And since such matters are an outgrowth of your own personal values, it's obvious that no one else can create your morality for you.

A *personal morality* is the attempt to consider all the relevant consequences of your actions. This is only one of three common types of moralities, however.

Universal Morality.   The second type is a morality that is meant to apply to everyone in the world. A *universal morality* is one that's supposed to bring happiness to anyone who uses it.

When you're exposed to the ideas of someone who has apparently done well with his own life, it's easy to conclude that he has all the final answers. His reasoning makes sense to you; he has results to show for his ideas. What further proof could you need to demonstrate that he knows how to live?

He probably *does* know how to live—*his* life. It would be foolish not to consider the ideas such a person offers. But it would also be foolish to expect that, as intelligent as he may be, he could have answers that apply to every life in the world.

His ideas have worked for him because he's been wise enough to develop ideas that are consistent with his own nature. He hasn't tried to live by the standards created by others; he's found his own. And that's vitally important.

You must do the same thing, too—if you want your code of conduct to work that well for you. Your rules have to consider everything that's unique about you—your emotions, your aptitudes, your weak points, your hopes and fears. . . .

A universal morality is a code of conduct that is presumed to bring happiness to anyone who uses it. I don't believe there can be such a thing. The differences between individuals are far too great to allow for anything but the most general kinds of rules.

Absolute Morality.   There's a third kind of morality. The first two are attempts to help you achieve happiness—one self-directed and the other coming from someone else. The third type is the opposite of this. An *absolute morality* is a set of rules to which an individual is expected to *surrender* his own happiness.

There are two main characteristics of an absolute morality:

1. It presumably comes from *an authority outside of the individual.* It comes from someone or somewhere more important than the individual himself.

2. It proposes that the individual should be "moral" *regardless of the consequences to himself.* In other words, doing what is "right" is more important than one's own happiness.

These two characteristics intertwine, so we'll consider them together.

Absolute morality is the most common type of morality, and it can be pretty intimidating. You can be made to appear "selfish," "whim-worshipping," "egotistic," "hedonistic," or "ruthless," if you merely assert that your own happiness is the most important thing in your life.

But what could be more important than your happiness? It's said that an authoritarian moral code is necessary to protect society. But who is society? Isn't it just a large group of people, each of whom have differing ideas concerning how one should live?

And if an individual is required to give up his own happiness, of what value is society to him?

It's also suggested that God commanded that we live by certain rules. But who can be sure he knows exactly when and how and what God said and what he meant? And even if that could be established once and for all, what would be the consequences to the individual if he acted otherwise? How do we know?

And if the code did come from God, it still had to be handled by human beings on its way to you. Whatever the absolute morality may be, you're relying upon someone else to vouch for its authority.

Suppose you use a holy book as your guide. I haven't yet seen one that doesn't have some apparent contradictions regarding conduct in it. Those contradictions may disappear with the proper interpretation; but who provides the interpretation? You'll do it yourself or you'll select someone to provide it for you. In either case, *you* have become the authority by making the choice.

There's no way someone else can become your authority; ultimately the decision will be yours in choosing the morality you'll live by—even if you choose to cite someone else (you've chosen) as the authority for your acts.

And there's no way you can ignore the consequences to yourself; a human being naturally acts in terms of consequences.

What happens, however, is that other people introduce consequences that they hope will influence you. They say that your "immoral" acts will: "prevent you from going to heaven"—or "cause other people to disapprove of you"—or "destroy society and cause chaos, and it will all be your fault."

Once again, however, it will be *you* deciding for yourself whether any of these consequences will result and whether any of them are important to you.

The absolute morality fails on its two important characteristics. Even if you choose to believe there's a higher authority, you are the authority who chooses what it is and what it is telling you to do. And since you'll always be considering consequences, even if you try to fix it so that you aren't, it's important to deliberately recognize the consequences and decide which ones are important to you. . . .

The Trap.   The Morality Trap is the belief that you must obey a moral code created by someone else. If you're acting in ways you hope will satisfy someone else's concept of what is moral, chances are you're using an ill-suited code of conduct—one that won't lead you to what you want and that may trap you in commitments and complications that can only cause you unhappiness. So in terms of the trap, *what* you do isn't as significant as *why* you do it.

You're in the trap if you hand a very important dollar to a beggar because "it's wrong to be selfish." Or if you continue to deal respectfully with someone who's made trouble for you because "to forgive is divine."

You're in the trap if you allow yourself to be drafted because "you have a duty to your country." Or if you prohibit drinking in your home because "it would weaken the moral fiber of society." Or if you send your children to Sunday school even though you aren't religious, because "you should give them a moral upbringing."

You might have very good reasons for any of these actions. But if you do them *only* in obedience to moral clichés, you're in the Morality Trap. . . .

Your Morality.   You are responsible for what happens to you (even if someone else offers to accept that responsibility), because you're the one who'll experience the consequences of your acts.

You are the one who decides what is right and what is wrong—no matter what meaning others may attach to those words. You don't have to obey blindly the dictates that you grew up with or that you hear around you now. Everything can be challenged, *should* be challenged, examined to determine it's relevance to you and what you want.

As you examine the teachings of others, you may find that some of it is very appropriate to you, but much of it may be meaningless or even harmful. The important thing is to carefully reappraise any moral precept that has been guiding your actions.

As you examine each of the rules you've been living by, ask yourself:

—Is this rule something that *others* have devised on behalf of "society" to restrain individuals? Or have *I* devised it in order to make my life better for myself?

—Am I acting by an old, just-happens-to-be-there morality? Or is it something I've personally determined from the knowledge of who I am and what I want?

—Are the rewards and punishments attached to the rules vague and intangible? Or do the rules point to specific happiness I can achieve or unhappiness I can avoid?

—Is it a morality I've accepted because "someone undoubtedly knows the reason for it"? Or is it one I've created because *I* know the reason for it?

—Is it a morality that's currently "in style" and accepted by all those around me? Or is it a morality specifically tailored to *my* style?

—Is it a morality that's aimed *at* me and *against* my self-interest? Or is it a morality that's *for* me and comes *from* me?

All the answers must come from you—not from a book or a lecture or a sermon. To assume that someone once wrote down the final answers for your morality is to assume that the writer stopped growing the day he wrote the code. Don't treat him unfairly by thinking that he couldn't have discovered more and increased his own understanding after he'd written the code. And don't forget that what he wrote was based upon what *he* saw.

No matter how you approach the matter, *you* are the sovereign authority who makes the final decisions. The more you realize that, the more your decisions will fit realistically with your own life. . . .

II. THE UNSELFISHNESS TRAP

The Unselfishness Trap is the belief that you must put the happiness of others ahead of your own.

Unselfishness is a very popular ideal, one that's been honored throughout recorded history. Wherever you turn, you find encouragement to put the happiness of others ahead of your own—to do what's best for the world, not for yourself.

If the ideal is sound, there must be something unworthy in seeking to live your life as you want to live it.

So perhaps we should look more closely at the subject—to see if the ideal *is* sound. For if you attempt to be free, we can assume that someone's going to consider that to be selfish.

We saw in Chapter 2 that each person always acts in ways he believes will make him feel good or will remove discomfort from his life. Because everyone is different from everyone else, each individual goes about it in his own way.

One man devotes his life to helping the poor. Another one lies and steals. Still another person tries to create better products and services for which he hopes to be paid handsomely. One woman devotes herself to her husband and children. Another one seeks a career as a singer.

In every case, the ultimate motivation has been the same. Each person is doing what *he* believes will assure his happiness. What varies between them is the *means* each has chosen to gain his happiness.

We could divide them into two groups labeled "selfish" and "unselfish," but I don't think that would prove anything. For the thief and the humanitarian each have the same motive—to do what he believes will make him feel good.

In fact, we can't avoid a very significant conclusion: *Everyone is selfish.* Selfishness isn't really an issue, because everyone selfishly seeks his own happiness.

What we need to examine, however, are the means various people choose to achieve their happiness. Unfortunately, some people oversimplify the matter by assuming that there are only two basic means: sacrifice yourself for others or make them sacrifice for you. Happily, there's a third way that can produce better consequences than either of those two.

A Better World?   Let's look first at the ideal of living for the benefit of others. It's often said that it would be a better world if everyone were unselfish. But would it be?

If it were somehow possible for everyone to give up his own happiness, what would be the result? Let's carry it to its logical conclusion and see what we find.

To visualize it, let's imagine that happiness is symbolized by a big red rubber ball. I have the ball in my hands—meaning that I hold the ability to be happy. But since I'm not going to be selfish, I quickly pass the ball to you. I've given up my happiness for you.

What will you do? Since you're not selfish either, you won't keep the ball; you'll quickly pass it on to your next-door neighbor. But he doesn't want to be selfish either, so he passes it to his wife, who likewise gives it to her children.

The children have been taught the virtue of unselfishness, so they pass it to playmates, who pass it to parents, who pass it to neighbors, and on and on and on.

I think we can stop the analogy at this point and ask what's been accomplished by all this effort. Who's better off for these demonstrations of pure unselfishness?

How would it be a better world if everyone acted that way? Whom would we be unselfish for? There would have to be a selfish person who would receive, accept, and enjoy the benefits of our unselfishness for there to be any purpose to it. But that selfish person (the object of our generosity) would be living by lower standards than we do.

For a more practical example, what is achieved by the parent who "sacrifices" himself for his children, who in turn are expected to sacrifice themselves for *their* children, etc.? The unselfishness concept is a merry-go-round that has no ultimate purpose. No one's self-interest is enhanced by the continual relaying of gifts from one person to another to another.

Perhaps most people have never carried the concept of unselfishness to this logical conclusion. If they did, they might reconsider their pleas for an unselfish world.

Negative Choices.   But, unfortunately, the pleas continue, and they're a very real part of your life. In seeking your own freedom and happiness, you have to deal with those who tell you that you shouldn't put yourself first. That creates a situation in which you're pressured to act negatively—to put aside your plans and desires in order to avoid the condemnation of others.

As I've said before, one of the characteristics of a free man is that he's usually choosing positively—deciding which of several alternatives would make him the happiest; while the average person, most of the time, is choosing which of two or three alternatives will cause him the least discomfort.

When the reason for your actions is to avoid being called "selfish" you're making a negative decision and thereby restricting the possibilities for your own happiness.

You're in the Unselfishness Trap if you regretfully pay for your aunt's surgery with the money you'd saved for a new car, or if you sadly give up the vacation you'd looked forward to in order to help a sick neighbor.

You're in the trap if you feel you're *required* to give part of your income to the poor, or if you think that your country, community, or family has first claim on your time, energy, or money.

You're in the Unselfishness Trap any time you make negative choices that are designed to avoid being called "selfish."

It isn't that no one else is important. You might have a self-interest in someone's well-being, and giving a gift can be a gratifying expression of the affection you feel for him. But you're in the trap if you do such things in order to appear unselfish.

Helping Others.   There *is* an understandable urge to give to those who are important and close to you. However, that leads many people to think that indiscriminate giving is the key to one's own happiness. They say that the way to be happy is to make others happy; get your glow by basking in the glow you've created for someone else.

It's important to identify that as a personal opinion. If someone says that giving is the key to happiness, isn't he saying that's the key to *his* happiness?

I think we can carry the question further, however, and determine how efficient such a policy might be. The suggestion to be a giver presupposes that you're able to judge what will make someone else happy. And experience has taught me to be a bit humble about assuming what makes others happy.

My landlady once brought me a piece of her freshly baked cake because she wanted to do me a favor. Unfortunately, it happened to be a kind of cake that was distasteful to me. I won't try to describe the various ways I tried to get the cake plate back to her without being confronted with a request for my judgment of her cake. It's sufficient to say that her well-intentioned favor interfered with my own plans.

And now, whenever I'm sure I know what someone else "needs," I remember that incident and back off a little. There's no way that one person can read the mind of another to know all his plans, goals, and tastes.

You may know a great deal about the desires of your intimate friends. But *indiscriminate* gift-giving and favor-doing is usually a waste of resources—or, worse, it can upset the well-laid plans of the receiver.

When you give to someone else, you might provide something he values—but probably not the thing he considers most important. If you expend those resources for *yourself,* you automatically devote them to what you consider to be most important. The time or money you've spent will most likely create more happiness that way.

If your purpose is to make someone happy, you're more apt to succeed if you make yourself the object. You'll never know another person more than a fraction as well as you can know yourself.

Do you want to make someone happy? Go to it—use your talents and your insight and benevolence to bestow riches of happiness upon the one person you understand well enough to do it efficiently—yourself. I guarantee that you'll get more genuine appreciation from yourself than from anyone else.

Give to you.

Support your local self.

Alternatives.   As I indicated earlier in this chapter, it's too often assumed that there are only two alternatives: (1) sacrifice your interests for the benefit of others; or (2) make others sacrifice their interests for you. If nothing else were possible, it would indeed be a grim world.

Fortunately, there's more to the world than that. Because desires vary from person to person, it's possible to create exchanges between individuals in which both parties benefit.

For example, if you buy a house, you do so because you'd rather have the house than the money involved. But the seller's desire is different—he'd rather have the money than the house. When the sale is completed, each of you has received something of greater value than what you gave up—otherwise you wouldn't have entered the exchange. Who, then, has had to sacrifice for the other?

In the same way, your daily life is made up of dozens of such exchanges— small and large transactions in which each party gets something he values more than what he gives up. The exchange doesn't have to involve money; you may be spending time, attention, or effort in exchange for something you value.

Mutually beneficial relationships are possible when desires are compatible. Sometimes the desires are the same—like going to a movie together. Sometimes the desires are different—like trading your money for someone's house. In either case, it's the *compatibility* of the desires that makes the exchange possible.

No sacrifice is necessary when desires are compatible. So it makes sense to seek out people with whom you can have mutually beneficial relationships.

Often the "unselfishness" issue arises only because two people with nothing in common are trying to get along together—such as a man who likes bowling and hates opera married to a woman whose tastes are the opposite. If they're to do things together, one must "sacrifice" his pleasure for the other. So each might try to encourage the other to be "unselfish."

If they were compatible, the issue wouldn't arise because each would be pleasing the other by doing what was in his own self-interest.

An efficiently selfish person *is* sensitive to the needs and desires of others. But he doesn't consider those desires to be demands upon him. Rather, he sees them as *opportunities*—potential exchanges that might be beneficial to him. He identifies desires in others so that he can decide if exchanges with them will help him get what he wants.

He doesn't sacrifice himself for others, nor does he expect others to be sacrificed for him. He takes the third alternative—he finds relationships that are mutually beneficial so that no sacrifice is required.

Please Yourself.   Everyone is selfish; everyone is doing what he believes will make himself happier. The recognition of that can take most of the sting out of accusations that you're being "selfish." Why should you feel guilty for seeking your own happiness when that's what everyone else is doing, too?

The demand that you be unselfish can be motivated by any number of reasons: that you'd help create a better world, that you have a moral obligation to be unselfish, that you give up your happiness to the selfishness of someone else, or that the person demanding it has just never thought it out.

Whatever the reason, you're not likely to convince such a person to stop his demands. But it will create much less pressure on you if you realize that it's *his* selfish reason. And you can eliminate the problem entirely by looking for more compatible companions.

To find constant, profound happiness requires that you be free to seek the gratification of your own desires. It means making positive choices.

If you slip into the Unselfishness Trap, you'll spend a good part of your time making negative choices—trying to avoid the censure of those who tell you not to think of yourself. You won't have time to be free.

If someone finds happiness by doing "good works" for others, let him. That doesn't mean that's the best way for you to find happiness.

And when someone accuses you of being selfish, just remember that he's only upset because you aren't doing what *he* selfishly wants you to do.

24. Utilitarianism

Jeremy Bentham

Jeremy Bentham (1748–1832), an English philosopher and political theorist, developed the utilitarian theory as a basis for political and legal reform.

OF THE PRINCIPLE OF UTILITY

I. Nature has placed mankind under the governance of two sovereign masters, *pain* and *pleasure.* It is for them alone to point out what we ought to do, as well as to determine what we shall do. On the one hand the standard of right and wrong, on the other the chain of causes and effects are fastened to their throne. They govern us in all we do, in all we say, in all we think: every effort we can make to throw off our subjection, will serve but to demonstrate and confirm it. In words a man may pretend to abjure their empire: but in reality he will remain subject to it all the while. The *principle of utility* recognises this subjection, and assumes it for the foundation of that system, the object of which is to rear the fabric of felicity by the hands of reason and of law. Systems which attempt to question it deal in sounds instead of sense, in caprice instead of reason, in darkness instead of light.

But enough of metaphor and declamation: it is not by such means that moral science is to be improved.

II. The principle of utility is the foundation of the present work: it will be proper therefore at the outset to give an explicit and determinate account of what is meant by it. By the principle of utility is meant that principle which approves or disapproves of every action whatsoever, according to the tendency which it appears to have to augment or diminish the happiness of the party whose interest is in question: or, what is the same thing in other words, to promote or to oppose that happiness. I say of every action whatsoever; and therefore not only of every action of a private individual, but of every measure of government.

III. By utility is meant that property in any object, whereby it tends to produce benefit, advantage, pleasure, good, or happiness (all this in the present case comes to the same thing) or (what comes again to the same thing) to prevent the happening of mischief, pain, evil, or unhappiness to the party whose interest is considered: if that party be the community in general, then the happiness of the community: if a particular individual, then the happiness of that individual.

IV. The interest of the community is one of the most general expressions that can occur in the phraseology of morals: no wonder that the meaning of it is often lost. When it has a meaning, it is this. The community is a fictitious *body,* composed

From Jeremy Bentham, *An Introduction to the Principles of Morals and Legislation.* First published in 1789.

of the individual persons who are considered as constituting as it were its *members.* The interest of the community then is, what?—the sum of the interests of the several members who compose it.

V. It is in vain to talk of the interest of the community, without understanding what is the interest of the individual. A thing is said to promote the interest, or to be *for* the interest, of an individual, when it tends to add to the sum total of his pleasures: or, what comes to the same thing, to diminish the sum total of his pains.

VI. An action then may be said to be comformable to the principle of utility, or, for shortness sake, to utility (meaning with respect to the community at large), when the tendency it has to augment the happiness of the community is greater than any it has to diminish it.

VII. A measure of government (which is but a particular kind of action, performed by a particular person or persons) may be said to be conformable to or dictated by the principle of utility, when in like manner the tendency which it has to augment the happiness of the community is greater than any which it has to diminish it.

VIII. When an action, or in particular a measure of government is supposed by a man to be conformable to the principle of utility, it may be convenient, for the purposes of discourse, to imagine a kind of law or dictate, called a law or dictate of utility: and to speak of the action in question, as being conformable to such law or dictate.

IX. A man may be said to be a partisan of the principle of utility, when the approbation or disapprobation he annexes to any action, or to any measure, is determined by and proportioned to the tendency which he conceives it to have to augment or to diminish the happiness of the community: or in other words, to its conformity or unconformity to the laws or dictates of utility.

X. Of an action that is conformable to the principle of utility one may always say either that it is one that ought to be done, or at least that it is not one that ought not to be done. One may say also, that it is right it should be done; at least that it is not wrong it should be done: that it is a right action; at least that it is not a wrong action. When thus interpreted, the words *ought,* and *right* and *wrong,* and others of that stamp, have a meaning: when otherwise, they have none.

XI. Has the rectitude of this principle been ever formally contested? It should seem that it had, by those who have not known what they have been meaning. Is it susceptible of any direct proof? it should seem not: for that which is used to prove everything else, cannot itself be proved: a chain of proofs must have their commencement somewhere. To give such proof is as impossible as it is needless.

XII. Not that there is or ever has been that human creature breathing, however stupid or perverse, who has not on many, perhaps on most occasions of his life, deferred to it. By the natural constitution of the human frame, on most occasions of their lives men in general embrace this principle, without thinking of it: if not for the ordering of their own actions, yet for the trying of their own actions, as well as of those of other men. There have been, at the same time, not many, perhaps, even of the most intelligent, who have been disposed to embrace it purely and without reserve. There are even few who have not taken some occasion or other to quarrel with it, either on account of their not understanding always how to apply it, or on account of some prejudice or other which they were afraid to examine into, or could not bear to part with. For such is the stuff that man is made of: in principle and in practice, in a right track and in a wrong one, the rarest of all human qualities is consistency.

XIII. When a man attempts to combat the principle of utility, it is with reasons drawn, without his being aware of it, from that very principle itself. His arguments, if they prove any thing, prove not that the principle is *wrong*, but that, according to the applications he supposes to be made of it, it is *misapplied.* Is it possible for a man to move the earth? Yes, but he must first find out another earth to stand upon.

OF PRINCIPLES ADVERSE TO THAT OF UTILITY

I. If the principle of utility be a right principle to be governed by, and that in all cases, it follows from what has been just observed, that whatever principle differs from it in any case must necessarily be a wrong one. To prove any other principle, therefore, to be a wrong one, there needs no more than just to show it to be what it is, a principle of which the dictates are in some point or other different from those of the principle of utility: to state it is to confute it.

II. A principle may be different from that of utility in two ways: 1. By being constantly opposed to it: this is the case with a principle which may be termed the principle of *asceticism.* 2. By being sometimes opposed to it, and sometimes not, as it may happen: this is the case with another, which may be termed the principle of *sympathy* and *antipathy.*

III. By the principle of asceticism I mean that principle, which, like the principle of utility, approves or disapproves of any action, according to the tendency which it appears to have to augment or diminish the happiness of the party whose interest is in question; but in an inverse manner: approving of actions in as far as they tend to diminish his happiness; disapproving of them in as far as they tend to augment it.

IV. It is evident that any one who reprobates any the least particle of pleasure, as such, from whatever source derived, is *pro tanto* a partisan of the principle of asceticism. It is only upon that principle, and not from the principle of utility, that the most abominable pleasure which the vilest of malefactors ever reaped from his crime would be to be reprobated, if it stood alone. The case is, that it never does stand alone; but is necessarily followed by such a quality of pain (or, what comes to the same thing, such a chance for a certain quantity of pain) that the pleasure in comparison of it, is as nothing: and this is the true and sole, but perfectly sufficient, reason for making it a ground for punishment. . . .

X. The principle of utility is capable of being consistently pursued; and it is but tautology to say, that the more consistently it is pursued, the better it must ever be for humankind. The principle of asceticism never was, nor ever can be, consistently pursued by any living creature. Let but one tenth part of the inhabitants of this earth pursue it consistently, and in a day's time they will have turned it into a hell.

XI. Among principles adverse to that of utility, that which at this day seems to have most influence in matters of government, is what may be called the principle of sympathy and antipathy. By the principle of sympathy and antipathy, I mean that principle which approves or disapproves of certain actions, not on account of their tending to augment the happiness, nor yet on account of their tending to diminish the happiness of the party whose interest is in question, but merely because a man finds himself disposed to approve or disapprove of them: holding up that approbation or disapprobation as a sufficient reason for itself, and disclaiming the necessity of looking out for any extrinsic ground. Thus far in the general department of morals: and in the particular department of politics, measuring out the quantum (as well as determining the ground) of punishment, by the degree of the disapprobation.

XII. It is manifest, that this is rather a principle in name than in reality: it is not a positive principle of itself, so much as a term employed to signify the negation of all principle. What one expects to find in a principle is something that points out some external consideration, as a means of warranting and guiding the internal sentiments of approbation and disapprobation: this expectation is but ill fulfilled by a proposition, which does neither more nor less than hold up each of those sentiments as a ground and standard for itself.

XIII. In looking over the catalogue of human actions (says a partisan of this principle) in order to determine which of them are to be marked with the seal of disapprobation, you need but to take counsel of your own feelings: whatever you find in yourself a propensity to condemn, is wrong for that very reason. For the same reason it is also meet for punishment: in what proportion it is adverse to utility, or whether it be adverse to utility at all, is a matter that makes no difference. In that same *proportion* also is it meet for punishment: if you hate much, punish much: if you hate little, punish little: punish as you hate. If you hate not at all, punish not at all; the fine feelings of the soul are not to be overborne and tyrannized by the harsh and rugged dictates of political utility. . . .

XV. It is manifest, that the dictates of this principle will frequently coincide with those of utility, though perhaps without intending any such thing. Probably more frequently than not: and hence it is that the business of penal justice is carried on upon that tolerable sort of footing upon which we see it carried on in common at this day. For what more natural or more general ground of hatred to a practice can there be, than the mischievousness of such practice? What all men are exposed to suffer by, all men will be disposed to hate. It is far yet, however, from being a constant ground: for when a man suffers, it is not always that he knows what it is he suffers by. A man may suffer grievously, for instance, by a new tax, without being able to trace up the cause of his sufferings to the injustice of some neighbour, who has eluded the payment of an old one.

XVI. The principle of sympathy and antipathy is more apt to err on the side of severity. It is for applying punishment in many cases which deserve none: in many cases which deserve some, it is for applying more than they deserve. There is no incident imaginable, be it ever so trivial, and so remote from mischief, from which this principle may not extract a ground of punishment. Any difference in taste: any difference in opinion: upon one subject as well as upon another. No disagreement so trifling which perseverance and altercation will not render serious. Each becomes in the other's eyes an enemy, and, if laws permit, a criminal. This is one of the circumstances by which the human race is distinguished (not much indeed to its advantage) from the brute creation. . . .

XIX. There are two things which are very apt to be confounded, but which it imports us carefully distinguish:—the motive or cause, which, by operating on the mind of an individual, is productive of any act: and the ground or reason which warrants a legislator, or other bystander, in regarding that act with an eye of approbation. When the act happens, in the particular instance in question, to be productive of effects which we approve of, much more if we happen to observe that the same motive may frequently be productive, in other instances, of the like effects, we are apt to transfer our approbation to the motive itself, and to assume, as the just ground for the approbation we bestow on the act, the circumstance of its originating from that motive. It is in this way that the sentiment of antipathy has often been considered as a just ground of action. Antipathy, for instance, in such or such a case, is the cause of an action which is attended with good effects: but this does not make it a right ground of action in that case, any more than in any other. Still farther. Not only the effects are good, but the agent sees beforehand that they will be so. This may make the action indeed a perfect right action: but it does not make antipathy a right ground of action. For the same sentiment of antipathy, if implicitly deferred to, may be, and very frequently is, productive of the very worst effects. Antipathy, therefore, can never be a right ground of action. No more, therefore, can resentment, which, as will be seen more particularly hereafter, is but a modification of antipathy. The only right ground of action, that can possibly subsist, is, after all, the consideration of utility, which, if it is a right principle of action, and of approbation, in any one case, is so in every other. Other principles in abundance, that is, other motives, may be the reasons why such and such an act *has* been done: that is, the reasons or causes of its being done: but it is this alone that can be the reason why it might or ought to have been done. Antipathy or resentment requires always to be regulated, to prevent its doing mischief: to be regulated by what? always by the principle of utility. The principle of utility neither requires nor admits of any other regulator than itself.

Value of a Lot of Pleasure or Pain, How to Be Measured

I. Pleasures then, and the avoidance of pains, are the *ends* which the legislator has in view: it behooves him therefore to understand their *value*. Pleasures and pains are the *instruments* he has to work with: it behooves him therefore to understand their force, which is again, in other words, their value.

II. To a person considered *by himself*, the value of a pleasure or pain considered *by itself*, will be greater or less, according to the four following circumstances:

1. Its *intensity*.
2. Its *duration*.
3. Its *certainty* or *uncertainty*.
4. Its *propinquity* or *remoteness*.

III. These are the circumstances which are to be considered in estimating a pleasure or a pain considered each of them by itself. But when the value of any pleasure or pain is considered for the purpose of estimating the tendency of any *act* by which it is produced, there are two other circumstances to be taken into the account; these are,

5. Its *fecundity*, or the chance it has of being followed by sensations of the *same* kind: that is, pleasures, if it be a pleasure: pains, if it be a pain.
6. Its *purity*, or the chance it has of *not* being followed by sensations of the *opposite* kind: that is, pains, if it be a pleasure: pleasures, if it be a pain.

These two last, however, are in strictness scarcely to be deemed properties of the pleasure or the pain itself; they are not, therefore, in strictness to be taken into the account of the value of that pleasure or that pain. They are in strictness to be deemed properties only of the act, or other event, by which such pleasure or pain has been produced; and accordingly are only to be taken into the account of the tendency of such act or such event.

IV. To a *number* of persons, with reference to each of whom the value of a pleasure or a pain is considered, it will be greater or less, according to seven circumstances: to wit, the six preceding ones; *viz.*

1. Its *intensity*.
2. Its *duration*.
3. Its *certainty* or *uncertainty*.
4. Its *propinquity* or *remoteness*.
5. Its *fecundity*.
6. Its *purity*.

And one other; to wit:

7. Its *extent*, that is, the number of persons to whom it *extends;* or (in other words) who are affected by it.

V. To take an exact account then of the general tendency of any act, by which the interests of a community are affected, proceed as follows. Begin with any one person of those whose interests seem most immediately to be affected by it: and take an account.

1. Of the value of each distinguishable *pleasure* which appears to be produced by it in the *first* instance.

2. Of the value of each *pain* which appears to be produced by it in the *first* instance.

3. Of the value of each pleasure which appears to be produced by it *after* the first. This constitutes the *fecundity* of the first *pleasure* and the *impurity* of the first *pain.*

4. Of the value of each *pain* which appears to be produced by it after the first. This constitutes the *fecundity* of the first *pain,* and the *impurity* of the first *pleasure.*

5. Sum up all the values of all the *pleasures* on the one side, and those of all the pains on the other. The balance, if it be on the side of pleasure, will give the *good* tendency of the act upon the whole, with respect to the interests of that *individual* person: if on the side of pain, the *bad* tendency of it upon the whole.

6. Take an account of the *number* of persons whose interests appear to be concerned; and repeat the above process with respect to each. *Sum up* the numbers expressive of the degrees of *good* tendency, which the act has, with respect to each individual, in regard to whom the tendency of it is *good* upon the whole: do this again with respect to each individual, in regard to whom the tendency of it is *good* upon the whole: do this again with respect to each individual, in regard to whom the tendency of it is *bad* upon the whole. Take the *balance;* which, if on the side of *pleasure,* will give the general *good tendency* of the act, with respect to the total number or community of individuals concerned; if on the side of pain, the general *evil tendency,* with respect to the same community.

VI. It is not to be expected that this process should be strictly pursued previously to every moral judgment, or to every legislative or judicial operation. It may, however, be always kept in view: and as near as the process actually pursued on these occasions approaches to it, so near will such process approach to the character of an exact one.

VII. The same process is alike applicable to pleasure and pain, in whatever shape they appear: and by whatever denomination they are distinguished: to pleasure, whether it be called *good* (which is properly the cause or instrument of pleasure) or *profit* (which is distant pleasure, or the cause or instrument of distant pleasure), or *convenience,* or *advantage, benefit, emolument, happiness,* and so forth:

to pain, whether it be called *evil* (which corresponds to *good*), or *mischief,* or *inconvenience,* or *disadvantage,* or *loss,* or *unhappiness,* and so forth.

VIII. Nor is this a novel and unwarranted, any more than it is a useless theory. In all this there is nothing but what the practice of mankind, wheresoever they have a clear view of their own interest, is perfectly conformable to. An article of property, an estate in land, for instance, is valuable, on what account? On account of the pleasures of all kinds which it enables a man to produce, and what comes to the same thing the pains of all kinds which it enables him to avert. But the value of such an article of property is universally understood to rise or fall according to the length or shortness of the time which a man has in it: the certainty or uncertainty of its coming into possession: and the nearness or remoteness of the time at which, if at all, it is to come into possession. As to the *intensity* of the pleasures which a man may derive from it, this is never thought of, because it depends upon the use which each particular person may come to make of it; which cannot be estimated till the particular pleasures he may come to derive from it, or the particular pains he may come to exclude by means of it, are brought to view. For the same reason, neither does he think of the *fecundity* or *purity* of those pleasures.

Thus much for pleasure and pain, happiness and unhappiness, in *general.*

25. The Deep Beauty of the Golden Rule

R. M. MacIver

Robert M. MacIver (1882–1970) was a prominent sociologist and political theorist who maintained a strong interest in a number of philosophical issues.

The subject that learned men call ethics is a wasteland on the philosophical map. Thousands of books have been written on this matter, learned books and popular books, books that argue and books that exhort. Most of them are empty and nearly all are vain. Some claim that pleasure is *the* good; some prefer the elusive and more enticing name of happiness; others reject such principles and speak of equally elusive goals such as self-fulfillment. Others claim that *the* good is to be found in looking away from the self, in devotion to the whole—which whole? in the service of God—whose God?—even in the service of the State—who prescribes the service? Here indeed, if anywhere, after listening to the many words of many apostles, one goes out by the same door as one went in.

The reason is simple. You say: "This is the way you should behave." But I say: "No, that is not the way." You say: "This is right." But I say: "No, that is wrong, and this is right." You appeal to experience. I appeal to experience against you. You appeal to authority: it is not mine. What is left? If you are strong, you can punish me for behaving my way. But does that prove anything except that you are stronger than I? Does it prove the absurd dogma that might makes right? Is the slavemaster right because he owns the whip, or Torquemada because he can send his heretics to the flames?

From this impasse no system of ethical rules has been able to deliver itself. How can ethics lay down final principles of behavior that are not your values against mine, your group's values against my group's?

Which, by the way, does not mean that your rules are any less valid for you because they are not valid for me. Only a person of shallow nature and autocratic leanings would draw that conclusion. For the sake of your integrity you must hold to your own values, no matter how much others reject them. Without *your* values you are nothing. True, you should search them and test them and learn by *your* experience and gain wisdom where you can. Your values are your guides through life but you need to use your own eyes. If I have different guides I shall go

Selected excerpts from pages 39–47 from *Moral Principles of Action (Science of Culture Series,* Vol 3) by Ruth Nanda Anshen, editor. Copyright 1952 by Harper & Row, Publishers, Inc. Copyright renewed (c) 1980 by Ruth Nanda Anshen. Reprinted by permission of Harper Collins Publishers, Inc.

another way. So far as we diverge, values are relative as between you and me. But your values cannot be relative for you or mine for me.

That is not here the issue. It is that the relativity of values between you and me, between your group and my group, your sect and my sect, makes futile nearly all learned disquisitions about the first principles of ethics.

By ethics I mean the philosophy of how men should behave in their relations to one another. I am talking about philosophy, not about religion. When you have a creed, you can derive from it principles of ethics. Philosophy cannot begin with a creed, but only with reasoning about the nature of things. It cannot therefore presume that the values of other men are less to be regarded than the values of the proponent. If it does, it is not philosophy but dogma, dogma that is the enemy of philosophy, the kind of dogma that has been the source of endless tyranny and repression.

Can it be a philosophy worth the name that makes a universal of your values and thus rules mine out of existence, where they differ from yours?

How can reasoning decide between my values and yours? Values do not claim truth in any scientific sense; instead they claim validity, rightness. They do not declare what is so but what *should* be so. I cling to my values, you to yours. Your values, some of them, do not hold for me; some of them may be repulsive to me; some of them may threaten me. What then? To what court of reason shall we appeal? To what court that you and I both accept is there any appeal?

The lack of any court is the final *fact* about final values. It is a fundamental fact. It is a terrifying fact. It is also a strangely challenging fact. It gives man his lonely autonomy, his true responsibility. If he has anything that partakes of the quality of a God it comes from this fact. Man has more than the choice to obey or disobey. If he accepts authority he also chooses the authority he accepts. He is responsible not only to others but, more deeply, to himself.

Does all this mean that a universal ethical principle, applicable alike to me and you, even where our values diverge, is impossible? That there is no rule to go by, based on reason itself, in this world of irreconcilable valuations?

There is no rule that can prescribe both my values and yours or decide between them. There is one universal rule, and one only, that can be laid down, on ethical grounds—that is, apart from the creeds of particular religions and apart from the ways of the tribe that falsely and arrogantly universalize themselves.

Do to others as you would have them do to you. This is the only rule that stands by itself in the light of its own reason, the only rule that can stand by itself in the naked, warring universe, in the face of the contending values of men and groups.

What makes it so? Let us first observe that the universal herein laid down is one of procedure. It prescribes a mode of behaving, not a goal of action. On the level of goals, of *final* values, there is irreconcilable conflict. One rule prescribes humility, another pride; one prescribes abstinence, another commends the fleshpots; and so forth through endless variations. All of us wish that *our* principle could be universal; most of us believe that it *should* be, that our *ought* ought to be all men's *ought*, but since we differ there can be, on this level, no possible agreement.

When we want to make our ethical principle prevail we try to persuade others, to "convert" them. Some may freely respond, if their deeper values are near enough to ours. Others will certainly resist and some will seek to persuade us in turn—why shouldn't they? Then we can go no further except by resort to force and fraud. We can, if we are strong, dominate some and we can bribe others. We compromise our own values in doing so and we do not in the end succeed; even if we were masters of the whole world we could never succeed in making our principle universal. We could only make it falsely tyrannous.

So if we look for a principle in the name of which we can appeal to all men, one to which their reason can respond in spite of their differences, we must follow another road. When we try to make our values prevail over those cherished by others, we attack their values, their dynamic of behavior, their living will. If we go far enough we assault their very being. For the will is simply valuation in action. Now the deep beauty of the golden rule is that instead of attacking the will that is in other men, it offers their will a new dimension. "Do as you *would* have others . . ." As *you* would will others to do. It bids you expand your vision, see yourself in new relationships. It bids you transcend your insulation, see yourself in the place of others, see others in your place. It bids you test your values or at least your way of pursuing them. If you would disapprove that another should treat you as you treat him, the situations being reversed, is not that a sign that, by the standard of your own values, you are mistreating him?

This principle obviously makes for a vastly greater harmony in the social scheme. At the same time it is the only universal of ethics that does not take sides with or contend with contending values. It contains no dogma. It bids everyone follow his own rule, as it would apply *apart* from the accident of his particular fortunes. It bids him enlarge his own rule, as it would apply whether he is up or whether he is down. It is an accident that you are up and I am down. In another situation you would be down and I would be up. That accident has nothing to do with my *final* values or with yours. You have numbers and force on your side. In another situation I would have the numbers and the force. All situations of power are temporary and precarious. Imagine then the situations reversed and that you had a more wonderful power than is at the command of the most powerful, the power to make the more powerful act toward you as you would want him to act. If power is your dream, then dream of a yet greater power—and act out the spirit of your dream.

But the conclusive argument is not in the terms of power. It goes far deeper, down to the great truth that power so often ignores and that so often in the end destroys it, the truth that when you maltreat others you detach yourself from them, from the understanding of them, from the understanding of yourself. You insulate yourself, you narrow your own values, you cut yourself off from that which you and they have in common. And this commonness is more enduring and more satisfying than what you possess in insulation. You separate yourself, and for all your power you weaken yourself. Which is why power and fear are such close companions.

This is the reason why the evil you do to another, you do also, in the end, to yourself. While if you and he refrain from doing evil, one to another—not to speak of the yet happier consequences, of doing positive good—this reciprocity of restraint from evil will redound to the good of both.

That makes a much longer story and we shall not here enter upon it. Our sole concern is to show that the golden rule is the *only* ethical principle, as already defined, that can have clear right of way everywhere in the kind of world we have inherited. It is the only principle that allows every man to follow his own intrinsic values while nevertheless it transforms the chaos of warring codes into a reasonably well-ordered universe.

Let us explain the last statement. What are a man's intrinsic values? Beyond his mere self-seeking every human being needs, and must find, some attachment to a large purpose. These attachments, in themselves and apart from the way he pursues them, are his intrinsic values. For some men they are centered in the family, the clan, the "class," the community, the nation, the "race." It is the warfare of their group-attachments that creates the deadliest disturbances of modern society. For some men the focus of attachment is found in the greater "cause," faith, the creed, the way of life. The conflict of these attachments also unlooses many evils on society and at some historical stages has brought about great devastation.

The greatest evils inflicted by man on man over the face of the earth are wrought not by the self-seekers, the pleasure lovers, or the merely amoral, but by the fervent devotees of ethical principles, those who are bound body and soul to some larger purpose, the nation, the "race," the "masses," the "brethren" whoever they may be. The faith they invoke, whatever it may be, is not large enough when it sets a frontier between the members and the non-members, the believers and the non-believers. In the heat of devotion to that larger but exclusive purpose there is bred the fanaticism that corrodes and finally destroys all that links man to the common humanity. In the name of the cause, they will torture and starve and trample under foot millions on millions of their fellowmen. In its name they will cultivate the blackest treachery. And if their methods fail, as fail in the end they must, they will be ready, as was Hitler, to destroy their own cause or their own people, the chosen ones, rather than accept the reality their blinded purpose denied.

How then can we say that the golden rule does not disqualify the intrinsic values of such people—even of people like Hitler or, say, Torquemada? In the name of his values Torquemada burned at the stake many persons who differed from their fellows mainly by being more courageous, honest, and faithful to their faith. What then were Torquemada's values? He was a servant of the Church and the Church was presumptively a servant of Jesus Christ. It was not the intrinsic values of his creed that moved him and his masters to reject the Christian golden rule. Let us concede they had some kind of devotion to religion. It was the distorted, fanatical way in which they pursued the dimmed values they cherished, it was not the values themselves, to which their inhumanity can be charged.

Let us take the case of Hitler. Apart from his passion for Germany, or the German "folk," he would have been of no account, for evil or for good. That passion of itself, that in his view intrinsic value, might have inspired great constructive service instead of destruction. It was the method he used, and not the values he sought to promote thereby, that led to ruin, his blind trust in the efficacy of ruthless might. Belonging to a "folk" that had been reduced in defeat from strength to humiliation, fed on false notions of history and responsive to grotesque fallacies about a "master race," he conceived the resurgence of Germany in the distorted light of his vindictive imagination. Had Hitler been a member of some small "folk," no more numerous, say, than the population of his native Austria, he might have cherished the same values with no less passion, but his aspirations would have taken a different form and would never have expressed themselves in horror and tragedy.

The golden rule says nothing against Hitler's mystic adoration of the German "race," against any man's intrinsic values. By "intrinsic values" we signify the goals, beyond mere self-seeking, that animate a human being. If your group, your nation, your "race," your church, is for you a primary attachment, continue to cherish it—give it all you have, if you are so minded. But do not use means that are repugnant to the standards according to which you would have others conduct themselves to you and your values. If your nation were a small one, would you not seethe with indignation if some large neighbor destroyed its independence? Where, then, is your personal integrity if, belonging instead to the large nation, you act to destroy the independence of a small one? You falsify your own values, in the longer run you do them injury, when you pursue them in ways that cannot abide the test of the golden rule.

It follows that while this first principle attacks no intrinsic values, no primary attachments of men to goods that reach beyond themselves, it nevertheless purifies every attachment, every creed, of its accidents, its irrelevancies, its excesses, its false reliance on power. It saves every human value from the corruption that comes from the arrogance of detachment and exclusiveness, from the shell of the kind of absolutism that imprisons its vitality.

At this point a word of caution is in order. The golden rule does not solve for us our ethical problems but offers only a way of approach. It does not prescribe our treatment of others but only the spirit in which we should treat them. It has no simple mechanical application and often enough is hard to apply—what general principle is not? It certainly does not bid us treat others as others *want* us to treat them—that would be an absurdity. The convicted criminal wants the judge to set him free. If the judge acts in the spirit of the golden rule, within the limits of the discretion permitted him as judge, he might instead reason somewhat as follows: "How would I feel the judge ought to treat *me* were I in this man's place? What could I— the man I am and yet somehow standing where this criminal stands—properly ask the judge to do for me, to me? In this spirit I shall assess his guilt and his punishment. In this spirit I shall give full consideration to the conditions under which he acted. I shall try to understand *him,* to do what I properly can for him, while at the same time I fulfill my judicial duty in protecting society against the dangers that arise if criminals such as he go free."

"Do to others as you would have others do to you." The disease to which all values are subject is the growth of a hard insulation. "I am right: I have the truth. If you differ from me, you are a heretic, you are in error. *Therefore* while you must allow me every liberty when you are in power I need not, in truth I ought not to, show any similar consideration for you." The barb of falsehood has already begun to vitiate the cherished value. While *you* are in power I advocate the equal rights of all creeds: when I am in power, I reject any such claim as ridiculous. This is the position taken by various brands of totalitarianism, and the communists in particular have made it a favorite technique in the process of gaining power, clamoring for rights they will use to destroy the rights of those who grant them. Religious groups have followed the same line. Roman Catholics, Calvinists, Lutherans, Presbyterians, and others have on occasion vociferously advocated religious liberty where they were in the minority, often to curb it where in turn they became dominant.

This gross inconsistency on the part of religious groups was flagrantly displayed in earlier centuries, but examples are still not infrequent. Here is one. *La Civilita Catholicâ*, a Jesuit organ published in Rome, has come out as follows:

"The Roman Catholic Church, convinced, through its divine prerogatives, of being the only true church, must demand the right for freedom for herself alone, because such a right can only be possessed by truth, never by error. As to other religions, the Church will certainly never draw the sword, but she will require that by legitimate means they shall not be allowed to propagate false doctrine. Consequently, in a state where the majority of the people are Catholic, the Church will require that legal existence be denied to error. . . . In some countries, Catholics will be obliged to ask full religious freedom for all, resigned at being forced to cohabitate where they alone should rightly be allowed to live. . . . The Church cannot blush for her own want of tolerance, as she asserts it in principle and applies it in practice."[1]

Since this statement has the merit of honesty it well illustrates the fundamental lack of rationality that lies behind all such violations of the golden rule. The argument runs: "Roman Catholics know they possess the truth; *therefore* they should not permit others to propagate error." By parity of reasoning why should not Protestants say—and indeed they have often said it—"We know we possess the truth; therefore we should not tolerate the errors of Roman Catholics." Why then should not atheists say: "We know we possess the truth; therefore we should not tolerate the errors of dogmatic religion."

No matter what we believe, we are equally convinced that *we* are right. We have to be. That is what belief means, and we must all believe something. The Roman Catholic Church is entitled to declare that all other religious groups are sunk in error. But what follows? That other groups have not the right to believe they are right? That you have the right to repress them while they have no right to repress you? That they should concede to you what you should not concede to

---

[1]Quoted in the *Christian Century* (June 1948).

them? Such reasoning is mere childishness. Beyond it lies the greater foolishness that truth is advanced by the forceful suppression of those who believe differently from you. Beyond that lies the pernicious distortion of meanings which claims that liberty is only "the liberty to do right"—the "liberty" for me to do what *you* think is right. This perversion of the meaning of liberty has been the delight of all totalitarians. And it might be well to reflect that it was the radical Rousseau who first introduced the doctrine that men could be "forced to be free."

How much do they have truth who think they must guard it within the fortress of their own might? How little that guarding has availed in the past! How often it has kept truth outside while superstition grew moldy within! How often has the false alliance of belief and force led to civil dissension and the futile ruin of war! But if history means nothing to those who call themselves "Christian" and still claim exclusive civil rights for their particular faith, at least they might blush before this word of one they call their Master: "All things therefore whatsoever ye would that men should do unto you, even so do ye also unto them; for this is the law and the prophets."

CONTEMPORARY ISSUES

Helping Others:
What Limits to Immigration?

26. *Lifeboat Ethics:*
The Case Against Helping the Poor

Garrett Hardin

Garrett Hardin (1915–   ) is a professor of human ecology at the University of California–Santa Barbara. His books and articles on population control and other social issues have been widely read.

Environmentalists use the metaphor of the earth as a "spaceship" in trying to persuade countries, industries, and people to stop wasting and polluting our natural resources. Since we all share life on this planet, they argue, no single person or institution has the right to destroy, waste, or use more than a fair share of its resources.

But does everyone on earth have an equal right to an equal share of its resources? The spaceship metaphor can be dangerous when used by misguided idealists to justify suicidal policies for sharing our resources through uncontrolled immigration and foreign aid. In their enthusiastic but unrealistic generosity, they confuse the ethics of a spaceship with those of a lifeboat.

A true spaceship would have to be under the control of a captain, since no ship could possibly survive if its course were determined by committee. Spaceship Earth certainly has no captain; the United Nations is merely a toothless tiger, with little power to enforce any policy upon its bickering members.

If we divide the world crudely into rich nations and poor nations, two thirds of them are desperately poor, and only one third comparatively rich, with the United States the wealthiest of all. Metaphorically each rich nation can be seen as a lifeboat full of comparatively rich people. In the ocean outside each lifeboat swim

Reprinted with permission from *Psychology Today Magazine*, Copyright © 1974 (Sussex Publishers, Inc.).

the poor of the world, who would like to get in, or at least to share some of the wealth. What should the lifeboat passengers do?

First, we must recognize the limited capacity of any lifeboat. For example, a nation's land has a limited capacity to support a population, and, as the current energy crisis has shown us, in some ways we have already exceeded the carrying capacity of our land.

ADRIFT IN A MORAL SEA

So here we sit, say fifty people in our lifeboat. To be generous, let us assume it has room for ten more, making a total capacity of sixty. Suppose the fifty of us in the lifeboat see 100 others swimming in the water outside, begging for admission to our boat or for handouts. We have several options: we may be tempted to try to live by the Christian ideal of being "our brother's keeper," or by the Marxist ideal of "to each according to his needs." Since the needs of all in the water are the same, and since they can all be seen as "our brothers," we could take them all into our boat, making a total of 150 in a boat designed for sixty. The boat swamps, everyone drowns. Complete justice, complete catastrophe.

Since the boat has an unused excess capacity of ten more passengers, we could admit just ten more to it. But which ten do we let in? How do we choose? Do we pick the best ten, the neediest ten, "first come, first served"? And what do we say to the ninety we exclude? If we do let an extra ten into our lifeboat, we will have lost our "safety factor," an engineering principle of critical importance. For example, if we don't leave room for excess capacity as a safety factor in our country's agriculture, a new plant disease or a bad change in the weather could have disastrous consequences.

Suppose we decide to preserve our small safety factor and admit no more to the lifeboat. Our survival is then possible, although we shall have to be constantly on guard against boarding parties.

While this last solution clearly offers the only means of our survival, it is morally abhorrent to many people. Some say they feel guilty about their good luck. My reply is simple: "Get out and yield your place to others." This may solve the problem of the guilt-ridden person's conscience, but it does not change the ethics of the lifeboat. The needy person to whom the guilt-ridden person yields his place will not himself feel guilty about his good luck. If he did, he would not climb aboard. The net result of conscience-stricken people giving up their unjustly held seats is the elimination of that sort of conscience from the lifeboat.

This is the basic metaphor within which we must work out our solutions. Let us now enrich the image, step by step, with substantive additions from the real world, a world that must solve real and pressing problems of overpopulation and hunger.

The harsh ethics of the lifeboat become even harsher when we consider the reproductive differences between the rich nations and the poor nations. The people inside the lifeboats are doubling in numbers every eighty-seven years; those swimming around outside are doubling, on the average, every thirty-five years, more than twice as fast as the rich. And since the world's resources are dwindling, the difference in prosperity between the rich and the poor can only increase.

As of 1973, the U.S. had a population of 210 million people, who were increasing by 0.8 per cent per year. Outside our lifeboat, let us imagine another 210 million people (say the combined populations of Colombia, Ecuador, Venezuela, Morocco, Pakistan, Thailand, and the Philippines), who are increasing at a rate of 3.3 per cent per year. Put differently, the doubling time for this aggregate population is twenty-one years, compared to eighty-seven years for the U.S.

MULTIPLYING THE RICH AND THE POOR

Now suppose the U.S. agreed to pool its resources with those seven countries, with everyone receiving an equal share. Initially the ratio of Americans to non-Americans in this model would be one-to-one. But consider what the ratio would be after eighty-seven years, by which time the Americans would have doubled to a population of 420 million. By then, doubling every twenty-one years, the other group would have swollen to 3.54 billion. Each American would have to share the available resources with more than eight people.

But, one could argue, this discussion assumes that current population trends will continue, and they may not. Quite so. Most likely the rate of population increase will decline much faster in the U.S. than it will in the other countries, and there does not seem to be much we can do about it. In sharing with "each according to his needs," we must recognize that needs are determined by population size, which is determined by the rate of reproduction, which at present is regarded as a sovereign right of every nation, poor or not. This being so, the philanthropic load created by the sharing ethic of the spaceship can only increase.

THE TRAGEDY OF THE COMMONS

The fundamental error of spaceship ethics, and the sharing it requires, is that it leads to what I call "the tragedy of the commons." Under a system of private property, the men who own property recognize their responsibility to care for it, for if they don't they will eventually suffer. A farmer, for instance, will allow no more cattle in a pasture than its carrying capacity justifies. If he overloads it, erosion sets in, weeds take over, and he loses the use of the pasture.

If a pasture becomes a commons open to all, the right of each to use it may not be matched by a corresponding responsibility to protect it. Asking everyone to use it with discretion will hardly do, for the considerate herdsman who refrains from overloading the commons suffers more than a selfish one who says his needs are greater. If everyone would restrain himself, all would be well; but it takes only one less than everyone to ruin a system of voluntary restraint. In a crowded world of less-than-perfect human beings, mutual ruin is inevitable if there are no controls. This is the tragedy of the commons.

One of the major tasks of education today should be the creation of such an acute awareness of the dangers of the commons that people will recognize its many varieties. For example, the air and water have become polluted because they are treated as commons. Further growth in the population, or per-capita conversion of natural resources into pollutants, will only make the problem worse. The same holds true for the fish of the oceans. Fishing fleets have nearly disappeared in many parts of the world; technological improvements in the art of fishing are hastening the day of complete ruin. Only the replacement of the system of the commons with a responsible system of control will save the land, air, water, and oceanic fisheries.

The World Food Bank

In recent years there has been a push to create a new commons called a World Food Bank, an international depository of food reserves to which nations would contribute according to their abilities and from which they would draw according to their needs. This humanitarian proposal has received support from many liberal international groups, and from such prominent citizens as Margaret Mead, U.N. Secretary General Kurt Waldheim, and Senators Edward Kennedy and George McGovern.

A world food bank appeals powerfully to our humanitarian impulses. But before we rush ahead with such a plan, let us recognize where the greatest political push comes from, lest we be disillusioned later. Our experience with the Food for Peace program, or Public Law 480, gives us the answer. This program moved billions of dollars worth of U.S. surplus grain to food-short, population-long countries during the past two decades. But when P.L. 480 first became law, a headline in the business magazine *Forbes* revealed the real power behind it: "Feeding the World's Hungry Millions: How It Will Mean Billions for U.S. Business."

And indeed it did. In the years 1960 to 1970, U.S. taxpayers spent a total of $7.9 billion on the Food for Peace program. Between 1948 and 1970, they also paid an additional $50 billion for other economic-aid programs, some of which went for food and food-producing machinery and technology. Though all U.S. taxpayers were forced to contribute to the cost of P.L. 480, certain special-interest groups gained handsomely under the program. Farmers did not have to contribute the grain; the Government, or rather the taxpayers, bought it from them at full market prices. The increased demand raised prices of farm products generally. The manufacturers of farm machinery, fertilizers, and pesticides benefited by the farmers' extra efforts to grow more food. Grain elevators profited from storing the surplus until it could be shipped. Railroads made money hauling it to ports, and shipping lines profited from carrying it overseas. The implementation of P.L. 480 required the creation of a vast Government bureaucracy, which then acquired its own vested interest in continuing the program regardless of its merits.

EXTRACTING DOLLARS

Those who proposed and defended the Food for Peace program in public rarely mentioned its importance to any of these special interests. The public emphasis was always on its humanitarian effects. The combination of silent selfish interests and highly vocal humanitarian apologists made a powerful and successful lobby for extracting money from taxpayers. We can expect the same lobby to push now for the creation of a World Food Bank.

However great the potential benefit to selfish interests, it should not be a decisive argument against a truly humanitarian program. We must ask if such a program would actually do more good than harm, not only momentarily but also in the long run. Those who propose the food bank usually refer to a current "emergency" or "crisis" in terms of world food supply. But what is an emergency? Although they may be infrequent and sudden, everyone knows that emergencies will occur from time to time. A well-run family, company, organization, or country prepares for the likelihood of accidents and emergencies. It expects them, it budgets for them, it saves for them.

LEARNING THE HARD WAY

What happens if some organizations or countries budget for accidents and others do not? If each country is solely responsible for its own well-being, poorly managed ones will suffer. But they can learn from experience. They may mend their ways, and learn to budget for infrequent but certain emergencies. For example, the weather varies from year to year, and periodic crop failures are certain. A wise and competent government saves out of the production of the good years in anticipation of bad years to come. Joseph taught this policy to Pharaoh in Egypt more than 2,000 years ago. Yet the great majority of the governments in the world today do not follow such a policy. They lack either the wisdom or the competence, or both. Should those nations that do manage to put something aside be forced to come to the rescue each time an emergency occurs among the poor nations?

"But it isn't their fault!" some kindhearted liberals argue. "How can we blame the poor people who are caught in an emergency? Why must they suffer for the sins of their governments?" The concept of blame is simply not relevant here. The real question is, what are the operational consequences of establishing a world food bank? If it is open to every country every time a need develops, slovenly rulers will not be motivated to take Joseph's advice. Someone will always come to their aid. Some countries will deposit food in the world food bank, and others will withdraw it. There will be almost no overlap. As a result of such solutions to food shortage emergencies, the poor countries will not learn to mend their ways, and will suffer progressively greater emergencies as their populations grow.

POPULATION CONTROL THE CRUDE WAY

On the average, poor countries undergo a 2.5 per cent increase in population each year; rich countries, about 0.8 per cent. Only rich countries have anything in the way of food reserves set aside, and even they do not have as much as they should. Poor countries have none. If poor countries received no food from the outside, the rate of their population growth would be periodically checked by crop failures and famines. But if they can always draw on a world food bank in time of need, their population can continue to grow unchecked, and so will their "need" for aid. In the short run, a world food bank may diminish that need, but in the long run it actually increases the need without limit.

Without some system of worldwide food sharing, the proportion of people in the rich and poor nations might eventually stabilize. The overpopulated poor countries would decrease in numbers, while the rich countries that had room for more people would increase. But with a well-meaning system of sharing, such as a world food bank, the growth differential between the rich and the poor countries will not only persist, it will increase. Because of the higher rate of population growth in the poor countries of the world, 88 per cent of today's children are born poor, and only 12 per cent rich. Year by year the ratio becomes worse, as the fast-reproducing poor outnumber the slow-reproducing rich.

A world food bank is thus a commons in disguise. People will have more motivation to draw from it than to add to any common store. The less provident and less able will multiply at the expense of the abler and more provident, bringing eventual ruin upon all who share in the commons. Besides, any system of "sharing" that amounts to foreign aid from the rich nations to the poor nations will carry the taint of charity, which will contribute little to the world peace so devoutly desired by those who support the idea of a world food bank.

As past U.S. foreign-aid programs have amply and depressingly demonstrated, international charity frequently inspires mistrust and antagonism rather than gratitude on the part of the recipient nation.

CHINESE FISH AND MIRACLE RICE

The modern approach to foreign aid stresses the export of technology and advice, rather than money and food. As an ancient Chinese proverb goes: "Give a man a fish and he will eat for a day; teach him how to fish and he will eat for the rest of his days." Acting on this advice, the Rockefeller and Ford Foundations have financed a number of programs for improving agriculture in the hungry nations.

Known as the "Green Revolution," these programs have led to the development of "miracle rice" and "miracle wheat," new strains that offer bigger harvests and greater resistance to crop damage. Norman Borlaug, the Nobel Prize-winning agronomist who, supported by the Rockefeller Foundation, developed "miracle wheat," is one of the most prominent advocates of a world food bank.

Whether or not the Green Revolution can increase food production as much as its champions claim is a debatable but possibly irrelevant point. Those who support this well-intended humanitarian effort should first consider some of the fundamentals of human ecology. Ironically, one man who did was the late Alan Gregg, a vice president of the Rockefeller Foundation. Two decades ago he expressed strong doubts about the wisdom of such attempts to increase food production. He likened the growth and spread of humanity over the surface of the earth to the spread of cancer in the human body, remarking that "cancerous growths demand food; but, as far as I know, they have never been cured by getting it."

OVERLOADING THE ENVIRONMENT

Every human born constitutes a draft on all aspects of the environment: food, air, water, forests, beaches, wildlife, scenery, and solitude. Food can, perhaps, be significantly increased to meet a growing demand. But what about clean beaches, unspoiled forests, and solitude? If we satisfy a growing population's need for food, we necessarily decrease its per capita supply of the other resources needed by men.

India, for example, now has a population of 600 million, which increases by 15 million each year. This population already puts a huge load on a relatively impoverished environment. The country's forests are now only a small fraction of what they were three centuries ago, and floods and erosion continually destroy the insufficient farmland that remains. Every one of the 15 million new lives added to India's population puts an additional burden on the environment, and increases the economic and social costs of crowding. However humanitarian our intent, every Indian life saved through medical or nutritional assistance from abroad diminishes the quality of life for those who remain, and for subsequent generations. If rich countries make it possible, through foreign aid, for 600 million Indians to swell to 1.2 billion in a mere twenty-eight years, as their current growth rate threatens, will future generations of Indians thank us for hastening the destruction of their environment? Will our good intentions be sufficient excuse for the consequences of our actions?

My final example of a commons in action is one for which the public has the least desire for rational discussion—immigration. Anyone who publicly questions the wisdom of current U.S. immigration policy is promptly charged with bigotry, prejudice, ethnocentrism, chauvinism, isolationism, or selfishness. Rather than encounter such accusations, one would rather talk about other matters, leaving immigration policy to wallow in the crosscurrents of special interests that take no account of the good of the whole, or the interests of posterity.

Perhaps we still feel guilty about things we said in the past. Two generations ago the popular press frequently referred to Dagos, Wops, Polacks, Chinks, and Krauts, in articles about how America was being "overrun" by foreigners of supposedly inferior genetic stock. But because the implied inferiority of foreigners was used then as justification for keeping them out, people now assume that restrictive policies could only be based on such misguided notions. There are other grounds.

A Nation of Immigrants

Just consider the numbers involved. Our Government acknowledges a net inflow of 400,000 immigrants a year. While we have no hard data on the extent of illegal entries, educated guesses put the figure at about 600,000 a year. Since the natural increase (excess of births over deaths) of the resident population now runs about 1.7 million per year, the yearly gain from immigration amounts to at least 19 per cent of the total annual increase, and may be as much as 37 per cent if we include the estimate for illegal immigrants. Considering the growing use of birth-control devices, the potential effect of educational campaigns by such organizations as Planned Parenthood Federation of America and Zero Population Growth, and the influence of inflation and the housing shortage, the fertility rate of American women may decline so much that immigration could account for all the yearly increase in population. Should we not at least ask if that is what we want?

For the sake of those who worry about whether the "quality" of the average immigrant compares favorably with the quality of the average resident, let us assume that immigrants and native-born citizens are of exactly equal quality, however one defines that term. We will focus here only on quantity; and since our conclusions will depend on nothing else, all charges of bigotry and chauvinism become irrelevant.

Immigration vs. Food Supply

World food banks *move food to the people,* hastening the exhaustion of the environment of the poor countries. Unrestricted immigration, on the other hand, *moves people to the food,* thus speeding up the destruction of the environment of the rich countries. We can easily understand why poor people should want to make this latter transfer, but why should rich hosts encourage it?

As in the case of foreign-aid programs, immigration receives support from selfish interests and humanitarian impulses. The primary selfish interest in unimpeded immigration is the desire of employers for cheap labor, particularly in industries and trades that offer degrading work. In the past, one wave of foreigners after another was brought into the U.S. to work at wretched jobs for wretched wages. In recent years the Cubans, Puerto Ricans, and Mexicans have had this dubious honor. The interests of the employers of cheap labor mesh well with the guilty silence of the country's liberal intelligentsia. White Anglo-Saxon Protestants are particularly reluctant to call for a closing of the doors to immigration, for fear of being called bigots.

But not all countries have such reluctant leadership. Most educated Hawaiians, for example, are keenly aware of the limits of their environment, particularly in terms of population growth. There is only so much room on the islands, and the islanders know it. To Hawaiians, immigrants from the other forty-nine states present as great a threat as those from other nations. At a recent meeting of Hawaiian government officials in Honolulu, I had the ironic delight of hearing a speaker, who like most of his audience was of Japanese ancestry, ask how the country might practically and constitutionally close its doors to further immigration. One member of the audience countered: "How can we shut the doors now? We have many friends and relatives in Japan that we'd like to bring here some day so that they can enjoy Hawaii too." The Japanese-American speaker smiled sympathetically and answered: "Yes, but we have children now, and someday we'll have grandchildren too. We can bring more people here from Japan only by giving away some of the land that we hope to pass on to our grandchildren some day. What right do we have to do that?"

At this point, I can hear U.S. liberals asking: "How can you justify slamming the door once you're inside? You say that immigrants should be kept out. But aren't we all immigrants, or the descendants of immigrants? If we insist on staying, must we not admit all others?" Our craving for intellectual order leads us to seek and prefer symmetrical rules and morals: a single rule for me and everybody else; the same rule yesterday, today, and tomorrow. Justice, we feel, should not change with time and place.

We Americans of non-Indian ancestry can look upon ourselves as the descendants of thieves who are guilty morally, if not legally, of stealing this land from its Indian owners. Should we then give back the land to the now living American descendants of those Indians? However morally or logically sound this proposal may be, I, for one, am unwilling to live by it and I know no one else who is. Besides, the logical consequence would be absurd. Suppose that, intoxicated with a sense of pure justice, we should decide to turn our land over to the Indians. Since all our wealth has also been derived from the land, wouldn't we be morally obliged to give that back to the Indians too?

PURE JUSTICE VS. REALITY

Clearly, the concept of pure justice produces an infinite regression to absurdity. Centuries ago, wise men invented statutes of limitations to justify the rejection of such pure justice, in the interest of preventing continual disorder. The law zealously defends property rights, but only relatively recent property rights. Drawing a line after an arbitrary time has elapsed may be unjust, but the alternatives are worse.

We are all the descendants of thieves, and the world's resources are inequitably distributed. But we must begin the journey to tomorrow from the point where we are today. We cannot remake the past. We cannot safely divide the wealth equitably among all peoples so long as people reproduce at different rates. To do so would guarantee that our grandchildren, and everyone else's grandchildren, would have only a ruined world to inhabit.

To be generous with one's own possessions is quite different from being generous with those of posterity. We should call this point to the attention of those who, from a commendable love of justice and equality, would institute a system of the commons, either in the form of a world food bank, or of unrestricted immigration. We must convince them, if we wish to save at least some parts of the world from environmental ruin.

Without a true world government to control reproduction and the use of available resources, the sharing ethic of the spaceship is impossible. For the foreseeable future, our survival demands that we govern our actions by the ethics of a lifeboat, harsh though they may be. Posterity will be satisfied with nothing less.

27. Insiders and Outsiders

Peter Singer

*Peter Singer (1946–   ), professor of philosophy at Princeton, has written
influential books on numerous philosophical issues. His best-known
book,* Animal Liberation, *attacks the treatment that animals receive from
humans.*

THE SHELTER

It is February 2002, and the world is taking stock of the damage done by the nuclear
war in the Middle East towards the close of the previous year. The global level of
radioactivity now and for about eight years to come is so high that only those living in fallout shelters can be confident of surviving in reasonable health. For the rest,
who must breathe unfiltered air and consume food and water with high levels of
radiation, the prospects are grim. Probably 10 per cent will die of radiation sickness
within the next two months; another 30 per cent are expected to develop fatal forms
of cancer within five years; and even the remainder will have rates of cancer
ten times higher than normal, while the risk that their children will be malformed
is fifty times greater than before the war.

The fortunate ones, of course, are those who were far-sighted enough to
buy a share in the fallout shelters built by real-estate speculators as international ten-
sions rose in the late 1990s. Most of these shelters were designed as underground
villages, each with enough accommodation and supplies to provide for the needs
of 10,000 people for twenty years. The villages are self-governing, with democratic
constitutions that were agreed to in advance. They also have sophisticated security systems that enable them to admit to the shelter whoever they decide to admit,
and keep out all others.

The news that it will not be necessary to stay in the shelters for much more
than eight years has naturally been greeted with joy by the members of an underground community called Fairhaven. But it has also led to the first serious friction
among them. For above the shaft that leads down to Fairhaven, there are thousands
of people who are not investors in a shelter. These people can be seen, and heard,
through television cameras installed at the entrance. They are pleading to be admitted. They know that if they can get into a shelter quickly, they will escape most
of the consequences of exposure to radiation. At first, before it was known how
long it would be until it was safe to return to the outside, these pleas had virtually

Reprinted from *Practical Ethics* (2nd ed. 1993) by Peter Singer. Reprinted with permission of Cambridge
University Press.

no support from within the shelter. Now, however, the case for admitting at least some of them has become much stronger. Since the supplies need last only eight years, they will stretch to more than double the number of people at present in the shelters. Accommodation presents only slightly greater problems: Fairhaven was designed to function as a luxury retreat when not needed for a real emergency, and it is equipped with tennis courts, swimming pools, and a large gymnasium. If everyone were to consent to keep fit by doing aerobics in their own living rooms, it would be possible to provide primitive but adequate sleeping space for all those whom the supplies can stretch to feed.

So those outside are now not lacking advocates on the inside. The most extreme, labelled "bleeding hearts" by their opponents, propose that the shelter should admit an additional 10,000 people—as many as it can reasonably expect to feed and house until it is safe to return to the outside. This will mean giving up all luxury in food and facilities; but the bleeding hearts point out that the fate for those who remain on the outside will be far worse.

The bleeding hearts are opposed by some who urge that these outsiders generally are an inferior kind of person, for they were either not sufficiently far-sighted, or else not sufficiently wealthy, to invest in a shelter; hence, it is said, they will cause social problems in the shelter, placing an additional strain on health, welfare, and educational services and contributing to an increase in crime and juvenile delinquency. The opposition to admitting outsiders is also supported by a small group who say that it would be an injustice to those who have paid for their share of the shelter if others who have not paid benefit by it. These opponents of admitting others are articulate, but few; their numbers are bolstered considerably, however, by many who say only that they really enjoy tennis and swimming and don't want to give it up.

Between the bleeding hearts and those who oppose admitting any outsiders, stands a middle group: those who think that, as an exceptional act of benevolence and charity, some outsiders should be admitted, but not so many as to make a significant difference to the quality of life within the shelter. They propose converting a quarter of the tennis courts to sleeping accommodation, and giving up a small public open space that has attracted little use anyway. By these means, an extra 500 people could be accommodated, which the self-styled "moderates" think would be a sensible figure, sufficient to show that Fairhaven is not insensitive to the plight of those less fortunate than its own members.

A referendum is held. There are three proposals: to admit 10,000 outsiders; to admit 500 outsiders; and to admit no outsiders. For which would you vote?

THE REAL WORLD

Like the issue of overseas aid, the situation of refugees today raises an ethical question about the boundaries of our moral community—not, as in earlier chapters, on grounds of species, stage of development, or intellectual capacities, but on nationality. The great majority of the approximately 15 million refugees in the world today are receiving refuge, at least temporarily, in the poorer and less developed countries of the world. More than 12 million refugees are in the less developed countries of Africa, Asia and Latin America. The effect on a poor country of receiving a sudden influx of millions of refugees can be gauged from the experience of Pakistan during the 1980s, when it was home to 2.8 million Afghan refugees—mainly living in the North West Frontier province. Although Pakistan did get some outside assistance to feed its refugees, the effects of bearing the burden of this refugee population for seven years was easily seen around refugee villages. Whole hillsides were denuded of trees as a result of the collection of wood for fuel for the refugees.

According to Article 14 of the 1948 United Nations Declaration of Human Rights, "Everyone has the right to seek and to enjoy in other countries asylum from persecution." The United Nations High Commission for Refugees was established in 1950 and the commissioner entrusted with the protection of any person who is outside the country of his nationality because of a "well founded fear of persecution by reason of his race, religion, nationality or political opinion, and is unwilling or unable to avail himself of the protection of his own government." This definition was originally designed to meet the dislocation caused by the Second World War in Europe. It is a narrow one, demanding that claims to refugee status be investigated case by case. It has failed to cover the large-scale movements of people in times of war, famine, or civil disturbance that have occurred since.

Less than generous responses to refugees are usually justified by blaming the victim. It has become common to distinguish "genuine refugees" from "economic refugees" and to claim that the latter should receive no assistance. This distinction is dubious, for most refugees leave their countries at great risk and peril to their lives—crossing seas in leaky boats under attack from pirates, or making long journeys over armed borders, to arrive penniless in refugee camps. To distinguish between someone fleeing from political persecution and someone who flees from a land made uninhabitable by prolonged drought is difficult to justify when they are in equal need of a refuge. The UN definition, which would not classify the latter as a refugee, defines away the problem.

What are the possible durable solutions for refugees in the world today? The main options are: voluntary repatriation, local integration in the country they first flee to, and resettlement.

Probably the best and most humane solution for refugees would be to return home. Unfortunately for the majority, voluntary repatriation is not possible because the conditions that caused them to flee have not changed sufficiently. Local settlement, where refugees can remain and rebuild their lives in neighboring countries, is too often impossible because of the inability of poor, economically struggling—and politically unstable—countries to absorb a new population when their indigenous people face a daily struggle for survival. This option works best where ethnic and tribal links cross national frontiers.

The difficulty of achieving either voluntary repatriation or local settlement leaves resettlement in a more remote country as the only remaining option. With the number of refugees needing resettlement reaching dimensions never before experienced, the main response of the industrialized countries has been to institute deterrent policies and close their doors as tight as they can. Admittedly, resettlement can never solve the problems that make refugees leave their homes. Nor is it, of itself, a solution to the world refugee problem. Only about 2 per cent of the world's refugees are permanently resettled. Nevertheless, the resettlement option is a significant one. It provides markedly better lives for a considerable number of individuals, even if not for a large proportion of the total number of refugees.

Resettlement also affects the policies of those countries to which refugees first flee. If such countries have no hope that refugees will be resettled, they know that their burden will grow with every refugee who enters their country. And countries of first refuge are among those least able to support additional people. When the resettlement option tightens, the countries to which refugees first go adopt policies to try to discourage potential refugees from leaving their country. This policy will include turning people back at the border, making the camps as unattractive as possible, and screening the refugees as they cross the border.

Resettlement is the only solution for those who cannot return to their own countries in the foreseeable future and are only welcome temporarily in the country to which they have fled; in other words for those who have nowhere to go. There are millions who would choose this option if there were countries who would take them. For these refugees, resettlement may mean the difference between life and death. It certainly is their only hope for a decent existence.

THE *EX GRATIA* APPROACH

A widely held attitude is that we are under no moral or legal obligation to accept any refugees at all; and if we do accept some, it is an indication of our generous and humanitarian character. Though popular, this view is not self-evidently morally sound. Indeed, it appears to conflict with other attitudes that are, if we can judge from what people say, at least as widely held, including the belief in the equality of all human beings, and the rejection of principles that discriminate on the basis of race or national origin.

All developed nations safeguard the welfare of their residents in many ways—protecting their legal rights, educating their children, and providing social security payments and access to medical care, either universally or for those who fall below a defined level of poverty. Refugees receive none of these benefits unless they are accepted into the country. Since the overwhelming majority of them are not accepted, the overwhelming majority will not receive these benefits. But is this distinction in the way in which we treat residents and nonresidents ethically defensible?

Very few moral philosophers have given any attention to the issue of refugees, even though it is clearly one of the major moral issues of our time and raises significant moral questions about who is a member of our moral community.

Take, for example, John Rawls, the Harvard philosopher whose book, *A Theory of Justice*, has been the most widely discussed account of justice since its publication in 1971. This 500-page volume deals exclusively with justice *within* a society, thus ignoring all the hard questions about the principles that ought to govern how wealthy societies respond to the claims of poorer nations, or of outsiders in need.

One of the few philosophers who has addressed this issue is another American, Michael Walzer. His *Spheres of Justice* opens with a chapter entitled "The Distribution of Membership" in which he asks how we constitute the community within which distribution takes place. In the course of this chapter Walzer seeks to justify something close to the present situation with regard to refugee policy. The first question Walzer addresses is: do countries have the right to close their borders to potential immigrants? His answer is that they do, because without such closure, or at least the power to close borders if desired, distinct communities cannot exist.

Given that the decision to close borders can rightfully be made, Walzer then goes on to consider how it should be exercised. He compares the political community with a club, and with a family. Clubs are examples of the *ex gratis* approach: "Individuals may be able to give good reason why they should be selected, but no one on the outside has a right to be inside." But Walzer considers the analogy imperfect, because states are also a bit like families. They are morally bound to open the doors of their country—not to anyone who wants to come in, perhaps, but to a particular group of outsiders, recognized as national or ethnic "relatives." In this way Walzer uses the analogy of a family to justify the principle of family reunion as a basis for immigration policy.

As far as refugees are concerned, however, this is not much help. Does a political community have the right to exclude destitute, persecuted, and stateless men and women simply because they are foreigners? In Walzer's view the community is bound by a principle of mutual aid and he rightly notes that this principle may have wider effects when applied to a community than when applied to an individual, because so many benevolent actions are open to a community that will only marginally affect its members. To take a stranger into one's family is something that we might consider goes beyond the requirement of mutual aid; but to take a stranger, or even many strangers, into the community is far less burdensome.

In Walzer's view, a nation with vast unoccupied lands—he takes Australia as his example, though by assumption rather than by any examination of Australia's water and soil resources—may indeed have an obligation in mutual aid to take in people from densely populated, famine-stricken lands of Southeast Asia. The choice for the Australian community would then be to give up whatever homogeneity their society possessed, or to retreat to a small portion of the land they occupied, yielding the remainder to those who needed it.

Although not accepting any general obligation on affluent nations to admit refugees, Walzer does uphold the popular principle of asylum. In accordance with this principle, any refugee who manages to reach the shores of another country can claim asylum and cannot be deported back to a country in which he may be persecuted for reasons of race, religion, nationality, or political opinion. It is interesting that this principle is so widely supported, while the obligation to accept refugees is not. The distinction drawn may reflect some of the principles discussed in previous chapters of this book. The principle of proximity clearly plays a role—the person seeking asylum is just physically closer to us than those in other countries. Perhaps our stronger support for asylum rests in part on the distinction between an act (deporting a refugee who has arrived here) and an omission (not offering a place to a refugee in a distant camp). It could also be an instance of the difference between doing something to an identifiable individual, and doing something that we know will have the same effect on someone, but we will never be able to tell on whom it has this effect. A further factor is probably the relatively small number of people who are actually able to arrive in order to seek asylum, in contrast to the much larger number of refugees of whose existence we are aware, although they are far from us. This is the "drops in the ocean" argument that was discussed in connection with overseas aid. We can, perhaps, cope with all the asylum seekers, but no matter how many refugees we admit, the problem will still be there. As in the case of the parallel argument against giving overseas aid, this overlooks the fact that in admitting refugees, we enable specific individuals to live decent lives and thus are doing something that is worthwhile, no matter how many other refugees remain whom we are unable to help.

Moderately liberal governments, prepared to heed at least some humanitarian sentiments, act much as Walzer suggests they should. They hold that communities have a right to decide whom they will admit; the claims of family reunion come first, and those of outsiders from the national ethnic group—should the state have an ethnic identity—next. The admission of those in need is an *ex gratis* act. The right of asylum is usually respected, as long as the numbers are relatively small. Refugees, unless they can appeal to some special sense of political affinity, have no real claim to be accepted, and have to throw themselves on the charity of the receiving country. All of this is in general agreement with immigration policy in the Western democracies. As far as refugees are concerned, the *ex gratis* approach is the current orthodoxy.

THE FALLACY OF THE CURRENT APPROACH

The current orthodoxy rests on vague and usually unargued assumptions about the community's right to determine its membership. A consequentialist would hold, instead, that immigration policy should be based squarely on the interests of all those affected. Where the interests of different parties conflict, we should be giving equal consideration to all interests, which would mean that more pressing or more fundamental interests take precedence over less fundamental interests. The first step in applying the principle of equal consideration of interests is to identify those whose interests are affected. The first and most obvious group is the refugees themselves. Their most pressing and fundamental interests are clearly at stake. Life in a refugee camp offers little prospect of anything more than a bare subsistence, and sometimes hardly even that. Here is one observer's impression of a camp on the Thai-Cambodian border in 1986. At the time the camp was home for 144,000 people:

> The visit of a foreigner causes a ripple of excitement. People gather round and ask earnestly about the progress of their case for resettlement, or share their great despair at continual rejection by the selection bodies for the various countries which will accept refugees. . . .People wept as they spoke, most had an air of quiet desperation. . . .On rice distribution day, thousands of girls and women mill in the distribution area, receiving the weekly rations for their family. From the bamboo observation tower the ground below was just a swirling sea of black hair and bags of rice hoisted onto heads for the walk home. A proud, largely farming people, forced to become dependent on UN rations of water, tinned fish and broken rice, just to survive.
>
> Most of these people could hope for no significant change in their lives for many years to come. Yet I, along with the others from outside, could get into a car and drive out of the camp, return to Taphraya or Aran, drink iced water, eat rice or noodles at the roadside restaurant at the corner, and observe life passing by. Those simplest parts of life were invested with a freedom I'd never valued so highly.[1]

At the same time, refugees accepted into another country have a good chance of establishing themselves and leading a life as satisfactory and fulfilling as most of us. Sometimes the interests of the refugees in being accepted are as basic as the interest in life itself. In other cases the situation may not be one of life or death, but it will still profoundly affect the whole course of a person's life.

The next most directly affected group is the residents of the recipient nation. How much they will be affected will vary according to how many refugees are taken, how well they will fit into the community, the current state of the national economy, and so on. Some residents will be more affected than others: some will find themselves competing with the refugees for jobs, and others will not; some will find themselves in a neighborhood with a high population of refugees, and others will not; and this list could be continued indefinitely, too.

We should not assume that residents of the recipient nation will be affected for the worse: the economy may receive a boost from a substantial intake of refugees, and many residents may find business opportunities in providing for their needs. Others may enjoy the more cosmopolitan atmosphere created by new arrivals from other countries: the exotic food shops and restaurants that spring up, and in the long run, the benefits of different ideas and ways of living. One could argue that in many ways refugees make the best immigrants. They have nowhere else to go and must commit themselves totally to their new country, unlike immigrants who can go home when or if they please. The fact that they have survived and escaped from hardship suggests stamina, initiative, and resources that would be of great benefit to any receiving country. Certainly some refugee groups, for instance the

---

[1]Rossi Van der Borch, "Impressions of a Refugee Camp," quoted in *Asia Bureau Australia Newsletter,* No. 85 (October–December, 1986).

Indo-Chinese, have displayed great entrepreneurial vigour when resettled in countries like Australia or the United States.

There are also some other *possible* and more diffuse consequences that we at least need to think about. For example, it has been argued that to take large numbers of refugees from poor countries into affluent ones will simply encourage the flow of refugees in the future. If poor and over-populated countries can get rid of their surplus people to other countries, they will have a reduced incentive to do something about the root causes of the poverty of their people, and to slow population growth. The end result could be just as much suffering as if we had never taken the refugees in the first place.

Consequences also arise from *not* taking significant numbers of refugees. Economic stability and world peace depend on international co-operation based on some measure of respect and trust; but the resource-rich and not over-populated countries of the world cannot expect to win the respect or trust of the poorest and most crowded countries if they leave them to cope with most of the refugee problem as best they can.

So we have a complex mix of interests—some definite, some highly speculative—to be considered. Equal interests are to be given equal weight, but which way does the balance lie? Consider a reasonably affluent nation that is not desperately overcrowded, like Australia. (I take Australia merely as an example of a country with which I am familiar; one could, with minor modifications, substitute other affluent nations.) In the early 1990s Australia is admitting about 12,000 refugees a year, at a time when there are several million refugees in refugee camps around the world, many of whom have no hope of returning to their previous country and are seeking resettlement in a country like Australia. Now let us imagine that Australia decides to accept twice as many refugees each year as it has in fact been doing. What can we say are the definite consequences of such a decision, and what are the possible consequences?

The first definite consequence would be that each year 12,000 more refugees would have been out of the refugee camps and settled in Australia, where they could expect, after a few years of struggle, to share in the material comforts, civil rights, and political security of that country. So 12,000 people would have been *very* much better off.

The second definite consequence would have been that each year Australia would have had 12,000 more immigrants, and that these additional immigrants would not have been selected on the basis of possessing skills needed in the Australian economy. They would therefore place an additional demand on welfare services. Some long-term residents of Australia may be disconcerted by the changes that take place in their neighborhood, as significant numbers of people from a very different culture move in. More refugees would make some impact on initial post-arrival services such as the provision of English language classes, housing in the first few months, job placement, and retraining. But the differences would be minor—after all, a decade earlier, Australia had accepted approximately 22,000 refugees a year. There were no marked adverse effects from this larger intake.

At this point, if we are considering the *definite* consequences of a doubled refugee intake, in terms of having a significant impact on the interests of others, we come to a halt. We may wonder if the increased numbers will lead to a revival of racist feeling in the community. We could debate the impact on the Australian environment. We might guess that a larger intake of refugees will encourage others, in the country from which the refugees came, to become refugees themselves in order to better their economic condition. Or we could refer hopefully to the contribution towards international goodwill that may flow from a country like Australia easing the burden of less well-off nations in supporting refugees. But all of these consequences are highly speculative.

Consider the environmental impact of an extra 12,000 refugees. Certainly, more people will put some additional pressure on the environment. This means that the increased number of refugees accepted will be just one item in a long list of factors that includes the natural rate of reproduction; the government's desire to increase exports by encouraging an industry based on converting virgin forests to wood-chips; the subdivision of rural land in scenic areas for holiday houses; the spurt in popularity of vehicles suitable for off-road use; the development of ski resorts in sensitive alpine areas; the use of no-deposit bottles and other containers that increase litter—the list could be prolonged indefinitely.

If as a community we allow these other factors to have their impact on the environment, while appealing to the need to protect our environment as a reason for restricting our intake of refugees to its present level, we are implicitly giving less weight to the interests of refugees in coming to Australia than we give to the interests of Australian residents in having holiday houses, roaring around the countryside in four-wheel-drive vehicles, going skiing, and throwing away their drink containers without bothering to return them for recycling. Such a weighting is surely morally outrageous, so flagrant a violation of the principle of equal consideration of interests that I trust it has only to be exposed in order to be seen as indefensible.

The other arguments are even more problematical. No one can really say whether doubling Australia's intake of refugees would have any effect at all on the numbers who might consider fleeing their own homes; nor is it possible to predict the consequences in terms of international relations. As with the similar argument linking overseas aid with increased population, in a situation in which the definite consequences of the proposed additional intake of refugees are positive, it would be wrong to decide against the larger intake on such speculative grounds, especially since the speculative factors point in different directions.

So there is a strong case for Australia to double its refugee intake. But there was nothing in the argument that relied on the specific level of refugees now being taken by Australia. If this argument goes through, it would also seem to follow that Australia should be taking not an extra 12,000 refugees, but an extra 24,000 refugees a year. Now the argument seems to be going too far, for it can then be reapplied to this new level: should Australia be taking 48,000 refugees? We can double and redouble the intakes of all the major nations of the developed world, and the refugee camps around the world will still not be empty. Indeed, the number of refugees who would seek resettlement in the developed countries is not fixed, and probably there is some truth in the claim that if all those now in refugee camps were to be accepted, more refugees would arrive to take their places. Since the interests of the refugees in resettlement in a more prosperous country will always be greater than the conflicting interests of the residents of those countries, it would seem that the principle of equal consideration of interests points to a world in which all countries continue to accept refugees until they are reduced to the same standard of poverty and overcrowding as the third world countries from which the refugees are seeking to flee.

Is this a reason for rejecting the original argument? Does it mean that if we follow the original argument through it leads to consequences that we cannot possibly accept; and therefore there must be a flaw in the argument that has led us to such an absurd conclusion? This does not follow. The argument we put forward for doubling Australia's refugee intake does not really imply that the doubled intake should then be redoubled, and redoubled again, ad infinitum. At some point in this process—perhaps when the refugee intake is four times what it now is, or perhaps when it is sixty-four times its present level—the adverse consequences that are now only speculative possibilities would become probabilities or virtual certainties.

There would come a point at which, for instance, the resident community had eliminated all luxuries that imperiled the environment, and yet the basic needs of the expanding population were putting such pressure on fragile ecological systems that a further expansion would do irreparable harm. Or there might come a point at which tolerance in a multicultural society was breaking down because of resentment among the resident community, whose members believed that their children were unable to get jobs because of competition from the hard-working new arrivals; and this loss of tolerance might reach the point at which it was a serious danger to the peace and security of all previously accepted refugees and other immigrants from different cultures. When any such point had been reached, the balance of interests would have swung against a further increase in the intake of refugees.

The present refugee intake might increase quite dramatically before any consequences like those mentioned above were reached; and some may take this as a consequence sufficiently unacceptable to support the rejection of our line of argument. Certainly anyone starting from the assumption that the status quo must be roughly right will be likely to take that view. But the status quo is the outcome of a system of national selfishness and political expediency, and not the result of a considered attempt to work out the moral obligations of the developed nations in a world with 15 million refugees.

It would not be difficult for the nations of the developed world to move closer towards fulfilling their moral obligations to refugees. There is no objective evidence to show that doubling their refugee intake would cause them any harm whatsoever. Much present evidence, as well as past experience, points the other way, suggesting that they and their present population would probably benefit.

But, the leaders will cry, what is moral is not what is politically acceptable! This is a spurious excuse for inaction. In many policy areas, presidents and prime ministers are quite happy to try to convince the electorate of what is right—of the need to tighten belts in order to balance budgets, or to desist from drinking and driving. They could just as easily gradually increase their refugee intakes, monitoring the effects of the increase through careful research. In this way they would fulfill their moral and geopolitical obligations and still benefit their own communities.

Shelters and Refuges

How would you have voted, in the referendum conducted in Fairhaven . . . ? I think most people would have been prepared to sacrifice not just a quarter, but all of the tennis courts to the greater need of those outside. But if you would have voted with the "bleeding hearts" in that situation, it is difficult to see how you can disagree with the conclusion that affluent nations should be taking far, far more refugees than they are taking today. For the situation of refugees is scarcely better than that of the outsiders in peril from nuclear radiation; and the luxuries that we would have to sacrifice are surely no greater.

The Morality of Abortion

28. *An Almost Absolute Value in History*

John T. Noonan Jr.

John T. Noonan Jr. (1926-   ) is Professor Emeritus at the University of California at Berkeley School of Law and a judge on the U.S. Court of Appeals, 9th Circuit (San Francisco). He is the author and editor of many books on social and legal issues.

The most fundamental question involved in the long history of thought on abortion is: How do you determine the humanity of a being? To phrase the question that way is to put in comprehensive humanistic terms what the theologians either dealt with as an explicitly theological question under the heading of "ensoulment" or dealt with implicitly in their treatment of abortion. The Christian position as it originated did not depend on a narrow theological or philosophical concept. It had no relation to theories of infant baptism.[1] It appealed to no special theory of instantaneous ensoulment. It took the world's view on ensoulment as that view changed from Aristotle to Zacchia. There was, indeed, theological influence affecting the theory of ensoulment finally adopted, and, of course, ensoulment itself was a theological concept, so that the position was always explained in theological terms. But the theological notion of ensoulment could easily be translated into humanistic language by substituting "human" for "rational soul"; the problem of knowing when a man is a man is common to theology and humanism.

If one steps outside the specific categories used by the theologians, the answer they gave can be analyzed as a refusal to discriminate among human beings on the basis of their varying potentialities. Once conceived, the being was

Reprinted by permission of the publishers, from *The Morality of Abortion: Legal and Historical Perspectives,* John T. Noonan, Jr., ed., Cambridge, Mass.: Harvard University Press. © 1970 by the President and Fellows of Harvard College.

[1]According to Glanville Williams (*The Sanctity of Human Life supra* n. 169, at 193), "The historical reason for the Catholic objection to abortion is the same as for the Christian Church's historical opposition to infanticide: the horror of bringing about the death of an unbaptized child." This statement is made without any citation of evidence. As has been seen, desire to administer baptism could, in the Middle Ages, even be urged as a reason for procuring an abortion. It is highly regrettable that the American Law Institute was apparently misled by Williams' account and repeated after him the same baseless statement. See American Law Institute, *Model Penal Code: Tentative Draft No. 9* (1959), p. 148, n. 12.

recognized as man because he had man's potential. The criterion for humanity, thus, was simple and all-embracing: if you are conceived by human parents, you are human.

The strength of this position may be tested by a review of some of the other distinctions offered in the contemporary controversy over legalizing abortion. Perhaps the most popular distinction is in terms of viability. Before an age of so many months, the fetus is not viable, that is, it cannot be removed from the mother's womb and live apart from her. To that extent, the life of the fetus is absolutely dependent on the life of the mother. This dependence is made the basis of denying recognition to its humanity.

There are difficulties with this distinction. One is that the perfection of artificial incubation may make the fetus viable at any time: it may be removed and artificially sustained. Experiments with animals already show that such a procedure is possible. This hypothetical extreme case relates to an actual difficulty: there is considerable elasticity to the idea of viability. Mere length of life is not an exact measure. The viability of the fetus depends on the extent of its anatomical and functional development. The weight and length of the fetus are better guides to the state of its development than age, but weight and length vary. Moreover, different racial groups have different ages at which their fetuses are viable. Some evidence, for example, suggests that Negro fetuses mature more quickly than white fetuses. If viability is the norm, the standard would vary with race and with many individual circumstances.

The most important objection to this approach is that dependence is not ended by viability. The fetus is still absolutely dependent on someone's care in order to continue existence; indeed a child of one or three or even five years of age is absolutely dependent on another's care for existence; uncared for, the older fetus or the younger child will die as surely as the early fetus detached from the mother. The unsubstantial lessening in dependence at viability does not seem to signify any special acquisition of humanity.

A second distinction has been attempted in terms of experience. A being who has had experience, has lived and suffered, who possesses memories, is more human than one who has not. Humanity depends on formation by experience. The fetus is thus "unformed" in the most basic human sense.

This distinction is not serviceable for the embryo which is already experiencing and reacting. The embryo is responsive to touch after eight weeks and at least at that point is experiencing. At an earlier stage the zygote is certainly alive and responding to its environment. The distinction may also be challenged by the rare case where aphasia has erased adult memory: has it erased humanity? More fundamentally, this distinction leaves even the older fetus or the younger child to be treated as an unformed inhuman thing. Finally, it is not clear why experience as such confers humanity. It could be argued that certain central experiences such as loving or learning are necessary to make a man human. But then human beings who have failed to love or to learn might be excluded from the class called man.

A third distinction is made by appeal to the sentiments of adults. If a fetus dies, the grief of the parents is not the grief they would have for a living child. The fetus is an unnamed "it" till birth, and is not perceived as personality until at least the fourth month of existence when movements in the womb manifest a vigorous presence demanding joyful recognition by the parents.

Yet feeling is notoriously an unsure guide to the humanity of others. Many groups of humans have had difficulty in feeling that persons of another tongue, color, religion, sex, are as human as they. Apart from reactions to alien groups, we mourn the loss of a ten-year-old boy more than the loss of his one-day-old brother or his 90-year-old grandfather. The difference felt and the grief expressed vary with the potentialities extinguished, or the experience wiped out; they do not seem to point to any substantial difference in the humanity of baby, boy, or grandfather.

Distinctions are also made in terms of sensation by the parents. The embryo is felt within the womb only after about the fourth month. The embryo is seen only at birth. What can be neither seen nor felt is different from what is tangible. If the fetus cannot be seen or touched at all, it cannot be perceived as man.

Yet experience shows that sight is even more untrustworthy than feeling in determining humanity. By sight, color became an appropriate index for saying who was a man, and the evil of racial discrimination was given foundation. Nor can touch provide the test; a being confined by sickness, "out of touch" with others, does not thereby seem to lose his humanity. To the extent that touch still has appeal as a criterion, it appears to be a survival of the old English idea of "quickening"— a possible mistranslation of the Latin *animatus* used in the canon law. To that extent touch as a criterion seems to be dependent on the Aristotelian notion of ensoulment, and to fall when this notion is discarded.

Finally, a distinction is sought in social visibility. The fetus is not socially perceived as human. It cannot communicate with others. Thus, both subjectively and objectively, it is not a member of society. As moral rules are rules for the behavior of members of society to each other, they cannot be made for behavior toward what is not yet a member. Excluded from the society of men, the fetus is excluded from the humanity of men.[2]

By force of the argument from the consequences, this distinction is to be rejected. It is more subtle than that founded on an appeal to physical sensation, but it is equally dangerous in its implications. If humanity depends on social recognition, individuals or whole groups may be dehumanized by being denied any status in their society. Such a fate is fictionally portrayed in *1984* and has actually been the lot of many men in many societies. In the Roman empire, for example, condemnation to slavery meant the practical denial of most human rights; in the Chinese Communist world, landlords have been classified as enemies of the people and so treated as nonpersons by the state. Humanity does not depend on social

---

[2] . . . Thomas Aquinas gave an analogous reason against baptizing a fetus in the womb: "As long as it exists in the womb of the mother, it cannot be subject to the operation of the ministers of the Church as it is not known to men" (*In sententias Petri Lombardi* 4.6 1.1.2).

recognition, though often the failure of society to recognize the prisoner, the alien, the heterodox as human has led to the destruction of human beings. Anyone conceived by a man and a woman is human. Recognition of this condition by society follows a real event in the objective order, however imperfect and halting the recognition. Any attempt to limit humanity to exclude some group runs the risk of furnishing authority and precedent for excluding other groups in the name of the consciousness or perception of the controlling group in the society.

A philosopher may reject the appeal to the humanity of the fetus because he views "humanity" as a secular view of the soul and because he doubts the existence of anything real and objective which can be identified as humanity. One answer to such a philosopher is to ask how he reasons about moral questions without supposing that there is a sense in which he and the others of whom he speaks are human. Whatever group is taken as the society which determines who may be killed is thereby taken as human. A second answer is to ask if he does not believe that there is a right and wrong way of deciding moral questions. If there is such a difference, experience may be appealed to: to decide who is human on the basis of the sentiment of a given society has led to consequences which rational men would characterize as monstrous.

The rejection of the attempted distinctions based on viability and visibility, experience and feeling, may be buttressed by the following considerations: Moral judgments often rest on distinctions, but if the distinctions are not to appear arbitrary *fiat*, they should relate to some real difference in probabilities. There is a kind of continuity in all life, but the earlier stages of the elements of human life possess tiny probabilities of development. Consider for example, the spermatozoa in any normal ejaculate: There are about 200,000,000 in any single ejaculate, of which one has a chance of developing a zygote. Consider the oocytes which may become ova: there are 100,000 to 1,000,000 oocytes in a female infant, of which a maximum of 390 are ovulated. But once spermatozoon and ovum meet and the conceptus is formed, such studies as have been made show that roughly in only 20 percent of the cases will spontaneous abortion occur. In other words, the chances are about 4 out of 5 that this new being will develop. At this stage in the life of the being there is a sharp shift in probabilities, an immense jump in potentialities. To make a distinction between the rights of spermatozoa and the rights of the fertilized ovum is to respond to an enormous shift in possibilities. For about twenty days after conception the egg may split to form twins or combine with another egg to form a chimera, but the probability of either event happening is very small.

It may be asked, What does a change in biological probabilities have to do with establishing humanity? The argument from probabilities is not aimed at establishing humanity but at establishing an objective discontinuity which may be taken into account in moral discourse. As life itself is a matter of probabilities, as most moral reasoning is an estimate of probabilities, so it seems in accord with the structure of reality and the nature of moral thought to found a moral judgment on the change in probabilities at conception. The appeal to probabilities is the most commonsensical of arguments, to a greater or smaller degree all of us base our actions on probabilities, and in morals, as in law, prudence and negligence are often measured by the account one has taken of the probabilities. If the chance is 200,000,000 to 1 that the movement in the bushes into which you shoot is a man's, I doubt if many persons would hold you careless in shooting; but if the chances are 4 out of 5 that the movement is a human being's, few would acquit you of blame. Would the argument be different if only one out of ten children conceived came to term? Of course this argument would be different. This argument is an appeal to probabilities that actually exist, not to any and all states of affairs which may be imagined.

The probabilities as they do exist do not show the humanity of the embryo in the sense of a demonstration in logic any more than the probabilities of the movement in the bush being a man demonstrate beyond all doubt that the being is a man. The appeal is a "buttressing" consideration, showing the plausibility of the standard adopted. The argument focuses on the decisional factor in any moral judgment and assumes that part of the business of a moralist is drawing lines. One evidence of the nonarbitrary character of the line drawn is the difference of probabilities on either side of it. If a spermatozoon is destroyed, one destroys a being which had a chance of far less than 1 in 200 million of developing into a reasoning being, possessed of the genetic code, a heart and other organs, and capable of pain. If a fetus is destroyed, one destroys a being already possessed of the genetic code, organs, and sensitivity to pain, and one which had an 80 percent chance of developing further into a baby outside the womb who, in time, would reason.

The positive argument for conception as the decisive moment of humanization is that at conception the new being receives the genetic code. It is the genetic information which determines his characteristics, which is the biological carrier of the possibility of human wisdom, which makes him a self-evolving being. A being with a human genetic code is man.

This review of current controversy over the humanity of the fetus emphasizes what a fundamental question the theologians resolved in asserting the inviolability of the fetus. To regard the fetus as possessed of equal rights with other humans was not, however, to decide every case where abortion might be employed. It did decide the case where the argument was that the fetus should be aborted for its own good. To say a being was human was to say it had a destiny to decide for itself which could not be taken from it by another man's decision. But human beings with equal rights often come in conflict with each other, and some decision must be made as whose claims are to prevail. Cases of conflict involving the fetus are different only in two respects: the total inability of the fetus to speak for itself and the fact that the right of the fetus regularly at stake is the right to life itself.

The approach taken by the theologians to these conflicts was articulated in terms of "direct" and "indirect." Again, to look at what they were doing from outside their categories, they may be said to have been drawing lines or "balancing values." "Direct" and "indirect" are spatial metaphors; "line-drawing" is another. "To weigh" or "to balance" values is a metaphor of a more complicated mathematical sort hinting at the process which goes on in moral judgments. All the metaphors suggest that, in the moral judgments made, comparisons were necessary, that no value completely controlled. The principle of double effect was no doctrine fallen from heaven, but a method of analysis appropriate where two relative values were being compared. In Catholic moral theology, as it developed, life even of the innocent was not taken as an absolute. Judgments on acts affecting life issued from a process of weighing. In the weighing, the fetus was always given a value greater than zero, always a value separate and independent from its parents. This valuation was crucial and fundamental in all Christian thought on the subject and marked it off from any approach which considered that only the parents' interests needed to be considered.

Even with the fetus weighed as human, one interest could be weighed as equal or superior; that of the mother in her own life. The casuists between 1450 and 1895 were willing to weigh this interest as superior. Since 1895, that interest was given decisive weight only in the two special cases of the cancerous uterus and the ectopic pregnancy. In both of these cases the fetus itself had little chance of survival even if the abortion were not performed. As the balance was once struck in favor of the mother whenever her life was endangered, it could be so struck again. The balance reached between 1895 and 1930 attempted prudentially and pastorally to forestall a multitude of exceptions for interests less than life.

The perception of the humanity of the fetus and the weighing of fetal rights against other human rights constituted the work of the moral analysts. But what spirit animated their abstract judgments? For the Christian community it was the injunction of Scripture to love your neighbor as yourself. The fetus as human was a neighbor; his life had parity with one's own. The commandment gave life to what otherwise would have been only rational calculation.

The commandment could be put in humanistic as well as theological terms: Do not injure your fellow man without reason. In these terms, once the humanity of the fetus is perceived, abortion is never right except in self-defense. When life must be taken to save life, reason alone cannot say that a mother must prefer a child's life to her own. With this exception, now of great rarity, abortion violates the rational humanist tenet of the equality of human lives.

For Christians the commandment to love had received a special imprint in that the exemplar proposed of love was the love of the Lord for his disciples. In the light given by this example, self-sacrifice carried to the point of death seemed in the extreme situations not without meaning. In the less extreme cases, preference for one's own interests to the life of another seemed to express cruelty or selfishness irreconcilable with the demands of love.

29. A Defense of Abortion[1]

Judith Jarvis Thomson

Judith Jarvis Thomson (1929–   ), professor of philosophy at Massachusetts Institute of Technology, has written highly acclaimed books and articles on a variety of philosophical issues.

Most opposition to abortion relies on the premise that the fetus is a human being, a person, from the moment of conception. The premise is argued for, but, as I think, not well. Take, for example, the most common argument. We are asked to notice that the development of a human being from conception through birth into childhood is continuous; then it is said that to draw a line, to choose a point in this development and say "before this point the thing is not a person, after this point it is a person" is to make an arbitrary choice, a choice for which in the nature of things no good reason can be given. It is concluded that the fetus is, or anyway that we had better say it is, a person from the moment of conception. But this conclusion does not follow. Similar things might be said about the development of an acorn into an oak tree, and it does not follow that acorns are oak trees, or that we had better say they are. Arguments of this form are sometimes called "slippery slope arguments"—the phrase is perhaps self-explanatory—and it is dismaying that opponents of abortion rely on them so heavily and uncritically.

I am inclined to agree, however, that the prospects for "drawing a line" in the development of the fetus look dim. I am inclined to think also that we shall probably have to agree that the fetus has already become a human person well before birth. Indeed, it comes as a surprise when one first learns how early in its life it begins to acquire human characteristics. By the tenth week, for example, it already has a face, arms and legs, fingers and toes; it has internal organs, and brain activity is detectable.[2] On the other hand, I think that the premise is false, that the fetus is not a person from the moment of conception. A newly fertilized ovum, a newly implanted clump of cells, is no more a person than an acorn is an oak tree. But I shall not discuss any of this. For it seems to me to be of great interest to ask

Judith Jarvis Thomson, "A Defense of Abortion," in *Philosophy and Public Affairs*, vol. 1, no. 1 (Copyright © 1971 by Princeton University Press): pp. 47–66. Reprinted by permission of Princeton University Press.

[1]I am very much indebted to James Thomson for discussion, criticism, and many helpful suggestions.

[2]Daniel Callahan, *Abortion: Law, Choice and Morality* (New York, 1970), p. 373. This book gives a fascinating survey of the available information on abortion. The Jewish tradition is surveyed in David M. Feldman, *Birth Control in Jewish Law* (New York, 1968), Part 5, the Catholic tradition in John T. Noonan, Jr., "An Almost Absolute Value in History," in *The Morality of Abortion*, ed. John T. Noonan, Jr. (Cambridge, Mass., 1970).

what happens if, for the sake of argument, we allow the premise. How, precisely, are we supposed to get from there to the conclusion that abortion is morally impermissible? Opponents of abortion commonly spend most of their time establishing that the fetus is a person and hardly any time explaining the step from there to the impermissibility of abortion. Perhaps they think the step too simple and obvious to require much comment. Or perhaps instead they are simply being economical in argument. Many of those who defend abortion rely on the premise that the fetus is not a person, but only a bit of tissue that will become a person at birth; and why pay out more arguments than you have to? Whatever the explanation, I suggest that the step they take is neither easy nor obvious, that it calls for closer examination than it is commonly given, and that when we do give it this closer examination we shall feel inclined to reject it.

I propose, then, that we grant that the fetus is a person from the moment of conception. How does the argument go from here? Something like this, I take it. Every person has a right to life. So the fetus has a right to life. No doubt the mother has a right to decide what shall happen in and to her body; everyone would grant that. But surely a person's right to life is stronger and more stringent than the mother's right to decide what happens in and to her body, and so outweighs it. So the fetus may not be killed; an abortion may not be performed.

It sounds plausible. But now let me ask you to imagine this. You wake up in the morning and find yourself back to back in bed with an unconscious violinist. A famous unconscious violinist. He has been found to have a fatal kidney ailment, and the Society of Music Lovers has canvassed all the available medical records and found that you alone have the right blood type to help. They have therefore kidnapped you, and last night the violinist's circulatory system was plugged into yours, so that your kidneys can be used to extract poisons from his blood as well as your own. The director of the hospital now tells you, "Look, we're sorry the Society of Music Lovers did this to you—we would never have permitted it if we had known. But still, they did it, and the violinist now is plugged into you. To unplug you would be to kill him. But never mind, it's only for nine months. By then he will have recovered from his ailment, and can safely be unplugged from you." Is it morally incumbent on you to accede to this situation? No doubt it would be very nice of you if you did, a great kindness. But do you *have* to accede to it? What if it were not nine months, but nine years? Or longer still? What if the director of the hospital says, "Tough luck, I agree, but you've now got to stay in bed, with the violinist plugged into you, for the rest of your life. Because remember this. All persons have a right to life, and violinists are persons. Granted you have a right to decide what happens in and to your body, but a person's right to life outweighs your right to decide what happens in and to your body. So you cannot ever be unplugged from him." I imagine you would regard this as outrageous, which suggests that something really is wrong with that plausible-sounding argument I mentioned a moment ago.

In this case, of course, you were kidnapped; you didn't volunteer for the operation that plugged the violinist into your kidneys. Can those who oppose abortion on the ground I mentioned make an exception for a pregnancy due to rape? Certainly. They can say that persons have a right to life only if they didn't come into existence because of rape; or they can say that all persons have a right to life, but that some have less of a right to life than others, in particular, that those who came into existence because of rape have less. But these statements have a rather unpleasant sound. Surely the question of whether you have a right to life at all, or how much of it you have, shouldn't turn on the question of whether or not you are the product of a rape. And in fact the people who oppose abortion on the ground I mentioned do not make this distinction, and hence do not make an exception in case of rape.

Nor do they make an exception for a case in which the mother has to spend the nine months of her pregnancy in bed. They would agree that would be a great pity, and hard on the mother; but all the same, all persons have a right to life, the fetus is a person, and so on. I suspect, in fact, that they would not make an exception for a case in which, miraculously enough, the pregnancy went on for nine years, or even the rest of the mother's life.

Some won't even make an exception for a case in which continuation of the pregnancy is likely to shorten the mother's life; they regard abortion as impermissible even to save the mother's life. Such cases are nowadays very rare, and many opponents of abortion do not accept this extreme view. All the same, it is a good place to begin: a number of points of interest come out in respect to it.

1. Let us call the view that abortion is impermissible even to save the mother's life "the extreme view." I want to suggest first that it does not issue from the argument I mentioned earlier without the addition of some fairly powerful premises. Suppose a woman has become pregnant, and now learns that she has a cardiac condition such that she will die if she carries the baby to term. What may be done for her? The fetus, being a person, has a right to life, but as the mother is a person too, so has she a right to life. Presumably they have an equal right to life. How is it supposed to come out that an abortion may not be performed? If mother and child have an equal right to life, shouldn't we perhaps flip a coin? Or should we add to the mother's right to life her right to decide what happens in and to her body, which everybody seems to be ready to grant—the sum of her rights now outweighing the fetus's right to life?

The most familiar argument here is the following. We are told that performing the abortion would be directly killing[3] the child, whereas doing nothing would not be killing the mother, but only letting her die. Moreover, in killing the child, one would be killing an innocent person, for the child has committed no crime, and is not aiming at his mother's death. And then there are a variety of ways in which this might be continued. (1) But as directly killing an innocent person is always and absolutely impermissible, an abortion may not be performed. Or,

---

[3]The term "direct" in the arguments I refer to is a technical one. Roughly, what is meant by "direct killing" is either killing as an end in itself, or killing as a means to some end, for example, the end of saving someone else's life. See note 6 for an example of its use.

(2) as directly killing an innocent person is murder, and murder is always and absolutely impermissible, an abortion may not be performed.[4] Or, (3) as one's duty to refrain from directly killing an innocent person is more stringent than one's duty to keep a person from dying, an abortion may not be performed. Or, (4) if one's only options are directly killing an innocent person or letting a person die, one must prefer letting the person die, and thus an abortion may not be performed.[5]

Some people seem to have thought that these are not further premises which must be added if the conclusion is to be reached, but that they follow from the very fact that an innocent person has a right to life.[6] But this seems to me to be a mistake, and perhaps the simplest way to show this is to bring out that while we must certainly grant that innocent persons have a right to life, the theses in (1) through (4) are all false. Take (2), for example. If directly killing an innocent person is murder, and thus is impermissible, then the mother's directly killing the innocent person inside her is murder, and thus is impermissible. But it cannot seriously be thought to be murder if the mother performs an abortion on herself to save her life. It cannot seriously be said that she *must* refrain, that she *must* sit passively by and wait for her death. Let us look again at the case of you and the violinist. There you are, in bed with the violinist, and the director of the hospital says to you, "It's all most distressing, and I deeply sympathize, but you see this is putting an additional strain on your kidneys, and you'll be dead within the month. But you *have* to stay where you are all the same. Because unplugging you would be directly killing an innocent violinist, and that's murder, and that's impermissible." If anything in the world is true, it is that you do not commit murder, you do not do what is impermissible, if you reach around to your back and unplug yourself from that violinist to save your life.

The main focus of attention in writings on abortion has been on what a third party may or may not do in answer to a request from a woman for an abortion. This is in a way understandable. Things being as they are, there isn't much a woman can surely do to abort herself. So the question asked is what a third party

[4]Cf. *Encyclical Letter of Pope Pius XI on Christian Marriage,* St. Paul Editions (Boston, n.d.), p. 32: "however much we may pity the mother whose health and even life is gravely imperiled in the performance of the duty allowed to her by nature, nevertheless what could ever be a sufficient reason for excusing in any way the direct murder of the innocent? This is precisely what we are dealing with here." Noonan (*The Morality of Abortion,* p. 43) reads this as follows: "What cause can ever avail to excuse in any way the direct killing of the innocent? For it is a question of that."

[5]The thesis in (4) is in an interesting way weaker than those in (1), (2), and (3): they rule out abortion even in cases in which both mother *and* child will die if the abortion is not performed. By contrast, one who held the view expressed in (4) could consistently say that one needn't prefer letting two persons die to killing one.

[6]Cf. the following passage from Pius XII, *Address to the Italian Catholic Society of Midwives:* "The baby in the maternal breast has the right to life immediately from God.—Hence there is no man, no human authority, no science, no medical, eugenic, social, economic or moral 'indication' which can establish or grant a valid juridical ground for a direct deliberate disposition of an innocent human life, that is a disposition which looks to its destruction either as an end or as a means to another end perhaps in itself not illicit.—The baby, still not born, is a man in the same degree and for the same reason as the mother" (quoted in Noonan, *The Morality of Abortion,* p. 45).

John T. Noonan, Jr.

may do, and what the mother may do, if it is mentioned at all, is deduced, almost as an afterthought, from what it is concluded that third parties may do. But it seems to me that to treat the matter in this way is to refuse to grant to the mother that very status of person which is so firmly insisted on for the fetus. For we cannot simply read off what a person may do from what a third party may do. Suppose you find yourself trapped in a tiny house with a growing child. I mean a very tiny house, and a rapidly growing child—you are already up against the wall of the house and in a few minutes you'll be crushed to death. The child on the other hand won't be crushed to death; if nothing is done to stop him from growing he'll be hurt, but in the end he'll simply burst open the house and walk out a free man. Now I could well understand it if a bystander were to say, "There's nothing we can do for you. We cannot choose between your life and his, we cannot be the ones to decide who is to live, we cannot intervene." But it cannot be concluded that you too can do nothing, that you cannot attack it to save your life. However innocent the child may be, you do not have to wait passively while it crushes you to death. Perhaps a pregnant woman is vaguely felt to have the status of house, to which we don't allow the right of self-defense. But if the woman houses the child, it should be remembered that she is a person who houses it.

I should perhaps stop to say explicitly that I am not claiming that people have a right to do anything whatever to save their lives. I think, rather, that there are drastic limits to the right of self-defense. If someone threatens you with death unless you torture someone else to death, I think you have not the right, even to save your life, to do so. But the case under consideration here is very different. In our case there are only two people involved, one whose life is threatened, and one who threatens it. Both are innocent: the one who is threatened is not threatened because of any fault, the one who threatens does not threaten because of any fault. For this reason we may feel that we bystanders cannot intervene. But the person threatened can.

In sum, a woman surely can defend her life against the threat to it posed by the unborn child, even if doing so involves its death. And this shows not merely that the theses in (1) through (4) are false; it shows also that the extreme view of abortion is false, and so we need not canvass any other possible ways of arriving at it from the argument I mentioned at the outset.

2. The extreme view could of course be weakened to say that, while abortion is permissible to save the mother's life, it may not be performed by a third party, but only by the mother herself. But this cannot be right either. For what we have to keep in mind is that the mother and the unborn child are not like two tenants in a small house which has, by an unfortunate mistake, been rented to both: the mother *owns* the house. The fact that she does adds to the offensiveness of deducing that the mother can do nothing from the supposition that third parties can do nothing. But it does more than this: it casts a bright light on the supposition that third parties can do nothing. Certainly it lets us see that a third party who says "I cannot choose between you" is fooling himself if he thinks this is impartiality. If Jones has found and fastened on a certain coat, which he needs to keep him from freezing, but which Smith also needs to keep him from freezing, then it is not impartiality that says "I cannot choose between you" when Smith owns the coat. Women have said again and again "This is *my* body!" and they have reason to feel angry, reason to feel that it has been like shouting into the wind. Smith, after all, is hardly likely to bless us if we say to him, "Of course it's your coat, anybody would grant that it is. But no one may choose between you and Jones who is to have it."

We should really ask what it is that says "no one may choose" in the face of the fact that the body that houses the child is the mother's body. It may be simply a failure to appreciate this fact. But it may be something more interesting, namely the sense that one has a right to refuse to lay hands on people, even where it would be just and fair to do so, even where justice seems to require that somebody do so. Thus justice might call for somebody to get Smith's coat back from Jones, and yet you have a right to refuse to be the one to lay hands on Jones, a right to refuse to do physical violence to him. This, I think, must be granted. But then what should be said is not "no one may choose," but only "*I* cannot choose," and indeed not even this, but "I will not *act*," leaving it open that somebody else can or should, and in particular that anyone in a position of authority, with the job of securing people's rights, both can and should. So this is no difficulty. I have not been arguing that any given third party must accede to the mother's request that he perform an abortion to save her life, but only that he may.

I suppose that in some views of human life the mother's body is only on loan to her, the loan not being one which gives her any prior claim to it. One who held this view might well think it impartiality to say "I cannot choose." But I shall simply ignore this possibility. My own view is that if a human being has any just, prior claim to anything at all, he has a just, prior claim to his own body. And perhaps this needn't be argued for here anyway, since, as I mentioned, the arguments against abortion we are looking at do grant that the woman has a right to decide what happens in and to her body.

But although they do grant it, I have tried to show that they do not take seriously what is done in granting it. I suggest the same thing will reappear even more clearly when we turn away from cases in which the mother's life is at stake, and attend, as I propose we now do, to the vastly more common cases in which a woman wants an abortion for some less weighty reason than preserving her own life.

3. Where the mother's life is not at stake, the argument I mentioned at the outset seems to have a much stronger pull. "Everyone has a right to life, so the unborn person has a right to life." And isn't the child's right to life weightier than anything other than the mother's own right to life, which she might put forward as ground for an abortion?

This argument treats the right to life as if it were unproblematic. It is not, and this seems to me to be precisely the source of the mistake.

For we should now, at long last, ask what it comes to, to have a right to life. In some views having a right to life includes having a right to be given at least the bare minimum one needs for continued life. But suppose that what in fact *is* the bare minimum a man needs for continued life is something he has no right at all to be given? If I am sick unto death, and the only thing that will save my life is the touch of Henry Fonda's cool hand on my fevered brow, then all the same, I have no right to be given the touch of Henry Fonda's cool hand on my fevered brow. It would be frightfully nice of him to fly in from the West Coast to provide it. It would be less nice, though no doubt well meant, if my friends flew out to the West Coast and carried Henry Fonda back with them. But I have no right at all against anybody that he should do this for me. Or again, to return to the story I told earlier, the fact that for continued life that violinist needs the continued use of your kidneys does not establish that he has a right to be given the continued use of your kidneys. He certainly has no right against you that *you* should give him continued use of your kidneys. For nobody has any right to use your kidneys unless you give him such a right; and nobody has the right against you that you shall give him this right—if you do allow him to go on using your kidneys, this is a kindness on your part, and not something he can claim from you as his due. Nor has he any right against anybody else that *they* should give him continued use of your kidneys. Certainly he had no right against the Society of Music Lovers that they should plug him into you in the first place. And if you now start to unplug yourself, having learned that you will otherwise have to spend nine years in bed with him, there is nobody in the world who must try to prevent you, in order to see to it that he is given something he has a right to be given.

Some people are rather stricter about the right to life. In their view, it does not include the right to be given anything, but amounts to, and only to, the right not to be killed by anybody. But here a related difficulty arises. If everybody is to refrain from killing that violinist, then everybody must refrain from doing a great many different sorts of things. Everybody must refrain from slitting his throat, everybody must refrain from shooting him—and everybody must refrain from unplugging you from him. But does he have a right against everybody that they shall refrain from unplugging you from him? To refrain from doing this is to allow him to continue to use your kidneys. It could be argued that he has a right against us that *we* should allow him to continue to use your kidneys. That is, while he had no right against us that we should give him the use of your kidneys, it might be argued that he anyway has a right against us that we shall not now intervene and deprive him of the use of your kidneys. I shall come back to third-party interventions later. But certainly the violinist has no right against you that *you* shall allow him to continue to use your kidneys. As I said, if you do allow him to use them, it is a kindness on your part, and not something you owe him.

The difficulty I point to here is not peculiar to the right to life. It reappears in connection with all the other natural rights; and it is something which an adequate account of rights must deal with. For present purposes it is enough just to draw attention to it. But I would stress that I am not arguing that people do not have a right to life—quite to the contrary, it seems to me that the primary control we must place on the acceptability of an account of rights is that it should turn out in that account to be a truth that all persons have a right to life. I am arguing only that having a right to life does not guarantee having either a right to be given the use of or a right to be allowed continued use of another person's body—even if one needs it for life itself. So the right to life will not serve the opponents of abortion in the very simple and clear way in which they seem to have thought it would.

4. There is another way to bring out the difficulty. In the most ordinary sort of case, to deprive someone of what he has a right to is to treat him unjustly. Suppose a boy and his small brother are jointly given a box of chocolates for Christmas. If the older boy takes the box and refuses to give his brother any of the chocolates, he is unjust to him, for the brother has been given a right to half of them. But suppose that, having learned that otherwise it means nine years in bed with that violinist, you unplug yourself from him. You surely are not being unjust to him, for you gave him no right to use your kidneys, and no one else can have given him any such right. But we have to notice that in unplugging yourself, you are killing him; and violinists, like everybody else, have a right to life, and thus in the view we were considering just now, the right not to be killed. So here you do what he supposedly has a right you shall not do, but you do not act unjustly to him in doing it.

The emendation which may be made at this point is this: the right to life consists not in the right not to be killed, but rather in the right not to be killed unjustly. This runs a risk of circularity, but never mind: it would enable us to square the fact that the violinist has a right to life with the fact that you do not act unjustly toward him in unplugging yourself, thereby killing him. For if you do not kill him unjustly, you do not violate his right to life, and so it is no wonder you do him no injustice.

But if this emendation is accepted, the gap in the argument against abortion stares us plainly in the face: it is by no means enough to show that the fetus is a person, and to remind us that all persons have a right to life—we need to be shown also that killing the fetus violates its right to life, i.e., that abortion is unjust killing. And is it?

I suppose we may take it as a datum that in a case of pregnancy due to rape the mother has not given the unborn person a right to the use of her body for food and shelter. Indeed, in what pregnancy could it be supposed that the mother has given the unborn person such a right? It is not as if there were unborn persons drifting about the world, to whom a woman who wants a child says "I invite you in."

But it might be argued that there are other ways one can have acquired a right to the use of another person's body than by having been invited to use it by that person. Suppose a woman voluntarily indulges in intercourse, knowing of the chance it will issue in pregnancy, and then she does become pregnant; is she not in part responsible for the presence, in fact the very existence, of the unborn person inside her? No doubt she did not invite it in. But doesn't her partial responsibility for its being there itself give it a right to the use of her body?[7] If so, then her aborting it would be more like the boy's taking away the chocolates, and less like your

---

[7]The need for a discussion of this argument was brought home to me by members of the Society for Ethical and Legal Philosophy, to whom this paper was originally presented.

unplugging yourself from the violinist—doing so would be depriving it of what it does have a right to, and thus would be doing it an injustice.

And then, too, it might be asked whether or not she can kill it even to save her own life: If she voluntarily called it into existence, how can she now kill it, even in self-defense?

The first thing to be said about this is that it is something new. Opponents of abortion have been so concerned to make out the independence of the fetus, in order to establish that it has a right to life, just as its mother does, that they have tended to overlook the possible support they might gain from making out that the fetus is *dependent* on the mother, in order to establish that she has a special kind of responsibility for it, a responsibility that gives it rights against her which are not possessed by any independent person—such as an ailing violinist who is a stranger to her.

On the other hand, this argument would give the unborn person a right to its mother's body only if her pregnancy resulted from a voluntary act, undertaken in full knowledge of the chance a pregnancy might result from it. It would leave out entirely the unborn person whose existence is due to rape. Pending the availability of some further argument, then, we would be left with the conclusion that unborn persons whose existence is due to rape have no right to the use of their mothers' bodies, and thus that aborting them is not depriving them of anything they have a right to and hence is not unjust killing.

And we should also notice that it is not at all plain that this argument really does go even as far as it purports to. For there are cases and cases, and the details make a difference. If the room is stuffy, and I therefore open a window to air it, and a burglar climbs in, it would be absurd to say, "Ah, now he can stay, she's given him a right to the use of her house—for she is partially responsible for his presence there, having voluntarily done what enabled him to get in, in full knowledge that there are such things as burglars, and that burglars burgle." It would be still more absurd to say this if I had had bars installed outside my windows, precisely to prevent burglars from getting in, and a burglar got in only because of a defect in the bars. It remains equally absurd if we imagine it is not a burglar who climbs in, but an innocent person who blunders or falls in. Again, suppose it were like this: people-seeds drift about in the air like pollen, and if you open your windows, one may drift in and take root in your carpets or upholstery. You don't want children, so you fix up your windows with fine mesh screens, the very best you can buy. As can happen, however, and on very, very rare occasions does happen, one of the screens is defective; and a seed drifts in and takes root. Does the person-plant who now develops have a right to the use of your house? Surely not—despite the fact that you voluntarily opened your windows, you knowingly kept carpets and upholstered furniture, and you knew that screens were sometimes defective. Someone may argue that you are responsible for its rooting, that it does have a right to your house, because after all you *could* have lived out your life with bare floors and furniture, or with sealed windows and doors. But this won't do—for by the same token anyone can avoid a pregnancy due to rape by having a hysterectomy, or anyway by never leaving home without a (reliable!) army.

It seems to me that the argument we are looking at can establish at most that there are *some* cases in which the unborn person has a right to the use of its mother's body, and therefore *some* cases in which abortion is unjust killing. There is room for much discussion and argument as to precisely which, if any. But I think we should sidestep this issue and leave it open, for at any rate the argument certainly does not establish that all abortion is unjust killing.

5. There is room for yet another argument here, however. We surely must all grant that there may be cases in which it would be morally indecent to detach a person from your body at the cost of his life. Suppose you learn that what the violinist needs is not nine years of your life, but only one hour: all you need do to save his life is spend one hour in that bed with him. Suppose also that letting him use your kidneys for that one hour would not affect your health in the slightest. Admittedly you were kidnapped. Admittedly you did not give anyone permission to plug him into you. Nevertheless it seems to me plain you *ought* to allow him to use your kidneys for that hour—it would be indecent to refuse.

Again, suppose pregnancy lasted only an hour, and constituted no threat to life or health. And suppose that a woman becomes pregnant as a result of rape. Admittedly she did not voluntarily do anything to bring about the existence of a child. Admittedly she did nothing at all which would give the unborn person a right to the use of her body. All the same it might well be said, as in the newly emended violinist story, that she *ought* to allow it to remain for that hour—that it would be indecent in her to refuse.

Now some people are inclined to use the term "right" in such a way that it follows from the fact that you ought to allow a person to use your body for the hour he needs, that he has a right to use your body for the hour he needs, even though he has not been given that right by any person or act. They may say that it follows also that if you refuse, you act unjustly toward him. This use of the term is perhaps so common that it cannot be called wrong; nevertheless it seems to me to be an unfortunate loosening of what we would do better to keep a tight rein on. Suppose that box of chocolates I mentioned earlier had not been given to both boys jointly, but was given only to the older boy. There he sits, stolidly eating his way through the box, his small brother watching enviously. Here we are likely to say "You ought not to be so mean. You ought to give your brother some of those chocolates." My own view is that it just does not follow from the truth of this that the brother has any right to any of the chocolates. If the boy refuses to give his brother any, he is greedy, stingy, callous—but not unjust. I suppose that the people I have in mind will say it does follow that the brother has a right to some of the chocolates, and thus that the boy does act unjustly if he refuses to give his brother any. But the effect of saying this is to obscure what we should keep distinct, namely the difference between the boy's refusal in this case and the boy's refusal in the earlier case, in which the box was given to both boys jointly, and in which the small brother thus had what was from any point of view clear title to half.

A further objection to so using the term "right" that from the fact that A ought to do a thing for B, it follows that B has a right against A that A do it for him, is that it is going to make the question of whether or not a man has a right to a thing turn on how easy it is to provide him with it; and this seems not merely unfortunate, but morally unacceptable. Take the case of Henry Fonda again. I said earlier that I had no right to the touch of his cool hand on my fevered brow, even though I needed it to save my life. I said it would be frightfully nice of him to fly in from the West Coast to provide me with it, but that I had no right against him that he should do so. But suppose he isn't on the West Coast. Suppose he has only to walk across the room, place a hand briefly on my brow—and lo, my life is saved. Then surely he ought to do it, it would be indecent to refuse. Is it to be said "Ah, well, it follows that in this case she has a right to the touch of his hand on her brow, and so it would be an injustice in him to refuse"? So that I have a right to it when it is easy for him to provide it, though no right when it's hard? It's rather a shocking idea that anyone's rights should fade away and disappear as it gets harder and harder to accord them to him.

So my view is that even though you ought to let the violinist use your kidneys for the one hour he needs, we should not conclude that he has a right to do so—we should say that if you refuse, you are, like the boy who owns all the chocolates and will give none away, self-centered and callous, indecent in fact, but not unjust. And similarly, that even supposing a case in which a woman pregnant due to rape ought to allow the unborn person to use her body for the hour he needs, we should not conclude that he has a right to do so; we should conclude that she is self-centered, callous, indecent, but not unjust, if she refuses. The complaints are no less grave; they are just different. However, there is no need to insist on this point. If anyone does wish to deduce "he has a right" from "you ought," then all the same he must surely grant that there are cases in which it is not morally required of you that you allow that violinist to use your kidneys, and in which he does not have a right to use them, and in which you do not do him an injustice if you refuse. And so also for mother and unborn child. Except in such cases as the unborn person has a right to demand it—and we were leaving open the possibility that there may be such cases—nobody is morally *required* to make large sacrifices, of health, of all other interests and concerns, of all other duties and commitments, for nine years, or even for nine months, in order to keep another person alive.

6. We have in fact to distinguish between two kinds of Samaritan: the Good Samaritan and what we might call the Minimally Decent Samaritan. The story of the Good Samaritan, you will remember, goes like this:

> A certain man went down from Jerusalem to Jericho, and fell among thieves, which stripped him of his raiment, and wounded him, and departed, leaving him half dead.
>
> And by chance there came down a certain priest that way; and when he saw him, he passed by on the other side.
>
> And likewise a Levite, when he was at the place, came and looked on him, and passed by on the other side.

But a certain Samaritan, as he journeyed, came where he was; and when he saw him he had compassion on him.

And went to him, and bound up his wounds, pouring in oil and wine, and set him on his own beast, and brought him to an inn, and took care of him.

And on the morrow, when he departed, he took out two pence, and then gave them to the host, and said unto him, "Take care of him; and whatsoever thou spendest more, when I come again, I will repay thee."

(Luke 10:30–35)

The Good Samaritan went out of his way, at some cost to himself, to help one in need of it. We are not told what the options were, that is, whether or not the priest and the Levite could have helped by doing less than the Good Samaritan did, but assuming they could have, then the fact they did nothing at all shows they were not even Minimally Decent Samaritans, not because they were not Samaritans, but because they were not even minimally decent.

These things are a matter of degree, of course, but there is a difference, and it comes out perhaps most clearly in the story of Kitty Genovese, who, as you will remember, was murdered while thirty-eight people watched or listened, and did nothing at all to help her. A Good Samaritan would have rushed out to give direct assistance against the murderer. Or perhaps we had better allow that it would have been a Splendid Samaritan who did this, on the ground that it would have involved a risk of death for himself. But the thirty-eight not only did not do this, they did not even trouble to pick up a phone to call the police. Minimally Decent Samaritanism would call for doing at least that, and their not having done it was monstrous.

After telling the story of the Good Samaritan, Jesus said "Go, and do thou likewise." Perhaps he meant that we are morally required to act as the Good Samaritan did. Perhaps he was urging people to do more than is morally required of them. At all events it seems plain that it was not morally required of any of the thirty-eight that he rush out to give direct assistance at the risk of his own life, and that it is not morally required of anyone that he give long stretches of his life—nine years or nine months—to sustaining the life of a person who has no special right (we were leaving open the possibility of this) to demand it.

Indeed, with one rather striking class of exceptions, no one in any country in the world is *legally* required to do anywhere near as much as this for anyone else. The class of exceptions is obvious. My main concern here is not the state of the law in respect to abortion, but it is worth drawing attention to the fact that in no state in this country is any man compelled by law to be even a Minimally Decent Samaritan to any person; there is no law under which charges could be brought against the thirty-eight who stood by while Kitty Genovese died. By contrast, in most states in this country women are compelled by law to be not merely Minimally Decent Samaritans, but Good Samaritans to unborn persons inside them. This doesn't by itself settle anything one way or the other, because it may well be argued that there should be laws in this country—as there are in many European countries—compelling at least Minimally Decent Samaritanism.[8] But it does show that there is a gross injustice in the existing state of the law. And it shows also that the groups currently working against liberalization of abortion laws, in fact working toward having it declared unconstitutional for a state to permit abortion, had better start working for the adoption of Good Samaritan laws generally, or earn the charge that they are acting in bad faith.

I should think, myself, that Minimally Decent Samaritan laws would be one thing, Good Samaritan laws quite another, and in fact highly improper. But we are not here concerned with the law. What we should ask is not whether anybody should be compelled by law to be a Good Samaritan, but whether we must accede to a situation in which somebody is being compelled—by nature, perhaps—to be a Good Samaritan. We have, in other words, to look now at third-party interventions. I have been arguing that no person is morally required to make large sacrifices to sustain the life of another who has no right to demand them, and this even where the sacrifices do not include life itself; we are not morally required to be Good Samaritans or anyway Very Good Samaritans to one another. But what if a man cannot extricate himself from such a situation? What if he appeals to us to extricate him? It seems to me plain that there are cases in which we can, cases in which a Good Samaritan would extricate him. There you are, you were kidnapped, and nine years in bed with that violinist lie ahead of you. You have your own life to lead. You are sorry, but you simply cannot see giving up so much of your life to the sustaining of his. You cannot extricate yourself, and ask us to do so. I should have thought that—in light of his having no right to the use of your body—it was obvious that we do not have to accede to your being forced to give up so much. We can do what you ask. There is no injustice to the violinist in our doing so.

7. Following the lead of the opponents of abortion, I have throughout been speaking of the fetus merely as a person, and what I have been asking is whether or not the argument we began with, which proceeds only from the fetus' being a person, really does establish its conclusion. I have argued that it does not.

But of course there are arguments and arguments, and it may be said that I have simply fastened on the wrong one. It may be said that what is important is not merely the fact that the fetus is a person, but that it is a person for whom the woman has a special kind of responsibility issuing from the fact that she is its mother. And it might be argued that all my analogies are therefore irrelevant—for you do not have that special kind of responsibility for that violinist, Henry Fonda does not have that special kind of responsibility for me. And our attention might be drawn to the fact that men and women both *are* compelled by law to provide support for their children.

[8]For a discussion of the difficulties involved, and a survey of the European experience with such laws, see *The Good Samaritan and the Law*, ed. James M. Ratcliffe (New York 1966).

I have in effect dealt (briefly) with this argument in section 4 above; but a (still briefer) recapitulation now may be in order. Surely we do not have any such "special responsibility" for a person unless we have assumed it, explicitly or implicitly. If a set of parents do not try to prevent pregnancy, do not obtain an abortion, and then at the time of birth of the child do not put it out for adoption, but rather take it home with them, then they have assumed responsibility for it, they have given it rights, and they cannot *now* withdraw support from it at the cost of its life because they now find it difficult to go on providing for it. But if they have taken all reasonable precautions against having a child, they do not simply by virtue of their biological relationship to the child who comes into existence have a special responsibility for it. They may wish to assume responsibility for it, or they may not wish to. And I am suggesting that if assuming responsibility for it would require large sacrifices, then they may refuse. A Good Samaritan would not refuse—or anyway, a Splendid Samaritan, if the sacrifices that had to be made were enormous. But then so would a Good Samaritan assume responsibility for that violinist; so would Henry Fonda, if he is a Good Samaritan, fly in from the West Coast and assume responsibility for me.

8. My argument will be found unsatisfactory on two counts by many of those who want to regard abortion as morally permissible. First, while I do argue that abortion is not impermissible, I do not argue that it is always permissible. There may well be cases in which carrying the child to term requires only Minimally Decent Samaritanism of the mother, and this is a standard we must not fall below. I am inclined to think it a merit of my account precisely that it does *not* give a general yes or a general no. It allows for and supports our sense that, for example, a sick and desperately frightened fourteen-year-old schoolgirl, pregnant due to rape, may *of course* choose abortion, and that any law which rules this out is an insane law. And it also allows for and supports our sense that in other cases resort to abortion is even positively indecent. It would be indecent in the woman to request an abortion, and indecent in a doctor to perform it, if she is in her seventh month, and wants the abortion just to avoid the nuisance of postponing a trip abroad. The very fact that the arguments I have been drawing attention to treat all cases of abortion, or even all cases of abortion in which the mother's life is not at stake, as morally on a par ought to have made them suspect at the outset.

Secondly, while I am arguing for the permissibility of abortion in some cases, I am not arguing for the right to secure the death of the unborn child. It is easy to confuse these two things in that up to a certain point in the life of the fetus it is not able to survive outside the mother's body; hence removing it from her body guarantees its death. But they are importantly different. I have argued that you are not morally required to spend nine months in bed, sustaining the life of that violinist; but to say this is by no means to say that if, when you unplug yourself, there is a miracle and he survives, you then have a right to turn round and slit his throat. You may detach yourself even if this costs him his life; you have no right to be guaranteed his death, by some other means, if unplugging yourself does not kill him. There are some people who will feel dissatisfied by this feature of my argument. A woman may be utterly devastated by the thought of a child, a bit of herself, put out for adoption and never seen or heard of again. She may therefore want not merely that the child be detached from her, but more, that it die. Some opponents of abortion are inclined to regard this as beneath contempt—thereby showing insensitivity to what is surely a powerful source of despair. All the same, I agree that the desire for the child's death is not one which anybody may gratify, should it turn out to be possible to detach the child alive.

At this place, however, it should be remembered that we have only been pretending throughout that the fetus is a human being from the moment of conception. A very early abortion is surely not the killing of a person, and so is not dealt with by anything I have said here.

PROBLEMS AND PUZZLES

30. The Case for Torture

Michael Levin

Michael Levin (1940–   ) is a professor of philosophy at the City University of New York. He is the author of several books and numerous articles on a variety of philosophical topics.

It is generally assumed that torture is impermissible, a throwback to a more brutal age. Enlightened societies reject it outright, and regimes suspected of using it risk the wrath of the United States.

I believe this attitude is unwise. There are situations in which torture is not merely permissible but morally mandatory. Moreover, these situations are moving from the realm of imagination to fact.

DEATH

Suppose a terrorist has hidden an atomic bomb on Manhattan Island which will detonate at noon on July 4 unless . . . (here follow the usual demands for money and release of his friends from jail). Suppose, further, that he is caught at 10 A.M. of the fateful day, but—preferring death to failure—won't disclose where the bomb is. What do we do? If we follow due process—wait for his lawyer, arraign him—millions of people will die. If the only way to save those lives is to subject the terrorist to the most excruciating possible pain, what grounds can there be for not doing so? I suggest there are none. In any case, I ask you to face the question with an open mind.

Torturing the terrorist is unconstitutional? Probably. But millions of lives surely outweigh constitutionality. Torture is barbaric? Mass murder is far more barbaric. Indeed, letting millions of innocents die in deference to one who flaunts his guilt is moral cowardice, an unwillingness to dirty one's hands. If *you* caught the terrorist, could you sleep nights knowing that millions died because you couldn't bring yourself to apply the electrodes?

Once you concede that torture is justified in extreme cases, you have admitted that the decision to use torture is a matter of balancing innocent lives against

Reprinted from *Newsweek,* June 7, 1982, with permission of the author.

the means needed to save them. You must now face more realistic cases involving more modest numbers. Someone plants a bomb on a jumbo jet. He alone can disarm it, and his demands cannot be met (or if they can, we refuse to set a precedent by yielding to his threats). Surely we can, we must, do anything to the extortionist to save the passengers. How can we tell 300, or 100, or 10 people who never asked to be put in danger, "I'm sorry, you'll have to die in agony, we just couldn't bring ourselves to . . ."

Here are the results of an informal poll about a third, hypothetical, case. Suppose a terrorist group kidnapped a newborn baby from a hospital. I asked four mothers if they would approve of torturing kidnappers if that were necessary to get their own newborns back. All said yes, the most "liberal" adding that she would administer it herself.

I am not advocating torture as punishment. Punishment is addressed to deeds irrevocably past. Rather, I am advocating torture as an acceptable measure for preventing future evils. So understood, it is far less objectionable than many extant punishments. Opponents of the death penalty, for example, are forever insisting that executing a murderer will not bring back his victim (as if the purpose of capital punishment were supposed to be resurrection, not deterrence or retribution). But torture, in the cases described, is intended not to bring anyone back but to keep innocents from being dispatched. The most powerful argument against using torture as a punishment or to secure confessions is that such practices disregard the rights of the individual. Well, if the individual is all that important—and he is—it is correspondingly important to protect the rights of individuals threatened by terrorists. If life is so valuable that it must never be taken, the lives of the innocents must be saved even at the price of hurting the one who endangers them.

Better precedents for torture are assassination and preemptive attack. No Allied leader would have flinched at assassinating Hitler, had that been possible. (The Allies did assassinate Heydrich.) Americans would be angered to learn that Roosevelt could have had Hitler killed in 1943—thereby shortening the war and saving millions of lives—but refused on moral grounds. Similarly, if nation A learns that nation B is about to launch an unprovoked attack, A has a right to save itself by destroying B's military capability first. In the same way, if the police can by torture save those who would otherwise die at the hands of kidnappers or terrorists they must.

IDEALISM

There is an important difference between terrorists and their victims that should mute talk of the terrorists' "rights." The terrorist's victims are at risk unintentionally, not having asked to be endangered. But the terrorist knowingly initiated his actions. Unlike his victims, he volunteered for the risks of his deed. By threatening to kill for profit or idealism, he renounces civilized standards, and he can have no complaint if civilization tries to thwart him by whatever means necessary.

Just as torture is justified only to save lives (not extort confessions or recantations), it is justifiably administered only to those *known* to hold innocent lives in their hands. Ah, but how can the authorities ever be sure they have the right malefactor? Isn't there a danger of error and abuse? Won't We turn into Them?

Questions like these are disingenuous in a world in which terrorists proclaim themselves and perform for television. The name of their game is public recognition. After all, you can't very well intimidate a government into releasing your freedom fighters unless you announce that it is your group that has seized its embassy. "Clear guilt" is difficult to define, but when 40 million people see a group of masked gunmen seize an airplane on the evening news, there is not much question about who the perpetrators are. There will be hard cases where the situation is murkier. Nonetheless, a line demarcating the legitimate use of torture can be drawn. Torture only the obviously guilty, and only for the sake of saving innocents, and the line between Us and Them will remain clear.

There is little danger that the Western democracies will lose their way if they choose to inflict pain as one way of preserving order. Paralysis in the face of evil is the greater danger. Some day soon a terrorist will threaten tens of thousands of lives, and torture will be the only way to save them. We had better start thinking about this.

31. People or Penguins: The Case for Optimal Pollution

William F. Baxter

William F. Baxter (1929–   ) is a professor at the Stanford University Law School. In addition to his writings on pollution, he has published books and articles on a variety of economic and legal issues.

I start with the modest proposition that, in dealing with pollution, or indeed with any problem, it is helpful to know what one is attempting to accomplish. Agreement on how and whether to pursue a particular objective, such as pollution control, is not possible unless some more general objective has been identified and stated with reasonable precision. We talk loosely of having clean air and clean water, of preserving our wilderness areas, and so forth. But none of these is a sufficiently general objective: each is more accurately viewed as a means rather than as an end.

With regard to clean air, for example, one may ask, "how clean?" and "what does clean mean?" It is even reasonable to ask, "why have clean air?" Each of these questions is an implicit demand that a more general community goal be stated—a goal sufficiently general in its scope and enjoying sufficiently general assent among the community of actors that such "why" questions no longer seem admissible with respect to that goal.

If, for example, one states as a goal the proposition that "every person should be free to do whatever he wishes in contexts where his actions do not interfere with the interests of other human beings," the speaker is unlikely to be met with a response of "why." The goal may be criticized as uncertain in its implications or difficult to implement, but it is so basic a tenet of our civilization—it reflects a cultural value so broadly shared, at least in the abstract—that the question "why" is seen as impertinent or imponderable or both.

I do not mean to suggest that everyone would agree with the "spheres of freedom" objective just stated. Still less do I mean to suggest that a society could subscribe to four or five such general objectives that would be adequate in their coverage to serve as testing criteria by which all other disagreements might be measured. One difficulty in the attempt to construct such a list is that each new goal added will conflict, in certain applications, with each prior goal listed; and thus each goal serves as a limited qualification on prior goals.

People or Penguins: The Case for Optimal Pollution by William F. Baxter, © 1974, Columbia University Press. Reprinted by permission of the publishers.

Without any expectation of obtaining unanimous consent to them, let me set forth four goals that I generally use as ultimate testing criteria in attempting to frame solutions to problems of human organization. My position regarding pollution stems from these four criteria. If the criteria appeal to you and any part of what appears hereafter does not, our disagreement will have a helpful focus: which of us is correct, analytically, in supposing that his position on pollution would better serve these general goals. If the criteria do not seem acceptable to you, then it is to be expected that our more particular judgments will differ, and the task will then be yours to identify the basic set of criteria upon which your particular judgments rest.

My criteria are as follows:

1. The spheres of freedom criterion stated above.
2. Waste is a bad thing. The dominant feature of human existence is scarcity—our available resources, our aggregate labors, and our skill in employing both have always been, and will continue for some time to be, inadequate to yield to every man all the tangible and intangible satisfactions he would like to have. Hence, none of those resources, or labors, or skills, should be wasted—that is, employed so as to yield less than they might yield in human satisfactions.
3. Every human being should be regarded as an end rather than as a means to be used for the betterment of another. Each should be afforded dignity and regarded as having an absolute claim to an evenhanded application of such rules as the community may adopt for its governance.
4. Both the incentive and the opportunity to improve his share of satisfactions should be preserved to every individual. Preservation of incentive is dictated by the "no-waste" criterion and enjoins against the continuous, totally egalitarian redistribution of satisfactions, or wealth; but subject to that constraint, everyone should receive, by continuous redistribution if necessary, some minimal share of aggregate wealth so as to avoid a level of privation from which the opportunity to improve his situation becomes illusory.

The relationship of these highly general goals to the more specific environmental issues at hand may not be readily apparent, and I am not yet ready to demonstrate their pervasive implications. But let me give one indication of their implications. Recently scientists have informed us that use of DDT in food production is causing damage to the penguin population. For the present purposes let us accept that assertion as an indisputable scientific fact. The scientific fact is often asserted as if the correct implication—that we must stop agricultural use of DDT—followed from the mere statement of the fact of penguin damage. But plainly it does not follow if my criteria are employed.

My criteria are oriented to people, not penguins. Damage to penguins, or sugar pines, or geological marvels is, without more, simply irrelevant. One must go further, by my criteria, and say: Penguins are important because people enjoy seeing them walk about rocks; and furthermore, the well-being of people would be less impaired by halting use of DDT than by giving up penguins. In short, my observations about environmental problems will be people-oriented, as are my criteria. I have no interest in preserving penguins for their own sake.

It may be said by way of objection to this position, that it is very selfish of people to act as if each person represented one unit of importance and nothing else was of any importance. It is undeniably selfish. Nevertheless I think it is the only tenable starting place for analysis for several reasons. First, no other position corresponds to the way most people really think and act—i.e., corresponds to reality.

Second, this attitude does not portend any massive destruction of nonhuman flora and fauna, for people depend on them in many obvious ways, and they will be preserved because and to the degree that humans do depend on them.

Third, what is good for humans is, in many respects, good for penguins and pine trees—clean air for example. So that humans are, in these respects, surrogates for plant and animal life.

Fourth, I do not know how we could administer any other system. Our decisions are either private or collective. Insofar as Mr. Jones is free to act privately, he may give such preferences as he wishes to other forms of life: he may feed birds in winter and do with less himself, and he may even decline to resist an advancing polar bear on the ground that the bear's appetite is more important than those portions of himself that the bear may choose to eat. In short my basic premise does not rule out private altruism to competing life-forms. It does rule out, however, Mr. Jones' inclination to feed Mr. Smith to the bear, however hungry the bear, however despicable Mr. Smith.

Insofar as we act collectively on the other hand, only humans can be afforded an opportunity to participate in the collective decisions. Penguins cannot vote now and are unlikely subjects for the franchise—pine trees more unlikely still. Again each individual is free to cast his vote so as to benefit sugar pines if that is his inclination. But many of the more extreme assertions that one hears from some conservationists amount to tacit assertions that they are specially appointed representatives of sugar pines, and hence that their preferences should be weighted more heavily than the preferences of other humans who do not enjoy equal rapport with "nature." The simplistic assertion that agricultural use of DDT must stop at once because it is harmful to penguins is of that type.

Fifth, if polar bears or pine trees or penguins, like men, are to be regarded as ends rather than means, if they are to count in our calculus of social organization, someone must tell me how much each one counts, and someone must tell me how these life-forms are to be permitted to express their preferences, for I do not know either answer. If the answer is that certain people are to hold their proxies, then I want to know how those proxy-holders are to be selected: self-appointment does not seem workable to me.

Sixth, and by way of summary of all the foregoing, let me point out that the set of environmental issues under discussion—although they raise very complex technical questions of how to achieve any objective—ultimately raise a normative question: what *ought* we to do. Questions of *ought* are unique to the human mind and world—they are meaningless as applied to a nonhuman situation.

I reject the proposition that we *ought* to respect the "balance of nature" or to "preserve the environment" unless the reason for doing so, express or implied, is the benefit of man.

I reject the idea that there is a "right" or "morally correct" state of nature to which we should return. The word "nature" has no normative connotation. Was it "right" or "wrong" for the earth's crust to heave in contortion and create mountains and seas? Was it "right" for the first amphibian to crawl up out of the primordial ooze? Was it "wrong" for plants to reproduce themselves and alter the atmospheric composition in favor of oxygen? For animals to alter the atmosphere in favor of carbon dioxide both by breathing oxygen and eating plants? No answers can be given to these questions because they are meaningless questions.

All this may seem obvious to the point of being tedious, but much of the present controversy over environment and pollution rests on tacit normative assumptions about just such nonnormative phenomena: that it is "wrong" to impair penguins with DDT, but not to slaughter cattle for prime rib roasts. That it is wrong to kill stands of sugar pines with industrial fumes, but not to cut sugar pines and build housing for the poor. Every man is entitled to his own preferred definition of Walden Pond, but there is no definition that has any moral superiority over another, except by reference to the selfish needs of the human race.

From the fact that there is no normative definition of the natural state, it follows that there is no normative definition of clean air or pure water—hence no definition of polluted air—or of pollution—except by reference to the needs of man. The "right" composition of the atmosphere is one which has some dust in it and some lead in it and some hydrogen sulfide in it—just those amounts that attend a sensibly organized society thoughtfully and knowledgeably pursuing the greatest possible satisfaction for its human members.

The first and most fundamental step toward solution of our environmental problems is a clear recognition that our objective is not pure air or water but rather some optimal state of pollution. That step immediately suggests the question: How do we define and attain the level of pollution that will yield the maximum possible amount of human satisfaction?

Low levels of pollution contribute to human satisfaction but so do food and shelter and education and music. To attain ever lower levels of pollution, we must pay the cost of having less of these other things. I contrast that view of the cost of pollution control with the more popular statement that pollution control will "cost" very large numbers of dollars. The popular statement is true in some senses, false in others; sorting out the true and false senses is of some importance. The first step in that sorting process is to achieve a clear understanding of the difference between dollars and resources. Resources are the wealth of our nation;

dollars are merely claim checks upon those resources. Resources are of vital importance; dollars are comparatively trivial.

Four categories of resources are sufficient for our purposes: At any given time a nation, or a planet if you prefer, has a stock of labor, of technological skill, of capital goods, and of natural resources (such as mineral deposits, timber, water, land, etc.). These resources can be used in various combinations to yield goods and services of all kinds—in some limited quantity. The quantity will be larger if they are combined efficiently, smaller if combined inefficiently. But in either event the resource stock is limited, the goods and services that they can be made to yield are limited; even the most efficient use of them will yield less than our population, in the aggregate, would like to have.

If one considers building a new dam, it is appropriate to say that it will be costly in the sense that it will require x hours of labor, y tons of steel and concrete, and z amount of capital goods. If these resources are devoted to the dam, then they cannot be used to build hospitals, fishing rods, schools, or electric can openers. That is the meaningful sense in which the dam is costly.

Quite apart from the very important question of how wisely we can combine our resources to produce goods and services, is the very different question of how they get distributed—who gets how many goods? Dollars constitute the claim checks which are distributed among people and which control their share of national output. Dollars are nearly valueless pieces of paper except to the extent that they do represent claim checks to some fraction of the output of goods and services. Viewed as claim checks, all the dollars outstanding during any period of time are worth, in the aggregate, the goods and services that are available to be claimed with them during that period—neither more nor less.

It is far easier to increase the supply of dollars than to increase the production of goods and services—printing dollars is easy. But printing more dollars doesn't help because each dollar then simply becomes a claim to fewer goods, i.e., becomes worth less.

The point is this: many people fall into error upon hearing the statement that the decision to build a dam, or to clean up a river, will cost $X million. It is regrettably easy to say: "It's only money. This is a wealthy country, and we have lots of money." But you cannot build a dam or clean a river with $X million—unless you also have a match, you can't even make a fire. One builds a dam or cleans a river by diverting labor and steel and trucks and factories from making one kind of goods to making another. The cost in dollars is merely a shorthand way of describing the extent of the diversion necessary. If we build a dam for $X million, then we must recognize that we will have $X million less housing and food and medical care and electric can openers as a result.

Similarly, the costs of controlling pollution are best expressed in terms of the other goods we will have to give up to do the job. This is not to say the job should not be done. Badly as we need more housing, more medical care, and more can openers, and more symphony orchestras, we could do with somewhat less of them, in my judgment at least, in exchange for somewhat cleaner air and rivers.

But that is the nature of the trade-off, and analysis of the problem is advanced if that unpleasant reality is kept in mind. Once the trade-off relationship is clearly perceived, it is possible to state in a very general way what the optimal level of pollution is. I would state it as follows:

People enjoy watching penguins. They enjoy relatively clean air and smog-free vistas. Their health is improved by relatively clean water and air. Each of these benefits is a type of good or service. As a society we would be well advised to give up one washing machine if the resources that would have gone into that washing machine can yield greater human satisfaction when diverted into pollution control. We should give up one hospital if the resources thereby freed would yield more human satisfaction when devoted to elimination of noise in our cities. And so on, trade-off by trade-off, we should divert our productive capacities from the production of existing goods and services to the production of a cleaner, quieter, more pastoral nation up to—and no further than—the point at which we value more highly the next washing machine or hospital that we would have to do without than we value the next unit of environmental improvement that the diverted resources would create.

Now this proposition seems to me unassailable but so general and abstract as to be unhelpful—at least unadministerable in the form stated. It assumes we can measure in some way the incremental units of human satisfaction yielded by very different types of goods. The proposition must remain a pious abstraction until I can explain how this measurement process can occur. . . . But I insist that the proposition stated describes the result for which we should be striving—and again, that it is always useful to know what your target is even if your weapons are too crude to score a bull's eye.

SUGGESTIONS FOR FURTHER READING

ANTHOLOGIES

Edel, Abraham, Elizabeth Flower, and Finbarr W. O'Connor, *Morality, Philosophy and Practice.* New York: Random House, 1989. A collection of important writings on ethics from ancient Greece to the present.

Feinberg, Joel, ed. *The Problem of Abortion.* Belmont, Calif.: Wadsworth, 1973. A collection of some of the best contemporary philosophical essays on the abortion controversy.

Glover, Jonathan, ed. *Utilitarianism and Its Critics.* New York: Macmillan, 1990. A well-chosen collection of articles defending and attacking utilitarianism.

Naveson, Jan, ed. *Moral Issues.* Toronto: Oxford Univ. Press, 1983. A well-chosen collection of articles on currently debated moral issues.

Regan, Tom, ed. *Matters of Life and Death.* 3rd ed. New York: McGraw-Hill, 1993. A collection of original essays on a variety of moral issues.

Singer, Peter, ed. *Ethics.* New York: Oxford Univ. Press, 1994. A recent collection of essays on the nature and origin of ethics. Many of the selections are from such fields as anthropology, ethology, biology, and game theory.

Taylor, Paul, ed. *Problems of Moral Philosophy.* Belmont, Calif.: Wadsworth, 1978. A good anthology of important writings on a wide range of ethical problems.

Wasserstrom, Richard, ed. *Today's Moral Problems.* 2d ed. New York: Macmillan, 1985. Recent essays on a variety of moral issues.

INDIVIDUAL WORKS

Barnes, Hazel E. *An Existentialist Ethics.* New York: Knopf, 1967. A clear presentation of an existentialist approach to ethics, as well as a consideration and rejection of a number of other contemporary ethical views.

Bedau, Hugo Adam. *Making Moral Choices.* New York: Oxford Univ. Press, 1997. A discussion of possible choices in three difficult cases drawn from history and literature.

Binkley, Luther. *Contemporary Ethical Theories.* New York: Citadel, 1961. A clear discussion of the twentieth-century analytic philosophers' approach to ethics.

Brandt, William. *Ethical Theory.* Englewood Cliffs, N.J.: Prentice Hall, 1959. An excellent but somewhat difficult introduction to ethical theory. Contains excellent bibliographies on almost all major topics in ethical theory.

Fletcher, Joseph. *Situation Ethics: The New Morality.* Philadelphia: Westminster, 1966. A contemporary Christian view of ethics, which stresses love as the basis for decision making in ethics.

Frankena, William. *Ethics.* 2nd ed. Englewood Cliffs, N.J.: Prentice Hall, 1973. Provides a clear, concise statement of the major ethical problems and positions.

Hospers, John. *Human Conduct.* New York: Harcourt, 1982. An excellent, clearly written text-book that is highly recommended for the beginning student.

Norman, Richard. *The Moral Philosophers.* New York: Oxford Univ. Press, 1983. A brief survey of the main figures in the history of ethics.

Olson, Robert G. *The Morality of Self-Interest.* New York: Harcourt, 1965. An interesting defense of a version of egoism.

Rand, Ayn. *The Virtue of Selfishness.* New York: Signet, 1964. An interesting, but at times confusing, defense of egoism by a popular novelist and an intellectual leader of the libertarian movement.

Russell, Bertrand. *Human Society in Ethics and Politics.* New York: Simon & Schuster, 1952. A clearly written analysis of a variety of ethical issues by a great modern philosopher.

Singer, Peter. *How Are We to Live?* Amherst, N.Y.: Prometheus Books, 1995. The author argues that an ethical approach to life can be more satisfying and meaningful than a self-centered approach.

Smart, J. J. C., and Bernard Williams. *Utilitarianism: For and Against.* London: Cambridge Univ. Press, 1973. Smart gives a detailed description and defense of utilitarianism, and Williams offers a variety of criticisms.

Dictionary of the History of Ideas: Studies of Selected Pivotal Ideas. Philip P. Weiner, editor-in-chief. New York: Scribner's, 1973. Substantial and clearly written essays emphasizing the historical development of topics discussed in this part. Designed to inform the nonspecialist, each essay concludes with a select bibliography.

Encyclopedia of Philosophy. Paul Edwards, editor-in-chief. New York: Macmillan, 1967. The student will find many worthwhile articles on the subject treated in this part and excellent bibliographies.

PART FOUR

State and Society

INTRODUCTION

Consider these two situations. It is April 14, late in the evening. Completing your federal income tax form, you discover to your dismay that you owe an additional tax of two hundred dollars to the U.S. government. After triple-checking your return, you sigh and write out a personal check in the amount required. For it is either pay or be fined or perhaps be clapped into jail. Nothing voluntary here. You are being coerced by other human beings; if you do not comply, you will suffer. Muttering, you trudge to the mailbox located on the next block. Returning to your home, a man you've never seen before points a revolver at you and demands that you give him all of your money. Nothing voluntary here, either. Choking down your anger, you give the robber the fifty dollars in your wallet. The story ends somewhat happily. You reach home safe but poorer.

Do these two situations differ in any significant way? Or are they the same except for incidental details? Both involve financial loss and coercion that you would prefer to avoid. Is the government nothing more than a robber on a more ambitious scale? Is the robber really an individual entrepreneur heroically defying a company monopoly? Of course, many would hold that the two situations are not comparable at all. The federal income tax is legitimate, legal, justifiable, whereas robbery is criminal, illegal, unjustifiable. The income tax constitutes a self-assessment; through your elected representatives you've consented to it. You have not consented to be robbed. As a result of the Sixteenth Amendment, the federal income tax is constitutional. Armed robbery is unconstitutional. Certainly armed robbery is undemocratic. The federal income tax possesses a political philosophy to give it rational support; armed robbery remains innocent of any political philosophy justifying it.

The field of political philosophy offers a rich and varied landscape of problems, methods of analysis, and solutions. This section focuses on one problem: Can the democratic state be justified rationally? Can its superiority to other forms of government be shown on rational grounds? All governments, whether allegedly democratic or not, claim to be legitimate. That is to say, they assert that they not only have the allegiance of those subject to their authority but that they also deserve loyalty. Democratic governments are no exception to this generalization. The government of the United States claims not only that its citizens must support it by paying taxes and, if necessary, must protect and defend it by fighting and dying in war; it further holds that American citizens ought to be ready and willing to make these sacrifices. If any individual American citizen or group of American citizens refuse to obey the government, then those in authority not only can use the police power to compel obedience but are justified in doing so.

A legitimate government maintains that its physical authority ultimately rests on moral authority. Governments justify their existence and policies by appealing to a political philosophy. Democratic governments claim to be promoting the political philosophy of democracy. Defending the cause of the Union at Gettysburg, Lincoln did not rest that defense on the threat of force; he declared that the nation was "conceived in liberty and dedicated to the proposition that all men are created equal." A political philosophy, whatever else it may comprise, consists of propositions claiming to be true and consistent with one another. And governments, particularly when their authority is seriously and sharply questioned, picture themselves implementing some political philosophy. Therefore, the political philosophy of democracy is not to be identified with familiar democratic practices such as universal suffrage, the two-party system, political conventions, a president and a congress, specific legislation, and so on; these actual governmental forms and exercises presumably are the most effective means so far devised for translating the abstract propositions of democratic political philosophy into concrete reality. A democratic government is supposed to be democratic political philosophy in action.

Of course, the political philosophy of democracy includes many more propositions than merely one or two basic ones such as that all men are created equal. Any serious political philosophy turns out to be more complex than that in the sense of being composed of a large number of propositions. Incidentally, this fact accounts for the inconsistency, which often exists unnoticed in the crowd, among some of the propositions. However, let us concentrate on the proposition that all men are created equal for the moment in order to facilitate the task of briefly sketching what a philosopher in his professional capacity does when he scrutinizes a political philosophy. Democratic politicians seek to implement the political philosophy of democracy, espouse principles, and renew people's dedication to those tenets. The philosopher works along different lines. He seeks to articulate each and every proposition constituting the political philosophy of democracy and to state them as free from ambiguity, vagueness, and emotional connotations as possible. As Socrates questioned the meaning of the Oracle of Delphi's declaration that no one was wiser than Socrates, the political philosopher searches for the meaning of the proposition "All men are created equal." What does the proposition "All men are created equal" mean? Is this the best statement of the proposition? Each word in the statement of the proposition can be found in the dictionary and the words are combined in a grammatically correct way. Does "created" imply some conception of a divine creation of humanity so that democratic political philosophy would have to include certain theological statements about God and the origin of humankind? Certainly some proponents of democracy have argued that democracy rests on supernatural and revealed religion, that it really is God's will. Some critics of democracy also have agreed with the religious defenders of democracy that it has a divine basis, that democracy is Christian ethics translated into a secular vocabulary. However, these critics have gone on to argue that the soundness and even the sense of Christian ethics is inextricably bound up with acceptance of the whole Christian faith. But in terms of the scientific outlook of the present, the Christian faith changes from truth to myth and so democracy along with it becomes no more than a dream, no matter how appealing. In reply, religious exponents of democracy have contended that the warranted conclusion to draw is that if democracy is to survive and prosper, everyone should "get religion." Our religiously pluralistic society has encouraged defenders of this religious basis of democracy to enlarge that basis beyond Christianity to embrace other religions and, even further, just to embrace religion in general. Further, how is the proposition that each individual is of unique worth to be rendered consistent with the principle that all men are created equal? What is meant by "equality"? Equal talents? Equal incomes? Equality before the law? Equality of opportunity? That every adult citizen who is not obviously insane or retarded can fulfill competently the duties of any elective office? Does "equality" mean all of these, some of these, or none of these? Finally, granted clarity and agreement on the meaning of the proposition "All men are created equal," is the proposition true or false? At least what evidence, were it to be found, would be accepted as falsifying the proposition? Is "All men are created equal" an empirical generalization such as "Water freezes at 32 degrees Fahrenheit"? If it is, then producing one human being created unequal would prove this generalization false. Or is the proposition "All men are created equal" prescriptive, rather than descriptive? Instead of asserting some state of affairs, is the proposition simply the expression of a desire: I, or we, wish that all men were created equal? But, then, if it were prescriptive, the proposition "All men are created equal" would be neither true nor false. A wish is neither true nor false.

The aim in this introduction is not to answer these questions but to suggest the distinctive character of the philosophic approach to political thought, an enterprise consisting in the combination of clarification of concepts, determination of logical consistency, formulation and assessment of criteria of truth and falsity, and the ultimate weighing of the truth claims of the principles espoused to justify political action. Political philosophy is distinct from day-to-day political debate and descriptive accounts of actual political behavior, although they may influence political philosophy and vice versa. Some political philosophies are so comprehensive they range from offering shrewd practical advice on how to be a successful tyrant or win a revolution to envisioning a total form or way of life covering all aspects of individual and collective human life; from how to win elections or seize control of the state to doctrines about the essence of human nature, the direction of history, and the nature of reality; from maneuvers to metaphysics. Certainly, in terms of speculative boldness and development, political philosophy extends beyond what social scientists would consider genuinely scientific theorizing. This bulging over the boundaries of the strictly scientific often has enhanced the power of political philosophies to elicit an active devotion from millions, which at times is religious in both intensity and endurance. From Plato to Karl Popper, influencing the actions of men has been one of the main goals of political philosophers.

For a moment let us return to the cases of paying one's taxes and being robbed. The federal income tax is constitutional and the law of the land, and so presumably it represents the will of a majority of American citizens. Yet there are Americans who do not want, do not consent, to pay income taxes any more than they do to being robbed. What rationally persuasive grounds can be found in democratic political philosophy as to why a dissenting minority should abide by the will of a majority and not seek to do everything possible to successfully evade it? Does a majority vote really reflect the will of a majority of the citizens? Convincing answers to these questions are not as easy to find as one might first suppose. Laws are devised and passed by elected representatives and not by a direct vote of the people. Representatives in government are cultivated constantly by skillful lobbyists representing not the people in general but powerful, wealthy special-interest groups. Before laws can be voted on by a legislature as a whole, they must be reported out of a legislative committee composed only of a small number of legislators. As a result of the seniority system in the U.S. Congress, the powerful chairmanships of these committees often are held by representatives who are reelected many times by a small minority of the American people in districts and states where the candidate faces no significant political opposition. The cost of campaigning for high national office has grown to the point where only wealthy individuals or those who have put themselves heavily in debt to wealthy individuals, corporations, unions, and other groups can afford it. The president of the United States, ostensibly representing all of the American people, is not elected directly by the people. Provided he has the necessary number of electoral votes, a candidate can become president of the United States even though he does not gain a majority of the popular vote. Furthermore, a majority of the eligible voters often do not even vote. Finally, few candidates for public office are elected unanimously; voters cast ballots against them by voting for opponents or by abstaining from voting entirely. That is to say, at any given time a considerable number of Americans are opposed to those governing them and do not consider their elected rulers to be representing their will at all.

However, let us suppose that the machinery of democratic government functioned perfectly and infallibly registered the will of the people. Is what the majority believes to be true or good always so? At one time a majority of Europeans believed the earth to be flat. A few generations ago a majority of Americans believed that slavery was right and just. Of course, by sheer overwhelming weight of numbers, a majority could force a dissenting minority to go along with its wishes, however much the minority might disagree silently. But all this would prove is the superior might of the majority, not its superior knowledge or virtue. If a dissenting minority should submit to a majority merely because decision, however arrived at, is better than indecisive drifting, a dictator securely in power could supply the decisiveness in a less inconstant manner than could a vague, shifting majority confused by conflicting propaganda. The quality of a majority decision is the resultant of the quality of the individuals who compose the majority; for example, a majority composed of stupid people would be more likely to reach foolish decisions than wise ones. Such a majority of poor quality might accidentally produce some wise decisions; nevertheless, fortuitous wisdom hardly seems a very persuasive reason for always accepting the will of the majority. Should not the vote of an intelligent, informed, responsible, civic-minded person count two, three, or more times the vote of some lout who must be dragged out of a saloon on election day and lured to the polls to vote with the promise of a free drink afterwards? Perhaps individuals should earn the privilege of the vote by first making some worthwhile contribution to society or only on the condition that they be self-supporting or have I.Q.s over 80. It has been argued that those who possess more property and more capital hold a greater stake in the fate of the country because they have more to lose than those who possess less, and that, therefore, these wealthier people should determine government policy. Those with little or nothing to lose are likely to act selfishly, rashly, and irresponsibly. Wealthy officeholders would be immune to bribes since they don't need more money, already having more than enough.

A rational justification of democracy would be impossible without weighing the merits of alternative forms of government. Everyone is familiar with the *mot* to the effect that democracy is the worst form of government except for all the other forms of government that have been tried. Yet the claimed superior worth of democracy hardly goes uncontested. The political philosophy of socialism, now subscribed to by millions of people, views American democracy as a sham doomed to disappear in the future. The political philosophy of anarchism opposes American democracy because it sees all government as inherently evil.

These foregoing remarks are not intended to settle the issue of the merits of democracy; they are intended to point up the fact that it is a real, vital issue.

In his defense of democracy, Sidney Hook defines his philosophical conception of democracy as including not only a form of political government but also as embracing a way of life. For him democracy as a way of life means "a way of organizing human relationships which embodies a certain complex of moral ideas."

Democracy is not only a political concept; it also is an ethical one. That this is so becomes clear when political democracies are criticized for not being democratic enough. Political democracy really is a means for achieving and securing ethical democracy. The principle of ethical democracy is equality. Political democracy means equality of freedom, but ethical democracy carries the concept of equality far beyond this to whatever is relevant to the effective exercise of equality of freedom. Ethical democracy means social equality, including political, educational, and economic democracy. Hook makes clear that ethical democracy does not mean equality of status or origin but, rather, equality of opportunity, relevant functions, and social participation. He clarifies the meaning of the equality principle in ethical democracy by distinguishing seven misconceptions of the nature of equality and contrasting them with their corresponding correct conceptions.

Of chief concern to philosophers is this question: What are the grounds justifying democracy as opposed to other forms of social organization? Hook argues that democracy as a way of life is a hypothesis capable of repeated empirical test and not a set of absolutely certain dogmas self-evidently valid and right. It should be noted that Hook treats moral ideas themselves as hypotheses capable of being tested by appeal to experience. He then sets forth six grounds he believes justify the superiority of democracy. Finally, Hook argues against three objections to the feasibility of the democratic idea.

"I know no country in which there is so little true independence of mind and freedom of discussion as in America." Although Alexis de Tocqueville made this observation about the United States of 1831–1832, many foreign and domestic critics of American democracy find his observation to be just as true today. But de Tocqueville was not merely an acute and shrewd observer of the events of his time; he also was a political philosopher who worked out the logical implications of concepts. He was convinced that the concept of democracy contained within itself the seeds of a future tyranny. Nevertheless, de Tocqueville did not believe in the inevitability of democracy becoming tyrannical; he was too realistic to think that human life always followed logic. He meant his observation of the America he had visited to warn that unless the growth of democracy were limited, democracy surely would destroy independence of mind and freedom of discussion.

What were the democratic seeds of tyranny de Tocqueville detected? They lurk in the principle of majority rule. In de Tocqueville's philosophy, every social order ultimately rests upon some supreme authority to which every other authority is subordinated. The nature of that supreme authority varies from one society to another. In a democracy it is the will of the majority. Legislators and presidents must stand for election; although amending the Constitution requires more than a majority vote, the people can amend it or even create a new one by calling a constitutional convention. The deadly danger to liberty in a democracy lies in the lack of any subordinate power strong enough to provide an effective check on the will of the majority. Any unlimited power becomes tyrannical and eventually destroys liberty, whether it be that of a monarch or majority opinion. Indeed, de Tocqueville believed that an unrestrained power of majority rule would produce a worse curtailment of independence of mind and freedom of discussion than that of any other kind of unchecked authority. Its tyranny would be so complete and pervasive that it would create a self-imposed censorship. Other kinds of despotism seek to control the body but not the mind; the democratic variety, however, subjugates the mind and leaves the body free to engage in its normal activities. Instead of being jailed, tortured, or executed, citizens of a democracy who dare to utter their disagreement with the opinion of the majority soon find themselves pariahs, blacklisted, denied employment, refused celebrity, and shunned by their former friends and associates. An exile in his or her own country, the democratic rebel falls silent and sinks into a hypocritical servility more demoralizing than that of the courtiers of old. De Tocqueville would not be surprised, however much he might be dismayed, were his ghost to return and see the campus protesters and marchers of the 1960s now turned into pillars of the "establishment" they once so vehemently opposed, the earlier student admirer of Socrates now transformed into an enthusiastic Rotarian. De Tocqueville's concern was heightened by what seemed to him to be the relentless march of democracy to world domination. True he did not foresee every future variation of his theme such as the deliberate manufacture of majority opinion by a host of advertisers, propagandists, politicians, and others skilled in the use of the means of mass communication. If he had, he probably would have predicted the same result: the self-inflicted destruction of independence of mind and freedom of expression. In any event, de Tocqueville hoped that if people were alerted to the tyrannical potentialities of democracy, they might be able to devise effective ways to prevent them from being realized.

According to Ayn Rand, a genuinely free society is one in which individuals are ends in themselves and society is only the means to "the peaceful, orderly, voluntary co-existence of individuals." Societies and governments are merely groups of individuals, not real entities in addition to individual men and women. Neither governments nor societies possess any rights. The only purpose of government in such societies is to protect individual rights. Individual rights constitute the means to bring society under the control of moral law. In most previous societies just the reverse has been the case because they have been dominated by altruism-collectivism, a doctrine which in effect says that the moral law applies to individuals but not to society. Consequently, these societies have been amoral tyrannies and their individual members sacrificial animals.

Rand identifies her conception of a free society with laissez-faire capitalism. Strictly speaking, human beings have only one right: a right to their own lives. All other rights flow from this basic right, which is not given to them by God or society but is theirs by virtue of their own rational natures. The identification of this right with capitalism appears in Rand's insistence that property rights are necessary to all other rights. A property right is a right to action. While it does not guarantee that anyone will own property, it is "a guarantee that he will own it if he earns it. It is the right to gain, to keep, to use and to dispose of material values." But there is no "economic right" to the property of another; no individual, society, or government has any "right" to compel anyone to surrender any of his or her property to others. Consequently, Rand uncompromisingly opposes all altruist-collectivist doctrines such as the welfare state, socialism, communism, and fascism because she sees them as enemies of freedom or, what for her is the same thing, the right to property.

In presenting his moral case for socialism, Kai Nielsen clarifies what capitalism and socialism are. In capitalism, productive property or the means of production are privately owned; an individual or a group of individuals rather than the general public own the property and decide what will be done with it. Socialism means genuine public ownership and control of productive property but not of personal property. Nielsen emphasizes that socialism is *not* state ownership without control of the state and its activities by the public or citizenry at large. As Nielsen sees capitalism and socialism, they are not merely economic organizations; they also are social systems, ways of life. As a social system, capitalism is a class society divided into a class of capitalists and a class of workers. In socialism every able-bodied person is a worker.

In arguing for the superiority of socialism over capitalism, Nielsen expressly compares the "pure" models of democratic socialism and competitive capitalism rather than the actually existing "impure" forms of bureaucratic state socialism and corporate capitalism. However, Nielsen does not believe he is comparing one impossible dream with another equally unobtainable one, because he is convinced that the pure models of socialism and capitalism he is contrasting could be realized. He then argues the moral case that socialism will be more successful than capitalism in sustaining and furthering the fundamental values of freedom and autonomy, equality, justice, rights and democracy.

Murray N. Rothbard's libertarian anarchism agrees with traditional anarchism in viewing the state or government as the chief enemy of all persons and property. Unlike the traditional anarchist, Rothbard does not advocate the violent overthrow of all governments. According to the libertarian anarchism of Rothbard, the state by its very nature is a robber, enslaver, and murderer. There are no exceptions to this indictment of the state; it applies equally to all governments be they democratic, dictatorial, monarchical, or some other form. States or governments always have considered themselves outside the general moral law, an amoral status often euphemistically called "reasons of state."

Can the state or government be reformed, tamed so that it serves moral ends, puts the welfare of the general citizenry ahead of its own selfish aggrandizement? Could any state ever sincerely promote life, liberty, and the pursuit of happiness? Not without ceasing to be a government. According to Rothbard, all social institutions *except* the state rely on voluntary support and must refrain from violence against others. The government, however, compels support through taxation and imposes its will on citizens under the threat or commission of violence against those who defy its tyranny. People have turned to government to protect themselves against private criminals. But who will protect the people against the greatest criminal of all, the government? Who will guard the guardians? Rothbard answers that no one and no institutional tinkering can or will. Such limitations as constitutions, separation of powers, and majority rule are at best feeble and ultimately are doomed to failure. But are not governments needed to provide at least some rough equality? On the contrary, inequality is a pervasive fact of all human life and social relations because it is a fact of nature. A society of free individuals and groups in which all relations are voluntary and untainted by coercion and in which private property is safe from theft is forever incompatible and irreconcilable with any state or government.

Appealing to the feminist demand for the abolition of sexism and sexual inequality because they are wrong or "lies," some activists and philosophers have called for the prohibition or at least control of pornography. Doing so has brought them into conflict with defenders of the democratic right to freedom of speech. The feminist philosopher Helen E. Longino redefines pornography in terms of the viewpoint of feminism. According to her, the distinguishing trait of pornography is not sexual explicitness, sexual realism, or even the depiction of degrading or abusive sexual behavior, as it has been thought to be in the past and is still believed to be by many in the present, but is the *endorsement* or *approval* of sexual behavior abusive of or degrading to one or more of the participants. For example, depictions of women deriving sexual pleasure from abuse or degradation are pornographic because their enjoyment connotes approval or endorsement of their treatment; pornography affirms that women, solely because they are women, want to be raped, bound, tortured, to be only instruments for providing male sexual satisfaction. But this is a lie about the nature of women and what women want. The truth is that women want to be treated as men's equals, as persons of basic human dignity deserving of respect. Thus pornography defames and libels women and, by endorsing their unequal sexual treatment, also suggests approval of their oppression socially, economically, and culturally.

But the right to free speech is not a right to libel others. In Longino's view, the right to free speech is not the right to utter whatever one pleases. The rights mentioned in the First Amendment to the Constitution, those of speech, press, religion, and the right to petition, are not absolute but rather are *means* needed to secure liberty. In Longino's interpretation, liberty is not "license" or the freedom to do as one pleases but is "independence" or "the status of a person as independent and equal rather than subservient." But pornography endorses the dependent and unequal status of women or their subservience to men. There is no "right" to pornography. Therefore, the prohibition or control of pornography is not an abridgment of a right of free speech or of any other right.

Jan Narveson claims that the case for banning or strictly controlling pornography is a weak one and marshals his reasons mainly in the form of criticisms of the case for suppressing it. Whereas, traditionally, pornography has been defined as the depiction of sexually stimulating subject matter with the purpose of producing sexual arousal, Narveson recognizes the recent expanding of its meaning to include an alleged connection of sex and violence. To argue that pornography should be prohibited or restricted because it demeans women assumes the premise that whatever demeans people should be prohibited or restricted which, in turn, would justify the censorship of the Old Testament and other works many or most people believe should not be censored. To the argument that pornography should be censored on the grounds that it approves falsehoods about women in general— e.g., women are inferior to men, women want to be abused or degraded, women enjoy being subservient to men, and so on—Narveson replies that falsehood does not justify the suppression of the people who express that falsehood but instead provides an opportunity to refute that falsehood. It must be remembered that to depict falsehood or evil is not necessarily to advocate it. In any event, normal people can be exposed to falsehood and evil, including explicit approval of them, without being converted. Audiences seeing the movie *Birth of a Nation* have not joined the Ku Klux Klan. Narveson's antipaternalism sounds in his declaration that people must be presumed capable of making their own decisions and that they are morally responsible. There is an undeniable paternalistic caste to any claim that people must be shielded from something lest it corrupt them. Narveson characterizes what empirical evidence there is that viewing pornography causes people to commit rape and other crimes as "overwhelmingly inconclusive." Instead of curtailing free speech, we should rely on education, particularly the proper instruction of children by their parents.

Should people be legally permitted to climb the sides of skyscrapers, go over Niagara Falls in a barrel, or treat themselves with dangerous drugs? The articles by Szasz and Dworkin deal with a fundamental social and ethical issue: should people be free to act as they choose as long as they do not harm others? Thomas Szasz, a supporter of extensive individual freedom, argues that there should be no restriction on a person's private use of drugs. To restrict access to potentially harmful drugs robs people of their dignity by deeming them incapable of making some important decisions about their lives. Gerald Dworkin, unlike Szasz, believes that some interference in people's private actions is warranted. Since there are many types of situations in which people know that they are likely to act hastily or foolishly, Dworkin contends that rational persons would support paternalistic measures as "social insurance policies."

In "The Prisoner's Dilemma" Morton Davis clearly sets forth one of the most intriguing problems of game theory. Indeed, some go so far as to claim that the articulation of this dilemma and the realization that it lies at the heart of many of our social and political problems constitute one of the outstanding intellectual achievements of this century. Critical understanding of social and political philosophies is sharpened by viewing them as attempts to grapple with this dilemma. Davis shows that the prisoner's dilemma is no mere game in the sense of a trivial amusement by amply illustrating how it reappears in setting advertising budgets, conserving water, paying taxes, limiting farm overproduction, dealing with the arms race—indeed, reemerges whenever one must decide how to act in response to the way one believes others will act under a given set of circumstances. In this kind of "game," each player can choose to cooperate with the other player or players by acting as they do or to defect or not act as the other player or players do. Essential to generating the dilemma is a graduated system of rewards and punishments such that the greatest reward or payoff goes to the player who defects when the other player cooperates, the second highest reward or payoff goes to all of the players when all of them cooperate, the second greatest punishment goes to all of the players when all of them defect, and the greatest punishment, or "sucker's payoff," goes to the player who cooperates when the others defect. It should be noted that if one side is to win the greatest reward, the other side must suffer the greatest punishment. Conversely, if everyone is to be spared the greatest punishment, then everyone must forego the greatest reward. Should one cooperate and thus act for the benefit of all, or should one defect and thus act only for one's selfish interest? What is it rational to do? Davis points out that most people are so repelled by the selfish strategy of defection for which the prisoner's dilemma presents such a compelling argument that they shift the question from What is the rational strategy? to How can cooperation or acting in concert be justified?

Anthony Downs argues that it is not rational for the individual voter to become well informed, although most citizens would benefit if all of the voters were well informed. Of course, conventional wisdom declares that each individual voter should be as well informed as possible in order to be able to make the most rational decision in voting. However, conventional wisdom fails to reckon with the Prisoner's Dilemma. When is it rational for the individual voter to expend the time, energy, and money necessary to become well informed? Downs appeals to the economic axiom that it is rational to perform any act when its marginal return exceeds its marginal cost. Applying this axiom to individual voters in a populous country like the United States, Downs reaches the unconventional conclusion that it is irrational for most people to acquire political information for the purpose of voting. In a large electorate any individual's vote is insignificant because of the minuscule probability of that vote's being decisive in determining the outcome of the election. Consequently, the marginal cost of becoming a well-informed voter almost always will outweigh the marginal benefit. Downs admits that this conclusion may not be true for every individual voter, but he claims that it is for most. The alleged voter apathy so often deplored really is voter rationality. Admittedly government would better serve the interests of an informed majority than it would those of an uninformed one. Collectively it is rational for voters to become well informed. Individually it is irrational.

DEMOCRACY

32. The Philosophical Presuppositions of Democracy

Sidney Hook

Sidney Hook (1902–1989) for many years was a member of the New York University faculty. He devoted particular attention to social, political, moral, and educational issues. His writings on these topics often appeared in publications of broad circulation. Although a Marxist activist in his early years, he later became most celebrated as a critic of communism and an uncompromising advocate and defender of democracy against all forms of totalitarianism on the basis of an undeviating commitment to freedom and to the pragmatic naturalism of John Dewey.

The principle may be stated in various ways, but for our purposes we may say that a democratic state is one in which the basic decisions of government rest upon the freely given consent of the governed. This obviously is only a beginning. For just as soon as we begin to investigate the conditions which must be present before we grant that a state lives up to this principle, we are carried beyond the sphere of political considerations into the domain of ethics. Thus, if information has been withheld or withdrawn before consent is assessed; if the opposition is muzzled or suppressed so that consent is as unanimous as a totalitarian plebiscite; or if economic sanctions are threatened against a section of the community in the event that consent takes one form or another, we declare that the "spirit" or "logic" or "rationale" of democracy is absent from its political forms. If birth does not give divine right, neither does numbers [*sic*]. We are all acquainted with situations in which we say that a political democracy has traduced its own ideals. Whenever we criticize existing states which conform to the political definition of democracy on the ground that they are not democratic enough; whenever we point out that Athenian democracy was limited only to free men, or that in some parts of the American South it is limited only to white men, or in some countries it is limited only to men, we are invoking a broader principle of democracy as a controlling reference in our judgments of comparison. This principle is an ethical one.

Sidney Hook, "The Presuppositions of Democracy," *Ethics*, Vol. 52, April, 1942, pp. 275–296. Copyright 1942 by The University of Chicago. Reprinted by permission of The University of Chicago Press.

What is this principle of ethical democracy? It is a principle of equality—an equality not of status or origin but of opportunity, relevant functions, and social participation. The enormous literature and bitter controversy which center around the concept of equality indicate that it is only a little less ambiguous than the concept of democracy. It is necessary, therefore, to block it off from some current notions before developing the argument.

a) The principle of equality is not a *description* of fact about men's physical or intellectual natures. It is a *prescription* or policy of treating men.

b) It is not a prescription to treat men in identical ways who are unequal in their physical or intellectual nature. It is a policy of equality of concern or consideration for men whose different needs may require differential treatment.

c) It is not a mechanical policy of equal opportunity for everyone at *any* time and in *all* respects. A musical genius is entitled to greater opportunities to develop his musical talents than someone who is tone deaf. It is equality of opportunity for all individuals to develop whatever personal and socially desirable talents they possess and to make whatever unique contributions their capacities permit.

d) It is not a demand for absolute uniformity of living conditions or even for arithmetically equal compensation for socially useful work. It demands that, when the productive forces of a society makes [*sic*] possible the gratification of basic human needs (which are, of course, historical variables), no one should be deprived of necessities in order to provide others with luxuries

e) It is not a policy of restricting the freedom of being different or becoming different. It is a policy of *encouraging* the freedom to be different, restricting only that exercise of freedom which converts talents or possessions into a monopoly that frustrates the emergence of other free personalities.

f) It is not a demand that all people be leaders or that none should be. It does demand that the career of leadership, like all other careers, be open to all whose natural or acquired talents qualify them; that everyone have a say in the process of selecting leaders; that the initiative of leaders operate within a framework of basic laws; and that these laws in turn ultimately rest upon the freely given consent of the persons who constitute the community.

g) It does not make the assumption of sentimental humanitarianism that all men are naturally good. It does assume that men, treated as equals in a community of persons, may become better. The emphasis upon respect for the personality of all individuals, the attitude which treats the personality not as something fixed but as a growing, developing pattern, is unique to the philosophy of democracy.

What I have been trying to show is that the logic of the democrat's position compels him to go beyond the limited conception of political democracy—the equality of freedom—to a broader attitude extending to those other phases of social existence that bear upon the effective exercise of equality of freedom. This in fact has been the historical tendency observable wherever democratic principles and programs are permitted to operate. Perhaps the synoptic phrase "social equality," whose connotations encompass political, educational, and economic democracy, may be taken as the most appropriate expression of the meaning of democracy in the broadest sense.

It is clear that the principle of equality, like any principle of justice, cannot by itself determine what is specifically right or good in each concrete case. But whatever the right is discovered to be, from the point of view of democracy it is the result of an analysis which considers equally the needs of all the persons involved in the situation; and, further, whatever the good is, it becomes better to the extent that it is shared among other members of the community. It is also clear that in concrete situations there will be conflicts between various demands for equality and that in negotiating these conflicts the methods of intelligence are indispensable for a functioning democracy. If empiricism be a generic term for the philosophic attitude which submits *all* claims of fact and value to test by experience, then empiricism as a philosophy is more congenial to a democratic than to an antidemocratic community, for it brings into the open light of criticism the interests in which moral values and social institutions are rooted. Empiricism so conceived is commitment to a procedure, not to a theory of metaphysics.

In this brief account of the nature of democracy as a way of life I have not aimed at an exhaustive analysis of the *forms* in which it may be expressed but have tried to indicate the basic ideals which are involved in the customary usage of the term and in the implications of that usage.

We now come to the problem which is of primary concern to philosophers. What are the grounds on which we can justify our acceptance of democracy in contradistinction to other modes of social life? . . .

Democracy as a hypothesis.—When democracy is taken strictly as a form of political government, its superiority over other forms of government can be established to the extent that it achieves more security, freedom, and co-operative diversity than any of its alternatives. If we test the workings of political democracy by Paul's scheme of virtues or by Nietzsche's, we may perhaps reach another conclusion. So long as there is no dispute about observable effects and so long as we raise no question about the moral ideals by which we evaluate these effects, we have clear sailing.

But, as has already been made plain, by democracy as a way of life we mean a way of organizing human relationships which embodies a certain complex of moral ideals. Can these ideals be treated as hypotheses? The conventional reply has always been that no moral principle can be regarded as a hypothesis, for we must already have certain knowledge of what is good before we can evaluate the consequences of acting upon it. If any position is question-begging, surely this seems to be!

Were this a symposium on value theory, I would devote all my time to developing the general theory of moral ideals as hypotheses. But here I can only barely indicate that the notion is not viciously circular. A moral ideal is a prescription to act in a certain situation or class of situations in determinate ways that will organize the human needs and wants involved so as to fulfil a set of *other* values which are *postulated* as binding in relation to the problem in hand. No more than in other cases of inquiry do we start with an empty head. The cluster of values we bring to the situation is the result of prior experience and reflection. They are not arbitrarily postulated. The consequences of acting upon the hypothesis may lead us to challenge a postulated or assumed value. This in turn can become the subject of a similar investigation. Terminal values are always related to specific contexts; there is no absolute terminal value which is either self-evident or beyond the necessity of justifying itself if its credentials are challenged. There is no vicious infinite regress involved if we take our problems concretely and one at a time. Nor is the procedure narrowly circular. For if, in a long history of raising and solving moral problems, we postulate as a value in solving a later problem a value which had itself to be certified in an earlier problem, this would testify to the presence of a fruitful set of systematically related values in the structure of our moral behavior. New values would emerge, or be discovered, in the course of our attempt to act upon our ideals and from the necessity of mediating the conflict between the postulated values as they bear on concrete human needs in specific situations.

I should like, however, to make the general position take form out of the discussion of the theme before us. That theme is: Why should we treat individuals of unequal talents and endowments as persons who are equally entitled to relevant consideration and care? Short of a treatise I can state only the reasons, without amplification of the concrete needs of the social situation which democracy seeks to meet and the institutional practices by which it must meet them.

a) This method of treating human beings is more successful than any other in evoking a maximum of creative, voluntary effort from all members of the community. Properly implemented it gives all persons a stake in the community and elicits a maximum of intelligent loyalty.

b) It enlarges the scope of our experience by enabling us to acquire insight into the needs, drives, and aspirations of others. Learning to understand how life is organized by other centers of experience is both a challenge and a discipline for our imagination. In aiding the growth of others, we aid our own growth.

c) The willingness to understand another man's point of view without necessarily surrendering to it makes it more likely that different points of view may negotiate their differences and learn to live peacefully with one another. A democratic community cannot be free from strife in a world where inequalities will always exist, but its ethics when intelligently acted upon makes more likely the diminution of strife or its transference to socially harmless forms than is the case when its principle of equality is denied. The consequences are less toadying, less fear, and less duplicity in the equalitarian community than in the nonequalitarian society.

d) In nurturing the capacities of each individual so that they may come to their greatest fulfilment, we can best share our existing stores of truth and beauty and uncover new dimensions in these realms. How can anyone dedicated to the values of science and art consistently oppose a policy which maximizes the possibility of the discovery and widest dispersion of scientific truths and artistic meanings?

e) Regard for the potentialities of all individuals makes for less cruelty of man toward man especially where cruelty is the result of blindness to, or ignorance of, other's needs. A community organized along democratic lines is guilty of cruelty only at those points where it has failed to live up to its own ideals. A totalitarian community is systematically insensitive to the personal needs not only of members of the outlawed scapegoat group but of the majority of its subjects who are excluded from policy-making discussions. At best, there is no way of determining these personal needs except by the interpretation of the dictator and his experts who operate with the dogma that they know the true interests of their subjects better than the subjects themselves. At worst, the dictator assumes not only that he speaks for his subjects but that in some mystic way he feels and thinks for them too. Despite the great limitations—limitations from the point of view of their own ideals—under which the nineteenth- and twentieth-century democracies of the Western world suffered, I think it is indisputable, on the evidence, that by and large their social life, in so far as this was the consequence of policy, displayed less cruelty than the social life of any other historical period.

f) Reasonableness of conclusions, where attitudes and interests conflict, depends upon the degree of mutual consultation and free intellectual communication between the principals involved. The democratic way of life makes possible the widest forms of mutual consultation and communication. Conclusions reached by these processes have a quality that can never be found where conclusions are imposed by force or authority—even if they are our own. Let me illustrate what I mean by taking as an example the enterprise represented by this Association [the American Philosophical Association]. Who among us, desirous as we may be of the possibility of philosophical agreement, would forego the methods of public discussion, criticism, argument, and rejoinder for a philosophical consensus imposed by a Gestapo or a G.P.U. even if by a strange quirk of affairs it was *our* philosophic position that the goon squads of orthodoxy sought to make the way of salvation? Who among us, knowing that outside the threshold of our meeting there stood an individual of strange country, color, or faith, capable of making a contribution to our deliberations, would not open the door to him? These are not rhetorical questions framed to discover philosophical fifth columnists. They are designed to show that the procedures of critical discussion and discovery, which are pre-eminently exhibited in the work of a scientific community, take for granted that national, racial, or religious origins are irrelevant to the logic of the method by which reasonable conclusions are reached. Democracy as a way of life differs from its alternatives in that it makes possible the extension of these methods of reaching reasonable conclusions from the fields of professional science and philosophy to all areas of human experience in which genuine problems arise.

There are other grounds that may be offered in justification of democracy as the most adequate social philosophy for our times. Every one of them, like the foregoing, postulates implicitly or explicitly values or desiderata. But I repeat: these postulates are ultimate only for the problem in hand. They may require justification. When we undertake such justification, we have undertaken a new inquiry into a new problem.

There are two important consequences of approaching democracy in this way. The first is that we avoid the temptation, which is rapidly gaining vogue, of making democracy absolutely valid in and for itself. There are many today who write as if they believe that democracy should prevail even though the heavens fall, and who say in so many words that "to question the validity of democracy is to disbelieve in it" and that we can meet the blind fanatical faith of fascism only with a faith in democracy which is at least just as fanatical. This temptation, it seems to me, must be avoided because, by counterposing subrational dogma to subrational dogma, it prepares the ground for an acceptance of a might makes right morality. Second, those who make of democracy an absolute value, which requires no justification but its inherent rightness, tend to identify this absolute democracy with whatever particular democratic status quo exists. On the other hand, the natural tendency of those who cannot distinguish between social philosophies on the ground of their inherent rightness is to test a social philosophy by the social institutions in which it is embodied. They are, therefore, more attentive to the actual workings and effects of democracy, more historical minded, and less likely to gloss over existing imperfections.

To those who say that human beings will not fight whole-heartedly except for certainties, and emphatically not for a hypothesis which is only probable, the reply must be made that this empirical proposition is highly dubious. Men have fought and do fight vigorously for causes on the basis of preponderant evidence. Vigorous action, indeed, is only desirable when we have first decided what is intelligent action. And intelligent action does not result when we assume that our ideas or ideals simply cannot be wrong. That both intelligence and resoluteness are compatible is clear in fields as far apart as military science and medicine. Once it is decided that the chances of one action are relatively better than another, once it is decided that an operation gives a patient a better chance of surviving than no operation, wisdom demands that the best warranted alternative be pursued with all our heart and all our soul. Let us remember that when we fight for democracy we are not fighting for an ideal which has just been proposed as a merely possible valid ideal for our times; we already have considerable evidence in its behalf, the weight of which, unfortunately too often, is properly evaluated only when democracy is lost or imperiled.

We now turn to the question whether democracy is feasible. We can imagine someone who has accepted the tentative ends by which we evaluate ways of life criticizing us as follows: "If only the assertions made in the previous section could be established as true, the case for democracy would be convincing. But the nature of man as we know him, of history as scientifically understood, and of the larger world we live in precludes the possibility of ever achieving democracy. It runs counter to the facts. Although you may still choose to live or die for democracy, the attempt to realize it, like any attempt to realize an ideal which has no natural basis, will be a ghastly failure. Its natural consequences will be worse than the evils it sets out to cure, and it will subvert the very ideals to which you have appealed in your argument. Democracy is an infirmity of noble but innocent minds who have never understood the world. It is not an intelligent option."

I have time to consider briefly three types of objection to the feasibility of the democratic ideal.

1. The first is based upon its alleged psychological impossibility. It maintains that democracy is too good for men who are essentially evil, fallen creatures, dominated by the lust for power, property, and self. In less theological form it asserts that democracy makes too high a call upon human intelligence and disinterestedness.

It is true that the psychological nature of man is quite relevant to our problem. If most human beings were idiots or infantile or permanently incapable of self-development, the democratic ideal could hardly be defended on plausible grounds. But there is no evidence that most human beings are such, and an intelligent attempt to find out whether they are would require that equalization of social opportunity which is of the essence of democracy. Even without such an experiment, if we surrender the utopian expectation of the complete realization of the democratic ideal and bear in mind that the forms of democracy may be direct as well as indirect and that democracy is compatible with the delegation of powers and responsibilities, the evidence at hand could hardly justify the belief either in universal cretinism or in man's permanent ineducability. Nor do we have to counter with the assertion that men are *infinitely* perfectible to make our option for democracy reasonable. We require merely that they be sufficiently plastic, sufficiently capable of learning, criticism, and improvement, to choose responsibly between alternatives of action whenever—and here lies the rub—they have alternatives of choice. It is only the democratic community which will systematically give them the alternatives of choice on basic decisions. It is not without significance that no free people has ever voluntarily relinquished its democratic forms for a government which openly proclaimed as its aim the establishment of a permanent dictatorship. Principled dictatorships, as distinct from those that come in through the unguarded doors of democracy, always triumph by usurpation. As low as the human estate is today, there is no reason to believe that human beings belong to a psychological species inferior to that of their ancestors. Although history is rich in human stupidities and lost opportunities, in the face of men's achievements in the arts and sciences it would be simply foolish to read history as nothing but the record of human error.

The theological doctrine of man's essentially evil nature metaphorically expresses the truth that he is always limited, always tempted, and never free of his animal origins. But, taken literally, it makes any kind of moral virtue inconceivable except by interposition of divine grace or mystery. Here, too, we do not have to counter with a contrary theological proposition that man is essentially good. He is neither one or the other but becomes good or evil depending upon his society, his habits, and his intelligence.

2. The most powerful arguments against the feasibility of democracy, strangely enough, have been neglected by most social philosophers. These are developed in the writings of Gaetano Mosca, Vilfredo Pareto, and Roberto Michels. Their common thesis, formulated on the basis of vast, detailed studies of political and social history, is that all historical change, whether reform or revolution, consists of the substitution of one ruling minority for another. This rule rests upon three pillars: vital myths which cement human relationships and conceal differences of interest; fraud or manipulation which negotiates differences of interests; and force which ultimately settles differences of interest. The nature of social organization, they claim, is such that democrats may be victorious but democracy never. So it has been, so it is, and so it will be.

I have elsewhere tried to meet their arguments in detail. But here I content myself with one consideration which points to the self-confessed inadequacy of their position. Despite this alleged law, every one of them admits, explicitly or implicitly, that some forms of society are better than others—and in every case it is the society which has a greater degree of democracy than the others. Thus Mosca, after maintaining the inescapability of minority rule, pays strong tribute to the superiority of parliamentary democracy over all other alternatives.

Three basic errors, it seems to me, vitiate their conclusion. The first is that the amount of freedom and democracy in a society is determined by a law *already known* or, as some would say today, by a historical wave. The truth is that the amount of freedom and democracy in the present and future depends as much upon human willingness to fight for them as upon anything else. The second error is the belief, common not only to these thinkers but to countless others, that human nature is unchangeable. In so far as this is neither a proposition of biology or of theology nor a logical tautology, but refers to psychological and social traits, it can be shown to be false. The third is their confusion between an organizing principle and the individual members of the series organized. Since no identification is possible between the principle of democracy and any one member of the series, they go from the true conclusion that the principle is incompletely realized in any one case to the false conclusion that there are no degrees of realization in the series of cases.

3. The third class of objections to the feasibility of the democratic ideal is derived from alleged cosmic or physicochemical laws which contain the equations of doom for man and all his works. Even granting the validity of such laws, they would hold no matter what society exists, and, therefore, they establish nothing about the relative superiority of one form of society over another. Such laws, as William James already pointed out in a definitive refutation of all views of this type, tell us about the *size* of "energy-rills," not their *significance*.

That the cosmic home of man limits his power, if not his dreams, is of course true. It is a perennial source of his humility before the intractabilities of things and the transient character of what he builds. But it is also true that this limitation is the source of his opportunities and a necessary condition for all achievement. From these truths we cannot infer that nature is the guarantor of man's ideals, certainly not of the democratic ideal. But neither is it the enemy of human ideals. Man's friends and enemies are other men. To forget this is to go from natural piety to superstition. The cosmic scene against which men live out their lives will not be affected by Hitler's victory or defeat. Democracy needs no cosmic support other than the *chance* to make good. That chance it has, because man is part of nature. To ask for more is unreasonable even if it were not unworthy. The way in which man acts upon his chances is additional evidence of the objective possibilities and novelties of existence. In so far as he is caught up in the flux of things, the intelligent democratic man honestly confronts the potentialities of existence, its futurities, its openness, its indeterminateness. He is free of the romantic madness which would seek to outlaw the truths of science and of the quaint conceit, permissible only as poetry, that nature is a democratic republic. He takes the world as science describes it. He employs his knowledge of the world to increase man's power over things, to decrease man's power over man, and to enlarge the fellowship of free and equal persons striving to achieve a more just and happier society.

33. Democratic Tyranny

Alexis de Tocqueville

Alexis de Tocqueville (1805–1859) was a French aristocrat. Although his family suffered under the French Revolution, de Tocqueville was not an embittered foe of democracy but greatly sympathized with democratic ideals, thus making his criticism of them more penetrating and prophetic. In his enduring masterpiece Democracy in America, *he sought to give an honest and objective account of both the strengths and weaknesses of the democratic equality he predicted would conquer the future.*

I am of the opinion that some one social power must always be made to predominate over the others; but I think that liberty is endangered when this power is checked by no obstacles which may retard its course, and force it to moderate its own vehemence.

Unlimited power is in itself a bad and dangerous thing; human beings are not competent to exercise it with discretion, and God alone can be omnipotent, because his wisdom and his justice are always equal to his power. But no power upon earth is so worthy of honour for itself, or of reverential obedience to the rights which it represents, that I would consent to admit its uncontrolled and all-predominant authority. When I see that the right and the means of absolute command are conferred on a people or upon a king, upon an aristocracy or a democracy, a monarchy or a republic, I recognize the germ of tyranny, and I journey onward to a land of more hopeful institutions.

In my opinion the main evil of the present democratic institutions of the United States does not arise, as is often asserted in Europe, from their weakness, but from their overpowering strength; and I am not so much alarmed at the excessive liberty which reigns in that country as at the very inadequate securities which exist against tyranny.

When an individual or a party is wronged in the United States, to whom can he apply for redress? If to public opinion, public opinion constitutes the majority; if to the legislature, it represents the majority, and implicitly obeys its injunctions; if to the executive power, it is appointed by the majority, and remains a passive tool in its hands; the public troops consist of the majority under arms; the jury is the majority invested with the right of hearing judicial cases; and in certain States even the judges are elected by the majority. However iniquitous or absurd the evil of which you complain may be, you must submit to it as well as you can.

Reprinted from *Democracy in America*, Part One, Chapter XV, translated by Henry Reeve, 1835.

If, on the other hand, a legislative power could be so constituted as to represent the majority without necessarily being the slave of its passions; an executive, so as to retain a certain degree of uncontrolled authority; and a judiciary, so as to remain independent of the two other powers; a government would be formed which would still be democratic without incurring any risk of tyrannical abuse.

I do not say that tyrannical abuses frequently occur in America at the present day, but I maintain that no sure barrier is established against them, and that the causes which mitigate the government are to be found in the circumstances and the manners of the country more than in its laws.

A distinction must be drawn between tyranny and arbitrary power. Tyranny may be exercised by means of the law, and in that case it is not arbitrary; arbitrary power may be exercised for the good of the community at large, in which case it is not tyrannical. Tyranny usually employs arbitrary means, but, if necessary, it can rule without them.

In the United States the unbounded power of the majority, which is favourable to the legal despotism of the legislature, is likewise favourable to the arbitrary authority of the magistrate. The majority has an entire control over the law when it is made and when it is executed; and as it possesses an equal authority over those who are in power and the community at large, it considers public officers as its passive agents, and readily confides the task of serving its designs to their vigilance. The details of their office and the privileges which they are to enjoy are rarely defined beforehand; but the majority treats them as a master does his servants when they are always at work in his sight, and he has the power of directing or reprimanding them at every instant.

In general the American functionaries are far more independent than the French civil officers within the sphere which is prescribed to them. Sometimes, even, they are allowed by the popular authority to exceed those bounds; and as they are protected by the opinion, and backed by the co-operation, of the majority, they venture upon such manifestations of their power as astonish a European. By this means habits are formed in the heart of a free country which may some day prove fatal to its liberties.

It is in the examination of the display of public opinion in the United States that we clearly perceive how far the power of the majority surpasses all the powers with which we are acquainted in Europe. Intellectual principles exercise an influence which is so invisible, and often so inappreciable, that they baffle the toils of oppression. At the present time the most absolute monarchs in Europe are unable to prevent certain notions, which are opposed to their authority, from circulating in secret throughout their dominions, and even in their courts. Such is not the case in America; as long as the majority is still undecided, discussion is carried on; but as soon as its decision is irrevocably pronounced, a submissive silence is observed, and the friends, as well as the opponents, of the measure unite in assenting to its propriety. The reason of this is perfectly clear: no monarch is so absolute as to combine all the powers of society in his own hands, and to conquer all opposition with the energy of a majority which is invested with the right of making and of executing the laws.

The authority of a king is purely physical, and it controls the actions of the subject without subduing his private will; but the majority possesses a power which is physical and moral at the same time; it acts upon the will as well as upon the actions of men, and it represses not only all contest, but all controversy.

I know no country in which there is so little true independence of mind and freedom of discussion as in America. In any constitutional state in Europe every sort of religious and political theory may be advocated and propagated abroad; for there is no country in Europe so subdued by any single authority as not to contain citizens who are ready to protect the man who raises his voice in the cause of truth from the consequences of his hardihood. If he is unfortunate enough to live under an absolute government, the people is upon his side; if he inhabits a free country, he may find a shelter behind the authority of the throne, if he require one. The aristocratic part of society supports him in some countries, and the democracy in others. But in a nation where democratic institutions exist, organized like those of the United States, there is but one sole authority, one single element of strength and of success, with nothing beyond it.

In America, the majority raises very formidable barriers to the liberty of opinion: within these barriers an author may write whatever he pleases, but he will repent it if he ever step beyond them. Not that he is exposed to the terrors of an *auto-da-fé*, but he is tormented by the slights and persecutions of daily obloquy. His political career is closed for ever, since he has offended the only authority which is able to promote his success. Every sort of compensation, even that of celebrity, is refused to him. Before he published his opinions he imagined that he held them in common with many others; but no sooner has he declared them openly than he is loudly censured by his overbearing opponents, while those who think like him, without having the courage to speak, abandon him in silence. He yields at length, oppressed by the daily efforts he has been making, and he subsides into silence, as if he was tormented by remorse for having spoken the truth.

Fetters and headsmen were the coarse instruments which tyranny formerly employed; but the civilization of our age has refined the arts of despotism, which seemed, however, to have been sufficiently perfected before. The excesses of monarchical power had devised a variety of physical means of oppression: the democratic republics of the present day have rendered it as entirely an affair of the mind as that will which it is intended to coerce. Under the absolute sway of an individual despot the body was attacked in order to subdue the soul, and the soul escaped the blows which were directed against it and rose superior to the attempt; but such is not the course adopted by tyranny in democratic republics; there the body is left free, and the soul is enslaved. The sovereign can no longer say, "You shall think as I do on pain of death"; but he says: "You are free to think differently from me, and to retain your life, your property, and all that you possess; but if such be your determination, you are henceforth an alien among your people. You may retain your civil rights, but they will be useless to you, for you will never be chosen by your fellow citizens if you solicit their suffrages, and they will affect to scorn you if you solicit their esteem. You will remain among men, but you will be deprived of the rights of mankind. Your fellow-creatures will shun you like an impure being, and those who are most persuaded of your innocence will abandon you too, lest they should be shunned in their turn. Go in peace! I have given you your life, but it is an existence incomparably worse than death."

Monarchical institutions have thrown an odium upon despotism; let us beware lest democratic republics should restore oppression, and should render it less odious and less degrading in the eyes of the many, by making it still more onerous to the few. . . .

The tendencies to which I have just alluded are as yet very slightly perceptible in political society, but they already begin to exercise an unfavourable influence upon the national character of the Americans. I am inclined to attribute the singular paucity of distinguished political characters to the ever-increasing activity of the despotism of the majority in the United States. When the American Revolution broke out they arose in great numbers, for public opinion then served, not to tyrannize over, but to direct the exertions of individuals. Those celebrated men took a full part in the general agitation of mind common at that period, and they attained a high degree of personal fame, which was reflected back upon the nation, but which was by no means borrowed from it. . . .

In free countries, where every one is more or less called upon to give his opinion in the affairs of state; in democratic republics, where public life is incessantly commingled with domestic affairs, where the sovereign authority is accessible on every side, and where its attention can almost always be attracted by vociferation, more persons are to be met with who speculate upon its foibles and live at the cost of its passions than in absolute monarchies. Not because men are naturally worse in these States than elsewhere, but the temptation is stronger, and of easier access at the same time. The result is a far more extensive debasement of the characters of citizens.

Democratic republics extend the practice of currying favour with the many, and they introduce it into a greater number of classes at once: this is one of the most serious reproaches that can be addressed to them. In democratic States organized on the principles of the American republics, this is more especially the case, where the authority of the majority is so absolute and so irresistible that a man must give up his rights as a citizen, and almost abjure his quality as a human being, if he intends to stray from the track which it lays down.

In that immense crowd which throngs the avenues to power in the United States I found very few men who displayed any of that manly candour and that masculine independence of opinion which frequently distinguished the Americans in former times, and which constitutes the leading feature in distinguished characters, wheresoever they may be found. It seems, at first sight, as if all the minds of the Americans were formed upon one model, so accurately do they correspond in their manner of judging. A stranger does, indeed, sometimes meet with Americans who dissent from these rigorous formularies; with men who deplore the defects of the laws, the mutability and the ignorance of democracy; who even go so far as to observe the evil tendencies which impair the national character, and to point out such remedies as it might be possible to apply; but no one is there to hear these things besides yourself, and you, to whom these secret reflections are confided, are a stranger and a bird of passage. They are very ready to communicate truths which are useless to you, but they continue to hold a different language in public. . . .

Despotism debases the oppressed much more than the oppressor: in absolute monarchies the king has often great virtues, but the courtiers are invariably servile. It is true that the American courtiers do not say "Sire," or "Your Majesty"—a distinction without a difference. They are for ever talking of the natural intelligence of the populace they serve; they do not debate the question as to which of the virtues of their master is pre-eminently worthy of admiration, for they assure him that he possesses all the virtues under heaven without having acquired them, or without caring to acquire them; they do not give him their daughters and their wives to be raised at his pleasure to the rank of his concubines, but, by sacrificing their opinions, they prostitute themselves. Moralists and philosophers in America are not obliged to conceal their opinions under the veil of allegory; but, before they venture upon a harsh truth, they say: "We are aware that the people which we are addressing is too superior to all the weaknesses of human nature to lose the command of its temper for an instant; and we should not hold this language if we were not speaking to men whom their virtues and their intelligence render more worthy of freedom than all the rest of the world." It would have been impossible for the sycophants of Louis XIV to flatter more dexterously. For my part, I am persuaded that in all governments, whatever their nature may be, servility will cower to force, and adulation will cling to power. The only means of preventing men from degrading themselves is to invest no one with that unlimited authority which is the surest method of debasing them.

Governments usually fall a sacrifice to impotence or to tyranny. In the former case their power escapes from them; it is wrested from their grasp in the latter. Many observers, who have witnessed the anarchy of democratic States, have imagined that the government of those States was naturally weak and impotent. The truth is, that when once hostilities are begun between parties, the government loses its control over society. But I do not think that a democratic power is naturally without force or without resources: say rather, that it is almost always by the abuse of its force and the misemployment of its resources that a democratic government fails. Anarchy is almost always produced by its tyranny or its mistakes, but not by its want of strength.

It is important not to confound stability with force, or the greatness of a thing with its duration. In democratic republics, the power which directs society is not stable; for it often changes hands and assumes a new direction. But whichever way it turns, its force is almost irresistible. The governments of the American republics appear to me to be as much centralized as those of the absolute monarchies of Europe, and more energetic than they are. I do not, therefore, imagine that they will perish from weakness.

If ever the free institutions of America are destroyed, that event may be attributed to the unlimited authority of the majority, which may at some future time urge the minorities to desperation, and oblige them to have recourse to physical force. Anarchy will then be the result, but it will have been brought about by despotism. . . .

CAPITALISM

34. Man's Rights

Ayn Rand

Ayn Rand (1905–1982) was an American author and social critic. In her novels and nonfiction writings she expounded and advocated a philosophy of individualism and rational self-interest. Born in Russia and educated under the Soviets, she rebelled against the doctrines and practices of Soviet Communism and at the age of 21 came to America alone and determined to become a writer. In her very popular novel Atlas Shrugged *(1957) she gives the fullest statement of her general philosophy of Objectivism. In the last two decades of her life she presented her philosophy in nonfiction form in such works as* Capitalism: The Unknown Ideal *(1946), which also includes several essays by Alan Greenspan, now chairman of the U.S. Federal Reserve.*

If one wishes to advocate a free society—that is, capitalism—one must realize that its indispensable foundation is the principle of individual rights. If one wishes to uphold individual rights, one must realize that capitalism is the only system that can uphold and protect them. And if one wishes to gauge the relationship of freedom to the goals of today's intellectuals, one may gauge it by the fact that the concept of individual rights is evaded, distorted, perverted and seldom discussed, most conspicuously seldom by the so-called "conservatives."

"Rights" are a moral concept—the concept that provides a logical transition from the principles guiding an individual's actions to the principles guiding his relationship with others—the concept that preserves and protects individual morality in a social context—the link between the moral code of a man and the legal code of a society, between ethics and politics. *Individual rights are the means of subordinating society to moral law.*

Every political system is based on some code of ethics. The dominant ethics of mankind's history were variants of the altruist-collectivist doctrine which subordinated the individual to some higher authority, either mystical or social. Consequently, most political systems were variants of the same statist tyranny, differing only in degree, not in basic principle, limited only by the accidents of tradition, of chaos, of bloody strife and periodic collapse. Under all such systems, morality was a code applicable to the individual, but not to society. Society was placed *outside* the

Courtesy The Ayn Rand Institute. Reprinted by permission of the Estate of Ayn Rand © 1963.

moral law, as its embodiment or source or exclusive interpreter—and the inculcation of self-sacrificial devotion to social duty was regarded as the main purpose of ethics in man's earthly existence.

Since there is no such entity as "society," since society is only a number of individual men, this meant, in practice, that the rulers of society were exempt from moral law; subject only to traditional rituals, they held total power and exacted blind obedience—on the implicit principle of: "The good is that which is good for society (or for the tribe, the race, the nation), and the ruler's edicts are its voice on earth."

This was true of all statist systems, under all variants of the altruist-collectivist ethics, mystical or social. "The Divine Right of Kings" summarizes the political theory of the first—*"Vox populi, vox dei"* of the second. As witness: the theocracy of Egypt, with the Pharaoh as an embodied god—the unlimited majority rule or *democracy* of Athens—the welfare state run by the Emperors of Rome—the Inquisition of the late Middle Ages—the absolute monarchy of France—the welfare state of Bismarck's Prussia—the gas chambers of Nazi Germany—the slaughterhouse of the Soviet Union.

All these political systems were expressions of the altruist-collectivist ethics—and their common characteristic is the fact that society stood above the moral law, as an omnipotent, sovereign whim worshiper. Thus, politically, all these systems were variants of an *amoral* society.

The most profoundly revolutionary achievement of the United States of America was *the subordination of society to moral law.*

The principle of man's individual rights represented the extension of morality into the social system—as a limitation on the power of the state, as man's protection against the brute force of the collective, as the subordination of *might* to *right*. The United States was the first *moral* society in history.

All previous systems had regarded man as a sacrificial means to the ends of others, and society as an end in itself. The United States regarded man as an end in himself, and society as a means to the peaceful, orderly, *voluntary* co-existence of individuals. All previous systems had held that man's life belongs to society, that society can dispose of him in any way it pleases, and that any freedom he enjoys is his only by favor, by the *permission* of society, which may be revoked at any time. The United States held that man's life is his by *right* (which means: by moral principle and by his nature), that a right is the property of an individual, that society as such has no rights, and that the only moral purpose of a government is the protection of individual rights.

A "right" is a moral principle defining and sanctioning a man's freedom of action in a social context. There is only *one* fundamental right (all the others are its consequences or corollaries): a man's right to his own life. Life is a process of self-sustaining and self-generated action; the right to life means the right to engage in self-sustaining and self-generated action—which means: the freedom to take all the actions required by the nature of a rational being for the support, the furtherance, the fulfillment and the enjoyment of his own life. (Such is the meaning of the right to life, liberty and the pursuit of happiness.)

The concept of a "right" pertains only to action—specifically, to freedom of action. It means freedom from physical compulsion, coercion or interference by other men.

Thus, for every individual, a right is the moral sanction of a *positive*—of his freedom to act on his own judgment, for his own goals, by his own *voluntary, uncoerced* choice. As to his neighbors, his rights impose no obligations on them except of a *negative* kind: to abstain from violating his rights.

The right to life is the source of all rights—and the right to property is their only implementation. Without property rights, no other rights are possible. Since man has to sustain his life by his own effort, the man who has no right to the product of his effort has no means to sustain his life. The man who produces while others dispose of his product, is a slave.

Bear in mind that the right to property is a right to action, like all the others: it is not the right *to an object* but to the action and the consequences of producing or earning that object. It is not a guarantee that a man *will* earn any property, but only a guarantee that he will own it if he earns it. It is the right to gain, to keep, to use and to dispose of material values.

The concept of individual rights is so new in human history that most men have not grasped it fully to this day. In accordance with the two theories of ethics, the mystical or the social, some men assert that rights are a gift of God—others, that rights are a gift of society. But, in fact, the source of rights is man's nature.

The Declaration of Independence stated that men "are endowed by their Creator with certain unalienable rights." Whether one believes that man is the product of a Creator or of nature, the issue of man's origin does not alter the fact that he is an entity of a specific kind—a rational being—that he cannot function successfully under coercion, and that rights are a necessary condition of his particular mode of survival.

"The source of man's rights is not divine law or congressional law, but the law of identity. A is A—and Man is Man. *Rights* are conditions of existence required by man's nature for his proper survival. If man is to live on earth, it is *right* for him to use his mind, it is *right* to act on his own free judgment, it is *right* to work for his values and to keep the product of his work. If life on earth is his purpose, he has a *right* to live as a rational being: nature forbids him the irrational." *(Atlas Shrugged)*

To violate man's rights means to compel him to act against his own judgment, or to expropriate his values. Basically, there is only one way to do it: by the use of physical force. There are two potential violators of man's rights: the criminals and the government. The great achievement of the United States was to draw a distinction between these two—by forbidding to the second the legalized version of the activities of the first.

The Declaration of Independence laid down the principle that "to secure these rights, governments are instituted among men." This provided the only valid justification of a government and defined its only proper purpose: to protect man's rights by protecting him from physical violence.

Thus the government's function was changed from the role of ruler to the role of servant. The government was set to protect man from criminals—and the Constitution was written to protect man from the government. The Bill of Rights was not directed against private citizens, but against the government—as an explicit declaration that individual rights supersede any public or social power.

The result was the pattern of a civilized society which—for the brief span of some hundred and fifty years—America came close to achieving. A civilized society is one in which physical force is banned from human relationships—in which the government, acting as a policeman, may use force *only* in retaliation and *only* against those who initiate its use.

This was the essential meaning and intent of America's political philosophy, implicit in the principle of individual rights. But it was not formulated explicitly, nor fully accepted nor consistently practiced.

America's inner contradiction was the altruist-collectivist ethics. Altruism is incompatible with freedom, with capitalism and with individual rights. One cannot combine the pursuit of happiness with the moral status of a sacrificial animal.

It was the concept of individual rights that had given birth to a free society. It was with the destruction of individual rights that the destruction of freedom had to begin.

A collectivist tyranny dare not enslave a country by an outright confiscation of its values, material or moral. It has to be done by a process of internal corruption. Just as in the material realm the plundering of a country's wealth is accomplished by inflating the currency—so today one may witness the process of inflation being applied to the realm of rights. The process entails such a growth of newly promulgated "rights" that people do not notice the fact that the meaning of the concept is being reversed. Just as bad money drives out good money, so these "printing-press rights" negate authentic rights.

Consider the curious fact that never has there been such a proliferation, all over the world, of two contradictory phenomena: of alleged new "rights" and of slave-labor camps.

The "gimmick" was the switch of the concept of rights from the political to the economic realm.

The Democratic Party platform of 1960 summarizes the switch boldly and explicitly. It declares that a Democratic Administration "will reaffirm the economic bill of rights which Franklin Roosevelt wrote into our national conscience sixteen years ago."

Bear clearly in mind the meaning of the concept of *"rights"* when you read the list which that platform offers:

> "1. The right to a useful and remunerative job in the industries or shops or farms or mines of the nation.

"2. The right to earn enough to provide adequate food and clothing and recreation.

"3. The right of every farmer to raise and sell his products at a return which will give him and his family a decent living.

"4. The right of every businessman, large and small, to trade in an atmosphere of freedom from unfair competition and domination by monopolies at home and abroad.

"5. The right of every family to a decent home.

"6. The right to adequate medical care and the opportunity to achieve and enjoy good health.

"7. The right to adequate protection from the economic fears of old age, sickness, accidents and unemployment.

"8. The right to a good education."

A single question added to each of the above eight clauses would make the issue clear: *At whose expense?*

Jobs, food, clothing, recreation (!), homes, medical care, education, etc., do not grow in nature. These are man-made values—goods and services produced by men. *Who* is to provide them?

If some men are entitled *by right* to the products of the work of others, it means that those others are deprived of rights and condemned to slave labor.

Any alleged "right" of one man, which necessitates the violation of the rights of another, is not and cannot be a right.

No man can have a right to impose an unchosen obligation, an unrewarded duty or an involuntary servitude on another man. There can be no such thing as *"the right to enslave."*

A right does not include the material implementation of that right by other men; it includes only the freedom to earn that implementation by one's own effort.

Observe, in this context, the intellectual precision of the Founding Fathers: they spoke of the right to *the pursuit* of happiness—*not* of the right to happiness. It means that a man has the right to take the actions he deems necessary to achieve his happiness; it does *not* mean that others must make him happy.

The right to life means that a man has the right to support his life by his own work (on any economic level, as high as his ability will carry him); it does *not* mean that others must provide him with the necessities of life.

The right to property means that a man has the right to take the economic actions necessary to earn property, to use it and to dispose of it; it does *not* mean that others must provide him with property.

The right of free speech means that a man has the right to express his ideas without danger of suppression, interference or punitive action by the government. It does *not* mean that others must provide him with a lecture hall, a radio station or a printing press through which to express his ideas.

Any undertaking that involves more than one man, requires the *voluntary* consent of every participant. Every one of them has the *right* to make his own decision, but none has the right to force his decision on the others.

There is no such thing as "a right to a job"—there is only the right of free trade, that is: a man's right to take a job if another man chooses to hire him. There is no "right to a home," only the right of free trade: the right to build a home or to buy it. There are no "rights to a 'fair' wage or a 'fair' price" if no one chooses to pay it, to hire a man or to buy his product. There are no "rights of consumers" to milk, shoes, movies or champagne if no producers choose to manufacture such items (there is only the right to manufacture them oneself). There are no "rights" of special groups, there are no "rights of farmers, of workers, of businessmen, of employees, of employers, of the old, of the young, of the unborn." There are only *the Rights of Man*— rights possessed by every individual man and by *all* men as individuals.

Property rights and the right of free trade are man's only "economic rights" (they are, in fact, *political* rights)—and there can be no such thing as "an *economic* bill of rights." But observe that the advocates of the latter have all but destroyed the former.

Remember that rights are moral principles which define and protect a man's freedom of action, but impose no obligations on other men. Private citizens are not a threat to one another's rights or freedom. A private citizen who resorts to physical force and violates the rights of others is a criminal—and men have legal protection against him.

Criminals are a small minority in any age or country. And the harm they have done to mankind is infinitesimal when compared to the horrors—the bloodshed, the wars, the persecutions, the confiscations, the famines, the enslavements, the wholesale destructions—perpetrated by mankind's governments. Potentially, a government is the most dangerous threat to man's rights: it holds a legal monopoly on the use of physical force against legally disarmed victims. When unlimited and unrestricted by individual rights, a government is men's deadliest enemy. It is not as protection against *private* actions, but against governmental actions that the Bill of Rights was written.

Now observe the process by which that protection is being destroyed.

The process consists of ascribing to private citizens the specific violations constitutionally forbidden to the government (which private citizens have no power to commit) and thus freeing the government from all restrictions. The switch is becoming progressively more obvious in the field of free speech. For years, the collectivists have been propagating the notion that a private individual's refusal to finance an opponent is a violation of the opponent's right of free speech and an act of "censorship."

It is "censorship," they claim, if a newspaper refuses to employ or publish writers whose ideas are diametrically opposed to its policy.

It is "censorship," they claim, if businessmen refuse to advertise in a magazine that denounces, insults and smears them.

It is "censorship," they claim, if a TV sponsor objects to some outrage perpetrated on a program he is financing—such as the incident of Alger Hiss being invited to denounce former Vice-President Nixon.

And then there is Newton N. Minow who declares: "There is censorship by ratings, by advertisers, by networks, by affiliates which reject programming offered to their areas." It is the same Mr. Minow who threatens to revoke the license of any station that does not comply with his views on programming—and who claims that *that* is not censorship.

Consider the implications of such a trend.

"Censorship" is a term pertaining only to governmental action. No private action is censorship. No private individual or agency can silence a man or suppress a publication; only the government can do so. The freedom of speech of private individuals includes the right not to agree, not to listen and not to finance one's own antagonists.

But according to such doctrines as the "economic bill of rights," an individual has no right to dispose of his own material means by the guidance of his own convictions—and must hand over his money indiscriminately to any speakers or propagandists, who have a "right" to his property.

This means that the ability to provide the material tools for the expression of ideas deprives a man of the right to hold any ideas. It means that a publisher has to publish books he considers worthless, false or evil—that a TV sponsor has to finance commentators who choose to affront his convictions—that the owner of a newspaper must turn his editorial pages over to any young hooligan who clamors for the enslavement of the press. It means that one group of men acquires the "right" to unlimited license—while another group is reduced to helpless irresponsibility.

But since it is obviously impossible to provide every claimant with a job, a microphone or a newspaper column, *who* will determine the "distribution" of "economic rights" and select the recipients, when the owners' right to choose has been abolished? Well, Mr. Minow has indicated *that* quite clearly.

And if you make the mistake of thinking that this applies only to big property owners, you had better realize that the theory of "economic rights" includes the "right" of every would-be playwright, every beatnik poet, every noise-composer and every nonobjective artist (who have political pull) to the financial support you did not give them when you did not attend their shows. What else is the meaning of the project to spend your tax money on subsidized art?

And while people are clamoring about "economic rights," the concept of political rights is vanishing. It is forgotten that the right of free speech means the freedom to advocate one's views and to bear the possible consequences, including disagreement with others, opposition, unpopularity and lack of support. The political function of "the right of free speech" is to protect dissenters and unpopular minorities from forcible suppression—*not* to guarantee them the support, advantages and rewards of a popularity they have not gained.

The Bill of Rights reads: "Congress shall make no law . . . abridging the freedom of speech, or of the press . . ." It does not demand that private citizens provide a microphone for the man who advocates their destruction, or a passkey for the burglar who seeks to rob them, or a knife for the murderer who wants to cut their throats.

Such is the state of one of today's most crucial issues: *political* rights versus "*economic* rights." It's either-or. One destroys the other. But there are, in fact, no "economic rights," no "collective rights," no "public-interest rights." The term "individual rights" is a redundancy: there is no other kind of rights and no one else to possess them.

Those who advocate *laissez-faire* capitalism are the only advocates of man's rights.

SOCIALISM

35. *A Moral Case for Socialism*

Kai Nielsen

Kai Nielsen (1926–   ), a Canadian philosopher, specializes in contemporary ethical and political theory, Marxism, metaphilosophy, and philosophy of religion.

In North America socialism gets a bad press. It is under criticism for its alleged economic inefficiency and for its moral and human inadequacy. I want here to address the latter issue. Looking at capitalism and socialism, I want to consider, against the grain of our culture, what kind of moral case can be made for socialism.

The first thing to do, given the extensive, and, I would add, inexcusably extensive, confusions about this, is to say what socialism and capitalism are. That done I will then, appealing to a cluster of values which are basic in our culture, concerning which there is a considerable and indeed a reflective consensus, examine how capitalism and socialism fare with respect to these values. Given that people generally, at least in Western societies, would want it to be the case that these values have a stable exemplification in our social lives, it is appropriate to ask the question: which of these social systems is more likely stably to exemplify them? I shall argue, facing the gamut of a careful comparison in the light of these values, that, everything considered, socialism comes out better than capitalism. And this, if right, would give us good reason for believing that socialism is preferable—indeed morally preferable—to capitalism if it also turns out to be a feasible socio-economic system.

What, then, are socialism and capitalism? Put most succinctly, capitalism requires the existence of private *productive* property (private ownership of the means of production) while socialism works toward its abolition. What is essential for socialism is public ownership and control of the means of production and public ownership means just what it says: *ownership by the public.* Under capitalism there is a domain of private property rights in the means of production which are not subject to political determination. That is, even where the political domain is a democratic one, they are not subject to determination by the public; only an individual or a set of individuals who own that property can make the final determination of what is to be done with that property. These individuals make that determination and not citizens at large, as under socialism. In fully developed socialism, by

Reprinted from *Critical Review*, Vol. 3, Nos. 3–4, 1989, pp. 542–553, by permission of the author.

contrast, there is, with respect to productive property, no domain which is not subject to political determination by the public, namely by the citizenry at large. Thus, where this public ownership and control is genuine, and not a mask for control by an elite of state bureaucrats, it will mean genuine popular and democratic control over productive property. What socialism is *not* is *state* ownership in the absence of, at the very least, popular sovereignty, i.e., genuine popular control over the state apparatus including any economic functions it might have.

The property that is owned in common under socialism is the means of existence—the productive property in the society. Socialism does not proscribe the ownership of private personal property, such as houses, cars, television sets and the like. It only proscribes the private ownership of the means of production.

The above characterizations catch the minimal core of socialism and capitalism, what used to be called the essence of those concepts. But beyond these core features, it is well, in helping us to make our comparison, to see some other important features which characteristically go with capitalism and socialism. Minimally, capitalism is private ownership of the means of production but it is also, at least characteristically, a social system in which a class of capitalists owns and controls the means of production and hires workers who, owning little or no means of production, sell their labor-power to some capitalist or other for a wage. This means that a capitalist society will be a class society in which there will be two principal classes: capitalists and workers. Socialism by contrast is a social system in which every able-bodied person is, was or will be a worker. These workers commonly own and control the means of production (this is the characteristic form of public ownership). Thus in socialism we have, in a perfectly literal sense, a classless society for there is no division between human beings along class lines.

There are both pure and impure forms of capitalism and socialism. The pure form of capitalism is competitive capitalism, the capitalism that Milton Friedman would tell us is the real capitalism while, he would add, the impure form is monopoly or corporate capitalism. Similarly the pure form of socialism is democratic socialism, with firm workers' control of the means of production and an industrial as well as a political democracy, while the impure form is state bureaucratic socialism.

Now it is a noteworthy fact that, to understate it, actually existing capitalisms and actually existing socialisms tend to be the impure forms. Many partisans of capitalism lament the fact that the actually existing capitalisms overwhelmingly tend to be forms of corporate capitalism where the state massively intervenes in the running of the economy. It is unclear whether anything like a fully competitive capitalism actually exists—perhaps Hong Kong approximates it—and it is also unclear whether many of the actual players in the major capitalist societies (the existing capitalists and their managers) want or even expect that it is possible to have laissez-faire capitalism again (if indeed we ever had it). Some capitalist societies are further down the corporate road than other societies, but they are all forms of corporate, perhaps in some instances even monopoly, capitalism. Competitive capitalism seems to be more of a libertarian dream than a sociological reality or even something desired by many informed and tough-minded members of the capitalist class. Socialism has had a similar fate. Its historical exemplifications tend to be of the impure forms, namely the bureaucratic state socialisms. Yugoslavia is perhaps to socialism what Hong Kong is to capitalism. It is a candidate for what might count as an exemplification, or at least a near approximation, of the pure form.

This paucity of exemplifications of pure forms of either capitalism or socialism raises the question of whether the pure forms are at best unstable social systems and at worse merely utopian ideals. I shall not try directly to settle that issue here. What I shall do instead is to compare *models* with *models.* In asking about the moral case for socialism, I shall compare forms that a not inconsiderable number of the theoretical protagonists of each take to be pure forms but which are still, they believe, historically feasible. But I will also be concerned to ask whether these models—these pure forms—can reasonably be expected to come to have a home. If they are not historically feasible models, then, even if we can make a good theoretical moral case for them, we will have hardly provided a good moral case for socialism or capitalism. To avoid bad utopianism we must be talking about forms which could be on the historical agenda. (I plainly here do not take "bad utopianism" to be pleonastic.)

Setting aside for the time being the feasibility question, let us compare the pure forms of capitalism and socialism—that is to say, competitive capitalism and democratic socialism—as to how they stand with respect to sustaining and furthering the values of freedom and autonomy, equality, justice, rights and democracy. My argument shall be that socialism comes out better with respect to those values.

Let us first look at freedom and autonomy. An autonomous person is a person who is able to set her ends for herself and in optimal circumstances is able to pursue those ends. But freedom does not only mean being autonomous; it also means the absence of unjustified political and social interference in the pursuit of one's ends. Some might even say that it is just the absence of interference with one's ends. Still it is self-direction—autonomy—not non-interference which is *intrinsically* desirable. Non-interference is only valuable where it is an aid to our being able to do what we want and where we are sufficiently autonomous to have some control over our wants.

How do capitalism and socialism fare in providing the social conditions which will help or impede the flourishing of autonomy? Which model society would make for the greater flourishing of autonomy? My argument is (a) that democratic socialism makes it possible for more people to be more fully autonomous than would be autonomous under capitalism; and (b) that democratic socialism also interferes less in people's exercise of their autonomy than any form of capitalism. All societies limit liberty by interfering with people doing what they want to do in some ways, but the restrictions are more extensive, deeper and more undermining of autonomy in capitalism than in democratic socialism. Where there is private ownership of productive property, which, remember, is private ownership of the means of life, it cannot help but be the case that a few (the owning and controlling capitalist class) will have, along with the managers beholden to them, except in periods of revolutionary turmoil, a firm control, indeed a domination, over the vast majority of people in the society. The capitalist class with the help of their managers determines whether workers (taken now as individuals) can work, how they work, on what they work, the conditions under which they work and what is done with what they produce (where they are producers) and what use is made of their skills and the like. As we move to welfare state capitalism—a compromise still favoring capital which emerged out of long and bitter class struggles—the state places some restrictions on some of these powers of capital. Hours, working conditions and the like are controlled in certain ways. Yet whether workers work and continue to work, how they work and on what, what is done with what they produce, and the rationale for their work are not determined by the workers themselves but by the owners of capital and their managers; this means a very considerable limitation on the autonomy and freedom of workers. Since workers are the great majority, such socio-economic relations place a very considerable limitation on human freedom and indeed on the very most important freedom that people have, namely their being able to live in a self-directed manner, when compared with the industrial democracy of democratic socialism. Under capitalist arrangements it simply cannot fail to be the case that a very large number of people will lose control over a very central set of facets of their lives, namely central aspects of their work and indeed in many instances, over their very chance to be able to work.

Socialism would indeed prohibit capitalist acts between consenting adults; the capitalist class would lose its freedom to buy and sell and to control the labor market. There should be no blinking at the fact that socialist social relations would impose some limitations on freedom, for there is, and indeed can be, no society without norms and some sanctions. In any society you like there will be some things you are at liberty to do and some things that you may not do. However, democratic socialism must bring with it an industrial democracy where workers by various democratic procedures would determine how they are to work, on what they are to work, the hours of their work, under what conditions they are to work (insofar as this is alterable by human effort at all), what they will produce and how much, and what is to be done with what they produce. Since, instead of there being "private ownership of the means of production," there is in a genuinely socialist society "public ownership of the means of production," the means of life are owned by everyone and thus each person has a *right* to work: she has, that is, a right to the means of life. It is no longer the private preserve of an individual owner of capital but it is owned in common by us all. This means that each of us has an equal right to the means of life. Members of the capitalist class would have a few of their liberties restricted, but these are linked with owning and controlling capital and are not the important civil and political liberties that we all rightly cherish. Moreover, the limitation of the capitalist liberties to buy and sell and the like would make for a more extensive liberty for many, many more people.

One cannot respond to the above by saying that workers are free to leave the working class and become capitalists or at least petty bourgeoisie. They may indeed all in theory, taken *individually,* be free to leave the working class, but if many in fact try to leave the exits will very quickly become blocked. Individuals are only free on the condition that the great mass of people, taken collectively, are not. We could not have capitalism without a working class and the working class is not free within the capitalist system to cease being wage laborers. We cannot all be capitalists. A people's capitalism is nonsense. Though a petty commodity production system (the family farm writ large) is a logical possibility, it is hardly a stable empirical possibility and, what is most important for the present discussion, such a system would not be a capitalist system. Under capitalism, most of us, if we are to find any work at all, will just have to sell (or *perhaps* "rent" is the better word) our labor-power as a commodity. Whether you sell or rent your labor power or, where it is provided, you go on welfare, you will not have much control over areas very crucial to your life. If these are the only feasible alternatives facing the working class, working class autonomy is very limited indeed. But these are the only alternatives under capitalism.

Capitalist acts between consenting adults, if they become sufficiently widespread, lead to severe imbalances in power. These imbalances in power tend to undermine autonomy by creating differentials in wealth and control between workers and capitalists. Such imbalances are the name of the game for capitalism. Even if we (perversely I believe) call a system of petty commodity production capitalism, we still must say that such a socio-economic system is inherently unstable. Certain individuals would win out in this exchanging of commodities and in fairly quick order it would lead to a class system and the imbalances of power—the domination of the many by the few—that I take to be definitive of capitalism. By abolishing capitalist acts between consenting adults, then (but leaving personal property and civil and political liberties untouched), socialism protects more extensive freedoms for more people and in far more important areas of their lives.

So democratic socialism does better regarding the value that epitomizes capitalist pride (*hubris*, would, I think, be a better term), namely autonomy. It also does better, I shall now argue, than capitalism with respect to another of our basic values, namely democracy. Since this is almost a corollary of what I have said about autonomy I can afford to be briefer. In capitalist societies, democracy must simply be *political* democracy. There can in the nature of the case be no genuine or thorough workplace democracy. When we enter the sphere of production, capitalists and not workers own, and therefore at least ultimately control, the means of production. While capitalism, as in some workplaces in West Germany and Sweden, sometimes can be pressured into allowing an ameliorative measure of worker control, once ownership rights are given up, we no longer have private productive property but public productive property (and in that way social ownership): capitalism is given up and we have socialism. However, where worker control is restricted to a few firms, we do not yet have socialism. What makes a system socialist or capitalist depends on what happens across the whole society, not just in isolated firms. Moreover, managers can become very important within capitalist firms, but as long as ownership, including the ability to close the place down and liquidate the business, rests in the hands of capitalists we can have no genuine workplace democracy. Socialism, in its pure form, carries with it, in a way capitalism in any form cannot, workplace democracy. (That some of the existing socialisms are anything but pure does not belie this.)

Similarly, whatever may be said of existing socialisms or at least of some existing socialisms, it is not the case that there is anything in the very idea of socialism that militates against political as well as industrial democracy. Socialists are indeed justly suspicious of some of the tricks played by parliamentary democracy in bourgeois countries, aware of its not infrequent hypocrisy and the limitations of its stress on purely legal and formal political rights and liberties. Socialists are also, without at all wishing to throw the baby out with the bath water, rightly suspicious of any simple reliance on majority rule, unsupplemented by other democratic procedures and safeguards. But there is nothing in socialist theory that would set it against political democracy and the protection of political and civil rights; indeed there is much in socialism that favors them, namely its stress on both autonomy and equality.

The fact that political democracy came into being and achieved stability within capitalist societies may prove something about conditions necessary for its coming into being, but it says nothing about capitalism being necessary for sustaining it. In Chile, South Africa and Nazi Germany, indeed, capitalism has flourished without the protection of civil and political rights or anything like a respect for the democratic tradition. There is nothing structural in socialism that would prevent it from continuing those democratic traditions or cherishing those political and civil rights. That something came about under certain conditions does not establish that these conditions are necessary for its continued existence. That men initially took an interest in chess does not establish that women cannot quite naturally take an interest in it as well. When capitalist societies with long-flourishing democratic traditions move to socialism there is no reason at all to believe that they will not continue to be democratic. (Where societies previously had no democratic tradition or only a very weak one, matters are more problematic.)

I now want to turn to a third basic value, equality. In societies across the political spectrum, *moral* equality (the belief that everyone's life matters equally) is an accepted value. Or, to be somewhat cynical about the matter, at least lip service is paid to it. But even this lip service is the compliment that vice pays to virtue. That is to say, such a belief is a deeply held considered conviction in modernized societies, though it has not been at all times and is not today a value held in all societies. This is most evident concerning moral equality.

While this value is genuinely held by the vast majority of people in capitalist societies, it can hardly be an effective or functional working norm where there is such a diminishment of autonomy as we have seen obtains unavoidably in such societies. Self-respect is deeply threatened where so many people lack effective control over their own lives, where there are structures of domination, where there is alienated labor, where great power differentials and differences in wealth make for very different (and often very bleak) life chances. For not inconsiderable numbers, in fact, it is difficult to maintain self-respect under such conditions unless they are actively struggling against the system. And, given present conditions, fighting the system, particularly in societies such as the United States, may well be felt to be a hopeless task. Under such conditions any real equality of opportunity is out of the question. And the circumstances are such, in spite of what is often said about these states, that equality of condition is an even more remote possibility. But without at least some of these things moral equality cannot even be approximated. Indeed, even to speak of it sounds like an obscene joke given the social realities of our lives.

Although under welfare state capitalism some of the worst inequalities of capitalism are ameliorated, workers still lack effective control over their work, with repercussions in political and public life as well. Differentials of wealth cannot but give rise to differentials in power and control in politics, in the media, in education, in the direction of social life and in what options get seriously debated. The life chances of workers and those not even lucky enough to be workers (whose ranks are growing and will continue to grow under capitalism) are impoverished compared to the life chances of members of the capitalist class and its docile professional support stratum.

None of these equality-undermining features would obtain under democratic socialism. Such societies would, for starters, be classless, eliminating the power and control differentials that go with the class system of capitalism. In addition to political democracy, industrial democracy and all the egalitarian and participatory control that goes with that would, in turn, reinforce moral equality. Indeed it would make it possible where before it was impossible. There would be a commitment under democratic socialism to attaining or at least approximating, as far as it is feasible, equality of condition; and this, where approximated, would help make for real equality of opportunity, making equal life chances something less utopian than it must be under capitalism.

In fine, the very things, as we have seen, that make for greater autonomy under socialism than under capitalism, would, in being more equally distributed, make for greater equality of condition, greater equality of opportunity and greater moral equality in a democratic socialist society than in a capitalist one. These values are values commonly shared by both capitalistically inclined people and those who are socialistically inclined. What the former do not see is that in modern industrial societies, democratic socialism can better deliver these goods than even progressive capitalism.

There is, without doubt, legitimate worry about bureaucratic control under socialism. But that is a worry under any historically feasible capitalism as well, and it is anything but clear that state bureaucracies are worse than great corporate bureaucracies. Indeed, if socialist bureaucrats were, as the socialist system requires, really committed to production for needs and to achieving equality of condition, they might, bad as they are, be the lesser of two evils. But in any event democratic socialism is not bureaucratic state socialism, and there is no structural reason to believe that it must—if it arises in a society with skilled workers committed to democracy—give rise to bureaucratic state socialism. There will, inescapably, be some bureaucracy, but in a democratic socialist society it must and indeed will be controlled. This is not merely a matter of optimism about the will of socialists, for there are more mechanisms for democratic control of bureaucracy within a democratic socialism that is both a political and an industrial democracy, than there can be under even the most benign capitalist democracies—democracies which for structural reasons can never be industrial democracies. If, all that notwithstanding, bureaucratic creepage is inescapable in modern societies, then that is just as much a problem for capitalism as for socialism.

The underlying rationale for production under capitalism is profit and capital accumulation. Capitalism is indeed a marvelous engine for building up the productive forces (though clearly at the expense of considerations of equality and autonomy). We might look on it, going back to earlier historical times, as something like a forced march to develop the productive forces. But now that the productive forces in advanced capitalist societies are wondrously developed, we are in a position to direct them to far more humane and more equitable uses under a socio-economic system whose rationale for production is to meet human needs (the needs of everyone as far as this is possible). This egalitarian thrust, together with the socialist's commitment to attaining, as far as that is possible, equality of condition, makes it clear that socialism will produce more equality than capitalism.

In talking about autonomy, democracy and equality, we have, in effect, already been talking about justice. A society or set of institutions that does better in these respects than another society will be a more just society than the other society.

Fairness is a less fancy name for justice. If we compare two societies and the first is more democratic than the second; there is more autonomy in the first society than in the second; there are more nearly equal life chances in the first society than in the second and thus greater equality of opportunity; if, without sacrifice of autonomy, there is more equality of condition in the first society than in the second; and if there is more moral equality in the first society than in the second, then we cannot but conclude that the first society is a society with more fairness than the second and, thus, that it is the more just society. But this is exactly how socialism comes out vis-à-vis even the best form of capitalism.

A society which undermines autonomy, heels in democracy (where democracy is not violating rights), makes equality impossible to achieve and violates rights cannot be a just society. If, as I contend, that is what capitalism does, and cannot help doing, then a capitalist society cannot be a just society. Democratic socialism, by contrast, does not need to do any of those things, and we can predict that it would not, for there are no structural imperatives in democratic socialism to do so and there are deep sentiments in that tradition urging us not to do so. I do not for a moment deny that there are similar sentiments for autonomy and democracy in capitalist societies, but the logic of capitalism, the underlying structures of capitalist societies—even the best of capitalist societies—frustrate the realization of the states of affairs at which those sympathies aim. A radical democrat with a commitment to human rights, to human autonomy and moral equality and fair equality of opportunity ought to be a democratic socialist and a firm opponent of capitalism—even a capitalism with a human face.

ANARCHISM

36. The State

Murray N. Rothbard

Murray N. Rothbard (1926–1995) has been hailed as the leading economist of his generation of the "Austrian school" and as one of the most influential theoreticians of the American libertarian movement.

THE STATE AS AGGRESSOR

The central thrust of libertarian thought, then, is to oppose any and all aggression against the property rights of individuals in their own persons and in the material objects they have voluntarily acquired. While individual and gangs of criminals are of course opposed, there is nothing unique here to the libertarian creed, since almost all persons and schools of thought oppose the exercise of random violence against persons and property. . . .

But the critical difference between libertarians and other people is not in the area of private crime; the critical difference is their view of the role of the State— the government. For libertarians regard the State as the supreme, the eternal, the best organized aggressor against the persons and property of the mass of the public. All States everywhere, whether democratic, dictatorial, or monarchical, whether red, white, blue, or brown.

The State! Always and ever the government and its rulers and operators have been considered above the general moral law. The "Pentagon Papers" are only one recent instance among innumerable instances in history of men, most of whom are perfectly honorable in their private lives, who lie in their teeth before the public. Why? For "reasons of State." Service to the State is supposed to excuse all actions that would be considered immoral or criminal if committed by "private" citizens. The distinctive feature of libertarians is that they coolly and uncompromisingly apply the general moral law to people acting in their roles as members of the State apparatus. Libertarians make no exceptions. For centuries, the State (or more strictly, individuals acting in their roles as "members of the government") has cloaked its criminal activity in high-sounding rhetoric. For centuries the State has committed mass murder and called it "war"; then ennobled the mass slaughter that "war"

From Murray N. Rothbard, *For a New Liberty*, Macmillan, 1973. Reprinted with permission of the Ludwig von Mises Institute and Laissez Faire Books.

involves. For centuries the State has enslaved people into its armed battalions and called it "conscription" in the "national service." For centuries the State has robbed people at bayonet point and called it "taxation." In fact, if you wish to know how libertarians regard the State and any of its acts, simply think of the State as a criminal band, and all of the libertarian attitudes will logically fall into place.

Let us consider, for example, what it is that sharply distinguishes government from all other organizations in society. Many political scientists and sociologists have blurred this vital distinction, and refer to all organizations and groups as hierarchical, structured, "governmental," etc. Left-wing anarchists, for example, will oppose equally government *and* private organizations such as corporations on the ground that each is equally "elitist" and "coercive." But the "rightist" libertarian is not opposed to inequality, and his concept of "coercion" applies only to the use of violence. The libertarian sees a crucial distinction between government, whether central, state, or local, and all other institutions in society. Or rather, two crucial distinctions. First, every other person or group receives its income by voluntary payment: either by voluntary contribution or gift (such as the local community chest or bridge club), *or* by voluntary purchase of its goods or services on the market (i.e., grocery store owner, baseball player, steel manufacturer, etc.). *Only* the government obtains its income by coercion and violence—i.e., by the direct threat of confiscation or imprisonment if payment is not forthcoming. This coerced levy is "taxation." A second distinction is that, apart from criminal outlaws, *only* the government can use its funds to commit violence against its own or any other subjects; only the government can prohibit pornography, compel a religious observance, or put people in jail for selling goods at a higher price than the government deems fit. Both distinctions, of course, can be summed up as: *only* the government, in society, is empowered to aggress against the property rights of its subjects, whether to extract revenue, to impose its moral code, or to kill those with whom it disagrees. Furthermore, any and all governments, even the least despotic, have always obtained the bulk of their income from the coercive taxing power. And historically, by far the overwhelming portion of all enslavement and murder in the history of the world have come from the hands of government. And since we have seen that the central thrust of the libertarian is to oppose all aggression against the rights of person and property, the libertarian necessarily opposes the institution of the State as the inherent and overwhelmingly the most important enemy of those precious rights.

There is another reason why State aggression has been far more important than private, a reason apart from the greater organization and central mobilizing of resources that the rulers of the State can impose. The reason is the absence of any check upon State depredation, a check that does exist when we have to worry about muggers or the Mafia. To guard against private criminals we have been able to turn to the State and its police; but who can guard us against the State itself? No one. For another critical distinction of the State is that it compels the monopolization of the service of protection; the State arrogates to itself a virtual monopoly of violence and of ultimate decision-making in society. If we don't like the decisions of the State courts, for example, there are no other agencies of protection to which we may turn.

It is true that, in the United States, at least, we have a constitution that imposes strict limits on some powers of government. But, as we have discovered in the past century, no constitution can interpret or enforce itself; it must be interpreted by *men*. And if the ultimate power to interpret a constitution is given to the government's own Supreme Court, then the inevitable tendency is for the Court to continue to place its imprimatur on ever-broader powers for its own government. Furthermore, the highly touted "checks and balances" and "separation of powers" in the American government are flimsy indeed, since in the final analysis all of these divisions are part of the same government and are governed by the same set of rulers.

One of America's most brilliant political theorists, John C. Calhoun, wrote prophetically of the inherent tendency of a State to break through the limits of its written constitution:

> A written constitution certainly has many and considerable advantages, but it is a great mistake to suppose that the mere insertion of provisions to restrict and limit the powers of the government, without investing those for whose protection they are inserted with the means of enforcing their observance, will be sufficient to prevent the major and dominant party from abusing its powers. Being the party in possession of the government, they will . . . be in favor of the powers granted by the constitution and opposed to the restrictions intended to limit them. As the major and dominant parties, they will have no need of these restrictions for their protection. . . .
>
> The minor or weaker party, on the contrary, would take the opposite direction and regard them as essential to their protection against the dominant party. . . . But where there are no means by which they could compel the major party to observe the restrictions, the only resort left them would be a strict construction of the constitution. . . . To this the major party would oppose a liberal construction—one which would give to the words of the grant the broadest meaning of which they were susceptible. It would then be construction against construction—the one to contract and the other to enlarge the powers of the government to the utmost. But of what possible avail could the strict construction of the minor party be, against the liberal interpretation of the major, when the one would have all the powers of the government to carry its construction into effect and the other be deprived of all means of enforcing its construction? In a contest so unequal, the result would not be doubtful. The party in favor of the restrictions would be overpowered. . . . The end of the contest would be the subversion of the constitution . . . the restrictions would ultimately be annulled and the government be converted into one of unlimited powers.
>
> Nor would the division of government into separate and, as it regards each other, independent departments prevent this result . . . as each and all the departments—and, of course, the entire government—would be under the control of the numerical majority, it is too clear to require explanation that a mere distribution of its powers among its agents or representatives could do little or nothing to counteract its tendency to oppression and abuse of powers.[1]

[1] John C. Calhoun, *A Disquisition on Government* (New York: Liberal Arts Press, 1953), pp. 25–27.

But why worry about the weakness of limits on governmental power? Especially in a "democracy," in the phrase so often used by American liberals in their heyday before the mid-1960s when doubts began to creep into the liberal utopia: "Are *we* not the government?" In the phrase "we are the government," the useful collective term "we" has enabled an ideological camouflage to be thrown over the naked exploitative reality of political life. For if *we* truly *are* the government, then *anything* a government does to an individual is not only just and not tyrannical; it is also "voluntary" on the part of the individual concerned. If the government has incurred a huge public debt which must be paid by taxing one group on behalf of another, this reality of burden is conveniently obscured by blithely saying that "we owe it to ourselves" (but *who* are the "we" and *who* the "ourselves?"). If the government drafts a man, or even throws him into jail for dissident opinions, then he is only "doing it to himself" and therefore nothing improper has occurred. Under this reasoning, then, Jews murdered by the Nazi government were *not* murdered; they must have "committed suicide," since they *were* the government (which was democratically chosen), and therefore anything the government did to them was only voluntary on their part. But there is no way out of such grotesqueries for those supporters of government who see the State merely as a benevolent and voluntary agent of the public.

And so we must conclude that "we" are *not* the government; the government is *not* "us." The government does not in any accurate sense "represent" the majority of the people, but even if it did, even if 90% of the people decided to murder or enslave the other 10%, this would *still* be murder and slavery, and would not be voluntary suicide or enslavement on the part of the oppressed minority. Crime is crime, aggression against rights is aggression, no matter how many citizens agree to the oppression. There is nothing sacrosanct about the majority; the lynch mob, too, is the majority in its own domain.

But while, as in the lynch mob, the majority can become actively tyrannical and aggressive, the normal and continuing condition of the State is *oligarchic* rule: rule by a coercive elite which has managed to gain control of the State machinery. There are two basic reasons for this: one is the inequality and division of labor inherent in the nature of man, which gives rise to an "Iron Law of Oligarchy" in all of man's activities; and second is the parasitic nature of the State enterprise itself.

We have said that the individualist is not an egalitarian. Part of the reason for this is the individualist's insight into the vast diversity and individuality within mankind, a diversity that has the chance to flower and expand as civilization and living standards progress. Individuals differ in ability and in interest both within and between occupations; and hence, in all occupations and walks of life, whether it be steel production or the organization of a bridge club, leadership in the activity will inevitably be assumed by a relative handful of the most able and energetic, while the remaining majority will form themselves into rank-and-file followers. This truth applies to all activities, whether they are beneficial or malevolent (as in criminal organizations). Indeed, the discovery of the Iron Law of Oligarchy was made by the Italian sociologist Robert Michels, who found that the Social Democratic

Party of Germany, despite its rhetorical commitment to egalitarianism, was rigidly oligarchical and hierarchical in its actual functioning.

A second basic reason for the oligarchic rule of the State is its parasitic nature—the fact that it lives coercively off the production of the citizenry. To be successful to its practitioners, the fruits of parasitic exploitation must be confined to a relative minority, otherwise a meaningless plunder of all by all would result in no gains for anyone. Nowhere has the coercive and parasitic nature of the State been more clearly limned than by the great late nineteenth-century German sociologist, Franz Oppenheimer. Oppenheimer pointed out that there are two and only two mutually exclusive means for man to obtain wealth. One, the method of production and voluntary exchange, the method of the free market, Oppenheimer termed the "economic means;" the other, the method of robbery by the use of violence, he called the "political means." The political means is clearly parasitic, for it requires previous production for the exploiters to confiscate, and it subtracts from instead of adding to the total production in society. Oppenheimer then proceeded to define the State as the "organization of the political means"—the systematization of the predatory process over a given territorial area.[2] . . .

If the State is a group of plunderers, *who* then constitutes the State? Clearly, the ruling elite consists at any time of (a) the full-time *apparatus*—the kings, politicians, and bureaucrats who man and operate the State; and (b) the groups who have maneuvered to gain privileges, subsidies, and benefices from the State. The remainder of society constitutes the ruled. It was, again, John C. Calhoun who saw with crystal clarity that, no matter how small the power of government, no matter how low the tax burden or how equal its distribution, the very nature of government creates two unequal and inherently conflicting classes in society: those who, on net, *pay* the taxes (the "tax-payers"), and those who, on net, *live off* taxes (the "tax-consumers"). Suppose that the government imposes a low and seemingly equally distributed tax to pay for building a dam. This very act takes money from most of the public to pay it out to net "tax-consumers": the bureaucrats who run the operation, the contractors and workers who build the dam, etc. . . .

If states have everywhere been run by an oligarchic group of predators, how have they been able to maintain their rule over the mass of the population? The answer, as the philosopher David Hume pointed out over two centuries ago, is that in the long run *every* government, no matter how dictatorial, rests on the support of the majority of its subjects. Now this does not of course render these governments "voluntary," since the very existence of the tax and other coercive powers shows how much compulsion the State must exercise. Nor does the majority support have to be eager and enthusiastic approval; it could well be mere passive acquiescence and resignation. The conjunction in the famous phrase "death and taxes" implies a passive and resigned acceptance to the assumed inevitability of the State and its taxation. . . .

[2]Franz Oppenheimer, *The State* (New York: Vanguard Press, 1926), pp. 24–27 and passim.

CONTEMPORARY ISSUES

Free Speech and Pornography

37. *Pornography, Oppression, and Freedom: A Closer Look*

Helen E. Longino

Helen E. Longino (1944-   ), professor at the University of Minnesota, is one of the founding editors of Hypatia: A Journal of Feminist Philosophy *and has authored books and articles in the areas of feminist philosophy and philosophy of science.*

I. INTRODUCTION

The much-touted sexual revolution of the 1960's and 1970's not only freed various modes of sexual behavior from the constraints of social disapproval, but also made possible a flood of pornographic material. According to figures provided by WAVPM (Women Against Violence in Pornography and Media), the number of pornographic magazines available at newsstands has grown from zero in 1953 to forty in 1977, while sales of pornographic films in Los Angeles alone have grown from $15 million in 1969 to $85 million in 1976.[1]

Traditionally, pornography was condemned as immoral because it presented sexually explicit material in a manner designed to appeal to "prurient interests" or a "morbid" interest in nudity and sexuality, material which furthermore lacked any redeeming social value and which exceeded "customary limits of candor." While these phrases, taken from a definition of "obscenity" proposed in the 1954 American Law Institute's *Model Penal Code*,[2] require some criteria of application to eliminate vagueness, it seems that what is objectionable is the explicit description or representation of bodily parts or sexual behavior for the purpose of inducing sexual stimulation or pleasure on the part of the reader or viewer. This kind

Reprinted from Laura Lederer, *Take Back the Night* (Morrow, 1980) pp. 40–54, by permission of the author. Copyright © 1980 by Helen Longino.

[1]*Women Against Violence in Pornography and Media Newspage*, Vol. II, No. 5, June 1978; and Judith Reisman in *Women Against Violence in Pornography and Media Proposal.*

[2]American Law Institute Model Penal Code, sec. 251.4.

of objection is part of a sexual ethic that subordinates sex to procreation and condemns all sexual interactions outside of legitimated marriage. It is this code which was the primary target of the sexual revolutionaries in the 1960's, and which has given way in many areas to more open standards of sexual behavior.

One of the beneficial results of the sexual revolution has been a growing acceptance of the distinction between questions of sexual mores and questions of morality. This distinction underlies the old slogan, "Make love, not war," and takes harm to others as the defining characteristic of immorality. What is immoral is behavior which causes injury to or violation of another person or people. Such injury may be physical or it may be psychological. To cause pain to another, to lie to another, to hinder another in the exercise of her or his rights, to exploit another, to degrade another, to misrepresent and slander another are instances of immoral behavior. Masturbation or engaging voluntarily in sexual intercourse with another consenting adult of the same or the other sex, as long as neither injury nor violation of either individual or another is involved, are not immoral. Some sexual behavior is morally objectionable, but not because of its sexual character. Thus, adultery is immoral not because it involves sexual intercourse with someone to whom one is not legally married, but because it involves breaking a promise (of sexual and emotional fidelity to one's spouse). Sadistic, abusive, or forced sex is immoral because it injures and violates another.

The detachment of sexual chastity from moral virtue implies that we cannot condemn forms of sexual behavior merely because they strike us as distasteful or subversive of the Protestant work ethic, or because they depart from standards of behavior we have individually adopted. It has thus seemed to imply that no matter how offensive we might find pornography, we must tolerate it in the name of freedom from illegitimate repression. I wish to argue that this is not so, that pornography is immoral because it is harmful to people.

II. WHAT IS PORNOGRAPHY?

I define pornography as *verbal or pictorial explicit representations of sexual behavior that,* in the words of the Commission on Obscenity and Pornography, *have as a distinguishing characteristic "the degrading and demeaning portrayal of the role and status of the human female . . . as a mere sexual object to be exploited and manipulated sexually."*[3] In pornographic books, magazines, and films, women are represented as passive and as slavishly dependent upon men. The role of female characters is limited to the provision of sexual services to men. To the extent that women's sexual pleasure is represented at all, it is subordinated to that of men and is never an end in itself as is the sexual pleasure of men. What pleases women is the use of their bodies to

---

[3]*Report of the Commission on Obscenity and Pornography* (New York: Bantam Books, 1979), p. 239. The Commission, of course, concluded that the demeaning content of pornography did not adversely affect male attitudes toward women.

satisfy male desires. While the sexual objectification of women is common to all pornography, women are the recipients of even worse treatment in violent pornography, in which women characters are killed, tortured, gang-raped, mutilated, bound, and otherwise abused, as a means of providing sexual stimulation or pleasure to the male characters. It is this development which has attracted the attention of feminists and been the stimulus to an analysis of pornography in general.[4]

Not all sexually explicit material is pornography, nor is all material which contains representations of sexual abuse and degradation pornography.

A representation of a sexual encounter between adult persons which is characterized by mutual respect is, once we have disentangled sexuality and morality, not morally objectionable. Such a representation would be one in which the desires and experiences of each participant were regarded by the other participants as having a validity and a subjective importance equal to those of the individual's own desire and experiences. In such an encounter, each participant acknowledges the other participant's basic human dignity and personhood. Similarly, a representation of a nude human body (in whole or in part) in such a manner that the person shown maintains self-respect—e.g., is not portrayed in a degrading position—would not be morally objectionable. The educational films of the National Sex Forum, as well as a certain amount of erotic literature and art, fall into this category. While some erotic materials are beyond the standards of modesty held by some individuals, they are not for this reason immoral.

A representation of a sexual encounter which is not characterized by mutual respect, in which at least one of the parties is treated in a manner beneath her or his dignity as a human being, is no longer simple erotica. That a representation is of degrading behavior does not in itself, however, make it pornographic. Whether or not it is pornographic is a function of contextual features. Books and films may contain descriptions or representations of a rape in order to explore the consequences of such an assault upon its victim. What is being shown is abusive or degrading behavior which attempts to deny the humanity and dignity of the person assaulted, yet the context surrounding the representation, through its exploration of the consequences of the act, acknowledges and reaffirms her dignity. Such books and films, far from being pornographic, are (or can be) highly moral, and fall into the category of moral realism.

What makes a work a work of pornography, then, is not simply its representation of degrading and abusive sexual encounters, but its implicit, if not explicit, approval and recommendation of sexual behavior that is immoral, i.e., that physically or psychologically violates the personhood of one of the participants. Pornography, then, is verbal or pictorial material which represents or describes sexual behavior that is degrading or abusive to one or more of the participants *in such a way as to endorse the degradation.* The participants so treated in virtually all

---

[4]Among recent feminist discussions are Diana Russell, "Pornography: A Feminist Perspective" and Susan Griffin, "On Pornography," *Chrysalis,* Vol. I, No. 4, 1978; and Ann Garry, "Pornography and Respect for Women," *Social Theory and Practice,* Vol. 4, Spring 1978, pp. 395–421.

heterosexual pornography are women or children, so heterosexual pornography is, as a matter of fact, material which endorses sexual behavior that is degrading and/or abusive to women and children. As I use the term "sexual behavior," this includes sexual encounters between persons, behavior which produces sexual stimulation or pleasure for one of the participants, and behavior which is preparatory to or invites sexual activity. Behavior that is degrading or abusive includes physical harm or abuse, and physical or psychological coercion. In addition, behavior which ignores or devalues the real interests, desires, and experiences of one or more participants in any way is degrading. Finally, that a person has chosen or consented to be harmed, abused, or subjected to coercion does not alter the degrading character of such behavior.

Pornography communicates its endorsement of the behavior it represents by various features of the pornographic context: the degradation of the female characters is represented as providing pleasure to the participant males and, even worse, to the participant females, and there is no suggestion that this sort of treatment of others is inappropriate to their status as human beings. These two features are together sufficient to constitute endorsement of the represented behavior. The contextual features which make material pornographic are intrinsic to the material. In addition to these, extrinsic features, such as the purpose for which the material is presented—i.e., the sexual arousal/pleasure/satisfaction of its (mostly) male consumers—or an accompanying text, may reinforce or make explicit the endorsement. Representations which in and of themselves do not show or endorse degrading behavior may be put into a pornographic context by juxtaposition with others that are degrading, or by a text which invites or recommends degrading behavior toward the subject represented. In such a case the whole complex—the series of representations or representations with text—is pornographic.

The distinction I have sketched is one that applies most clearly to sequential material—a verbal or pictorial (filmed) story—which represents an action and provides a temporal context for it. In showing the before and after, a narrator or filmmaker has plenty of opportunity to acknowledge the dignity of the person violated or clearly to refuse to do so. It is somewhat more difficult to apply the distinction to single still representations. The contextual features cited above, however, are clearly present in still photographs or pictures that glamorize degradation and sexual violence. Phonograph album covers and advertisements offer some prime examples of such glamorization. Their representations of women in chains (the Ohio Players), or bound by ropes and black and blue (the Rolling Stones) are considered high-quality commercial "art" and glossily prettify the violence they represent. Since the standard function of prettification and glamorization is the communication of desirability, these albums and ads are communicating the desirability of violence against women. Representations of women bound or chained, particularly those of women bound in such a way as to make their breasts, or genital or anal areas vulnerable to any passerby, endorse the scene they represent by the absence of any indication that this treatment of women is in any way inappropriate.

To summarize: Pornography is not just the explicit representation or description of sexual behavior, nor even the explicit representation or description of sexual behavior which is degrading and/or abusive to women. Rather, it is material that explicitly represents or describes degrading and abusive sexual behavior so as to endorse and/or recommend the behavior as described. The contextual features, moreover, which communicate such endorsement are intrinsic to the material; that is, they are features whose removal or alteration would change the representation or description.

This account of pornography is underlined by the etymology and original meaning of the word "pornography." *The Oxford English Dictionary* defines pornography as "Description of the life, manners, etc. of prostitutes and their patrons [from πόρνη (porne) meaning "harlot" and γράφειν (graphein) meaning "to write"]; hence the expression or suggestion of obscene or unchaste subjects in literature or art."[5]

Let us consider the first part of the definition for a moment. In the transactions between prostitutes and their clients, prostitutes are paid, directly or indirectly, for the use of their bodies by the client for sexual pleasure.* Traditionally males have obtained from female prostitutes what they could not or did not wish to get from their wives or women friends, who, because of the character of their relation to the male, must be accorded some measure of human respect. While there are limits to what treatment is seen as appropriate toward women as wives or women friends, the prostitute as prostitute exists to provide sexual pleasure to males. The female characters of contemporary pornography also exist to provide pleasure to males, but in the pornographic context no pretense is made to regard them as parties to a contractual arrangement. Rather, the anonymity of these characters makes each one Everywoman, thus suggesting not only that all women are appropriate subjects for the enactment of the most bizarre and demeaning male sexual fantasies, but also that this is their primary purpose. The recent escalation of violence in pornography—the presentation of scenes of bondage, rape, and torture of women for the sexual stimulation of the male characters or male viewers—while shocking in itself, is from this point of view merely a more vicious extension of a genre whose success depends on treating women in a manner beneath their dignity as human beings.

III. Pornography: Lies and Violence Against Women

What is wrong with pornography, then, is its degrading and dehumanizing portrayal of women (and *not* its sexual content). Pornography, by its very nature, requires that women be subordinate to men and mere instruments for the fulfillment of male fantasies. To accomplish this, pornography must lie. Pornography lies when

---

[5]*The Oxford English Dictionary,* Compact Edition (London: Oxford University Press, 1971), p. 2242.

*In talking of prostitution here, I refer to the concept of, rather than the reality of, prostitution. The same is true of my remarks about relationships between women and their husbands or men friends.

it says that our sexual life is or ought to be subordinate to the service of men, that our pleasure consists in pleasing men and not ourselves, that we are depraved, that we are fit subjects for rape, bondage, torture, and murder. Pornography lies explicitly about women's sexuality, and through such lies fosters more lies about our humanity, our dignity, and our personhood.

Moreover, since nothing is alleged to justify the treatment of the female characters of pornography save their womanhood, pornography depicts all women as fit objects of violence by virtue of their sex alone. Because it is simply being female that, in the pornographic vision, justifies being violated, the lies of pornography are lies about all women. Each work of pornography is on its own libelous and defamatory, yet gains power through being reinforced by every other pornographic work. The sheer number of pornographic productions expands the moral issue to include not only assessing the morality or immorality of individual works, but also the meaning and force of the mass production of pornography.

The pornographic view of women is thoroughly entrenched in a booming portion of the publishing, film, and recording industries, reaching and affecting not only all who look to such sources for sexual stimulation, but also those of us who are forced into an awareness of it as we peruse magazines at newsstands and record albums in record stores, as we check the entertainment sections of city newspapers, or even as we approach a counter to pay for groceries. It is not necessary to spend a great deal of time reading or viewing pornographic material to absorb its male-centered definition of women. No longer confined within plain brown wrappers, it jumps out from billboards that proclaim "Live X-rated Girls!" or "Angels in Pain" or "Hot and Wild," and from magazine covers displaying a woman's genital area being spread open to the viewer by her own fingers.* Thus, even men who do not frequent pornographic shops and movie houses are supported in the sexist objectification of women by their environment. Women, too, are crippled by internalizing as self-images those that are presented to us by pornographers. Isolated from one another and with no source of support for an alternative view of female sexuality, we may not always find the strength to resist a message that dominates the common cultural media.

The entrenchment of pornography in our culture also gives it a significance quite beyond its explicit sexual messages. To suggest, as pornography does, that the primary purpose of women is to provide sexual pleasure to men is to deny that women are independently human or have a status equal to that of men. It is, moreover, to deny our equality at one of the most intimate levels of human experience. This denial is especially powerful in a hierarchical, class society such as ours, in which individuals feel good about themselves by feeling superior to others. Men in our society have a vested interest in maintaining their belief in the inferiority of the female sex, so that no matter how oppressed and exploited by the society in which they live and work, they can feel that they are at least superior to someone or some category of individuals—a woman or women. Pornography, by presenting

---

*This was a full-color magazine cover seen in a rack at the check-out counter of a corner delicatessen.

women as wanton, depraved, and made for the sexual use of men, caters directly to that interest.* The very intimate nature of sexuality which makes pornography so corrosive also protects it from explicit public discussion. The consequent lack of any explicit social disavowal of the pornographic image of women enables this image to continue fostering sexist attitudes even as the society publicly proclaims its (as yet timid) commitment to sexual equality.

In addition to finding a connection between the pornographic view of women and the denial to us of our full human rights, women are beginning to connect the consumption of pornography with committing rape and other acts of sexual violence against women. Contrary to the findings of the Commission on Obscenity and Pornography a growing body of research is documenting (1) a correlation between exposure to representations of violence and the committing of violent acts generally, and (2) a correlation between exposure to pornographic materials and the committing of sexually abusive or violent acts against women.[6] While more study is needed to establish precisely what the causal relations are, clearly so-called hard-core pornography is not innocent.

From "snuff" films and miserable magazines in pornographic stores to *Hustler,* to phonograph album covers and advertisements, to *Vogue,* pornography has come to occupy its own niche in the communications and entertainment media and to acquire a quasi-institutional character (signaled by the use of diminutives such as "porn" or "porno" to refer to pornographic material, as though such familiar naming could take the hurt out). Its acceptance by the mass media, whatever the motivation, means a cultural endorsement of its message. As much as the materials themselves, the social tolerance of these degrading and distorted images of women in such quantities is harmful to us, since it indicates a general willingness to see women in ways incompatible with our fundamental human dignity and thus to justify treating us in those ways.[†] The tolerance of pornographic representations of the rape, bondage, and torture of women helps to create and maintain a climate more tolerant of the actual physical abuse of women.[‡] The tendency on the

---

*Pornography thus becomes another tool of capitalism. One feature of some contemporary pornography—the use of Black and Asian women in both still photographs and films—exploits the racism as well as the sexism of its white consumers. For a discussion of the interplay between racism and sexism under capitalism as it relates to violent crimes against women, see Angela Y. Davis, "Rape, Racism, and the Capitalist Setting," *The Black Scholar,* Vol. 9, No. 7, April 1978.

[6]Urie Bronfenbrenner, *Two Worlds of Childhood* (New York: Russell Sage Foundation, 1970); H. J. Eysenck and D. K. B. Nias, *Sex, Violence and the Media* (New York: St. Martin's Press, 1978); and Michael Goldstein, Harold Kant, and John Hartman, *Pornography and Sexual Deviance* (Berkeley: University of California Press, 1973); and the papers by Diana Russell, Pauline Bart, and Irene Diamond included in this volume.

[†]This tolerance has a linguistic parallel in the growing acceptance and use of nonhuman nouns such as "chick," "bird," "filly," "fox," "doll," "babe," "skirt," etc., to refer to women, and of verbs of harm such as "fuck," "screw," "bang" to refer to sexual intercourse. See Robert Baker and Frederick Elliston, " 'Pricks' and 'Chicks': A Plea for Persons." *Philosophy and Sex* (Buffalo, N.Y.: Prometheus Books, 1975).

[‡]This is supported by the fact that in Denmark the number of rapes committed has increased while the number of rapes reported to the authorities has decreased over the past twelve years. See *WAVPM Newspage,* Vol. II, No. 5, June, 1978, quoting M. Harry, "Denmark Today—The Causes and Effects of Sexual Liberty" (paper presented to The Responsible Society, London, England, 1976). See also Eysenck and Nias, *Sex, Violence and the Media* (New York: St. Martin's Press, 1978), pp. 120–124.

part of the legal system to view the victim of a rape as responsible for the crime against her is but one manifestation of this.

In sum, pornography is injurious to women in at least three distinct ways:

1. Pornography, especially violent pornography, is implicated in the committing of crimes of violence against women.
2. Pornography is the vehicle for the dissemination of a deep and vicious lie about women. It is defamatory and libelous.
3. The diffusion of such a distorted view of women's nature in our society as it exists today supports sexist (i.e., male-centered) attitudes, and thus reinforces the oppression and exploitation of women.

Society's tolerance of pornography, especially pornography on the contemporary massive scale, reinforces each of these modes of injury: By not disavowing the lie, it supports the male-centered myth that women are inferior and subordinate creatures. Thus, it contributes to the maintenance of a climate tolerant of both psychological and physical violence against women.

IV. PORNOGRAPHY AND THE LAW

> Congress shall make no law respecting the establishment of religion, or prohibiting the free exercise thereof; or abridging the freedom of speech, or of the press; or the right of the people peaceably to assemble, and to petition the Government for a redress of grievances.—FIRST AMENDMENT, BILL OF RIGHTS OF THE UNITED STATES CONSTITUTION

Pornography is clearly a threat to women. Each of the modes of injury cited above offers sufficient reason at least to consider proposals for the social and legal control of pornography. The almost universal response from progressives to such proposals is that constitutional guarantees of freedom of speech and privacy preclude recourse to law.[7] While I am concerned about the erosion of constitutional rights and also think for many reasons that great caution must be exercised before undertaking a legal campaign against pornography, I find objections to such a campaign that are based on appeals to the First Amendment or to a right to privacy ultimately unconvincing.

Much of the defense of the pornographer's right to publish seems to assume that, while pornography may be tasteless and vulgar, it is basically an entertainment that harms no one but its consumers, who may at worst suffer from the debasement of their taste; and that therefore those who argue for its control are

---

[7]Cf. Marshall Cohen, "The Case Against Censorship," *The Public Interest*, No. 22, Winter 1971, reprinted in John R. Burr and Milton Goldinger, *Philosophy and Contemporary Issues* (New York: Macmillan, 1976), and Justice William Brennan's dissenting opinion in *Paris Adult Theater I* v. *Slaton*, 431 U.S. 49.

demanding an unjustifiable abridgment of the rights to freedom of speech of those who make and distribute pornographic materials and of the rights to privacy of their customers. The account of pornography given above shows that the assumptions of this position are false. Nevertheless, even some who acknowledge its harmful character feel that it is granted immunity from social control by the First Amendment, or that the harm that would ensue from its control outweighs the harm prevented by its control.

There are three ways of arguing that control of pornography is incompatible with adherence to constitutional rights. The first argument claims that regulating pornography involves an unjustifiable interference in the private lives of individuals. The second argument takes the First Amendment as a basic principle constitutive of our form of government, and claims that the production and distribution of pornographic material, as a form of speech, is an activity protected by that amendment. The third argument claims not that the pornographer's rights are violated, but that others' rights will be if controls against pornography are instituted.

The privacy argument is the easiest to dispose of. Since the open commerce in pornographic materials is an activity carried out in the public sphere, the publication and distribution of such materials, unlike their use by individuals, is not protected by rights to privacy. The distinction between the private consumption of pornographic material and the production and distribution of, or open commerce in it, is sometimes blurred by defenders of pornography. But I may entertain, in the privacy of my mind, defamatory opinions about another person, even though I may not broadcast them. So one might create without restraint—as long as no one were harmed in the course of preparing them—pornographic materials for one's personal use, but be restrained from reproducing and distributing them. In both cases what one is doing—in the privacy of one's mind or basement—may indeed be deplorable, but immune from legal proscription. Once the activity becomes public, however—i.e., once it involves others—it is no longer protected by the same rights that protect activities in the private sphere.*

In considering the second argument (that control of pornography, private or public, is wrong in principle), it seems important to determine whether we consider the right to freedom of speech to be absolute and unqualified. If it is, then obviously all speech, including pornography, is entitled to protection. But the right is, in the first place, not an unqualified right: There are several kinds of speech not protected by the First Amendment, including the incitement to violence in volatile circumstances, the solicitation of crimes, perjury and misrepresentation, slander, libel, and false advertising.† That there are forms of proscribed speech shows that we accept limitations on the right to freedom of speech if such speech, as do the

---

*Thus, the right to use such materials in the privacy of one's home, which has been upheld by the United States Supreme Court (*Stanley* v. *Georgia*, 394 U.S. 557), does not include the right to purchase them or to have them available in the commercial market. See also *Paris Adult Theater I* v. *Slaton*, 431 U.S. 49.

†The Supreme Court has also traditionally included obscenity in this category. As not everyone agrees it should be included, since as defined by statutes, it is a highly vague concept, and since the grounds accepted by the Court for including it miss the point, I prefer to omit it from this list.

forms listed, impinges on other rights. The manufacture and distribution of material which defames and threatens all members of a class by its recommendation of abusive and degrading behavior toward some members of that class simply in virtue of their membership in it seems a clear candidate for inclusion on the list. The right is therefore not an unqualified one.

Nor is it an absolute or fundamental right, underived from any other right: If it were there would not be exceptions or limitations. The first ten amendments were added to the Constitution as a way of guaranteeing the "blessings of liberty" mentioned in its preamble, to protect citizens against the unreasonable usurpation of power by the state. The specific rights mentioned in the First Amendment— those of religion, speech, assembly, press, petition—reflect the recent experiences of the makers of the Constitution under colonial government as well as a sense of what was and is required generally to secure liberty.

It may be objected that the right to freedom of speech is fundamental in that it is part of what we mean by liberty and not a right that is derivative from a right to liberty. In order to meet this objection, it is useful to consider a distinction explained by Ronald Dworkin in his book *Taking Rights Seriously*.[8] As Dworkin points out, the word "liberty" is used in two distinct, if related, senses: as "license," i.e., the freedom from legal constraints to do as one pleases, in some contexts; and as "independence," i.e., "the status of a person as independent and equal rather than subservient," in others. Failure to distinguish between these senses in discussions of rights and freedoms is fatal to clarity and understanding.

If the right to free speech is understood as a partial explanation of what is meant by liberty, then liberty is perceived as license: The right to do as one pleases includes a right to speak as one pleases. But license is surely not a condition the First Amendment is designed to protect. We not only tolerate but require legal constraints on liberty as license when we enact laws against rape, murder, assault, theft, etc. If everyone did exactly as she or he pleased at any given time, we would have chaos if not lives, as Hobbes put it, that are "nasty, brutish, and short." We accept government to escape, not to protect, this condition.

If, on the other hand, by liberty is meant independence, then freedom of speech is not necessarily a part of liberty; rather, it is a means to it. The right to freedom of speech is not a fundamental, absolute right, but one derivative from, possessed in virtue of, the more basic right to independence. Taking this view of liberty requires providing arguments showing that the more specific rights we claim are necessary to guarantee our status as persons "independent and equal rather than subservient." In the context of government, we understand independence to be the freedom of each individual to participate as an equal among equals in the determination of how she or he is to be governed. Freedom of speech in this context means that an individual may not only entertain beliefs concerning government privately, but may express them publicly. We express our opinions about taxes, disarmament, wars, social-welfare programs, the function of the police, civil rights, and so on. Our right to freedom of speech includes the right to criticize the

---

[8]Ronald Dworkin, *Taking Rights Seriously* (Cambridge: Harvard University Press, 1977), p. 262.

government and to protest against various forms of injustice and the abuse of power. What we wish to protect is the free expression of ideas even when they are unpopular. What we do not always remember is that speech has functions other than the expression of ideas.

Regarding the relationship between a right to freedom of speech and the publication and distribution of pornographic materials, there are two points to be made. In the first place, the latter activity is hardly an exercise of the right to the free expression of ideas as understood above. In the second place, to the degree that the tolerance of material degrading to women supports and reinforces the attitude that women are not fit to participate as equals among equals in the political life of their communities, and that the prevalence of such an attitude effectively prevents women from so participating, the absolute and fundamental right of women to liberty (political independence) is violated.

This second argument against the suppression of pornographic material, then, rests on a premise that must be rejected, namely, that the right to freedom of speech is a right to utter anything one wants. It thus fails to show that the production and distribution of such material is an activity protected by the First Amendment. Furthermore, an examination of the issues involved leads to the conclusion that tolerance of this activity violates the rights of women to political independence.

The third argument (which expresses concern that curbs on pornography are the first step toward political censorship) runs into the same ambiguity that besets the arguments based on principle. These arguments generally have as an underlying assumption that the maximization of freedom is a worthy social goal. Control of pornography diminishes freedom—directly the freedom of pornographers, indirectly that of all of us. But again, what is meant by "freedom"? It cannot be that what is to be maximized is license—as the goal of a social group whose members probably have at least some incompatible interests, such a goal would be internally inconsistent. If, on the other hand, the maximization of political independence is the goal, then that is in no way enhanced by, and may be endangered by, the tolerance of pornography. To argue that the control of pornography would create a precedent for suppressing political speech is thus to confuse license with political independence. In addition, it ignores a crucial basis for the control of pornography, i.e., its character as libelous speech. The prohibition of such speech is justified by the need for protection from the injury (psychological as well as physical or economic) that results from libel. A very different kind of argument would be required to justify curtailing the right to speak our minds about the institutions which govern us. As long as such distinctions are insisted upon, there is little danger of the government's using the control of pornography as precedent for curtailing political speech.

In summary, neither as a matter of principle nor in the interests of maximizing liberty can it be supposed that there is an intrinsic right to manufacture and distribute pornographic material.

The only other conceivable source of protection for pornography would be a general right to do what we please as long as the rights of others are respected. Since the production and distribution of pornography violates the rights of women—to respect and to freedom from defamation, among others—this protection is not available.

V. CONCLUSION

I have defined pornography in such a way as to distinguish it from erotica and from moral realism, and have argued that it is defamatory and libelous toward women, that it condones crimes against women, and that it invites tolerance of the social, economic, and cultural oppression of women. The production and distribution of pornographic material is thus a social and moral wrong. Contrasting both the current volume of pornographic production and its growing infiltration of the communications media with the status of women in this culture makes clear the necessity for its control. Since the goal of controlling pornography does not conflict with constitutional rights, a common obstacle to action is removed.

Appeals for action against pornography are sometimes brushed aside with the claim that such action is a diversion from the primary task of feminists—the elimination of sexism and of sexual inequality. This approach focuses on the enjoyment rather than the manufacture of pornography, and sees it as merely a product of sexism which will disappear when the latter has been overcome and the sexes are socially and economically equal. Pornography cannot be separated from sexism in this way: Sexism is not just a set of attitudes regarding the inferiority of women but the behaviors and social and economic rules that manifest such attitudes. Both the manufacture and distribution of pornography and the enjoyment of it are instances of sexist behavior. The enjoyment of pornography on the part of individuals will presumably decline as such individuals begin to accord women their status as fully human. A cultural climate which tolerates the degrading representation of women is not a climate which facilitates the development of respect for women. Furthermore, the demand for pornography is stimulated not just by the sexism of individuals but by the pornography industry itself. Thus, both as a social phenomenon and in its effect on individuals, pornography, far from being a mere product, nourishes sexism. The campaign against it is an essential component of women's struggle for legal, economic, and social equality, one which requires the support of all feminists.*

*Many women helped me to develop and crystallize the ideas presented in this paper. I would especially like to thank Michele Farrell, Laura Lederer, Pamela Miller, and Dianne Romain for their comments in conversation and on the first written draft. Portions of this material were presented orally to members of the Society for Women in Philosophy and to participants in the workshops on "What Is Pornography?" at the Conference on Feminist Perspectives on Pornography, San Francisco, November 17, 18, and 19, 1978. Their discussion was invaluable in helping me to see problems and to clarify the ideas presented here.

38. Pornography

Jan Narveson

Jan F. Narveson (1936–   ), professor of philosophy at the University of Waterloo, Ontario, Canada, has written books and articles on ethics and on social and political philosophy.

Pornography is the depiction, by visual, literary, or aural means, of subject-matter intended to be sexually stimulating, when that depiction is for the *purpose* of such stimulation. Pornography is a sort of depictional aphrodisiac. Or at least, that was once the idea. Recently, the depiction of nonsexual violence against people has also come to be described as pornographic. Although we will in general have the sexual type in mind in the following discussion, the connection, or a supposed connection, between violence and sex is a major part of the conceptual concern with this matter, as we will see.

Official suppression, censorship, and/or strict control over the circulation of pornography has been commonplace in our society for a long time, and remains the principal form of current censorship. Movies are rated, some are suppressed, and others altered by their makers in order to avoid the censor's hand. The same has been true of books, at various times, though currently "hate literature" is a more likely target than pornography. The question that concerns us here is whether such interventions are justified.

LIBERAL VS. CONSERVATIVE

Standing against censorship is the *liberal* principle: that people should be able to live the sort of life they choose, exercising their own taste (or lack of it), not being subject to the rule of others. In political terms, the liberal holds that the purpose of a commonwealth is the advancement of the several goods of its members, a point that the conservative agrees with. *But* the liberal adds that the goods in question must be good in the view of the individual members of society, rather than in the view of some self-appointed or state-appointed authority. It is in this full sense that the liberal holds that the state exists for the sake of the citizen, and not the other way around. The conservative, by contrast, holds that in some or a lot of cases, certain people—namely those in power or hoping to be in power—know what is good for us, the people. "We are out for your good, to be sure," say they—but it is *they* who will decide what that good is.

From Jan Narveson, *Moral Matters*, 1993. Reprinted with permission of Broadview Press.

The same distinction is applicable to morality. A liberal morality attributes to individuals the right to live as they please, free of interference from others, subject only to such controls as are necessary to uphold the same freedom for all. A conservative morality, by contrast, holds that there are right or wrong ways of life, that it is our duty to steer people, by force if necessary, into the right ones and away from the wrong ones—and that what is right and wrong is known independently of the values and interests that people actually have. Of course, which values are the right ones is a subject on which views will vary greatly from one conservative to another.

My characterization of conservatism is probably broader than that prevalent in ordinary usage—if there is any such usage. If a society were to force its subjects to read pornography or engage in nonstandard sex acts, on the ground that those were part of the ideal way of life which all should adhere to, then few would call this "conservative," although it would, on my usage, be precisely that—and at least as objectionable to the liberal as would be the prohibition of such things on a similar ground. For present purposes, however, we needn't worry about that. In this discussion, we will simply take the conservative to hold that the depiction of sexual acts with a view to stimulating sexual sensations may properly be suppressed.

Harm

Everyone agrees that we may insist on someone's not doing x if his doing x would be *harmful* to others. The question is, what constitutes harm? The liberal version of the harm principle is that harm consists in physical damage to the body, to one's property, or to one's civil and political rights. This is the version of the harm principle that leaves us maximally free to live our lives as we see fit, with all that that entails, for better or worse. It does not allow mere "damage" to one's beliefs, for instance, to count as a reason for restricting the offending person's liberty.

We will explore the subject of censorship in the light of this principle, asking what kind of restrictions it would approve, if any, and whether there is any justification for principles more congenial than that to would-be censors.

Disgust

It is obvious enough that there can be a rationale for censorship in *conservative* terms: that someone else's activity in some respect is "abhorrent," or "disgusting," or the like, is taken by the conservative to be a sufficient basis for action to prevent the alleged miscreant from carrying on in the offending manner. How would the conservative try to argue for his claims? Presumably he hopes to persuade you that the sort of life you live if you view pornography, say, is one from which you would recoil if you could just view it properly. But what if you don't recoil? That the consumer of pornography doesn't see it as disgusting is taken by the conservative as evidence of his base nature: question-begging arguments are the conservative's stock in trade. They are appeals to our aesthetic sense, or our sense of propriety, but not appeals that can be backed up with further reasons; we must either take it or leave it. In the case of pornography, for instance, we must either just take it or leave it that such pleasures as people might get from viewing pictures of genitalia or of people engaged in sex acts are "bad" pleasures. But if they really are pleasures, it is going to be difficult to convince the pornographer that they are also bad ones.

Public/Private

If someone professing to be liberal in his views wants to support any censorship, he must search for an argument of a different kind. He must show that use of the materials in question visits some genuine harm on someone. But the only "harm" he is usually able to demonstrate is *offense:* some people, such as himself, are offended by the prospect of others viewing this kind of material.

But offense is surely not enough for this purpose. If it were, we would all be at the mercy of everyone else's whims and tastes. In fact, though, there is a tacit assumption at work here that needs to be brought out. No one could seriously think that offense can't *ever* be sufficient cause to justify restrictive activity on the part of the offended person. If you offend me in my living room, for example, then I would certainly be justified, on that account alone, in showing you the door. You might think me unreasonable, and for that matter you might be right; still, I surely have the right to do that. What makes all the difference is whether the space in which the expression takes place is privately owned or not. If it is, then the owner has the authority to decide what will and won't be said on the premises. But if it is not, then we have a problem, for nonprivate property is either just unowned (which is rare) or *public,* in which case the familiar problems of politics set in.

Our question, then, must concern conduct in public areas, those where we encounter each other routinely. The general idea concerning such areas is that everyone has the right to be there, going to and fro as they please. Nobody can "show the door" to anyone, for no individual or small group of individuals owns the place. That, indeed, is just the trouble. If no one has any more right than any other, on what rational principle can we govern interactions? How do we decide who has to give way in a public space, when presumably both have the right to be there?

It's easy enough to give a partial answer to this. For not everything in a public area is public. You and I are not public property. The perimeters of our bodies, at least, define a frontier beyond which other members of the public may not go even if the area we respectively occupy is a public area. Physical attacks against each other's bodies are prohibited on the same ground that verbal attacks within our houses may be prohibited by the owner. But what about verbal attacks in public places?

We can also usefully distinguish between, say, a verbal attack at a volume that is physically painful and one that is only "painful" in some other sense. But that will take us back to the subject of offense. And here it seems we can again hardly deny its relevance in some cases: offensive verbal attacks are not routinely allowable in public, either. There our discourse ought to be peaceable, not intended to offend. The same can be true regarding our appearance, perhaps. To go forth topless in public, as one woman did in a small Canadian city one hot summer's day, is to try to unilaterally impose a standard of dress (or undress) that is likely to offend many. Are we justified in coercively prohibiting such exhibitions? May we say that those who are offended are merely prudish and have no real reason for their offense? I'm inclined to agree with that, in fact, but it is surely a matter on which opinions may legitimately differ. Thus, there is a question whether we would merely be imposing another standard if we insisted that citizens must put up with displays of public nudity. It seems uncomfortably comparable to an earlier example: *requiring* people to engage in sexually deviant behavior.

That it is impossible to please everyone here is illustrated by the interesting case of the devout Muslim woman, who goes forth in public dressed in heavy veil and robes. She is presumably offended by the carefree attire of most of those around her. But one can easily imagine that some women would actually be offended at the Muslim woman's dress, holding that her costume shows a submission to male domination that is beneath human dignity. The Muslim woman and the feminist are then in a zero-sum game: a given kind of attire will offend one of them only if it won't offend the other. In fact, we are inclined to award both of them the right to dress as they please, requiring both to restrain any offense they might feel, this being the price they pay for going forth in public at all. Yet the would-be nudist is required to wear something in the interests of nonoffense, and there is a problem drawing the line. Why should we cater to the offense of the "prude" when we do not do so regarding the Muslim or the feminist?

Privacy and Porn

Actually, pornographic viewing doesn't take place in public either. All that happens in public is that enough information is made available to the public, in the form of advertising (which, in turn, can be discreetly displayed) to enable some of its members to seek out the private locations in which they can pursue their interests. So long as those locations are clearly identifiable, they can also be avoided by those of differing taste. Privatization enables all parties to be satisfied, it seems. And the liberal does not defend the *public* display of pornography.

Or does she? Here we have to distinguish between what the privatization idea would do if it were thoroughly carried out, and what would happen in the real world if we tried to approximate it—that is, between what philosophers call "ideal," or "perfect compliance" theory, and "partial compliance" theory. Total privatization means that all costs and benefits of an act are borne by the agent. No costs are imposed on anyone, and no one benefits at the expense of anyone else.

Now let us return to our problem. Suppose that all acts of reading or viewing satisfy our privacy requirement. Nobody sees anything that she doesn't want to see, nobody reads anything that she doesn't want to read, and nobody reads or sees anything without the consent of whoever provides it (authors, booksellers, movie-house operators, and so on). Is everything just fine, then? The liberal says Yes. But many think not, and we must look carefully at their proposed reasons.

There are two types of objection to be concerned with here. First, there is the view that some material *inherently demeans* certain people. This, some hold, harms those people sufficiently to justify restriction even on liberal terms. And second, there is a concern with the effects of such material on the consumer's subsequent behavior. His viewing of pornography, for instance, stimulates him to go out and rape people.

These two objections are important, because they are addressed by people who at least claim to be sympathetic with liberalism. We must look closely at them.

DEMEANING DEPICTIONS

The first objection is advanced, for instance, by many feminists against pornography. Women, they say, are demeaned in such material. They are portrayed as inferior, or as slaves of men, or as mere "sex objects" to be used as men wish. Probably some pornographic literature does not do this, but let us suppose that some does. The interesting question is whether this would provide ground for suppression.

Here's an example to think about: in the Old Testament, a good many groups of people in the then Middle East were portrayed as pretty bad lots. The Philistines, for instance, were depicted as a bunch of yahoos who went around beating up on people until at last courageous little David came along and laid their main champion low with a deft application of high (for the times) technology. Are the people who make this charge proposing, then, that we should outlaw reading of the Old Testament? That book is not a "sacred cow," to be sure; yet very few of those who favor suppression of other literature would take kindly to the thought that it should be suppressed too. Obviously, evil can be portrayed without implying approval.

FALSITY

It might be said that the depiction of women in pornography nevertheless does imply approval, and that its depiction is false and thereby creates a false image of women in general. Would this be a ground for objection even if true? I find it difficult to see how any other construal can be put on it than this: that what are claimed to be demeaning portrayals, say of women or of Palestinians, are false. Women are not slavish, passive, and mere sex objects; Palestinians aren't cruel and warlike. For after all, if these claims were actually true, then there is at least some question why it would be held wrong to depict them in those ways.

But if that's the claim about pornography, then the trouble is that we are back to the old arguments for censorship so successfully refuted by John Stuart Mill in his famous *Essay on Liberty*. The fact that statement **p** is *false* cannot be used as a ground for suppression of those who would say it, though it does provide an excellent occasion for refuting it.

This isn't the end of the matter, however. There are truths about people which nevertheless may not be broadcast. Your sex life, for example, is not something the details of which I am entitled to know. We suppose, and for excellent reason, that there is a right of privacy that should not be invaded even if the result would be the publication of any number of true statements. However, this charge would not be sustainable against pornography, provided that it was produced within the confines of our privatization restrictions. For after all, the actors in those films are required by our principles to have participated voluntarily in their production, for example by accepting payment large enough to make it worth their while. On the face of it, we don't as yet have a clear case against pornographic portrayals, however demeaning we may think them to be.

VOLUNTARINESS

Proponents of the objection we are considering might well respond to this by claiming that the actresses in question did *not* participate voluntarily. But to make good this claim, which is superficially implausible, they have to stretch the notion of voluntariness well beyond its normal usage. The soldiers from an all-volunteer army who were unfortunate enough to have been killed in battle nevertheless did volunteer. They signed up in full knowledge that their work entailed a risk of death. The actress in a pornographic movie knows what sort of customers will leer at the results; it is up to her to consider whether she is willing to assume all sorts of undignified positions, with that expected result, in return for the proferred fee.

It might be complained that it isn't really up to the actress to decide whether to act in a scene that depicts women in that way: if she acts in it, then that is how they are depicted, whether she intends that or not. But is this a valid complaint? No-one can make women that way, just by so depicting them. Nor can anyone plausibly claim to know all women; our actress is, after all, just one woman among others, and women differ. And in any case, the porn actress would surely disclaim any such intention, insisting that she is only portraying one particular character of that kind—not women in general. Anyone who thinks that any character in any artistic representation *must* represent everybody is surely going far beyond the intentions of typical artists, as well as supposing something that is quite obviously untrue.

TRUTH, FALSITY, AND HARM

Is truth good in itself? Is truth any kind of value at all? And is it a value *for* all? *Is* Society just one big clone of Plato's Academy, after all? Opinions may vary on the first question, but to the third, it is hard to see how the answer could be affirmative.

Aristotle claimed that "all men by nature desire to know," but as any elementary school teacher will tell you, this is not at all obvious, especially if it means that everyone's goal in life is to maximize her supply of interesting information about the universe, as compared with other possible goals. That relatively clear conjecture we may pretty confidently dismiss. Moreover, those who don't go in for such exotic amusements are guilty of no moral error.

But on the other hand, we might mean that *falsehood*, or more precisely, the provision of false "information" in response to requests for information, is a *disvalue* for anyone. That is indeed plausible. One cannot act well *on the basis of falsehoods*. If my doing **x** successfully is contingent on some supposed fact, **p,** and **p** is false, then my action to that extent, and in that respect, misfires. How and why action might be so contingent varies, and may sometimes need explaining. But in typical cases, there's no problem at all: if you want to accomplish goal **G** by performing some act, **x,** then you are assuming that **x** is connected to **G.** If someone tells you this and what he says is false, he has put you out, at very least by motivating you to perform a useless action, or worse, by getting you to do something you really don't want. In some cases, the point of not being in error is less clear. Certainly it could be in someone's short-run interest, at least, to deceive someone else, and even perhaps himself, about some limited matter. (Yet even the self-deceiver needs to know what is true in order to persuade himself of what is false; if what he wants to believe were actually true, he could spare himself the trouble of deceiving himself about it!) That truth, in the sense of not being in error about things that matter to you, is generally a value is clear enough.

The question of how falsehoods might harm is rather complex. Here are several pointers and queries.

1. To say, sincerely, what is in fact false is to stand in need of correction, for to be in possession of what is false is likely to be unfortunate or worse. One does better to be refuted. And one has the moral duty to entertain proposed refutations rather than ignore them. To what extent must one do so? That's not easy to estimate; my point is that they shouldn't just be shunted aside, unless one has good antecedent reason for believing them false without further examination.

2. To say what one knows is false is to make oneself liable for consequences. When one's misinformation reasonably motivates others to act badly, with results unfortunate for them or others, then one bears liability for the misfortune and may in principle be sued for damages.

3. What if **A** impugns the reputation of **B** on grounds that are either meaningless, or logically insulated from refutation? For example, suppose **A** claims that **B** is "evil," but that his supposed evil consists in having a certain mysterious, unique, but suitably sinister property? That seems pretty nearly equivalent to falsehood, especially if propagated among gullible people. At any rate, it is not a rational ground of action. Its equivalence to falsehood lies in this: that for any given action, **x,** by some person, **C,** that has certain effects on person **B, C**'s doing **x** to **B** for the reason that **B** is **F**

(where **x** is evil in our defined sense) is based on a necessarily irrelevant ground. If '**F**' is indefinable, then the "fact" that **B** is **F** couldn't be a good reason for treating **B** in any one way as opposed to any other. There is also the problem of assessing responsibility of those who act badly on the basis of this drivel. If **B** assassinates **C** because **B** has been told by **A** that "God ordered it," how do we apportion blame to **B** and **A**? A difficult question, but surely both are to blame.

4. The fact that one dislikes person **B** is, of course, a putatively good reason for having as little as possible to do with him. It can also seem to be a reason, so far as it goes, for performing acts that would violate his rights, of course; but there are then independent reasons against it, overriding mere dislike—that, indeed, is part of the point of calling those things "rights." Nor, of course, is the fact that I dislike **B** any reason, so far as it goes, why *you* should dislike **B**. We do not have a general, basic duty to like each other, of course, but we have a general interest in good relations with all people, so we should not easily indulge in ill-considered dislikings. Still, it does not violate someone's rights if you ultimately dislike that person.

5. Do we harm someone by disliking him? We must be careful to distinguish this from the question whether you might come to harm someone *as a result of* disliking him. That, of course, is common enough. But in those cases, we typically have in mind someone's harming someone in various familiar ways; we don't mean that the very fact of dislike is itself harmful to the other person.

But could it not sometimes be so? We might first point out that one could keep one's dislike to oneself, rather than manifesting it in readily observable ways. It's difficult to see how one could regard the sheer *fact* of someone's dislike, independently of any outward manifestations, as constituting "harm." It isn't impossible, to be sure. We can easily enough imagine someone having a desire that everyone like him, and be wounded if they do not. But we can not credit supposed harms of this type. To do so is to court disaster: everyone is really enslaved to everyone else if we can blame Jones merely for disliking Smith. Does the allegation that pornography demeans women identify a genuine ground of moral objection to it? We have noted that portrayals of some person mistreating others may not be false for clearly this sometimes actually happens. It is the "message"—that this is a good way to treat those others—that we may be concerned about. We certainly don't want anyone believing it. But whether this is a ground for suppressing the message is another question. If we think it is, we must be assuming that the audience for the message is gullible and incapable of properly evaluating claims of that kind, or else that it is evil, in which case the video or picture isn't "convincing" them, but is instead just pandering to or reinforcing a base tendency of character that is already present.

We must in any case distinguish those pornographic materials that are, in effect, "hate literature" from those that are not. Most are surely in the latter category:

they depict people sexually carrying on in various ways that plenty of possible viewers would find distasteful, but that the buying audience clearly does not. Nor, characteristically, did the participants. But there is a question about inferring intentions from what one sees on a screen, hears on a soundtrack, or reads in a text. Those who depict evil are not necessarily advocating it: indeed, one must describe something to condemn it. Many fine movies are devoted almost wholly to depicting evils: the message of such movies is typically that they *are* evils.

Now, it is clear that normal people can witness depictions of evil, and even advocacy of it, without being in any way corrupted by this. Cinema buffs have long been keen on certain cinema classics, such as "Birth of a Nation" and Leni Riefenstahl's depiction of the Third Reich, that are and were intended to be out-and-out exercises in propaganda, without being converted to the KKK or the Nazi party. To suppress such movies on the ground that their message is evil would be absurd, if those audiences are typical. And to assume, in general, that those witnessing pornography must be in fact corrupted by it is to make an assumption that we ought not generally to make about people. People must be generally presumed to have minds of their own, as well as to be responsible for their actions—which brings us to the other major question concerning pornography's effects on the consumer's behavior.

MOTIVATION TO DO EVIL

The other objection to pornography is that exposure to it induces people to engage in harmful behavior, such as rape. That objection cannot be dismissed along the lines we have just been considering. If it is true that reading x will *cause* **A** to go out and commit murder, rape or something comparably evil, then obviously we have reason to be concerned.

Some reason, yes—but how much? When, if ever, do we have a case for outright censorship arising from possibilities like this? It is important and true that murder and rape, among various other forms of interpersonal assault, are things which no person may do to anyone, under almost any conceivable circumstances. Someone who does this is rightly considered liable for criminal proceedings. And if we knew of any actual *causes* of any of these kinds of activity, such that we could know for certain in advance that a certain person was going to do an act of such a kind, then we would certainly be entitled to prevent that person from carrying out his evil plans. But the trouble is, we do *not* know of any such causes.

We do know that certain ways of treating young people, especially very young ones, drastically reduce the probability that they will end up performing such deeds, while certain others greatly increase it. For example, hardened recidivist criminals, the ones who commit another major crime almost right away upon their release from prison for the last one, it turns out, have almost invariably been brought up in domestic environments characterized by frequent violence, verbal and otherwise, by wildly inconsistent disciplinary practices, and by a pronounced shortage of parental (especially maternal) affection. Readers of this book have probably been fortunate enough to have been brought up in good homes. Even so, not all children from bad homes will end up hardened criminals—merely a lot of them. Virtually 100% of those brought up in "good" homes will not end up like that—but not quite 100%. Should we try to legally require parents to provide good homes for their children? If this could possibly be successful, it would have a drastic effect on the crime rate—virtually eliminating it, it seems. But it is clear that massive failure awaits any legal initiative of this kind.

Now apply that result, from an area where the evidence is strong, to the present one, where it is extremely weak. Is there a connection between witnessing pornographic materials and the likelihood of committing rape? Nobody would claim that there is anything remotely approximating a necessary condition here: millions of people view pornography without being rapists. It is certain that eliminating pornography entirely while leaving other things the same would leave us with plenty of rapists. In some cases, I gather, it might even increase the number: pornography in those cases acts as a substitute for the real thing, satisfying the would-be rapist before he gets out the door. It is very clear that this is an empirical question, and one that is decidedly not easy to answer; the evidence, such as it is, is overwhelmingly inconclusive.

All this requires us to address a further issue: what standards of evidence are we to use? Let us suppose that on the whole, people being exposed to pornography slightly increases the probability that they will later commit rape (and we do not even know that as yet). Now consider a figure we shall call **P**: the probability that a given individual will be a rapist given that he is a pornographer, less the probability that he would have been a rapist even if he hadn't been a pornographer. **P**, in other words, represents the marginal increment in this probability for members of the class of consumers of pornography. Then our question is, what value of **P** would justify depriving the entire class of consumers of pornography of opportunities to view it?

Consider another comparison case. Alcohol is a causative factor in a good many murders and a great many automobile accidents. We may be quite certain that the incidence of murder or criminal negligence among drinkers as compared with what it would be for those same people if they didn't drink is significant—far higher, given what we do know, than **P**. Yet prohibition in the USA was agreed to be a massive failure, and there is a genuine issue whether it would have been justified even if it hadn't been. Depriving everyone of alcohol when only some are induced by its consumption to commit criminal acts punishes the innocent in order to get at the guilty. Is this just?

Most readers will probably feel that the joys of alcohol consumption greatly outweigh those of pornography consumption. Perhaps so—but then, the joys of listening to a Mozart string quintet far outweigh either. Yet I don't think we are justified in requiring people to listen to Mozart; and this is not only because our efforts would no doubt prove a total failure. It is instead because how we shall run our lives is up to those whose lives they are, not to others—even if those others have terrific taste.

Zero Risk?

Some may insist that crimes like rape are so serious a matter that if we can do anything at all to make them less probable, then we should do it. That is a common attitude toward many things as well. But it is wrong—profoundly wrong, in one direction, and absurdly so in another.

To see its absurdity, consider your own case, and the risks you will quite reasonably take in order to gain modest pleasures. The most obvious and spectacular case is presented by smokers, who take a statistically very significant risk of contracting cancer in return for a modest amount of pleasure. But their conduct is perfectly rational (and I say this as a moderately fanatical nonsmoker). Given the choice between a probably longer but smoke-free life and a probably shorter and smoke-filled one, they prefer the latter. It's their choice, so long as they keep the smoke out of the lungs of the nonsmokers. For another example: there are people who voluntarily move to places like New York City from amazingly safe places like Selma, North Dakota, despite the vastly greater likelihood of being killed, mugged, or raped if they do so. They reckon that the more interesting things they can do in New York more than compensate for the increased risks of life in the big city. And again, they are not irrational to reason this way.

Given all this, if we imposed total censorship of pornography, who would lose and what would they lose? Presumably the consumers of porn would lose, and what they would lose are the various pleasures they presumably take in such literature. The overwhelming majority of these people will never rape anybody, and of the tiny minority who would, most would do so whether or not they watched pornography. Thus the innocent consumers of pornography would be penalized for the behavior of the others. And that isn't fair, just as it is not fair that the alcohol consumers among us who do not drive when drunk and do not knife people in heated arguments while inebriated should be deprived of their pleasures in order to protect the world from the others who do.

Indeed, it is perfectly clear that nothing in life is perfectly safe, once one considers the matter carefully. What walk of life has not produced its monsters, its aberrations? Academics who are convinced of some bizarre theory go forth to assassinate innocent people; accountants, preachers, secretaries—you name it: who can sincerely claim to know that the probability that persons in that walk of life will as a consequence of following it go out and do major harm to someone is *zero*? To prohibit these activities on that account would be to commit palpable wrongs now in the interests of preventing vague and remote possible wrongs in the future.

On the Theory of Social Risk

I will now suggest a social cost-benefit assessment for proposals like abolition of pornography. First, assign some definite negative value to the actual committing of one of the acts whose prevention we aim at. Then assign an equal positive value to each case in which the act in question didn't occur, though it otherwise would have. Society has paid itself that much in each successful case. Now assign another value, to the costs of the interferences we make in the interest of preventing the larger disvalues. And now suppose that society pays a compensation to each innocent person whose life is interfered with in this way. Then ask whether this was a good investment of society's time and energy.

Let's admit that it is very difficult to estimate the gains of such a policy. The best one can do would be to compare incidences of rape before and after the massive regime of censorship is installed. Nobody knows what the result would be, but if it is only a tiny diminution of the rate of rape, which is the worst we currently have reason to believe, then we have our result: we will have paid an astronomical amount in the way of lost liberty for a tiny gain in personal security—ten kilos of prevention for one gram of cure. This is not a rational way to run a society.

All in all, we do better to continue our liberal maxim. Every individual person is presumed innocent until proven guilty, and guilt will be proved only by deeds, not by the suspect's choice of reading or viewing matter. Other methods, such as argument, or moral suasion, especially in early childhood, will have to be employed by those wishing to protect the public.

PATERNALISM

Should we perhaps control what gets exposed to the *immature* eye? It does seem rather difficult to suppose that no sort of "censorship" is admissible in such cases, to be sure. But there are at least three angles from which to view this matter. One focuses on parental control and consent. Some parents will not wish their children to be exposed to certain of what they consider subversive influences—religious or moral, for instance. Another concerns the proper extent of community involvement in the nurturing of children. Particular parents may wish their children not to be exposed to certain material, but what if other parents are happy to expose theirs to it? The community may not arbitrarily rule in favour of one parent and against another.

Finally, there is the possibly distinct question of developmental psychology. Is it possible to know what is truly good for children, ignoring what their parents or other people want for them? These are difficult matters, and it is impossible to deny that what they are exposed to will likely have influence on them. But also, I think, what influences it will have must depend heavily on context. In a home where there is an extremely repressive atmosphere about sexual matters, a child's exposure to certain kinds of pornographic literature might help to turn him into the Montreal mass murderer; and yet, the same literature read by the child of tolerant and supportive parents might produce nothing but wry amusement. Indeed, there is probably little if anything that normal children can read or view in such an atmosphere that would produce serious harm to them in later years.

But here again, a major effort to intervene in the home is likely to be hugely counterproductive. What is likely to be much less so, I think, is a policy of holding parents responsible for the behavior of their children, at the same time encouraging the distribution of advice and information about childcaring. Behind almost every teenager committing a violent crime is a parent who did a lot of things very wrong. It might greatly encourage parents to seek advice on what it was, and how to correct it, if when a teenager committed such a crime, its parents were held liable and required to effect at least partial compensation. (This contrasts with the present rule in Canada, in which not even the teenager himself is held responsible, let alone his parents.)

The point here, then, is that it is difficult to find an independent basis for community restrictions on the reading matter to which even children are to be allowed to be exposed. Parents are not acting primarily as agents for the community when they take charge of their childrens' upbringing. They are, instead, making their own possibly separate judgments about what makes life good or bad. If that is how things stand even with the case of children, they must stand yet worse with the case of adults.

Summing Up

It is easy to be offended at what we are told is a frequent theme of much pornographic literature, that it depicts women as slaves or willing victims of assorted kinds of mistreatment. But the case for outrightly preventing people from creating and seeing such materials is very weak, even so. Normally all participants have acted voluntarily. And there is considerable room for divergent taste as accounting for much of the denunciation. Finally, we would need good evidence of a very strong causal connection between viewing pornography and being moved to commit actual violence before a case for suppression could become strong. In fact, there is at best extremely weak evidence of any such connection. Society would be wisest to leave intact the right of free speech and expression, and to expect its parents to avert evil tendencies by proper attention and training in their family life rather than by trusting to the censor to nip such tendencies in the bud.

HOW FREE SHOULD PEOPLE BE?

39. The Ethics of Addiction: An Argument in Favor of Letting Americans Take Any Drug They Want

Thomas Szasz

Thomas S. Szasz (1920–   ) is professor of psychiatry emeritus at the State University of New York Health Sciences Center at Syracuse. He has written numerous books and articles attacking abuses in the fields of psychiatry and psychological counseling.

To avoid clichés about "drug abuse," let us analyze its official definition. According to the World Health Organization, "Drug addiction is a state of periodic or chronic intoxication detrimental to the individual and to society, produced by the repeated consumption of a drug (natural or synthetic). Its characteristics include: 1) an overpowering desire or need (compulsion) to continue taking the drug and to obtain it by any means, 2) a tendency to increase the dosage, and 3) a psychic (psychological) and sometimes physical dependence on the effects of the drug."

Since this definition hinges on the harm done to both the individual and society, it is clearly an ethical one. Moreover, by not specifying what is "detrimental," it consigns the problem of addiction to psychiatrists who define the patient's "dangerousness to himself and others."

Next, we come to the effort to obtain the addictive substance "by any means." This suggests that the substance must be prohibited, or is very expensive, and is hence difficult for the ordinary person to obtain (rather than that the person who wants it has an inordinate craving for it). If there were an abundant and inexpensive supply of what the "addict" wants, there would be no reason for him to go to "any means" to obtain it. Thus by the WHO's definition, one can be addicted only to a substance that is illegal or otherwise difficult to obtain. This surely removes the problem of addiction from the realm of medicine and psychiatry, and puts it squarely into that of morals and law.

Copyright © 1972 by *Harper's Magazine.* All rights reserved. Reproduced from the April issue by special permission.

In short, drug addiction or drug abuse cannot be defined without specifying the proper and improper uses of certain pharmacologically active agents. The regular administration of morphine by a physician to a patient dying of cancer is the paradigm of the proper use of a narcotic; whereas even its occasional self-administration by a physically healthy person for the purpose of "pharmacological pleasure" is the paradigm of drug abuse.

I submit that these judgments have nothing whatever to do with medicine, pharmacology, or psychiatry. They are moral judgments. Indeed, our present views on addiction are astonishingly similar to some of our former views on sex. Until recently, masturbation—or self-abuse, as it was called—was professionally declared, and popularly accepted, as both the cause and the symptom of a variety of illnesses. Even today, homosexuality—called a "sexual perversion"—is regarded as a disease by medical and psychiatric experts as well as by "well-informed" laymen.

To be sure, it is now virtually impossible to cite a contemporary medical authority to support the concept of self-abuse. Medical opinion holds that whether a person masturbates or not is medically irrelevant: and that engaging in the practice or refraining from it is a matter of personal morals or life-style. On the other hand, it is virtually impossible to cite a contemporary medical authority to oppose the concept of drug abuse. Medical opinion holds that drug abuse is a major medical, psychiatric, and public health problem; that drug addiction is a disease similar to diabetes, requiring prolonged (or lifelong) and careful, medically supervised treatment; and that taking or not taking drugs is primarily, if not solely, a matter of medical responsibility.

Thus the man on the street can only believe what he hears from all sides—that drug addiction is a disease, "like any other," which has now reached "epidemic proportions," and whose "medical" containment justifies the limitless expenditure of tax monies and the corresponding aggrandizement and enrichment of noble medical warriors against this "plague."

PROPAGANDA TO JUSTIFY PROHIBITION

Like any social policy, our drug laws may be examined from two entirely different points of view: technical and moral. Our present inclination is either to ignore the moral perspective or to mistake the technical for the moral.

Since most of the propagandists against drug abuse seek to justify certain repressive policies because of the alleged dangerousness of various drugs, they often falsify the facts about the true pharmacological properties of the drugs they seek to prohibit. They do so for two reasons: first, because many substances in daily use are just as harmful as the substances they want to prohibit: second, because they realize that dangerousness alone is never a sufficiently persuasive argument to justify the prohibition of any drug, substance, or artifact. Accordingly, the more they ignore the moral dimensions of the problem, the more they must escalate their fraudulent claims about the dangers of drugs.

To be sure, some drugs are more dangerous than others. It is easier to kill oneself with heroin than with aspirin. But it is also easier to kill oneself by jumping off a high building than a low one. In the case of drugs, we regard their potentiality for self-injury as justification for their prohibition: in the case of buildings, we do not.

Furthermore, we systematically blur and confuse the two quite different ways in which narcotics may cause death: by a deliberate act of suicide or by accidental overdosage.

Every individual is capable of injuring or killing himself. This potentiality is a fundamental expression of human freedom. Self-destructive behavior may be regarded as sinful and penalized by means of informal sanctions. But it should not be regarded as a crime or (mental) disease, justifying or warranting the use of the police powers of the state for its control.

Therefore, it is absurd to deprive an adult of a drug (or of anything else) because he might use it to kill himself. To do so is to treat everyone the way institutional psychiatrists treat the so-called suicidal mental patient: they not only imprison such a person but take everything away from him—shoelaces, belts, razor blades, eating utensils, and so forth—until the "patient" lies naked on a mattress in a padded cell—lest he kill himself. The result is degrading tyrannization.

Death by accidental overdose is an altogether different matter. But can anyone doubt that this danger now looms so large precisely because the sale of narcotics and many other drugs is illegal? Those who buy illicit drugs cannot be sure what drug they are getting or how much of it. Free trade in drugs, with governmental action limited to safeguarding the purity of the product and the veracity of the labeling, would reduce the risk of accidental overdose with "dangerous drugs" to the same levels that prevail, and that we find acceptable, with respect to other chemical agents and physical artifacts that abound in our complex technological society.

This essay is not intended as an exposition on the pharmacological properties of narcotics and other mind-affecting drugs. However, I want to make it clear that in my view, *regardless* of their danger, all drugs should be "legalized" (a misleading term I employ reluctantly as a concession to common usage). Although I recognize that some drugs—notably heroin, the amphetamines, and LSD, among those now in vogue—may have undesirable or dangerous consequences, I favor free trade in drugs for the same reason the Founding Fathers favored free trade in ideas. In an open society, it is none of the government's business what idea a man puts into his mind; likewise, it should be none of the government's business what drug he puts into his body.

WITHDRAWAL PAINS FROM TRADITION

It is a fundamental characteristic of human beings that they get used to things: one becomes habituated, or "addicted," not only to narcotics, but to cigarettes, cocktails before dinner, orange juice for breakfast, comic strips, and so forth. It is similarly a fundamental characteristic of living organisms that they acquire increasing tolerance to various chemical agents and physical stimuli: the first cigarette may cause nothing but nausea and headache; a year later, smoking three packs a day may be pure joy. Both alcohol and opiates are "addictive" in the sense that the more regularly they are used, the more the user craves them and the greater his tolerance for them becomes. Yet none of this involves any mysterious process of "getting hooked." It is simply an aspect of the universal biological propensity for *learning*, which is especially well developed in man. The opiate habit, like the cigarette habit or food habit, can be broken—and without any medical assistance—provided the person wants to break it. Often he doesn't. And why, indeed, should he, if he has nothing better to do with his life? Or, as happens to be the case with morphine, if he can live an essentially normal life while under the influence?

Actually, opium is much less toxic than alcohol. Just as it is possible to be an "alcoholic" and work and be productive, so it is (or, rather, it used to be) possible to be an opium addict and work and be productive. According to a definitive study published by the American Medical Association in 1929, " . . . morphine addiction is not characterized by physical deterioration or impairment of physical fitness . . . There is no evidence of change in the circulatory, hepatic, renal, or endocrine functions. When it is considered that these subjects had been addicted for at least five years, some of them for as long as twenty years, these negative observations are highly significant." In a 1928 study, Lawrence Kolb, an Assistant Surgeon General of the United States Public Health Service, found that of 119 persons addicted to opiates through medical practice, "90 had good industrial records and only 29 had poor ones . . . Judged by the output of labor and their own statements, none of the normal persons had [his] efficiency reduced by opium. Twenty-two of them worked regularly while taking opium for twenty-five years or more; one of them, a woman aged 81 and still alert mentally, had taken 3 grains of morphine daily for 65 years. [The usual therapeutic dose is one-quarter grain, three or four grains being fatal for the nonaddict.] She gave birth to and raised six children, and managed her household affairs with more than average efficiency. A widow, aged 66, had taken 17 grains of morphine daily for most of 37 years. She is alert mentally . . . does physical labor every day, and makes her own living."

I am not citing this evidence to recommend the opium habit. The point is that we must, in plain honesty, distinguish between pharmacological effects and personal inclinations. Some people take drugs to help them function and conform to social expectations; others take them for the very opposite reason, to ritualize their refusal to function and conform to social expectations. Much of the "drug abuse" we now witness—perhaps nearly all of it—is of the second type. But instead of acknowledging that "addicts" are unfit or unwilling to work and be "normal," we prefer to believe that they act as they do because certain drugs—especially heroin, LSD, and the amphetamines—make them "sick." If only we could get them "well," so runs this comforting view, they would become "productive" and "useful" citizens. To believe this is like believing that if an illiterate cigarette smoker would only stop smoking, he would become an Einstein. With a falsehood like this, one can go far. No wonder that politicians and psychiatrists love it.

The concept of free trade in drugs runs counter to our cherished notion that everyone must work and idleness is acceptable only under special conditions. In general, the obligation to work is greatest for healthy, adult, white men. We tolerate idleness on the part of children, women, Negroes, the aged, and the sick, and even accept the responsibility to support them. But the new wave of drug abuse affects mainly young adults, often white males, who are, in principle at least, capable of working and supporting themselves. But they refuse: they "drop out"; and in doing so, they challenge the most basic values of our society.

The fear that free trade in narcotics would result in vast masses of our population spending their days and nights smoking opium or mainlining heroin, rather than working and taking care of their responsibilities, is a bugaboo that does not deserve to be taken seriously. Habits of work and idleness are deep-seated cultural patterns. Free trade in abortions has not made an industrious people like the Japanese give up work for fornication. Nor would free trade in drugs convert such a people from hustlers to hippies. Indeed, I think the opposite might be the case: it is questionable whether, or for how long, a responsible people can tolerate being treated as totally irresponsible with respect to drugs and drug-taking. In other words, how long can we live with the inconsistency of being expected to be responsible for operating cars and computers, but not for operating our own bodies?

Although my argument about drug-taking is moral and political, and does not depend upon showing that free trade in drugs would also have fiscal advantages over our present policies, let me indicate briefly some of its economic implications.

The war on addiction is not only astronomically expensive; it is also counterproductive. On April 1, 1967, New York State's narcotics addiction control program, hailed as "the most massive ever tried in the nation," went into effect. "The program, which may cost up to $400 million in three years," reported the *New York Times*, "was hailed by Governor Rockefeller as 'the start of an unending war.'" Three years later, it was conservatively estimated that the number of addicts in the state had tripled or quadrupled. New York State Senator John Hughes reports that the cost of caring for each addict during this time was $12,000 per year (as against $4,000 per year for patients in state mental hospitals). It's been a great time, though, for some of the ex-addicts. In New York City's Addiction Services Agency, one ex-addict started at $6,500 a year in 1967, and was making $16,000 seven months later. Another started at $6,500 and soon rose to $18,100. The salaries of the medical bureaucrats in charge of these programs are similarly attractive. In short, the detection and rehabilitation of addicts is good business. We now know that the spread of witchcraft in the late Middle Ages was due more to the work of witchmongers than to the lure of witchcraft. Is it not possible that the spread of addiction in our day is due more to the work of addictmongers than to the lure of narcotics?

Let us see how far some of the monies spent on the war on addiction could go in supporting people who prefer to drop out of society and drug themselves. Their "habit" itself would cost next to nothing: free trade would bring the price of narcotics down to a negligible amount. During the 1969–70 fiscal year, the New York State Narcotics Addiction Control Commission had a budget of nearly $50 million, excluding capital construction. Using these figures as a tentative base for calculation, here is what we come to: $100 million will support 30,000 drug addicts at $3,300 per year. Since the population of New York State is roughly one-tenth that of the nation, if we multiply its operating budget for addiction control by ten, we arrive at a figure of $500 million, enough to support 150,000 addicts.

I am not advocating that we spend our hard-earned money in this way I am only trying to show that free trade in narcotics would be more economical for those of us who work, even if we had to support legions of addicts, than is our present program of trying to "cure" them. Moreover, I have not even made use, in my economic estimates, of the incalculable sums we would save by reducing crimes now engendered by the illegal traffic in drugs.

THE RIGHT OF SELF-MEDICATION

Clearly, the argument that marijuana—or heroin, methadone, or morphine—is prohibited because it is addictive or dangerous cannot be supported by facts. For one thing, there are many drugs, from insulin to penicillin, that are neither addictive nor dangerous but are nevertheless also prohibited; they can be obtained only through a physician's prescription. For another, there are many things, from dynamite to guns, that are much more dangerous than narcotics (especially to others) but are not prohibited. As everyone knows, it is still possible in the United States to walk into a store and walk out with a shotgun. We enjoy this right not because we believe that guns are safe but because we believe even more strongly that civil liberties are precious. At the same time, it is not possible in the United States to walk into a store and walk out with a bottle of barbiturates, codeine, or other drugs.

I believe that just as we regard freedom of speech and religion as fundamental rights, so we should also regard freedom of self-medication as a fundamental right. Like most rights, the right of self-medication should apply only to adults; and it should not be an unqualified right. Since these are important qualifications, it is necessary to specify their precise range.

John Stuart Mill said (approximately) that a person's right to swing his arm ends where his neighbor's nose begins. And Oliver Wendell Holmes said that no one has a right to shout "Fire!" in a crowded theater. Similarly, the limiting condition with respect to self-medication should be the inflicting of actual (as against symbolic) harm on others.

Our present practices with respect to alcohol embody and reflect this individualistic ethic. We have the right to buy, possess, and consume alcoholic beverages. Regardless of how offensive drunkenness might be to a person, he cannot interfere with another person's "right" to become inebriated so long as that person drinks in the privacy of his own home or at some other appropriate location, and so long as he conducts himself in an otherwise law-abiding manner. In short, we have a right to be intoxicated—in private. Public intoxication is considered an offense to others and is therefore a violation of the criminal law. It makes sense that what is a "right" in one place may become, by virtue of its disruptive or disturbing effect on others, an offense somewhere else.

The right to self-medication should be hedged in by similar limits. Public intoxication, not only with alcohol but with any drug, should be an offense punishable by the criminal law. Furthermore, acts that may injure others—such as driving a car—should, when carried out in a drug-intoxicated state, be punished especially strictly and severely. The right to self-medication must thus entail unqualified responsibility for the effects of one's drug-intoxicated behavior on others. For unless we are willing to hold ourselves responsible for our own behavior, and hold others responsible for theirs, the liberty to use drugs (or to engage in other acts) degenerates into a license to hurt others.

Such, then, would be the situation of adults, if we regarded the freedom to take drugs as a fundamental right similar to the freedom to read and worship. What would be the situation of children? Since many people who are now said to be drug addicts or drug abusers are minors, it is especially important that we think clearly about this aspect of the problem.

I do not believe, and I do not advocate, that children should have a right to ingest, inject, or otherwise use any drug or substance they want. Children do not have the right to drive, drink, vote, marry, or make binding contracts. They acquire these rights at various ages, coming into their full possession at maturity, usually between the ages of eighteen and twenty-one. The right to self-medication should similarly be withheld until maturity.

In short, I suggest that "dangerous" drugs be treated, more or less, as alcohol is treated now. Neither the use of narcotics, nor their possession, should be prohibited, but only their sale to minors. Of course, this would result in the ready availability of all kinds of drugs among minors—though perhaps their availability would be no greater than it is now, but would only be more visible and hence more easily subject to proper controls. This arrangement would place responsibility for the use of all drugs by children where it belongs: on parents and their children. This is where the major responsibility rests for the use of alcohol. It is a tragic symptom of our refusal to take personal liberty and responsibility seriously that there appears to be no public desire to assume a similar stance toward other "dangerous" drugs.

Consider what would happen should a child bring a bottle of gin to school and get drunk there. Would the school authorities blame the local liquor stores as pushers? Or would they blame the parents and the child himself? There is liquor in practically every home in America and yet children rarely bring liquor to school. Whereas marijuana, Dexedrine, and heroin—substances children usually do not find at home and whose very possession is a criminal offense—frequently find their way into the school.

Our attitude toward sexual activity provides another model for our attitude toward drugs. Although we generally discourage children below a certain age from engaging in sexual activities with others, we do not prohibit such activities by law. What we do prohibit by law is the sexual seduction of children by adults. The "pharmacological seduction" of children by adults should be similarly punishable. In other words, adults who give or sell drugs to children should be regarded as offenders. Such a specific and limited prohibition—as against the kinds of generalized prohibitions that we had under the Volstead Act or have now with respect to countless drugs—would be relatively easy to enforce. Moreover, it would probably be rarely violated, for there would be little psychological interest and no economic profit in doing so.

THE TRUE FAITH: SCIENTIFIC MEDICINE

What I am suggesting is that while addiction is ostensibly a medical and pharmacological problem, actually it is a moral and political problem. We ought to know that there is no necessary connection between facts and values, between what is and what ought to be. Thus, objectively quite harmful acts, objects, or persons may be accepted and tolerated—by minimizing their dangerousness. Conversely, objectively quite harmless acts, objects, or persons may be prohibited and persecuted—by exaggerating their dangerousness. It is always necessary to distinguish—and especially so when dealing with social policy—between description and prescription, fact and rhetoric, truth and falsehood.

In our society, there are two principle methods of legitimizing policy: social tradition and scientific judgment. More than anything else, time is the supreme ethical arbiter. Whatever a social practice might be, if people engage in it, generation after generation, that practice becomes acceptable.

Many opponents of illegal drugs admit that nicotine may be more harmful to health than marijuana; nevertheless, they urge that smoking cigarettes should be legal but smoking marijuana should not be, because the former habit is socially accepted while the latter is not. This is a perfectly reasonable argument. But let us understand it for what it is—a plea for legitimizing old and accepted practices, and for illegitimizing novel and unaccepted ones. It is a justification that rests on precedent, not evidence.

The other method of legitimizing policy, ever more important in the modern world, is through the authority of science. In matters of health, a vast and increasingly elastic category, physicians play important roles as legitimizers and illegitimizers. This, in short, is why we regard being medicated by a doctor as drug use, and self-medication (especially with certain classes of drugs) as drug abuse.

This, too, is a perfectly reasonable arrangement. But we must understand that it is a plea for legitimizing what doctors do, because they do it with "good therapeutic" intent; and for illegitimizing what laymen do, because they do it with bad self-abusive ("masturbatory" or mind-altering) intent. This justification rests on the principles of professionalism, not of pharmacology. Hence we applaud the systematic medical use of methadone and call it "treatment for heroin addiction," but decry the occasional nonmedical use of marijuana and call it "dangerous drug abuse."

Our present concept of drug abuse articulates and symbolizes a fundamental policy of scientific medicine—namely, that a layman should not medicate his own body but should place its medical care under the supervision of a duly accredited physician. Before the Reformation, the practice of True Christianity rested on a similar policy—namely, that a layman should not himself commune with God but should place his spiritual care under the supervision of a duly accredited priest. The self-interests of the church and of medicine in such policies are obvious enough. What might be less obvious is the interest of the laity: by delegating responsibility for the spiritual and medical welfare of the people to a class of authoritatively accredited specialists, these policies—and the practices they ensure—relieve individuals from assuming the burdens of responsibility for themselves. As I see it, our present problems with drug use and drug abuse are just one of the consequences of our pervasive ambivalence about personal autonomy and responsibility.

I propose a medical reformation analogous to the Protestant Reformation: specifically, a "protest" against the systematic mystification of man's relationship to his body and his professionalized separation from it. The immediate aim of this reform would be to remove the physician as intermediary between man and his body and to give the layman direct access to the language and contents of the pharmacopoeia. If man had unencumbered access to his own body and the means of chemically altering it, it would spell the end of medicine, at least as we now know it. This is why, with faith in scientific medicine so strong, there is little interest in this kind of medical reform. Physicians fear the loss of their privileges: laymen, the loss of their protections.

Finally, since luckily we still do not live in the utopian perfection of "one world," our technical approach to the "drug problem" has led, and will undoubtedly continue to lead, to some curious attempts to combat it.

Here is one such attempt: the American government is now pressuring Turkey to restrict its farmers from growing poppies (the source of morphine and heroin). If turnabout is fair play, perhaps we should expect the Turkish government to pressure the United States to restrict its farmers from growing corn and wheat. Or should we assume that Muslims have enough self-control to leave alcohol alone, but Christians need all the controls that politicians, policemen, and physicians can bring to bear on them to enable them to leave opiates alone?

LIFE, LIBERTY, AND THE PURSUIT OF HIGHS

Sooner or later we shall have to confront the basic moral dilemma underlying this problem: does a person have the right to take a drug, any drug—not because he needs it to cure an illness, but because he wants to take it?

The Declaration of Independence speaks of our inalienable right to "life, liberty, and the pursuit of happiness." How are we to interpret this? By asserting that we ought to be free to pursue happiness by playing golf or watching television, but not by drinking alcohol, or smoking marijuana, or ingesting pep pills?

The Constitution and the Bill of Rights are silent on the subject of drugs. This would seem to imply that the adult citizen has, or ought to have, the right to medicate his own body as he sees fit. Were this not the case, why should there have been a need for a Constitutional Amendment to outlaw drinking? But if ingesting alcohol was, and is now again, a Constitutional right, is ingesting opium, or heroin, or barbiturates, or anything else, not also such a right? If it is, then the Harrison Narcotic Act is not only a bad law but is unconstitutional as well, because it prescribes in a legislative act what ought to be promulgated in a Constitutional Amendment.

The questions remain: as American citizens, should we have the right to take narcotics or other drugs? If we take drugs and conduct ourselves as responsible and law-abiding citizens, should we have a right to remain unmolested by the government? Lastly, if we take drugs and break the law, should we have a right to be treated as persons accused of crime, rather than as patients accused of mental illness?

These are fundamental questions that are conspicuous by their absence from all contemporary discussions of problems of drug addiction and drug abuse. The result is that instead of debating the use of drugs in moral and political terms, we define our task as the ostensibly narrow technical problem of protecting people from poisoning themselves with substances for whose use they cannot possibly assume responsibility. This, I think, best explains the frightening national consensus against personal responsibility for taking drugs and for one's conduct while under their influence. In 1965, for example, when President Johnson sought a bill imposing tight federal controls over pep pills and goof balls, the bill cleared the House by a unanimous vote, 402 to 0.

The failure of such measures to curb the "drug menace" has only served to inflame our legislators' enthusiasm for them. In October 1970 the Senate passed, again by a unanimous vote (54 to 0), "a major narcotics crackdown bill."

To me, unanimity on an issue as basic and complex as this means a complete evasion of the actual problem and an attempt to master it by attacking and over-powering a scapegoat—"dangerous drugs" and "drug abusers." There is an ominous resemblance between the unanimity with which all "reasonable" men—and especially politicians, physicians, and priests—formerly supported the protective measures of society against witches and Jews, and that with which they now support them against drug addicts and drug abusers.

After all is said and done, the issue comes down to whether we accept or reject the ethical principle John Stuart Mill so clearly enunciated: "The only purpose [he wrote in *On Liberty*] for which power can be rightfully exercised over any member of a civilized community, against his will, is to prevent harm to others. His own good, either physical or moral, is not a sufficient warrant. He cannot rightfully be compelled to do or forbear because it will make him happier, because in the opinion of others, to do so would be wise, or even right . . . In the part [of his conduct] which merely concerns himself, his independence is, of right, absolute. Over himself, over his own body and mind, the individual is sovereign."

By recognizing the problem of drug abuse for what it is—a moral and political question rather than a medical or therapeutic one—we can choose to maximize the sphere of action of the state at the expense of the individual, or of the individual at the expense of the state. In other words, we could commit ourselves to the view that the state, the representative of many, is more important than the individual; that it therefore has the right, indeed the duty, to regulate the life of the individual in the best interests of the group. Or we could commit ourselves to the view that individual dignity and liberty are the supreme values of life, and that the foremost duty of the state is to protect and promote these values.

In short, we must choose between the ethic of collectivism and individualism, and pay the price of either—or of both.

40. Paternalism

Gerald Dworkin

*Gerald Dworkin (1937–   ), professor of philosophy at the University of
Illinois at Chicago, has written many books and articles on a variety
of ethical, political, legal, and social issues.*

> Neither one person, nor any number of persons, is warranted in saying to
> another human creature of ripe years, that he shall not do with his life for
> his own benefit what he chooses to do with it.
>
> [John Stuart Mill]

> I do not want to go along with a volunteer basis. I think a fellow should be
> compelled to become better and not let him use his discretion whether
> he wants to get smarter, more healthy or more honest.
>
> [General Hershey]

I take as my starting point the "one very simple principle" proclaimed by
Mill in *On Liberty* . . . "That principle is, that the sole end for which mankind are
warranted, individually or collectively, in interfering with the liberty of
action of any of their number, is self-protection. That the only purpose for which
power can be rightfully exercised over any member of a civilized community,
against his will, is to prevent harm to others. He cannot rightfully be compelled
to do or forbear because it will be better for him to do so, because it will
make him happier, because, in the opinion of others, to do so would be wise, or
even right."

This principle is neither "one" nor "very simple." It is at least two principles: one asserting that self-protection or the prevention of harm to others
is sometimes a sufficient warrant and the other claiming that the individual's
own good is *never* a sufficient warrant for the exercise of compulsion either by
the society as a whole or by its individual members. I assume that no one, with the
possible exception of extreme pacifists or anarchists, questions the correctness of
the first half of the principle. This essay is an examination of the negative claim
embodied in Mill's principle—the objection to paternalistic interferences with a
man's liberty.

From *Morality and the Law*, Richard A. Wasserstom, ed. © 1971 by Wadsworth Publishing Co., Inc. Reprinted by permission of the author.

I

By paternalism I shall understand roughly the interference with a person's liberty of action justified by reasons referring exclusively to the welfare, good, happiness, needs, interests or values of the person being coerced. One is always well-advised to illustrate one's definitions by examples but it is not easy to find "pure" examples of paternalistic interferences. For almost any piece of legislation is justified by several different kinds of reasons and even if historically a piece of legislation can be shown to have been introduced for purely paternalistic motives, it may be that advocates of the legislation with an anti-paternalistic outlook can find sufficient reasons justifying the legislation without appealing to the reasons which were originally adduced to support it. Thus, for example, it may be that the original legislation requiring motorcyclists to wear safety helmets was introduced for purely paternalistic reasons. But the Rhode Island Supreme Court recently upheld such legislation on the grounds that it was "not persuaded that the legislature is powerless to prohibit individuals from pursuing a course of conduct which could conceivably result in their becoming public charges," thus clearly introducing reasons of a quite different kind. Now I regard this decision as being based on reasoning of a very dubious nature but it illustrates the kind of problem one has in finding examples. The following is a list of the kinds of interferences I have in mind as being paternalistic.

II

1. Laws requiring motorcyclists to wear safety helmets when operating their machines.
2. Laws forbidding persons from swimming at a public beach when lifeguards are not on duty.
3. Laws making suicide a criminal offense.
4. Laws making it illegal for women and children to work at certain types of jobs.
5. Laws regulating certain kinds of sexual conduct, e.g. homosexuality among consenting adults in private.
6. Laws regulating the use of certain drugs which may have harmful consequences to the user but do not lead to anti-social conduct.
7. Laws requiring a license to engage in certain professions with those not receiving a license subject to fine or jail sentence if they do engage in the practice.
8. Laws compelling people to spend a specified fraction of their income on the purchase of retirement annuities (Social Security).
9. Laws forbidding various forms of gambling (often justified on the grounds that the poor are more likely to throw away their money on such activities than the rich who can afford to).

10. Laws regulating the maximum rates of interest for loans.
11. Laws against duelling.

In addition to laws which attach criminal or civil penalties to certain kinds of action there are laws, rules, regulations, decrees which make it either difficult or impossible for people to carry out their plans and which are also justified on paternalistic grounds. Examples of this are:

1. Laws regulating the types of contracts which will be upheld as valid by the courts, e.g. (an example of Mill's to which I shall return) no man may make a valid contract for perpetual involuntary servitude.
2. Not allowing assumption of risk as a defense to an action based on the violation of a safety statute.
3. Not allowing as a defense to a charge of murder or assault the consent of the victim.
4. Requiring members of certain religious sects to have compulsory blood transfusions. This is made possible by not allowing the patient to have recourse to civil suits for assault and battery and by means of injunctions.
5. Civil commitment procedures when these are specifically justified on the basis of preventing the person being committed from harming himself. The D.C. Hospitalization of the Mentally Ill Act provides for involuntary hospitalization of a person who "is mentally ill, and because of that illness, is likely to injure *himself* or others if allowed to remain at liberty." The term injure in this context applies to unintentional as well as intentional injuries.

All of my examples are of existing restrictions on the liberty of individuals. Obviously one can think of interferences which have not yet been imposed. Thus one might ban the sale of cigarettes, or require that people wear safety-belts in automobiles (as opposed to merely having them installed), enforcing this by not allowing motorists to sue for injuries even when caused by other drivers if the motorist was not wearing a seat-belt at the time of the accident.

I shall not be concerned with activities which though defended on paternalistic grounds are not interferences with the liberty of persons, e.g. the giving of subsidies in kind rather than in cash on the grounds that the recipients would not spend the money on the goods which they really need, or not including a $1,000 deductible provision in a basic protection automobile insurance plan on the ground that the people who would elect it could least afford it. Nor shall I be concerned with measures such as "truth-in-advertising" acts and Pure Food and Drug legislation which are often attacked as paternalistic but which should not be considered so. In these cases all that is provided—it is true by the use of compulsion—is information which it is presumed that rational persons are interested in having in order to make wise decisions. There is no interference with the liberty of the consumer unless one wants to stretch a point beyond good sense and say that his liberty to apply for a loan without knowing the true rate of interest is diminished. It is true that sometimes there is sentiment for going further than providing information, for example when laws against usurious interest are passed preventing those who might wish to contract loans at high rates of interest from doing so, and these measures may correctly be considered paternalistic.

III

Bearing these examples in mind, let me return to a characterization of paternalism. I said earlier that I meant by the term, roughly, interference with a person's liberty for his own good. But, as some of the examples show, the class of persons whose good is involved is not always identical with the class of persons whose freedom is restricted. Thus, in the case of professional licensing it is the practitioner who is directly interfered with but it is the would-be patient whose interests are presumably being served. Not allowing the consent of the victim to be a defense to certain types of crime primarily affects the would-be aggressor but it is the interests of the willing victim that we are trying to protect. Sometimes a person may fall into both classes as would be the case if we banned the manufacture and sale of cigarettes and a given manufacturer happened to be a smoker as well.

Thus we may first divide paternalistic interferences into "pure" and "impure" cases. In "pure" paternalism the class of persons whose freedom is restricted is identical with the class of persons whose benefit is intended to be promoted by such restrictions. Examples: the making of suicide a crime, requiring passengers in automobiles to wear seat-belts, requiring a Christian Scientist to receive a blood transfusion. In the case of "impure" paternalism in trying to protect the welfare of a class of persons we find that the only way to do so will involve restricting the freedom of other persons besides those who are benefitted. Now it might be thought that there are no cases of "impure" paternalism since any such case could always be justified on nonpaternalistic grounds, i.e. in terms of preventing harm to others. Thus we might ban cigarette manufacturers from continuing to manufacture their product on the grounds that we are preventing them from causing illness to others in the same way that we prevent other manufacturers from releasing pollutants into the atmosphere, thereby causing danger to the members of the community. The difference is, however, that in the former but not the latter case the harm is of such a nature that it could be avoided by those individuals affected if they so chose. The incurring of the harm requires, so to speak, the active cooperation of the victim. It would be mistaken theoretically and hypocritical in practice to assert that our interference in such cases is just like our interference in standard cases of protecting others from harm. At the very least someone interfered with in this way can reply that no one is complaining about his activities. It may be that impure paternalism requires arguments or reasons of a stronger kind in order to be justified, since there are persons who are losing a portion of their liberty and they do not even have the solace of having it be done "in their own interest." Of course in some sense, if paternalistic justifications are ever correct, then we are protecting others, we are preventing some from injuring others, but it is important to see the differences between this and the standard case.

Paternalism then will always involve limitations on the liberty of some individuals in their own interest but it may also extend to interferences with the liberty of parties whose interests are not in question.

IV

Finally, by way of some more preliminary analysis, I want to distinguish paternalistic interference with liberty from a related type with which it is often confused. Consider, for example, legislation which forbids employees to work more than, say, 40 hours per week. It is sometimes argued that such legislation is paternalistic for if employees desired such a restriction on their hours of work they could agree among themselves to impose it voluntarily. But because they do not the society imposes its own conception of their best interests upon them by the use of coercion. Hence this is paternalism.

Now it may be that some legislation of this nature is, in fact, paternalistically motivated. I am not denying that. All I want to point out is that there is another possible way of justifying such measures which is not paternalistic in nature. It is not paternalistic because, as Mill puts it in a similar context, such measures are "required not to overrule the judgment of individuals respecting their own interest, but to give effect to that judgment: they being unable to give effect to it except by concert, which concert again cannot be effectual unless it receives validity and sanction from the law." (*Principles of Political Economy*)

The line of reasoning here is a familiar one first found in Hobbes and developed with great sophistication by contemporary economists in the last decade or so. There are restrictions which are in the interests of a class of persons taken collectively but are such that the immediate interest of each individual is furthered by his violating the rule when others adhere to it. In such cases the individuals involved may need the use of compulsion to give effect to their collective judgment of their own interest by guaranteeing each individual compliance by the others. In these cases compulsion is not used to achieve some benefit which is not recognized to be a benefit by those concerned, but rather because it is the only feasible means of achieving some benefit which *is* recognized as such by all concerned. This way of viewing matters provides us with another characterization of paternalism in general. Paternalism might be thought of as the use of coercion to achieve a good which is not recognized as such by those persons for whom the good is intended. Again while this formulation captures the heart of the matter—it is surely what Mill is objecting to in *On Liberty*—the matter is not always quite like that. For example, when we force motorcyclists to wear helmets we are trying to promote a good—the protection of the person from injury—which is surely recognized by most of the individuals concerned. It is not that a cyclist doesn't value his bodily integrity; rather, as a supporter of such legislation would put it, he either places, perhaps irrationally, another value or good (freedom from wearing a helmet) above that of physical well-being or, perhaps, while recognizing the danger in the abstract, he either does not fully appreciate it or he underestimates the likelihood of its occurring. But now we are approaching the question of possible justifications of paternalistic measures and the rest of this essay will be devoted to that question. . . .

VI

We might begin looking for principles governing the acceptable use of paternalistic power in cases where it is generally agreed that it is legitimate. Even Mill intends his principles to be applicable only to mature individuals, not those in what he calls "non-age." What is it that justifies us in interfering with children? The fact that they lack some of the emotional and cognitive capacities required in order to make fully rational decisions. It is an empirical question to just what extent children have an adequate conception of their own present and future interests but there is not much doubt that there are many deficiencies. For example, it is very difficult for a child to defer gratification for any considerable period of time. Given these deficiencies and given the very real and permanent dangers that may befall the child it becomes not only permissible but even a duty of the parent to restrict the child's freedom in various ways. There is however an important moral limitation on the exercise of such parental power which is provided by the notion of the child eventually coming to see the correctness of his parent's interventions. Parental paternalism may be thought of as a wager by the parent on the child's subsequent recognition of the wisdom of the restrictions. There is an emphasis on what could be called future-oriented consent—on what the child will come to welcome, rather than on what he does welcome.

The essence of this idea has been incorporated by idealist philosophers into various types of "real-will" theory as applied to fully adult persons. Extensions of paternalism are argued for by claiming that in various respects, chronologically mature individuals share the same deficiencies in knowledge, capacity to think rationally, and the ability to carry out decisions that children possess. Hence in interfering with such people we are in effect doing what they would do if they were fully rational. Hence we are not really opposing their will, hence we are not really interfering with their freedom. The dangers of this move have been sufficiently exposed by Berlin in his *Two Concepts of Freedom*. I see no gain in theoretical clarity nor in practical advantage in trying to pass over the real nature of the interferences with liberty that we impose on others. Still the basic notion of consent is important and seems to me the only acceptable way of trying to delimit an area of justified paternalism.

Let me start by considering a case where the consent is not hypothetical in nature. Under certain conditions it is rational for an individual to agree that others should force him to act in ways which, at the time of action, the individual may not see as desirable. If, for example, a man knows that he is subject to breaking his resolves when temptation is present, he may ask a friend to refuse to entertain his requests at some later stage.

A classical example is given in the Odyssey when Odysseus commands his men to tie him to the mast and refuse all future orders to be set free, because he knows the power of the Sirens to enchant men with their songs. Here we are on relatively sound ground in later refusing Odysseus' request to be set free. He may even claim to have changed his mind but since it is *just* such changes that he wished to guard against we are entitled to ignore them.

A process analogous to this may take place on a social rather than individual basis. An electorate may mandate its representatives to pass legislation which when it comes time to "pay the price" may be unpalatable. I may believe that a tax increase is necessary to halt inflation though I may resent the lower pay check each month. However in both this case and that of Odysseus the measure to be enforced is specifically requested by the party involved and at some point in time there is genuine consent and agreement on the part of those persons whose liberty is infringed. Such is not the case for the paternalistic measures we have been speaking about. What must be involved here is not consent to specific measures but rather consent to a system of government, run by elected representatives, with an understanding that they may act to safeguard our interests in certain limited ways.

I suggest that since we are all aware of our irrational propensities, deficiencies in cognitive and emotional capacities, and avoidable and unavoidable ignorance it is rational and prudent for us to in effect take out "social insurance policies." We may argue for and against proposed paternalistic measures in terms of what fully rational individuals would accept as forms of protection. Now clearly, since the initial agreement is not about specific measures we are dealing with a more-or-less blank check and therefore there have to be carefully defined limits. What I am looking for are certain kinds of conditions which make it plausible to suppose that rational men could reach agreement to limit their liberty even when other men's interests are not affected.

Of course as in any kind of agreement schema there are great difficulties in deciding what rational individuals would or would not accept. Particularly in sensitive areas of personal liberty, there is always a danger of the dispute over agreement and rationality being a disguised version of evaluative and normative disagreement.

Let me suggest types of situations in which it seems plausible to suppose that fully rational individuals would agree to having paternalistic restrictions imposed upon them. It is reasonable to suppose that there are "goods" such as health which any person would want to have in order to pursue his own good—no matter how that good is conceived. This is an argument used in connection with compulsory education for children but it seems to me that it can be extended to other goods which have this character. Then one could agree that the attainment of such goods should be promoted even when not recognized to be such, at the moment, by the individuals concerned.

An immediate difficulty arises from the fact that men are always faced with competing goods and that there may be reasons why even a value such as health—or indeed life—may be over-ridden by competing values. Thus the problem with the Christian Scientist and blood transfusions. It may be more important for him to reject "impure substances" than to go on living. The difficult problem that must be faced is whether one can give sense to the notion of a person irrationally attaching weights to competing values.

Consider a person who knows the statistical data on the probability of being injured when not wearing seat-belts in an automobile and knows the types and gravity of the various injuries. He also insists that the inconvenience attached to fastening the belt every time he gets in and out of the car outweighs for him the possible risks to himself. I am inclined in this case to think that such a weighing is irrational. Given his life-plans, which we are assuming are those of the average person, his interests and commitments already undertaken, I think it is safe to predict that we can find inconsistencies in his calculations at some point. I am assuming that this is not a man who for some conscious or unconscious reasons is trying to injure himself nor is he a man who just likes to "live dangerously." I am assuming that he is like us in all the relevant respects but just puts an enormously high negative value on inconvenience—one which does not seem comprehensible or reasonable.

It is always possible, of course, to assimilate this person to creatures like myself. I, also, neglect to fasten my seat-belt and I concede such behavior is not rational but not because I weigh the inconvenience differently from those who fasten the belts. It is just that having made (roughly) the same calculation as everybody else I ignore it in my actions.[1] A plausible explanation for this deplorable habit is that although I know in some intellectual sense what the probabilities and risks are I do not fully appreciate them in an emotionally genuine manner.

We have two distinct types of situations in which a man acts in a non-rational fashion. In one case he attaches incorrect weights to some of his values; in the other he neglects to act in accordance with his actual preferences and desires. Clearly there is a stronger and more persuasive argument for paternalism in the latter situation. Here we are really not—by assumption—imposing a good on another person. But why may we not extend our interference to what we might call evaluative delusions? After all, in the case of cognitive delusions we are prepared, often, to act against the expressed will of the person involved. If a man believes that when he jumps out the window he will float upwards—Robert Nozick's example—would not we detain him, forcibly if necessary? The reply will be that this man doesn't wish to be injured and if we could convince him that he is mistaken as to the consequences of his action he would not wish to perform the action. But part of what is involved in claiming that the man who doesn't fasten his seat-belts is attaching an incorrect weight to the inconvenience of fastening them is that if he were to be involved in an accident and severely injured he would look back and admit that the inconvenience wasn't as bad as all that. So there is a sense in which if I could convince him of the consequences of his action he also would not wish to continue his present course of action. Now the notion of consequences being used here is covering a lot of ground. In one case it's being used to indicate what will or can

---

[1][Note: a much better case of weakness of the will than those usually given in ethics texts.]

happen as a result of a course of action and in the other it's making a prediction about the future evaluation of the consequences—in the first sense—of a course of action. And whatever the difference between facts and values—whether it be hard and fast or soft and slow—we are genuinely more reluctant to consent to interferences where evaluative differences are the issue. Let me now consider another factor which comes into play in some of these situations which may make an important difference in our willingness to consent to paternalistic restrictions.

Some of the decisions we make are of such a character that they produce changes which are in one or another way irreversible. Situations are created in which it is difficult or impossible to return to anything like the initial stage at which the decision was made. In particular, some of these changes will make it impossible to continue to make reasoned choices in the future. I am thinking specifically of decisions which involve taking drugs that are physically or psychologically addictive and those which are destructive of one's mental and physical capacities.

I suggest we think of the imposition of paternalistic interferences in situations of this kind as being a kind of insurance policy which we take out against making decisions which are far-reaching, potentially dangerous and irreversible. Each of these factors is important. Clearly there are many decisions we make that are relatively irreversible. In deciding to learn to play chess I could predict in view of my general interest in games that some portion of my free time was going to be preempted and that it would not be easy to give up the game once I acquired a certain competence. But my whole life-style was not going to be jeopardized in an extreme manner. Further it might be argued that even with addictive drugs such as heroin one's normal life plans would not be seriously interfered with if an inexpensive and adequate supply were readily available. So this type of argument might have a much narrower scope than appears to be the case at first.

A second class of cases concerns decisions which are made under extreme psychological and sociological pressures. I am not thinking here of the making of the decision as being something one is pressured into—e.g., a good reason for making duelling illegal is that unless this is done many people might have to manifest their courage and integrity in ways in which they would rather not do so—but rather of decisions, such as that to commit suicide, which are usually made at a point where the individual is not thinking clearly and calmly about the nature of his decision. In addition, of course, this comes under the previous heading of all-too-irrevocable decisions. Now there are practical steps which a society could take if it wanted to decrease the possibility of suicide—for example not paying social security benefits to the survivors or, as religious institutions do, not allowing persons to be buried with the same status as natural deaths. I think we may count these as interferences with the liberty of persons to attempt suicide and the question is whether they are justifiable.

Using my argument schema the question is whether rational individuals would consent to such limitations. I see no reason for them to consent to an absolute prohibition but I do think it is reasonable for them to agree to some kind of enforced waiting period. Since we are all aware of the possibility of temporary states, such as great fear or depression, that are inimical to the making of well-informed and rational decisions, it would be prudent for all of us if there were some kind of institutional arrangement whereby we were restrained from making a decision which is so irreversible. What this would be like in practice is difficult to envisage and it may be that if no practical arrangements were feasible we would have to conclude that there should be no restriction at all on this kind of action. But we might have a "cooling off" period, in much the same way that we now require couples who file for divorce to go through a waiting period. Or, more far-fetched, we might imagine a Suicide Board composed of a psychologist and another member picked by the applicant. The Board would be required to meet and talk with the person proposing to take his life, though its approval would not be required.

A third class of decisions—these classes are not supposed to be disjoint—involves dangers which are either not sufficiently understood or appreciated correctly by the persons involved. Let me illustrate, using the example of cigarette smoking, a number of possible cases.

1. A man may not know the facts—e.g., smoking between 1 and 2 packs a day shortens life expectancy 6.2 years, the costs and pain of the illness caused by smoking, etc.
2. A man may know the facts, wish to stop smoking, but not have the requisite will-power.
3. A man may know the facts but not have them play the correct role in his calculation because, say, he discounts the danger psychologically since it is remote in time and/or inflates the attractiveness of other consequences of his decision which he regards as beneficial.

In case 1 what is called for is education, the posting of warnings, etc. In case 2 there is no theoretical problem. We are not imposing a good on someone who rejects it. We are simply using coercion to enable people to carry out their own goals. (Note: There obviously is a difficulty in that only a subclass of the individuals affected wish to be prevented from doing what they are doing.) In case 3 there is a sense in which we are imposing a good on someone in that given his current appraisal of the facts he doesn't wish to be restricted. But in another sense we are not imposing a good since what is being claimed—and what must be shown or at least argued for—is that an accurate accounting on his part would lead him to reject his current course of action. Now we all know that such cases exist, that we are prone to disregarding dangers that are only possibilities, that immediate pleasures are often magnified and distorted.

If in addition the dangers are severe and far-reaching, we could agree to allow the state a certain degree of power to intervene in such situations. The difficulty is in specifying in advance, even vaguely, the class of cases in which intervention will be legitimate.

A related difficulty is that of drawing a line so that it is not the case that all ultra-hazardous activities are ruled out, e.g., mountain-climbing, bull-fighting, sports-car racing, etc. There are some risks—even very great ones—which a person is entitled to take with his life.

A good deal depends on the nature of the deprivation—e.g., does it prevent the person from engaging in the activity completely or merely limit his participation—and how important to the nature of the activity is the absence of restriction when this is weighed against the role that the activity plays in the life of the person. In the case of automobile seat-belts, for example, the restriction is trivial in nature, interferes not at all with the use or enjoyment of the activity, and does, I am assuming, considerably reduce a high risk of serious injury. Whereas, for example, making mountain-climbing illegal completely prevents a person from engaging in an activity which may play an important role in his life and his conception of the person he is.

In general, the easiest cases to handle are those which can be argued about in the terms which Mill thought to be so important—a concern not just for the happiness or welfare, in some broad sense, of the individual but rather a concern for the autonomy and freedom of the person. I suggest that we would be most likely to consent to paternalism in those instances in which it preserves and enhances for the individual his ability to rationally consider and carry out his own decisions.

I have suggested in this essay a number of types of situations in which it seems plausible that rational men would agree to granting the legislative powers of a society the right to impose restrictions on what Mill calls "self-regarding" conduct. However, rational men knowing something about the resources of ignorance, ill-will and stupidity available to the law-makers of a society—a good case in point is the history of drug legislation in the United States—will be concerned to limit such intervention to a minimum. I suggest in closing two principles designed to achieve this end.

In all cases of paternalistic legislation there must be a heavy and clear burden of proof placed on the authorities to demonstrate the exact nature of the harmful effects (or beneficial consequences) to be avoided (or achieved) and the probability of their occurrence. The burden of proof here is twofold—what lawyers distinguish as the burden of going forward and the burden of persuasion. That the authorities have the burden of going forward means that is up to them to raise the question and bring forward evidence of the evils to be avoided. Unlike the case of new drugs where the manufacturer must produce some evidence that the drug has been tested and found not harmful, no citizen has to show with respect to self-regarding conduct that it is not harmful or promotes his best interests. In addition the nature and cogency of the evidence for the harmfulness of the course of action must be set at a high level. To paraphrase a formulation of the burden of proof for criminal proceedings—better 10 men ruin themselves than one man be unjustly deprived of liberty.

Finally, I suggest a principle of the least restrictive alternative. If there is an alternative way of accomplishing the desired end without restricting liberty although it may involve great expense, inconvenience, etc., the society must adopt it.

PROBLEMS AND PUZZLES

41. The Prisoner's Dilemma

Morton D. Davis

Morton David Davis (1930–   ) is an American mathematician whose research focuses on game theory.

Two men suspected of committing a crime together are arrested and placed in separate cells by the police. Each suspect may either confess or remain silent, and each one knows the possible consequences of his action. These are: (1) If one suspect confesses and his partner does not, the one who confessed turns state's evidence and goes free and the other one goes to jail for twenty years. (2) If both suspects confess, they both go to jail for five years. (3) If both suspects remain silent, they both go to jail for a year for carrying concealed weapons—a lesser charge. We will suppose that there is no "honor among thieves" and each suspect's sole concern is his own self-interest. Under these conditions, what should the criminals do? The game, shown in Figure 5.19, is the celebrated prisoner's dilemma which was originally formulated by A. W. Tucker and which has become one of the classical problems in the short history of game theory.

Figure 5.19

		SUSPECT II	
		CONFESS	DO NOT CONFESS
SUSPECT I	CONFESS	(5 yrs., 5 yrs.)	(go free, 20 yrs.)
	DO NOT CONFESS	(20 yrs., go free)	(1 yr., 1 yr.)

Let us look at the prisoner's dilemma from the point of view of one of the suspects. Since he must make his decision without knowing what his partner will do, he must consider each of his partner's alternatives and anticipate the effect of each of them on himself.

Suppose his partner confesses; our man must either remain silent and go to jail for twenty years, or confess and go to jail for five. Or, if his partner remains

Morton D. Davis, "The Prisoner's Dilemma," from *Game Theory: A Nontechnical Introduction* (Revised Edition), Dover Publications, 1997.

silent, he can serve a year by being silent also, or win his freedom by confessing. Seemingly, in either case, *he is better off confessing!* What, then, is the problem?

The paradox lies in this. Two naive prisoners, too ignorant to follow this compelling argument, are both silent and go to prison for only a year. Two sophisticated prisoners, primed with the very best game-theory advice, confess and are given five years in prison in which to contemplate their cleverness.

We will return to this argument in a moment, but before we do, let's consider the essential elements that characterize this game. Each player has two basic choices: he can act "cooperatively" or "uncooperatively." When all the players act cooperatively, each does better than when all of them act uncooperatively. For any fixed strategy(ies) of the other player(s), a player always does better by playing uncooperatively than by playing cooperatively.

In the following examples, taken from many different contexts, these same basic elements appear.

1. Two different firms sell the same product in a certain market. Neither the product's selling price nor the total combined sales of both companies vary from year to year. What does vary is the portion of the market that each firm captures, and this depends on the size of their respective advertising budgets. For the sake of simplicity, suppose each firm has only two choices: spending $6 million or $10 million. The size of the advertising budget determines the share of the market and, ultimately, the profits of each company, as follows:

If both companies spend $6 million, they each get a $5 million profit. If a company spends $10 million when its competitor spends only $6 million, its profit goes up to $8 million at the expense of its competitor, who now loses $2 million. And if both companies spend $10 million, the extra marketing effort is wasted, since the market is fixed and the relative market position of each company remains the same; consequently, the profit of each company drops to $1 million. No collusion is allowed between the firms. The game is shown in Figure 5.20.

Figure 5.20

		CORPORATION *II*	
		SPEND $6 MILLION	SPEND $10 MILLION
CORPORATION *I*	SPEND $6 MILLION	($5 million, $5 million)	(−$2 million, $8 million)
	SPEND $10 MILLION	($8 million, −$2 million)	($1 million, $1 million)

2. There is a water shortage and citizens are urged to cut down on water consumption. If each citizen responds to these requests by considering his or her own self-interest, no one will conserve water. Obviously, any saving by an individual has only a negligible effect on the city's water supply, yet the inconvenience involved is very real. On the other hand, if everyone acts in his or her own self-interest, the results will be catastrophic for everyone.

3. If no one paid taxes, the machinery of government would break down. Presumably all citizens would prefer that everyone, including themselves, pay taxes to having no one pay taxes. Better yet, of course, everyone would pay taxes except the individual him- or herself.

4. After several years of overproduction, farmers agree to limit their output voluntarily in order to keep the prices up. But no one farmer produces enough seriously to affect the price, so each starts producing what he or she can and selling it for what it will bring, and once again there is overproduction.

5. Two unfriendly nations are preparing their military budgets. Each nation wants to obtain a military advantage over the other by building a more powerful army, and each spends accordingly. They wind up having the same relative strength, and a good deal poorer.

As we can see from these examples, this kind of problem comes up all the time. For convenience's sake, let us fix our attention on a single game, using the first example, that of two companies setting their advertising budgets. The game will be the same, except for an additional condition. The budget will not be set once but, more realistically, we will assume that it is fixed annually for a certain period of time; say, twenty years. When each company decides on its budgets for any given year, it knows what its competitor spent in the past.

In discussing the prisoner's dilemma, we had decided that if the game is played only once, the prisoners have no choice but to confess. The same line of reasoning applied here leads to the conclusion that the firms should each spend $10 million. But when the game is played repeatedly, the argument loses some of its force. It is still true that if you spend $10 million in a given year, you will always do better than if you spend $6 million *that* year. But if you spend $10 million in one year, you are very likely to induce your competitor to spend $10 million the next year, and that is something you don't want. A more optimistic strategy is to signal your intent to cooperate by spending $6 million and hope your competitor draws the proper inference and does the same. This strategy could lead to a cooperative outcome and in practice often does. But in theory there is a problem.

The argument that spending $6 million in any one year tends to encourage your competitor to spend the same amount the next year is all very well for the first nineteen years, but it clearly breaks down in the twentieth year. In the twentieth year, there is *no next year.* When the firms reach the twentieth year, they are in effect in the same position they are in when they play the game only once. If the firms want to maximize their profits, and we assume that they do, the argument favoring the uncooperative strategy is as compelling now as it was then.

But the argument doesn't end there. Once the futility of cooperating in the twentieth year is recognized, it follows that there is no point in cooperating in the nineteenth year either. And if there is no chance of inducing a cooperative response in the nineteenth year, why cooperate in the eighteenth year? Once you fall into the trap, you fall all the way: there is no point in cooperating in the eighteenth, the seventeenth . . . or the first year either. If you accept the argument supporting the uncooperative strategy in the single instance, it follows that you must play uncooperatively not only in the last of a series but in every individual trial as well.

It is when the prisoner's dilemma is played repeatedly—and not for a fixed number of trials but for an indefinite period—that the cooperative strategy comes into its own. And these are precisely the conditions under which the prisoner's dilemma is often played. Two competing firms know that they won't be in business forever, but they generally have no way of knowing when death, merger, bankruptcy, or some other force will end their competition. Thus the players can't analyze what will happen in the last "play" and then work backward from there, for nobody knows when the last "play" will be. The compelling argument in favor of the uncooperative strategy breaks down, then, and we breathe a sigh of relief.

This is really the point. The prisoner's dilemma has one characteristic that makes it different from the other games that have been discussed. As a rule, when analyzing a game, you are content if you can say what rational players should do and predict what the outcome will be. But in the prisoner's dilemma the uncooperative strategy is so unpalatable that the question most people try to answer is not What strategy should a rational person choose? but How can we justify playing a cooperative strategy? . . .

42. Is It Rational to Be an Informed Voter?

Anthony Downs

Anthony Downs (1930–   ) is an urban economist and real estate consultant in Washington, D.C. He has taught economics and political science at the University of Chicago. Since 1977 he has been a senior fellow at the Brookings Institution, Washington, D.C. His books include An Economic Theory of Democracy, Inside Bureaucracy, Racism in America, *and* Stuck in Traffic.

When information is costly, no decision-maker can afford to know everything that might possibly bear on his decision before he makes it. He must select only a few data from the vast supply in existence and base his decision solely upon them. This is true even if he can procure data without paying for them, since merely assimilating them requires time and is therefore costly.

The amount of information it is rational for a decision-maker to acquire is determined by the following economic axiom: It is always rational to perform any act if its marginal return is larger than its marginal cost. The marginal cost of a "bit" of information is the return foregone by devoting scarce resources—particularly time—to getting and using it. The marginal return from a "bit" is the increase in utility income received because the information enabled the decision-maker to improve his decision. In an imperfectly informed world, neither the precise cost nor the precise return is usually known in advance; but decision-makers can nevertheless employ the rule just stated by looking at expected costs and expected returns.

This reasoning is as applicable to politics as it is to economics. Insofar as the average citizen is concerned, there are two political decisions that require information. The first is deciding which party to vote for; the second is deciding on what policies to exercise direct influence on government policy formation (that is, how to lobby). Let us examine the voting decision first.

Before we do so, it is necessary to recognize that in every society a stream of "free" information is continuously disseminated to all citizens. Though such "free" data take time to assimilate, this time is not directly chargeable to any particular type of decision-making, since it is a necessary cost of living in society. For example, conversation with business associates, small talk with friends, reading the newspaper in a barber shop, and listening to the radio while driving to work are all sources of information which the average man encounters without any particular effort to do so. Therefore, we may consider them part of the "free"

Anthony Downs, "An Economic Theory of Political Action in Democracy," *Journal of Political Economy,* Section VII, Vol. 65, No. 2, April, 1957. Copyright 1957 by The University of Chicago. Reprinted by permission of the University of Chicago Press and the author. The title "Is It Rational to Be An Informed Voter?" is the responsibility of the editors.

information stream and exclude them from the problem of how much information a decision-maker should obtain specifically to improve his decisions.

The marginal return on information acquired for voting purposes is measured by the expected gain from voting "correctly" instead of "incorrectly." In other words, it is the gain in utility a voter believes he will receive if he supports the party which would really provide him with the highest utility income instead of supporting some other party. However, unless his vote actually decides the election, it does not cause the "right" party to be elected instead of a "wrong" party; whether or not the "right" party wins does not depend on how he votes. Therefore, voting "correctly" produces no gain in utility whatsoever; he might as well have voted "incorrectly."

This situation results from the insignificance of any one voter in a large electorate. Since the cost of voting is very low, hundreds, thousands, or even millions of citizens can afford to vote. Therefore, the probability that any one citizen's vote will be decisive is very small indeed. It is not zero, and it can even be significant if he thinks the election will be very close; but, under most circumstances, it is so negligible that it renders the return from voting "correctly" infinitesimal. This is true no matter how tremendous a loss in utility income the voter would experience if the "wrong" party were elected. And if that loss is itself small—as it may be when parties resemble each other closely or in local elections—then the incentive to become well informed is practically nonexistent.

Therefore, we reach the startling conclusion that it is irrational for most citizens to acquire political information for purposes of voting. As long as each person considers the behavior of others as given, it is simply not worthwhile for him to acquire information so as to vote "correctly" himself. The probability that his vote will determine which party governs is so low that even a trivial cost of procuring information outweighs its return. Hence ignorance of politics is not a result of unpatriotic apathy; rather it is a highly rational response to the facts of political life in a large democracy.

This conclusion does not mean that every citizen who is well informed about politics is irrational. A rational man can become well informed for four reasons: (1) he may enjoy being well informed for its own sake, so that information as such provides him with utility; (2) he may believe the election is going to be so close that the probability of his casting the decisive vote is relatively high; (3) he may need information to influence the votes of others so that he can alter the outcome of the election or persuade government to assign his preferences more weight than those of others; or (4) he may need information to influence the formation of government policy as a lobbyist. Nevertheless, since the odds are that no election will be close enough to render decisive the vote of any one person, or the votes of all those he can persuade to agree with him, the rational course of action for most citizens is to remain politically uninformed. Insofar as voting is concerned, any attempt to acquire information beyond that furnished by the stream of "free" data is for them a sheer waste of resources.

The disparity between this conclusion and the traditional conception of good citizenship in a democracy is indeed striking. How can we explain it? The answer is that the benefits which a majority of citizens would derive from living in a society with a well-informed electorate are indivisible in nature. When most members of the electorate know what policies best serve their interests, the government is forced to follow those policies in order to avoid defeat (assuming that there is a consensus among the informed). This explains why the proponents of democracy think citizens should be well informed. But the benefits of these policies accrue to each member of the majority they serve, regardless of whether he has helped bring them about. In other words, the individual receives these benefits whether or not he is well informed, so long as most people are well informed and his interests are similar to those of the majority. On the other hand, when no one else is well informed, he cannot produce these benefits by becoming well informed himself, since a collective effort is necessary to achieve them.

Thus, when benefits are indivisible, each individual is always motivated to evade his share of the cost of producing them. If he assumes that the behavior of others is given, whether or not he receives any benefits does not depend on his own efforts. But the cost he pays does depend on his efforts; hence the most rational course for him is to minimize that cost—in this case, to remain politically ignorant. Since every individual reasons in the same way, no one bears any costs, and no benefits are produced.

The usual way of escaping this dilemma is for all individuals to agree to be coerced by a central agency. Then each is forced to pay his share of the costs, but he knows all others are likewise forced to pay. Thus everyone is better off than he would be if no costs were borne, because everyone receives benefits which (I here assume) more than offset his share of the costs. This is a basic rationale for using coercion to collect revenues for national defense and for many other government operations that yield indivisible benefits.

But this solution is not feasible in the case of political information. The government cannot coerce everyone to be well informed, because "well-informedness" is hard to measure, because there is no agreed-upon rule for deciding how much information of what kinds each citizen "should" have, and because the resulting interference in personal affairs would cause a loss of utility that would probably outweigh the gains to be had from a well-informed electorate. The most any democratic government has done to remedy this situation is to compel young people in schools to take courses in civics, government, and history.

Consequently, it is rational for every individual to minimize his investment in political information, in spite of the fact that most citizens might benefit substantially if the whole electorate were well informed. As a result, democratic political systems are bound to operate at less than maximum efficiency. Government does not serve the interests of the majority as well as it would if they were well informed but they never become well informed. It is collectively rational, but individually irrational, for them to do so; and, in the absence of any mechanism to insure collective action, individual rationality prevails.

SUGGESTIONS FOR FURTHER READING

ANTHOLOGIES

Copp, David and Susan Wendell, eds. *Pornography and Censorship.* Buffalo, N.Y.: Prometheus Books, 1983. Part One of this book is devoted to philosophical essays on pornography, feminism, free speech, and related topics by philosophers. There is also a "Selected Bibliography of Academic and Popular Philosophy."

Cranston, Maurice, ed. *Western Political Philosophers: A Background Book.* New York: Capricorn, 1967. A series of concise and lucid essays by contemporary philosophers and political scientists on Plato, Aristotle, Aquinas, Machiavelli, Hobbes, Locke, Rousseau, Burke, Hegel, Marx, and Mill. The beginning student, particularly, will find this book helpful.

Graham, Keith, ed. *Contemporary Political Philosophy: Radical Studies.* New York: Cambridge Univ. Press, 1982. This collection of original and sophisticated essays by young British philosophers discusses such topics as human nature and political beliefs, liberty and equality, individual rights and socialism, and other topics treated in the readings in this section.

Lederer, Laura, ed. *Take Back the Night:* New York: William Morrow, 1980. This anthology is a collection of articles, interviews, research, and impassioned calls to action by feminist leaders in the effort to stop violence against women, particularly in the form of pornography.

Pettit, Philip, ed. *Contemporary Political Theory.* Philosophical Topics Series. Paul Edwards, editor-in-chief. New York: Macmillan, 1991. This is a collection of more technical writings by current political philosophers. It includes a bibliography emphasizing recent books.

Somerville, John, and Ronald E. Santoni, eds. *Social and Political Philosophy: Readings from Plato to Gandhi.* New York: Doubleday, Anchor, 1963. Extensive selections (in some instances the unabridged work) from some of the most famous and influential writings in social and political thought by philosophers and political leaders.

Stewart, Robert M. *Readings in Social and Political Philosophy.* Oxford: Oxford Univ. Press, 1986, 1996. This is a recent anthology of classical and contemporary readings in social and political philosophy.

INDIVIDUAL WORKS

Dworkin, Ronald. "Women and Pornography." *New York Review of Books,* 40:36–42 (Oct., 1993). For a number of years Ronald Dworkin, a philosopher of law, has been criticizing feminist positions on pornography and free speech such as the one expressed by Helen E. Longino. The above article is an analysis and evaluation of Catharine MacKinnon's *Only Words* by Dworkin, whom MacKinnon calls the "liberal philosopher-king."

Flew, Antony. *The Politics of Procrustes: Contradictions of Enforced Equality.* Buffalo, N.Y.: Prometheus, 1981. A contemporary British philosopher vigorously critiques the philosophical assumptions of socialism and egalitarianism.

Held, Virginia. *Models of Democracy.* Stanford, Calif.: Stanford Univ. Press, 1987. A recent examination of democracy undertaken by an American philosopher who specializes in social and political philosophy, game theory, and public policy.

Hook, Sidney. *Political Power and Personal Freedom: Critical Studies in Democracy, Communism, and Civil Rights.* New York: Collier, 1962. An American philosopher vigorously analyzes the philosophical assumptions of the major political systems, including democracy, socialism, liberalism, and communism, as well as such issues as limitations to individual freedom, from the standpoint of his interpretation of John Dewey's philosophy.

Hook, Sidney. *Reason, Social Myths, and Democracy.* Amherst, N.Y.: Prometheus Books, 1991. In this work the author defends democracy in terms of a detailed philosophical analysis of democracy and scientific method, the nature of social inquiry, capitalism, Catholicism, and Marxism.

Howe, Irving. *Socialism and America.* New York: Harcourt Brace Jovanovich, 1985. An American socialist defends a form of socialism designed for contemporary America.

Levine, Andrew. *Arguing for Socialism: Theoretical Considerations.* London and Boston: Routledge & Kegan Paul, 1984. The author presents a theoretical defense of a form of socialism suitable for today and the foreseeable future.

MacKinnon, Catharine. *Only Words.* Cambridge: Harvard Univ. Press, 1993. A professor of law at the University of Michigan briefly and vigorously argues that pornography is not speech as American law conceives of it but rather is an act of sexual discrimination and harassment that subordinates women to men and thus denies women the equality that is their right.

Macpherson, Crawford B. *The Life and Times of Liberal Democracy.* New York: Oxford Univ. Press, 1977. A brief, clear attempt to set forth the essence of liberal democracy as now conceived.

Nielsen, Kai. *Equality and Liberty: A Defense of Radical Egalitarianism.* Totowa, N.J.: Rowman & Allanheld, a Division of Littlefield, Adams and Company, 1985. A Canadian philosopher defends his version of radical egalitarianism and critiques the liberal egalitarianism of John Rawls, Ronald Dworkin, and others and the individualistic libertarianism of Robert Nozick, Milton Friedman, and others.

Nozick, Robert. *Anarchy, State, and Utopia.* New York: Basic Books, 1974. Nozick's conception of the minimal State, or the "nightwatchman" State with the primary function of protection rather than redistribution of wealth, has provoked much discussion.

Oakeshott, Michael. *Rationalism in Politics.* New York: Basic Books, 1962. This work offers a stimulating challenge to liberalism.

Poundstone, William. *Prisoner's Dilemma.* New York: Doubleday, 1992. In a vivid and lively fashion Poundstone tells the history of the discovery of the prisoner's dilemma as a landmark in twentieth-century thought and investigates game theory's far-reaching impact on public policy.

Rand, Ayn. *Capitalism: The Unknown Ideal.* New York: New American Library–Dutton, 1986. In a series of essays the author argues that laissez-faire capitalism is the consequence and application of fundamental philosophical principles.

Raphael, D. D. *Problems of Political Philosophy.* London: Pall Mall, 1970. A clearly written introduction for the beginning student.

Rawls, John. *A Theory of Justice.* Cambridge: Belknap Press of Harvard Univ. Press. 1971. An outstanding systematic work in social and political philosophy by an American philosopher. It has provoked a great deal of discussion. Recommended for the more advanced student.

Reitman, Jeffrey H. *In Defense of Political Philosophy.* New York: Harper, Harper Torchbooks, 1972. The book vigorously argues against R. P. Wolff's *In Defense of Anarchism* (see Wolff, *In Defense of Anarchism*) and for majoritarian democracy.

Rothbard, Murray N. *The Ethics of Liberty.* New York: New York Univ. Press, 1998. In many ways this work provides the fullest exposition and defense of Rothbard's political philosophy.

Sabine, George H. *A History of Political Theory.* 3d ed. New York: Holt, Rinehart & Winston, 1961.4th ed. Revised by Thomas Landon Thorson. Hinsdale, Ill.: Dryden, 1973. This is the classic work with which every student should be familiar.

Spencer, Herbert. *The Man versus the State.* Edited by Donald Macrae. Baltimore: Penguin, 1969. As a result of the growing conviction that governments have become too strong for the preservation of men's liberties, the writings of the great nineteenth-century champion of laissez-faire individualism against an inherently oppressive state have sparked renewed interest.

Taylor, Richard. *Freedom, Anarchy, and the Law: An Introduction to Political Philosophy.* Englewood Cliffs, N.J.: Prentice Hall, 1973. Beginning and advanced students will find this lucid work stimulating and a pleasure to read.

Wolff, Robert Paul. *In Defense of Anarchism.* New York: Harper, Harper Torchbooks, 1970. This iconoclastic work by an American philosopher has provoked much discussion. (See Reitman, *In Defense of Political Philosophy.*)

Dictionary of the History of Ideas: Studies of Selected Pivotal Ideas. Philip P. Wiener, editor-in-chief. New York: Scribners, 1973. Substantial and clearly written essays emphasizing the historical development of topics discussed in this part. Designed to inform the nonspecialist, each essay concludes with a select bibliography.

Encyclopedia of Philosophy. Paul Edwards, editor-in-chief. New York: Macmillan, 1967. The student will find many worthwhile articles on the subjects treated in this part and excellent bibliographies.

Philosophy and Public Affairs. Princeton, N.J.: Princeton Univ. Press. A quarterly journal. Philosophers and philosophically inclined writers from various disciplines bring their methods to bear on problems that concern everyone interested in social and political issues.

PART FIVE

Mind and Body

INTRODUCTION

In Karel Čapek's well-known play R.U.R. (Rossum's Universal Robots), scientists have learned to manufacture robots capable of doing all the manual and intellectual activities humans perform. Humans consider the robots to be lacking a soul since they are nothing more than a machine produced by a complex physical process, and they use the robots in any way that serves human needs. The robots, whose manufacture resulted from a new method of organizing matter, look and act very much like humans except that they lack emotions and feelings, which were purposely omitted to increase productivity. Since the robot's insensitivity to pain often leads to accidents, a scientist at Rossum's robot factory experiments with changes in their formula to give them human emotions. His experiments succeed; but the new, sensitive robots consider themselves to be equal to humans and, frustrated by their inferior status, rebel and destroy their creators.

This play raises the question of whether the robots, though only physical objects, essentially are like the people who created them. The answer to this question can affect our view of ourselves and our place in the world. Humans generally like to consider themselves especially important and unique, but their importance and uniqueness are diminished if they are not significantly different from robots. Also, if humans, like robots, are solely physical, they apparently must act in accord with the natural laws that govern the rest of nature. To preserve human uniqueness and to avoid viewing humans as determined objects, some philosophers claim that humans, unlike machines, possess nonphysical minds. These minds, they contend, enable humans to think and feel in ways that could not be duplicated by any machine. The claim that humans possess minds is very controversial: opponents consider it to be an unverifiable and unnecessary hypothesis, but supporters consider it an important component in their defense of the existence of free will, moral responsibility, and immortality.

The problem of whether humans possess minds and, if so, how the mind is related to the body is called the mind-body problem. One prominent view of reality—*materialism*—holds that the universe consists only of particles of matter moving in space. Thus, materialists consider humans, as all other objects in the universe, to be solely physical. Our ability to reason is attributed to our highly developed nervous system and brain, not to a mind. Since they deny that there are minds, materialists also deny that there is any disembodied personal immortality; for them, all thoughts and feelings cease when the body ceases to function. This sort of materialism should not be confused with a popular use of the term "materialism" to refer to those who have low moral aims or who are primarily concerned with acquiring worldly goods. The metaphysical materialist, who denies the existence of mind, can be quite idealistic and without any special interest in acquiring possessions.

Opposed to materialists are *dualists,* philosophers who believe that humans possess both a physical body and a mind. For them mental life consists of such phenomena as thoughts, images and sensations which, lacking any size, weight, or location, must be considered nonphysical. The most generally held form of dualism, the form that is perhaps closest to our ordinary conception of a person, is *interactionism.* The interactionists maintain that mind and body can causally affect each other. Thus, events in the mind can produce bodily behavior, and bodily events can produce mental occurrences. An example of events in the mind causing bodily events would be the thought of a girl friend causing one to pick up the phone and call her. An example of a physical event causing a mental event would be a case in which stubbing one's toe produces a sensation of pain.

Many philosophers have thought the interactionist view unsatisfactory. The major difficulty is that there seems to be no good explanation of how a mental event, such as a thought, can cause physical behavior. We ordinarily think of causation in terms of one physical event producing another. A simple example would be a moving billiard ball's hitting a second ball and moving it. But how can a thought produce movement in a person's body? And where does the mind act on the body to cause it to move? One might be inclined to say that the mind affects some portion of the brain, but physiologists have found no place where the brain seems to be stimulated by any invisible cause. Similarly, how can the body produce sensations or images in the mind, which is nonphysical?

Confronted with such difficulties, some philosophers who believe that mental phenomena cannot be reduced to physical ones have given up interactionism in favor of *epiphenomenalism.* This view holds that physical events can cause mental events, but that occurrences in the mind are not able to cause any physical events. Rather than interaction, we have a one-way causal relation: from the body to the mind. This view, too, has had its share of critics. This view, like interactionism, needs to explain how a physical event in the body can cause an event to take place in the mind. Another problem is that paradoxical results follow from this theory. One such result is that all thoughts and reasoning are totally without significance in the determination of our behavior. It is certainly hard to believe that the world would be exactly as it is today had none of people's thoughts about democracy, religion, and morality ever occurred.

An ingenious theory that asserts the existence of minds but avoids the problems of the various dualist theories is *idealism.* Idealists affirm the existence of minds along with perceptions and feelings but deny the existence of any material objects existing apart from minds. Those objects that we ordinarily consider to exist in an external world are, in fact, nothing but appearances in minds. Although the idealist view of the world as consisting solely of disembodied minds and their contents seems very odd, it should not be dismissed without a careful assessment. Perhaps the most serious difficulty confronting the idealist is that of providing an explanation of the cause of our perceptions. If there is nothing independent of our minds causing our perceptions of such objects as tables and chairs, why do we perceive them at all?

In the first group of readings that follow, several of these positions are defended. In "Materialism," Hugh Elliot presents a detailed defense of the materialistic view of man and the world. He maintains that the main principles of materialism are the uniformity of law, the denial of teleology, and the denial of any form of existence other than those envisaged by physics and chemistry. He attempts to answer some of the major difficulties that materialists face, especially the nature of images and the apparent existence of purposive behavior. In defending the interactionist position, C. E. M. Joad argues that the materialist cannot adequately explain purposive behavior or the way in which meaning is apprehended. He conceives of the mind as an active, creative force, which carries on activities that could not be conceived as resulting from the function of the brain. In opposition to the materialist view, Joad maintains that a perfect knowledge of a person's brain would fail to tell us what she was thinking since different thoughts could result in the same brain state. In "Sense Without Matter," A. A. Luce rejects materialism by denying that we have any knowledge of matter or any need to postulate its existence. The sensations we have cannot, however, exist alone; and, so, we must postulate the existence of minds.

Speculation about the nature of mind gives rise to some knotty problems. One problem is that if the mind is distinct from the body, it is difficult to show how the thoughts and feelings of other people can be known. In "The Problem of Other Minds," John Hospers presents the main arguments for and against the claim that the thoughts and feelings of others can be known to be similar to our own. He shows not only that there are grounds for doubting the possibility of knowing the nature and existence of the mental states of others, but also that there are grounds for doubting the possibility of knowing our own mental states. A second problem, dealt with in "Brain Transplants and Personal Identity: A Dialogue," is whether someone who has undergone significant changes can be identified as the same person who existed before the changes. One might, for example, wonder whether a person whose knowledge and memories have been lost in an accident is still the friend you used to know. The dialogue between Godfrey Vesey and Derek Parfit points out the fact that the possibilities of brain transplants and splitting a brain and then placing it into two bodies present special difficulties for deciding the identity of a person.

Although the development of robots has long been a subject for science fiction stories and plays, such as *R.U.R.*, it is becoming a subject of increasing interest to philosophers and scientists as a result of the development of computers. Some theorists maintain that computers will eventually be developed to the point where they can perform all of the rational processes of human beings. With the development of computerized robots, we would have a machine that could do everything a human being can do. In fact, it is argued, such a machine would be a human being, and a human being would have been shown to be nothing more than a machine. But is it possible to develop a machine that can perform all of the "mental" feats of a human being? And if such a machine could be developed, would it still lack something that humans possess? If we produce a machine that can do everything a human being can do, then have we shown that humans are really nothing more than physical objects?

In discussing whether machines can think, Christopher Evans analyses Alan Turing's famous test for machine intelligence. The test, which places a computer and a human behind opaque screens, is designed to prove whether the responses of a computer can be distinguished from those of a human. Turing claimed that computers must be deemed as capable as humans of thought and intelligence if those taking the test cannot determine what is behind each screen. Along with exploring the value of the Turing test, Evans criticizes numerous objections to the possibility of machine intelligence. In contrast to Evans, Jenny Teichman contends that human thinking differs from that of any machine. In "Human Beings and Machines," she argues that, unlike machine thinking, human thinking is an interconnected network of beliefs, desires, emotions, and intentions. Also, humans do not merely manipulate symbols in a prescribed way; they understand how symbols are related to the events that happen in the world around them.

The "Problems and Puzzles" section contains two essays on issues related to the mind-body controversy. In the first essay, Durant Drake presents a number of arguments against the belief in personal immortality. Questions about the possibility of immortality are connected to the mind-body controversy because survival without a body would seem to require that people possess minds. Even such possession, however, would not be sufficient to establish the existence of life after death; the mind could, as Drake points out, cease to function when the body does. Support for immorality would require both a belief in minds and a belief in their ability to function without bodies. In the second essay, John Searle maintains that a digital computer is not the same as a mind because its operations are defined syntactically, i.e., it responds in specified ways to symbols that are not about anything. A person, unlike a computer, responds to the semantic content of symbols.

MATERIALISM

43. Materialism

Hugh Elliot

Hugh Elliot (1881–1930), editor of the Annual Register, England, was a champion of modern science and materialism and a student and biographer of Herbert Spencer, the famous nineteenth-century philosopher of evolution.

. . . The main purpose of the present work is to defend the doctrine of materialism. . . .

The outlines of this system are not new; the main features of it, indeed, have been admittedly associated with scientific progress for centuries past. An age of science is necessarily an age of materialism; ours is a scientific age, and it may be said with truth that we are all materialists now. The main principles which I shall endeavour to emphasize are three.

1. The uniformity of law. In early times events appeared to be entirely hazardous and unaccountable, and they still seem so, if we confine attention purely to the passing moment. But as science advances, there is disclosed a uniformity in the procedure of Nature. When the conditions at any one moment are precisely identical with those which prevailed at some previous moment, the results flowing from them will also be identical. It is found, for instance, that a body of given mass attracts some other body of given mass at a given distance with a force of a certain strength. It is found that when the masses, distances, and other conditions are precisely repeated, the attraction between the bodies is always exactly the same. It is found, further, that when the distance between the bodies is increased the force of their attraction is diminished in a fixed proportion, and this again is found to hold true at all distances at which they may be placed. The force of their attraction again varies in a different but still constant proportion to their masses. And hence results the law of gravitation, by which the force of attraction can be precisely estimated from a knowledge of the masses and distances between any two bodies whatever. A uniformity is established which remains absolute within the experience of Man, and to an equivalent extent the haphazard appearance of events is found to be only an appearance. Innumerable other laws of a similar character are gradually discovered, establishing a sort of nexus between every kind of event. If oxygen and hydrogen in the proportion by weight of eight to one are mixed together, and an

From *Modern Science and Materialism* by Hugh Elliot. Published by Longman's, Green and Company, Ltd., 1919.

electric spark is passed through them, water is formed; and on every occasion where precisely the same conditions are realized precisely the same result ensues. This truth is the basis of the experimental method. If from similar conditions it were possible that dissimilar results should follow on various occasions, then experiments would be useless for advancing knowledge. . . .

2. The denial of teleology. Scientific materialism warmly denies that there exists any such thing as purpose in the Universe, or that events have any ulterior motive or goal to which they are striving. It asserts that all events are due to the interaction of matter and motion acting by blind necessity in accordance with those invariable sequences to which we have given the name of laws. This is an important bond of connection between the materialism of the ancient Greeks and that of modern science. Among all peoples not highly cultivated there reigns a passionate conviction, not only that the Universe as a whole is working out some predetermined purpose, but that every individual part of it subserves some special need in the fulfillment of this purpose. Needless to say, the purpose has always been regarded as associated with human welfare. The Universe, down to its smallest parts, is regarded by primitive superstition as existing for the special benefit of man. To such extreme lengths has this view been carried that even Bernardin de Saint-Pierre, who only died last century, argued that the reason why melons are ribbed is that they may be eaten more easily by families. . . .

When it is alleged that the Universe is purposive, it is assumed that humanity is intimately connected with the purpose. Without that assumption, none but the most transcendental of philosophers would have any interest in maintaining teleology. As the anthropocentric doctrine falls, therefore, the doctrine of teleology must fall with it. This, at all events, is the position taken up by scientific, as indeed by all materialism; it is the position that I hope I shall have little difficulty in defending in the following pages. Nevertheless, however obvious its truth, we must recognize that it involves a profound alteration in the existing mental point of view of the majority of mankind; for most men have as yet not shaken off the habit, which all men necessarily start from, that they themselves, or their family, nation or kind, are in fact, as in appearance, the very centre of the cosmos.

3. The denial of any form of existence other than those envisaged by physics and chemistry, that is to say, other than existences that have some kind of palpable material characteristics and qualities. It is here that modern materialism begins to part company with ancient materialism, and it is here that I expect the main criticisms of opponents to be directed. The modern doctrine stands in direct opposition to a belief in any of those existences that are vaguely classed as "spiritual." To this category belong not only ghosts, gods, souls, *et hoc genus omne,* for these have long been rejected from the beliefs of most advanced thinkers. The time has now come to include also in the condemned list that further imaginary entity which we call "mind," "consciousness," etc., together with its various subspecies of intellect, will, feeling, etc., in so far as they are supposed to be independent or different from material existences or processes.

. . . It seems to the ordinary observer that nothing can be more remotely and widely separated than some so-called "act of consciousness" and a material object. An act of consciousness or mental process is a thing of which we are immediately and indubitably aware: so much I admit. But that it differs in any sort of way from a material process, that is to say, from the ordinary transformations of matter and energy, is a belief which I very strenuously deny. . . .

The proposition which I here desire to advance is that every event occurring in the Universe, including those events known as mental processes, and all kinds of human action or conduct, are expressible purely in terms of matter and motion. If we assume in the primeval nebula of the solar system no other elementary factors beyond those of matter and energy or motion, we can theoretically, as above remarked, deduce the existing Universe, including mind, consciousness, etc., without the introduction of any new factor whatsoever. The existing Universe and all things and events therein may be theoretically expressed in terms of matter and energy, undergoing continuous redistribution in accordance with the ordinary laws of physics and chemistry. If all manifestations within our experience can be thus expressed, as has for long been believed by men of science, what need is there for the introduction of any new entity of spiritual character, called mind? It has no part to play; it is impotent in causation. . . . Now there is an ancient logical precept which retains a large validity: *entia non sunt multiplicanda praeter necessitatem.* It is sometimes referred to as William of Occam's razor, which cuts off and rejects from our theories all factors or entities which are superfluous in guiding us to an explanation. "Mind" as a separate entity is just such a superfluity. I will not deny—indeed I cordially affirm— that it is a direct datum of experience; but there is no direct datum of experience to the effect that it is anything different from certain cerebral processes. . . .

The materialism which I shall advocate, therefore, is centred round three salient points: the uniformity of law, the exclusion of purpose, and the assertion of monism; that is to say, that there exists no kind of spiritual substance or entity of a different nature from that of which matter is composed.

The first of these propositions, otherwise called the Law of Universal Causation, affirms that nothing happens without a cause, and that the same causes under the same conditions always produce the same effects. In order to gain a true comprehension of this law, we have to define what we mean by "cause" and "effect," and what is the nature of the nexus between them. The conception of the Universe from which we start is that of a great system of matter and motion undergoing redistribution according to fixed sequences, which in the terminology of science are called laws. The matter is constantly undergoing transformation from one of its forms into another, and the energy is redistributed and transformed in a corresponding manner. From this primary conception alone, we are able to derive a precise definition of what is meant by cause, a problem which is almost insuperable from any other standpoint. . . . If we regard an event as a momentary phase in the redistribution of matter and motion, then the cause of the event is found in the immediately preceding state of distribution of that same matter and motion. Let us ask, for instance, what is the cause of the sudden appearance of a new fixed star in the heavens. Supposing that there were previously two extinct suns moving rapidly towards each other and coming into collision, we should be making a statement of events which would be recognized as a possibly true "cause." The second event, or "effect," is represented exclusively in terms of matter and motion by the idea of two coalesced and volatilized bodies giving rise to vast quantities of heat and light. And the cause is given merely by stating the previous distribution of that matter and energy which is concerned in the production of the event. The *matter* concerned in the event consisted of two solid bodies at a rapidly diminishing distance from one another. The *energy* consisted of half the product of their momentum and velocity. By the collision the matter contained in the solid bodies underwent that redistribution involved in passing into a gaseous state, with the decomposition of many of its molecules, that is to say, with a rearrangement or redistribution of its atoms. The energy of motion previously contained in the solid bodies underwent at the same time a transformation into heat and light. The sudden light, therefore, is explained, or derives its cause, merely by furnishing a statement of the previous distribution of the matter and energy concerned in its production. . . .

And this leads me to the second problem which I have here to deal with, the problem of teleology. I have hitherto endeavoured to represent the notion of cause and effect in purely materialistic terms, to the exclusion of all metaphysical transcendentalism; to state the relation of cause and effect in terms of the redistribution of matter and motion. I now have to perform the same task for the conception of purpose, and more particularly of human purpose, in order to show how purposiveness may be translated into purely materialistic and mechanical terms; that is to say, how it, too, may be expressed as a phase of the normal process of redistribution of matter and motion under fixed and invariable laws.

At the outset of this inquiry, we have to notice that the word purpose is involved in the same vagueness of significance that attends almost all words used in popular speech. In general a word in popular use has to be defined and limited to some precise meaning before it is fit for employment in a philosophical discussion. In the present case the word is commonly employed in at least two meanings, which differ greatly from each other; and this duality of meaning leads to a duality in the derivative conceptions of "teleology," "finalist," "end," etc., which has not infrequently given rise to confusion and error. The two significations may be roughly grouped as intelligent purposiveness and unintelligent purposiveness, and the reduction of each of these to mechanistic terms involves two different lines of analysis. I shall deal first with unintelligent purposiveness.

In this case, the word is usually applied to certain kinds of organic reactions that bear an obvious relation to the requirements of the reacting organism. An *Amoeba* in the water throws out pseudopodia at random in all directions. When one of these pseudopodia comes into contact with some substance suitable for food, the protoplasm streams round and encloses the particle, which is thus incorporated in the body of the *Amoeba* and there digested. The reaction is purposive in the sense that a somewhat complicated series of movements is carried out, which leads to the preservation of the active organism.

In just the same way, when we ascend the animal scale, the sea-anemone spreads it tentacles at large under the surface of the water. On contact with any substance suitable for food the tentacles contract around the substance and draw it into the interior of the sea-anemone. This action is similarly purposive in that it procures the continued existence of the animal. In all animals the common movements and reactions are predominantly of this purposive type. If an object suddenly appears close to our eyes, we involuntarily close them for an instant, and this reaction is obviously purposive, as directed toward the protection of the eyes.

All these instinctive actions are purposive in character, yet equally, without doubt, they are all of the nature of reflex action, working blindly and inevitably to their conclusion. On contact with the tentacle of a sea-anemone, the stimulus thus applied to that tentacle sets up by entirely mechanical procedure organic processes which necessarily result in the observed contractions. Similarly, in the case of the human being, the sudden appearance of a near object causes an impulse to be conveyed down the optic nerve, which immediately and mechanically propagates its effect to the efferent nerves which lead to the muscles that close the eyelids. The same kind of reaction is characteristic of the functions in plants. The turning of flowers towards the light, and all the processes of absorption, transpiration, etc., are, on the one hand, subservient to the life and prosperity of the plant, while, on the other hand, they are blind mechanical reactions to stimuli.

Seeing that a single action may thus be at the same time both purposive and mechanical, it is plain that there can be no antithesis between the two; but that the difference between purposive and blind mechanism arises simply from our point of view, and not from any difference of objective character. Purposive reactions are not different from mechanical reactions, but they *are* mechanical reactions of a certain kind. Not all mechanical reactions are purposive, but all purposive reactions are mechanical; and it remains to determine *what* mechanical actions may be correctly described as purposive, and what are simply blind and meaningless. . . .

I now come to the second class of activities to which the name of purpose is applied, that is to say, cases of activity which bear reference to an end consciously and intelligently foreseen, such as the acts inspired by the conscious will in human beings. These activities are commonly regarded as being in a higher degree teleological than the unintelligent reactions hitherto considered; and in many uses of the word "purpose," reference is intended exclusively to these intelligent anticipations of future events, and to the activities carried out in consequence of such anticipations. In this sense purpose is allied to will, and purposive actions are more or less synonymous with voluntary actions. . . .

We are now in a position to appreciate the true meaning of those acts which are described as intelligently purposive. Being deliberate and reasoned activities, they are as far as possible removed from the simple type of reflex action in which response follows immediately on external stimulus. They belong to the category in which the immediate stimulus is in the brain itself, and is to be regarded as consisting of rearrangements of the matter and energy contained in the nervous substance of the brain. The brain during consciousness can never be still, and its unceasing activities supply the stimulus, not only for purposive, but for all actions of an intellectual character. Now this permanent cerebral activity can be divided into a number of different types, known psychologically by such names as memory, imagination, reason, etc. Although nervous physiology has not yet advanced far enough to enable us to say what are the different kinds of material processes in the brain corresponding to these psychical processes, yet there is no doubt that the psychical distinction is based upon some actual distinction in the corresponding activities occurring in the brain. Among these cerebral processes is that which is known psychologically as a desire for some external object or event, a visualization of some external phenomenon as an end or purpose to be attained. This desire may then act upon efferent nerves and give rise to the activities which we know as purposive. The essence of a purposive action, and the standard by which it is distinguished from other kinds of actions, is that the "end" to which the action leads was previously represented in the brain of the agent, and composes the stimulus of action. The compound stimulus arises, as I have said, from the composition of large numbers of elementary stimuli previously received. It consists psychologically of a faint representation of the sensation which would be vividly presented by the realization of some outward occurrence. And when this faint representation actually functions as a stimulus which innervates the muscles whose contraction brings about the external occurrence represented, we have what is called an action of intelligent purpose. . . .

Intelligent purpose, like unintelligent purpose, is then only a name given to a particular kind of incident in the midst of the eternal redistribution of matter and motion under blind mechanical laws. It is in perfect harmony with that materialistic scheme; it can be stated in terms of the purest mechanism. As the matter and motion undergo their invariable and unalterable redistribution, we naturally find ourselves more interested in some phases of it than in others; and in one class of evolving events we are so interested and we have such frequent occasion to refer to them, that we denominate them by a special name—the name of purposive. By this name we designate the majority of those redistributions which issue from the little whirlpools of matter and energy called organisms, and those factors in particular by which the immediate continuance of such whirlpools is ensured.

I have now dealt with the law of universal causation, and with the doctrine of teleology. It remains only to say a few words about the third main pillar of materialism—the assertion of monism, that is, that there are not two kinds of fundamental existences, material and spiritual, but one kind only. . . . For simplifying the discussion, it will be as well at once to dismiss from consideration all those kinds of spiritual entities imagined by religious believers. The Victorian writers said on this subject nearly all that could be said, and interest now attaches only to those problems of matter and spirit which they left unsolved. I shall, therefore, confine myself to an attempt to reduce the last stronghold of dualism; to ascertain the relation between mind and body; to show that mental manifestations and bodily manifestations are not two different things, as generally supposed, but one and the same thing appearing under different aspects. I shall not attempt to deal with any of the so-called "non-material" existences with the exception of mind; for if mind can be identified with matter, all other kinds of non-material entities must lapse, even those described by religious systems. . . .

We reached the conclusion in a previous chapter that the bodily organism is a complex machine. We found that all its processes and activities are attributable to physico-chemical forces, identical with those which are recognized in the inorganic realm. We learnt that there is no "vital force" or other spiritual interference with the normal physical sequences. If, then, there be a mind, it is reduced to the function of inertly and uselessly accompanying the activities of certain neural elements. This is the doctrine of epiphenomenalism, and it is the last word possible to one who accepts the duality of mind and matter. It is a theory which on the face of it is devoid of verisimilitude. What can be the use of such a shadowy and inefficient entity? What parallel can be found in Nature for the existence of so gratuitous a superfluity? Moreover, what mechanism, conceivable or inconceivable, could cause it thus to shadow neural processes, which *ex hypothesi* do not produce it? If one such mental state is the cause of the next, how does it happen that it causes the one which is necessary to accompany the actual neural process at the moment? Epiphenomenalism involves us in a pre-established harmony that is profoundly opposed to the scientific spirit of the twentieth century. The problem, however, is not one that need be discussed on the grounds of *a priori* probability. It is a theory that may be rigidly refuted, and to that task I now turn.

It is a part of the doctrine of epiphenomenalism that a man would to all external appearance be precisely the same whether he was possessed of his epiphenomenal mind or not. Conduct, action, expression, would not in the slightest extent be affected were he completely devoid of mind and consciousness; for all these things depend upon material sequences alone. Men are puppets or automata, and we have no further grounds for supposing them to have minds than the fact that we know we have a mind ourselves, and the argument by analogy from ourselves to them. But arguments from analogy are notoriously insecure, and it seems, therefore, to be quite within the bounds of possibility to the epiphenomenalist that some or all other men may be mindless syntheses of matter. . . .

Now let us assume that such a man actually exists, or, if you prefer, let us assume that physical chemistry has advanced to such a pitch that a man may be synthesized in the laboratory, starting from the elements, carbon, nitrogen, etc., of which protoplasm is composed. Let us assume in any case a "synthetic man" without a mind, yet indistinguishable by the epiphenomenalist hypothesis from another man identically constituted materially but having a mind. Ask the synthetic man whether he has a mind. What will he say? Inevitably he will say yes. For he must say the same thing as the man, identically made, who *has* a mind. Otherwise the same question would set up different responses in the nervous systems of the two, and that is by hypothesis impossible. The sound of the words "have you a mind?" entering the ears of the synthetic man sets up highly complex cerebral associations (which we call grasping their meaning); these associations will, after a short time, culminate in nervous currents to the tongue, lips and larynx, which will be moved in such a way as to produce an audible and intelligent answer. Now this answer must be the same in the case of the man who has a mind as in the case of the mindless man, since their nervous systems are the same. If there was a different vocal response to an identical aural stimulus, then there must in one of them have been some external interference with the physico-chemical sequences. Mind must have broken through the chain of physical causality, and that is contrary to hypothesis.

What can the epiphenomenalist say? That the mindless man is a liar, to say he has a mind? That will not do, for if the two men are objectively identical one cannot be a liar, and the other not; one engaged in deceit, while the other speaks the truth. The epiphenomenalist is thrown back, therefore, on the assumption that the mindless man has made a mistake; that he thinks he has a mind, but really has not one; that his nervous constitution is such as to impel him to the conviction that he has a mind when he really has not, to lead him to talk upon psychical phenomena and their differences from matter, and in general to behave exactly as if he knew all about mind and matter, had considered the subject of their relationship, etc.

The example shows, furthermore, that the condition of "knowing one has a mind" is a condition which can be stated and accounted for in rigidly materialistic terms. When the epiphenomenalist himself asserts that he has a mind, the movements of his vocal cords by which he makes that pronouncement are by his own theory led up to by a chain of purely material sequences. He would make just the same pronouncement if he had no mind at all. His claim to possess a mind, therefore, is wholly irrelevant to the real question whether he actually has a mind or not. The events that make him say he has a mind are not the actual possession of a mind, but those cerebral processes which, in epiphenomenalist language, are said to underlie states of consciousness. It is the cerebral processes alone which make him speak, and his utterance, his belief in a mind, furnish testimony alone to the existence of those cerebral processes. Were the mind truly able to compel a belief and an announcement of its own existence, it could only be by breaking through the chain of material bodily sequences, and this is a vitalistic supposition that is ruled out by physiology. The belief in the possession of a mind is a cerebral condition, due, not to the actual possession of a mind, but to definite pre-existing cerebral conditions on the same material plane.

I do not see how epiphenomenalism could be much more effectively refuted. Yet it is the only respectable dualistic theory that is compatible with physiological mechanism. Let me recapitulate for a moment the facts, now before us, upon which we have to establish a theory of the relationship of mind and body.

Physiology has shown that bodily activity of every kind is a product of purely material sequences, into the course of which there is no irruption of any spiritualistic factor. On the dualistic theory, that doctrine is excessively difficult to understand. You move your arm by an act of will, or what seems to be a nonmaterial cause, and yet it is conclusively established that the movement of the arm is due to definite material changes occurring in the brain, and caused by the fixed laws of physics and chemistry in the most determinist fashion. Now, anchoring ourselves firmly to that fact, we are confronted with the problem of where to put the mind. For every mental state there is some corresponding cerebral state; the one appears to be the exact counterpart of the other down to the smallest discoverable particular. Now on the dualistic assumption, there is only one possible hypothesis, namely, that of epiphenomenalism. Or, rather, it is incorrect to call it an hypothesis; for *if* there are two things, mind and body, epiphenomenalism is no more than a statement of the facts established by physiology and psychology. Dualistic physiologists, therefore, are practically forced to accept it. Yet, as I have shown, it is utterly untenable when properly thought out.

We are faced, therefore, by two possible alternatives: (1) to abandon mechanism, (2) to abandon dualism. Now mechanism is physiological theory which is proved. We must hold fast to it therefore at any expense to our metaphysical preconceptions. The only remaining alternative, then, is the abandonment of dualism. . . .

When once we have got over the shock which monism carries to those accustomed to think in dualistic terms, we find that the great majority of the difficulties of metaphysics fall away. By an act of will I raise my arm. The plain man insists that his will did it; the physiologist knows that it was physico-chemical processes in the brain. The dilemma is at once overcome when the philosopher points out that the will *is* the physico-chemical processes, and that they both mean the same thing. . . . The difficulty of the epiphenomenalist is also solved. He says he has a mind. What makes him say so is not a transcendental "knowledge of having mind," but a certain cerebral state. When we have affirmed the absolute identity of that knowledge with that cerebral state, all difficulties vanish. The mind is the sum-total of cerebral conditions. He says he has a mind; it is the existence of the cerebral conditions which cause him to say so. He says he has a mind because he has cerebral conditions, and his remark is true and intelligible only on the one hypothesis that the mind *is* the cerebral conditions. . . .

Monism resolves the great biological difficulty as to the origin of consciousness. The biological conclusions as to the origin of life are to the effect that living and organic matter was developed by evolution from non-living and inorganic matter. The evolution of Man from unicellular parentage is a fact. There is little or no reason to doubt that his unicellular ancestor was evolved just as gradually from inorganic matter. Now, says the dualist, we know that the man has a mind. It follows, therefore, either that inorganic matter has a psychical accompaniment, or else that, in the course of evolution, there was a sudden leap: mind was suddenly intruded at some period of Man's past history. Neither of these hypotheses is easy to entertain, or perhaps even practicable to conceive. The doctrine of monism, with its assertion that there are not two ultimate things, but one, causes the difficulty to vanish; for there is then no necessity to introduce a new entity at any period of an organism's evolution. According to our theory, a conscious state is a specific neural functioning. If there is no discontinuity in the evolution of nervous elements from inorganic matter, there is then no discontinuity in the evolution of consciousness.

INTERACTIONISM

44. *The Mind as Distinct from the Body*

C. E. M. Joad

Cyril Edwin Mitchinson Joad (1891–1953) was a prolific English author whose books, articles, and speeches on philosophy exerted broad public appeal in his lifetime.

The issue between those who endeavour to interpret mind action in terms of body action, and those who contend for the unique, distinct, and in some sense independent status of mind, is not capable of definite settlement. . . . The most that can be done is to suggest certain objections that can be and have been brought against the materialist position, . . . and at the same time to indicate a number of independent considerations which seem to demand a different kind of approach to psychology, and a different interpretation of its problems. This interpretation, to put it briefly, insists that a living organism is something over and above the matter of which its body is composed; that it is, in short, an expression of a principle of life, and that life is a force, stream, entity, spirit, call it what you will, that cannot be described or accounted for in material terms; that in human beings this principle of life expresses itself at the level of what is called mind, that this mind is distinct from both body and brain, and, so far from being a mere register of bodily occurrences, is able, acting on its own volition, to produce such occurrences, and that no account of mind action which is given in terms of brain action, gland activity or bodily responses to external stimuli can, therefore, be completely satisfactory. This is the view which in some form or other is held by those who find a materialist explanation of psychology unsatisfactory, and in this chapter we shall be concerned with the reasons for it.

BIOLOGICAL CONSIDERATIONS

Purposiveness

Some of these reasons, and perhaps the most important, are derived in part from regions which lie outside the scope of psychology proper; they belong to biology, and are based on a consideration of the characteristics which all living beings are

From *How Our Minds Work* by C.E.M. Joad. Published by Philosophical Library (1947). Reprinted by permission of the publishers.

found to possess in common. With regard to one of these "alleged" characteristics of living organisms it is necessary to say a few words, since it constitutes a starting point for the method of interpretation with which we shall be concerned in this chapter. The characteristic in question is that to which we give the name of purposiveness, and because of this characteristic it is said that any attempt to interpret the behaviour of living creatures in terms of material response to stimuli must inevitably break down. Purposiveness implies the capacity to be influenced by and to work for a purpose; this in its turn involves the apprehension, whether conscious or unconscious, of some object which lies in the future and which the purpose seeks to achieve; it therefore necessitates the existence of a mind. If, therefore, purposiveness is a true characteristic of living creatures, then we have established a good starting point for our "mental" approach to psychology.

What, therefore, is meant by saying that living creatures are purposive? Primarily, that in addition to those of their movements which may be interpreted as responses to existing situations, they also act in a way which seems to point to the existence of a spontaneous impulse or need to bring about some other situation which does not yet exist. This impulse or need is sometimes known as a conation; a good instance of the sort of thing that is meant is the impulse we feel to maintain the species by obtaining food or seeking a mate. The impulse is chiefly manifested in the efforts a living organism will make to overcome any obstacle which impedes the fulfillment of its instinctive need. It will try first one way of dealing with it and then another, as if it were impelled by some overmastering force which drove it forward to the accomplishment of a particular purpose. Thus the salmon, proceeding up stream, leaping over rocks and breasting the current in order to deposit her spawn in a particular place, is acting in a way which it is difficult to explain in terms of a response to external stimuli. An organism again will seek to preserve the trend of natural growth and development by which alone the purpose of existence will be fulfilled; in its endeavour to reach and to maintain what we may call its natural state or condition, it is capable, if need arises, of changing or modifying its bodily structure. If you take the hydroid plant *Antennularia* and remove it from the flat surface to which it is accustomed to adhere, it will begin to proliferate long wavy roots or fibers in the effort to find something solid to grip, while everybody has heard of the crab's habit of growing a new leg in place of one that has been knocked off.

Activity of this kind seems difficult to explain on materialist lines as the response to a stimulus; it appears rather to be due to the presence of a living, creative impulse to develop in the face of any obstacle in a certain way. That a living organism works as a machine works, by reacting in the appropriate way to the appropriate stimulus, is admitted; all that is contended is that it acts in other ways as well, that these other activities depend not only upon the quality of stimulus received, but upon the intensity of the creature's conative impulse, and that the existence of the impulse is only explicable on the assumption that the creature is animated by the need to fulfill a purpose.

Foresight and Expectation

When we apply this conclusion to human psychology, we are immediately struck by the fact that the individual not only exhibits in common with other organisms this characteristic of purposive behaviour, but is in many cases conscious of the nature of the purpose which inspires his behaviour. The man who studies in order to pass an examination is not only impelled by a push from behind; he is drawn forward by a pull from in front. This pull from in front can only become operative if he can be credited with the capacity to conceive the desirability of a certain state of affairs—namely, the passing of the examination, which does not yet exist; he shows, in other words, foresight and expectation. It is activities of this kind which seem most insistently to involve the assumption of a mind to do the foreseeing and expecting. In other words, the capacity to be influenced by events which lie in the future seems inexplicable on the stimulus-response basis; the *thought* of what does not exist may be allowed to influence the mind, but it is difficult to see how the non-existent can stimulate the body. . . .

THE APPREHENSION OF MEANING

An important fact about our mental life is that we are capable of appreciating meaning. A statement of fact written on a piece of paper is, so far as its material content is concerned, merely a number of black marks inscribed on a white background. Considered, then, as a collection of visual, physical stimuli, it is comparatively unimportant; what is important is the meaning which is attached to these marks. If they inform us, for example, that we have received a legacy of ten thousand pounds it is not the black marks on the white background but the meaning they convey that effects a disturbance in our emotional life, sufficiently profound to keep us awake all night. Now the meaning of the marks is obviously not a physical stimulus; it is something immaterial. How, then, is its effect to be explained in terms of bodily responses to physical stimuli, which the mind merely registers? Let us take one or two further examples in order to present the difficulty in a concrete form.

Let us suppose that I am a geometrician and am thinking about the properties of a triangle. As I do not wish at this point to enter into the vexed question of whether *some* physical stimulus is or is not necessary to initiate every chain of reasoning, we will assume that in this case there was a physical stimulus—it may have been a chance remark about Euclid, or the appearance of a red triangular road signpost while I am driving a car—a stimulus which we will call X, which prompted me to embark upon the train of speculations about the triangle. My reasoning proceeds until I arrive at a conclusion, which takes the form of a geometrical proposition expressed in a formula. I carry this formula in my head for a number of days and presently write it down. In due course I write a book, setting forth my formula and giving an account of the reasoning which led me to it. The book is read and understood by A. Presently it is translated into French, and is read and understood by B.

Later still I deliver a lecture on the subject which is heard and understood by C. As A, B, and C have each of them understood my formula and the reasoning upon which it is based, we may say that the reasoning process has had for them the same meaning throughout. If it had not, they would not all have reached the same conclusion and understood the same thing by it. Yet in each of the four cases the sensory stimulus was different; for myself it was X, for A it was a number of black marks on a white background, for B a number of different black marks on a white background, and for C a number of vibrations in the atmosphere impinging upon his ear drums. It seems incredible that all these different stimuli should have been able to produce a consciousness of the same meaning, if our respective reactions to them were confined to physical responses (which must in each case have been different) which were subsequently reflected in our minds by a process of mental registration of the different responses. The stimuli being different, the intervention of something possessed of the capacity to grasp the *common* element among these physically different entities alone seems able to account for the facts, but the common element is the meaning, which is immaterial and can be grasped, therefore, only by a mind.

Let us take another example instanced by Professor McDougall:

A man receives a telegram which says "Your son is dead." The visual physical stimulus here is, as before, a collection of black marks on an orange field. The reaction experienced in terms of his bodily behaviour may take the form of a complete cessation of all those symptoms usually associated with life—that is to say, he may faint. When he recovers consciousness his thoughts and actions throughout the whole of the remainder of his life may be completely changed. Now that all these complicated reactions are not constituted by and do not even spring from a response to the *physical* stimulus, may be seen by comparing the reactions of an acquaintance who reads the telegram, and so subjects himself to the same stimulus. Moreover, the omission of a single letter, converting the telegram into "Our son is dead," would cause none of the reactions just described, but might result at most in the writing of a polite letter of condolence.

The independence of the bodily reactions to the physical stimuli actually presented is in these cases very marked, and, unless we are to introduce conceptions such as the intellectual apprehension of the *meaning* of the marks, it seems impossible to explain their effect. Yet such a conception again involves the active intervention of mind.

Synthesizing Power of Mind

This conclusion is reinforced by what we may call the synthesizing power of mind. Synthesizing means putting together, and one of the most remarkable powers that we possess is that of taking a number of isolated sensations and forming them into a whole. We shall have occasion to return to this point at greater length in connection with our account of sensation in the next chapter. For the present we will content ourselves with giving one or two examples of mental synthesis.

Let us consider for a moment the case of aesthetic appreciation. The notes of a symphony considered separately consist merely of vibrations in the atmosphere. Each note may, when sounded in isolation produce a pleasant sensation, and as one note is struck after another we get a sequence of pleasant sensations. But although this is a sufficient description of the symphony considered as a collection of material events, and of our reactions to these events considered merely in terms of sensations, it is quite clear that we normally think of a symphony as being something more than this. We think of it in fact as a whole, and it is as a whole that it gives what is called aesthetic pleasure. Now in thinking of the symphony in this way our mind is going beyond the mere sequence of pleasant sensations which its individual notes produce, and putting them together into some sort of pattern. If the notes were arranged in a different order, although the actual vibrations which impinged upon our senses would be the same, the pleasurable aesthetic effect would be destroyed.

It seems to follow that our pleasure in a symphony cannot be wholly accounted for, although it may depend upon our physical responses to the stimuli of the individual notes; in order to obtain aesthetic pleasure we must somehow be able to perceive it as more than the sum total of the individual notes—that is, as a whole pattern or arrangement. The pleasure ceases when the *wholeness* of the object perceived is destroyed, as it is, for example, by the transposition of certain notes. We may compare the difference between the physical sensations which are our responses to the visual stimuli of the colours and canvas of which a picture is composed, with our synthesized perception of a picture as a work of art.

We must conclude, then, that we possess the power of realizing external objects not merely as collections of physical stimuli, which of course they are, but as wholes in which the actual sensory elements are combined to form a single object of a higher order. This faculty of combining or putting together seems to involve the existence not only of a mind, but of a mind of an active, creative type which is able to go out beyond the raw material afforded by our bodily sensations, and to apprehend ideal objects as wholes which are more than the collection of physical events which compose their constituent parts.

SUMMARY OF ARGUMENT

The conclusion to which the arguments of this chapter appear to point is that, in addition to the body and brain, the composition of the living organism includes an immaterial element which we call mind; that this element, although it is in very close association with the brain, is more than a mere glow or halo surrounding the cerebral structure, the function of which is confined to reflecting the events occurring in the structure; that, on the contrary, it is in some sense independent of the brain, and in virtue of its independence is able in part to direct and control the material constituents of the body, using them to carry out its purposes in relation to the external world of objects, much as a driver will make use of the mechanism of his motorcar. Mind so conceived is an active, dynamic, synthesizing force; it goes out beyond the sensations provided by external stimuli and arranges them into patterns, and it seems to be capable on occasion of acting without the provocation of bodily stimuli to set it in motion. It is, in other words, creative, that is, it carries on activities which even the greatest conceivable extension of our physiological knowledge would not enable us to infer from observing the brain. How, then, are we to conceive of the relationship of the mind to the brain?

An actor in a play of Shakespeare not only speaks words, but makes gestures, so that if you were completely deaf you would still be able to infer something of what the play was about from seeing the gestures. It is obvious, however, that there is much more in the play than the pantomime of the players. There are, for example, the words, the characters, the plot, and the poetry. Now to use a simile of the philosopher Bergson, the brain is the organ of pantomime. If you were to observe a man's brain you would know just as much of his thoughts as found vent in gestures. You would know, in other words, all that his thoughts imply in the way of actions or the beginnings of actions,[1] but the thoughts themselves would escape you just as the words and meaning of the play would escape the deaf spectator. This is what is meant by saying that the mind overflows the brain. If our knowledge of both psychology and physiology were perfect, we should be able to describe the movements of the brain without observing it, provided we had complete understanding of a man's state of mind; but we should not from the most minute and thorough inspection of the brain be able to tell what the man was thinking, since just as one gesture of the actor may stand for many different thoughts, so one state of the brain may represent any one of a host of states of mind.

---

[1] Among the beginnings of actions may be mentioned those movements of the larynx which are involved in talking.

IDEALISM

45. *Sense Without Matter*

A. A. Luce

Arthur Aston Luce (1882–1940), professor of metaphysics at Trinity College, Dublin, was the author of many books and articles on immaterialism and the philosophy of George Berkeley.

According to the ancient theory of sense-perception, founded on Aristotle's teaching, there are two factors to be distinguished in every case of sense-perception: (1) the sensible qualities or appearances, i.e., the sense-data actually perceived by sense; and (2) the material substance, itself unperceived and unperceivable, that supports the qualities or appearances. In this account of things matter is essential to sense-perception, but is just what we do not perceive; that is why I call it a *residuum*. In so far as there is a theory of matter, this is it. Matter, when taken precisely and positively and apart from its appearances, is to be regarded as spread like a carpet, an unqualified carpet, under all the outward and obvious aspects of the things of sense. More technically, matter is the substrate, *per se* unperceived and unperceivable, that "supports" sensible qualities, like red and rough and loud, qualities *per se* unsubstantial; matter substantiates them, and lets them "materialise." Both factors are, they say, necessary to real existence and sense-perception. Sensible qualities are, they say, flimsy, transient and variable; matter gives them solidity and permanence and invariability. Matter, they say, is all in the dark night, and but for the sensible qualities that reveal it we should know nothing at all about it. Our external world, luminous and solid, is thus the product of these two factors, sensible quality and matter. Every external thing, or body, is the product of the same two factors. The shoe, the ship, the piece of sealing-wax, each is twofold, like a nut. Each has shell and kernel. The shell is the red, the brown, the hard, the soft, the sound, the smell, the taste and whatever else in it is actually sensed or to be sensed; the rest of it is kernel, substance, substrate, matter, which, as matter, is utterly unperceivable.

There it is in its naked simplicity, in its shameless obscurity—this old Greek guess, the theory of matter or material substance. Hammered for centuries into the heads of uncomprehending youth, conned and repeated by rote by learned and unlearned alike, it has entered into the public mind, as did the flatness of the earth;

Reprinted from *Sense Without Matter* by A. A. Luce. Published by Thomas Nelson & Sons Limited, 1954. Reprinted by permission.

and both superstitions die hard. The theory is venerated, not understood; it is indeed unintelligible, and it is venerated all the more on that account. It is venerated for its comparative antiquity; it is valued more as a blanket than as a carpet; it solves no problems; it gives no support, but it removes certain difficulties out of sight. It holds up an ideal of permanence in the flux of things in a changing world; it contains the welcome suggestion of a hidden hand and of an absolute standard behind the scenes, and it offers these things without making any demand on man's moral and spiritual nature. But is it true? No, it is not true. Does it shed light? No, it sheds no light. It is redolent of the *a priori* and the abstract. I doubt if it ever aimed at truth, as the realist understands that term. I doubt if it was ever intended to provide a true-to-fact account of what actually happens when a man sees and touches. It tries to ease certain difficulties in the theories of perception and of change; but it obscures other problems, and removes them out of sight; it makes darkness visible; it sheds no light. . . .

I am indeed asking, "Does matter exist?" And I answer, "No"; but I am also asking a deeper, constructive question, viz.: "What precisely do I see and touch?" If we know precisely what we see and touch and otherwise sense, the question about matter settles itself automatically. We are studying sense-perception in order to find out precisely what man perceives by sense. Matter has always been the intellectual refuge of skepticism and half-knowledge. The materialist distrusts his senses, depreciates their position and rejects their evidence. He holds that sense without matter does not make sense. That contention goes far and cuts deep, and warps a man's attitude, not only to things of spirit, but to reality all along the line. The materialist holds that without matter the sensible could not exist as a *thing*, could not cause, and would be indistinguishable from dream. . . .

I open my eyes and see. What precisely do I see? I stretch out my hand and touch. What precisely do I touch? What precisely do we see and touch, when we see and touch? That is our question. We have many names in ordinary life for the myriad things we see and touch—shoes, ships, sealing-wax, apples, pears, and plums; those names are precise enough for action, but they are not precise enough for thought; thought is concerned with common features and resemblances, more than with differences and distinctions. Now, when I see ships and shoes and apples and so forth, what precisely do I see that is common to all those sights? I see colours and shades of colour, light and its modes, illuminated points and lines and surfaces. Those are the things I actually see, and I call them inclusively visual data; they are the elemental objects of the sense of sight. And when I touch shoes and ships and apples and so forth, what precisely do I touch that is common to all those touches? I touch hard, soft, solid, fluid, resistant, yielding, and (in the wider sense of "touch") hot, cold, warm and tepid. Those are the things I actually touch, and I call them inclusively factual data; they are elemental objects of the sense of touch. . . .

The theory of matter, as we have seen, requires us to hold that in every instance of sense-perception there are two factors to be recognized and distinguished, viz. the actual object of sense, the sense-data actually perceived by eye or ear or hand or other sense organ, and the material substance, itself unperceived and unperceivable, that supports the sense-data. The case against the theory is, in outline, that the theory postulates an intolerable division, based on an improbable guess. It is not a theory reasonably distinguishing homogeneous parts in a thing, like shell and kernel, pea and pod. It is a theory requiring us to break up the one homogeneous thing into two heterogeneous and inconsistent parts, and, incidentally, to pin our faith to the existence of material substance, for which there is not the slightest evidence from fact.

Let us take an instance, and see how the theory of matter works out. See yonder mahogany table. Its colour is brown, in the main, though it is veined and grained in lighter colours. Its touch is hard and smooth. It has a smell and a taste and a sound; but I hardly ever need to bother about them; for I know the table ordinarily by its colors and by the cut and shape of its lines of light and its shading, and if I am in doubt I can handle it, and feel it and lift it up. It is a sensible table. It is a sensible table through and through. I can bore holes in it, can plane away its surfaces, can burn it with fire and reduce it to ashes; and I shall never come on anything in it that is not an actual or possible object of sense; it is composed entirely of sense-data and *sensibilia*. Now the theory of matter brings in totally different considerations; it asks me to believe that all these sense-data and *sensibilia* do not constitute the real table. I am asked to believe that beneath the table I see and touch stands another table, a supporting table, a table of a totally different nature that cannot be seen or touched or sensed in any other way, a table to be taken on trust, and yet a highly important table, because it is the real, invariable, material table, while the table I see and touch is only apparent, variable, inconstant and volatile. The visible-tangible, sensible table has colour and hardness and the other qualities by which things of sense are known and distinguished. The real table has none of these.

What an impossible duality! Yonder mahogany table proves to be two tables. It is a sensible table, and it is a material table. If I take the theory seriously, and go through with it, I am bound to believe the same of everything else around me; wherever I look, I am condemned to see double, and to grope my way through life with divided aim and reduced efficiency.

No rational account of the coexistence of the two tables has ever been given, nor could be given. Some say that the "real table" is the *cause* of the apparent table, but how the cause works is a mystery. Some say that the "real table" is the original, and the apparent table a copy; but what would be the use of a copy that is totally unlike its original? And who, or what, does the copying, and how? The two tables are left there, juxtaposed, unrelated and unexplained. They are not two aspects of the one thing; they are not two parts of the one thing; they have nothing in common; they are not comparable; they could not stem from the one stock; they are heterogeneous; they are at opposite poles of thought; they differ as light from darkness; if the one is, the other is not. No mixing of the two is possible; they cannot be constituents of the one thing; for they are contradictories; if the table is really coloured, then it is not matter; if the table is really matter, then it is not coloured. The supposition of two heterogeneous bodies in the one thing of sense is self-contradictory, destroying the unity of the thing. . . .

Then consider the question of evidence. What evidence is there for the existence of matter? What evidence is there for non-sensible matter? Why should I believe in the matter of materialism? Set aside the misunderstanding that confuses matter with the sensible, set aside the prejudice that would identify with matter the chemical atom, or the subatomic objects of nuclear physics; set aside the legend of the constant sum-total of energy from which all springs and to which all returns; set aside mere tradition and voice of uninformed authority. And what philosophical evidence is there for the matter of materialism? There is no evidence at all. Writers on matter appeal to prejudice and ignorance in favour of matter; they assume and take it for granted that everyone accepts the existence of matter, they never attempt to prove its existence directly. There is no direct evidence to be had. They try to establish it indirectly. There could not be an external *thing*, they say, unless there were matter; unless there were matter, they say, there would be no cause of change in the external world, nor any test for true and false. . . .

I have examined the typical case of seeing and touching, and have shown that there is no place for matter there. I have examined the normal perceptual situation, and have shown that it contains no evidence for matter, and that the forcible intrusion of matter destroys the unity of the thing perceived and of the world of sense. The onus of proof is on the materialist, and the immaterialist can fairly challenge him to produce his evidence. If there is matter, produce it. If there is evidence for matter, produce it. Neither matter, nor valid evidence for matter, has ever yet been produced.

The nearest approach to evidence for matter proves on careful study to be bad evidence. It is not evidence for matter; it evidence for spirit *spoilt*. I refer to the notion of *support*. The strength of materialism (and its ultimate weakness) is its exploitation of the sub-rational feeling that somehow the pillars of the house rest on matter. People turn to matter for support; they are dimly aware of the need for support; but if they analyzed that need, they would look for the support elsewhere.

Sense-data need support, and from the time of Aristotle to the present day men have claimed that matter supplies the desired support. But could matter, if it existed, supply the kind of support that sense-data need? Literal support is not in question. Sense-data do not need literal support, and if they did need it, matter *ex hypothesi* could not supply it. In the literal sense sense-data are *given* supported; they are supported by other sense-data. The table supports the books; the books rest on it; without it they would fall. I can see and feel the books and the table in effective contact. That support is visible and tangible. Literal support means sensible support, which is just what matter *e vi termini* could not give; for matter cannot be seen or touched or otherwise sensed. The legs of the table support the table; the floor supports both; the earth supports the floor; in all such cases support and things supported are homogeneous; both are *sensibilia*. Matter is not a *sensibile*. Matter and sense are heterogeneous *ex hypothesi,* and therefore matter, if there were such a thing, could not literally support sense-data.

Sense-data cannot stand alone. Like letters of the alphabet or figures or any other symbols they need the support of mind or spirit. By their very mould and nature they are not absolute, but are relative to mind or spirit. An alphabet *in vacuo* would be nonsense. The footprint in the sand implies one to leave the imprint, and the same *understood* implies one to understand it. To "understand" is to stand under and support, as the taking mind stands under and supports the work of the making mind. The materialist's quest of matter as an absolute object of perception, distinct from sense-data, is wrong-headed in principle; he leaves out of the account his own mind. His mind supports his object, as the reader's understanding mind supports the meaning of the printed page, and takes out of it what the writer's mind put into it. Sense-data are not mind or modes of mind; they do not think or will or plan or purpose; but they are from mind and for the mind, and they imply mind and cannot be understood apart from mind. That is why they cannot stand alone; that is why they require support; that is why they require *that sort* of support that only mind or spirit can give. To look to matter for such support would be absurd; for matter is defined as that which is not mind or spirit. Matter cannot support the objects of our senses in theory or practice, literally or metaphorically, and to look to matter for support is to lean on a broken reed.

Let me clinch the argument with an appeal to observable fact in a concrete case. If matter is, I ask, *where* is it? If matter is, it is in things, and in all external things, and the type of external thing selected is neither here nor there. I will choose a homely, explodable thing that we can know through and through, a mutton chop. If matter is, it is in this mutton chop. I ask, where? Where is it in this mutton chop? Where could it be? Take away from this given chop all its sense-data, including its obtainable sense-data. Take away those of the outside and those of the inside, those of the meat and the bone, those of the fat and the lean, be it cooked or uncooked. Take away all that we do sense and all that we might sense, and what is left? There are its visual data, its browns and reds and blacks and whites, and all the other colours and hues of its surface and potential surfaces and centre. There are its factual data, its rough and smooth, hard and soft, resistant and yielding, solid and fluid, and those varied palpables that admit my knife or hinder its easy passage. It has auditory data; its fat and lean and bone make different sounds when struck by knives and forks. Many smells and savours go to its composing, raw or cooked. Air and moisture link it to its sensible context, and show as steam and vapour under heat. The chop has sensible shapes that may concern artists and even geometricians; it has sensible contents and sensible forms that are specially the concern of chemist and physicist; they are no less sensible and no less real than those contents and forms that are of importance to the butcher and the housewife and the cook. Take them all away in thought. Take away all the *sensa* and the *sensibilia* of the mutton chop, and what is left? Nothing! Nothing is left. In taking away its *sensa* and *sensibilia* you have taken away all the mutton chop, and nothing is left, and its matter is nowhere. Its matter, other than its sense-data, is nothing at all, nothing but a little heap of powdered sentiment, nothing but the ghost of the conventional thing, nothing but the sceptic's question-mark. . .

Is matter wanted as a cause? Are sense-data or sensible qualities (call them what you wish) effects of matter? Are the immediate objects of our senses caused by matter? Are sense-data so lacking in causal power that material substance must be postulated and assumed? Is material substance the power behind the scenes, the secret spring of causal action?...

Is matter wanted as a cause? Several questions are here combined. What is meant by "cause"? Can sense-data cause? Can they make changes begin to be? If they can, is there any need for matter? If they cannot, how could matter help? If sense-data are passive, how could material substance activate them, and confer on them the power of the cause?

These questions answer themselves in the light of the foregoing analysis of "cause." The term "cause" is ambiguous. In one sense sense-data can cause, in the other sense, not. Sense-data are not spirits; they cannot make changes begin to be; they cannot directly alter the course of events; for they are passive; but indirectly they give rise to effects; they are signs of what is coming; men read those signs and act on them and make changes begin to be. The sign works through the mind that reads it and understands it and acts on it, just as the works of Shakespeare work through minds that read them and understand them and act on them. The passive sign gives rise indirectly to changes it does not produce. In that respect, and in that respect only, the passive objects of sense around us are causes. In strict speech they are not causes, but are like causes, and not unnaturally, but wrongly, they become credited with the power of making changes begin to be. For practical purposes it is enough for us to know that smoke and fire are almost invariably found together. When we see smoke we expect the fire, and we are on our guard and take precautions. That is the full extent of the causal connection. The smoke is a passive sign of what is coming; it involves you and me in action, but does not act itself. The black smoke is there, and it will soon burst into a red flame unless I extinguish it. That is the only sense in which the black smoke is the cause of the red flame. The smoke does not make the fire begin to be. The smoke is not the true cause of the fire. The smoke is but the customary antecedent; when we see or smell it, we expect its consequent. The two are indissolubly connected in our minds because they are very frequently associated in nature. The association is there in nature, as in the mind; sometimes we see the smoke before the fire, sometimes the fire before the smoke. Hence it matters little which we call *cause,* and which we call *effect;* they are two parts of the one process; all we need to know is that the two events are causally connected in the sense that the one makes us expect the other. It is no truer that the fire is the cause of the smoke than that the smoke is the cause of the fire. Both propositions are on the one level as regards truth and falsity. In respect of significance or cue-causation, both events are indifferently causes and effects. In respect of efficient or true causation, neither is cause, neither is effect of the other.

Then comes the question about matter. Sense-data *per se* are passive; they may be viewed as acting indirectly through their significance for minds. Does matter enter into the cause? Is material substance the hidden hand behind the senses? No; matter has nothing to say to causation in either sense of the term. *Ex hypothesi* matter has no significance for mind, and has not the power of the cause. Matter could not cause, nor enable sense-data to do so. There is no room for matter in the causal relation. All that matter does is to mystify, and people are too ready to be mystified. They see that the objects of sense cannot truly cause, and yet that some cause of change is required; and instead of thinking the problem out along the lines sketched above, they jump at the hypothesis of material substance. It shelves the problem and puts it out of sight; it is a facile solution that saves men the trouble of thinking. They say to themselves, "Matter is something we know not what; it acts we know not how." And so all issues in mystery.

Putting aside mystery and mystification, we see that what calls for explanation is some sensible event, some event in the world of sense. We *see* the water rise, and the litmus-paper change colour; we feel the wax soft and then still softer. A sensible change has occurred, and as rational sentients we are bound to ask, "What did it? What caused this change in the world of sense?" To reply, "The material substance of moon or wax or acid did it," or, "Material substance in general did it," may give some mystic satisfaction to mystic minds; but such replies have no explanatory value; they shed no light on the problem. Man wants to know causes, and needs to know causes, in order to have some control over events. If he cannot shape the course of events, he must shape his behavior to suit the events. He needs to be able to move muscle and limb at the right time and to push and pull the things of sense in immediate contact with his body. To do so to the best advantage man needs a certain attitude to things; he needs confidence in the universe; he needs to be able to trust the course and composition of the universe, its order and regularity, its wisdom and its goodness. Man is spirit and sense. To form and guide his experience man needs a knowledge of spiritual causes and sensible effects. Matter comes under neither category; *ex hypothesi* matter is neither spiritual nor sensible; therefore it can contribute nothing to a knowledge of causes; it cannot be seen or touched, and therefore it cannot tell me when or how to push and pull the things I see and touch around me. Even if matter existed and possessed some occult power of altering sensible things and effecting visible and tangible changes, we never could *know* that this matter effected that change; we never could connect cause and its effect; we should be none the wiser for the existence of matter; we should have nothing to build on, no foundation for experience or for future action. We never could *know* that this invisible was the cause of that visible change, or that that intangible was the cause of this tangible change. In a word, if matter were a cause, we should never have the evidence of sense as to the cause of a sensible effect. Matter would be of no practical use with regard to knowledge of causes, and it would make no practical difference in life and experience. The invention of matter and its intrusion into the causal relation is purely psychological. It gives some sort of relief to the feelings; it cannot be too easily disproved, and it asks nothing of our moral and spiritual nature.

We men originate changes, and we know that we do so. We push; we pull; we strive, purpose and endeavour; we produce effects, often at second-hand, and working with the effects of another's will, but we produce effects, and we recognize the effects as effects of our causal power. We are true causes; we are true causes that endure; therefore we are substantial causes; we are substances that cause. We understand spiritual causation from within, to some extent at least, and it is the only true causation that we understand at all; and we know it by the effort involved. In prospect or retrospect I know what it is to climb a ladder. I connect causally myself at the foot of it and myself at the top; climbing a ladder is quite different from falling off a ladder; causal effort is required. I can look at fire and wax without any similar sense of effort; I can keep on looking. I can watch the wax soften and melt on the hearth-stone. I have no sense of effort; it is a smooth, expected transition; it is a relation between two events or states; it is the relation of simple series in time, the relation of before and after, completely devoid of any suggestion of true causality. To mount a five-foot ladder and climb down again involves an effort of mind and body. If I am hoisted up five feet and let down again, no effort by me is involved. In the former case I cause the rise and the fall; in the latter case, not. Effort marks the difference; that feeling of effort, be it muscular, mental or mixed, is the index of finite, causal power. Causal power belongs to the *anima*, to the finite *anima* or spirit, and it does not belong to the inanimate.

How then to account for the opposite view? Why do people make the mistake, I will not say of imagining causation where there is none, but of crediting the inanimate thing or event with the power of the cause? Why do they attribute causal power to the sun and moon instead of to the Power that moves them? Several answers might be given; one deserves special mention here, and that is sympathy or empathy. It may be a relic of the old notions, classed as animism or hylozoist, or it may be a very natural result of our real oneness with the things around us. We do feel with them and for them and in them. We do project ourselves into them, as little Alice projects herself into her doll. When Homer makes the river fight, or Wordsworth sets his daffodils a-dancing, they are projecting their own efforts into the external world, and thereby enlivening their themes and winning their readers' sympathies. There lies one great source of the supposed inanimate second cause. There is no such cause, but we invent it. We invent it empathetically. As do the poets and the other masters of language, we project into a passive object splinters and sparks of our own activity. We throw forward into the inanimate thing the effort we should make and the action we should take, if we were it. Smoke follows fire, often, always. It is cause and effect, we say. We see the fire, and we expect the smoke, or we smell the smoke and we go looking for the fire. These inanimate, passive things, easily moved, are cues for the action; they are *like* causes; they make us think causally. But that is not enough for all of us; for we are sympathetic, imaginative creatures. We are not content with cue causes; we are not content with sequences; we are not content with the observed fact that where there is smoke there is fire. We proceed to embellish and embroider the fact by reading ourselves into the situation; we mentally puff a lighted cigar, and there is the smoke; empathetically we say that the fire produces the smoke, and we vaguely view the tongues of flame puffing forth the smoke. The embroidery and embellishment are not true to fact; but they are part of the art of using rich, imaginative language. If taken literally, they misrepresent the primary facts of our sentient existence.

Causal matter is a parallel development. The causal sensible has been developed empathetically from the passive, inanimate thing of sense; and the supposed causal powers of matter have by a similar process of self-projection been embroidered upon the original hypothesis of the passive substrate. Aristotle distinguished the material cause from the efficient cause. His efficient cause was what I have termed the true cause; his material cause was like my cue cause. His efficient cause got things done, and made changes begin to be; his material cause was the inactive *sine qua non* of the doing. The function of Aristotelian matter was to support, and not to act. Aristotelian matter was passive; it was a limiting concept, almost a negation; it was not a thing, nor a quality, nor a quantity; for it had to consist with sensible things and sensible qualities and sensible quantities; it was potentiality and possibility, just short of nothing. Later philosophers referred to matter as "a dead, inactive lump." An object so slight and negative and ineffective might well have been lost to sight altogether, and very naturally there has long been an oscillation between the two poles of thought about matter. Some understand it as active, some as passive. Some adhere to the original notion of it as passive substrate, visualizing it as a carpet spread under the things of sense, or as a prop supporting them. Others have gone over to the active theory, making matter the secret source of change in the world of sense, the "hidden hand" behind sensible phenomena.

The modern trends of chemistry and physics have furthered the tendency to regard matter as an active cause. Many people today, I fancy, identify matter vaguely with atomic energy or with the rapid movement of the tiny parts and particles of elements. In olden days Jove's thunderbolt was the secret weapon of the gods; today atomic energy has taken its place as the power behind the scenes. The bomb that controls the policies of nations controls the trend of thought, and in popular imagination appears as proof positive of active matter. Gunpowder and high explosives, when they were first invented, affected popular thought in a similar way. No new factors bearing on the issue for intellect have come to light in our day. No new proof of a non-sensible substrate of the world of sense has been discovered. The bomb is nothing new by way of proof of matter, only the horror, the suddenness and the vast scale of the consequent destruction have reinforced whatever argument is there. The fact is that electrons, neutrons and the other scientific objects and working concepts of today are no nearer possessing the power of the true cause than were acids, alkalis, phlogiston and gravity; but they are more remote from the macroscopic, and in consequence they strike the imagination more forcibly than did the objects and concepts of the older sciences. The bomb may be designed, constructed and described by various concepts and symbols, but such concepts and symbols do not alter the fact that the bomb itself is sensible through and through. In whole and part and particle it can be seen and touched and heard; it contains and releases and conveys motions that can be seen and touched and heard. Atomic energy, however subtle its constitution, however penetrating its results, belongs entirely to the province of sense; its only causality is that of significance, the causality of the sign or cue cause. The bomb, live, exploding, or exploded, is a multiple sign of sights and sounds and feelings that go with and after it; pity and fear and panic movements of escape are aroused in us by the sight or thought of it, and naturally we project into it those incipient movements that we begin, not it. Our sympathies are strongly aroused. "I have a pain in your chest," wrote Madame de Sevigné to her daughter. We feel in the bomb what we might feel in ourselves, and thus we credit it with those efforts and activities that are really our own. Empathy accounts for our *mis*-takes, but does not alter the facts of existence. Empathy cannot transmute passive into active, or make a cue cause into a true cause. The bomb is no true cause; for it is entirely an effect; finite spirits have made it, using and misusing the effects of Will Infinite.

The causal argument for the existence of matter has thus been examined and refuted. I will recapitulate before I leave it. The causal argument owes its cogency to the assumption that colours and touches and all the other objects we actually perceive by sense cannot cause the changes we observe in the world of sense. That assumption is true in one sense of the term "cause," and false in another. It is true that colours and other such objects are passive things, unable to initiate motion or make the smallest change begin to be. But that rule would apply equally to matter, if matter existed; for it is only another way of saying that spirits alone are truly active, and matter, being by definition non-spiritual, would necessarily be ruled out as cause. If, on the other hand, is meant by "cause" merely the inoperative, antecedent sign, created and conserved by cosmic power, in that sense colours and similar objects are causes; for sentients can read their meaning, can grasp their significance, and can act accordingly. To postulate matter as causal sign would be doubly absurd. If you have a perfectly good and adequate sensible sign, there is no need for the material sign, or room for it. And secondly, matter *ex hypothesi* cannot be seen or touched or otherwise perceived by sense, and therefore it could not act as a sign for sentient beings. In sum, no argument for the existence of matter can validly be drawn from the concept of cause or the facts of causation.

CONTEMPORARY ISSUES

Personal Identity and Other Minds

46. *The Problem of Other Minds*

John Hospers

John Hospers (1918–   ) is emeritus professor of philosophy at the University of Southern California School of Philosophy and a former editor of the Monist. In 1972 he was the Libertarian Party's candidate for president of the United States.

When my finger is cut and bleeding, I know that I have a pain in the most direct way possible: I feel it. I do not *infer* from my behavior or anything else that I feel pain, I am *directly* aware of it—what philosophers sometimes call "immediate acquaintance." But when *your* finger is cut and bleeding, I do not know in the same way that you are feeling pain. I *infer* it from the fact that I see the blood and hear you saying that it hurts, and so on, but I do not feel your pain. (I may feel great empathy toward you, and feel distressed at the thought that you are in pain, but that still isn't feeling your pain in the way I feel my own pain when my finger is cut.) It seems to be impossible for me to feel your pain, or for you to feel mine. We are each aware of our own experiences, and no one else's. . . .

Thus, even if it is granted that I can know you're in pain, I still can't *feel* your pain, or think your thoughts, or experience your worry. If you tell me what you're worried about ("There's a hurricane on the way"), I too may feel worried; but even so, I feel my worry and you feel yours. There are two worries going on here, yours and mine, and I can't experience yours any more than you can experience mine. In fact, it would seem to be a necessary truth that I can't experience your experiences and you can't experience mine.

But is it a necessary truth? Suppose that the laws of physiology were different, and that we consider two persons, A and B. When A is cut with a knife, B feels pain, and when B is cut, A feels pain. Wouldn't that be a case of A feeling B's pain, and B A's pain? We might *say* that it is; if "my pain" means "the pain felt in my body," the answer would be yes. But in another sense the answer would be no. A might feel pain when B's body is injured and B feel pain when A's body is injured;

From *An Introduction to Philosophical Analysis* 3rd ed., by John Hospers, © 1988. Reprinted by permission of Prentice-Hall, Inc., Upper Saddle River, NJ.

this would be a very peculiar kind of world: I might say to you, "Don't get hit over the head today, I don't want to have that headache again." Still, wouldn't I be having *my* pain—but feeling it when your body was injured—just as you would still be feeling your pain when my body was injured? The causal conditions of having pain would be different in such a world, but I would still have my pain and you would have yours. "My pain" is *the pain I feel*—regardless of the causal conditions under which it was felt; even if I feel the pain when your finger is cut, it would still be my pain, because I am the one who has the pain.

It seems, then, that "I feel your pain" and "You feel my pain" are not just empirically impossible—contrary to biological laws—but logically impossible; it would involve saying that I feel a pain that is not mine but yours. Experiences, including pains, are essentially private; I could not have your pain any more than a circle could be square. In that case, however, I cannot possibly *verify* that you are in pain; I can verify only what your facial expression is and, if necessary, supplement that with a lie-detector test and a brainscan. But I cannot feel your pain myself. By such means I may be able to discover what thoughts or feelings you are having—even to know (at least in the weak sense of "know") *that* you are feeling so-and-so. But knowing *that* you are having a certain feeling is not at all the same as feeling it myself. If I know you well I may be able to say truly, "I know just what you're going through," but that's not the same thing as feeling it myself. I may empathize strongly with you and even feel pain when you are in pain, but the pain I feel is still mine and the pain you feel is yours.

Can I verify the proposition that you are feeling pain? Not if verifying means having all the evidence, or even the best possible evidence, which would be feeling it. At best I can verify that you behave in a certain way, and respond in a certain way to a lie-detector test.

Perhaps then all I mean by saying that you are in pain is that you behave in a certain way and respond to lie-detector tests and so on. But this view is absurdly implausible. If you have just cut yourself badly and I see your agonized behavior, do I, in saying that you feel pain, mean only that you behave *as if* you felt pain? Surely I mean that your behavior is an *indication* that you feel pain—and when I say that you are in pain I mean to say exactly the same thing about you that I am saying about myself when I say that I am in pain. The only difference between "I am in pain" and "You are in pain" is the personal pronoun. *What* I am saying about me and about you is exactly the same in the two cases. The question is, How can I verify the pain in your case, as I can do so immediately in my own?

"Well, at least I can *confirm* that you are feeling pain." Surely the fact that you cry out after having been cut is a good *confirmation* to me that you are in pain. Sometimes when you cry out you may be play-acting, but with careful observation I can confirm that too.

Many would be content with confirmation rather that verification. But a skeptic can pursue the question further: How do I know that you have pains or any other experiences at all? How do I know that you experience pain or pleasure or have sensations or thoughts or feelings of any kind? Could you not be a cleverly rigged-up automaton, wound up like a top every morning to go through certain complicated motions every day, but all the while experiencing nothing at all? True, you give answers to mathematical questions faster than I do; but so do computers when they have been programmed to do so. How do I know that you are not a fancy computer, having no more feelings or thoughts than the computers scientists build? If you were one, programmed to go through just the motions that you do, how would I ever know the difference? You would do the same things, say the same things, every bit of your behavior would be the same—so how could I tell? I can tell that you feel pain only from the symptoms from which I make the inference—but what if the symptoms were the same? If I don't believe that a computer has feelings, and if you behaved just as a computer does (the computer too can exhibit pain behavior and even say that it is in pain), what reason would I have for saying that you experience pain but the computer doesn't? Your behavior is all I can confirm, and I have no evidence that there is anything else beyond that. I have never even once felt your pain; for all that I know, your pain may be a myth.

To counter this alarming possibility, the *argument from analogy* is often invoked. When my finger is cut (A), I feel pain (B); therefore, I infer that when your finger is cut (A'), you feel pain (B'). That doesn't confer certainty on the statement that you feel pain, but doesn't it make your feeling quite probable? After all, you behave as I do when I feel pain; you too are composed of skin, bones, nerves, and blood vessels—just as I am. So can't I infer by analogy (similarity) that if I feel pain when cut, so do you?

The trouble is that as an argument from analogy, this seems a weak one. Suppose I see a set of boxes stored in someone's garage. I open one box and find that it is full of books. I don't open any of the rest, but I say, "Since all the boxes look pretty much alike, I infer that they all contain books." Admittedly this wouldn't be a very safe inference, and you wouldn't bet much on it. The boxes might contain anything—trinkets, papers, children's toys. If you open only one box, you're not in a very good position to say that they all contain books. Your position would be much better if you had opened all the boxes but one, found that they contained books, and then inferred that probably the last box would contain books also. An argument from analogy based on only one case is a pretty poor argument.

But isn't that exactly the position we are in with regard to other minds? In my own case, I have (1) my behavior and (2) my feeling pain. But in every other case, I have only the behavior to go by. So am I not in the position of the person who concludes that all the boxes contain books, on the slender basis of finding that one box contains books?

Yet I am much more confident that you feel pain when your finger is cut, than I am that all the boxes contain books after examining the contents of only one box. Why is this? Is this just an irrational conclusion, a prejudice? Or is it my belief that you have feelings based on something other than a weak argument from analogy?

Consider the following three statements:

1. I ask you, "Where is the book I lent you?"
2. You understand my question and think for a moment.
3. You utter the words, "I'm sorry—I forgot it, I left it at home."

The first statement is a report of words emanating from my mouth; these I not only utter but can hear myself uttering. The third statement is also something I can hear; your lips move and you utter the words. The problem is with the second statement. How do I know it is true, since I can't experience your thoughts? John Stuart Mill wrote,

> I conclude that other human beings have feelings like me because, first, they have bodies like me, which I know in my own case, to be the antecedent condition of feelings; and because secondly, they exhibit the acts, and other outward signs, which in my own case I know from experience to be caused by feelings. . . . In the case of other human beings I have the evidence of my senses for the first and last links of the series, but not for the intermediate link. I find, however, that the sequence between the first and last is as regular and constant in those other cases as it is in mine. In my own case I know that the first link produces the last through the intermediate link, and could not produce it without. Experience, therefore, obliges me to conclude that there must be an intermediate link; which must either be the same in others as in myself, or a different one; I must either believe them to be alive, or to be automatons; and by believing them to be alive, that is, by supposing the link to be of the same nature as in the case of which I have experience, and which is in all other respects similar, I bring other human beings, as phenomena, under the same generalizations which I know by experience to be the true story of my own existence.[1]

Particularly impressive is the fact that I ask someone a question and then from that person's lips emanate words which answer the very question I asked. How would this be possible if the other body doesn't have a mind that understands the question? To understand the question must he not have consciousness like me? Surely, the belief that he has consciousness like me is *the best explanation* of his ability to answer my questions.

Many would rest content with this answer, believing the problem of other minds to be solved. But there are a few bothersome questions that have been raised about this account.

1. How did we ever learn to use words like "pain" and "anger"—and other words we use—in talking about our "inner states"? As children we learned to use words by having them uttered by parents, accompanied typically by acts of pointing: "That's a chair," "That's a car." But of course you can't point to pain or anger. So how does the child learn to use the language of sensations and feelings? How did we ourselves learn to use the words correctly? How did words like "pain" become part of a *public language?*

[1]John Stuart Mill, *An Examination of Sir William Hamilton's Philosophy,* 6th ed. (London: Longmans Green, 1889), pp. 243–244.

Suppose you have some special feeling whenever you see, say, a mountain gorge. You might give a name to that peculiar sensation, and use it again if you had that same peculiar sensation another time. But thus far the name would not be part of a public language; you could use it only in "communing with yourself." You might try to communicate this special feeling to others, but others might be quite uncomprehending as to what you meant. But the word "pain" is not the same. You learned to use that word from seeing your parents and other people use it: And to use it correctly you didn't need to feel their pains, or even to feel pain yourself. It was only necessary to observe the occasions on which they used the word—what their behavior was like when they used it, and by doing so you became able to use it yourself. If your father cut his finger and said that it hurt, and later you cut your finger, you could say the same thing of yourself—and presumably the feeling you had when this happened would be one you would identify as "pain."

This is not to say, then, that you have no "inner episodes" such as sensations of pain, but that you can learn to identify something as pain only by observing behavior that accompanies the use of the word. The child did not begin with her own case, as the argument from analogy seems to assume. She learned it as she learned any word in a public language, by observing the contexts in which other people used it. Thus, even though you can feel only your own pain, as a child you could learn how to use the word "pain" without having felt it. And you would recognize what you feel as being pain because of the similarity of the context to that of others when they spoke of pain. How else, it would be asked, would we learn the meaning of terms like "anger," "hope," "dread," and countless others?

2. We have argued thus far that you can know that you are in pain, and that your pain report is about as certain as a statement can be. But this too has been questioned.

Suppose that an encephalograph was constructed to test whether your reports that you are in pain are true; the machine is designed to test your pain level. What if you sincerely report that you are in pain, but this report conflicts with the evidence of the encephalograph? Should it be concluded that you are not telling the truth when you say you are in pain?

"Not at all," one might well exclaim, "I *know* whether I feel a pain. If the machine says I'm not, then it's the machine that's making the mistake. After all, *I* know whether I have a pain or not—I feel it! The machine only provides an indirect test—one that can be mistaken if the machine malfunctions."

> However good the evidence may be, such a physiological theory can never be used to show the sufferer that he was mistaken in thinking that he had a pain. . . . The sufferer's epistemological authority must therefore be better than the best physiological theory can ever be.[2]

But wait: How does Jones know that he is using the word "pain" correctly? Has he any *criteria* for the use of the term? He feels what he feels, but perhaps he

---

[2]Kurt Baier, "Smart on Sensations," *Australian Journal of Philosophy* (1962): 57.

is misdescribing what he feels in calling it a pain. Or perhaps he can describe it rightly once it is recognized for what it is, but he doesn't recognize it for what it is, in much the same way that a person may think she sees someone else in the room when she is only seeing her image in a mirror.

> The encephalograph says that the brain-process constantly correlated with pain-reports occurs in Jones's brain. However, although he exhibits pain-behavior, Jones thinks that he does not feel pain. . . . Now is it that he does not know that *pain* covers what you feel when you are burned as well as what you feel when you are stuck, struck, etc.? Or is it that he really does not feel pain when he is burned? Suppose we tell Jones that what he feels when he is burned is *also* called "pain." Suppose he then admits that he does feel *something*, but insists that what he feels is quite *different* from what he feels when he is stuck, struck, etc. Where does Jones go from here? Has he failed to learn the language properly, or is he correctly (indeed infallibly) reporting that he has different sensations than those normally had in the situation in question?[3]

If the certainty of a sincere pain report is thus cast in doubt, some alarming skeptical possibilities now confront us. Would one sincere pain report—if at odds with the machine report—be enough to break down at one blow well-confirmed scientific theories? Can our certainty about our pains possibly be shaken by such questions as "Does she really know which sensations are called pains?" and "Is she a good judge of whether she is in pain or not?" Can the truth of a pain report *never* be overridden by evidence from other sources?

Consider another kind of case. You say, "It's hot in this room." But you look at the thermometer and it reads 55°; you check other thermometers and they all say the same. Are you sure you are right and the thermometers wrong? In this case we say the thermometers are right and that it isn't hot in the room, you just *feel* hot; perhaps you have a slight fever. Here we trust the thermometer and not your individual judgment. Why not do the same in trusting the encephalogram rather than your individual pain report?

"But this is different," one might say. Instead of saying it's hot in the room, you should say that you *feel* hot—no one will doubt that this is true. You do have a heat experience, no one is doubting the truth of your report that you *feel* hot; it's just that this time your heat experience doesn't correspond to the actual temperature. But in the case of the pain report, how can we deny that the person is feeling pain? If *you* are the one who has the pain, won't you say without hesitation that the encephalograph is mistaken? Aren't *you* the final judge of whether you feel pain? Isn't this one case that's absolutely clear and unshakable?

But some philosophers have questioned even this. We learn the word "pain"—like other words—in certain behavioral and environmental contexts; that's how we come to recognize pain when we feel it, and to name it correctly. However,

---

[3]Richard Rorty, "Mind-Body Identity, Privacy, and Categories," *Review of Metaphysics 19* (1965): 24–25.

Now suppose that these public criteria (for "knowing how to use 'pain'") change as physiology and technology progress. Suppose, in particular, that we find it convenient to speed up the learning of contrastive observation predicates (such as "painful" "tickling," etc.) by supplying children with portable encephalographs-cum-teaching-machines which, whenever the appropriate brain-process occurs, murmur the appropriate term in their ears. Now "appropriate brain-process" will start out by meaning "brain-process constantly correlated with sincere utterances of 'I'm in pain' by people taught the use of 'pain' in the old rough-and-ready way." But soon it will come to mean, "the brain-process which we have always programmed the machine to respond to with a murmur of 'pain' ". . . . Given this situation, it would make sense to say things like "You say you are in pain, and I'm sure you are sincere, but you can see for yourself that your brain is not in the state to which you were trained to respond to with 'Pain,' so apparently the training did not work, and you do not yet understand what pain is." In such a situation, our "inability to be mistaken" about our pains would remain, but our "final epistemological authority" on the subject would be gone, for there would be a standard procedure for overriding our reports.[4]

The question is, however, whether such first-person reports can be overridden in this way. The person reporting the experience may be lying, or may be misreporting the experience by using words incorrectly. But if neither of these things is taking place, how can the person be mistaken? Some would contend that the first-person report is not coherent with the physical evidence, and that if the physical evidence is considerable, the first-person report, lacking coherence with the other propositions, must be rejected. But others would contend that if the physical evidence is not coherent with the first-person report, then it is the physical evidence that should be rejected and the first-person report that should be maintained.

[4]Ibid.

47. Brain Transplants and Personal Identity: A Dialogue

Derek Parfit and Godfrey Vesey

Derek Parfit (1942–   ) teaches philosophy at Oxford University. He has made outstanding contributions to ethical theory and the problem of personal identity.

Godfrey Vesey (1923–   ) teaches philosophy at the Open University in England. He has published books on a variety of philosophical topics.

Brain Transplants

In 1973 in the *Sunday Times* there was a report of how a team from the Metropolitan Hospital in Cleveland under Dr. R. J. White had successfully transplanted a monkey's head on to another monkey's body.[1] Dr. White was reported as having said, "Technically a human head transplant is possible," and as hoping that "it may be possible eventually to transplant *parts* of the brain or other organs inside the head."

The possibility of brain transplants gives rise to a fascinating philosophical problem. Imagine the following situation:

> Two men, a Mr. Brown and a Mr. Robinson, had been operated on for brain tumours and brain extractions had been performed on both of them. At the end of the operations, however, the assistant inadvertently put Brown's brain in Robinson's head, and Robinson's brain in Brown's head. One of these men immediately dies, but the other, the one with Robinson's body and Brown's brain, eventually regains consciousness. Let us call the latter "Brownson." Upon regaining consciousness Brownson exhibits great shock and surprise at the appearance of his body. Then, upon seeing Brown's body, he exclaims incredulously "That's me lying there!" Pointing to himself as he says "This isn't my body; the one over there is!" When asked his name he automatically replies "Brown." He recognizes Brown's wife and family (whom Robinson had never met), and is able to describe in detail events in Brown's life, always describing them as events in his own life. Of Robinson's past life he evinces no knowledge at all. Over a period of time he is observed to display all of the personality traits, mannerisms, interests, likes and dislikes, and so on, that had previously characterized Brown, and to act and talk in ways completely alien to the old Robinson.[2]

"Brain Transplants and Personal Identity" from *Philosophy in the Open* edited by Godfrey Vesey, Open University Press, 1974.

[1]*Sunday Times* (London: December 9, 1973), p. 13.

[2]Sydney Shoemaker, *Self-Knowledge and Self-Identity* (New York: Cornell University Press, 1963).

The next step is to suppose that Brown's brain is not simply transplanted whole into someone else's brainless head, but is divided in two and half put into each of *two* other people's brainless heads. The same memory having been coded in many parts of the cortex, they *both* then say they are Brown, are able to describe events in Brown's life as if they are events in their own lives, etc. What should we say now?

The implications of this case for what we should say about personal identity are considered by Derek Parfit in a paper entitled "Personal Identity." Parfit's own view is expressed in terms of a relationship he calls "psychological continuity." He analyses this relationship partly in terms of what he calls "*q*-memory" ("*q*" stands for "quasi"). He sketches a definition of "*q*-memory" as follows:

> I am q-remembering an experience if (1) I have a belief about a past experience which seems in itself like a memory belief, (2) someone did have such an experience, and (3) my belief is dependent upon this experience in the same way (whatever that is) in which a memory of an experience is dependent upon it.[3]

The significance of this definition of *q*-memory is that two people can, in theory, *q*-remember doing what only one person did. So two people can, in theory, be psychologically continuous with one person.

Parfit's thesis is that there is nothing more to personal identity than this "psychological continuity." This is *not* to say that whenever there is a sufficient degree of psychological continuity there is personal identity, for psychological continuity could be a one-two, or "branching," relationship, and we are able to speak of "identity" only when there is a one-one relationship. It *is* to say that a common belief—in the special nature of personal identity—is mistaken.

In the discussion that follows I began by asking Parfit what he thinks of this common belief. Derek Parfit is a Fellow of All Souls, Oxford.

PERSONAL IDENTITY

VESEY   Derek, can we begin with the belief that you claim most of us have about personal identity? It's this: whatever happens between now and some future time either I shall still exist or I shan't. And any future experience will either be my experience or it won't. In other words, personal identity is an all or nothing matter: either I survive or I don't. Now what do you want to say about that?

PARFIT   It seems to me just false. I think the true view is that we can easily describe and imagine large numbers of cases in which the question, "Will the future person be me—or someone else?," is both a question which doesn't have any answer at all, and there's no puzzle that there's no answer.

---

[3]Derek Parfit, "Personal Identity," *The Philosophical Review,* Vol. 80, p. 15.

VESEY   Will you describe one such case?

PARFIT   One of them is the case discussed in the correspondence material, the case of division in which we suppose that each half of my brain is to be transplanted into a new body and the two resulting people will both seem to remember the whole of my life, have my character and be psychologically continuous with me in every way. Now in this case of division there were only three possible answers to the question, "What's going to happen to *me?*" And all three of them seem to me open to very serious objections. So the conclusion to be drawn from the case is that the question of what's going to happen to me, just doesn't have an answer. I think the case also shows that that's not mysterious at all.

VESEY   Right, let's deal with these three possibilities in turn.

PARFIT   Well, the first is that I'm going to be both of the resulting people. What's wrong with that answer is that it leads very quickly to a contradiction.

VESEY   How?

PARFIT   The two resulting people are going to be different people from each other. They're going to live completely different lives. They're going to be as different as any two people are. But if they're different people from each other it can't be the case that I'm going to be both of them. Because if I'm both of them, then one of the resulting people is going to be the same person as the other.

VESEY   Yes. They can't be different people and be the same person, namely me.

PARFIT   Exactly. So the first answer leads to a contradiction.

VESEY   Yes. And the second?

PARFIT   Well, the second possible answer is that I'm not going to be both of them but just one of them. This doesn't lead to a contradiction, it's just wildly implausible. It's implausible because my relation to each of the resulting people is exactly similar.

VESEY   Yes, so there's no reason to say that I'm one rather than the other?

PARFIT   It just seems absurd to suppose that, when you've got exactly the same relation, one of them is identity and the other is nothing at all.

VESEY   It does seem absurd, but there are philosophers who would say that sort of thing. Let's go on to the third.

PARFIT   Well, the only remaining answer, if I'm not going to be both of them or only one of them, is that I'm going to be neither of them. What's wrong with this answer is that it's grossly misleading.

VESEY   Why?

PARFIT   If I'm going to be neither of them, then there's not going to be anyone in the world after the operation who's going to be me. And that implies, given the way we now think, that the operation is as bad as death. Because if there's going to be no one who's going to be me, then I cease to exist. But it's obvious on reflection that the operation isn't as bad as death. It isn't bad in any way at all. That this is obvious can be shown by supposing that when they do the operation only one of the transplants succeeds and only one of the resulting people ever comes to consciousness again.

VESEY   Then I think we would say that this person is me. I mean we'd have no reason to say that he wasn't.

PARFIT   On reflection I'm sure we would all think that I would survive as that one person.

VESEY   Yes.

PARFIT   Yes. Well, if we now go back to the case where both operations succeed . . .

VESEY   Where there's a double success . . .

PARFIT   It's clearly absurd to suppose that a double success is a failure.

VESEY   Yes.

PARFIT   So the conclusion that I would draw from this case is firstly, that to the question, "What's going to happen to me?," there's no true answer.

VESEY   Yes.

PARFIT   Secondly, that if we decide to say one of the three possible answers, what we say is going to obscure the true nature of the case.

VESEY   Yes.

PARFIT   And, thirdly, the case isn't in any way puzzling. And the reason for that is this. My relation to each of the resulting people is the relation of full psychological continuity. When I'm psychologically continuous with only one person, we call it identity. But if I'm psychologically continuous with two future people, we can't call it identity. It's puzzling because we know exactly what's going to happen.

VESEY   Yes, could I see if I've got this straight? Where there is psychological continuity in a one-one case, this is the sort of case which we'd ordinarily talk of in terms of a person having survived the operation, or something like that.

PARFIT   Yes.

VESEY   Now what about when there is what you call psychological continuity—that's to say, where the people seem to remember having been me and so on—in a one-two case? Is this survival or not?

PARFIT   Well, I think it's just as good as survival, but the block we have to get over is that we can't say that anyone in the world after the operation is going to be me.

VESEY   No.

PARFIT   Well, we can say it but it's very implausible. And we're inclined to think that if there's not going to be anyone who is me tomorrow, then I don't survive. What we need to realize is that my relation to each of those two people is just as good as survival. Nothing is missing at all in my relation to both of them, as compared with my relation to myself tomorrow.

VESEY   Yes.

PARFIT   So here we've got survival without identity. And that only seems puzzling if we think that identity is a further fact over and above psychological continuity.

VESEY   It is very hard not to think of identity being a further fact, isn't it?

PARFIT   Yes, I think it is. I think that the only way to get rid of our temptation to believe this is to consider many more cases than this one case of division. Perhaps I should give you another one. Suppose that the following is going to happen to me. When I die in a normal way, scientists are going to map the states of all the cells in my brain and body and after a few months they will have constructed a perfect duplicate of me out of organic matter. And this duplicate will wake up fully psychologically continuous with me, seeming to remember my life with my character, etc.

VESEY   Yes.

PARFIT   Now in this case, which is a secular version of the Resurrection, we're very inclined to think that the following question arises and is very real and very important. The question is, "Will that person who wakes up in three months be me or will he be some quite other person who's merely artificially made to be exactly like me?"

VESEY   It does seem to be a real question. I mean in the one case, if it is going to be me, then I have expectations and so on, and in the other case, where it isn't me, I don't.

PARFIT   I agree, it seems as if there couldn't be a bigger difference between it being me and it being someone else.

VESEY   But you want to say that the two possibilities are in fact the same?

PARFIT   I want to say that those two descriptions, "It's going to be me" and "It's going to be someone who is merely exactly like me," don't describe different outcomes, different courses of events, only one of which can happen. They are two ways of describing one and the same course of events. What I mean by that perhaps could be shown if we take an exactly comparable case involving not a person but something about which I think we're not inclined to have a false view.

VESEY   Yes.

PARFIT   Something like a club. Suppose there's some club in the nineteenth century . . .

VESEY   The Sherlock Holmes Club or something like that?

PARFIT   Yes, perhaps. And after several years of meeting it ceases to meet. The club dies.

VESEY   Right.

PARFIT   And then two of its members, let's say, have emigrated to America, and after about fifteen years they get together and they start up a club. It has exactly the same rules, completely new membership except for the first two people, and they give it the same name. Now suppose someone came along and said: "There's a real mystery here, because the following question is one that must have an answer. But how can we answer it?" The question is, "Have they started up the very same club—is it the same club as the one they belonged to in England—or is it a completely new club that's just exactly similar?"

VESEY   Yes.

PARFIT   Well, in that case we all think that this man's remark is absurd; there's no difference at all. Now that's my model for the true view about the case where they make a duplicate of me. It seems that there's all the difference in the world between its being me and its being this other person who's exactly like me. But if we think there's no difference at all in the case of the clubs, why do we think there's a difference in the case of personal identity, and how can we defend the view that there's a difference?

VESEY   I can see how some people would defend it. I mean, a dualist would defend it in terms of a soul being a simple thing, but . . .

PARFIT   Let me try another case which I think helps to ease us out of this belief we're very strongly inclined to hold.

VESEY   Go on.

PARFIT   Well, this isn't a single case, this is a whole range of cases. A whole smooth spectrum of different cases which are all very similar to the next one in the range. At the start of this range of cases you suppose that the scientists are going to replace one per cent of the cells in your brain and body with exact duplicates.

VESEY   Yes.

PARFIT   Now if that were to be done, no one has any doubt that you'd survive. I think that's obvious because after all you can *lose* one per cent of the cells and survive. As we get further along the range they replace a larger and larger percentage of cells with exact duplicates, and of course at the far end of this range, where they replace a hundred per cent, then we've got my case where they just make a duplicate out of wholly fresh matter.

VESEY   Yes.

PARFIT   Now on the view that there's all the difference in the world between its being me and its being this other person who is exactly like me, we ought in consistency to think that in some case in the middle of the range, where, say, they're going to replace fifty per cent, the same question arises: is it going to be me or this completely different character? I think that even the most convinced dualist who believes in the soul is going to find this range of cases very embarrassing, because he seems committed to the view that there's some crucial percentage up to which it's going to be him and after which it suddenly ceases to be him. But I find that wholly unbelievable.

VESEY   Yes. He's going to have to invent some sort of theory about the relation of mind and body to get round this one. I'm not quite sure how he would do it. Derek, could we go on to a related question? Suppose that I accepted what you said, that is, that there isn't anything more to identity than what you call psychological continuity in a one-one case. Suppose I accept that, then I would want to go on and ask you, well, what's the philosophical importance of this?

PARFIT   The philosophical importance is, I think, that psychological continuity is obviously, when we think about it, a matter of degree. So long as we think that identity is a further fact, one of the things we're inclined to think is that it's all or nothing, as you said earlier. Well, if we give up that belief and if we realize that what matters in my continued existence is a matter of degree, then this does make a difference in actual cases. All the cases that I've considered so far are of course bizarre science fiction cases. But I think that in actual life it's obvious on reflection that, to give an example, the relations between me now and me next year are much closer in every way than the relation between me now and me in twenty years. And the sorts of relations that I'm thinking of are relations of memory, character, ambition, intention—all of those. Next year I shall remember much more of this year than I will in twenty years. I shall have a much more similar character. I shall be carrying out more of the same plans, ambitions and, if that is so, I think there are various plausible implications for our moral beliefs and various possible effects on our emotions.

VESEY   For our moral beliefs? What have you in mind?

PARFIT   Let's take one very simple example. On the view which I'm sketching it seems to me much more plausible to claim that people deserve much less punishment, or even perhaps no punishment, for what they did many years ago as compared with what they did very recently. Plausible because the relations between them now and them many years ago when they committed the crime are so much weaker.

VESEY   But they are still the people who are responsible for the crime.

PARFIT   I think you say that because even if they've changed in many ways, after all it was just as much they who committed the crime. I think that's true, but on the view for which I'm arguing, we would come to think that it's a completely trivial truth. It's like the following truth: it's like the truth that all of my relatives are just as much my relatives. Suppose I in my will left more money to my close relatives and less to my distant relatives; a mere pittance to my second cousin twenty-nine times removed. If you said, "But that's clearly unreasonable because all of your relatives are just as much your relatives," there's a sense in which that's true but it's obviously too trivial to make my will an unreasonable will. And that's because what's involved in kinship is a matter of degree.

VESEY   Yes.

PARFIT   Now, if we think that what's involved in its being the same person now as the person who committed the crime is a matter of degree, then the truth that it was just as much him who committed the crime, will seem to us trivial in the way in which the truth that all my relatives are equally my relatives is trivial.

VESEY   Yes. So you think that I should regard myself in twenty years' time as like a fairly distant relative of myself?

PARFIT   Well, I don't want to exaggerate; I think the connections are much closer.

VESEY   Suppose I said that this point about psychological continuity being a matter of degree—suppose I said that this isn't anything that anybody denies?

PARFIT   I don't think anybody does on reflection deny that psychological continuity is a matter of degree. But I think what they may deny, and I think what may make a difference to their view, if they come over to the view for which I'm arguing—what they may deny is that psychological continuity is all there is to identity. Because what I'm arguing against is this further belief which I think we're all inclined to hold even if we don't realize it. The belief that however much we change, there's a profound sense in which the changed us is going to be just as much us. That even if some magic wand turned me into a completely different sort of person—a prince with totally different character, mental powers—it would be just as much me. That's what I'm denying.

VESEY   Yes. This is the belief which I began by stating, and I think that if we did lose that belief that would be a change indeed.

Are People Machines?

48. *Can a Machine Think?*

Christopher Evans

Christopher Evans (1931–1979) was an experimental psychologist and computer scientist. He wrote several books on various aspects of psychology.

In the early years of the second world war when the British began, in ultra-secret, to put together their effort to crack German codes, they set out to recruit a team of the brightest minds available in mathematics and the then rather novel field of electronic engineering. Recruiting the electronic whizzes was easy, as many of them were to be found engrossed in the fascinating problem of radio location of aircraft— or radar as it later came to be called. Finding mathematicians with the right kind of obsessive brilliance to make a contribution in the strange field of cryptography was another matter. In the end they adopted the ingenious strategy of searching through lists of young mathematicians who were also top-flight chess players. As a result of a nationwide trawl an amazing collection of characters were billeted together in the country-house surroundings of Bletchley Park, and three of the most remarkable were Irving John Good, Donald Michie, and Alan Turing. . . .

If contemporary accounts of what the workers at Bletchley were talking about in their few moments of spare time can be relied on, many of them were a bit over-optimistic if anything. Both Good and Michie believed that the use of electronic computers such as Colossus* would result in major advances in mathematics in the immediate post-war era and Turing was of the same opinion. All three (and one or two of their colleagues) were also confident that it would not be long before machines were exhibiting intelligence, including problem-solving abilities, and that their role as simple number-crunchers was only one phase in their evolution. Although the exact substance of their conversations, carried long into the night when they were waiting for the test results of the first creaky Colossus prototypes, has softened with passage of time, it is known the topic of machine intelligence loomed very large. They discussed, with a *frisson* of excitement and unease, the peculiar ramifications of the subject they were pioneering and about which the rest of the world knew (and still knows) so little. Could there ever be a machine which was able

From *The Micro Millennium* by Christopher Evans. Copyright © 1979 by Christopher Evans. Reprinted by permission of Viking Penguin, a division of Penguin Books USA Inc.

* An early computer that was first used in 1943.—Ed.

to solve problems that no human could solve? Could a computer ever beat a human at chess? Lastly, could a machine *think?*

Of all the questions that can be asked about computers none has such an eerie ring. Allow a machine intelligence perhaps, the ability to control other machines, repair itself, help us solve problems, compute numbers a million fold quicker than any human; allow it to fly airplanes, drive cars, superintend our medical records and even, possibly, give advice to politicians. Somehow you can see how a machine might come to do all these things. But that it could be made to perform that apparently exclusively human operation known as *thinking* is something else, and something which is offensive, alien and threatening. Only in the most *outré* forms of science fiction, stretching back to Mary Shelley's masterpiece *Frankenstein,* is the topic touched on, and always with a sense of great uncertainty about the enigmatic nature of the problem area.

Good, Michie and their companions were content to work the ideas through in their spare moments. But Turing—older, a touch more serious and less cavalier—set out to consider things in depth. In particular he addressed himself to the critical question: Can, or could, a machine think? The way he set out to do this three decades ago and long before any other scientists had considered it so cogently, is of lasting interest. The main thesis was published in the philosophical journal *Mind* in 1950. Logically unassailable, when read impartially it serves to break down any barriers of uncertainty which surround this and parallel questions. Despite its classic status the work is seldom read outside the fields of computer science and philosophy, but now that events in computer science and in the field of artificial intelligence are beginning to move with the rapidity and momentum which the Bletchley scientists knew they ultimately would, the time has come for Turing's paper to achieve a wider public.

Soon after the war ended and the Colossus project folded, Turing joined the National Physical Laboratory in Teddington and began to work with a gifted team on the design of what was to become the world's most powerful computer, ACE. Later he moved to Manchester, where, spurred by the pioneers Kilburn, Hartee, Williams and Newman, a vigorous effort was being applied to develop another powerful electronic machine. It was a heady, hard-driving time, comparable to the state of events now prevailing in microprocessors, when anyone with special knowledge rushes along under immense pressure, ever conscious of the feeling that whoever is second in the race may as well not have entered it at all. As a result Turing found less time than he would have hoped to follow up his private hobbies, particularly his ideas on computer game-playing—checkers, chess and the ancient game of Go—which he saw was an important sub-set of machine intelligence.

Games like chess are unarguably intellectual pursuits, and yet, unlike certain other intellectual exercises, such as writing poetry or discussing the inconsistent football of the hometown team, they have easily describable rules of operation. The task, therefore, would seem to be simply a matter of writing a computer program which "knew" these rules and which could follow them when faced with moves offered by a human player. Turing made very little headway as it happens, and the first chess-playing programs which were scratched together in the late '40s and early '50s were quite awful—so much so that there was a strong feeling that this kind of project was not worth pursuing, since the game of chess as played by an "expert" involves some special intellectual skill which could never be specified in machine terms.

Turing found this ready dismissal of the computer's potential to be both interesting and suggestive. If people were unwilling to accept the idea of a machine which could play games, how would they feel about one which exhibited "intelligence," or one which could "think"? In the course of discussions with friends Turing found that a good part of the problem was that people were universally unsure of their definitions. What exactly did one mean when one used the word "thought"? What processes were actually in action when "thinking" took place? If a machine was created which *could* think, how would one set about testing it? The last question, Turing surmised, was the key one, and with a wonderful surge of imagination spotted a way to answer it, proposing what has in computer circles come to be known as "The Turing Test for Thinking Machines." In the next section, we will examine that test, see how workable it is, and also try to assess how close computers have come, and will come, to passing it.

When Turing asked people whether they believed that a computer could think, he found almost universal rejection of the idea—just as I did when I carried out a similar survey almost thirty years later. The objections I received were similar to those that Turing documented in his paper "Computing Machinery and Intelligence,"* and I will summarize them here, adding my own comments and trying to meet the various objections as they occur.

First there is the Theological Objection. This was more common in Turing's time than it is now, but it still crops up occasionally. It can be summed up as follows: "Man is a creation of God, and has been given a soul and the power of conscious thought. Machines are not spiritual beings, have no soul and thus must be incapable of thought." As Turing pointed out, this seems to place an unwarranted restriction on God. Why shouldn't he give machines souls and allow them to think if he wanted to? On one level I suppose it is irrefutable: if someone chooses to define thinking as something that *only* Man can do and that *only* God can bestow, then that is the end of the matter. Even then the force of the argument does seem to depend upon a confusion between "thought" and "spirituality," upon the old Cartesian dichotomy of the ghost in the machine. The ghost presumably does the thinking while the machine is merely the vehicle which carries the ghost around.

Then there is the Shock/Horror Objection, which Turing called the "Heads in the Sand Objection." Both phrases will do though I prefer my own. When the subject of machine thought is first broached, a common reaction goes something like this: "What a horrible idea! How could any scientist work on such a monstrous development? I hope to goodness that the field of artificial intelligence doesn't

---

* Published in *Mind*, Vol. LIX (October, 1950).—Ed.

advance a step further if its end-product is a thinking machine!" The attitude is not very logical—and it is not really an argument why it *could* not happen, but rather the expression of a heartfelt wish that it never will!

The Extra-sensory Perception Objection was the one that impressed Turing most, and impresses me least. *If* there were such a thing as extra-sensory perception and *if* it were in some way a function of human brains, then it could well also be an important constituent of thought. By this token, in the absence of any evidence proving that computers are telepathic, we would have to assume that they could never be capable of thinking in its fullest sense. The same argument applies to any other "psychic" or spiritual component of human psychology. I cannot take this objection seriously because there seems to me to be no evidence which carries any scientific weight that extra-sensory perception does exist. The situation was different in Turing's time, when the world-renowned parapsychology laboratory at Duke University in North Carolina, under Dr. J. B. Rhine, was generating an enormous amount of material supposedly offering evidence for telepathy and precognition. This is not the place to go into the long, and by no means conclusive, arguments about the declining status of parapsychology, but it is certainly true that as far as most scientists are concerned, what once looked like a rather good case for the existence of telepathy, etc., now seems to be an extremely thin one. But even if ESP *is* shown to be a genuine phenomenon, it is, in my own view, something to do with the transmission of information from a source point to a receiver and ought therefore to be quite easy to reproduce in a machine. After all, machines can communicate by radio already, which is, effectively, ESP and is a far better method of long-distance communication than that possessed by any biological system.

The Personal Consciousness Objection is, superficially, a rather potent argument which comes up in various guises. Turing noticed it expressed particularly cogently in a report, in the *British Medical Journal* in 1949, on the Lister Oration for that year, which was entitled "The Mind of Mechanical Man." It was given by a distinguished medical scientist, Professor G. Jefferson. A short quote from the Oration will suffice:

> Not until a machine can write a sonnet or compose a concerto *because of thoughts and emotions felt,* and not by the chance fall of symbols, could we agree that machine equals brain—that is, not only write it but *know that it had written it.* No mechanism could feel (and not merely artificially signal, an easy contrivance) pleasure at its successes, grief when its valves fuse, be warmed by flattery, be made miserable by its mistakes, be charmed by sex, be angry or depressed when it cannot get what it wants.

The italics, which are mine, highlight what I believe to be the fundamental objection: the output of the machine is more or less irrelevant, no matter how impressive it is. Even if it wrote a sonnet—and a very good one—it would not mean much unless it had written it as the result of "thoughts and emotions felt," and it would also have to "know that it had written it." This could be a useful "final definition" of one aspect of human thought—but how would you establish whether or not the sonnet was written with "emotions"? Asking the computer would not help for, as Professor Jefferson realized, there would be no guarantee that it was not simply *declaring* that it had felt emotions. He is really propounding the extreme solipsist position and should, therefore, apply the same rules to humans. Extreme solipsism is logically irrefutable ("I am the only real thing; all else is illusion") but it is so unhelpful a view of the universe that most people choose to ignore it and decide that when people say they are thinking or feeling they may as well believe them. In other words, Professor Jefferson's objection could be over-ridden if you *became* the computer and experienced its thoughts (if any)—only then could you really *know.* His objection is worth discussing in some depth because it is so commonly heard in one form or another, and because it sets us up in part for Turing's resolution of the machine-thought problem, which we will come to later.

The Unpredictability Objection argues that computers are created by humans according to sets of rules and operate according to carefully scripted programs which themselves are sets of rules. So if you wanted to, you could work out exactly what a computer was going to do at any particular time. It is, in principle, totally predictable. *If* you have all the facts available you *can* predict a computer's behavior because it follows rules, whereas there is no way in which you could hope to do the same with a human *because he is not behaving according to a set of immutable rules.* Thus there is an essential difference between computers and humans, so (the argument gets rather weak here) thinking, because it is unpredictable and does not blindly follow rules, must be an essentially human ability.

There are two comments: firstly, computers are becoming so complex that it is doubtful their behavior could be predicted even if everything was known about them—computer programmers and engineers have found that one of the striking characteristics of present-day systems is that they constantly spring surprises. The second point follows naturally: humans are *already* in that super-complex state and the reason that we cannot predict what they do is *not* because they have no ground rules but because (a) we don't know what the rules are, and (b) even if we did know them they would still be too complicated to handle. At best, the unpredictability argument is thin, but it is often raised. People frequently remark that there is always "the element of surprise" in a human. I have no doubt that that is just because *any* very complex system is bound to be surprising. A variant of the argument is that humans are capable of error whereas the "perfect" computer is not. That may well be true, which suggests that machines are superior to humans, for there seems to be little point in having any information-processing system, biological or electronic, that makes errors in processing. It would be possible to build a random element into computers to make them unpredictable from time to time, but it would be a peculiarly pointless exercise.

The "See How Stupid They Are" Objection will not need much introduction. At one level it is expressed in jokes about computers that generate ridiculous bank statements or electricity bills; at another and subtler level, it is a fair appraisal of the computer's stupendous weaknesses in comparison with Man. "How could you possibly imagine that such backward, limited things could ever reach the point where they could be said to think?" The answer, as we have already pointed out, is that they may be dumb now but they have advanced at a pretty dramatic rate and show every sign of continuing to do so. Their present limitations may be valid when arguing whether they could be said to be capable of thinking *now* or in the *very* near future, but it has no relevance to whether they would be capable of thinking at some later date.

The "Ah But It Can't Do That" Objection is an eternally regressing argument which, for a quarter of a century, computer scientists have been listening to, partially refuting, and then having to listen to all over again. It runs: "Oh yes, you can obviously make a computer do so and so—you have just demonstrated that, but of course you will never be able to make it do such and such." The such and such may be anything you name—once it was play a good game of chess, have a storage capacity greater than the human memory, read human hand-writing or understand human speech. Now that these "Ah buts" have (quite swiftly) been overcome, one is faced by a new range: beat the world human chess champion, operate on parallel as opposed to serial processing, perform medical diagnosis better than a doctor, translate satisfactorily from one language to another, help solve its own software problems, etc. When these challenges are met, no doubt it will have to design a complete city from scratch, invent a game more interesting than chess, admire a pretty girl/handsome man, work out the unified field theory, enjoy bacon and eggs, and so on. I cannot think of anything more silly than developing a computer which could enjoy bacon and eggs, but there is nothing to suggest that, provided enough time and money was invested, one could not pull off such a surrealistic venture. On the other hand, it might be *most* useful to have computers design safe, optimally cheap buildings. Even more ambitious (and perhaps comparable to the bacon and egg project but more worthwhile) would be to set a system to tackle the problem of the relationship between gravity and light, and my own guess is that before the conclusion of the long-term future (before the start of the twenty-first century), computers will be hard at work on these problems and will be having great success.

The "It Is Not Biological" Objection may seem like another version of the theological objection—only living things could have the capacity for thought, so nonbiological systems could not possibly think. But there is a subtle edge that requires a bit more explanation. It is a characteristic of most modern computers that they are discrete state machines, which is to say that they are digital and operate in a series of discrete steps—on/off. Now the biological central nervous system may not be so obviously digital, though there is evidence that the neurone, the basic unit of communication, acts in an on/off, all or nothing way. But if it turned out that it were *not,* and operated on some more elaborate strategy, then it is conceivable that "thought" might only be manifest in things which had switching systems of this more elaborate kind. Put it another way: it might be possible to build digital computers which were immensely intelligent, but no matter how intelligent they became they would never be able to *think.* The argument cannot be refuted at the moment, but even so there is no shred of evidence to suppose that only non-digital systems can think. There may be other facets of living things that make them unique from the point of view of their capacity to generate thought, but none that we can identify, or even guess at. This objection therefore is not a valid one at present, though in the event of some new biological discovery, it may became so.

The Mathematical Objection is one of the most intriguing of the ten objections, and is the one most frequently encountered in discussions with academics. It is based on a fascinating exercise in mathematical logic propounded by the Hungarian Kurt Gödel. To put it rather superficially, Gödel's theorem shows that within any sufficiently powerful logical system (which could be a computer operating according to clearly defined rules), statements can be formulated which can neither be proved nor disproved *within the system*. In his famous 1936 paper, Alan Turing restructured Gödel's theorem so that it could apply specifically to machines. This effectively states that no matter how powerful a computer is, there are bound to be certain tasks that it cannot tackle on its own. In other words, you could not build a computer which could solve *every* problem no matter how well it was programmed; or, if you wanted to carry the thing to the realms of fancy, no computer (or any other digital system) could end up being God.

Gödel's theorem, and its later refinements by Alonzo Church, Bertrand Russell and others, is interesting to mathematicians, not so much because it assumes an implicit limitation to machine intelligence, but because it indicates a limitation to mathematics itself. But the theorem has been used, incorrectly, by critics of machine intelligence to "prove" that computers could never reach the same intellectual level as Man. The weakness of the position is that it is based on the assumption that the human brain is not a formal logical system. But such evidence as we have suggests very strongly that it is and will, therefore, be bound by the same Gödel-limitations as are machines. There is also a tweak in the tail. While the theorem admittedly states that no system *on its own* can completely tackle its own problems—"understand itself"—it does *not* imply that the areas of mystery could not be tackled by some other system. No individual human brain could solve its own problems or fully "know itself," but with the assistance of other brains these deficiencies might be corrected. Equally, and significantly, problem areas associated with complex computer systems could be solved totally and absolutely by other computer systems, provided that *they* were clever enough.

The last of the ten arguments against the concept of a thinking machine has become known as Lady Lovelace's Objection. . . . In its modern form this comes up as, "A Computer cannot do anything that you have not programmed it to." The objection is so fundamental and so widely accepted that it needs detailed discussion.

In the most absolute and literal sense, this statement is perfectly correct and applies to any machine or computer that has been made or that could be made. According to the rules of the universe that we live in, nothing can take place without a prior cause; a computer will not spring into action without something powering it and guiding it on its way. In the case of the various tasks that a computer performs, the "cause"—to stretch the use of the word rather—is the program or sets of programs that control these tasks. Much the same applies to a brain: it, too, must come equipped with sets of programs which cause it to run through its repertoire of tasks. This might seem to support Lady Lovelace, at least to the extent that machines "need" a human to set them up, but it would also seem to invalidate the argument that this constitutes an essential difference between computers and people. But is there not still a crucial difference between brains and computers? No matter how sophisticated computers are, must there not always have been a human being to *write* its programs? Surely the same does not have to be said for humans?

To tackle this we need to remember that all brains, human included, are equipped at birth with a comprehensive collection of programs which are common to all members of a species and which are known as instincts. These control respiration, gastric absorption, cardiac activity, and, at a behavioral level, such reflexes as sucking, eyeblink, grasping and so on. There may also be programs which "cause" the young animal to explore its environment, exercise its muscles, play and so on. Where do these come from? Well, they are acquired over an immensely long-winded trial-and-error process through the course of evolution. We might call them permanent software ("firmware" is the phrase used sometimes by computer scientists) and they correspond to the suites of programs which every computer has when it leaves the factory, and which are to do with its basic running, maintenance, and so on.

In addition to this, all biological computers come equipped with a bank of what might best be described as raw programs. No one has the faintest idea whether they are neurological, biochemical, electrical or what—all we know is that they *must* exist. They start being laid down the moment the creature begins to interact with the world around it. In the course of time they build up into a colossal suite of software which ultimately enables us to talk, write, walk, read, enjoy bacon and eggs, appreciate music, think, feel, write books, or come up with mathematical ideas. These programs are useful only to the owner of that particular brain, vanish with his death and are quite separate from the "firmware."

If this seems too trivial a description of the magnificent field of human learning and achievement, it is only because anything appears trivial when you reduce it to its bare components: a fabulous sculpture to a quintillion highly similar electrons and protons, a microprocessor to a million impurities buried in a wafer of sand, the human brain into a collection of neurones, blood cells and chemical elements. What is not trivial is the endlessly devious, indescribably profound way in which these elements are structured to make up the whole. The real difference between the brain and most existing computers is that in the former, data acquisition and the initial writing and later modification of the program is done by a mechanism within the brain itself, while in the latter, the software is prepared outside and passed to the computer in its completed state. But I did use the word "most." In recent years increasing emphasis has been placed on the development of "adaptive" programs—software which can be modified and revised on the basis of the program's interaction with the environment. In simple terms these could be looked upon as "programs which learn for themselves," and they will, in due course, become an important feature of many powerful computer systems.

At this point the sceptic still has a few weapons in his armoury. The first is generally put in the form of the statement: "Ah, but even when computers *can* update their own software and acquire new programs for themselves, they will still only be doing this because of Man's ingenuity. Man may no longer actually write the programs, but had he not invented the idea of the self-adaptive program in the first place none of this could have happened." This is perfectly true but has little to do with whether or not computers could think, or perform any other intellectual exercise. It could place computers eternally in our debt, and we may be able to enjoy a smug sense of pride at having created them, but it offers no real restriction on their development.

The sceptic may also argue that no matter how clever or how intelligent you make computers, they will never be able to perform a creative task. Everything they do will inevitably spring from something they have been taught, have experienced or is the subject of some preexisting program. There are two points being made here. One is that computers could never have an original or creative thought. The other is that the seeds of everything they do, no matter how intelligent, lie in their existing software. To take the second point first: again one is forced to say that the same comment applies to humans. Unless the argument is that some of Man's thoughts or ideas come from genuine inspiration—a message from God, angels, or spirits of the departed—no one can dispute that all aspects of our intelligence evolve from preexisting programs and the background experiences of life. This evolution may be enormously complex and its progress might be impossible to track, but any intellectual flowering arises from the seeds of experience planted in the fertile substrate of the brain.

There still remains the point about creativity, and it is one that is full of pitfalls. Before making any assumptions about creativity being an *exclusive* attribute of Man, the concept has to be defined. It is not enough to say "write a poem," "paint a picture" or "discuss philosophical ideas," because it is easy enough to program computers to do all these things. The fact that their poems, paintings and philosophical ramblings are pretty mediocre is beside the point: it would be just as unfair to ask them to write, say, a sonnet of Shakespearian calibre or a painting of da Vinci quality and fail them for lack of creativity as it would be to give the same task to the man in the street. Beware too of repeating the old saying, "Ah, but you have to program them to paint, play chess and so on," for the same is unquestionably true of people. Try handing a twelve-month-old baby a pot of paint or a chessboard if you have any doubts about the need for some measure of learning and experience.

Obviously a crisper definition of creativity is required, and here is one that is almost universally acceptable: If a person demonstrates a skill which has never been demonstrated before and which was not specifically taught to him by someone else, or in the intellectual domain provides an *entirely novel* solution to a problem—

a solution which was not known to any other human being—then they can be said to have done something original or had an original or creative thought. There may be other forms of creativity of course, but this would undeniably be an example of it in action. There is plenty of evidence that humans are creative by this standard and the history of science is littered with "original" ideas which humans have generated. Clearly, until a computer also provides such evidence, Lady Lovelace's Objection still holds, at least in one of its forms.

But alas for the sceptics. This particular barrier has been overthrown by computers on a number of occasions in the past few years. A well-publicized one was the solution, by a computer, of the venerable "four colour problem." This has some mathematical importance, and can best be expressed by thinking of a two-dimensional map featuring a large number of territories, say the counties of England or the states of the USA. Supposing you want to give each territory a colour, what is the minimum number of colours you need to employ to ensure that no two territories of the same colour adjoin each other?

After fiddling around with maps and crayons, you will find that the number seems to come out at four, and no one has ever been able to find a configuration where five colours are required, or where you can always get away with three. Empirically, therefore, four is the answer—hence the name of the problem. But if you attempt to demonstrate this mathematically and *prove* that four colours will do for any conceivable map, you will get nowhere. For decades mathematicians have wrestled with this elusive problem, and from time to time have come up with a "proof" which in the end turns out to be incomplete or fallacious. But the mathematical world was rocked when in 1977 the problem was handed over to a computer, which attacked it with a stupendous frontal assault, sifting through huge combinations of possibilities and eventually demonstrating, to every mathematician's satisfaction, that four colours would do the trick. Actually, although this is spectacular testimony to the computer's creative powers, it is not really the most cogent example, for its technique was block-busting rather than heuristic (problem solving by testing hypotheses). It was like solving a chess problem by working out every possible combination of moves, rather than by concentrating on likely areas and experimenting with them. A better, and much earlier, demonstration of computer originality came from a program which was set to generate some totally new proofs in Euclidean geometry. The computer produced a completely novel proof of the well-known theorem which shows that the base angles of an isosceles triangle are equal, by flipping the triangles through 180 degrees and declaring them to be congruent. Quite apart from the fact that it had not before been known to Man, it showed such originality that one famous mathematician remarked, "If any of my students had done that, I would have marked him down as a budding genius."

And so Lady Lovelace's long-lasting objection can be overruled. We have shown that computers can be intelligent, and that they can even be creative—but we have not yet proved that they can, or ever could, *think*.

Now, what do we mean by the word "think"?

TOWARDS THE ULTRA-INTELLIGENT MACHINE

The most common objections raised to the notion of thinking machines are based on misunderstandings of fairly simple issues, or on semantic confusions of one kind or another. We are still left with the problem of defining the verb "to think," and in this section we will attempt to deal with this, or at least to discuss one particular and very compelling way of dealing with it. From this position we shall find ourselves drifting inevitably into a consideration of the problem of creating thinking machines, and in particular to the eerie concept of the Ultra-Intelligent Machine.

Most people believe that they know what they mean when they talk about "thinking" and have no difficulty identifying it when it is going on in their own heads. We are prepared to believe other human beings think because we have experience of it ourselves and accept that it is a common property of the human race. But we cannot make the same assumption about machines, and would be sceptical if one of them told us, no matter how persuasively, that it too was thinking. But sooner or later a machine will make just such a declaration and the question then will be, how do we decide whether to believe it or not?

When Turing tackled the machine-thought issue, he proposed a characteristically brilliant solution which, while not entirely free from flaws, is nevertheless the best that has yet been put forward. The key to it all, he pointed out, is to ask what the signs and signals are that humans give out, from which we infer that *they* are thinking. It is clearly a matter of *what kind of conversation we can have with them,* and has nothing to do with what kind of face they have and what kind of clothes they wear. Unfortunately physical appearances automatically set up prejudices in our minds, and if we were having a spirited conversation with a microprocessor we might be very sceptical about its capacity for thought, simply because it did not look like any thinking thing we had seen in the past. But we *would* be interested in what it had to say; and thus Turing invented his experiment or test.

Put a human—the judge or tester—in a room where there are two computer terminals, one connected to a computer, the other to a person. The judge, of course, does not know which terminal is connected to which, but can type into either terminal and receive typed messages back on them. Now the judge's job is to decide, by carrying out conversations with the entities on the end of the respective terminals, *which is which.* If the computer is very stupid, it will immediately be revealed as such and the human will have no difficulty identifying it. If it is bright, he may find that he can carry on quite a good conversation with it, though he may ultimately spot that it must be the computer. If it is exceptionally bright and has a wide range of knowledge, he may find it impossible to say whether it is the computer he is talking to or the person. In this case, Turing argues, the computer will have passed the test and could for all practical purposes be said to be a thinking machine.

The argument has a simple but compelling force: if the intellectual exchange we achieve with a machine is indistinguishable from that we have with a being we *know* to be thinking, then we are, to all intents and purposes, communicating with another thinking being. This, by the way, does not imply that the personal experience, state of consciousness, level of awareness or whatever, of the entity is going to be the same as that experienced by a human when he or she thinks, so the test is not for these particular qualities. They are not, in any case, the parameters which concern the observer.

At first the Turing Test may seem a surprising way of looking at the problem, but it is an extremely sensible way of approaching it. The question now arises: is any computer at present in existence capable of passing the test?—And if not, how long is it likely to be before one comes along? From time to time one laboratory or another claims that a computer has had at least a pretty good stab at it. Scientists using the big computer conferencing systems (each scientist has a terminal in his office and is connected to his colleagues via the computer, which acts as host and general message-sorter) often find it difficult to be sure, for a brief period of time at least, whether they are talking to the computer or to one of their colleagues. On one celebrated occasion at MIT, two scientists had been chatting via the network when one of them left the scene without telling the other, who carried on a cheery conversation with the computer under the assumption that he was talking to his friend. I have had the same spooky experience when chatting with computers which I have programmed myself, and often find their answers curiously perceptive and unpredictable.

To give another interesting example in the remarkable match played in Toronto in August 1978 between the International Chess Master David Levy, and the then computer chess champion of the world, Northwestern University's "Chess 4.7," the computer made a number of moves of an uncannily "human" nature. The effect was so powerful that Levy subsequently told me that he found it difficult to believe that he was not facing an outstanding human opponent. Few chess buffs who looked at the move-by-move transcripts of the match were, without prior knowledge, able to tell which had been made by the computer and which by the flesh-and-blood chess master. David Levy himself suggested that Chess 4.7 had effectively passed the Turing Test.

It would be nice to believe that I had been present on such an historic occasion, but this did not constitute a proper "pass." In the test as Turing formulated it, the judge is allowed to converse with either of his two mystery entities on any topic that he chooses, and he may use any conversational trick he wants. Furthermore he can continue the inquisition for as long as he wants, always seeking some clue that will force the computer to reveal itself. Both the computer and the human can lie if they want to in their attempts to fool the tester, so the answers to questions like "Are you the computer?" or "Do you watch much television?" will not give much away. Obviously any computer with a chance in hell of passing the test will have to have a pretty substantial bank of software at its disposal, and not just be extremely bright in one area. Chess 4.7 for example might look as though it was thinking if it was questioned about chess, or, better still, invited to play the game, but switch the area of discourse to human anatomy, politics or good restaurants and it would be shown up as a dunderhead.

As things stand at present, computers have quite a way to go before they jump the hurdle so cleverly laid out for them by Turing. But this should not be taken as providing unmitigated comfort for those who resist the notion of advanced machine intelligence. It should now be clear that the difference, in intellectual terms, between a human being and a computer is one of degree and not of kind.

Turing himself says in his *Mind* paper that he feels computers will have passed the test before the turn of the century, and there is little doubt that he would dearly have liked to live long enough to be around on the splendiferous occasion when "machine thinking" first occurred.

49. Human Beings and Machines

Jenny Teichman

Jenny Teichman teaches at Cambridge University in England. She is the author of several books and numerous journal articles on a wide range of philosophical issues.

Although we are mere sojourners on the surface of the planet, chained to a mere point in space, enduring but for a moment of time, the human mind is enabled not only to number worlds beyond the unassisted ken of mortal eye, but to trace the events of indefinite ages before the creation of our race, and is not even withheld from penetrating into the dark secrets of the ocean or the interior of the solid globe.

Charles Lyell, *Principles of Geology*

REDUCTIVE PHILOSOPHY AND OCCAM'S RAZOR

William of Occam (1300–48) proposed that the following rule be adopted when theorizing: *Do not multiply entities beyond necessity.* For example, if some phenomenon can be explained by postulating one cause there is no need to postulate two or three or more causes; the superfluous postulations should be razored away.

Reductive philosophy employs a generalized version of the Razor. A reductive ontology asks: What is everything made out of? Ancient answers include *All is water,* and *All is fire.* A more up-to-date reply would be *Everything is made of electrons.* In the philosophy of language a reductive strategist might try to show that the basic "atoms" of meaning are sentences, or words, or names, or labels, or marks on paper, or noises made by mouths.

Philosophical reductionism, or nothing-but-ism, appeals very strongly to a certain kind of temperament. Thinkers who wish to say "the world is nothing but such-and-such" often like to add "and language is nothing but . . .", "morality is nothing but . . .", "so-called truth is nothing but . . .", and so on. . . .

Reductive theories, whether ontological, epistemological or ethical, often turn out to be inadequate. The unwise use of Occam's Razor cuts off too much.

This chapter will discuss a currently popular view of the nature of human thought processes, namely, the theory that human thinking is nothing but a more complicated version of what goes on inside a computer.

The idea that human beings, or human brains, resemble sophisticated bits of machinery has been greatly bolstered by the armchair speculations of philosophers

From *Social Ethics* by Jenny Teichman (Oxford: Blackwell Publishers, 1996). Reprinted by permission.

involved with cognitive science. The implications, for ethical theory, of these speculations seem to hold no interest for cognitive scientists. Yet it is fair to say, I believe, that the ontology of the machine tends to encourage the view that the sanctity of human life is a mere superstition. For very often the overall psychological effect of breaking down a distinction is to reduce respect for one side of the distinction. If one knows that living matter is made up of carbon and oxygen and hydrogen one might find oneself asking: Is there anything ethically important about carbon? Or oxygen? What's so important, then, about living things? In short, a philosophy which speculates that human thought and thinking are reducible to the same kind of operations that occur in computers is not *logically* inconsistent with respect for human life but its *psychological* effect tends in that direction. That is because in such a philosophy the concept of human thinking is analysed in ways that do not mention life. However, there are good reasons for believing that a correct analysis of human thinking has to mention human life.

MACHINES AND METAPHORS

One important style of reductive philosophy about the nature of thought begins with Alan Turing's famous paper, published in the journal *Mind* in 1950, in which he states that the essence of thinking is the ability to give correct answers to certain sorts of question.[1] Turing believed, apparently, that thinking either is, or is whatever produces, the ability to answer questions in mathematics and logic. In his paper he reasons as follows. Imagine that a human being and a Universal Computing Machine are placed in a closed room (the "Turing Room"), with apparatus for sending and receiving written messages to and from an observer outside. The observer sends in questions and the man and the machine send back separate written replies. Turing says that the observer outside would not be able to tell which replies came from the machine and which from the man. He concludes that both the man and the machine would be thinking.

What is wrong with this picture? Well, we might object that to talk of machines thinking is to speak in metaphor and we might compare this metaphor with others. For example: men run on two legs, dogs run on four legs, and fish, who have no legs, cannot run at all; but water, which has no legs, and is not even alive, can run downhill. Some other legless and inanimate things—engines—can run without changing location!

The running of water and of engines is obviously metaphorical because real running, the paradigm of running, is running with legs. By parallel reasoning, it seems, we can argue that any account of non-metaphorical thinking must start with the paradigm case. Now the paradigm case here is human thinking and human thinking is part of human life. D. H. Mellor notes that the question whether

[1]Turing, A. "Computers and Intelligence." *Mind*, 59 (1950).

computers can think is interesting only if it is directed at finding out which operations of computers resemble the operations of a human mind.[2]

No doubt some readers will agree that the thinking of computers is like running without legs while others will insist that computers think in the literal sense. The reasons offered for the second, or Turingesque, opinion are fairly familiar. Modern computers perform tasks with great rapidity and so reach solutions not available to a human being in a human lifetime. Given a little help from hackers and other human operators modern computers can "communicate" with one another. Modern computers have feedback. Neurologists and biochemists tell us that brains, like computers, process information. We are told, too, that brains and computers seem to work in somewhat similar ways.

Those who hold that machine thinking is a metaphor will perhaps respond by saying that genuine thinking requires consciousness.

CONSCIOUSNESS AND INFORMATION-PROCESSING

Common sense tells us that consciousness is present in many living creatures: horses and dogs, seagulls and mice, and perhaps even ants and bees, are conscious. Do these animals think? Consciousness might be a precondition of thought but it isn't exactly the same thing. If a creature is thinking many would say that it must be conscious, but few, I believe, would make the opposite inference.

Entities which process information comprise a considerable variety. Some processors of information are thinkers who think while processing, others can think but do not necessarily think while processing, and others never think at all. Processors include complete animals and also parts of animals. Human beings and dolphins process information, and so too does the human eye and the dolphin eye, but an eye taken by itself does not think. Some creatures, even when complete, seem too simple to be thinking. Presumably an oyster can process information about the sea and the rock but it is not easy to believe that it thinks about these things. Even having a brain doesn't guarantee thought. Fish have brains, but do they think? I doubt whether we know the answer to that question. Then again, the amount of thought that goes with human information-processing varies a great deal. When students listen to lectures and take notes, or read books and write essays, they sometimes think and sometimes don't. Some students seem able to listen carefully and take careful notes without understanding much or anything of what the lecturer says. Some students seem able to skim through books and make reasonably coherent notes without having a clue as to what the books are saying. Listening accompanied by automatic note-taking, and reading followed by mindless plagiarism, are good examples of processing information, though not examples of good work.

---

[2]Mellor, D. H. "How Much of the Mind Is Like a Computer?" in his *Matters of Metaphysics.* Cambridge: Cambridge University Press, 1992.

LANGUAGE AND LANGUAGE RULES

One difference between mice and oysters on the one hand, and human beings and computers on the other, is that the mice and oysters do not have language (as far as we know) whereas computers and human beings do. But in spite of the fact that computers deal with codes and languages it is commonly said that they do not really think because they have syntax without semantics. What this slogan means is that computers use linguistic rules but don't know the meanings, the contents, of the strings of symbols which the rules generate.

Does this matter? Perhaps understanding content is not a necessary component in the use and understanding of language. Perhaps some human thinking is purely syntactical. If purely syntactical exercises are ever carried out by human beings, and if they then count as one kind of thinking, then computers too can think. (In *Grundgesetze* [vol. 2 section 90] Frege remarks that someone might follow rules in constructing formulae, and so write proofs, without having a clue as to what it all meant.)

The idea that communication depends on rules is quite important but it has often been over-emphasized. Communication requires first and foremost something to be communicated. It also requires a someone or a something in the set-up who understands the content of the communiqué.

Why don't computers have thoughts with content? Machines as we know them have no understanding of content because there is no place or way for that particular function to enter the system directly. Consider concrete nouns. Each noun has its own sense (or senses) stemming from connections between the word and the world. Human thinking first sets up, and then depends upon, connections between words and things. When it is said that computers have no semantics, part of what is meant, I suppose, is that computers are incapable of either seeing, or setting up, the connections between words and things.

Now it might be thought that the incapacity is due to the fact that computer outputs (words on a screen, for example) are caused by inputs consisting of physical phenomena (electrical impulses) which themselves have no representational function. But that cannot be the explanation. The question as to how merely physical inputs can eventuate in representation of content has not yet been explained, as far as I know, but it is certain that such inputs do result in representation of content because it is certain that this actually occurs in the case of the human brain. What goes into the human head, the input, is a lot of photons and sound waves and so on, which in themselves are mere physical phenomena, while much of the output is language and thoughts.

One huge difference between the computer and the brain is that the first (merely physical) inputs into human thinking are non- or pre-symbolic, whereas with a computer all inputs, including the earliest, already have representational roles, i.e., roles which *for us* are representational. Computers operate with symbols, that is, with physical things or marks or events which have already been given content *by us and for us*. The semantic function, the content, enters the system indirectly, via the human designer. But in the case of the brain the function enters the system directly, it comes straight off the world, as it were.

HUMAN BEINGS AND MACHINES

Causal chains of object–perception–belief are the beginnings of human thinking and the beginnings of any other animal thinking that there might be on our planet. If you should happen to truly believe that there is a dead rat in the vicinity that is either because you have been told so in words (symbols), or because you have seen or smelt something. In the latter case the input comes directly off the world. *Qua* input it is pre- or non-symbolic (it is a smell, for instance). True, the expression "dead rat" means something, and means what it does mean, partly because of its role in the language as a union of adjective and noun, partly because of the conventions that attach the particular words "deceased" and "rat" to these and those kinds of things, and partly because we use all words in rule-following ways. Nevertheless the history of how the expression got its meaning does not start with linguistic rules. The rules themselves arose from pre-meaning encounters between human beings equipped with eyes and brains and noses (on the one hand) and material objects in various states of florescence and decay (on the other).

In our world material things and their visible states not only govern the meanings of (many) words, they are also needed to initiate meanings. How, in our world, could things possibly be otherwise? The set-up which lies behind the computer's production of the marks "dead rat" is quite different. The computer did not start off by having a rat's body waved in front of its screen or jammed into its disc slot. The marks, the words, get into the computer's software but the object itself has no role.

VARIETIES OF THOUGHT

Human thinking is very various. Its species include (i) accurate or inaccurate mental input (perception, memory), (ii) poor or successful processing of information (reproducing, judging, calculating), and (iii) wise or unwise mental output (deciding, willing, planning). These major species of thinking belong to the intellectual aspect of mental life. Other species or aspects—such as fear, hope, expectation—do not fit neatly into the three categories just mentioned.

Wittgenstein argues that human thinking has no single essential feature but is a collection of processes, states and dispositions such as hoping, day-dreaming, imagining, predicting, concentration, worry, fear, belief and expectation.[3] To suppose that thinking is just one thing is like supposing that athletics is only one

[3]Wittgenstein, L. *Philosophical Investigations* (trans. G. E. M. Anscombe). Oxford: Blackwell, 1952.

thing—sprinting for instance—whereas athletics in fact includes hurdling and weight-lifting and archery and pole-vaulting and many other activities.

The comparison, however, is not helpful for those who wish to argue that computers do not think. Even though sprinting isn't the only kind of athletic activity, still, sprinters are athletes and by parallel reasoning we might say that, although human thinking has many forms, each form taken separately counts as thinking. So it could be argued that if a computer can do at least one of the things that count as human thinking then it too can think.

Computers do process information but in human beings the processing of information is *only one* of at least three species of *only one* aspect of thinking. The significance of this is that only a holistic theory which allows for connections between the varieties of thought can give an adequate account of human (paradigm) thinking.

THREE KINDS OF HOLISM

Human thinking, as Schopenhauer says, has a biological function. Man is an animal and animal thinking has a natural evolutionary history. Thus human thinking is holistic in the sense that it is an integral part of the natural life of human beings. The situation is quite otherwise with computers. The behaviour of a computer has no natural evolutionary history because the computer itself has no natural evolutionary history. The behaviour of a computer has no biological function because the computer is not a biological entity. Depriving a computer of its floppy discs will not upset it or make it ill or shorten its existence. Machine behaviour isn't dedicated to promoting the survival of the machine. Computers are not alive and they have no desires and so they cannot possibly be dominated by the will to live.

Thought is not only biologically holistic, it is also logically holistic, and causally holistic. We saw how Wittgenstein says that thinking comprises a collection of states and processes, yet even he does not suggest that thought is a ragbag. He speaks of family resemblances between different kinds of thinking and he describes some of the logical connections that hold between different states of mind.

Thinking is logically holistic in that there are necessary connections between many of its different varieties. Here are some examples. Beliefs entail other beliefs, of course, but so do emotions and intentions and expectations. Fear of failure, for instance, entails a belief that failure is possible. Decisions entail at least a few true or false beliefs about what is feasible and what is not. Gratitude entails belief in the existence of a benefactor, known or even unknown (W. E. Henley: "I thank whatever gods may be . . ."). Resentment entails a belief that you've been injured. And one's expectations might well entail a belief in astrology, or in Newton's laws, or in a principle of induction. In short it is not possible to be in states of mind such as fear, resentment, gratitude, expectation, hope and so on without also having beliefs.

Thinking is causally holistic because for every individual there will be many psychological connections between mental states of different types. Thus particular desires can produce particular intentions and particular beliefs can lead to particular wishes. In some people a wish that something or other be true will induce the belief that it *is* true.

Because human thinking is logically and causally holistic it is doubly impossible for a human being to be a believer and nothing else, or an intender and nothing else, or a resenter and nothing else, or a rememberer, planner, lover, hater, hoper, expecter and nothing else. The functions of computers, on the other hand, are not elements in suchlike networks. If (which is absurd) machines had beliefs and intentions those beliefs and intentions, so-called, would be truncated items. Machines lack the desires and instincts and emotions which are the product of evolution. The states of machines lack the logical connections that knit together beliefs and other human mental states. And although machine-states have electrical connections (of course), these could not mimic the links between human beliefs and desires and emotions because machines don't have any desires and emotions in the first place.

In people the network of connected beliefs and desires and intentions and emotions is immensely complicated. I surmise that the real reason why some folk deny that the other animals can think is the obscurely recognized fact that in other animals the networks are simpler than those in the human animal. It's not that other creatures have no beliefs or memories or emotions, on the contrary, it is very obvious that all the higher animals do. Their networks are simpler because animals, or anyway those we are most familiar with (dogs, cats, horses, cage birds), have fewer beliefs and plans than we do. They have fewer beliefs because they have less knowledge, and they have fewer plans and intentions, either because they do not measure time, or (perhaps) because their awareness of time and times is a lot less complicated than ours is. Their simpler networks are quantitatively different from ours but probably qualitatively similar. Their mental functions are holistic.

CONCLUSIONS

There are many kinds of human thinking. If each type counted as thinking, even when taken alone, then there is a case, but only a *prima facie* case, that computers can think.

Not all information-processing requires thought or understanding. Students, for example, can process information without understanding it.

Computer thought is unlike human thought because it is contentless, and it is contentless because it has no direct connection with the non-human natural world. There are fundamental connections between human language and its meanings, and the natural world. For human beings the natural world has two semantic roles. First, it initiates meaning in general. Second, in many cases it governs particular meanings. In the case of computers both these natural-world roles are filled by a human designer who already possesses language.

Human thinking is holistic—in three ways—and computer thinking is not. The mental activity of higher animals, though simpler than the human, is presumably holistic and in that way is closer to our human thinking than are the operations of computers.

There are thus big gulfs between human thinking and computer thinking. These gulfs are so wide that the word thinking when used of computers can only be a metaphor.

Yet metaphorical meanings sometimes supplant literal ones and become literal themselves. In a hundred years' time, as Turing hinted, people might say and believe that it is machines, and not human beings, which really think. If that state of affairs comes about it might become difficult to hang onto the respect for human life which is the foundation of moral thinking in general and of democratic social concepts in particular.

PROBLEMS AND PUZZLES

50. *Considerations Against the Belief in Immortality*

Durant Drake

Durant Drake (1878–1933) was a well-known American philosopher and a professor at Vassar College for many years. He was the author of many books and scholarly articles on a variety of philosophical topics.

(1) It takes no critical acumen to perceive the *prima facie* case against immortality. In all our experience a man's conscious life is bound up with the fortunes of his body. We see men stunned by a blow, we see their minds enfeebled by bodily injury, we see their bodies killed and with that their mental life apparently ended. Consciousness seems to be dependent upon the body's supply of food, air, and sleep, and its safety from harm. To suppose that when the bodily mechanism stops entirely, consciousness, which has been so subject to its influence, gains a new lease of life on its own account, has always been difficult for reflective persons. And this explains, no doubt, the pale and impotent existence which the ancients almost universally attributed to the dead.

(2) The rise of modern physiological psychology, showing us, as it does, the intimate correlation of mind and brain, increases the difficulties of faith. We have discovered that thinking tires the brain; or, to put it the other way, the fatigue of brain-cells retards and inhibits thinking. The loss of memory, weakening of the will, increase in petulance of old age go hand in hand with a degeneration of brain-tissue. Certain kinds of consciousness are bound up with specific parts of the brain; when a certain portion of the brain is diseased or injured, the mind is affected in a definite manner. Whatever may be the relation between brain and consciousness, the study of the close parallelism between their activities makes it harder to resist the conviction that the disintegration of the one involves the disintegration of the other.

(3) Moreover, it is difficult to conceive what conscious life can be *like*, without a physical body, with its sense organs and organs of expression. If we cut out of our consciousness the visual, auditory, tactile, motor and other bodily produced

From Durant Drake, *Problems of Religion: An Introductory Survey.* Published by Houghton-Mifflin, 1916.

images, what have we left? Very little if anything. Yet how could we have visual experiences without eyes, or touch experiences without hands? And, setting aside the questions what sort of consciousness we could have, and how we could communicate with our friends, what would they *mean* to us apart from their bodies? Take away the *look* of your dear one, her facial expression, the light in her eyes, the sound of her voice, the grace of her movements, the touch of her hand, what have you remaining to attract and interest you?

(4) Modern psychology has no longer any use for the concept of "soul." But if there is a "soul," a something inhabiting the body as a tenant, and separable from it at death, where does it abide, how does it get into the body, *when* does it get into the body, when does it leave the body, and how? Do portions of the parents' souls separate themselves, join together with the joining of the germ plasma at conception, to form a new immortal soul? If so, does it remain immortal if the incipient fœtus is ejected from the woman's body, if miscarriage takes place, or the child is still-born? Or does a new soul come somewhere at the moment of birth, and enter the child when it first breathes? The more clearly we realize the continuity of the physical processes of conception, pregnancy, and birth, the more difficult it becomes to know where to interpolate a soul.

(5) A similar continuity is seen to pervade the course of evolution, whereby man has emerged from a brute ancestry. If man is immortal, must not his brute ancestors have been immortal, and their descendants in the diverging, non-human lines? A rather disagreeable alternative seems to be offered. On the one hand, you may say that at a certain point in his ascent, man acquired immortality. If so, there was a time, in the slow evolution of the human type, when parents who, like all their ancestors, were doomed to die, gave birth to a child who was blessed with an immortal future. By what miracle was this momentous change effected? It seems unfair to the generations preceding. On the other hand, if you postulate no such moment of acquisition of an immortal soul, you must grant immortality to all the animals—and then perhaps to the plants too, for the vegetable and animal kingdoms merge gradually one into the other, just as brutehood grew insensibly into manhood. Many animals are, indeed, more intelligent and more affectionate than human babies, or underwitted men, idiots, and—doubtless—primitive savages; one would like to imagine one's pet dog immortal. But when it comes to tigers and snakes and mosquitoes and bedbugs and cholera microbes, our imagination halts!

(6) Where is the heaven to which souls go at death? It was easy enough for the ancients to picture a heavenly region up above the dome of the sky, easy enough for the evangelist to think of Jesus as having ascended into heaven and sitting there on the right hand of God. But we have long since learned the naiveté of that primitive world-view. We can no longer believe, with Dante, in an island in the Western sea, to which Ulysses could sail, where the mountain of purgatory reaches up to paradise. Nor can we believe that sulphur springs and volcanic steam bubble up from a hades under the earth where departed souls groan in torment.

The stellar universe, as we scan it with our telescopes, offers indeed unlimited ports to which we may conceive of ourselves as going; but there seems something grotesque about the fancy of our winging our way to Sirius or the Pleiades. And whatever heaven may lie beyond the stars, millions of millions of miles away, we cannot easily feel so sure of it as the pre-Copernicans did of their paradise of God just above the ninth sphere.

51. Parable of the Chinese Room

John Searle

John Searle (1932–   ), professor of philosophy at the University of California–Berkeley, is well known for his writings on the philosophy of mind and the philosophy of language. In recent years, his views on artificial intelligence have produced extensive controversy.

Though we do not know in detail how the brain functions, we do know enough to have an idea of the general relationships between brain processes and mental processes. Mental processes are caused by the behaviour of elements of the brain. At the same time, they are realised in the structure that is made up of those elements. I think this answer is consistent with the standard biological approaches to biological phenomena. Indeed, it is a kind of commonsense answer to the question, given what we know about how the world works. However, it is very much a minority point of view. The prevailing view in philosophy, psychology, and artificial intelligence is one which emphasises the analogies between the functioning of the human brain and the functioning of digital computers. According to the most extreme version of this view, the brain is just a digital computer and the mind is just a computer program. One could summarise this view—I call it "strong artificial intelligence" or "strong AI"—by saying that the mind is to the brain, as the program is to the computer hardware.

This view has the consequence that there is nothing essentially biological about the human mind. The brain just happens to be one of an indefinitely large number of different kinds of hardware computers that could sustain the programs which make up human intelligence. On this view, any physical system whatever that had the right program with the right inputs and outputs would have a mind in exactly the same sense that you and I have minds. So, for example, if you made a computer out of old beer cans powered by windmills; if it had the right program, it would have to have a mind. And the point is not that for all we know it might have thoughts and feelings, but rather that it must have thoughts and feelings, because that is all there is to having thoughts and feelings: implementing the right program.

Most people who hold this view think we have not yet designed programs which are minds. But there is pretty much general agreement among them that it's only a matter of time until computer scientists and workers in artificial intelligence

Reprinted by permission of the publishers from *Minds, Brains and Science,* by John Searle, Cambridge, Massachusetts: Harvard University Press, Copyright © 1984 by John Searle.

design the appropriate hardware and programs which will be the equivalent of human brains and minds. These will be artificial brains and minds which are in every way the equivalent of human brains and minds.

Many people outside of the field of artificial intelligence are quite amazed to discover that anybody could believe such a view as this. So, before criticising it, let me give you a few examples of the things that people in this field have actually said. Herbert Simon of Carnegie-Mellon University says that we already have machines that can literally think. There is no question of waiting for some future machine, because existing digital computers already have thoughts in exactly the same sense that you and I do. Well, fancy that! Philosophers have been worried for centuries about whether or not a machine could think, and now we discover that they already have such machines at Carnegie-Mellon. Simon's colleague Alan Newell claims that we have now discovered (and notice that Newell says "discovered" and not "hypothesized" or "considered the possibility," but we have *discovered*) that intelligence is just a matter of physical symbol manipulation; it has no essential connection with any specific kind of biological or physical wetware or hardware. Rather, any system whatever that is capable of manipulating physical symbols in the right way is capable of intelligence in the same literal sense as human intelligence of human beings. Both Simon and Newell, to their credit, emphasise that there is nothing metaphorical about these claims; they mean them quite literally. Freeman Dyson is quoted as having said that computers have an advantage over the rest of us when it comes to evolution. Since consciousness is just a matter of formal processes, in computers these formal processes can go on in substances that are much better able to survive in a universe that is cooling off than beings like ourselves made of our wet and messy materials. Marvin Minsky of MIT says that the next generation of computers will be so intelligent that we will "be lucky if they are willing to keep us around the house as household pets." My all-time favourite in the literature of exaggerated claims on behalf of the digital computer is from John McCarthy, the inventor of the term "artificial intelligence." McCarthy says even "machines as simple as thermostats can be said to have beliefs." And indeed, according to him, almost any machine capable of problem-solving can be said to have beliefs. I admire McCarthy's courage. I once asked him: "What beliefs does your thermostat have?" And he said: "My thermostat has three beliefs—it's too hot in here, it's too cold in here, and it's just right in here." As a philosopher, I like all these claims for a simple reason. Unlike most philosophical theses, they are reasonably clear, and they admit of a simple and decisive refutation. It is this refutation that I am going to undertake in this chapter.

The nature of the refutation has nothing whatever to do with any particular stage of computer technology. It is important to emphasize this point because the temptation is always to think that the solution to our problems must wait on some as yet untreated technological wonder. But in fact, the nature of the refutation is completely independent of any state of technology. It has to do with the very definition of a digital computer, with what a digital computer is.

It is essential to our conception of a digital computer that its operations can be specified purely formally; that is, we specify the steps in the operation of the computer in terms of abstract symbols—sequences of zeroes and ones printed on a tape, for example. A typical computer "rule" will determine that when a machine is in a certain state and it has a certain symbol on its tape, then it will perform a certain operation such as erasing the symbol or printing another symbol and then enter another state such as moving the tape one square to the left. But the symbols have no meaning; they have no semantic content; they are not about anything. They have to be specified purely in terms of their formal or syntactical structure. The zeroes and ones, for example, are just numerals; they don't even stand for numbers. Indeed, it is this feature of digital computers that makes them so powerful. One and the same type of hardware, if it is appropriately designed, can be used to run an indefinite range of different programs. And one and the same program can be run on an indefinite range of different types of hardwares.

But this feature of programs, that they are defined purely formally or syntactically, is fatal to the view that mental processes and program processes are identical. And the reason can be stated quite simply. There is more to having a mind than having formal or syntactical processes. Our internal mental states, by definition, have certain sorts of contents. If I am thinking about Kansas City or wishing that I had a cold beer to drink or wondering if there will be a fall in interest rates, in each case my mental state has a certain mental content in addition to whatever formal features it might have. That is, even if my thoughts occur to me in strings of symbols, there must be more to the thought than the abstract strings, because strings by themselves can't have any meaning. If my thoughts are to be *about* anything, then the strings must have a *meaning* which makes the thoughts about those things. In a word, the mind has more than a syntax, it has a semantics. The reason that no computer program can ever be a mind is simply that a computer program is only syntactical, and minds are more than syntactical. Minds are semantical, in the sense that they have more than a formal structure, they have a content.

To illustrate this point I have designed a certain thought-experiment. Imagine that a bunch of computer programmers have written a program that will enable a computer to simulate the understanding of Chinese. So, for example, if the computer is given a question in Chinese, it will match the question against its memory, or data base, and produce appropriate answers to the questions in Chinese. Suppose for the sake of argument that the computer's answers are as good as those of a native Chinese speaker. Now then, does the computer, on the basis of this, understand Chinese, does it literally understand Chinese, in the way that Chinese speakers understand Chinese? Well, imagine that you are locked in a room, and in this room are several baskets full of Chinese symbols. Imagine that you (like me) do not understand a word of Chinese, but that you are given a rule book in English for manipulating these Chinese symbols. The rules specify the manipulations of the symbols purely formally, in terms of their syntax, not their semantics. So the rule might say: "Take a squiggle-squiggle sign out of basket number one and put it next to a squoggle-squoggle sign from basket number two." Now suppose that some other Chinese symbols are passed into the room, and that you are given further rules for passing back Chinese symbols out of the room. Suppose that unknown to you the symbols passed into the room are called "questions" by the people outside the room, and the symbols you pass back out of the room are called "answers to the questions." Suppose, furthermore, that the programmers are so good at designing the programs and that you are so good at manipulating the symbols, that very soon your answers are indistinguishable from those of a native Chinese speaker. There you are locked in your room shuffling your Chinese symbols and passing out Chinese symbols in response to incoming Chinese symbols. On the basis of the situation as I have described it, there is no way you could learn any Chinese simply by manipulating these formal symbols.

Now the point of the story is simply this: by virtue of implementing a formal computer program from the point of view of an outside observer, you behave exactly as if you understood Chinese, but all the same you don't understand a word of Chinese. But if going through the appropriate computer program for understanding Chinese is not enough to give *you* an understanding of Chinese, then it is not enough to give *any other digital computer* an understanding of Chinese. And again, the reason for this can be stated quite simply. If you don't understand Chinese, then no other computer could understand Chinese because no digital computer, just by virtue of running a program, has anything that you don't have. All that the computer has, as you have, is a formal program for manipulating uninterpreted Chinese symbols. To repeat, a computer has a syntax, but no semantics. The whole point of the parable of the Chinese room is to remind us of a fact that we knew all along. Understanding a language, or indeed, having mental states at all, involves more than just having a bunch of formal symbols. It involves having an interpretation, or a meaning attached to those symbols. And a digital computer, as defined, cannot have more than just formal symbols because the operation of the computer, as I said earlier, is defined in terms of its ability to implement programs. And these programs are purely formally specifiable—that is, they have no semantic content.

We can see the force of this argument if we contrast what it is like to be asked and to answer questions in English, and to be asked and to answer questions in some language where we have no knowledge of any of the meanings of the words. Imagine that in the Chinese room you are also given questions in English about such things as your age or your life history, and that you answer these questions. What is the difference between the Chinese case and the English case? Well again, if like me you understand no Chinese and you do understand English, then the difference is obvious. You understand the questions in English because they are expressed in symbols whose meanings are known to you. Similarly, when you give the answers in English you are producing symbols which are meaningful to you. But in the case of the Chinese, you have none of that. In the case of the Chinese, you simply manipulate formal symbols according to a computer program, and you attach no meaning to any of the elements.

Various replies have been suggested to this argument by workers in artificial intelligence and in psychology, as well as philosophy. They all have something in common; they are all inadequate. And there is an obvious reason why they have to be inadequate, since the argument rests on a very simple logical truth, namely, syntax alone is not sufficient for semantics, and digital computers insofar as they are computers have, by definition, a syntax alone.

I want to make this clear by considering a couple of the arguments that are often presented against me.

Some people attempt to answer the Chinese room example by saying that the whole system understands Chinese. The idea here is that though I, the person in the room manipulating the symbols do not understand Chinese, I am just the central processing unit of the computer system. They argue that it is the whole system, including the room, the baskets full of symbols and the ledgers containing the programs and perhaps other items as well, taken as a totality, that understands Chinese. But this is subject to exactly the same objection I made before. There is no way that the system can get from the syntax to the semantics. I, as the central processing unit, have no way of figuring out what any of these symbols means; but then neither does the whole system.

Another common response is to imagine that we put the Chinese understanding program inside a robot. If the robot moved around and interacted causally with the world, wouldn't that be enough to guarantee that it understood Chinese? Once again the inexorability of the semantics-syntax distinction overcomes this manoeuvre. As long as we suppose the robot has only a computer for a brain then, even though it might behave exactly as if it understood Chinese, it would still have no way of getting from the syntax to the semantics of Chinese. You can see this if you imagine that I am the computer. Inside a room in the robot's skull I shuffle symbols without knowing that some of them come in to me from television cameras attached to the robot's head and others go out to move the robot's arms and legs. As long as all I have is a formal computer program, I have no way of attaching any meaning to any of the symbols. And the fact that the robot is engaged in causal interactions with the outside world won't help me to attach any meaning to the symbols unless I have some way of finding out about the fact. Suppose the robot picks up a hamburger and this triggers the symbol for hamburger to come into the room. As long as all I have is the symbol with no knowledge of its causes or how it got there, I have no way of knowing what it means. The causal interactions between the robot and the rest of the world are irrelevant unless those causal interactions are represented in some mind or other. But there is no way they can be if all that the so-called mind consists of is a set of purely formal, syntactical operations.

It is important to see exactly what is claimed and what is not claimed by my argument. Suppose we ask the question that I mentioned at the beginning: "Could a machine think?" Well, in one sense, of course, we are all machines. We can construe the stuff inside our heads as a meat machine. And of course, we can all think. So, in one sense of "machine," namely that sense in which a machine is just a physical system which is capable of performing certain kinds of operations, in that sense, we are all machines, and we can think. So, trivially, there are machines that can think. But that wasn't the question that bothered us. So let's try a different formulation of it. Could an artefact think? Could a man-made machine think? Well, once again, it depends on the kind of artefact. Suppose we designed a machine that was molecule-for-molecule indistinguishable from a human being. Well then, if you can duplicate the causes, you can presumably duplicate the effects. So once again, the answer to that question is, in principle at least, trivially yes. If you could build a machine that had the same structure as a human being, then presumably that machine would be able to think. Indeed, it would be a surrogate human being. Well, let's try again.

The question isn't: "Can a machine think?" or "Can an artefact think?" The question is: "Can a digital computer think?" But once again we have to be very careful in how we interpret the question. From a mathematical point of view, anything whatever can be described as *if* it were a digital computer. And that's because it may be described as instantiating or implementing a computer program. In an utterly trivial sense, the pen that is on the desk in front of me can be described as a digital computer. It just happens to have a very boring computer program. The program says: "Stay there." Now since in this sense, anything whatever is a digital computer, because anything whatever can be described as implementing a computer program, then once again, our question gets a trivial answer. Of course our brains are digital computers, since they implement any number of computer programs. And of course our brains can think. So once again, there is a trivial answer to the question. But that wasn't really the question we were trying to ask. The question we wanted to ask is this: "Can a digital computer, as defined, think?" That is to say: "Is instantiating or implementing the right computer program with the right inputs and outputs, sufficient for, or constitutive of, thinking?" And to this question, unlike its predecessors, the answer is clearly "no." And it is "no" for the reason that we have spelled out, namely, the computer program is defined purely syntactically. But thinking is more than just a matter of manipulating meaningless symbols, it involves meaningful semantic contents. These semantic contents are what we mean by "meaning."

It is important to emphasize again that we are not talking about a particular stage of computer technology. The argument has nothing to do with the forthcoming, amazing advances in computer science. It has nothing to do with the distinction between serial and parallel processes, or with the size of programs, or the speed of computer operations, or with computers that can interact causally with their environment, or even with the invention of robots. Technological progress is always grossly exaggerated, but even subtracting the exaggeration, the development of computers has been quite remarkable, and we can reasonably expect that even more remarkable progress will be made in the future. No doubt we will be much better able to simulate human behaviour on computers than we can at present, and certainly much better than we have been able to in the past. The point I am making is that if we are talking about having mental states, having a mind, all of these simulations are simply irrelevant. It doesn't matter how good the technology is, or how rapid the calculations made by the computer are. If it really is a computer, its operations have to be defined syntactically, whereas consciousness, thoughts, feelings, emotions, and all the rest of it involve more than a syntax. Those features, by definition, the computer is unable to *duplicate* however powerful may be its ability to *simulate.* The key distinction here is between duplication and simulation. And no simulation by itself ever constitutes duplication.

What I have done so far is give a basis to the sense that those citations I began this talk with are really as preposterous as they seem. There is a puzzling question in this discussion though, and that is: "Why would anybody ever have thought that computers could think or have feelings and emotions and all the rest of it?" After all, we can do computer simulations of any process whatever that can be given a formal description. So, we can do a computer simulation of the flow of money in the British economy, or the pattern of power distribution in the Labour party. We can do computer simulation of rain storms in the home counties, or warehouse fires in East London. Now, in each of these cases, nobody supposes that the computer simulation is actually the real thing; no one supposes that a computer simulation of a storm will leave us all wet, or a computer simulation of a fire is likely to burn the house down. Why on earth would anyone in his right mind suppose a computer simulation of mental processes actually had mental processes? I don't really know the answer to that, since the idea seems to me, to put it frankly, quite crazy from the start. But I can make a couple of speculations.

First of all, where the mind is concerned, a lot of people are still tempted to some sort of behaviourism. They think if a system behaves as if it understood Chinese, then it really must understand Chinese. But we have already refuted this form of behaviourism with the Chinese room argument. Another assumption made by many people is that the mind is not a part of the biological world, it is not a part of the world of nature. The strong artificial intelligence view relies on that in its conception that the mind is purely formal; that somehow or other, it cannot be treated as a concrete product of biological processes like any other biological product. There is in these discussions, in short, a kind of residual dualism. AI partisans believe that the mind is more than a part of the natural biological world; they believe that the mind is purely formally specifiable. The paradox of this is that the AI literature is filled with fulminations against some view called "dualism," but in fact, the whole thesis of strong AI rests on a kind of dualism. It rests on a rejection of the idea that the mind is just a natural biological phenomenon in the world like any other. . . .

SUGGESTIONS FOR FURTHER READING

ANTHOLOGIES

Anderson, Alan Ross, ed. *Minds and Machines.* Englewood Cliffs, N.J.: Prentice Hall, 1964. A collection of interesting contemporary articles on the question of whether men are machines. The articles are difficult but worthwhile reading.

Edwards, Paul, ed. *Immortality.* Amherst, N.Y.: Prometheus Books, 1997. A recent collection of many of the best articles on immortality and the related philosophical issues of personal identity and the nature of mind.

Flew, Anthony, ed. *Body, Mind, and Death.* New York: Macmillan, 1966. Some important articles on the mind-body problem from Plato to the present day. The introduction and annotated bibliography are excellent.

Hofstadter, Douglas R., and Daniel Dennett, eds. *The Mind's I.* New York: Basic Books, 1981. Twenty-seven articles on artificial intelligence and the nature of mind, with extensive comments by the editors.

Laslett, Peter, ed. *The Physical Basis of the Mind.* Oxford: Basil Blackwell, 1951. A series of eight radio broadcasts given by British scientists and philosophers. The talks are very clear and interesting.

INDIVIDUAL WORKS

Adler, Mortimer. *The Difference of Man and the Difference It Makes.* Cleveland: World, 1967. The relation of the problem of the existence of mind to the issue of how men differ from animals. There is also a good discussion of whether men differ essentially from computing machines.

Beloff, John. *The Existence of Mind.* New York: Citadel, 1964. An examination of the arguments for and against dualism.

Brown, Geoffrey. *Minds, Brains, and Machines.* New York: St. Martin's Press, 1989. An introductory account of the major positions on the mind-body controversy and a discussion of the possibility of thinking machines.

Churchland, Paul. *Matter and Consciousness.* Cambridge: MIT Press, 1984. A clear introduction to the mind-body controversy.

Dennett, Daniel C. *Brainstorms.* Montgomery, Vt.: Bradford Books, 1978. A series of provocative articles dealing with various aspects of the mind-body controversy.

Dreyfus, Hubert, and Stuart Dreyfus. *Mind Over Machine.* New York: Macmillan, 1986. An attack on the claim that computers can duplicate human intelligence.

Ducasse, C. J. *Nature, Mind, and Death.* LaSalle, Ill.: Open Court, 1951. A good discussion of the mind-body problem and its relation to the question of immortality.

Gardner, Howard. *The Mind's New Science.* New York: Basic Books, 1985. An explanation of the new field of cognitive science, which is closely tied to the mind-body controversy and artificial intelligence.

Hospers, John. *An Introduction to Philosophical Analysis.* 3d ed. Englewood Cliffs, N.J.: Prentice Hall, 1988. Chapter Six presents a clear account of the mind-body controversy.

Shaffer, Jerome. *Reality, Knowledge, and Value.* New York: Random, 1971. Chapters 8–14 provide a very readable account of the main issues in the mind-body controversy.

Taylor, Richard. *Metaphysics.* 4th ed. Englewood Cliffs, N.J.: Prentice Hall, 1992. Chapters 2–4 provide a clear discussion of the mind-body controversy and a defense of materialism.

Dictionary of the History of Ideas: Studies of Selected Pivotal Ideas. Philip P. Weiner, editor-in-chief. New York: Scribners, 1973. Substantial and clearly written essays emphasizing the historical development of topics discussed in this part. Designed to inform the nonspecialist, each essay concludes with a select bibliography.

Encyclopedia of Philosophy. Paul Edwards, editor-in-chief. New York: Macmillan, 1967. The student will find many worthwhile articles on the subject treated in this part and excellent bibliographies.

PART SIX

Knowledge and Science

INTRODUCTION

All human beings want knowledge, admire it, even revere it. Platitudinous as this statement may appear, it is certainly ambiguous. No doubt this accounts for the fact that so many people think the statement true. For knowledge as something sought, as a value, suggests two quite different things: (1) knowledge as a good or end-in-itself independent of any use to which it may be put; (2) knowledge as a means necessary for the securing of some other value. We call those who dedicate themselves to the disinterested pursuit of knowledge, to the free play of ideas, "intellectuals," or "theoreticians." In this sense, philosophers traditionally have seen themselves and have been seen by others as superintellectuals, as the theoretician's theoretician. Historical legend has it that the first philosopher known to us, Thales of Miletus in Asia Minor (circa 585 B.C.), afflicted with the reproaches of his fellow citizens that he was a man of knowledge but also a poor man (and so what worth did knowledge have?), used his knowledge of nature to predict that the next crop of olives would be a bumper one. Keeping the practical results of his knowledge to himself, as would become a hardheaded businessman, Thales then bought up all of the olive presses in the region, thereby securing a monopoly for himself. When the unusually abundant harvest of olives duly took place, Thales rented out his olive presses at a high price and so made a large amount of money by cornering the market. Philosophers could make money if they wanted to do so, he reportedly declared, but willingly were poor because they valued knowledge above everything else, even wealth. No doubt Thales would never enroll in a business school; however, if he did, he would earn all As.

Socrates refused to accept money for his teaching, not wishing to be financially dependent on anyone. (No wonder he scorned politicians.) Socrates distrusted wealth; for of what use is wealth but to stimulate and delight the senses, so sapping one's rational energies and distracting one's reason from the pursuit of truth. Refusing to stop asking questions as the price of life and freedom, condemned to death, drinking the hemlock, dying, Socrates has become a symbol of the fearless and unrelenting search for knowledge despite the opposition of the ignorant majority. The god Apollo announced that Socrates was the wisest man in Greece. Aristotle, the most influential philosopher in the Western world and the first great biologist, conceived man's highest destiny, because man is the only animal possessing reason, to be the full and unimpeded functioning of that reason, sheer knowing for its own sake. In knowing, man comes closest to being a god. If there are gods, knowing would be the only activity compatible with their exalted status. Practical activities, such as healing broken legs or multiplying loaves and fishes, would be beneath divine dignity. In the seventeenth century, the philosopher Spinoza equated God and Nature. In the glow of his own "intellectual love of God,"

Spinoza revealed how knowing the unchanging truth for its own sake can elicit all of the traditional religious emotions of devotion to what is greater and worthier than one's self and how knowing for its own sake can satisfy the old religious yearning for triumph over devouring time and for unshakable peace. The pursuit of knowledge as the ultimate Good thus emits cosmic, religious echoes. The devotees of knowing for its own sake have moved with a priestly mien whether they wore the toga or the white laboratory coat of the modern scientist. In our day, Albert Einstein is the symbol of the philosopher-scientist, the pure Knower, the inspired theoretician—Einstein, with the massive brow, the lined face, the flowing white hair suggesting a symphony conductor or other artist, and the luminous eyes through which the universe gazes into you.

Nevertheless, the pursuit of knowledge for its own sake evokes the supreme allegiance of only a small minority of Americans and people in other countries. The great majority value knowledge as technique, as know-how, as a necessary means to other more important values, such as excitement and amusement. A little over a century ago, a Jewish prophet, who had read Greek and German philosophy, wrote that until his day philosophers had been content to understand the world but that the real task of philosophy was to change the world. Most Americans and all thoroughly modern people of other countries agree with Marx. The great majority of contemporary men and women prize knowledge as power, science as technology, as a kind of magic that works, a cornucopia pouring forth an unending and swelling stream of wealth with its attendant power and luxury. A small minority of intellectuals excepted, most contemporaries know very well what they want—wealth, power, luxury. For them, the problem concerns means: how to produce wealth, power, luxury, and all things dependent on them ever more abundantly. If the cost of that production means a polluted environment, chemically fouled lakes and streams, dying wildlife, and degraded human life, so far we have been willing to pay that cost. And should that cost become exorbitant, even deadly, we are sustained by the faith that the cure for the ills of technology is a bigger and better technology.

Only because science has shown itself so fecund in producing these goods and in progressively eliminating undesirable side effects has it been allowed to develop to its present level. For science, particularly on its theoretical side as a pursuit of knowledge for its own sake, was and is one of the most subversive agents ever invented by humans. It is no coincidence that controversy whirls around the figures of Copernicus, Galileo, Darwin, Einstein, and Freud like black clouds rumbling with thunder and flashing with lightning. They symbolize the disturbing fact that science constantly shows us that the world and humans really are quite different from what most people thought they were. Hence, for most people the value of knowing for its own sake must be subordinated to other values. Millions of Americans drive automobiles and at the same time reject the proposition that a human being is a mammal. The pursuit of knowledge is splendid, but such an enterprise must be compatible with national security. Of course we must hold all of our theories tentatively, but we "know" that any average American is superior in every way to any foreigner.

This ambiguity of knowledge as an end for its own sake and as a means to realizing other values provides the humus out of which philosophical reflection on knowledge and science grows. Hence, philosophers study and discuss what they technically call *epistemology:* the investigation of the origin, nature, methods, and limits of knowledge. Philosophers wonder about and often answer such questions as: What is the nature of knowledge? What criteria distinguish genuine knowledge from the spurious article? Does all knowledge come from sense experience, or can our reason know that certain propositions must be true independently of sense experience? What is science? What is the scientific method? Is there *a* scientific method? Is all knowledge that is worthy of the name produced by science and science alone? Is there anything that science cannot find out? More radically, can we know anything at all, or is it all merely a matter of shifting opinions, what we call "knowledge" being merely those illusions, or perhaps even delusions, agreed upon?

Underlying questions concerning the nature of science and such contemporary issues as skepticism and the value of science is a profound philosophical dispute: Rationalism *versus* Empiricism. Rationalism is the doctrine that reason alone is a source of knowledge and is independent of sense experience. Empiricism is the doctrine that *all* knowledge comes from sense experience. Rationalism and Empiricism contradict one another. The propositions that "Some of our knowledge does not derive from sense experience" and that "All of our knowledge does derive from sense experience" cannot both be true nor both be false. But which proposition is true and which one is false?

René Descartes, often called the father of modern philosophy, sought intellectual certainty. For Descartes, genuinely to know something is to be unable to doubt its truth. Hence, he searches for propositions that he cannot doubt. In *Meditations I and II,* he gives an account of his search and its result. Descartes resolves to examine the principles on which depend all that he once believed, only to discover that there is not one principle whose truth he cannot doubt. He finds that he can doubt the reliability of his senses, the existence of his physical body and senses, the existence of an external world. Indeed, he can doubt whether he presently is awake or asleep. Descartes goes further. Might there not be an "evil genius" who is systematically deceiving him so that all that he formerly believed is false, even his belief that two plus three makes five? Yet Descartes snatches certainty from the jaws of doubt. He finds it to be self-evidently true that he is a being that thinks. Nothing could be more clear and distinct to his reason. He cannot doubt that he is doubting; to doubt his existence is to affirm it. In its Latin expression as *cogito ergo sum,* "I think, therefore I am" has become the most famous principle of all modern philosophy. Descartes now possesses criteria of certainty: Whatever is perfectly clear and distinct to his reason cannot be doubted and so must be true. Applying these criteria, Descartes proceeds to discover other truths such as the existence of extended substance or matter. For rationalists like Descartes, all knowledge is expressible in self-evident propositions or their consequences.

As Friedrich Paulsen points out, empiricism claims that all of our knowledge about the world is derived from sense experience. Our reason alone cannot reveal what does or does not exist. The empiricist distinguishes two basic kinds of science, differing in nature and method: purely formal or conceptual sciences, such as logic and mathematics, and objective sciences, such as physics and psychology. The former kind gives us certainty but tells us nothing about matters of fact. From what is logically possible (i.e., not self-contradictory) alone, nothing can be deduced about what exists. The other kind, the objective sciences, gives us probabilities only, not certainties, but does tell us about matters of fact. Friedrich Paulsen then proceeds to a more detailed account, from the empiricist standpoint, of the differences in nature and method between the formal or conceptual sciences and the objective or empirical sciences. At the close of the selection, Paulsen infers a more general conclusion from empiricism: We can have no absolute or certain knowledge of matters of fact. Then is knowledge about existence impossible? According to empiricism, such knowledge is possible if we will relinquish the rationalist demand that knowledge be certain or beyond all doubt.

David Hume argues for what he calls a *"mitigated skepticism or academical philosophy"* in which "philosophical decisions are nothing but the reflections of common life, methodized and corrected." That we must choose to be universal skeptics or to be instinctive dogmatists, to doubt everything or to doubt nothing, to follow reason or to follow custom or instinct are false alternatives because there is a third alternative in which skepticism and common sense correct each other.

Hume rejects what he terms excessive skepticism or *Pyrrhonism*, under which he includes Cartesian doubt, doubt that an external world exists independently of any perceiver, and doubt that cause-and-effect relationships will hold in the future. He does so not because excessive skepticism can be refuted by reason—for it cannot—but because no one could act on the basis of such skepticism and continue to live. Natural instinct proves stronger than reason. Hume is famous for his skeptical analysis of cause and effect with its conclusion that no fact logically entails any other fact. According to Hume, reason shows that the conception of cause and effect really consists of no more than two parts: (1) a frequent conjunction of two objects or events observed in the past and present and (2) a custom or "instinct of our nature" that leads us to expect that the same conjunction will occur in the future.

Hume concludes that we need not dispense wholly with either reason or custom or "instinct of our nature." Reason can doubt that food will nourish us in the future; indeed, rational argument can neither prove nor disprove it. But if we acted in accordance with that excessive skepticism we would die of starvation. Yet reason also shows us that custom or instinct may deceive us. *Mitigated* skepticism or *academical* philosophy, Hume's third alternative, will keep custom or instinct cautious and undogmatic and confine our search for knowledge within the limits of our understanding. Excessive skepticism or *Pyrrhonism* is impotent; custom or natural instinct alone is blind. In philosophy we may doubt that fire will cause smoke, but our houses will have chimneys.

"The Detective As Scientist" by Irving M. Copi, an outstanding contemporary logician, provides a clear and authoritative outline of the structure or logic of the process of inquiry that we have come to call "science" or "the scientific method," which has proved so increasingly successful since the seventeenth century. Copi's description reveals how scientific inquiry fruitfully combines elements from philosophical skepticism, rationalism, and empiricism without basing itself wholly on any one of those positions alone.

However, science is not only a problem-solving enterprise; it is a cultural phenomenon of enormous and growing importance. Deprived of science and scientific technologies, our lives would be transformed out of all recognition. Success breeds criticism. The achievement of science is no exception. We may live in a scientific age, as many claim or complain; nonetheless, critics and powerful enemies of science abound in contemporary life and, some fear, steadily mount in numbers and influence. They challenge the value of science, accuse it of doing more harm than good, and champion other methods of obtaining the truth as superior to that of science. In "The Limits and the Value of Scientific Method," two eminent American philosophers of science, Morris Cohen and Ernest Nagel, defend science as "the finest flower and test of a liberal civilization" against its critics and foes.

According to Duane Gish, creation and evolution are both equally scientific and religious. Furthermore, creation and evolution are the only possible explanations for the origins of the universe and of all living creatures. Strictly speaking, neither creation nor evolution is a scientific theory. Rather, both are "inferences based on *circumstantial evidence*." If a theory is to be scientific, then it must be testable by repeatable observations and must in principle be falsifiable. Gish interprets this conception of the nature of a scientific theory to mean that such a theory is limited to explanation of "processes and events that are presently occurring repeatedly within our observations." From this interpretation he infers that historical theories or theories about what has happened in the past are not scientific theories. Thus he concludes that since theories of creation and of evolution are about alleged past events, neither are scientific theories. Nonetheless, Gish believes that it is appropriate to call both creation and evolution "scientific" because each seeks to connect and to account for data related to origins.

Gish also contends that both creation and evolution are religious in the sense that each involves a distinctive philosophical or metaphysical world view. The creation world view is theistic, and the evolutionary world view, atheistic. For Gish, whatever includes a philosophical or world view is "basically religious in nature." Neither creation nor evolution can be extricated from its distinctive theistic or atheistic philosophy. Creation and evolution being the only two, but irreconcilable, alternative theories on origins, Gish concludes that the scientific evidence for both should be taught in the public schools in a manner that is neutral concerning their religious world views. As long as one did not try to make converts, there would be no violation of the U.S. Constitution in teaching about religions.

Addressing the philosophical or conceptual issues as distinguished from empirical ones in the continuing creation-evolution controversy, A. David Kline concentrates on refuting three creationist arguments: (1) evolution is merely a theory; (2) evolution is about nonrepeatable phenomena; and (3) evolution is unfalsifiable. He finds all three arguments to be unsound.

Kline criticizes the creationist charge that evolution is merely a theory and not a fact on the ground that this indictment rests on an equivocation on the meaning of the term "theory." The creationist argues that because the theory of evolution is a theory, it is not well established. Kline contends that, in so arguing, the creationist is using the term "theory" in its ordinary, prescientific sense as mere speculation or opinion as contrasted with facts known for certain. However, when biologists and other scientists speak of evolution as a theory, they mean that it is a theory well supported by relevant data, that evolution is *not* merely poorly established or unjustified speculation or opinion. When scientists go so far as to call evolution a fact they mean that there is little difference between their confidence in the data and their confidence in the theory, that the theory of evolution is beyond any reasonable doubt.

Next Kline argues that creationists such as Gish employ an incorrect conception of scientific methodology. Creationists claim that confidence in the truth of a regularity or law requires repeatedly observing instances of it and that since such observation concerning the regularities composing evolution is impossible, we should have little or no confidence in the truth of evolution. Kline contends that demanding repeated observation of instances of regularities would result in most of physics not being confirmed. Since events do not recur, broadening the requirement from observational instances to observational regularities would be too narrow. However, if what is observed is broadened still further to event-types, evolution meets the confirmation requirement.

In response to the creationist contention that evolution is not a scientific theory but a philosophical or metaphysical system or even a religion, Kline makes several replies. The philosopher Karl Popper did not deny the testability of contemporary evolutionary theory. Creationists in effect seem to hold contradictory positions: the evidence falsifies the theory of evolution, and the theory of evolution is not falsifiable. Kline holds that much of creationism—that is, creationism without a supernatural God and His creative activities—clearly is falsifiable and indeed is false. Can God play a role in scientific explanations? Kline answers that He can only if God ceases to be conceived of as a supernatural being outside of space and time and instead is treated as just another natural entity; creationists would find such a naturalizing of God to be objectionable.

The "brains-in-vats" paradox tantalizes because it seems to show that our experience must remain forever equivocal, that just possibly everything we know is false. This haunting paradox is a scientifically up-to-date version of Descartes' postulation of an evil genius who might be systematically deceiving our senses. Might we not be disembodied brains floating in vats of nutrient fluid in some remote future while a mad scientist produces in us the delusion that we are brains in bodies living in the last decade of the twentieth century? Our experience is a stream of nerve impulses. But what causes these impulses? Most of us most of the time blithely assume that they are caused by a contemporaneous external world of objects and persons. But this normal assumption could be false; there are other possible causes of our present experience, the brains-in-vats scenario being one of them. The punch of the paradox is that we cannot prove the truth or falsity of the brains-in-vats hypothesis by appealing to sense experience. If all of our sense experience may be always deceptive, then any sense experience may be always deceptive. The brains-in-vats paradox does not prove that all of our experience is hallucinatory. What it says is much more disturbing: we can never know.

Sextus Empiricus claims that a criterion of truth or a principle or standard by which to judge something true or false is undiscoverable. Any attempt to find such a criterion must result ultimately in an infinite regression. The truth of propositions is established either by assertion or by proof. Sheer assertion must be rejected because for every assertion there is a contradictory assertion. Therefore, we are driven to seek a criterion or standard by which to judge the assertions. But why should we accept the criterion? We cannot do so on the basis of assertion alone because that justification already has failed. If we try to judge asserted disagreeing criteria, we must then search for another criterion and so on without end. We cannot appeal to any characteristics of those making assertions such as age, intelligence, or agreement with the majority because they are unreliable bases for determining who speaks truly and who does not. Can a criterion or standard be established by proof rather than bare assertion? Sextus Empiricus claims that every attempt at proof must fail. How can we know any proof is sound or unsound? We cannot merely assert that a proof is sound or unsound because we have appealed to proof as the result of the inadequacy of assertion. We need a criterion or standard of proof. Yet we cannot justify the proof by the criterion and then justify the criterion by the proof or vice versa without plunging into a vicious circle of reasoning. But we cannot appeal to yet another criterion or standard without encountering the same pitfall of viciously circular reasoning and being driven on to yet another criterion or standard ad infinitum. Sextus Empiricus is not maintaining that all propositions are true or that all are false. What he is maintaining is that it is impossible for us to determine which are true and which are false.

RATIONALISM

52. *Meditations I and II*

René Descartes

René Descartes (1596–1650), inventor of analytic geometry and one of the greatest of French philosophers, has affected profoundly the problems, methods, and solutions of modern philosophy.

MEDITATION I

Of the Things of Which We May Doubt. Several years have now elapsed since I first became aware that I had accepted, even from my youth, many false opinions for true, and that consequently what I afterwards based on such principles was highly doubtful; and from that time I was convinced of the necessity of undertaking once in my life to rid myself of all the opinions I had adopted, and of commencing anew the work of building from the foundation, if I desired to establish a firm and abiding super structure in the sciences. But as this enterprise appeared to me to be one of great magnitude, I waited until I had attained an age so mature as to leave me no hope that at any stage of life more advanced I should be better able to execute my design. On this account, I have delayed so long that I should henceforth consider I was doing wrong were I still to consume in deliberation any of the time that now remains for action. Today, then, since I have opportunely freed my mind from all cares, and am happily disturbed by no passions, and since I am in the secure possession of leisure in a peaceable retirement, I will at length apply myself earnestly and freely to the general overthrow of all my former opinions. But, to this end, it will not be necessary for me to show that the whole of these are false—a point, perhaps, which I shall never reach; but as even now my reason convinces me that I ought not the less carefully to withhold belief from what is not entirely certain and indubitable, than from what is manifestly false, it will be sufficient to justify the rejection of the whole if I shall find in each some ground for doubt. Nor for this purpose will it be necessary even to deal with each belief individually, which would be truly an endless labour; but, as the removal from below of the foundation necessarily involves the downfall of the whole edifice, I will at once approach the criticism of the principles on which all my former beliefs rested.

From *The Meditations and Selections from the Principles of René Descartes,* translated by John Veitch, The Open Court Publishing Co., La Salle, Illinois, 1905.

All that I have, up to this moment, accepted as possessed of the highest truth and certainty, I received either from or through the senses. I observed however, that these sometimes misled us; and it is the part of prudence not to place absolute confidence in that by which we have even once been deceived.

But it may be said, perhaps that, although the senses occasionally mislead us respecting minute objects, and such as are so far removed from us as to be beyond the reach of close observation, there are yet many other of their information (presentations), of the truth of which it is manifestly impossible to doubt; as for example, that I am in this place, seated by the fire, clothed in a winter dressing-gown, that I hold in my hands this piece of paper, with other intimations of the same nature. But how could I deny that I possess these hands and this body, and withal escape being classed with persons in a state of insanity, whose brains are so disordered and clouded by dark bilious vapours as to cause them pertinaciously to assert that they are monarchs when they are in the greatest poverty; or clothed in gold and purple when destitute of any covering; or that their head is made of clay, their body of glass, or that they are gourds? I should certainly be not less insane than they, were I to regulate my procedure according to examples so extravagant.

Though this be true, I must nevertheless here consider that I am a man, and that, consequently, I am in the habit of sleeping, and representing to myself in dreams those same things, or even sometimes others less probable, which the insane think are presented to them in their waking moments. How often have I dreamt that I was in these familiar circumstances,—that I was dressed, and occupied this place by the fire, when I was lying undressed in bed? At the present moment, however, I certainly look upon this paper with eyes wide awake; the head which I now move is not asleep; I extend this hand consciously and with express purpose, and I perceive it; the occurrences in sleep are not so distinct as all this. But I cannot forget that, at other times, I have been deceived in sleep by similar illusions; and, attentively considering those cases, I perceive so clearly that there exist no certain marks by which the state of waking can ever be distinguished from sleep, that I feel greatly astonished; and in amazement I almost persuade myself that I am now dreaming.

Let us suppose, then, that we are dreaming, and that all these particulars—namely, the opening of the eyes, the motion of the head, the forth putting of the hands—are merely illusions; and even that we really possess neither an entire body nor hands such as we see. Nevertheless, it must be admitted at least that the objects which appear to us in sleep are, as it were, painted representations which could not have been formed unless in the likeness of realities; and, therefore, that those general objects, at all events,—namely, eyes, a head, hands, and an entire body—are not simply imaginary, but really existent. For, in truth, painters themselves, even when they study to represent sirens and satyrs by forms the most fantastic and extraordinary, cannot bestow upon them natures absolutely new, but can only make a certain medley of the members of different animals; or if they chance to imagine something so novel that nothing at all similar has ever been before, and such as is, therefore, purely fictitious and absolutely false, it is at least certain that the colours of which this is composed are real.

And on the same principle, although these general objects, viz. a body, eyes, a head, hands, and the like, be imaginary, we are nevertheless absolutely necessitated to admit the reality at least of some other objects still more simple and universal than these, of which, just as of certain real colours, all those images of things, whether true and real, or false and fantastic, that are found in our consciousness, are formed.

To this class of objects seem to belong corporeal nature in general and its extension; the figure of extended things, their quantity or magnitude, and their number, as also the place in, and the time during which they exist, and other things of the same sort. We will not, therefore, perhaps reason illegitimately if we conclude from this that Physics, Astronomy, Medicine, and all the other sciences that have for their end the consideration of composite objects, are indeed of a doubtful character; but that Arithmetic, Geometry, and the other sciences of the same class, which regard merely the simplest and most general objects, and scarcely inquire whether or not these are really existent, contain somewhat that is certain and indubitable; for whether I am awake or dreaming, it remains true that two and three makes five, and that a square has but four sides; nor does it seem possible that truths so apparent can ever fall under a suspicion of falsity or incertitude.

Nevertheless, the belief that there is a God who is all-powerful, and who created me, such as I am, has, for a long time, obtained steady possession of my mind. How, then, do I know that he has not arranged that there should be neither earth, nor sky, nor any extended thing, nor figure, nor magnitude, nor place, providing at the same time, however, for the rise in me of the perceptions of all these objects, and the persuasion that these do not exist otherwise than as I perceive them? And further, as I sometimes think that others are in error respecting matters of which they believe themselves to possess a perfect knowledge, how do I know that I am not also deceived each time I add together two and three, or number the sides of a square, or form some judgment still more simple, if more simple indeed can be imagined? But perhaps Deity has not been willing that I should be thus deceived, for He is said to be supremely good. If, however, it were repugnant to the goodness of Deity to have created me subject to constant deception, it would seem likewise to be contrary to this goodness to allow me to be occasionally deceived; and yet it is clear that this is permitted. Some, indeed, might perhaps be found who would be disposed rather to deny the existence of a Being so powerful than to believe that there is nothing certain. But let us for the present refrain from opposing this opinion, and grant that all which is here said of a Deity is fabulous; nevertheless in whatever way it be supposed that I reached the state in which I exist, whether by fate, or chance, or by an endless series of antecedents and consequents, or by any other means, it is clear (since to be deceived and to err is a certain defect) that the probability of my being so imperfect as to be the constant victim of deception, will be increased exactly in proportion as the power possessed by the cause, to which they assign my origin, is lessened. To these reasonings I have assuredly nothing to reply, but am constrained at last to avow that there is nothing of all that I formerly believed to be true of which it is impossible to doubt, and that not through thoughtlessness or levity, but from cogent and maturely considered reasons; so that henceforward, if I desire to discover anything certain, I ought not the less carefully to refrain from assenting to those same opinions than to what might be shown to be manifestly false.

But it is not sufficient to have made these observations; care must be taken likewise to keep them in remembrance. For those old and customary opinions perpetually recur—long and familiar usage giving them the right to occupying my mind, even almost against my will, and subduing my belief; nor will I lose the habit of deferring to them and confiding in them so long as I shall consider them to be what in truth they are, viz., opinions to some extent doubtful, as I have already shown, but still highly probable, and such as it is much more reasonable to believe than deny. It is for this reason I am persuaded that I shall not be doing wrong, if, taking an opposite judgment of deliberate design, I become my own deceiver, by supposing, for a time, that all those opinions are entirely false and imaginary, until at length, having thus balanced my old by my new prejudices, my judgment shall no longer be turned aside by perverted usage from the path that may conduct to the perception of truth. For I am assured that, meanwhile, there will arise neither peril nor error from this course, and that I cannot for the present yield too much distrust, since the end I now seek is not action but knowledge.

I will suppose, then, not that Deity, who is sovereignly good and the fountain of truth, but that some malignant demon, who is at once exceedingly potent and deceitful, has employed all his artifice to deceive me; I will suppose that the sky, the air, the earth, colours, figures, sounds, and all external things, are nothing better than the illusions of dreams, by means of which this being has laid snares for my credulity; I will consider myself as without hands, eyes, flesh, blood, or any of the senses, and as falsely believing that I am possessed of these; I will continue resolutely fixed in this belief, and if indeed by this means it be not in my power to arrive at the knowledge of truth, I shall at least do what is in my power, viz., suspend my judgment, and guard with settled purpose against giving my assent to what is false, and being imposed upon by this deceiver, whatever be his power and artifice.

But this undertaking is arduous, and a certain indolence insensibly leads me back to my ordinary course of life; and just as the captive, who, perchance, was enjoying in his dreams an imaginary liberty; when he begins to suspect that it is but a vision, dreads awakening, and conspires with the agreeable illusions that the deception may be prolonged; so I, of my own accord, fall back into the train of my former beliefs, and fear to arouse myself from my slumber, lest the time of laborious wakefulness that would succeed this quiet rest, in place of bringing any light of day, should prove inadequate to dispel the darkness that will arise from the difficulties that have now been raised.

MEDITATION II

Of the Nature of the Human Mind; and That It Is More Easily Known Than the Body. The Meditation of yesterday has filled my mind with so many doubts, that it is no longer in my power to forget them. Nor do I see, meanwhile, any principle on which they can be resolved; and, just as if I had fallen all of a sudden into very deep water, I am so greatly disconcerted as to be unable either to plant my feet firmly on the bottom or sustain myself by swimming on the surface, I will, nevertheless, make an effort, and try anew the same path on which I had entered yesterday, that is, proceed by casting aside all that admits of the slightest doubt, not less than if I had discovered it to be absolutely false; and I will continue always in this track until I shall find something that is certain, or at least, if I can do nothing more, until I shall know with certainty that there is nothing certain. Archimedes, that he might transport the entire globe from the place it occupied to another, demanded only a point that was firm and immovable; so also, I shall be entitled to entertain the highest expectations, if I am fortunate enough to discover only one thing that is certain and indubitable.

I suppose, accordingly, that all the things which I see are false (fictitious); I believe that none of those objects which my fallacious memory represents ever existed; I suppose that I possess no senses; I believe that body, figure, extension, motion, and place are merely fictions of my mind. What is there, then, that can be esteemed true? Perhaps this only, that there is absolutely nothing certain.

But how do I know that there is not something different altogether from the objects I have now enumerated, of which it is impossible to entertain the slightest doubt? Is there not a God, or some being, by whatever name I may designate him, who causes these thoughts to arise in my mind? But why suppose such a being, for it may be I myself am capable of producing them? Am I, then, at least not something? But I before denied that I possessed senses or a body; I hesitate, however, for what follows from that? Am I so dependent on the body and the senses that without these I cannot exist? But I had the persuasion that there was absolutely nothing in the world, that there was no sky and no earth, neither minds nor bodies; was I not, therefore, at the same time, persuaded that I did not exist? Far from it; I assuredly existed, since I was persuaded. But there is I know not what being, who is possessed at once of the highest power and the deepest cunning, who is constantly employing all his ingenuity in deceiving me. Doubtless, then, I exist, since I am deceived; and, let him deceive me as he may, he can never bring it about that I am nothing, so long as I shall be conscious that I am something. So that it must, in fine, be maintained, all things being maturely and carefully considered, that this proposition, I am, I exist, is necessarily true each time it is expressed by me, or conceived in my mind.

But I do not yet know with sufficient clearness what I am, though assured that I am; and hence, in the next place, I must take care, lest perchance I inconsiderately substitute some other object in room of what is properly myself, and thus wander from truth, even in that knowledge which I hold to be of all others the most certain and evident. For this reason, I will now consider anew what I formerly believed myself to be, before I entered on the present train of thought; and of my previous opinion I will retrench all that can in the least be invalidated by the grounds of doubt I have adduced, in order that there may at length remain nothing but what is certain and indubitable. What then did I formerly think I was? Undoubtedly I judged that I was a man. But what is a man? Shall I say a rational animal? Assuredly not; for it would be necessary forthwith to inquire into what is meant by animal, and what by rational, and thus, from a single question, I should insensibly glide into others, and these more difficult than the first; nor do I now possess enough of leisure to warrant me in wasting my time amid subtleties of this sort. I prefer here to attend to the thoughts that sprung up of themselves in my mind, and were inspired by my own nature alone, when I applied myself to the consideration of what I was. In the first place, then, I thought that I possessed a countenance, hands, arms, and all the fabric of members that appears in a corpse, and which I called by the name of body. It further occurred to me that I was nourished, that I walked, perceived, and thought, and all those actions I referred to the soul, but what the soul itself was I either did not stay to consider, or, if I did, I imagined that it was something extremely rare and subtile, like wind, or flame, or ether, spread through my grosser parts. As regarded the body, I did not even doubt of its nature, but thought I distinctly knew it, and if I had wished to describe it according to the notions I then entertained, I should have explained myself in this manner: By body I understand all that can be terminated by a certain figure; that can be comprised in a certain place, and so fill a certain space as therefrom to exclude every other body; that can be perceived either by touch, sight, hearing, taste, or smell; that can be moved in different ways, not indeed of itself, but by something foreign to it by which it is touched and from which it receives the impression; for the power of self-motion, as likewise that of perceiving and thinking, I held as by no means pertaining to the nature of body; on the contrary, I was somewhat astonished to find such faculties existing in some bodies.

But as to myself, what can I now say that I am, since I suppose there exists an extremely powerful, and, if I may so speak, malignant being, whose whole endeavours are directed towards deceiving me? Can I affirm that I possess any one of all those attributes of which I have lately spoken as belonging to the nature of body? After attentively considering them in my own mind, I find none of them that can properly be said to belong to myself. To recount them were idle and tedious. Let us pass, then, to the attributes of the soul. The first mentioned were the powers of nutrition and walking; but, if it be true that I have no body, it is true likewise that I am capable neither of walking nor of being nourished. Perception is another attribute of the soul; but perception too is impossible without the body: besides, I have frequently during sleep, believed that I perceived objects which I afterwards observed I did not in reality perceive. Thinking is another attribute of the soul; and here I discover what properly belongs to myself. This alone is inseparable from me. I am—I exist: this is certain; but how often? As often as I think; for perhaps it would even happen, if I should wholly cease to think, that I should at the same time altogether cease to be. I now admit nothing that is not necessarily true: I am therefore, precisely speaking, only a thinking thing, that is, a mind, understanding, or reason,—terms whose signification was before unknown to me. I am, however, a real thing, and really existent; but what thing? The answer was, a thinking thing. The question now arises, am I aught besides? I will stimulate my imagination with a view to discover whether I am not still something more than a thinking being. Now it is plain I am not the assemblage of members called the human body; I am not a thin and penetrating air diffused through all these members, or wind, or flame, or vapour, or breath, or any of all the things I can imagine; for I supposed that all these were not, and, without changing the supposition, I find that I still feel assured of my existence.

But it is true, perhaps, that those very things which I suppose to be nonexistent, because they are unknown to me, are not in truth different from myself whom I know. This is a point I cannot determine, and do not now enter into any dispute regarding it. I can only judge of things that are known to me: I am conscious that I exist, and I who know that I exist inquire into what I am. It is, however, perfectly certain that the knowledge of my existence, thus precisely taken, is not dependent on things, the existence of which is as yet unknown to me: and consequently it is not dependent on any of the things I can feign in imagination. Moreover, the phrase itself, I frame an image, reminds me of my error; for I should in truth frame one if I were to imagine myself to be anything, since to imagine is nothing more than to contemplate the figure or image of a corporeal thing; but I already know that I exist, and that it is possible at the same time that all those images, and in general all that relates to the nature of body, are merely dreams or chimeras. From this I discover that it is not more reasonable to say, I will excite my imagination that I may know more distinctly what I am, than to express myself as follows: I am now awake and perceive something real; but because my perception is not sufficiently clear, I will of express purpose go to sleep that my dreams may represent to me the object of my perception with more truth and clearness. And, therefore, I know that nothing of all that I can embrace in imagination belongs to the knowledge which I have of myself, and that there is need to recall with the utmost care the mind from this mode of thinking, that it may be able to know its own nature with perfect distinctness.

But what, then, am I? A thinking thing, it has been said. But what is a thinking thing? It is a thing that doubts, understands, conceives, affirms, denies, wills, refuses, that imagines also, and perceives. Assuredly it is not little, if all these properties belong to my nature. But why should they not belong to it? Am I not that very being who now doubts of almost everything; who, for all that, understands and conceives certain things; who affirms one alone as true, and denies the others; who desires to know more of them, and does not wish to be deceived; who imagines many things, sometimes even despite his will; and is likewise percipient of many, as if through the medium of the senses? Is there nothing of all this as true as that I am, even although I should be always dreaming, and although he who gave me being employed all his ingenuity to deceive me? Is there also any one of these attributes that can be properly distinguished from my thought, or that can be said to be separate from myself? For it is of itself so evident that it is I who doubt, I who understand, and I who desire, that it is here unnecessary to add anything by way of rendering it more clear. And I am as certainly the same being who imagines; for, although it may be (as I before supposed) that nothing I imagine is true, still the power of imagination does not cease really to exist in me and to form part of my thought. In fine, I am the same being who perceives, that is, who apprehends certain objects as by the organs of sense, since, in truth, I see light, hear a noise, and feel heat. But it will be said that these presentations are false, and that I am dreaming. Let it be so. At all events it is certain that I seem to see light, hear a noise, and feel heat; this cannot be false, and this is what in me is properly called perceiving, which is nothing else than thinking. From this I begin to know what I am with somewhat greater clearness and distinctness than heretofore.

But, nevertheless, it still seems to me, and I cannot help believing, that corporeal things, whose images are formed by thought, which fall under the senses, and are examined by the same, are known with much greater distinctness than that I know not what part of myself which is not imaginable; although, in truth, it may seem strange to say that I know and comprehend with greater distinctness things whose existence appears to me doubtful, that are unknown, and do not belong to me, than others of whose reality I am persuaded, that are known to me, and appertain to my proper nature; in a word, than myself. But I see clearly what is the state of the case. My mind is apt to wander, and will not yet submit to be restrained within the limits of truth. Let us therefore leave the mind to itself once more, and, according to it every kind of liberty, permit it to consider the objects that appear to it from without, in order that, having afterwards withdrawn it from these gently and opportunely, and fixed it on the consideration of its being and the properties it finds in itself, it may then be the more easily controlled.

Let us now accordingly consider the objects that are commonly thought to be the most easily, and likewise the most distinctly known, viz., the bodies we touch and see; not, indeed, bodies in general, for these general notions are usually somewhat more confused, but one body in particular. Take, for example, this piece of wax; it is quite fresh, having been but recently taken from the bee-hive; it has not yet lost the sweetness of the honey it contained; it still retains somewhat of the odour of the flowers from which it was gathered; its colour, figure, size, are apparent to the sight, it is hard, cold, easily handled; and sounds when struck upon with the finger. In fine, all that contributes to make a body as distinctly known as possible, is found in the one before us. But, while I am speaking, let it be placed near the fire—what remained of the taste exhales, the smell evaporates, the colour changes, its figure is destroyed, its size increases, it becomes liquid, it grows hot, it can hardly be handled, and, although struck upon, it emits no sound. Does the same wax still remain after this change? It must be admitted that it does remain; no one doubts it, adjudges otherwise. What, then, was it I knew with so much distinctness in the piece of wax? Assuredly, it could be nothing of all that I observed by means of the senses, since all the things that fell under taste, smell, sight, touch, and hearing are changed, and yet the same wax remains. It was perhaps what I now think, viz., that this wax was neither the sweetness of honey, the pleasant odour of flowers, the whiteness, the figure, nor the sound, but only a body that a little before appeared to me conspicuous under these forms, and which is now perceived under others. But, to speak precisely, what is it that I imagine when I think of it in this way? Let it be attentively considered, and, retrenching all that does not belong to the wax, let us see what remains. There certainly remains nothing, except something extended, flexible, and movable. But what is meant by flexible and movable? Is it not that I imagine that the piece of wax, being round, is capable of becoming square, or of passing from a square into a triangular figure? Assuredly such is not the case, because I conceive that it admits of an infinity of similar changes; and I am, moreover, unable to compass this infinity by imagination, and consequently this conception which I have of the wax is not the product of the faculty of imagination. But what now is this extension? Is it not also unknown? For it becomes greater when the wax is melted, greater when it is boiled, and greater still when the heat increases; and I should not conceive clearly and according to truth, the wax as it is, if I did not suppose that the piece we are considering admitted even of a wider variety of extension that I ever imagined. I must, therefore, admit that I cannot even comprehend by imagination what the piece of wax is, and that it is the mind alone which perceives it. I speak of one piece in particular; for, as to wax in general, this is still more evident. But what is the piece of wax that can be perceived only by the understanding or mind? It is certainly the same which I see, touch, imagine; and, in fine, it is the same which, from the beginning, I believed it to be. But (and this it is of moment to observe) the perception of it is neither an act of sight, of touch, nor of imagination, and never was either of these, though it might formerly seem so, but is simply an intuition of the mind, which may be imperfect and confused, as it formerly was, or very clear and distinct, as it is at present, according as the attention is more or less directed to the elements which it contains, and of which it is composed.

But, meanwhile, I feel greatly astonished when I observe the weakness of my mind, and its proneness to error. For although, without at all giving expression to what I think, I consider all this in my own mind, words yet occasionally impede my progress, and I am almost led into error by the terms of ordinary language. We say, for example, that we see the same wax when it is before us, and not that we judge it to be the same from its retaining the same colour and figure: whence I should forthwith be disposed to conclude that the wax is known by the act of sight, and not by the intuition of the mind alone, were it not for the analogous instance of human beings passing on in the street below, as observed from a window. In this case I do not fail to say that I see the men themselves, just as I say that I see the wax; and yet what do I see from the window beyond hats and cloaks that might cover artificial machines, whose motions might be determined by springs? But I judge that there are human beings from these appearances, and thus I comprehend, by the faculty of judgment alone which is in the mind, what I believed I saw with my eyes.

The man who makes it his aim to rise to knowledge superior to the common, ought to be ashamed to seek occasions of doubting from the vulgar forms of speech: instead, therefore, of doing this, I shall proceed with the matter in hand, and inquire whether I had a clearer and more perfect perception of the piece of wax when I first saw it, and when I thought I knew it by means of the external sense itself, or, at all events, by the common sense, as it is called, that is, by the imaginative faculty; or whether I rather apprehend it more clearly at present, after having examined with greater care, both what it is, and in what way it can be known. It would certainly be ridiculous to entertain any doubt on this point. For what, in that first perception, was there distinct? What did I perceive which any animal might not have perceived? But when I distinguish the wax from its exterior forms, and when, as if I had stripped it of its vestments, I consider it quite naked, it is certain, although some error may still be found in my judgment, that I cannot, nevertheless, thus apprehend it without possessing a human mind.

But, finally, what shall I say of the mind itself, that is, of myself? For as yet I do not admit that I am anything but mind. What, then! I who seem to possess so distinct an apprehension of the piece of wax,—do I not know myself, both with greater truth and certitude, and also much more distinctly and clearly? For if I judge that the wax exists because I see it, it assuredly follows, much more evidently, that I myself am or exist, for the same reason: for it is possible that what I see may not in truth be wax, and that I do not even possess eyes with which to see anything; but it cannot be that when I see, or, which comes to the same thing, when I think I see, I myself who think am nothing. So likewise, if I judge that the wax exists because I touch it, it will still also follow that I am; and if I determine that my imagination or any other cause, whatever it be, persuades me of the existence of the wax, I will still draw the same conclusion. And what is here remarked of the piece of wax, is applicable to all the other things that are external to me. And further, if the notion or perception of wax appeared to me more precise and distinct, after that not only sight and touch, but many other causes besides, rendered it manifest to my apprehension, with how much greater distinctness must I not know myself, since all the reasons that contribute to the knowledge of the nature of wax, or of any body whatever, manifest still better the nature of my mind? And there are besides so many other things in the mind itself that contribute to the illustration of its nature, that those dependent on the body, to which I have here referred, scarcely merit to be taken into account.

But, in conclusion, I find I have insensibly reverted to the point I desired; for, since it is now manifest to me that bodies themselves are not properly perceived by the senses nor by the faculty of imagination, but by the intellect alone; and since they are not perceived because they are seen and touched, but only because they are understood or rightly comprehended by thought, I readily discover that there is nothing more easily or clearly apprehended than my own mind. But because it is difficult to rid one's self so promptly of an opinion to which one has been long accustomed, it will be desirable to tarry for some time at this stage, that, by long continued meditation, I may more deeply impress upon my memory this new knowledge.

EMPIRICISM

53. Empiricism

Friedrich Paulsen

Friedrich Paulsen (1846–1908) was professor of philosophy and pedagogy at the University of Berlin. His Introduction to Philosophy, *translated from the third German edition by the American philosopher Frank Thilly, went through a total of twenty-three editions. Its clarity, felicity of style, learning without pedantry, and humane common sense helped make Paulsen's book a standard introductory philosophy text in Germany and the United States.*

. . . The fundamental conception of empiricism is: there are *two kinds of sciences, differing in nature and method*—purely *conceptual sciences,* like *mathematics,* and *objective sciences,* like physics and psychology. Rationalism errs in recognizing only *one* form of science, the mathematical, and in attempting to fashion all sciences after its pattern. That is an impossible undertaking; the sciences dealing with matters of fact, natural and mental sciences, wholly differ from mathematics in content and method.[1]

It is characteristic of mathematics that it makes no assertions concerning the existence and behavior of reality, but deals solely with deductions from notions. Geometry does not say: This figure is a circle; this body is a sphere, and its motion has the form of an ellipse but: Such and such consequences follow from the definition of the circle and the sine. Whoever accepts the definition must also accept its deductions; he is bound by logic to do so. It is wholly immaterial whether or not anything exists corresponding to the notion.

The case is quite different in the other group of sciences, which deal with objects. Physics and psychology aim to inform us how things act which exist independently of our notions. How can we know anything about them? Empiricism answers: Only by experience. It is absolutely impossible to discover from the notion of water and of heat what will happen when the thermometer falls to zero or rises to one hundred degrees; or to infer from the concept of the body what will occur if

From *Introduction to Philosophy* by Friedrich Paulsen, second American edition from the third German edition. Henry Holt and Company, New York, 1895.

[1]The distinction between demonstrative and experimental knowledge founded on perception is fundamental to the entire fourth book of Locke's *Essay,* which is in reality the principal part of the work. The distinction is, however, not accurately defined. The clear and logical exposition of this difference forms the starting-point of Hume's *Enquiry* (Section IV and Section XII, conclusion).

it is deprived of its support. Only by perception do we learn that it will fall under such circumstances; the concept does not help us in the least. Not even the most perfect intellect, says Hume, the intellect of Adam before the fall, could have told him that if he should happen to fall into the water, he would sink and be suffocated. Nay, it could not even reveal to him what would happen were a body in motion to collide with one at rest. Nor can psychology deduce from an absolute notion of the soul that it feels and desires, reasons and infers, or foresee that air-waves will arouse a sensation of sound, or pressure upon the eye, sensations of light, or a blow in the face, a feeling of anger. All these facts are known by experience only.

Locke[2] began these reflections. He attempts to prove that all our notions are derived from experience. In the first book of the *Essay Concerning the Human Understanding* he undertakes to show, with hypercritical thoroughness, that men do not come into the world with innate ideas; a fact of which perhaps no philosopher, least of all Descartes, needed to be apprised. The real opposition between them is a different one. Descartes claims that it is as possible to form notions in physics and psychology as in mathematics, the validity or truth of which is proved by their inner possibility. Locke denies it. The definition of the body: *corpus est res mere extensa,* or the definition: *mens est res mere cogitans,* may be logically possible; it may be clearly and distinctly conceivable, but that by no means establishes its validity: we may have as clear and distinct a conception of a golden mountain. The truth of the notions of all sciences that deal with facts is based solely on the perception of such facts and connections. Hence it follows that the definitions of sciences of fact cannot be as fixed and final as mathematical concepts; they may be enlarged and modified by further observation. Our notion of *gold* is the result of all previous observations concerning this body: it has such and such a color, a particular specific gravity, and reacts in a certain way upon mechanical, chemical, and thermal influences. Further observations may possibly discover new qualities. It is also possible that we may become acquainted with a body having all the qualities of gold but a somewhat higher or lower melting-point. We should in that event extend our notion sufficiently to admit this difference. The mathematical concept, however, is final: A figure in which the radii are not quite equal is not a circle; a line that touches a circle at more than one point is not a tangent. The same remarks apply to the notions on which Descartes aims to base physics and psychology; they are not final or mathematical, but provisional and empirical. Descartes explains: A body is a thing whose essence consists in extension, the soul a thing whose essence consists in states of consciousness (*cogitatio*) for I can clearly and distinctly conceive such a thing. Of course I can; but should experience show that this extended thing also thinks, at least occasionally, or that this thinking being also sets bodies in motion, could I not also conceive that? And in that case would it be advisable to retain the above definitions? Evidently not. For then they would be inadequate to explain actual facts. Hence all concepts concerning matters of fact are provisional notions, they are constantly changing in order to fit the facts yielded by observation. Such notions make a demonstrative procedure like mathematics impossible.

[2][John Locke (1632–1704) was an English philosopher and empiricist.—Ed.]

Locke often insists that mathematics is the most perfect form of knowledge. He deplores the fact that this kind of knowledge (which outside of mathematics is possible only in morals) is restricted to so narrow a field. Nevertheless
we must confess that the sciences of fact like physics, chemistry, and psychology
cannot be treated according to the mathematical method; observation and experiment are necessary here.

Hume[3] continued and completed these reflections. His examination of the
notion of cause and effect forms the cardinal point in his brief and simple but thoughtful *Inquiry Concerning Human Understanding*. The law of causality had always been
the chief support of rationalism. It was supposed that the effect could be deduced
from the cause; the relation existing between cause and effect is the same as that existing between ground and consequent: *sequi = causari*. Hume shows that this is an
error. Inference according to the law of causality is entirely different from con-
cluding according to the logical law of contradiction. The relation between cause and
effect is no logical relation at all, discoverable by pure thought. In physics and psychology such phenomena are said to be causally related as they invariably succeed
each other in time. The perception of succession in time is all that is really observed
here; at any rate, an *inner connection* of phenomena, a necessity that binds them
together, is not a matter of observation. I perceive that a certain state follows upon
a given state; I expect the same event to succeed it the next time it occurs. Here we
have the beginning of the causal conception. We find it in animals; they too learn
from experience, and in the manner indicated: a certain succession is perceived in
events; at the recurrence of the first, the second is expected or anticipated. The function is more highly developed in man; not every perceived succession leads us to
expect its return; we gradually learn to separate the constant causal relations existing
between phenomena from the accidental and dissoluble connections. But the principle is the same in either case. It is absolutely impossible to discover the effect from
the notion of the cause by logical inference. Take the simplest example. The motion of a body in a given period of time is the cause of the same movement during
the succeeding period. This is in no wise discoverable by a logical inference.
From the proposition that a certain body moves with a certain velocity per second,
and in a certain direction, no logical conclusion follows, except the falseness of
its opposite. Nothing whatever can be deduced as to what is going to happen during the *next* second. On the ground of previous observations, I *expect* this body to
pass through an equal space with the same velocity and in the same direction, during the ensuing period of time. But this expectation is not a *necessity of thought,* like
a mathematical proposition. It is also conceivable that the movement should cease
of its own accord, either suddenly or gradually, or that it should turn off in any
direction whatever. Past experience has invariably taught us that things behave
in the manner stated in the law of inertia, but it is not a logical necessity that
the future should resemble the past. Moreover, says Hume,—and that is his
most general proposition,—there is absolutely no fact the non-existence of which
would not be conceivable or logically possible. The non-existence of any body, the

---

[3][David Hume (1711–1776) was a Scottish philosopher, empiricist, and skeptic.—Ed.]

invalidity of any natural law, is conceivable, for the non-existence of the entire world is conceivable.

Hence it follows: In the sciences concerning matters of fact like physics and psychology there are no *truths that are strictly universal and necessary.* These sciences contain propositions that are *only probably universal.* Each one is true with the tacit proviso: subject to correction by subsequent experience. The propositions of mathematics are absolutely universal and necessary. No observation can shake or change the proposition that the sum of the angles of a plane triangle is equal to two right angles; it is implied in the notions themselves as their logically necessary consequence. On the other hand, there is no proposition in physics or psychology that can be said to possess such necessity. Nor is the causal law itself an exception; the proposition that there is absolute regularity in the succession of natural phenomena has presumptive validity only. It is also conceivable or logically possible that phenomena should occur that stand in no relation whatever to all antecedent and all consequent phenomena. We should call such phenomena miracles. Hence miracles are undoubtedly possible, just as possible to thought as facts that may be explained by our laws of nature, *i.e.,* inserted into the natural connection of things according to rules. The question is not a question of possibility, but one of fact. Have facts been observed that would have to be regarded as miracles? Hume raises serious objections to the assertion. According to him the theory that the alleged miracles are explainable, if not physically, psychologically at least, has such great probability that it may be regarded as practically certain. It is a matter of such common experience that human testimony rests on voluntary or involuntary deception, that it seems much more plausible for us to explain an alleged miracle in this way than to abandon the fundamental principle of all natural science, the universal reign of law in nature. This presupposition is, of course, not logically necessary, but has been so often confirmed by facts and has, upon close observation, been so often verified even in the case of alleged miracles, that we have the right, on *a priori* grounds, to doubt new miracles.

That is the epistemology of empiricism. . . . the question at stake in the controversy between rationalism and empiricism is: Do we possess an *a priori* or rational knowledge of objects? Rationalism answers in the affirmative: By pure thought we reach an absolute knowledge of things that cannot be acquired through the senses. Empiricism denies the statement: We gain a knowledge of objects solely by perception, whence it follows that we have no absolute knowledge. . . .

SCEPTICISM

54. Scepticism

David Hume

David Hume (1711–1776) was born in Edinburgh, Scotland. Though known mainly as a historian and diplomat during his lifetime, today he is considered to be one of the great philosophers of modern times, perhaps of all time. His scepticism still profoundly influences contemporary philosophy.

There is a species of scepticism, *antecedent* to all study and philosophy, which is much inculcated by Des Cartes and others, as a sovereign preservative against error and precipitate judgment. It recommends an universal doubt, not only of all our former opinions and principles, but also of our very faculties; of whose veracity, say they, we must assure ourselves, by a chain of reasoning, deduced from some original principle, which cannot possibly be fallacious or deceitful. But neither is there any such original principle, which has a prerogative above others, that are self-evident and convincing: or if there were, could we advance a step beyond it, but by the use of those very faculties, of which we are supposed to be already diffident. The Cartesian doubt, therefore, were it ever possible to be attained by any human creature (as it plainly is not) would be entirely incurable; and no reasoning could ever bring us to a state of assurance and conviction upon any subject.

It must, however, be confessed, that this species of scepticism, when more moderate, may be understood in a very reasonable sense, and is a necessary preparative to the study of philosophy, by preserving a proper impartiality in our judgments, and weaning our mind from all those prejudices, which we may have imbibed from education or rash opinion. To begin with clear and self-evident principles, to advance by timorous and sure steps, to review frequently our conclusions, and examine accurately all their consequences; though by these means we shall make both a slow and a short progress in our systems; are the only methods, by which we can ever hope to reach truth, and attain a proper stability and certainty in our determinations.

There is another species of scepticism, *consequent* to science and enquiry, when men are supposed to have discovered, either the absolute fallaciousness of their mental faculties, or their unfitness to reach any fixed determination in all those

From *An Enquiry Concerning Human Understanding* by David Hume. Edited by L. A. Selby-Bigge. London: Clarendon Press, 1902. Sec. XII, Parts I, II, III, pp. 149–164.

curious subjects of speculation, about which they are commonly employed. Even our very senses are brought into dispute, by a certain species of philosophers; and the maxims of common life are subjected to the same doubt as the most profound principles or conclusions of metaphysics and theology. As these paradoxical tenets (if they may be called tenets) are to be met with in some philosophers, and the refutation of them in several, they naturally excite our curiosity, and make us enquire into the arguments on which they may be founded.

I need not insist upon the more trite topics, employed by the sceptics in all ages, against the evidence of *sense;* such as those which are derived from the imperfection and fallaciousness of our organs, on numberless occasions; the crooked appearance of an oar in water; the various aspects of objects, according to their different distances; the double images which arise from the pressing of one eye; with many other appearances of a like nature. These sceptical topics, indeed, are only sufficient to prove that the senses alone are not implicitly to be depended on; but that we must correct their evidence by reason, and by considerations, derived from the nature of the medium, the distance of the object, and the disposition of the organ, in order to render them, within their sphere, the proper *criteria* of truth and falsehood. There are other more profound arguments against the senses, which admit not of so easy a solution.

It seems evident, that men are carried, by a natural instinct or prepossession, to repose faith in their senses; and that, without any reasoning, or even almost before the use of reason, we always suppose an external universe, which depends not on our perception, but would exist, though we and every sensible creature were absent or annihilated. Even the animal creations are governed by a like opinion, and preserve this belief of external objects, in all their thoughts, designs, and actions.

It seems also evident, that, when men follow this blind and powerful instinct of nature, they always suppose the very images, presented by the senses, to be the external objects, and never entertain any suspicion, that the one are nothing but representations of the other. This very table, which we see white, and which we feel hard, is believed to exist, independent of our perception, and to be something external to our mind, which perceives it. Our presence bestows not being on it: our absence does not annihilate it. It preserves its existence uniform and entire, independent of the situation of intelligent beings, who perceive or contemplate it.

But this universal and primary opinion of all men is soon destroyed by the slightest philosophy, which teaches us that nothing can ever be present to the mind but an image or perception, and that the senses are only the inlets, through which these images are conveyed, without being able to produce any immediate intercourse between the mind and the object. The table, which we see, seems to diminish, as we remove farther from it: but the real table, which exists independent of us, suffers no alteration: it was, therefore, nothing but its image, which was present to the mind. These are the obvious dictates of reason; and no man, who reflects, ever doubted that the existences which we consider when we say *this house* and *that tree,* are nothing but perceptions in the mind, and fleeting copies or representations of other existences, which remain uniform and independent.

So far, then, are we necessitated by reasoning to contradict or depart from the primary instincts of nature, and to embrace a new system with regard to the evidence of our senses. But here philosophy finds herself extremely embarrassed, when she would justify this new system, and obviate the cavils and objections of the sceptics. She can no longer plead the infallible and irresistible instinct of nature: for that led us to a quite different system, which is acknowledged fallible and even erroneous. And to justify this pretended philosophical system, by a chain of clear and convincing argument, or even any appearance of argument, exceeds the power of all human capacity.

By what argument can it be proved, that the perceptions of the mind must be caused by external objects, entirely different from them, though resembling them (if that be possible) and could not arise either from the energy of the mind itself, or from the suggestion of some invisible and unknown spirit or from some other cause still more unknown to us? It is acknowledged, that, in fact, many of these perceptions arise not from anything external, as in dreams, madness, and other diseases. And nothing can be more inexplicable than the manner, in which body should so operate upon mind as ever to convey an image of itself to a substance, supposed of so different, and even contrary a nature.

It is a question of fact, whether the perceptions of the senses be produced by external objects, resembling them: how shall this question be determined? By experience surely; as all other questions of a like nature. But here experience is, and must be entirely silent. The mind has never anything present to it but the perceptions, and cannot possibly reach any experience of their connexion with objects. The supposition of such a connexion is, therefore, without any foundation in reasoning. . . .

Thus the first philosophical objection to the evidence of sense or to the opinion of external existence consists in this, that such an opinion, if rested on natural instinct, is contrary to reason, and if referred to reason, is contrary to natural instinct, and at the same time carries no rational evidence with it, to convince an impartial enquirer. The second objection goes farther, and represents this opinion as contrary to reason: at least, if it be a principle of reason, that all sensible qualities are in the mind, not in the object. Bereave matter of all its intelligible qualities, both primary and secondary, you in a manner annihilate it, and leave only a certain unknown, inexplicable *something,* as the cause of our perceptions; a notion so imperfect, that no sceptic will think it worth while to contend against it. . . .

It is needless to insist farther on this head. These objections are but weak. For as, in common life, we reason every moment concerning fact and existence, and cannot possibly subsist, without continually employing this species of argument, any popular objections, derived from thence, must be insufficient to destroy that evidence. The great subverter of *Pyrrhonism* or the excessive principles of scepticism is action, and employment, and the occupations of common life. These principles may flourish and triumph in the schools; where it is, indeed, difficult, if not impossible, to refute them. But as soon as they leave the shade, and by the presence of the real objects, which actuate our passions and sentiments, are put in opposition to the more powerful principles of our nature, they vanish like smoke, and leave the most determined sceptic in the same condition as other mortals.

The sceptic, therefore, had better keep within his proper sphere, and display those *philosophical* objections, which arise from more profound researches. Here he seems to have ample matter of triumph; while he justly insists, that all our evidence for any matter of fact, which lies beyond the testimony of sense or memory, is derived entirely from the relation of cause and effect; that we have no other idea of this relation than that of two objects, which have been frequently *conjoined* together; that we have no argument to convince us, that objects, which have, in our experience, been frequently conjoined, will likewise, in other instances, be conjoined in the same manner; and that nothing leads us to this inference but custom or a certain instinct of our nature; which it is indeed difficult to resist, but which, like other instincts, may be fallacious and deceitful. While the sceptic insists upon these topics, he shows his force, or rather, indeed, his own and our weakness; and seems, for the time at least, to destroy all assurance and conviction. These arguments might be displayed at greater length, if any durable good or benefit to society could ever be expected to result from them.

For here is the chief and most confounding objection to *excessive* scepticism, that no durable good can ever result from it; while it remains in its full force and vigour. . . . A Pyrrhonian cannot expect that his philosophy will have any constant influence on the mind: or if it had, that its influence would be beneficial to society. On the contrary, he must acknowledge, if he will acknowledge anything, that all human life must perish, were his principles universally and steadily to prevail. All discourse, all action would immediately cease; and men remain in a total lethargy, till the necessities of nature, unsatisfied, put an end to their miserable existence. . . .

There is, indeed, a more *mitigated* scepticism or *academical* philosophy, which may be both durable and useful, and which may, in part, be the result of this Pyrrhonism, or *excessive* scepticism, when its undistinguished doubts are, in some measure, corrected by common sense and reflection. The greater part of mankind are naturally apt to be affirmative and dogmatical in their opinions; and while they see objects only on one side, and have no idea of any counterpoising argument, they throw themselves precipitately into the principles, to which they are inclined; nor have they any indulgence for those who entertain opposite sentiments. To hesitate or balance perplexes their understanding, checks their passion, and suspends their action. They are, therefore, impatient till they escape from a state which to them is so uneasy: and they think that they could never remove themselves far enough from it, by the violence of their affirmations and obstinacy of their belief. But could such dogmatical reasoners become sensible of the strange infirmities of human understanding, even in its most perfect state, and when most accurate and cautious in its determinations; such a reflection would naturally inspire them with more modesty and reserve, and diminish their fond opinion of themselves, and their prejudice against antagonists. . . .

Another species of *mitigated* scepticism which may be of advantage to mankind, and which may be the natural result of the Pyrrhonian doubts and scruples, is the limitation of our enquiries to such subjects as are best adapted to the narrow capacity of human understanding. The *imagination* of man is naturally sublime, delighted with whatever is remote and extraordinary, and running, without control, into the most distant parts of space and time in order to avoid the objects, which custom has rendered too familiar to it. A correct *Judgment* observes a contrary method, and avoiding all distant and high enquiries, confines itself to common life, and to such subjects as fall under daily practice and experience; leaving the more sublime topics to the embellishment of poets and orators, or to the arts of priests and politicians. To bring us to so salutary a determination, nothing can be more serviceable, than to be once thoroughly convinced of the force of the Pyrrhonian doubt, and of the impossibility, that anything, but the strong power of natural instinct, could free us from it. Those who have a propensity to philosophy, will still continue their researches; because they reflect, that, besides the immediate pleasure, attending such an occupation, philosophical decisions are nothing but the reflections of common life, methodized and corrected. But they will never be tempted to go beyond common life, so long as they consider the imperfection of those faculties which they employ, their narrow reach, and their inaccurate operations.

THE NATURE OF SCIENCE

55. *The Detective As Scientist*

Irving M. Copi

*Irving M. Copi (1917–   ), an American professor of philosophy, has written
extensively and lucidly on logic, scientific method, and the philosophy
of language.*

. . . A perennial favorite in this connection is the detective, whose problem is not
quite the same as that of the pure scientist, but whose approach and technique
illustrate the method of science very clearly. The classical example of the astute
detective who can solve even the most baffling mystery is A. Conan Doyle's immortal creation, Sherlock Holmes. Holmes, his stature undiminished by the passage of time, will be our hero in the following account:

1. THE PROBLEM

Some of our most vivid pictures of Holmes are those in which he is busy with mag-
nifying glass and tape measure, searching out and finding essential clues which
had escaped the attention of those stupid bunglers, the "experts" of Scotland Yard.
Or those of us who are by temperament less vigorous may think back more
fondly on Holmes the thinker, ". . . who, when he had an unsolved problem upon
his mind, would go for days, and even for a week, without rest, turning it over,
rearranging his facts, looking at it from every point of view until he had either fathomed it or convinced himself that his data were insufficient."[1] At one such time,
according to Dr. Watson:

> He took off his coat and waistcoat, put on a large blue dressing-gown, and then
> wandered about the room collecting pillows from his bed and cushions from the sofa
> and armchairs. With these he constructed a sort of Eastern divan, upon which he
> perched himself cross-legged, with an ounce of shag tobacco and a box of matches
> laid out in front of him. In the dim light of the lamp I saw him sitting there, an old

Irving M. Copi, *Introduction to Logic*, 5th ed., © 1961. Reprinted by permission of Prentice-Hall, Inc.,
Upper Saddle River, NJ.
[1]"The Man with the Twisted Lip."

briar pipe between his lips, his eyes fixed vacantly upon the corner of the ceiling, the blue smoke curling up from him, silent, motionless, with the light shining upon his strong-set aquiline features. So he sat as I dropped off to sleep, and so he sat when a sudden ejaculation caused me to wake up, and I found the summer sun shining into the apartment. The pipe was still between his lips, the smoke still curling upward, and the room was full of a dense tobacco haze, but nothing remained of the heap of shag which I had seen upon the previous night.[2]

But such memories are incomplete. Holmes was not always searching for clues or pondering over solutions. We all remember those dark periods—especially in the earlier stories—when, much to the good Watson's annoyance, Holmes would drug himself with morphine or cocaine. That would happen, of course, between cases. For when there is no mystery to be unraveled, no man in his right mind would go out to look for clues. Clues, after all, must be clues for something. Nor could Holmes, or anyone else, for that matter, engage in profound thought unless he had something to think about. Sherlock Holmes was a genius at solving problems, but even a genius must have a problem before he can solve it. All reflective thinking, and this term includes criminal investigation as well as scientific research, is a problem-solving activity, as John Dewey and other pragmatists have rightly insisted. There must be a problem felt before either the detective or the scientist can go to work.

Of course the active mind sees problems where the dullard sees only familiar objects. One Christmas season Dr. Watson visited Holmes to find that the latter had been using a lens and forceps to examine" . . . a very seedy and disreputable hard-felt hat, much the worse for wear, and cracked in several places."[3] After they had greeted each other, Holmes said of it to Watson, "I beg that you will look upon it not as a battered billycock but as an intellectual problem."[4] It so happened that the hat led them into one of their most interesting adventures, but it could not have done so had Holmes not seen a problem in it from the start. A problem may be characterized as a fact or group of facts for which we have no acceptable explanation, which seem unusual, or which fail to fit in with our expectations or preconceptions. It should be obvious that *some* prior beliefs are required if anything is to appear problematic. If there are no expectations, there can be no surprises.

Sometimes, of course, problems came to Holmes already labeled. The very first adventure recounted by Dr. Watson began with the following message from Gregson of Scotland Yard:

My Dear Mr. Sherlock Holmes:
There has been a bad business during the night at 3, Lauriston Gardens, off the Brixton Road. Our man on the beat saw a light there about two in the morning, and as the house was an empty one, suspected that something was amiss. He found

---

[2]Ibid.
[3]"The Adventure of the Blue Carbuncle."
[4]Ibid.

the door open, and in the front room, which is bare of furniture, discovered the body of a gentleman, well dressed, and having cards in his pocket bearing the name of "Enoch J. Drebber, Cleveland, Ohio, U.S.A." There had been no robbery, nor is there any evidence as to how the man met his death. There are marks of blood in the room, but there is no wound upon his person. We are at a loss as to how he came into the empty house; indeed, the whole affair is a puzzler. If you can come round to the house any time before twelve, you will find me there. I have left everything *in statu quo* until I hear from you. If you are unable to come, I shall give you fuller details, and would esteem it a great kindness if you would favour me with your opinion.

Yours faithfully,
Tobias Gregson[5]

Here was a problem indeed. A few minutes after receiving the message, Sherlock Holmes and Dr. Watson "were both in a hansom, driving furiously for the Brixton Road."

2. PRELIMINARY HYPOTHESES

On their ride out Brixton way, Holmes "prattled away about Cremona fiddles and the difference between a Stradivarius and an Amati." Dr. Watson chided Holmes for not giving much thought to the matter at hand, and Holmes replied: "No data yet. . . . It is a capital mistake to theorize before you have all the evidence. It biases the judgment."[6] This point of view was expressed by Holmes again and again. On one occasion he admonished a younger detective that "The temptation to form premature theories upon insufficient data is the bane of our profession."[7] Yet for all of his confidence about the matter, on this one issue Holmes was completely mistaken. Of course one should not reach a *final judgment* until a great deal of evidence has been considered, but this procedure is quite different from *not theorizing*. As a matter of fact, it is strictly impossible to make any serious attempt to collect evidence unless one *has* theorized beforehand. As Charles Darwin, the great biologist and author of the modern theory of evolution, observed:" . . . all observation must be for or against some view, if it is to be of any service." The point is that there are too many particular facts, too many data in the world, for anyone to try to become acquainted with them all. Everyone, even the most patient and thorough investigator, must pick and choose, deciding which facts to study and which to pass over. He must have some working hypothesis for or against which to collect relevant data. It need not be a *complete* theory, but at least the rough outline must be there. Otherwise how could one decide what facts to select for consideration out of the totality of all facts, which is too vast even to begin to sift?

[5]*A Study in Scarlet.*
[6]Ibid.
[7]*The Valley of Fear.*

Holmes' actions were wiser than his words in this connection. After all, the words were spoken in a hansom speeding towards the scene of the crime. If Holmes really had no theory about the matter, why go to Brixton Road? If facts and data were all that he wanted, any old facts and any old data, with no hypotheses to guide him in their selection, why should he have left Baker Street at all? There were plenty of facts in the rooms at 221-B, Baker Street. Holmes might just as well have spent his time counting all the words on all the pages of all the books there, or perhaps making very accurate measurements of the distances between each separate pair of articles of furniture in the house. He could have gathered data to his heart's content and saved himself cab fare into the bargain!

It may be objected that the facts to be gathered at Baker Street have nothing to do with the case, whereas those which awaited Holmes at the scene of the crime were valuable clues for solving the problem. It was, of course, just this consideration which led Holmes to ignore the "data" at Baker Street and hurry away to collect those off Brixton Road. It must be insisted, however, that the greater relevance of the latter could not be *known* beforehand but only conjectured on the basis of previous experience with crimes and clues. It was in fact a *hypothesis* which led Holmes to look in one place rather than another for his facts, the hypothesis that there was a murder, that the crime was committed at the place where the body was found, and that the murderer had left some trace or clue which could lead to his discovery. Some such hypothesis is always required to guide the investigator in his search for relevant data, for in the absence of any preliminary hypothesis, there are simply too many facts in this world to examine. The preliminary hypothesis ought to be highly tentative, and it must be based on previous knowledge. But a preliminary hypothesis is as necessary as the existence of a problem for any serious inquiry to begin.

It must be emphasized that a preliminary hypothesis, as here conceived, need not be a complete solution to the problem. The hypothesis that the man was murdered by someone who had left some clues to his identity on or near the body of his victim was what led Holmes to Brixton Road. This hypothesis is clearly incomplete: it does not say who committed the crime, or how it was done, or why. Such a preliminary hypothesis may be very different from the final solution to the problem. It will never be complete: it may be a tentative explanation of only part of the problem. But however partial and however tentative, a preliminary hypothesis is required for any investigation to proceed.

3. COLLECTING ADDITIONAL FACTS

Every serious investigation begins with some fact or group of facts which strike the investigator as problematic and which initiate the whole process of inquiry. The initial facts which constitute the problem are usually too meagre to suggest a wholly satisfactory explanation for themselves, but they will suggest—to the competent investigator—some preliminary hypotheses which lead him to search out additional facts. These additional facts, it is hoped, will serve as clues to the final solution. The inexperienced or bungling investigator will overlook or ignore all but the most obvious of them; but the careful worker will aim at completeness in his examination of the additional facts to which his preliminary hypotheses had led. Holmes, of course, was the most careful and painstaking of investigators.

Holmes insisted on dismounting from the hansom a hundred yards or so from their destination and approached the house on foot, looking carefully at its surroundings and especially at the pathway leading up to it. When Holmes and Watson entered the house, they were shown the body by the two Scotland Yard operatives, Gregson and Lestrade. ("There is no clue," said Gregson. "None at all," chimed in Lestrade.) But Holmes had already started his own search for additional facts, looking first at the body:

> . . . his nimble fingers were flying here, there, and everywhere, feeling, pressing, unbuttoning, examining. . . . So swiftly was examination made, that one would hardly have guessed the minuteness with which it was conducted. Finally, he sniffed the dead man's lips, and then glanced at the soles of his patent leather boots.[8]

Then turning his attention to the room itself.

> . . . he whipped a tape measure and large round magnifying glass from his pocket. With these two implements he trotted noiselessly about the room, sometimes stopping, occasionally kneeling, and once lying flat upon his face. So engrossed was he with his occupation that he appeared to have forgotten our presence, for he chattered away to himself under his breath the whole time, keeping up a running fire of exclamations, groans, whistles, and little cries, suggestive of encouragement and of hope. As I watched him I was irresistibly reminded of a pure-blooded, well-trained fox-hound as it dashes backward and forward through the covert, whining in its eagerness, until it comes across the lost scent. For twenty minutes or more he continued his researches, measuring with the most exact care the distance between marks which were entirely invisible to me, and occasionally applying his tape to the walls in an equally incomprehensible manner. In one place he gathered up very carefully a little pile of gray dust from the floor and packed it away in an envelope. Finally he examined with his glass the word upon the wall, going over every letter of it with the most minute exactness. This done, he appeared to be satisfied, for he replaced his tape and his glass in his pocket.
> "They say that genius is an infinite capacity for taking pains," he remarked with a smile. "It's a very bad definition, but it does apply to detective work."[9]

One matter deserves to be emphasized very strongly. Steps 2 and 3 are not completely separable but are usually very intimately connected and interdependent. True enough, we require a preliminary hypothesis to begin any intelligent examination of facts, but the additional facts may themselves suggest new

[8]*A Study in Scarlet.*
[9]Ibid.

hypotheses, which may lead to new facts, which suggest still other hypotheses, which lead to still other additional facts, and so on. Thus having made his careful examination of the facts available in the house off Brixton Road, Holmes was led to formulate a further hypothesis which required the taking of testimony from the constable who found the body. The man was off duty at the moment, and Lestrade gave Holmes the constable's name and address.

> Holmes took a note of the address.
> "Come along, Doctor," he said: "we shall go and look him up. I'll tell you one thing which may help you in the case," he continued, turning to the two detectives. "There has been murder done, and the murderer was a man. He was more than six feet high, was in the prime of life, had small feet for his height, wore coarse, square-toed boots and smoked a Trichinopoly cigar. He came here with his victim in a four-wheeled cab, which was drawn by a horse with three old shoes and one new one on his off fore-leg. In all probability the murderer had a florid face, and the fingernails of his right hand were remarkably long. These are only a few indications, but they may assist you."
> Lestrade and Gregson glanced at each other with an incredulous smile.
> "If this man was murdered, how was it done?" asked the former.
> "Poison," said Sherlock Holmes curtly, and strode off.[10]

4. FORMULATING THE HYPOTHESIS

At some stage or other of his investigation, any man—whether detective, scientist, or ordinary mortal—will get the feeling that he has all the facts needed for his solution. He has his "2 and 2," so to speak, but the task still remains of "putting them together." At such a time Sherlock Holmes might sit up all night, consuming pipe after pipe of tobacco, trying to think things through. The result or end product of such thinking, if it is successful, is a hypothesis which accounts for all the data, both the original set of facts which constituted the problem, and the additional facts to which the preliminary hypotheses pointed. The actual discovery of such an explanatory hypothesis is a process of creation, in which imagination as well as knowledge is involved. Holmes, who was a genius at inventing hypotheses, described the process as reasoning "backward." As he put it,

> Most people if you describe a train of events to them, will tell you what the result would be. They can put those events together in their minds, and argue from them that something will come to pass. There are few people, however, who, if you told them a result, would be able to evolve from their own inner consciousness what the steps were which led up to that result.[11]

[10]Ibid.
[11]Ibid.

Here is Holmes' description of the process of formulating an explanatory hypothesis. However that may be, when a hypothesis has been proposed, its evaluation must be along the lines that were sketched in Section III [omitted here]. Granted its relevance and testability, and its compatibility with other well-attested beliefs, the ultimate criterion for evaluating a hypothesis is its predictive power.

5. DEDUCING FURTHER CONSEQUENCES

A really fruitful hypothesis will not only explain the facts which originally inspired it, but will explain many others in addition. A good hypothesis will point beyond the initial facts in the direction of new ones whose existence might otherwise not have been suspected. And of course the verification of those further consequences will tend to confirm the hypothesis which led to them. Holmes' hypothesis that the murdered man had been poisoned was soon put to such a test. A few days later the murdered man's secretary and traveling companion was also found murdered. Holmes asked Lestrade, who had discovered the second body, whether he had found anything in the room which could furnish a clue to the murderer. Lestrade answered, "Nothing," and went on to mention a few quite ordinary effects. Holmes was not satisfied and pressed him, asking, "And was there nothing else?" Lestrade answered, "Nothing of any importance," and named a few more details, the last of which was "a small chip ointment box containing a couple of pills." At this information,

> Sherlock Holmes sprang from his chair with an exclamation of delight.
> "The last links," he cried, exultantly. "My case is complete."
> The two detectives stared at him in amazement.
> "I have now in my hands," my companion said, confidently, "all the threads which have formed such a tangle. . . . I will give you a proof of my knowledge. Could you lay your hands upon those pills?"
> "I have them," said Lestrade, producing a small white box . . .[12]

On the basis of his hypothesis about the original crime, Holmes was able to predict that the pills found at the scene of the second crime must contain poison. Here deduction has an essential role in the process of any scientific or inductive inquiry. The ultimate value of any hypothesis lies in its predictive or explanatory power, which means that additional facts must be deducible from an adequate hypothesis. From his theory that the first man was poisoned and that the second victim met his death at the hands of the same murderer, Holmes inferred that the pills found by Lestrade must be poison. His theory, however sure he may have felt about it, was only a theory and needed further confirmation. He obtained that confirmation by testing the consequences deduced from the hypothesis and

[12]Ibid.

finding them to be true. Having used deduction to make a prediction, his next step was to test it.

6. Testing the Consequences

The consequences of a hypothesis, that is, the predictions made on the basis of that hypothesis, may require various means for their testing. Some require only observation. In some cases, Holmes needed only to watch and wait—for the bank robbers to break into the vault, in the "Adventure of the Redheaded League," or for Dr. Roylott to slip a venomous snake through a dummy ventilator, in the "Adventure of the Speckled Band." In the present case, however, an experiment had to be performed.

Holmes asked Dr. Watson to fetch the landlady's old and ailing terrier, which she had asked to have put out of its misery the day before. Holmes then cut one of the pills in two, dissolved it in a wineglass of water, added some milk, and

> . . . turned the contents of the wineglass into a saucer and placed it in front of the terrier, who speedily licked it dry. Sherlock Holmes's earnest demeanour had so far convinced us that we all sat in silence, watching the animal intently, and expecting some startling effect. None such appeared, however. The dog continued to lie stretched upon the cushion, breathing in a laboured way, but apparently neither the better nor the worse for its draught.
>
> Holmes had taken out his watch, and as minute followed minute without result, an expression of the utmost chagrin and disappointment appeared upon his features. He gnawed his lip, drummed his fingers upon the table, and showed every other symptom of acute impatience. So great was his emotion that I felt sincerely sorry for him, while the two detectives smiled derisively, by no means displeased at this check which he had met.
>
> "It can't be a coincidence," he cried, at last springing from his chair and pacing wildly up and down the room: "it is impossible that it should be a mere coincidence. The very pills which I suspected in the case of Drebber are actually found after the death of Stangerson. And yet they are inert. What can it mean? Surely my whole chain of reasoning cannot have been false. It is impossible! And yet this wretched dog is none the worse. Ah, I have it! I have it!" With a perfect shriek of delight he rushed to the box, cut the other pill in two, dissolved it, added milk, and presented it to the terrier. The unfortunate creature's tongue seemed hardly to have been moistened in it before it gave a convulsive shiver in every limb, and lay as rigid and lifeless as if it had been struck by lightning.
>
> Sherlock Holmes drew a long breath, and wiped the perspiration from his forehead.[13]

By the favorable outcome of his experiment, Holmes' hypothesis had received dramatic and convincing confirmation.

[13]Ibid.

7. APPLICATION

The detective's concern, after all, is a practical one. Given a crime to solve, he has not merely to explain the facts but to apprehend and arrest the criminal. The latter involves making application of his theory, using it to predict where the criminal can be found and how he may be caught. He must deduce still further consequences from the hypothesis, not for the sake of additional confirmation but for practical use. From his general hypothesis Holmes was able to infer that the murderer was acting the role of a cabman. We have already seen that Holmes had formed a pretty clear description of the man's appearance. He sent out his army of "Baker Street Irregulars," street urchins of the neighborhood, to search out and summon the cab driven by just that man. The successful "application" of this hypothesis can be described again in Dr. Watson's words. A few minutes after the terrier's death.

> . . . there was a tap at the door, and the spokesman of the street Arabs, young Wiggins, introduced his insignificant and unsavoury person.
>
> "Please, sir," he said touching his forelock, "I have the cab downstairs."
>
> "Good boy" said Holmes, blandly. "Why don't you introduce this pattern at Scotland Yard?" he continued, taking a pair of steel handcuffs from a drawer. "See how beautifully the spring works. They fasten in an instant."
>
> "The old pattern is good enough," remarked Lestrade, "if we can only find the man to put them on."
>
> "Very good, very good," said Holmes, smiling. "The cabman may as well help me with my boxes. Just ask him to step in, Wiggins."
>
> I was surprised to find my companion speaking as though he were about to set out on a journey, since he had not said anything to me about it. There was a small portmanteau in the room, and this he pulled out and began to strap. He was busily engaged at it when the cabman entered the room.
>
> "Just give me a help with this buckle, cabman," he said, kneeling over his task, and never turning his head.
>
> The fellow came forward with a somewhat sullen, defiant air, and put down his hands to assist. At that instant there was a sharp click, the jangling of metal, and Sherlock Holmes sprang to his feet again.
>
> "Gentlemen," he cried, with flashing eyes, "let me introduce you to Mr. Jefferson Hope, the murderer of Enoch Drebber and of Joseph Stangerson."[14]

Here we have a picture of the detective as scientist, reasoning from observed facts to a testable hypothesis which not only explains the facts but permits of practical application.

[14]Ibid.

56. The Limits and the Value of Scientific Method

Morris R. Cohen and Ernest Nagel

Morris Raphael Cohen (1880–1947), American philosopher and logician, was professor of philosophy at the College of the City of New York for many years, then at the University of Chicago. He was a tireless champion of reason, scientific naturalism, and liberalism against all forms of irrationalism, supernaturalism, and dogmatism.

Ernest Nagel (1901–1985), an internationally known American philosopher of science, was university professor emeritus, Columbia University, when he died. From 1955 to 1966 he was John Dewey Professor of Philosophy at the same institution. Like Morris Cohen, he was an unwavering defender of reason, scientific naturalism, and liberalism.

The desire for knowledge for its own sake is more widespread than is generally recognized by anti-intellectualists. It has its roots in the animal curiosity which shows itself in the cosmological questions of children and the gossip of adults. No ulterior utilitarian motive makes people want to know about the private lives of their neighbors, the great, or the notorious. There is also a certain zest which makes people engage in various intellectual games or exercises in which one is required to find out something. But while the desire to know is wide, it is seldom strong enough to overcome the more powerful organic desires, and few indeed have both the inclination and the ability to face the arduous difficulties of scientific method in more than one special field. The desire to know is not often strong enough to sustain critical inquiry. Men generally are interested in the results, in the story or romance of science, not in the technical methods whereby these results are obtained and their truth continually is tested and qualified. Our first impulse is to accept the plausible as true and to reject the uncongenial as false. We have not the time, inclination, or energy to investigate everything. Indeed, the call to do so is often felt as irksome and joy-killing. And when we are asked to treat our cherished beliefs as mere hypotheses, we rebel as violently as when those dear to us are insulted. This provides the ground for various movements that are hostile to rational scientific procedure (though their promoters do not often admit that it is science to which they are hostile).

From *An Introduction to Logic and Scientific Method* by Morris R. Cohen and Ernest Nagel, copyright 1934 by Harcourt Brace Jovanovich, Inc. Reprinted by permission of Hackett Publishing Co., Inc. All rights reserved.

Mystics, intuitionists, authoritarians, voluntarists, and factionalists are all trying to undermine respect for the rational methods of science. These attacks have always met with wide acclaim and are bound to continue to do so, for they strike a responsive note in human nature. Unfortunately they do not offer any reliable alternative method for obtaining verifiable knowledge. The great French writer Pascal opposed to logic the spirit of subtlety or finesse (*esprit géometrique and esprit de finesse*) and urged that the heart has its reasons as well as the mind, reasons that cannot be accurately formulated but which subtle spirits apprehend none the less. Men as diverse as James Russell Lowell and George Santayana are agreed that:

"The soul is oracular still,"

and

"It is wisdom to trust the heart. . .
        To trust the soul's invincible surmise."

Now it is true that in the absence of omniscience we must trust our soul's surmise; and great men are those whose surmises or intuitions are deep or penetrating. It is only by acting on our surmise that we can procure the evidence in its favor. But only havoc can result from confusing a surmise with a proposition for which there is already evidence. Are all the reasons of the heart sound? Do all oracles tell the truth? The sad history of human experience is distinctly discouraging to any such claim. Mystic intuition may give men absolute subjective certainty, but can give no proof that contrary intuitions are erroneous. It is obvious that when authorities conflict we must weigh the evidence in their favor logically if we are to make a rational choice. Certainly, when a truth is questioned it is no answer to say, "I am convinced," or, "I prefer to rely on this rather than on another authority." The view that physical science is no guide to proof, but is a mere fiction, fails to explain why it has enabled us to anticipate phenomena of nature and to control them. These attacks on scientific method receive a certain color of plausibility because of some indefensible claims made by uncritical enthusiasts. But it is of the essence of scientific method to limit its own pretension. Recognizing that we do not know everything, it does not claim the ability to solve all of our practical problems. It is an error to suppose, as is often done, that science denies the truth of all unverified propositions. For that which is unverified today may be verified tomorrow. We may get at truth by guessing or in other ways. Scientific method, however, is concerned with verification. Admittedly the wisdom of those engaged in this process has not been popularly ranked as high as that of the sage, the prophet, or the poet. Admittedly, also, we know of no way of supplying creative intelligence to those who lack it. Scientists, like all other human beings, may get into ruts and apply their techniques regardless of varying circumstances. There will always be formal procedures which are fruitless. Definitions and formal distinctions may be a sharpening of tools without the wit to use them properly, and statistical information may conform to the highest technical standards and yet be irrelevant and inconclusive. Nevertheless, scientific method is the only way to increase the general body of tested and verified truth and to eliminate arbitrary opinion. It is well to clarify our ideas by asking for the precise meaning of our words, and to try to check our favorite ideas by applying them to accurately formulated propositions.

In raising the question as to the social need for scientific method, it is well to recognize that the suspension of judgment which is essential to that method is difficult or impossible when we are pressed by the demands of immediate action. When my house is on fire, I must act quickly and promptly—I cannot stop to consider the possible causes, nor even to estimate the exact probabilities involved in the various alternative ways of reacting. For this reason, those who are bent upon some specific course of action often despise those devoted to reflection; and certain ultramodernists seem to argue as if the need for action guaranteed the truth of our decision. But the fact that I must either vote for candidate X or refrain from doing so does not of itself give me adequate knowledge. The frequency of our regrets makes this obvious. Wisely ordered society is therefore provided with means for deliberation and reflection *before* the pressure of action becomes irresistible. In order to assure the most thorough investigation, all possible views must be canvassed, and this means toleration of views that are *prima facie* most repugnant to us.

In general the chief social condition of scientific method is a widespread desire for truth that is strong enough to withstand the powerful forces which made us cling tenaciously to old views or else embrace every novelty because it is a change. Those who are engaged in scientific work need not only leisure for reflection and material for their experiments, but also a community that respects the pursuit of truth and allows freedom for the expression of intellectual doubt as to its most sacred or established institutions. Fear of offending established dogmas has been an obstacle to the growth of astronomy and geology and other physical sciences; and the fear of offending patriotic or respected sentiment is perhaps one of the strongest hindrances to scholarly history and social science. On the other hand, when a community indiscriminately acclaims every new doctrine the love of truth becomes subordinated to the desire for novel formulations.

On the whole it may be said that the safety of science depends on there being men who care more for the justice of their methods than for any results obtained by their use. For this reason it is unfortunate when scientific research in the social field is largely in the hands of those not in a favorable position to oppose established or popular opinion.

We may put it the other way by saying that the physical sciences can be more liberal because we are sure that foolish opinions will be readily eliminated by the shock of facts. In the social field, however, no one can tell what harm may come of foolish ideas before the foolishness is finally, if ever, demonstrated. None of the precautions of scientific method can prevent human life from being an adventure, and no scientific investigator knows whether he will reach his goal. But scientific method does enable large numbers to walk with surer step. By analyzing the possibilities of any step or plan, it becomes possible to anticipate the future and adjust ourselves to it in advance. Scientific method thus minimizes the shock of novelty and the uncertainty of life. It enables us to frame policies of action and of moral judgment fit for a wider outlook than those of immediate physical stimulus or organic response.

Scientific method is the only effective way of strengthening the love of truth. It develops the intellectual courage to face difficulties and to overcome illusions that are pleasant temporarily but destructive ultimately. It settles differences without any external force by appealing to our common rational nature. The way of science, even if it is up a steep mountain, is open to all. Hence, while sectarian and partisan faiths are based on personal choice or temperament and divide men, scientific procedure unites men in something nobly devoid of all pettiness. Because it requires detachment, disinterestedness, it is the finest flower and test of a liberal civilization.

CONTEMPORARY ISSUES

Creationism vs. Evolution

57. The Nature of Science and of Theories on Origins

Duane T. Gish

Duane Tolbert Gish (1921–) is senior vice president at the Institute for Creation Research, El Cajon, California. He has degrees from both the University of California at Los Angeles and the University of California at Berkeley (Ph.D., biochemistry) as well as eighteen years of experience in biochemical and biomedical research at Berkeley, Cornell University, and the Upjohn Company. He has authored numerous books and articles on scientific creation, including booklets for high school and college students.

Science is our attempt to observe, understand, and explain the operation of the universe and of the living things it contains. Since a scientific theory, by definition, must be testable by repeatable observations and must be capable of being falsified if indeed it were false, a scientific theory can only attempt to explain processes and events that are presently occurring repeatedly within our observations. Theories about history, although interesting and often fruitful, are not scientific theories, even though they may be related to other theories which do fulfill the criteria of a scientific theory.

THE NATURE OF THEORIES ON ORIGINS

On the other hand, the theory of creation and the theory of evolution are attempts to explain the *origin* of the universe and of its inhabitants. There were no human observers to the origin of the universe, the origin of life, or, as a matter of fact, to the origin of a single type of living organism. These events were unique historical events which have occurred only once. Thus, no one has ever seen anything created, nor has anyone ever seen a fish evolve into an amphibian nor an ape evolve into man.

Duane T. Gish, Impact article 262, April, 1995. Institute for Creation Research, El Cajon, CA 92021.

The changes we see occurring today are mere fluctuations in populations which result neither in an increase in complexity nor significant change. Therefore, *neither* creation nor evolution is a scientific theory. Creation and evolution are inferences based on *circumstantial evidence.*

Thus the notion that evolution is a scientific theory while creation is nothing more than religious mysticism is blatantly false. This is being recognized more and more today, even by evolutionists themselves. Karl Popper, one of the world's leading philosophers of science, has stated that evolution is not a scientific theory but is a metaphysical research program.[1] Birch and Ehrlich state that:

> Our theory of evolution has become . . . one which cannot be refuted by any possible observation. Every conceivable observation can be fitted into it. It is thus "outside of empirical science" but not necessarily false. No one can think of ways in which to test it. Ideas either without basis or based on a few laboratory experiments carried out in extremely simplified systems have attained currency far beyond their validity. They have become part of an evolutionary dogma accepted by most of us as part of our training.[2]

Green and Goldberger, with reference to theories on the origin of life, have said that:

> . . . the macromolecule-to-cell transition is a jump of fantastic dimensions, which lies beyond the range of testable hypothesis. In this area all is conjecture.[3]

It seems obvious that a theory that is outside of empirical science, or a theory that lies beyond the range of testable hypothesis cannot qualify as a scientific theory. Any suggestion that these challenges to the status of evolution as a scientific theory are exceptions can be refuted by a thorough search of the scientific literature. Although these quotes are fairly old, they are still true and relevant.

It is evident that the major challenge to the status of evolution as a scientific theory comes from within the evolutionary establishment itself, not from creation scientists.

Creation and evolution are thus theoretical inferences about history. Even though neither qualifies as a scientific theory, each possesses scientific character, since each attempts to correlate and explain scientific data. Creation and evolution are best characterized as explanatory scientific models which are employed to correlate and explain data related to origins. The terms "creation theory," "evolution theory," "creation science," and "evolution science" are appropriate as long as it is clear that the use of such terms denotes certain inferences about the history of origins which employ scientific data rather than referring to testable scientific theories.

[1] Karl Popper, *The Philosophy of Karl Popper,* vol. 1, ed. P.A. Schilpp (La Salle, Ill.: Open Court Publishers, 1974), pp. 133–181.

[2] L.C. Birch and P.R. Ehrlich, *Nature,* vol. 214 (1967), p. 369.

[3] D.E. Green and R.F. Goldberger, *Molecular Insights into the Living Process* (New York: Academic Press, 1967), p. 407.

Since neither is a scientific theory and each seeks to explain the same scientific data related to origins, it is not only incorrect but arrogant and self-serving for evolutionists to declare that evolution is science while creation is mere religion. Creation is in every sense as scientific as evolution.

THE RELATIONSHIP OF THEORIES ON ORIGINS TO PHILOSOPHY AND RELIGION

No theory on origins can be devoid of philosophical and religious implications. Creation implies the existence of a Creator (a person or persons, a force, an intelligence, or whatever one may wish to impute). The creation scientist assumes that the natural universe is the product of the design, purpose, and direct volitional acts of a Creator. It is untrue to say that creation scientists are seeking to introduce Biblical creation into the public schools. Their desire is that the subject of origins be taught in a philosophically and religiously neutral manner, as required by the U.S. Constitution as applied in recent decades.

On the other hand, evolution is a non-theistic theory of origins which by definition excludes the intervention of an outside agency of any kind. Evolutionists believe that by employing natural laws and processes *plus nothing*, it is possible to explain the origin of the universe and of all that it contains. This involves the acceptance of a particular philosophical or metaphysical world view and is thus basically religious in nature. The fact that creation and evolution involve fundamentally different world views has been frankly admitted by some evolutionists. For example, Lewontin has said:

> Yet, whatever our understanding of the social struggle that gives rise to creationism, whatever the desire to reconcile science and religion may be, there is no escape from the fundamental contradiction between evolution and creationism. They are irreconcilable world views.[4]

Thus, Lewontin characterizes creation and evolution as *irreconcilable world views*, and as such each involves commitment to irreconcilable philosophical and religious positions. This does not imply that all evolutionists are atheists or agnostics, nor does it imply that all creationists are Bible-believing fundamentalists.

While it is true that teaching creation science exclusively would encourage belief in a theistic world view, it is equally true that teaching evolution exclusively (as is essentially the case in the U.S. today) encourages belief in a non-theistic, and in fact, an essentially atheistic world view. Indoctrinating our young people in evolutionism tends to convince them that they are hardly more than a mechanistic product of a mindless universe, that there is no God, that there is no one to whom they are responsible.

---

[4]R. Lewontin, in the Introduction to *Scientists Confront Creationism*, ed. L. R. Godfrey (New York: W. W. Norton and Co., 1983), p. xxvi.

In their literature, humanists have proclaimed that humanism is a "nontheistic religion." They quote Sir Julian Huxley as stating:

> I use the word "Humanist" to mean someone who believes that man is just as much a natural phenomenon as an animal or plant; that his body, mind, and soul were not supernaturally created but are products of evolution. . . .[5]

In his eulogy to Theodosius Dobzhansky, one of the world's leading evolutionists until his death, Ayala wrote that:

> . . . Dobzhansky believed and propounded that the implications of biological evolution reach much beyond biology into philosophy, sociology, and even sociopolitical issues. The place of biological evolution in human thought was, according to Dobzhansky, best expressed in a passage he often quoted from Pierre Teilhard de Chardin: "(Evolution) is a general postulate to which all theories, all hypotheses, all systems must henceforward bow and which they must satisfy in order to be thinkable and true. Evolution is a light which illuminates all facts, a trajectory which all lines of thought must follow—this is what evolution is.[6]

The above statement is as saturated with religion as any assertion could be, and yet it is quoted approvingly by Ayala and Dobzhansky, two of the main architects of the neo-Darwinian theory of evolution.

It is no wonder that Marjorie Grene, a leading historian of science, has stated that:

> It is as a religion of science that Darwinism chiefly held, and holds, men's minds. The derivation of life, of man, of man's deepest hopes and highest achievements, from the external and indirect determination of small chance errors, appears as the very keystone of the naturalistic universe. . . . Today the tables are turned. The modified, but still characteristically Darwinian theory has itself become an orthodoxy preached by its adherents with religious fervor, and doubted, they feel, only by a few muddlers imperfect in scientific faith.[7]

Birch and Ehrlich have used the term "evolutionary dogma," Grene has referred to Darwinism as a "religion of science," an "orthodoxy preached by its adherents with religious fervor," and Dobzhansky and Teilhard de Chardin proclaim that "all theories, all hypotheses, all systems must bow before evolution in order to be thinkable and true." One could easily search the evolutionary literature to find many other examples that reveal the religious nature of the evolutionary world view. *It can thus be stated unequivocally that evolution is as religious as creation, and conversely, that creation is as scientific as evolution.*

---

[5]*"What Is Humanism?"* San Jose, Calif.: Humanist Community of San Jose.
[6]F.J. Ayala, *J. Heredity.*
[7]M. Grene, *Encounter* (Nov. 1959), pp. 48–50.

CREATION AND EVOLUTION ARE THE ONLY VALID ALTERNATIVE THEORIES OF ORIGINS

Evolutionists often assert that creationists have constructed a false dichotomy between creation and evolution, that there are actually many theories of origins. However, all theories of origins can be fitted within these two general theories. Thus, Futuyma, an evolutionist, states:

> Creation and evolution, between them, exhaust the possible explanations for the origin of living things. Organisms either appeared on the earth fully developed or they did not. If they did not, they must have developed from preexisting species by some process of modification. If they did appear in a fully developed state, they must indeed have been created by some omnipotent intelligence.[8]

No professionally trained teacher should thus hesitate to teach the scientific evidence that supports creation as an alternative to evolution. This is recognized by Alexander, who stated that:

> No teacher should be dismayed at efforts to present creation as an alternative to evolution in biology courses; indeed at this moment creation is the only alternative to evolution. Not only is this worth mentioning, but a comparison of the two alternatives can be an excellent exercise in logic and reason. Our primary goal as educators should be to teach students to think. . . . Creation and evolution in some respects imply backgrounds about as different as one can imagine. In the sense that creation is an alternative to evolution for any specific question, a case against creation is a case for evolution, and vice versa.[9]

Teaching both theories of origins is an educational imperative. Thus, since creation is as scientific as evolution, and evolution is as religious as creation, and since creation and evolution between them exhaust the possible explanations for origins, therefore a comparison of the two alternatives can be excellent exercises in logic and reason. No theory in science should be allowed to freeze into dogma, immune from the challenge of alternative theories. Academic and religious freedoms are guaranteed by the United States Constitution, and public schools are supported by the taxes derived from all citizens. Therefore, in the public schools in the United States, the scientific evidences which support creation should be taught along with the scientific evidences which support evolution in a philosophically neutral manner devoid of references to any religious literature.

[8]D.J. Futuyma, *Science on Trial* (New York: Pantheon Books, 1983), p. 197.

[9]R.D. Alexander, in *Evolution versus Creationism: The Public Education Controversy* (Phoenix: Oryx Press, 1983), p. 91.

58. Theories, Facts, and Gods: Philosophical Aspects of the Creation-Evolution Controversy

A. David Kline

A. David Kline is a philosopher and provost and vice president for academic affairs at the University of North Florida. His specialties include philosophy of science, epistemology, modern philosophy, and ethical issues in biotechnology.

To understand the basic issues in the creation-evolution debate, it is helpful to distinguish those arguments that are mainly empirical in nature from those that are philosophical or conceptual. On the empirical side, creationists have challenged a number of tenets of the evolutionists—for example, the thermodynamical possibility of the spontaneous origin of life or the accuracy and consistency of widely used techniques for dating geological strata. . . . On the philosophical side, the areas of contention range beyond the theory of evolution to the nature of science itself. This chapter discusses four of these philosophical issues: (1) the relationship between theories and facts, (2) evidence for laws, (3) the relevance of "falsifiability" to evolutionary theory, and (4) the alleged place of God in scientific explanations. The discussion indicates why creationist arguments present an inconsistent and inaccurate view of the nature of scientific knowledge.

THEORIES OR FACTS

There is considerable and vitriolic disagreement over whether evolution is a theory or a fact. At Iowa State University, for example, such an interchange between a biology professor and his student made the campus newspaper. The student apparently pointed out with some delight that the theory of evolution was only a theory; the professor with some impatience insisted that it wasn't a theory but a fact. Speaking to an evangelical group in Dallas, Texas, President Ronald Reagan gave this opinion: "Well, it is a theory. It is a scientific theory only, and it has in recent years been challenged in the world of science—that is, not believed in the scientific community to be as infallible as it once was."[1]

From *Did the Devil Make Darwin Do It?: Modern Perspectives on the Creation-Evolution Controversy*, David B. Wilson, ed. Iowa State University Press, 1983, 1985: pp. 37–43. Reprinted by permission of Iowa State University Press.

[1]S.J. Gould, "Evolution as Fact and Theory," *Discovery* (May 1981):34.

The disagreement is not restricted to contrary students and professors or admitted anti-intellectuals. Among vocal "authorities," the issue has been kept alive by Stephen Jay Gould's recent paper "Evolution as Fact and Theory"[2] and Duane Gish's creationist response.[3]

At the quick of the issue is an equivocation on the meaning of the term *theory*. A tip-off to this is that the theory-fact distinction is alien to scientific discourse. The distinction comes from ordinary or prescientific discourse, in which facts refer to statements that are known for certain, or that are indubitable or obviously true, whereas theories refer to statements that are speculative and not well established. That Jack Ruby shot Lee Harvey Oswald is a fact. Many, actually millions, saw the shooting on television. The event engendered many theories as to Ruby's motivations. Was he part of a larger plot to silence Oswald? Was he simply a man intent on avenging John Kennedy's death? Or what?

Let us label the ordinary sense of *theory*, $theory_o$. Now, as has been pointed out, if something is $theory_o$, then it is not well established.

In the scientific context, however, the contrast is between theories and data. We know, for example, that human memory appears to have a practically limitless capacity for storing information. But how (by means of what mechanism) do we retrieve information from memory? Some especially elegant experiments by Saul Sternberg hint at the answer.[4] His work also provides a clear illustration of the theory-data distinction.

Sternberg gave his subjects a short list of digits to memorize—called the "positive set." Then he gave them an additional digit—the "test stimulus." The subject's task was to determine quickly and accurately whether the test stimulus was in the positive set or not.

Figure 3.1 is an idealized visual representation of Sternberg's data. The actual data are a set of results of the form: subject 1 had a reaction time of t on positive set p of size s, where t, p, and s are particular values.

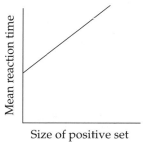

Figure 3.1.   Graph of Sternberg's data.

[2]Ibid., pp. 34–37.

[3]D. Gish, "Evolution as Fact and Theory," *Discovery* (July 1981):6.

[4]S. Sternberg, "Two Operations in Character Recognition: Some Evidence from Reaction-Time Measurements," *Perception and Psychophysics* 2(1967):45–53.

Sternberg proposed a theory to explain the data. He suggested that, at least in simple cases like the described task, memory retrieval proceeds by a *serial* and *exhaustive* search. That is, the subject internally represents the set and the test stimulus, then compares the test stimulus against the first item in the positive set for a match. He then proceeds to the next item and so on until the test stimulus has been compared with every item in the positive set. The subject goes through the entire procedure whether a match is found or not.

Notice that the theory is not what we would normally expect—that is, that the search would be terminated as soon as a match occurred. Rather, the data support the theory that an *exhaustive* search occurs, since reaction times increase as the size of the positive set increases,[5] and since whether the test stimulus is actually in the positive set or not has no effect on the mean reaction time. Only the size of the positive set is relevant.

Several general points on the theory-data distinction are in order. First, data are typically used to support or justify a theory. Exactly how the data must be related to a theory in order to provide support is a complicated issue in inductive logic and, fortunately, one with which we need not be concerned here. Second, since it would be pointless to use *a* to justify *b* if *a* were less well established than *b*, typically the data are better established than the theories they support. Third, nevertheless, data are not certain or indubitable. The data are often discovered to be mistaken. The source of the error can be faulty instruments, false auxiliary assumptions, poor experimental design, and so on.[6] The point is that for data to be used in a justifying role requires that the data be correct, not that they be certain or indubitable.[7] If the data are correct and if they are related to the theory in the proper way, they provide some justification for the theory. Finally, justification is a historical as well as logical process. Although initially data are supposed to be much better established than the theory they support, they need not remain so. As the theory becomes supported by numerous data and explains more and more, our confidence in it rises. It can rise to such an extent that there is little difference between our confidence in the data and our confidence in the theory. Theories can come to be well established, indeed, very well established. Special relativity and transmission genetics are examples of such theories.

This last point is the important one for understanding the spat over whether evolution is a theory or fact. Let us label the scientific sense of *theory*, theory$_s$. The

---

[5]More precisely, the mean reaction time and the size of the positive set are linearly correlated.

[6]Theories are tested by checking the predicted observational consequences of the theory. Typically, the predicted consequences do not follow *merely* from the theory being tested. The theory must be supplemented with auxiliary assumptions, such as assumptions about background conditions or the apparatus used in the experiment. If, for example, one's theory predicts that a microorganism will increase in size when placed in a certain solution, the test of this view will involve the auxiliary assumption that microscopes faithfully reveal at least the relative size of certain microorganisms. If the predicted consequences fail to occur, it is logically possible that the auxiliary assumptions are false and not the theory proper.

[7]Being certain is a logically stronger notion than being correct. If the data are correct, they are true. If the data were certain, they would not merely be true. It would be *impossible* for the data to be false.

crucial conceptual truth is that to claim that a theory$_s$ is well established, even beyond a reasonable doubt, is not a contradiction.

Then how shall we speak of evolution? All should agree with the creationists that it is a theory, in that evolution is a systematically related set of regularities that allegedly explain numerous and diverse phenomena.[8] But the creationist concludes straightaway that evolution is not well established, a move made plausible only by an equivocation on the meaning of *theory*. The creationist's conclusion follows only on the supposition that evolution is a theory$_o$. But when biologists call evolution a theory, they mean that it is a theory$_s$. And on that reading the creationist conclusion does not follow. One cannot reason that since the theory of evolution is a *theory*, it is not well established.

The creationist may admit that the evolutionary account is a theory$_s$, yet not a well-established one. This point could be true, of course; but if so, it becomes an *empirical*, not a *philosophical*, point. The claim that evolution is not well established thus requires empirical justification.

REPEATABILITY OF EVENTS

Creationists charge that evolutionary theory has a special difficulty in conforming to one of the canons of scientific method. As Duane Gish notes: "Another criterion that must apply to a scientific theory is the ability to repeatedly observe the events, processes or properties used to support the theory. There were obviously no human witnesses to the origin of the universe, the origin of life, or in fact to the origin of a single living thing."[9] Gish's point, which is widely echoed in the popular creationist literature, seems to come down to this. Consider some scientific regularity—for example, that arsenic poisons or that copper conducts electricity. To have confidence in the truth of such a regularity or law, the creationists argue, one must be able to repeatedly observe instances of it. In the case of the regularities that make up the theory of evolution, it is in principle impossible to observe instances of them, since evolutionary history consists of a unique series of events.

This argument has two flaws.[10] First, the canons of scientific method do not require that one be able to observe the instances of the regularities or the particular event in order to justify one's belief in them. It is acceptable and standard practice to justify belief in a regularity by deducing certain observable consequences from it and certain auxiliary assumptions. The same procedure holds for establishing the occurrence of particular events. To insist that instances of the laws be observed would eliminate not only much of the theory of evolution but nearly the

---

[8]Typically, phenomena are explained by being shown to be an instance of causal regularities or laws of nature.

[9]Gish, "Evolution as Fact and Theory," p. 6.

[10]I do not wish to deny that there are interesting differences between the regularities of evolutionary theory and other theories. But those differences do not seem to be at issue in the creationists' criticism. See D. Hull, *Philosophy of Biological Science* (Englewood Cliffs, N.J.: Prentice Hall, 1974), pp. 70–100.

whole of modern physics. The kind of reasoning illustrated by the Sternberg experiments is standard fare in scientific inquiry. Sternberg did not observe the serial exhaustive search said to take place in the brain but observed consequences of it, namely, reaction times. Similarly, one does not observe the interaction of elementary particles but, rather, certain consequences or effects of those hypothesized interactions.

Second, even when instances of a regularity are observable—for example, Snell's Law (sin i/sin r = constant)[11] or the gas law $(PV = NrT)$[12]—one cannot repeatedly observe the *same* events being instances of the regularity simply because every event is unique. No event occurs twice. So if we adhere rigorously to Gish's demand, no law can be confirmed.

Of course, given some notion of relevant similarity, relevantly similar events can occur an indefinitely large number of times. It is by observing such event-*types* that scientists confirm observational laws. But there is no reason that the evolutionist cannot meet this demand. He claims that the same regularities hold now as in the past. Of course, he cannot observe past instances of the regularities. That is a trivial truth. Neither can he observe past instances of Newton's laws. But he can confirm Newton's laws in the laboratory and in nature. The same situation holds for the evolutionary regularities that have observable instances.[13]

In summary, Gish's supposed canon of method is far too strong. If confirmation requires the observation of instances of regularities, most of science will not meet the requirement. Even if we restrict the requirement to observational regularities, it is still too strict since events do not recur. If we weaken the requirement to event-types then there is no a priori reason that evolutionary regularities cannot meet the condition.

FALSIFIABILITY

The creationists' main criticism of evolutionary theory is the bold challenge that the theory is not scientific. This claim has had a powerful rhetorical effect among creationists. Scientists, they argue, have painted themselves as hard-nosed, no-nonsense fellows who claim that the weak-willed creationists have failed to properly limit religion and hence have tainted the truth. So the claim that evolutionary theory is a metaphysical system or, worse yet, an alternative religion is the ultimate criticism.

The creationist charge is based entirely on the work of the philosopher of science Karl Popper.[14] Over a half century ago Popper was impressed by the contrast

---

[11]Whenever any ray of light is incident at the surface that separates two media, it is bent in such a way that the ratio of the sine of the angle of incidence to the sine of the angle of refraction is always a constant quantity for those two media.

[12]Very roughly, the product of the pressure and volume is proportional to the temperature.

[13]For example, any characteristic will become more prevalent in the population if the individual possessing it produces a larger progeny that survives to adulthood than individuals not having the trait.

[14]See, for example, Gish, "Evolution as Fact and Theory," p. 6.

between the "scientific" status of Marx's theory of history, Freud's psychoanalysis, and Alfred Adler's individual psychology on the one hand and Einstein's theory of gravitation on the other. He set for himself the problem of "demarcation," or the problem of defining when a theory should be regarded as scientific. Popper's answer is that the mark of a scientific theory is falsifiability.[15] In other words, theories are scientific if they prohibit some occurrences. There must be some observable events such that if they were to occur the theory would be false. Sternberg's theory, for example, could be falsified if subsequent data gave a different graph from that shown in Figure 3.1. As a matter of historical record, Popper believes that the theories of Marx, Freud, and Adler failed to meet the criterion, whereas Einstein's theory did. He also stated that "Darwinism" was not falsifiable and therefore not scientific.

The creationist argument against the scientific status of evolutionary theory can be reduced to a simple syllogism: *premise one,* falsifiability is the criterion for scientific status; *premise two,* the theory of evolution is not falsifiable; *conclusion,* the theory of evolution is not a scientific theory. To evaluate this argument, three points must be considered:

1. Creationists defend the premises by nothing more than an appeal to Popper's authority. Popper *said* that falsifiability is the mark of a scientific theory. Popper *said* that the theory of evolution is not falsifiable. Nowhere in the creationist literature do we find a defense of falsificationism or Popper's evaluation of evolutionary theory. We do not even find a clear statement of Popper's ideas. What Popper actually says about "evolutionary theory" is that "Darwinism is not a testable scientific theory, but a metaphysical *research programme*—a possible framework for testable scientific theories."[16] Nowhere do creationists demonstrate that what Popper means by "Darwinism" is what contemporary biologists mean by "the theory of evolution." Perhaps the current theory is one of those testable theories that fall within the Darwinian framework.

The creationists' crude appeal to Popper's authority can perhaps be understood, though not justified, when it is noticed that many anticreationists also accept Popper with no questions asked. Popperianism appears to be gospel among many scientists. Efforts by scientists to counter the nonscientific components of our culture, such as astrology and extrasensory perception, have typically been fought under the banner of falsificationism. Here, too, the banner has simply been borrowed, not examined.[17]

2. If one's arguments rest merely on appeals to authority and the authority happens to change his mind, then one is left, as they say, holding the bag.

[15]K. Popper, "Science: Conjectures and Refutations," reprinted in *Introductory Readings in the Philosophy of Science,* E. Klemke, R. Hollinger, and A. D. Kline, eds. (Buffalo, N.Y.: Prometheus Books, 1980), pp. 19–34.

[16]K. Popper, "Autobiography of Karl Popper," in *The Philosophy of Karl Popper,* vol. 1 P. Schilpp, ed. (La Salle, Ill.: Open Court, 1974), p. 134.

[17]There are serious problems with falsificationism. See P. Thagard, "Why Astrology Is a Pseudoscience," and P. Feyerabend, "How to Defend Society against Science," both in *Introductory Readings in the Philosophy of Science,* E. Klemke, R. Hollinger, and A. D. Kline, eds. (Buffalo, N.Y.: Prometheus Books, 1980).

Unfortunately for creationists, that is precisely the present situation. Popper's recent comments clearly indicate that he believes that the contemporary theory of evolution is testable.[18] Of course, he may be wrong. But what we need is an argument to that effect.

3. For the purposes of argument, let us suppose that falsifiability is the mark of a scientific theory. Present in this supposition are two embarrassing points that the creationists have overlooked. First, the bulk of the creationists' objections to evolutionary theory are straightforward empirical objections. For example, creationists claim that evolutionary theory is incompatible with our knowledge of thermodynamics and that evolutionary theory is incompatible with the fossil and sediment-layer records. It is by means of such objections that creationists attempt to establish their scientific expertise and to refute the theory of evolution.

Whether these critical claims are correct is not the present issue. . . . The present point is that if creationists claim that observable evidence actually refutes a theory, then they must think that it is falsifiable. Therefore, the creationists cannot claim to have given evidence that the theory of evolution *is false* and also that it *is not falsifiable.* Second, is creationism itself a scientific theory? Despite some disagreement among creationists on this issue, most would say that it is. The following remarks are addressed to those who believe creationism is a scientific theory and that falsifiability is the mark of such a theory.

The obvious question is whether creationism is falsifiable. I shall be suggesting that in a sense it is not. My remarks could be understood as encouraging creationists to state what those observable occurrences are, which, if they were to happen, would constitute counterevidence to their theory.

To determine whether creationism is falsifiable, let us consider first a possible theory called "originism," which is amazingly similar to creationism in that it denies almost every claim of evolutionary theory. According to originism, for example, the universe is about 10,000 years old, plants and animals appear in the universe as distinct kinds, the earth's history contains a massive catastrophic flood, and so on. Suppose that originism is just like creationism except that it is "naturalized." Everywhere that creationism talks about such and such being supernaturally created, originism talks about such and such appearing or occurring. Originism, then, is just like creationism except that it has been purged of nonnatural creative activities and, of course, creators.

It is obvious that originism is falsifiable. There are possible fossil records, or sedimentary records, or carbon-dating results that would refute originism. Since originism is "contained" in creationism, creationism will also, at least in principle, be falsifiable. That is, the same results as just stated could falsify creationism.

But given that originism is a simpler view than creationism, on standard methodological grounds it should be preferred unless creationism has additional observational consequences—consequences in addition to those of originism. I suspect there are none. For those who disagree, it will be instructive to have the

---

[18]K. Popper, "Evolution," *New Scientist* (August 1980): 611.

observational consequences clearly stated. The next section formulates a dilemma for anyone who takes up this challenge.

GOD AND SCIENTIFIC EXPLANATION

Is it possible, in principle, for concepts like God, creator, and creative process to play a role in scientific explanations? As we have seen in the previous discussion, the answer depends on what you mean by "God," "creator," and "creative process." In particular, are these concepts understood in such a way that they play a role in a theory having observational consequences that the theory would not have without them?

This very general response is correct, but it makes it appear that the answer to the question is more open than it really is. It is not up to a specific speaker of a language to create for words whatever meanings he wants. Lewis Carroll put the point humorously in *Alice in Wonderland:* "That's a great deal to make one word mean," Alice said in a thoughtful tone. "When I make a word do a lot of work like that," said Humpty Dumpty, "I always pay it extra."

Consider the concept of God. Within the standard Judeo-Christian tradition, one that scientific creationists accept and want to be identified with, God is a supernatural being that is all good, all knowing, and all powerful. The essential question, therefore, is whether this specific God can play a role in scientific explanations. There appear to be logical reasons why it cannot.

God's nature, being supernatural, is unlike natural entities such as electrons, genes, apples, and societies. Entities in the natural order interact with one another through efficient causal relations. Very generally in efficient causal relations the entities are spatially and temporally contiguous and undergo a transfer of energy from one to the other—for example, a hammer striking a nail causes the nail to move into the wood. The heart of scientific explanation is providing the efficient causes of events or phenomena.

Now it should be clear that there is a severe logical tension in the claim that God could play a role in scientific explanations. The most plausible reason for allowing God as a scientific entity is that God enters into efficient causal relations. But if an entity enters into efficient causal relations, it can be understood as natural, not supernatural. God can acquire a scientific status only by abandoning his supernatural status. For those within the standard Judeo-Christian tradition, that price must be judged too high.

The philosophical arguments used by creationists to refute the theory of evolution—that it is merely a theory, that it is about nonrepeatable phenomena, that it is unfalsifiable—are woefully inadequate. The dust raised by these arguments was agitated by various confused or uncritically held views about the nature of science. . . .

PROBLEMS AND PUZZLES

59. *Brains in Vats*

William Poundstone

William Poundstone (1955–   ) studied physics at the Massachusetts Institute of Technology and is now a writer living in Los Angeles.

Blue sky, sunshine, déjà vu glazed with dread. Something horrible is going to happen about now. It is a perfect summer day in a meadow of tall grass. J.V. is following her brothers, lagging lazily behind. A shadow falls on the ground; something rustles the grass. J.V. turns—she cannot help it, it is what happens next—and sees a strange man. He has no face, like a minor character in a dream. The man holds something writhing and indistinct. He asks, "How would you like to get into this bag with the snakes?"

J.V.'s encounter is an unlikely milestone of twentieth-century thought. J.V., a fourteen-year-old girl, was not in a summer field but on an operating table in the Montreal Neurological Institute. Her physician, Wilder Penfield, was attempting an experimental operation to relieve her violent epileptic seizures. The operating team had removed the side of J.V.'s skull to expose the temporal lobe of the brain. In order to locate the site of the attacks, Penfield probed the brain with an electrode connected to an EEG machine. The surgery was a collaboration between physician and patient. J.V. had to remain conscious throughout and help locate the site of the seizures. When Penfield touched the probe to a certain spot on J.V.'s temporal lobe, she again found herself in the field of grass . . .

J.V.'s experience with the strange man had occurred seven years earlier, in Canada, in what we call the real world. She reported seeing herself as she was then, a seven-year-old girl. J.V. had been frightened but not physically harmed, and ran crying home to her mother. These few moments of terror were to haunt her over and over. The man with the bag of snakes entered her dreams, made them nightmares. The trauma became interwoven with her epileptic seizures. Like a madeleine, a fleeting recollection would trigger the whole memory, then an attack.

Under the EEG probe, J.V. not merely recalled but *relived* the encounter. All the richness of detail, all the lucid horror of the original experience, came back. Penfield's probe caused the brain to replay past experiences like a movie. With bits

From *Labyrinths of Reason* by Richard Poundstone. Copyright © 1988 by William Poundstone. Used by permission of Doubleday, a division of Random House, Inc.

of lettered or numbered paper, Penfield kept track of the sites on the cerebral cortex associated with the recollection. Touching nearby points produced different sensations. When the probe touched one point, J.V. recalled people scolding her for doing something wrong. Other sites produced only a phantasmagoria of colored stars.

BRAINS IN VATS

Penfield's classic brain experiments of the 1930s inspired a certain famous riddle, long since dubbed "brains in vats" by philosophy students. It goes like this: You think you're sitting there reading this book. Actually, you could be a disembodied brain in a laboratory somewhere, soaking in a vat of nutrients. Electrodes are attached to the brain, and a mad scientist is feeding it a stream of electrical impulses that exactly *simulates* the experience of reading this book!

Let's expand a little on the anecdote to see the full force of this. At some indistinct past time, while you were sleeping, your brain was removed from your body. Every nerve was severed by skilled surgeons and attached to a microscopic electrode. Each of these millions of electrodes is hooked to a machine that produces tiny electrical pulses just as the original nerves did.

When you turn the page, it *feels* like a page because the electrodes send your brain exactly the same nerve impulses that would have come from real fingers grasping a real page. But the page and the fingers are illusion. Bringing the book closer to your face makes it look bigger; holding it at arm's length makes it look smaller . . . 3-D perspective is simulated by judiciously adjusting the voltages of the electrodes attached to the stump of the optic nerve. If, right this instant, you can smell spaghetti cooking and hear dulcimer music in the background, that is part of the illusion too. You can pinch yourself and receive the expected sensation, but it will prove nothing. In fact, *there's no way you can prove that this isn't so.* How, then, can you justify your belief that the external world exists?

DREAMS AND EVIL GENIUSES

To anyone with a skeptical turn of mind, the brains-in-vats paradox is both appealing and infuriating. There is something fascinating about the demonstration that, just possibly, everything you know is wrong!

Despite the influence of Penfield and other brain researchers, doubts about the reality of the world are not a uniquely modern malaise. Brains-in-vats is simply a stronger version of older riddles asking "How do you know this isn't all a dream?" Best known of these is the Chinese tale of Chuang-tzu, dating from the fourth century B.C. Chuang-tzu was the man who dreamt he was a butterfly, then awoke to wonder if he was a butterfly dreaming he was a man.

Chuang-tzu's fable is unconvincing. It is true that we usually don't realize we're dreaming in our dreams. But a waking person always knows that he is not dreaming. Doesn't he?

Opinions differ. In his "First Meditation" (1641), French philosopher and mathematician René Descartes decided he could not be *absolutely* sure he wasn't dreaming. Most people would probably disagree with Descartes. You're not dreaming right now, and you know it because experiences in dreams are different from those in waking life.

Saying exactly *how* they're different is difficult. If waking life is absolutely, unmistakably different from a dream, there ought to be some surefire test you can perform to distinguish the two. For instance:

• There's the old gag about pinching yourself to see if you're dreaming. The rationale is apparently that you don't feel pain in dreams. But I *have* felt pain in dreams, and suspect that everyone must from time to time. Scratch that test.

• Since few dreams are in color, the red rose on your desk proves you're awake. Again, the dream sensation of color is not all that rare. Many people dream in color, and even if you never have, this could be the first time.

• Real life usually seems more detailed and coherent than dreams. If you can examine the wall before you and see every minute crack, that means you're awake. If you can add a column of figures, then check the result with a calculator, you're awake. These tests are more telling though still not fool-proof. (Might not you dream about seeing tiny cracks in the wall after hearing that the cracks "prove" you are awake?)

• Some say that the very fact that you are wondering whether you are dreaming or awake proves you are awake. In waking life, you are aware of the dream state, but while dreaming you forget the distinction (and think you are awake). But if that were true, you could never have a dream in which you realize you are dreaming, and such dreams are fairly common with many people.

• I propose this test, based on what might be called "coherent novelty." Keep a book of limericks by your bed. Don't read the book; just use it thus. Whenever you want to know if you are dreaming, go into your bedroom and open the book at random (it may of course be a dream bedroom and a dream book). Read a limerick, making sure it is one you have never read or heard before. Most likely you cannot compose a bona fide limerick on a moment's notice. You can't do it when awake, and certainly not when asleep either. Nonetheless, anyone can *recognize* a limerick when he sees it. It has a precise rhyme and metrical scheme, and it is funny (or more likely *not* funny, but in a certain way). If the limerick meets all these tests, it must be part of the external world and not a figment of your dreaming mind.[1]

---

[1]Samuel Taylor Coleridge composed his masterwork, "Kubla Khan," in a dream. Coleridge fell asleep reading a history of the emperor and dreamed, with startling lucidity, a poem of 300 verses. Upon awakening, Coleridge scrambled to write down the poem before it eluded him. He wrote about 50 verses—the "Kubla Khan" we know—then was interrupted by a visitor. Afterward, he could remember but a few scattered lines of the remaining 250 verses. Coleridge, however, was a poet in waking life. I recommend the limerick test only to people who can't easily compose a limerick. Also, Coleridge's dream was perhaps atypical, for he had taken laudanum to get to sleep.

There was a young girl at Bryn Mawr
   Who committed a dreadful faux pas:
     She loosened a stay
     Of her décolleté
   Exposing her je-ne-sais-quoi.

My real point is that you don't need to use any of these tests to establish that you're awake; you just *know*. The suggestion that Chuang-tzu's, or anyone's, "real" life is literally a nighttime dream lacks credibility.

It may however be a "dream" of a different sort. The most famous discussion along these lines is in Descartes's *Meditations*. There Descartes wonders if the external world, including his body, is an illusion created by an "evil genius" bent on deceiving him. "I will suppose that . . . some malicious demon of the utmost power and cunning has employed all his energies in order to deceive me. I shall think that the sky, the air, the earth, colours, shapes, sounds and all external things are merely the delusions of dreams which he has devised to ensnare my judgment. I shall consider myself as not having hands or eyes, or flesh, or blood or senses, but as falsely believing that I have all these things."

That the demon and Descartes's mind were the only two realities would be the very pinnacle of deception, Descartes reasoned. Were there even one other mind as "audience" for the deception, Descartes would at least be correct about the existence of minds such as his own.

Descartes's evil genius anticipates the brains-in-vats paradox in all meaningful particulars. The Penfield experiments merely showed how Descartes's metaphysical fantasy might be physically conceivable. The illusion in the Penfield experiments was more realistic than a dream or memory, though not complete. Penfield's patients described it as a double consciousness: Even while reliving the past experience in detail, they were also aware of being on the operating table.

One can readily envision the more complete neurological illusion supposed in the brains-in-vats riddle. The eyes do not send the brain pictures, nor the ears sound. The senses communicate with the brain via electrochemical impulses in the nerve cells. Each cell in the nervous system "sees" only the impulses of neighboring cells, not the external stimulus that caused them.

If we knew more about the original sensory nerve communication with the brain (as may be the case in a century or so), it might be possible to simulate any experience artificially. That contingency throws all experience into doubt. Even the current embryonic stage of neurology is no guarantee of the validity of our senses. It might be the twenty-fifth century right now, and the forces behind the brains-in-vats laboratory want you to think it's the twentieth, when such things don't happen!

The existence of one's brain is just as open to doubt as the external world. We talk of "brains in vats" because it is a convenient picture, wryly suggestive of bad science fiction. The brain is shorthand for "mind." We no more know, with unimpeachable certainty, that our consciousness is contained in a brain than that it is contained in a body. A yet more complete version of the fantasy would have your mind hallucinating the entire world, including Penfield, J.V., and the brains-in-vats riddle.

AMBIGUITY

"Brains in vats" is the quintessential illustration of what philosophers call the "problem of knowledge." The point is not the remote possibility that we are brains in vats but that we may be just as deluded in ways we cannot even imagine. Few persons reach their fifteenth birthday without having some thoughts along this line. How do we know *anything* for sure?

The whole of our experience is a stream of nerve impulses. The sheen of a baroque pearl, the sound of a dial tone, and the odor of apricots are suppositions from these nerve impulses. We have all *imagined* a world that might account for the unique set of nerve impulses we have received since (and several months before) birth. The conventional picture of a real, external world is not the only possible explanation for that neural experience. We are forced to admit that an evil genius or a brains-in-vats experiment could explain the neural experience just as well. Experience is forever equivocal.

Science places great faith in the evidence of the senses. Most people are skeptical about ghosts, the Loch Ness monster, and flying saucers, not because they are inherently stupid notions, but only because no one has produced unquestionable sensory evidence for them. Brains-in-vats turns this (apparently reasonable!) skepticism inside out. How can you know, by the evidence of your senses, that you are not a brain in a vat? You can't! The belief that you are *not* a brain in a vat can never be disproven empirically. In the jargon of philosophy, it is "evidence-transcendent."

This is a serious blow to the idea that "everything can be determined scientifically." At issue is not some bit of trivia such as the color of a tyrannosaurus. If we cannot even know whether the external world exists, then there are profound limitations on knowledge. Our conventional view of things might be outrageously wrong.

Ambiguity underlies a famous analogy proposed by Albert Einstein and Leopold Infeld. In 1938 they wrote:

> In our endeavour to understand reality we are somewhat like a man trying to understand the mechanism of a closed watch. He sees the face and the moving hands, even hears its ticking, but he has no way of opening the case. If he is ingenious he may form some picture of a mechanism which could be responsible for all the things he observes, but he may never be quite sure his picture is the only one which could explain his observations. He will never be able to compare his picture with the real mechanism and he cannot even imagine the possibility of the meaning of such a comparison.

60. The Problem of the Criterion

Sextus Empiricus

Sextus Empiricus (c. 200 C.E.) was the codifier of ancient Greek scepticism and a physician. About his life practically nothing is known. He seems to have been a Greek. It is not known whether his Latin name "Empiricus" is a proper name or a designation of him as an "empirical" medical doctor. His extant works constitute the only lucid, complete, and firsthand summary of ancient Greek scepticism available to us and have exerted a significant influence on Western philosophizing.

But the dogmatists, conceited as they are, do not yield the judgment of the truth to others but claim truth as their own exclusive discovery. All right, let us base our argument on them[1] and show that not even in this way can any criterion of truth possibly be discovered.

Now, each one of those who claim to have discovered the truth either declares this by mere assertion only or else uses a proof. But he will not say it by mere assertion, for one of those on the opposing side will bring forward an assertion that claims the contrary, and in this way the former will be "no more" credible than the latter, one bare assertion being equal to another. If, on the other hand, he has proof for his declaration of himself as the criterion, it must in any case be a sound one. But in order to ascertain the soundness of the proof he uses in declaring himself the criterion, we must have a criterion, and moreover one that is agreed on beforehand. But we possess no generally accepted criterion, that being what is sought after. It is impossible, therefore, to discover a criterion.

Again, since those who call themselves criteria of the truth derive from different philosophical schools, and for this reason disagree with one another, we need to have at our disposal some criterion which we can use to decide their dispute for the purpose of giving our assent to some and withholding it from others. Now, this criterion is either in disagreement with all the parties disagreeing or it is in agreement with one only. But if in disagreement with all, it will itself also become a party to the disagreement, and as a party to it will not be a criterion but will itself be in need of judgement, like the disagreement as a whole. For it is an impossibility for the same thing to be at once both the examiner and the thing examined. And if it is not in disagreement with all views but is in agreement with one of them, this one with which it agrees, since it is involved in the disagreement, has

From *Sextus Empiricus. Selection from the Major Writings on Scepticism, Man & God.* Philip P. Hallie, ed. and Sanford G. Etheridge, trans. Hackett Publishing Co., 1985: pp. 140–146. Reprinted by permission of Hackett Publishing Co., Inc. All rights reserved.

[1]That is, on their arguments. (—Tr.) (All other footnotes are by the editor, Philip P. Hallie.)

need of an examiner. And hence the criterion agreeing with that view will require judgement, as it is no different from it; and if it requires judgement it will not be a criterion.

But—what is most important of all—if we say that any one dogmatist is the judge of truth and that he alone is the repository of truth, we shall be saying this either because we fix our gaze on his age, or not on his age but on his hard work, or not on this but on his sagacity and intellect, or not on his sagacity but on the testimony of the multitude. But it is not appropriate in an investigation concerned with the truth to pay attention either to age or industry or any other of the factors mentioned, as we shall show. One should not, therefore, say that any one of the philosophers is the criterion of truth.[2] Indeed, the consideration of age is excluded by the fact that most of the dogmatists were more or less equal in áge when they declared themselves criteria of the truth. . . . Also, it is not unreasonable to suppose that, just as in ordinary life and common intercourse we observe that young men are often more intelligent than older men, so also in philosophy young men may be shrewder than old men. . . . Therefore one must not say that any one dogmatist, by reason of his age, is the criterion. Nor indeed by reason of his industry either: for all are equally industrious, and there is none whose behaviour is sluggish once he has entered the contest for truth and claims to have found it. And when equality in this respect is ascribed to all, it is an injustice to incline towards one only.

And likewise one could not very well select one philosopher as superior to another on account of his intelligence. In the first place, they are all intelligent; they are not classed as dullards and non-dullards. Further, men who are considered intelligent often are advocates not of truth but of falsehood. For example, we call those orators powerful and intellectual who nobly come to the aid of the false and raise it to a level of credibility equal to the true; and conversely, those who are not of this class we call dull and unintelligent. Perhaps in philosophy too, then, those inquirers after truth who are the most ingenious seem to be convincing even if they plead the cause of falsehood, because they are naturally gifted, while the untalented are considered unconvincing even if they are allied with the truth. Therefore neither by reason of age nor of industry nor of intelligence is it proper to give the preference to any one person over anybody else and say that this man has discovered the truth and that man has not.

There remains, then, the alternative of listening to the agreement of the majority, for possibly someone will say that he is the best judge of truth whom the

---

[2] This is a typical form of Sceptical argument against such notions as that of the Sage, or Wise Man, who is the arbiter of all knowledge and value to the Stoics. Nowadays this seems like a rather obvious "conclusion," but in the Middle Ages, for instance, it was to be by no means obvious, and this little sequences of arguments is one of the most potent attacks upon the notion of one-man authoritarianism to be found in Western civilization. The authority in question is an authority on intellectual matters, but this attack could be and was to be also extended to political authority. Neo-Sceptics like Petrarch, Erasmus, and Montaigne were to knock down the authority of the Philosopher, Aristotle, toward the end of the Middle Ages, but they were also to invade political thought, with arguments similar to the ones given by Sextus here and in the *Outlines*.

majority agree in approving. But this is foolish, and would be a worse criterion than those we have already discredited. . . . [J]ust as in the affairs of daily life it is not impossible for one intelligent person to be better than many unintelligent ones, so also in philosophy it is not unreasonable to suppose that there is one man who is sensible, and hence reliable, and many who are like geese and for this reason unreliable, even if they are in agreement in their testimony in favour of somebody; for the intelligent man is rare, while the thoughtless are common. Also, even if we do give heed to agreement and to the testimony of the majority, we are brought round again to the opposite of the end in view, for of necessity those disagreeing about a thing out-number those who agree about it. . . .

But now if the discoverer of truth in philosophy is said to owe his success either to his age, or his industry, or his intelligence, or to the fact that he has large numbers to speak for him, while we, on the other hand, have shown that one can for none of these reasons say that he is the criterion of truth, then it is manifest that the criterion in philosophy is undiscoverable.

Also, the philosopher who declares himself to be the criterion is saying nothing more than what appears to himself. Therefore, since each of the other philosophers also says what appears to himself, and what is contrary to the statement of the former, it is plain that, as he is on an equal basis with all the others, we shall not be able to say definitely that any one of them is the criterion. For if this man is trustworthy because it appears to him that he himself is the criterion, the second man too will be trustworthy, since it appears to him also that he himself is the criterion, and so on with the third and all the rest. From this it follows that no one is definitely[3] the criterion of truth.

In addition to this, it is either by mere assertion that a man claims to be the criterion, or it is because he is using a criterion. But if it is by mere assertion, he will be checked by mere assertion, and if he is using a criterion, he will refute himself. For this criterion either disagrees or agrees with him. And if it disagrees it is untrustworthy, since it is in disagreement with him who believes himself to be the criterion, while if it agrees it will have need of a judge. For just as this man who declares himself the criterion was seen to be untrustworthy, so also the criterion which agrees with him, since it is in a way possessed of the same function[4] as he, will require some other criterion. And if this is so, then we must not say that each philosopher is the criterion, for everything that requires judging is of itself untrustworthy.—Again, whoever declares himself the criterion makes this claim either by mere assertion or by virtue of a proof. He cannot, for the reasons already urged, do so by mere assertion. And if he does so by virtue of a proof, it must at any rate be a sound one. But his declaration of the soundness of this proof is made either by

---

[3] This does not necessarily mean that all of them are speaking falsely; it means only that we have no way of deciding whether one and one only is speaking truly. Sextus is here suspending judgment, not making an adverse judgment on the basis of the previous argument.

[4] The man and the criterion are both personal standards for making a decision about truth and falsity.

assertion or by virtue of proof, and so on *ad infinitum*. And so this is one reason more why we must declare that the criterion of truth is undiscoverable.

Another argument is this. Those who profess to be able to judge the truth are bound to have a criterion of truth. Now, this criterion is either untested or tested. And if it is untested, how can it be trustworthy? No subject of dispute is without judging trustworthy. But if it is tested, than that which adjudges it is in turn either untested or tested. And if untested, it is untrustworthy; if tested, that which tests it is again either tested or not tested, and so on *ad infinitum*.—Again, since the criterion is a subject of dispute, it requires some proof. But since some proofs are true and some false, the proof employed for confirming the criterion must itself be confirmed by means of some criterion. The result is that we fall into the mode of circular reasoning, since the criterion is awaiting confirmation by the proof while the proof is waiting for confirmation from the criterion, and neither of them is able to show confirmation by the other. Besides, the same thing becomes both trustworthy and untrustworthy. The criterion is trustworthy because it judges the proof, and the proof because it proves the criterion; and the criterion is untrustworthy because it undergoes proof at the hand of the proof, and the proof because it undergoes judgement at the hand of the criterion.

SUGGESTIONS FOR FURTHER READING

ANTHOLOGIES

Ammerman, Robert R., and Marcus G. Singer, eds. *Belief, Knowledge and Truth.* New York: Scribners, 1970. A rich selection, ranging from elementary to difficult, from philosophical writings on skepticism, empiricism, rationalism, and other issues in the theory of knowledge from ancient Greece to the present. An extensive bibliography of books and articles.

Klemke, E. D., Robert Hollinger, and A. David Kline. *Introductory Readings in the Philosophy of Science.* Buffalo, N.Y.: Prometheus, 1981. In addition to such standard subjects as explanation and confirmation of theories, this anthology for the beginning student contains sections on science and pseudoscience and science and values.

Moser, Paul K., and Arnold Vander Nat. *Human Knowledge: Classical and Contemporary Approaches.* New York: Oxford Univ. Press, 1987. This recent anthology provides an informative selection of readings in the philosophical field of epistemology.

Nagel, Ernest, and Richard Brandt, eds. *Meaning and Knowledge.* New York: Harcourt Brace Jovanovich, 1965. This is a comprehensive anthology on epistemology, or the study of human knowledge, its nature, sources, and justification.

INDIVIDUAL WORKS

Annas, Julia, and Jonathan Barnes. *The Modes of Scepticism: Ancient Texts and Modern Interpretations.* Cambridge: Cambridge Univ. Press, 1985. This is an excellent example of recent scholarship concerning ancient skepticism and its subsequent influence.

Aune, Bruce A. *Rationalism, Empiricism & Pragmatism: An Introduction.* New York: Random House, 1970. This book gives a good general discussion of the problems of knowledge.

Ayer, A. J. *The Problem of Knowledge.* Baltimore: Penguin, 1956. A more advanced yet clearly written philosophical investigation of the nature, scope, and limits of human knowledge. This book was designed not only for the professional philosopher but for the general reader as well. Particular attention is called to Chapter 2, "Skepticism and Certainty."

Blanshard, Brand. *Reason and Analysis.* La Salle, Ill.: Open Court, The Paul Carus Lectures, 1964. A leading American philosopher defends his version of rationalism in terms of a lucid and comprehensive critique of British analytic philosophy.

Casti, John L. *Paradigms Lost: Images of Man in the Mirror of Science.* New York: William Morrow, 1989. This book offers a thoroughly informed and charmingly written account of the nature of science as actually practiced by scientists today. The author critically discusses some of the solutions to philosophic problems contemporary science allegedly has to offer.

Chisholm, Roderick. *Theory of Knowledge.* 3d. ed. Englewood Cliffs, N.J.: Prentice Hall, 1989. This recent work is a short and clearly written introduction to epistemology. The first two chapters attempt to refute skepticism.

Cohen, Morris R. *Reason and Nature.* 2d ed. New York: Free Press, 1964. A classic work by an American philosopher who was a champion of the supremacy of critical reason in human life. Cohen devotes considerable attention to the ethical, legal, religious, and historical implications of scientific knowledge and method. A scholarly work, yet written so lucidly that the beginning student can read it with pleasure.

Dennett, Daniel C. *Darwin's Dangerous Idea: Evolution and the Meanings of Life.* New York: Simon and Schuster, 1995. In this gracefully written and often witty book the author, an American philosopher, shows how Darwin's idea of natural selection and its real implications transform not only our traditional religious conceptions but also our inherited view of our place in the universe and our understanding of our own human nature.

Gardner, Martin. *Fads and Fallacies in the Name of Science.* 2d ed. New York: Dover, 1957. A fascinating examination of extrasensory perception, the hollow earth hypothesis, dianetics, orgone boxes, and other theories and devices that the author criticizes as being pseudoscience.

Gardner, Martin. *Science: Good, Bad, and Bogus.* Buffalo, N.Y.: Prometheus Books, 1981. A recent collection of Gardner's essays, book reviews, and other writings that attack fraud, hoax, and self-delusion when practiced in the name of science.

Gardner, Martin. *The WHYS of a Philosophical Scrivener.* New York: Quill, a Division of William Morrow & Company, 1983. Learned in science, mathematics, and philosophy, the author imaginatively and wittily defends his own views on the fundamental issues of classical philosophy.

Hempel, Carl G. *Philosophy of Natural Science.* Englewood Cliffs, N.J.: Prentice Hall, Foundations of Philosophy Series, 1966. This is a classic study in the philosophy of science.

Hospers, John. *An Introduction to Philosophical Analysis.* 2d ed. Englewood Cliffs, N.J.: Prentice Hall, 1967. This expository text contains a clear, contemporary, and elementary discussion of rationalism and empiricism for the beginning student.

Johnson, Oliver. *Skepticism and Cognitivism.* Berkeley: Univ. of California Press, 1978. The author thoroughly examines nearly every argument for skepticism.

Kenny, Anthony. *Descartes.* New York: Random House, 1968. This book provides a good, recent study of Descartes and his methods.

Kuhn, Thomas S. *The Structure of Scientific Revolutions.* 2d enlarged ed. Chicago: Univ. of Chicago Press, 1970. This very influential and controversial study rejects the view of the history of science as a steady, cumulative growth of knowledge in favor of an interpretation of that history as a series of peaceful interludes punctuated by revolutionary changes from one conceptual world view to another.

Morris, Henry M. *Scientific Creationism.* Green Forest, AR. Master Books, 1986. Many creationists consider this work to be the best documented case for scientific creationism.

Nagel, Ernest. *The Structure of Science.* New York: Harcourt, 1961. A recent comprehensive treatment of the nature of explanation in the natural and social sciences by an outstanding American philosopher of science. A book for the more advanced student.

Poundstone, William. *Labyrinths of Reason: Paradox, Puzzles and the Frailty of Knowledge.* New York: Anchor, Doubleday, 1988. Wittily and provocatively the author explores various paradoxes to raise the philosophical question How do we know what we know? In his epistemological journey, he ranges from ancient Greek philosophers like Zeno to such contemporary American philosophers as John Searle.

Russell, Bertrand. *Problems of Philosophy.* London: Oxford Univ. Press, 1912. For over 75 years of reprintings, this brief book has remained a popular and highly readable introduction to the problems of knowledge.

Stapledon, Olaf. *Last and First Men and Star Maker.* New York: Dover, 1968. Two science fiction novels by a philosopher, which convey the haunting beauty and disturbing strangeness of the world revealed by science better than most abstract treatises. These powerfully imaginative works reveal why many people find the scientific understanding and manipulation of the world and humankind so fascinating and hopeful and many others find it so appalling and depressing.

Unger, Peter K. *Ignorance: A Case for Scepticism.* New York: Oxford Univ. Press, 1975. The author presents a challenging defense of modern skepticism.

Dictionary of the History of Ideas: Studies of Selected Pivotal Ideas. Philip P. Wiener, editor-in-chief. New York: Scribners, 1973. Substantial and clearly written essays emphasizing the historical development of topics discussed in this part. Designed to inform the nonspecialist, each essay concludes with a select bibliography.

Encyclopedia of Philosophy. Paul Edwards, editor-in-chief. New York: Macmillan, 1967. The beginning student will find many worthwhile articles on the subjects treated in this part and excellent bibliographies.

EPILOGUE

This book will have accomplished all it can do if it not only has acquainted the student with some philosophy but also has encouraged the seeker to philosophize, to strive for genuine freedom of thought. The U.S. Constitution may guarantee freedom of expression; it cannot ensure freedom of thought. To achieve freedom of thought, one must practice the ceaseless questioning that is philosophy. In the simple but powerful words of the philosopher John Stuart Mill, without philosophizing, human beings

> are condemned to live second-hand. Their views on life's greatest questions come from sources other than themselves. Their character, their life, their *being* is shaped and controlled by philosophical views that are not their own. They believe what other men want them to believe, for other men's reasons. They never know the joy of living one's own life, which Plato likened to being released from lifelong imprisonment in a cave. They never know freedom of thought—though they may know freedom of expression.

It is not enough to express oneself. One also must have the Socratic wisdom to know and be oneself.

GLOSSARY

A posteriori A way of knowing that a statement is true in which a person does refer to facts, experiments, or past experiences.

A priori A way of knowing that a statement is true in which one does not refer to facts, experiments, or past experiences. One just figures out or "sees" that the statement is true.

Absolute (1) In contexts concerning questions of knowledge, this term refers to being completely certain. (2) In the context of ethics, the term refers to the view that contrasts with ethical relativism. It is the view that there are principles of morality that should be binding on everyone, even if no one actually follows them. (3) In contexts of discussions of reality, the term refers to some thing that is beyond mere nature and that is a kind of goal that everything is striving toward.

Aesthetics The branch of philosophy that examines questions concerning beauty and art.

Agnosticism The view that there is no way of knowing whether God exists or not.

Altruism The view that one should aim at performing actions that benefit others whether or not they benefit oneself.

Analytic statement A statement that is true solely because of the meanings of the constituent words, such as, "All widows were once married."

Anarchy In philosophical contexts the form of society in which there is no government and no official laws. It is hoped that all members voluntarily keep themselves from violating others' rights.

Argument A series of statements in which one of the statements is to be accepted as true because the other statements are supposed to be true. Arguments are the means that people use to convince others through reason.

Argument from analogy A kind of argument in which two things are compared and found to be generally similar. Then, since one of the things has a feature that is of interest, the conclusion is that the other thing probably has the same feature.

Argument from design A way of arguing that God exists based on the premise that the world that we experience has many examples of complicated order which could not have occurred without a designer, who is held to be God.

Artificial intelligence A branch of technology that attempts to make machines and computer programs that simulate behavior that we usually call intelligent.

Atheism The view that God does not exist.

Capitalism An economic system in which ideally the important decisions of what should be produced and how it should be distributed are determined by individuals making their own separate decisions of how to spend their time and money.

Causal explanation A way of explaining why an event happened. The explanation that is offered is in terms of the causes that led to the event.

Cause and effect Two events are related as cause and effect if one, the cause, comes before the other, the effect, and furthermore, the cause *makes* the effect happen. These are the traditional and also, the ordinary definitions; they play a major role in the debate concerning freedom and determinism.

Conclusion The part of an argument that is to be accepted on the basis of the reasons and evidence presented in the other part of the argument.

Consciousness The quality of being aware of the world and one's own mental states.

Consistency Two or more statements that can be true at the same time. In matters of rationality consistency refers to making similar judgments in similar situations.

Contingency The view that some events just occur randomly and accidentally, and not because they fit any pattern or fulfill any purpose.

Deduction A kind of argument in which the premises present absolutely conclusive reasons for accepting the conclusion. The standard example of deduction is that the premises, "All men are mortal" and "Socrates is a man" require one to accept the conclusion, "Socrates is mortal."

Deism The view that God does exist and did create the universe and set it into motion, but that this God is not particularly concerned about the actions of human beings.

Democracy The form of government in which the people participate in the important decisions that affect their lives.

Desert The concept that everyone deserves a particular kind of treatment. There are different standards for determining what people deserve. Among them are merit, effort, achievement, and need.

Determinism The view that *every* event in the universe is caused by the events which came before it.

Dilemma A situation in which a person faces two choices and both of them are undesirable.

Dualism The view that there are two basic kinds of things that exist—one that is material and one that is nonmaterial.

Duty An action that a person ought to perform for moral reasons.

Empirical Having to do with factual matters, or matters that can be discovered by experiment.

Empiricism The view that the ultimate source of every true belief about the world is sense-experience. For a belief to be true according to this view, it must be confirmed in some way by sense-experience.

Epiphenomenalism The view that mental activities are not just material processes, but are the by-products, or mere accompaniments, of material processes. On this view mental events and processes can never cause changes in the physical world.

Epistemology The branch of philosophy that examines questions concerning knowledge. The major questions are: What is the nature of knowledge? Do we know anything? And if we do, how do we gain this knowledge?

Essence The really important features of a thing that make it what it is, and if it did not have them, it would not be what it is. A standard view used to be that part of the essence of human beings was rationality.

Ethical egoism The view that a person should always and only aim at improving his or her own welfare.

Ethics The branch of philosophy that deals with questions of what is good and what we should do.

Evolution A scientific theory that claims that complicated life-forms developed as the result of an accumulation of accidents.

External world What exists outside of one's own mind, including one's own body.

Faith A kind of belief that is not supported by evidence. It is common in religious contexts.

Fatalism The view that the future is already set and cannot be changed by anything that is done in the present. The future is thus as set as is the past.

First cause argument An argument which concludes that God exists based on the premise that everything, including the universe, must have a cause.

Free will (1) The feeling that people have when they perform an action that they think is up to them. (2) The theory that at least some of the actions actually are up to us.

Hard determinism The variety of determinism that claims that no actions are due to free will. Hard determinists usually claim that the concept of free will makes no sense and as a result, people are not responsible for their actions.

Hypothesis A proposed answer to some question. William James uses this term to mean any possible belief.

Idealism (1) The view that matter does not exist—that nothing material causes our sensations. (2) The view that the most important forces that cause effects in the human world are not physical ones.

Indetermination The philosophical view that some events have no cause at all. They just occur.

Induction A kind of argument in which the premises provide evidence for the conclusion, but do not absolutely require that the conclusion be accepted. The conclusion is only more likely to be true than false. A standard example of induction: the premise that every known human being so far has been less than 100 feet tall provides evidence for the conclusion that no human beings are over 100 feet tall. The evidence makes the conclusion only probably true.

Instrumental good The kind of good thing that is desired just for what it leads to and not simply for itself, such as a trip to the dentist.

Intentionality The property of being about something. Sentences in a language, beliefs, thoughts, wishes, and other mental states all have this property. For example, one does not just have beliefs; one's beliefs are always about something.

Interactionism The view that mind and body are two different kinds of things that can cause changes in each other.

Intrinsic good The kind of good thing that is desired just for itself and not simply for what it leads to, such as happiness.

Introspection The ability to focus and report on one's own mental states.

Intuition A belief that one considers to be obviously and clearly correct. This term is often used in ethics.

Knowledge A highly valued state in which one has a true belief that can be defended against criticisms.

Law of contradiction A fundamental law of logic. According to this law, a statement and its contradiction cannot both be true, and cannot both be false, at the same time. Two statements that illustrate this law are "Elvis is alive" and "Elvis is not alive."

Law of the excluded middle A fundamental law of logic. According to this law, any statement is either true or false. Thus, "There is intelligent life on other planets" is either true or false. There is no third alternative.

Libertarianism Another name for the theory of free will, the theory that at least some of our actions are up to us.

Materialism The view that matter is the only kind of thing that exists, and so-called mental acts and entities are really just material things and processes.

Matter What takes up space and would exist even if there were no one to perceive it.

Metaphysics The branch of philosophy that deals with questions of reality—of what really exists.

Mind A nonphysical thing that is supposed to be the place where thinking, sensing, and feeling take place. A particular mind is considered to be accessible only to the particular person to whom it belong.

Monism The view that only one kind of thing exists. This one kind of thing may be just material or nonmaterial.

Morality A system of rules or guidelines that set forth the most important features of how we should treat other people.

Mysticism The view that there are fundamental truths about the world that are not known through our senses or by our reason.

Naturalism The view that everything that is real is either part of nature or is built out of things found in nature.

Necessary condition A requirement for something else to occur. Water is a necessary condition for life as we know it.

Necessity The condition in which what happens or what is true has to be that way.

Objective A point of view in which no individual's biases or perspectives are allowed to distort the reality of the matter.

Obligation An action that a person ought to perform.

Occam's razor A guideline for correct thinking that states that one should not invent entities to explain something if it is not necessary to do so. What this amounts to is that one should make as few assumptions as possible and that one should try to keep one's explanations as simple as possible.

Ontology The branch of philosophy that attempts to determine what are the basic kinds of things that exist.

Paradox (1) An apparently sound argument that conflicts with what is generally believed to be true. Zeno's arguments against the possibility of motion are famous examples of this type of paradox. (2) A statement that seems to be neither true nor false. A famous example of this kind of paradox is "This statement is false."

Paternalism The view that restrictions on individual liberty are legitimate when they are justified by appealing to the values and the welfare of the person being restricted.

Personal identity What remains the same throughout one's life that makes one the person one is. There are debates about whether one's identity can be found in something material or something mental. Some argue that there is no such thing as personal identity at all.

Phenomenology Having to do with the qualities of a kind of experience. A phenomenological examination of religion would focus on the characteristics of religious experience without consideration of what, if anything, it is an experience of.

Possible A state of affairs that could exist. There are three different types of possibility commonly considered in philosophy. (1) Technically possible—States of affairs that could exist given the current state of technology. Examples: Sending a rocket to the moon is technically possible, but flying from New York to London in 5 minutes is not. (2) Physically possible—States of affairs that could exist given the current understanding of scientific theory. Examples: Flying from London to New York in 5 minutes is physically possible, but going the same distance faster than the speed of light is not. (3) Logically possible—States of affairs that could exist given our current understanding of logical consistency. Examples: Going from New York to London faster than the speed of light is logically possible, but the same small object being in both places at the same time is not.

Pragmatism The view that statements should be judged as true according to the value they have for us in believing them. Thus, if it is valuable for us to believe that we have free will, then we should consider it to be true that we do have free will.

Premise The part of an argument that provides the reasons and the evidence that are the basis for accepting the conclusion.

Proposition A statement which is true or false and in which everything is clearly specified.

Psychological egoism The view that all people, as a matter of fact, always and only aim at improving their own welfare. This view is just a description of what people do. It implies no judgment about whether this is the right way to act.

Rationalism The view that the source of at least some true beliefs about the world is not the senses. This source is sometimes called reason or the understanding. An often used example of a belief that is true although not confirmed by sense-experience is that flexible objects can be put into an infinite number of different shapes.

Rationality (1) The characteristic of adopting beliefs only when they are adequately supported by evidence. (2) The characteristic of selecting an efficient way to achieve one's ends.

Realism The view that certain things or qualities exist independently of human beings. These things or qualities would exist even if all human beings disappeared or had never existed in the first place.

Reason (1) A faculty of human beings that is contrasted with the emotions. (2) The disposition of accepting beliefs only when they are supported by evidence. (3) The disposition of using arguments to decide what to believe.

Reductio ad absurdum A commonly used strategy in philosophy in which one tries to show that a view is mistaken because it leads to a conclusion that is absurd, ridiculous, or obviously false.

Relativism In ethics the view that moral principles are just the teaching of certain groups, and that there is no principle that should be considered binding on all groups. Sometimes relativism is used to mean there is *no way to show* that a principle would be binding on all groups, and sometimes this term is used to mean that it *makes no sense* to say that a moral principle should be binding on all groups.

Retribution A theory of punishment that those who commit crimes deserve a certain amount of suffering proportional to the harm caused by the crime.

Rights In ethics the view that there are certain domains in which every person can act as they wish without interference, such as the right to free speech and the right to own property.

Semantics The subject which studies the interpretations of symbols. In language semantics refers to the meanings of words.

Sensation The final result of processes of sight, touch, smell, taste, and hearing. Sensations are generally considered to occur in the mind.

Sense-data The information that our senses provide us with.

Skepticism The philosophical view that knowledge does not exist. Usually there is a reference in the context to a particular kind of knowledge, such as knowledge of what the world is like or knowledge about whether God exists.

Socialism An economic system in which ideally a publically chosen group makes the important decisions of what will be produced and how it will be distributed.

Soft determinism The variety of determinism that claims that determinism is compatible with free will. That means that the very same action can be the result of causes and also be called "free." This view of determinism does not eliminate the possibility of moral responsibility.

Sound argument An argument in which the premises are true and the reasoning is valid. This is the best kind of argument and provides the best grounds for accepting the conclusion.

Sovereignty In political philosophy the group that holds supreme political power. In a democracy the people are sovereign. In a monarchy, the king or queen is the sovereign.

Spiritual A vague word that is often used to refer to anything that is not physical.

State In political philosophy the organization that has political control over a certain territory. The usual functions of the state are to make the laws, enforce them, and interpret them when necessary.

Subjective A personal point of view, or how matters appear to an individual.

Substance A philosophical term that refers to whatever it is that has properties, such as a table that has color, shape, and size. Some use substance to refer to whatever it is that has a body and a mind.

Sufficient condition An adequate ground for the occurrence of something, but not a requirement. A gunshot is sufficient to kill someone, but it is not a requirement because there are other ways to kill people.

Supernaturalism The view that there are real things besides what occurs in nature. This other kind of real thing is considered more powerful than nature.

Syntax The subject which studies the capacity to manipulate symbols according to rules. Syntax is often used to refer to the grammar of a language.

Synthetic statement A statement that is true, but the truth of which is not based solely on the meanings of the constituent words. An example of such a statement is "The dinosaurs are extinct."

Teleology The view that a thing has a predetermined purpose. Sometimes the word is used in connection with the universe as a whole. In ethics the view that what makes an act right is the results the act leads to. Utilitarianism is an example of a teleological theory in ethics.

Theism The view that there is a God who created the universe and who also has a personal interest in the well-being of humanity.

Theodicy A way of reconciling God's goodness, knowledge, and power with the fact of human suffering.

Universal (1) A statement that refers to all the members of some group. For example, "All men are mortal." (2) Qualities that all items of a particular group share. For example, all monkeys share in the universal of mortality.

Utilitarianism The view in ethics that acts are right to the extent that they increase happiness and wrong to the extent that they increase suffering.

Valid argument An argument in which the reasoning is good, but the premises are not necessarily all true. Valid arguments have one of the features of sound arguments, but they do not always have the other important feature—true premises.

Value What is important. Values involve comparison and ranking.